D1737958

THE ENCYCLOPEDIA OF PAKISTAN

THE ENCYCLOPEDIA OF PAKISTAN

Editors-in-Chief
Hafeez Malik
Yuri V. Gankovsky

OXFORD
UNIVERSITY PRESS

OXFORD
UNIVERSITY PRESS

Great Clarendon Street, Oxford OX2 6DP

Oxford University Press is a department of the University of Oxford.
It furthers the University's objective of excellence in research, scholarship,
and education by publishing worldwide in

Oxford New York

Auckland Cape Town Dar es Salaam Hong Kong Karachi
Kuala Lumpur Madrid Melbourne Mexico City Nairobi
New Delhi Shanghai Taipei Toronto

with offices in

Argentina Austria Brazil Chile Czech Republic France Greece
Guatemala Hungary Italy Japan South Korea Poland Portugal
Singapore Switzerland Thailand Turkey Ukraine Vietnam

Oxford is a registered trade mark of Oxford University Press
in the UK and in certain other countries

First published 2006

ISBN-13: 978-0-19-597735-6
ISBN-10: 0-19-597735-1

Cover design by K.B. Abro

Typeset in Times
Printed in Pakistan by
New Sketch Graphics, Karachi.
Published by
Ameena Saiyid, Oxford University Press
Plot No. 38, Sector 15, Korangi Industrial Area, PO Box 8214
Karachi-74900, Pakistan.

INTRODUCTION

Hafeez Malik

This first ever edition of the *Encyclopedia of Pakistan* can make no claim to finality. In fact no encyclopedia ever does.

In the future scholars will, through their collective endeavors, compile encyclopedias of Pakistan, and present more detailed information about the country, which by virtue of societal development and geostrategic importance is destined to be in the eye of international storms, and internal socio-political upheavals.

(I)

Planning for this encyclopedia started nearly twenty years ago. In one of Moscow city's parks, where my dear friend, the late Professor Yuri V. Gankovsky and I spent one afternoon in the summer of 1981 exchanging ideas on Pakistan and its relations with the Soviet Union. This was supposedly the most stable, predictable and quiescent period of Leonid Brezhnev's rule (1964-82). At this time, neither Professor Gankovsky nor I realized that the Soviet Union would cease to exist in December 1991. He informed me that he had planned to initiate a one volume project of *Soviet Encyclopedia of Pakistan*, which would be published in Moscow. He invited me to be one of the three editors, the other two being himself and a mutual friend, Igor Khalevinsky, who was then a member of the Soviet Foreign Service, and a respected Pakistan Specialist.

I accepted his invitation, but suggested that I would rather be the editor-in-chief of the encyclopedia, if it were published in English. This proposal was accepted. Then by mutual agreement an outline was drawn, including the topics, scholars in Russia were identified, and a general agreement was reached on the selection of facts. (Very generously, Villanova University and Pakistan-American Foundation paid the substantial cost of translation of the Russian draft into readable English). While emphasizing the objective and unbiased presentation of social, economic and political developments in Pakistan, we ran into the problem of running the Soviet Censors' gauntlet. Soviet Censorship had established the rule that all historical, economic, political and ethnic developments must be analyzed within the framework of Marxism and Leninism. In fact the insertion of appropriate quotations from the patron saints of the Soviet Union was mandatory for every chapter and verse of any publication. Russian scholars had conformed to this requirement repeatedly and unquestionably for such a long period of time that the so-called Marxist-Leninist mould of thinking and writing had become their thinking habit.

Could the framework be avoided? A tacit understanding was reached that the Russian edition of the *Encyclopedia of Pakistan* would be published conforming to the Russian Censors' 'scientific standards,' while I would have to edit the total English version of the manuscript, eliminating the Soviet 'scientific' approach. One year before Professor Gankovsky's death in 2001 the Russian edition of this encyclopedia was published in Moscow.

I spent nearly five years in editing the English draft of the encyclopedia improving the language style and eliminating Soviet terminology. Finally the manuscript was submitted to Oxford University Press in May, 1997. As a matter of policy Oxford University Press logically divided the manuscript into six sections, 1. history, 2. politics and parties, 3. geography, 4. foreign policy, 5. the arts, 6. and religions. Oxford submitted the respective section to six outstanding Pakistani scholars and faculty members of the University of Karachi, for their critical reviews: 1. Fazle Karim Khan, Professor of Geography, 2. S.H.M. Jafri, former Director of Pakistan Studies Center, 3. Mehrunnisa Ali, Professor (emeritus) of Political Science, 4. Mohammad Reza Kazimi, Associate Professor of Religion, 5. Jaffar Ahmad, Director of Pakistan Studies

Center, and 6. Musaddiq Sawwal, Creative Director of Pakistan Institute of Labor Education and Research.

These respected scholars subjected the manuscript to detailed scrutiny, and made exceptionally constructive suggestions to improve the contents and timeliness. Subsequently, Oxford University Press engaged Dr Muhammad Reza Kazimi as an editorial consultant, who meticulously supervised the insertion of appropriate improvements in various items, which the six scholars had proposed. He added several items, whose inclusion had become essential with the passage of time, or which had been inadvertently overlooked. Moreover, Dr Kazimi invited additional scholars in Pakistan to write articles on topics of their specialization. In consequence the quality of the encyclopedia improved immeasurably.

The section on economic development presented another problem. Since the advent of Pakistan, American economic development specialists, and economic scholars had close collaborative relationship with the Pakistan government, which have enabled them to amass a vast amount of economic data on Pakistan's economy. This advantage in economic data was not available to Russian scholars.

(II)

The object of this *Encyclopedia* is to present, within the relatively brief space of a single volume, a mass of useful information on Pakistan. It is not a compilation of scholarly articles to sustain an international discourse among scholars. Nevertheless, as a matter of policy an attempt has been made to maintain a high level of scholarship without being too technical, and to present the material in a clear and readable style. The amount of information that can be included in one volume is necessarily limited, yet we think that the coverage is broad and comprehensive. It is the editors' expectation that the *Encyclopedia* will meet a need of the general public, journalists, and students in the universities and colleges.

In the preparation of this *Encyclopedia* seventy Russian scholars made, some small and some major, contributions. Against this extensive number of Russian contributors nearly twenty Pakistani scholars contributed a fairly sizeable number of articles. Consequently, the *Encyclopedia of Pakistan* is truly an international scholarly endeavor. Practically all the Russian scholars belonged to the Soviet, now the Russian Institute of Oriental Studies where Professor Gankovsky spent most years of his academic career as Head of the Department of the Middle East, Afghanistan and Pakistan.

Established during the Czarist period in the nineteenth century, the Institute of Oriental Studies employed in 1979, when I first visited it, at least 300 scholars. Under Professor Gankovsky's leadership the Pakistan Studies Center flourished not only in the Russian Federation, but also in Central Asia and the Caucasus. The Pakistan Department, which is now headed by Professor V.N. Moskalenko, and the Middle East Department by Professor Vyacheslav Y. Belokrenitsky, are the best source of knowledge about Pakistan for the Russian government, and the media, which now plays a significant role in informing the Russian public.

This *Encyclopedia* is a tribute to Professor Gankovsky, and his colleagues at the Institute of Oriental Studies who have demonstrated profound scholarly interest in Pakistan's development. In addition to his numerous publications, Professor Gankovsky was the President of Soviet, and then after December 1991 Russian Pakistan Friendship Society for many years. Also, he was the Vice President of Scientific Council for the coordination of Oriental Studies in the Soviet/Russian Academy of Sciences. Despite these devoted services to Russia, including a soldierly duty in the Armed Forces during World War II, the KGB imprisoned him for seven years. Pakistan became his academic passion since December 1956, when he joined the Institute of Oriental Studies. Unfortunately, neither Russia nor Pakistan extended the recognition or honour that he deserved. Of course his friends of longstanding, including myself, would cherish his memory with tender loving care.

(III)

Compiled with the help of Russian scholars, the *Encyclopedia of Pakistan* lights up the possibility of additional cooperation between Pakistan and Russia. Historically, Pakistan's relations with the Soviet have oscillated from indifference to estrangement, and even hostility. Granted that Pakistan has substantially benefited in its close relations with the United States, but it must be recognized that indifferent or antagonistic policy toward Russia has damaged Pakistan's vital national interests, as was the case in 1970-71. Pakistan had the window of opportunity wide open to significantly improve its relations with Russia in 1991, 1992 and even in 1993. Pakistan squandered that opportunity, and India moved in skillfully to sign another Treaty of Friendship with Russia. Prudently Russia signed the new treaty without the military clause, which had been incorporated in the 1971 Treaty of Friendship with India. Clearly this prudent approach indicated that Russia valued its 'friendship' with India, but not at the expense of relations with China and Pakistan.

Despite Russia's decline as a superpower, it is still a major Eurasian state, and destined to play a significant role within the region of Pakistan's security. Moreover Russia is a bi-religious state (especially in the Volga-Ural Basin) consisting of Russian Orthodox Christians and Muslims. Tatars, Bashkorts, and other Caucasian Muslims flourish in the traditional Islamic belt, which extends along the Volga River from Ufa-Kazan region to Samara, Saratov to Astrakhan. Located here are the Republics of Tatarstan and Bashkortastan. These regions are highly industrialized and developed, and can serve as bridges of understanding and co-operation between Russia and Pakistan in matters of trade, commerce and even security. The *Encyclopedia of Pakistan* should lead the way, hopefully, to better relations with Russia as well as with other regional states.

(IV)

In closing these introductory remarks it is my delightful obligation to express sincere appreciation of the supportive role of those individuals, who were involved in the preparation of the of the *Encyclopedia of Pakistan*. They cheerfully tolerated my unavoidable delaying performance as editor-in-chief.

Villanova University has not only been an intellectual haven for me, but it has also generously supported the *Encyclopedia of Pakistan*, over the last twenty-six years the *Journal of South Asian and Middle Eastern Studies,* the Pakistan-American Foundation, and the American Institute of Pakistan Studies, which have also received generous support from the Ministry of Education of the Government of Pakistan. I am equally indebted to Fr. Edmund J. Dobbin (President), Dr John R. Johannes (Vice President of Academic Affairs), and Fr. Kail C. Ellis (Dean of Arts and Sciences, and Founder-Director of the Center for Contemporary Arab and Islamic Studies) of Villanova University.

Among my friends, I single out Nadia Barsoum, who helped me in many ways to make this publication a successful enterprise. Also, thanks to my former graduate assistant, Murtaza (Sunny) Razvi, who is now a noted journalist in Pakistan, helped me in editing this *Encyclopedia*. Some of my friends, both in the United States and abroad, have always been a source of encouragement and support: Muhammad Rafiq Tarar, my childhood friend, (who later became the President of Pakistan for three years), Yuri V. Gankovsky, Afaq Haydar, Jack Schrems, Zaheer Chaudhry, Kamran Khan, Stanley Wolpert, M. Imtiaz Ali, Igor V. Khalevinsky, Vyacheslav Ya. Belokrinitsky, Anwar Aziz Chaudhry, Ralph Braibanti, Akbar S. Ahmad, Syed Jamil Shah, Sharif al-Mujahid, (Akhuna) Khalil Ilyas, Jawahirah and Rashid Makhdoomi, Aiyesha and Muhammad Latib, and Syed Abid Ali, and his devoted wife, Naznin Syed.

Special mention must be made of three very dear families—Sadaqat Gul and Waqar Asim Mansuri; Nasira and Javid Iqbal; and Nuria and Walid Iqbal, the latter graduated from the position of a 'nephew' to a dear friend. I value their friendship and cherish their affection. Always a source of encouragement and help, Javid Iqbal is really a soul mate. A dynamic educator in her own time, Amina (Begum) Majeed Malik, my aunt, was a source of inspiration, and always admiringly supportive of my endeavors. My program coordinator, Susan K. Hausman, who retired in 2001, handled the details of the *Encyclopedia* with her usual efficiency and imaginative skills. Last, but not least, a colleague at Villanova University, my wife, Lynda P. Malik, a sociologist specializing on Islamic societies, was supportive and helpful in many ways.

(V)

The names of Russian and Pakistani scholars follow this introduction. The biographical descriptions of 20 Russian scholars whose entries in the *Encyclopedia* are extensive are included; for others the names are mentioned.

MAIN CONTRIBUTORS

1. Leonid B. Alaev, Professor, Ph.D., is a specialist in the history of India and South Asia. His scholarly interest is in the structure and specific features of the Indian village communities of South and North India. His latest publication on the village societies is a compilation of articles and unpublished monographs on the subject (Moscow Nauka Publishing House, 2000). His other works deal with theories of feudalism in the East and the ideological and political currents in the Colonial and Independent India. At present he is Chief Research Associate, at the Institute of Oriental Studies (IOS), Russian Academy of Sciences, Moscow and Professor of the MGIMO University in Moscow.
2. Luidmila B. Aristova, Ph.D., is a Senior Researcher at the IOS. Her field of research is economics, particularly productive and social infrastructure of Pakistan, Afghanistan and Central Asia. She has authored a book and a number of articles on these issues.
3. Vyacheslav Ya. Belokrenitsky, Professor, Ph.D. is Head, Near and Middle East Department, IOS, and Professor, South Asian Politics, MGIMO University, Moscow. His scholarly interest includes economy, demography, socio-economic and political problems of Pakistan. He is the author of several books, including the English edition of *Capitalism in Pakistan,* (New Delhi: People's Publishing House, 1991). He also writes on international politics of South and Central Asia. In 2001, Edwin Mellen Press, USA, published his book (co-authored by Vladimir Moscalenko and Tatiana Shaumian), *South Asia in the Contemporary Political World* (in the Russian Language Series).
4. Djoy I. Edelman, Prof. Ph.D., is a specialist in the South Asian philology, and is at present Head of Department of the Institute of Languages, Russian Academy of Sciences. Her scholarly interest is focussed on Dardic languages, especially Kashmiri. She has contributed a number of works on these and various related subjects.
5. Yuri V. Gankovsky's whole life (1921-2001) was devoted to the Institute of Oriental Studies in Moscow. In 1958 he earned his Candidate of Science (Ph.D.) degree in History. Simultaneously his first book *The Durrani Empire* was published. With basic knowledge of Persian, some Arabic and Urdu, he was attracted to scholarly studies on Pakistan. With Alexei D'yakov and Luidmila Gordon-Polonskaya he laid the foundation of the Pakistani studies in the USSR. His book *History of Pakistan* (co-authored with Gordon-Polonskaya), published first in Russian and then in English, became one of the reference works on the history of Pakistan. Subsequently his second book *The Peoples of Pakistan* (Russian edition of 1964, English edition printed in Pakistan in 1972) attracted wide attention. In 1967 Professor Gankovsky presented his second dissertation and earned the Doctor of Science degree, soon after he became full Professor at the Institute of Oriental Studies. In 1964 he was appointed Head of the newly created Section for Pakistan Studies and then in 1969 of the Department of Pakistan (later Pakistan and Bangladesh) Studies. In 1978 the Pakistan Section was joined with the Department of Near and Middle East, and Professor Gankovsky became its Head. In 1987 at age 65 he became the chairman of a section, *Encyclopedia of Asia*, and till the last days of his life remained responsible for its program. In 1991 Professor Yuri Gankovsky was a Visiting Distinguished Professor at Villanova University. He had many good friends among colleagues in the United States, Pakistan and other countries.

6. Irina V. Jhmuida, Ph.D., is a Senior Researcher, IOS. An expert on the economy of Pakistan, she is the author of three books dealing with industrial development, home savings and investments, and foreign economic relations. She has also contributed works on Islamic economics and regional economic policy in Pakistan.
7. Sergey N. Kamenev, Ph.D., is a Researcher, IOS. He analyses economic and financial problems of Pakistan and Central Asian States, particularly Turkmenistan. One of his books on Pakistani economy, *Economic Growth in Pakistan* was translated into English and published by Vanguard Books, Lahore, in 1986.
8. Vladimir P. Liperovsky, Ph.D., is a Researcher, IOS. He is a well-known specialist on Urdu and Hindi languages, their semantics and syntax. Some of his works were published in English.
9. Boris A. Litvinsky, Professor, Ph.D., is an accomplished historian and archaeologist who worked for many years in Tajikistan and Northern Afghanistan and made several well known archaeological discoveries. He is co-author of *The History of Tajikistan* (with Academician Bobojan Gafurov) and was elected Corresponding Member of the Tajikistan Academy of Sciences. He is currently Chief Research Associate, IOS, and also a member of several American and European academic and scholarly organizations.
10. Marina Yu. Morozova, Ph.D., is a Senior Research Associate, IOS. Geographer by training, she specialises in the economic geography and economy of Pakistan, especially the agriculture and social structure of the Pakistani rural society. Her other scholarly interests are the political parties and Islamic political forces in Pakistan.
11. Vladimir N. Moscalenko, Professor, Ph.D., is Chairman of Pakistan Section, IOS. He is a leading expert on the Pakistani political history, constitutional and administrative structure, socio-political development, and history of the Pakistani Studies in Russia. His book *The Three Constitutions of Pakistan* (co-author-Yu.V. Gankovsky) was published by People's Publishing House, Lahore, in 1977. His other main interest is the foreign policy of Pakistan. He has authored a number of monographs and articles on this subject, in particular the issue of Kashmir and of nuclear weapons in South Asia.
12. Railya M. Mukimjanova, Professor, Ph.D., is a Researcher, IOS. An Uzbek scholar who has contributed substantially to the study of the Pakistani foreign policy from the 1950s to the present time. She is the author of three monographs and a large number of scholarly articles on Pakistani-American and Pakistani-Indian Relations. Since 1991 her interest has shifted to the study of relations between Pakistan and the new Central Asian states, Afghanistan, Iran and Arab states. She is a leading expert on the history and the contemporary state of affairs between Russia and Pakistan.
14. Aziz Niyazi, Ph.D., is a Senior Researcher, IOS, and also Director, Institute of Central Asia Development in Moscow. Hailing from Tajikistan, he is a leading authority on the political situation in Central Asia. He is a well-known specialist on the issues of Islam and Islamic ideology in Pakistan and South Asia, and on the role of religious political parties and their organizations.
15. Oleg V. Pleshov, Ph.D., is a Senior Researcher, IOS. A well-known journalist, turned scholar has special interest in Pakistani Islam, and its role in the political system. His book *Islam and Democracy: The Pakistan Experience* (in Russian) is followed by the forthcoming extended edition in both Russian and English.
16. Natalya I. Prigarina, Professor, Ph.D., is a Researcher, IOS. She is an expert on the philosophy and literary works of Allama Muhammad Iqbal. She has published several books on Iqbal. Persian and Urdu Literature are her main scholarly interest. She regularly participates in international conferences and seminars.

17. Anna A. Suvorova, Professor, Ph.D., is Head, Department of Literature, IOS. She is a well-known authority on the classical Urdu literature and also the history of Islam, especially Sufism in South Asia. Her book in Russian *Muslim Saints of South Asia* (Moscow, 1999) is a bestseller. She is known also as a translator of Urdu poetry into Russian.
18. Luidmila A. Vasilyeva, Ph.D., is a Senior Researcher, IOS. A specialist in Urdu literature and cultural history of Pakistan, she is well known as a participant of international conferences on Iqbal, and Faiz Ahmad Faiz. Her latest book is devoted to the life and creative activities of the famous poet and educationist Altaf Husain Hali.
19. Alexei A. Vigasin, Ph.D., is Professor of Ancient History at the Institute of Asian and African countries, M. V. Lomonosov Moscow National University. He specialises in the ancient history of India and southern Asia and has authored many books and articles on the history of primordial societies, material and spiritual culture of the peoples of the region.
20. Alexander V. Zabolotsky, Ph.D., is a Senior Researcher, IOS. He is a well-known specialist of the demography of Pakistan and some other Asian countries. He authored a book, and a number of articles in different scholarly journals.

CONTRIBUTORS

Editors-in-Chief:

Hafeez Malik
Yuri V. Gankovsky

Subject Editors and Contributors:

F. A. Abdrakhmanova
M. S. Adrona
L. B. Alayev
N. N. Alexeeva
M. Ali
A. S. Alpatova
S. Amin
Yu. V. Areshko
V. P. Baidakov
V. Ya. Belokrenitsky
S. A. Bhutto
O. N. Bobyleva
V. A. Chernyshev
L. M. Chevkina
O. A. Druzhinina
D. I. Edelman
N. Farrukh
A. Farrukhi
E. V. Ganevskaya
Yu V. Gankovsky
A. S. Gerasimova
N. V. Glebov
Ye. M. Gorokhovik
E. M. Gorokhovik
A. M. Goryacheva
I. S. Graginsky
N. V. Gurov
N. R. Guseva
R. Husain
A. Hussain
M. I. Karatygina
N. K. Karpova
M. R. Kazimi
A. M. Khazanov
B. I. Klyuev
N. P. Kochergina
S. T. Kureishi
S. F. Levin
V. P. Liperovsky
B. A. Litvinsky
O. V. Lustsova
O. V. Lystgova
A. H. Mallik
A. M. Melnikov
M. Yu. Morozova
V. V. Moshkalo
S. Mujahid
R. M. Mukimjanova
K. K. Mumtaz
T. K. Naim
D. B. Novosyolov
F. N. Ogureeva
M. M. Osipova
I. Piracha
O. V. Pleshov
N. I. Prigarina
Rafi Peer Theatre Workshop
T. Rahman
A. V. Raikov
A. A. Rallev
V. A. Ranov
T. J. Roberts
S. B. Rostotsky
M. K. Safolov
L. V. Savelyeva
A. M. Scheglova
S. D. Serebryani
Shahnawaz
M. Shamsie
P. M. Shastitko
A. Ya. Shchetenko
B. Ya. Stavisky
M. Stoney
A. S. Sukhochev
A. A. Suvorova
R. Symonds
N. I. Tolstaya
Yu. V. Tsvetsov
E. Yu. Vanina
L. A. Vasilyeva
A. A. Vigasin
N. M. Vinogradova
S. Wolpert
V. A. Yefimov
T. Ya. Yelizarenkova
M. Yousaf
A. V. Zabolotsky
R. Zafar
N. A. Zamaraeva
G. A. Zograf
I. V. Zotova

CONTENTS

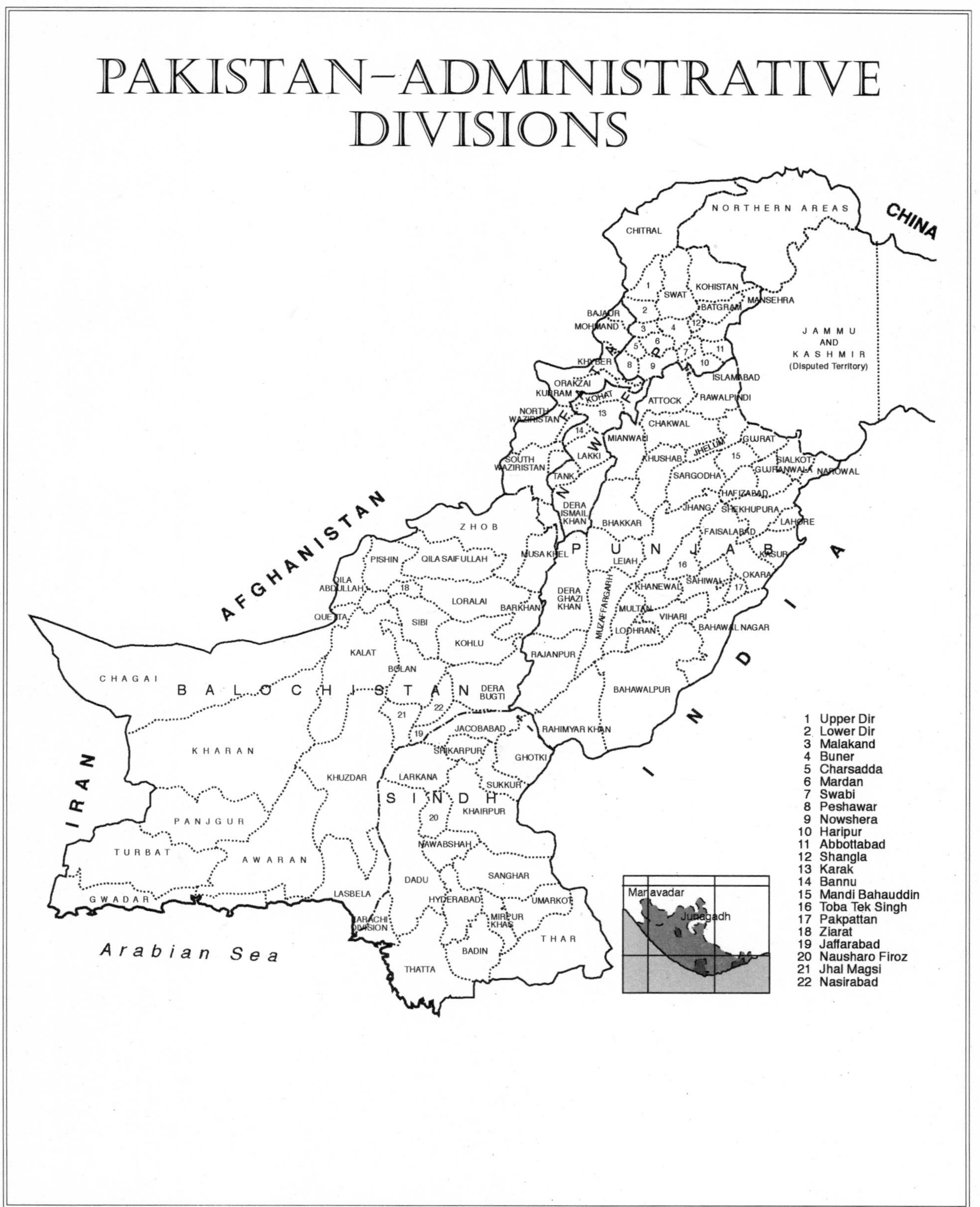

Source: Fazle Karim Khan, '*Pakistan Geography, Economy and People*', 2002.

Aali, Jamiluddin (1926–)

Poet. His real name is Mirza Jamiluddin Ahmad Khan. Born in Delhi, son of Nawab Sir Amiruddin Khan of Loharu, he joined the government service after coming to Pakistan, first as an Income Tax Officer, then as Officer on Special Duty in the President's House. He later became Secretary of the *National Press Trust and subsequently worked in the Ministry of Finance. Aali was the founding Honorary Secretary-General of the *Pakistan Writers Guild (1959–62), and Secretary-General of the *Anjuman Tarraqi-i-Urdu* (Society for the Progress of Urdu) after that. He was awarded the President's Pride of Performance Medal in 1991 and the *Hilal-i-Imtiaz* (Crescent of Distinction) in 1996. A D. Litt. *Honoris Causa* from the University of Karachi (1996), he served as senator from 1996–99.

Jamiluddin Aali has written **ghazals* and **geets*, but his popularity was built up mostly on his **dohas*. Drawing on vernacular traditions and a sub-continental vocabulary, he has written on patriotic themes, declaring that 'his muse was accountable to the people and nation of Pakistan'. These patriotic *geets* have enjoyed immense popularity, some of them, such as *Jeeway Jeeway Pakistan,* almost acquiring the status of an anthem. His war poems (1965) and his lyric *Ham Mustafavi Hain* composed on the occasion of the second Islamic Summit (Lahore, 1974), are among his claims to immortality. The culmination of his poetic works has come together in an epic called *Insan* (Human).

Apart from three volumes of poetry, Aali has published several travelogues, volumes of prefaces, and writes a weekly column for **Jang,* the largest circulating Urdu newspaper.

WORKS: *'Ghazlen'; 'Dohey Geet Karachi', 1957; 'La Hasil', Karachi, 1974; 'Ai Meri Dasht-i-Sukhan', Lahore, 1995.*

BIBLIOGRAPHY: *Mehrunnisa Aziz, 'Jamiluddin Aali Ki Tahriron Mien Pakistaniat', Karachi, 2000 (in Urdu); Auj-i-Kamal, ed. 'Dunya-i-Adab', Aali Number, Karachi, 2001 (in Urdu).*

M.R. KAZIMI

Abbas, Ghulam (1909–82)

Writer. Ghulam Abbas was an *Urdu language novelist and short story writer. Educated in Lahore and subsequently working out of that city, he edited a number of literary journals from 1927 onwards. His publications include collections of stories *Anandi, Jare ki Chandni* (Winter Moonlight) in 1961, *Jazira-i-Sukhanwaran* (The Island of Poets), a novel about everyday life in the urban middle class, and *Zindagi, Chehre, aur Naqab* (Life, Faces, and Masks) published posthumously.

Ghulam Abbas belongs to the literary trend known as 'critical realism'. He made a notable contribution to Urdu literature for children.

BIBLIOGRAPHY: *R.A. Elizarova, A.S. Sukhochev, 'Pakistan's Progressive Writers', Tashkent, 1978 (in Russian); Syed Ehtisham Husain, 'Urdu Sahitiya ka Itihas', Delhi, 1954 (in Urdu); Shahzad Manzar, 'Ghulam Abbas - Ek Mutalia', Lahore, 1991 (in Urdu); Soyamane Yasir, 'Ghulam Abbas—Sawanh O Fan ka Tahqiqui Jaiza', Lahore, 1995 (in Urdu).*

A.S. SUKHOCHEV

Abbasi, Tanvir, Dr (1934–99)

Writer. A medical doctor by profession, Tanvir Abbasi was one of the most versatile and accomplished literary luminaries of the *Sindhi language. In poetry, he wrote in every form, **nazm,* **ghazal* and **geet*; in prose he wrote literary criticism, travelogues, character sketches, memoirs, and fiction. Tanvir Abbasi was an author involved in contemporary issues and submerged in classical lore. He began composing poetry during the time the Sindhi intelligentsia were protesting against the imposition of One Unit. Since Sindh's identity had become an issue, Abbasi began addressing Shah Abdul Latif *Bhitai in his poems. This evocation of the Bhitai personae gave his symbolism a perspective not found in the works of other poets of the time.

Ideologically a progressive writer, Tanvir Abbasi nevertheless took to *ghazal*, bringing about some innovations in the form. Although it is as a poet that he is best known, his contribution to prose, especially literary criticism, is also commendable. His works on the classical greats such as Shah Abdul Latif Bhitai and Sachal *Sarmast are well known. In addition, his essays in *Narwar* show him at his best as a prose stylist. He has also written in the pattern of Japanese *Haiku* poems.

In the mid-fifties Abbasi wrote two memorable short stories, *Wand Khai* (1955) and *Loni* (1956).

S.A. BHUTTO

Abdus Salam (1926–96)

Scientist. Abdus Salam is Pakistan's only Nobel Laureate (Physics, 1979). The citation with the award mentioned his 'achieving an enormous step in the search for the underlying principle of the Universe through his contribution to the theory of unified and weak electromagnetic interaction between elementary particles'. In other words, identifying the unity in the basic forces of nature. The 'unification theory' has become a very important part of modern physics.

Dr Abdus Salam computed the precise relations between the electromagnetic and the weak nuclear force which, among other functions, enables the sun to convert its hydrogen into nuclear energy. The search for the Higgs Particle, predicted by him, remains a top priority of physics research.

Salam was educated in Government College, Jhang, and Government College, Lahore (1946). He obtained his MSc and PhD degrees from the University of Cambridge (1949). From 1954-56 he was Professor of Mathematics at Imperial College, London. He became Advisor for Science to the President of Pakistan in 1974. He founded SUPARCO in 1961. He was also a Member (Technical) of the *Pakistan Atomic Energy Commission. He founded and funded the Third World Academy of Sciences in Trieste, Italy.

V.N. MOSCALENKO

Abjad

See, Tarikh.

Achaemenids

Royal dynasty of ancient Iran, 558-330 BC. In the rule of Darius I (522-486 BC), the Achaemenid Empire embraced the present-day territory of Iran, Turkey, Iraq, Syria, Egypt, Central Asia and the northwest of Pakistan.

The Achaemenids were defeated by Alexander of Macedonia (ruled 336-323 BC).

YU.V. GANKOVSKY

Achkan

See, Sherwani.

Adib, Mirza (1914–99)

Writer. Dilawar Ali, who adopted the pen name of Mirza Adib, was an *Urdu language author. He was educated at the Islamia College in Lahore. He was first published in 1935. He edited the magazines *Adab-i-Latif* (Belle Letters), *Musawwir* (Artist) and *Kalamkar* (Master of the Pen). After 1962 *Kalamkar* became the official organ of the *Pakistan Writers' Guild.

Adib's main works include several collections of plays, including *Ansu aur Sitare* (Tears and Stars), *Lohu aur Kalin* (Blood and the Carpet), *Fasil-i-Shab* (The Wall of Night); He also has some collections of stories, including *Jangal* (Jungle), *Kambal* (Blanket); and collections of critical essays: *Fan aur Fankar* (Art and Artist), and some children's stories.

Mirza Adib's realistic work depicts the urban lower class and is permeated with compassion for man, which he believed is a victim of social inequality. Mirza Adib died in Lahore, on 31 July 1999.

WORKS: *'Sehranaward ke Khutut' (Letters of the Lonely Wanderer), 1939; 'Satwan Chiragh' (The Seventh Lamp), 1983; 'Selected Stories', 1966; 'Collections of plays: Shishe-o-Sang' (Glass and Stone), 1979; 'Lamhon ki Rakh' (The Ashes of Moments), 1988; (autobiography) 'Mitti ka Diya' (Clay Lamp), 1981.*

A.S. SUKHOCHEV

Afghanistan-Pakistan Relations

Afghanistan and Pakistan share a long border called the *Durand Line. Although there are religious and ethnic affinities between the people of these two countries, relations between the two neighbours were less than cordial throughout the Cold War. Acute differences developed between the two states, even to the point of diplomatic relations being terminated (in 1961). These were restored in 1963 by virtue of the Shah of Iran's successful mediation. Being a landlocked country, Afghanistan had no access to the sea. Consequently most of its foreign trade is routed through Pakistan's port of Karachi. This factor has significant importance in the development of bilateral relations between the two countries.

From 1976 to 1978 Pak-Afghan high-level contacts tended to mend relations. However, in the late 1970s fellowship began to deteriorate rapidly. Pakistan's territory became the principal base for the Afghan opposition forces against the Soviet supported Kabul government.

The war in Afghanistan gave rise to a number of destructive developments for Pakistan, such as the spread of drugs, terrorism, and violence, social difficulties resulting from the presence of three million Afghan refugees. The desire to stabilize the position of Pakistan's foreign and domestic relations led Islamabad, in the early 1980s, to seek a negotiated settlement of the Afghan War. Pakistan supported the proposal of the UN Secretary General, in May 1981, i.e. to settle the problem by political means. This led to the *Geneva Agreement in 1988, facilitating the withdrawal of Soviet troops from Afghanistan in early 1989. Subsequently a Soviet-American agreement was reached on the simultaneous cessation of weapons deliveries to all warring Afghan forces, as of 1 January 1992.

Pakistan's relations with Afghanistan had an inauspicious beginning. Afghanistan was the only country to oppose Pakistan's membership of the UN in September 1947. It belatedly refused to recognize the Durand Line (1893) as the common frontier between the two countries, and claimed territories lying in Pakistan to be its own. The Afghan government had insisted in 1947 that the people of the NWFP be given a chance to vote in the referendum on union with Pakistan or Afghanistan or, alternatively, on the founding of an independent state of Pakhtunistan. This demand ran contrary to the terms of reference of the Partition Plan. The prime minister designate of India, Pandit Jawaharlal Nehru, had ruled out the third option, that is, independence in the case of *Bengal, therefore it could not be introduced anywhere else in the country.

It was after the Soviet withdrawal from Afghanistan that the Taliban, an Islamist party that is usually labelled 'fundamentalist', acquired strength. The Taliban's success in Herat (in Afghanistans Herat province) resulted in the ransacking of the Pakistan Embassy by the forces of Ahmad Shah Masood. On 27 September 1996 the Taliban entered Kabul and executed Dr Najibullah, who had been the president during the Soviet dominated era. On 25 May 1997, Pakistan, along with Saudi Arabia and the United Arab Emirates, recognized the Taliban regime led by Mullah Muhammad Umar.

Pakistan's recognition of the Taliban regime caused a setback to the relations held with the Central Asian States as well as with the United States of America, who were pressurizing Pakistan to use its influence with the Taliban to track down Osama Bin Laden, a Saudi citizen suspected of terrorism. Following the 11 September 2001 terrorist attacks on the United States, Osama Bin Laden, harboured by the Taliban, became the prime suspect. After promising the US that it would help in the fight against terrorism, Pakistan-Taliban relations became practically nil, and were later completely cut off.

The US attacked Afghanistan on 7 October 2001 with full intelligence and logistical help from Pakistan. The interim regime set up under Hamid Karzai took Kandahar on 7 December 2001, paving his way to becoming president on 13 June 2002. Pakistan and Afghanistan were further alienated because of terrorism within Pakistan's territory, for which Afghans were held responsible. As a result of this the Pakistani Embassy in Kabul was closed down. It was reopened on 14 January 2002 after Afghan authorities gave assurance of safety. On 8 February of the same year, Presidents Karzai and *Musharraf met in Islamabad and talked about improvement of bilateral ties. On 2 April President Musharraf visited Kabul. On 2 May 2002, Air Services between Afghanistan and Pakistan resumed after twenty-three years. Pakistan turned down Afghanistan's request to allow Indian goods through its territory on 13 May 2002. On 22 December 2002, Pakistan signed a pact with Afghanistan not to interfere in its internal affairs. On 22 April 2003 Pakistani and Afghan presidents met again in Islamabad to normalize relations. On 8 July 2003, the Pakistan Mission to Afghanistan again became the victim of a Kabul mob attack and closed down. 25 October 2003 saw Pakistan set up a large number of check posts on the Pak-Afghan border.

Relations were once again damaged when President Hamid Karzai accused Pakistan on 23 November 2004 of harbouring and promoting Taliban elements for attacks in his country. The Pakistan Foreign Office issued a rebuttal the same day, saying that Afghanistan should improve internal security by curbing warlords in its territory, control factional fighting and the production and trafficking of drugs. Prime Minister Mian Zafarullah Jamali visited Kabul on 12 January 2003 and vowed to fight terrorists together with the Afghans and both monitoring their respective borders more closely.

R.M. MUKIMJANOVA

Afkar

(in Urdu: thoughts, ideas) An *Urdu language literary journal, founded in 1945 in Bhopal (India). Since 1951, the journal was published in Karachi. Its main principles and tasks remained unchanged, that is, development of *Urdu literature, recognition of its social role and non-confessional nature, and publication of selected works by the best writers. The editors always attempted to attract writers and poets of different trends. Many famous Pakistani authors were first published in *Afkar*. The journal followed literary developments in various regions of Pakistan and publishes reviews, essays, and literary criticism. To mark anniversaries of major writers, *Afkar* devoted special issues to them. The journal commanded authority and a good reputation as an independent organ with a distinct policy of its own. It was intended for a broad circle of creative intelligentsia and academics.*

BIBLIOGRAPHY: *A.S. Sukhochev, 'Anniversary Issue of Afkar', Afro-Asian Peoples, No. 4, 1971, Moscow (in Russian).*

A.S. SUKHOCHEV

Afridi (also Apridi)

A *Pashtun tribe belonging to the Kerlarni group of tribes. They are divided into 'lowland' Afridi, who inhabit the Bara Valley in Kohat district, NWFP (the main clan: Adam Khel); and 'mountain' Afridi, who inhabit the political agency of Khyber (the main clans are Mir Ahmad Khel, Kuki Khel, Zakka Khel, Sepai or Sepahi).

BIBLIOGRAPHY: *L. Temirkhanow, 'Eastern Pashtuns and the New times (Ethno-Social Characteristics)', Moscow, 1984 (in Russian); 'Eastern Pashtuns: Main Issues of Modern History', Moscow, 1987 (in Russian); Akbar S. Ahmed, 'Social and Economic Changes in the Tribal Areas', Karachi, 1977.*

YU.V. GANKOVSKY

Aga Khan

(also: Agha Khan; *aga* is a Turkic word for elder brother, master; *Khan* is a Turkic word derived from the Mongolian *haqan, hagan* meaning ruler, master) A hereditary title for the *Ismaili spiritual leader, the word came to be used in Iran in the first half of the 19th century as a shortened name of the forty-sixth Ismaili imam, Agha Hasan Ali Shah (d. 1881). He served at the court of the Iranian Shah, Fath Ali Shah Qajar (1797–1834). Aga Khan was married to the shah's daughter and occupied important government posts (such as governor of Qum). In 1838, accompanied by numerous followers, he left Iran to travel through Afghanistan and *Sindh. He settled in Bombay in what was then *British India. After his death, the title of Aga Khan passed on to his son, the forty-seventh imam, Aga Khan II Aga Ali Shah (d. 1885). It was later transferred to his grandson, the forty-eighth imam, *Aga Khan III Sultan Muhammad Shah (d. 1975), and then on to the forty-ninth imam, *Aga Khan IV Prince Karim Aga (1936–).

BIBLIOGRAPHY: *M.D. Naoroji, A Brief History of Aga Khan, Bombay, 1903; A.Sh. Iqbal, The Prince Aga Khan: An Authentic Life Story, London, 1933.*

YU.V. GANKOVSKY

Aga Khan III, Sultan Muhammad Shah, Prince Sir (1877–1957)

Religious Leader. The forty-eighth hereditary spiritual leader of the Ismailis, he succeeded his father to the *Ismaili Imamate in 1885 and was awarded the title 'His Highness' by the British authorities in 1886. Aga Khan III was a member of the Imperial Legislative Council under the Viceroy Lord Minto (1906), and president of the *All-India Muslim League from 1907 to 1912. He became Vice-Chancellor of the Muslim University in Aligarh in 1921 and took part in the *Round Table Conference (1932) in London and the World Conference on Disarmament in Geneva in the same year. He was a member of the British Privy Council in 1934. In 1937, he became president of the League of Nations Assembly.

Prince Sir Sultan Muhammad Shah.

Among the many honours bestowed upon him are Commander of the Order of the Indian Empire, the Stars of India, Victoria, St Michael, and St George. He had two sons, Prince Ali Khan and Prince Sadruddin Khan.

WORKS: *'India in Transition', London-Bombay, 1918; 'The Memoirs of Aga Khan: World Enough and Time', London, 1954.*

YU.V. GANKOVSKY

Aga Khan IV, Karim Al-Hussaini, Prince (1936–)

Religious Leader. The forty-ninth hereditary spiritual leader of the *Ismailis, he was the son of Prince Ali Khan, the elder son of *Aga Khan III Sultan Muhammad

Shah and the Princess Tajudaullah, daughter of Lord Churston.

Aga Khan IV graduated from Harvard University, USA (1957). On his initiative, the Industrial Promotion Service of Pakistan (1966) and the International Aga Khan Foundation (1983) were founded. The latter institution and its related institutions are responsible for promoting and funding a number of outstanding social, educational and philanthropic projects in Pakistan. He has founded the Aga Khan University and Medical Centre in Karachi as a centre of excellence, as well as health care projects in different parts of the country. His titles include: His Highness, granted by Queen Elizabeth II in 1957; and His Imperial Highness, granted by the Shah of Iran in 1959.

YU.V. GANKOVSKY

Agent, Agency

See, Political Agency.

Agha, Wazir (1922–)

Writer. Hailing from Sargodha, Wazir Agha is a poet, critic and journalist, writing in *Urdu. He graduated from Government College, Lahore, with a degree in economics, and holds a Doctorate in Literature from Punjab University. Wazir Agha started writing poetry in his student days, when he came under the influence of the creative ideas of the founders of modern poetry in Pakistan: Miraji, Muhammad Din Taseer and Noon Meem *Rashid.

Wazir Agha uses European styles and forms in his work, such as ballads, sonnets and *vers libre*. He also experiments with rhymes and metres. From 1960 to 1963, he edited the left-wing literary journal *Adabi Duniya* (The World of Literature). He lives in Lahore and Sargodha, where he owns a publishing house.

Since 1966, he has edited the magazine **Auraq* (Pages). An accomplished literary scholar, he promotes new ideas and techniques in writing, while respecting classical literary traditions. His critical treatises are well known, not only in Pakistan and India, but also in Western academic circles. His work won him several prestigious literary prizes.

WORKS: *'Urdu Shairi ka Mizaj' (The Temperament of Urdu Poetry), Lahore, 1965; 'Chahak Uthi Lafzon ki Chagul' (Collected Works) Lahore, 1991; 'Selected Poems', Sargodha, 1978; 'Half a Century Later', Lahore, 1989 (in English).*

BIBLIOGRAPHY: *Muhammad Husain, 'Jadid Urdu Adab' (Contemporary Urdu Literature), Delhi, 1975; Anwar, Sadid, 'Wazir Agha, Ek Mutalia', Lahore, 1982.*

N.V. GLEBOV

Agha, Zubeida (1922–97)

Artist. Zubeida Agha was a painter and sculptor who lived and worked in Islamabad. She learned painting in Europe. Between 1949 and 1988, there were numerous personal exhibitions of her work in Pakistan and abroad. From 1961 to 1977, she remained director of the Modern Art Gallery in Rawalpindi. She was awarded the President's Medal for the best work of art in 1965, and the Shakir Ali Prize at the National Exhibition in Pakistan in 1982.

Zubeida Agha is regarded as the founder of abstract art in Pakistan although she painted only a few purely abstract canvases.

In earlier works, Agha stressed primarily on the line, intending to embody a certain abstract idea; colour played a secondary role. Her later works displayed masterful technique, smooth lines and carefully balanced drawing to create a rhythmic effect, combining form and colour in a single whole.

Her work and its influence on art in Pakistan caused her to be regarded among the best colourists in Pakistan.

WORKS: *'The Clown', 'A Bouquet of Flowers in a Vase Before a Window' (1977); 'A Red Flower, A Landscape' (1981).*

BIBLIOGRAPHY: *Paintings from Pakistan, Islamabad, 1988.*

N. FARRUKH

Agricultural research

Pakistan's economy is largely based on agriculture. This sector employs almost 44 per cent of the labour

Wheat Crop.

force and directly or indirectly supports 70 per cent of the population. *British India was endowed with many agricultural colleges and research institutions. Of these, Pakistan inherited an Agricultural College at Faisalabad, a Veterinary College at Lahore, and three small research stations. Major research organizations remained in India.

From the outset, the Government of Pakistan considered the development of agriculture important, but regarded it as a provincial responsibility. In 1948, a Food and Agriculture Committee was set up to coordinate provincial research. This committee was later reconstituted as a full-fledged Agriculture Research Council. The government's commitment to agricultural development has continued and grown since then. Almost 35 per cent of the total budget allocated for scientific research is provided to agriculture. At present, there are 64 major research institutions, four universities, and over 200 research stations/laboratories dedicated to agriculture. Due to its importance to Pakistan's population, the government has given agricultural research high priority, and various experts and scientists have been called upon to help solve important problems.

T.K. NAIM

Ahl-i-Hadith

(In Arabic: people of the tradition) A puritanical movement in South Asian Islam which began in 19th century *Punjab. Its founders, Siddiq Hasan Khan (d. 1890) and Nazir Husayn (d. 1902), were influenced by the reformist ideas of Shah Waliullah (1703-62) and the Indian *Wahhabis. They did not recognize the doctrine known as **Ijma*, a consensus of the major theologian jurists concerning questions not covered by the Quran and the *Sunna*. They believed that the holy books contain answers to every conceivable question, without exception. *Ahl-i-Hadith* reject or minimize the authority of the main Sunnite **madhabs* (denominations) and recognize each Muslim's right to **ijtihad*. They believe that each Muslim can find instructions in the **hadith* for public and private life. The word and deed of the Prophet (PBUH) are ideal guidance for each believer. Any innovation (*bidah*) not based on the sources approved by the theologians of *Ahl-i-Hadith*, are considered to be deviations from Islam.

The first annual meeting of the *Ahl-i-Hadith* in India was held in Delhi in 1912. The Central Society of *Ahl-i-Hadith* (*Markazi Jamiat-i Ahl-i-Hadith*), set up in Pakistan by its leaders with their centre in Lahore, has been playing an increasingly important role in the country's political life since the 1960s. In 1988, *Ahl-i-Hadith* participated in parliamentary elections within the coalition of Islamic Democratic Alliance (*Islami Jamhuri Ittehad*). They were represented in parliament by Prof. Sajid Mir.

A. NIYAZI

Ahl-i-Quran

(In Arabic: people of the Quran) A puritanical movement in South Asian Islam whose followers emphasized the absolute authority of the Quran. The movement was formed in the early 20th century.

One of the first preachers, Abdullah Chakralawi, believed that most *ahadiths (*plural of **hadith)* are unreliable (because they come from word-of-mouth) and, therefore, cannot be used as precedents for solving legal problems. Therefore socio-political development of Muslim societies must be based exclusively on the Quran, the perfect source of Muslim tradition.

Ahl-i-Quran recognize the right of Muslims to **ijtihad* and maintain that the Muslim holy book, by avoiding direct answers to many personal problems, gives one the freedom of choice in one's actions. In Pakistan, the followers of *Ahl-i-Quran* are united into a public organization known as *Tulu-i-Islam* (The Dawn of Islam).

The guiding leader of the movement, until recently, was Ghulam Ahmad Pervaiz. Parvaiz did not believe in the private ownership of the factors of productions (money, buildings or labour). According to him, they should be the responsibility of those who distribute according to the laws of God. He was careful to distance himself from the atheistic ideology of communism. Parvaiz asserts that neither capitalism nor priesthood were prevalent in the lifetime of the Holy Prophet (PBUH) and belong to the later dynastic kingdoms. *Tulu-i-Islam* is also the name of the journal which disseminates the views supported by *Ahl-i-Quran*.

M.R. KAZIMI

Ahmad, Aftab (1924–2005)

Literary Critic. Aftab Ahmad was educated at the Government College, Lahore, where he earned his MA in *English Literature in 1947. In 1965, he was awarded a PhD in Public Administration by George Washington University.

A career civil servant by profession, Dr Aftab Ahmad started writing literary criticism in 1946, with an article on 'The Romantic Poetry of Ghalib'; he later went on to become one of the most influential critics of *Ghalib. Aftab Ahmad was closely associated with the celebrated literary critic Muhammad Hasan *Askari and their correspondence forms one of the major tracts of informal criticism. From Ghalib, Aftab Ahmad turned his attention to Noon Meem *Rashid, who is also well known (like Ghalib) for his metaphysical themes and an innovative mode of expression. He then turned to another contemporary, Faiz Ahmad *Faiz, whose life and works form the subject of his latest work.

WORKS: *'Ghalib-e-Ashufta Nawa', Karachi, 1989; 'N.M. Rashid, Shakhs aur Shair', Lahore 1989; Isharat, Karachi, 1996; 'Faiz Ahmad Faiz, Shakhs aur Shair', Karachi, 1999.*

M.R. KAZIMI

Ahmad, Aziz (1913–78)

Writer. Aziz Ahmad was born in Barabanki, India, and was educated in Hyderabad (India) at the Osmania University. After teaching there, he joined the Information Ministry of Pakistan. In 1957 he joined the School of Oriental and African Studies, University of London as a teacher. In 1962 he moved to the University of Toronto, Canada eventually retiring from there as Professor of Islamic Studies.

Aziz Ahmad was an outstanding literary critic in *Urdu with landmark publications on *Iqbal and Progressive Literature. He was one of the more successful novelists in Urdu, but even established a name through his English language contributions to South Asian studies, specially in the religious, social, and cultural spheres.

WORKS: *'Studies in Islamic Culture in the Indian Environment', Oxford, 1964; 'Islamic Modernism in India and Pakistan', Oxford, 1967.*

BIBLIOGRAPHY: *Milton Israel and N.K. Wagle (eds.) 'Islamic Society and Culture: Studies in Honour of Aziz Ahmad', New Delhi, 1983.*

M.R. KAZIMI

Ahmad, Jamiluddin (1914–70)

Political Writer. Jamiluddin Ahmad passed his MA in English from Aligarh Muslim University in 1936. He was a member of the All India Muslim Students Federation and the *All-India Muslim League. He was personally close to the founders of Pakistan, and in 1942 and 1960 published two volumes of the 'Speeches and Writings of M.A. Jinnah'. After partition, he joined Emerson College, Multan as lecturer, but soon became Public Relations Officer to Liaquat Ali *Khan, the then prime minister of Pakistan. From 1968 to 1970, he served as the co-editor of 'Contemporary Affairs'.

WORKS: *'Glimpses of Quaid-i-Azam', Karachi, 1960 (ed.); 'Quaid-i-Azam as seen by his contemporaries', Karachi, 1966; 'The Creation of Pakistan', Lahore, 1976; 'Early Phase of Muslim Political Movement', Lahore, 1960; 'Middle Phase of Muslim Political Movement', Lahore, 1969; 'Final Phase of Struggle for Pakistan', Karachi, 1964.*

YU.V. GANKOVSKY

Ahmad, Mushtaq (1919–98)

Political Writer. A Pakistani political scientist, historian and journalist, Mushtaq Ahmad graduated from the Department of Economics and Political Sciences, Bombay University, then studied at the London School of Economics, London and at Columbia University, New York. For more than ten years he was editor of the *Morning News* (Karachi).

WORKS: *'The United Nations and Pakistan', Karachi, 1955; 'Government and Politics in Pakistan', Karachi, 1963; 'Pakistan's Foreign Policy', Karachi, 1968; 'Politics Without Social Change', Karachi, 1971.*

YU.V. GANKOVSKY

Ahmadiya

Religious Sect. Founded in *Punjab in 1889 by Mirza Ghulam Ahmad, who is revered by his followers as **Mahdi*, a prophet and a reincarnation of Krishna and Jesus Christ. Following the death of Mirza Ghulam Ahmad in 1908, the sect was led by his successors (*Khalifahs*). From 1898 to 1947, the city of Qadian (Punjab state, India) was the religious centre of this sect and the seat of its authority. After 1947, it moved to the town of Rabwah (Punjab Province, Pakistan).

The sect is based on strict centralism. All members donate no less than 4 per cent of their annual income to the sects fund. Their doctrine rejects the finality of Muhammad's (PBUH) prophethood which inspired the harsh criticism of orthodox **ulema*, both **Shia* and **Sunni*. Ahmadiya also preach the equality of all people before God, the peaceful nature of *jihad,* which they regard as a movement for the spread of Ahmadiya teaching, and obedience to authorities.

In 1914, a group of Lahori Ahmadiyas refused to recognize the leadership of Nuruddin, the first successor of Mirza Ghulam Ahmad, and broke away from the sect. Though they refused to recognize Ahmad as a prophet, they saw him as a reformer and a renovator of Islam (*mujaddid*).

The Ahmadiyas were repeatedly and voilently denounced in Pakistan in the years 1953, 1974, and 1984. In 1974 they were proclaimed a non-Muslim religious minority.

There are more than two hundred Ahmadiya centers in Europe, Africa, Asia, Oceania and America conducting active missionary work.

YU.V. GANKOVSKY

Ahmed, Akbar S. (1943–)

Sociologist. Salahuddin Ahmed Akbar is a sociologist and ethnologist who studied the *Pashtun tribes of Pakistan. He graduated from the University of Punjab in Lahore, then continued his education in Britain (at the universities of Birmingham, Cambridge, and London). In 1971, he joined the *Civil Service of Pakistan.

WORKS: *'Millennium and Charisma Among Pathans', London, 1976; 'Pakhtun Economy and Society', London, 1980; 'Religion and Politics in Muslim Society', Cambridge, 1983; 'Discovering Islam', London, 1988; 'Jinnah, Pakistan and Islamic Identity: Searching for Saladin', Karachi, 1997.*

YU.V. GANKOVSKY

Ahmed, Nazir, 'Deputy' (1836–1912)

Writer. The pioneer of the *Urdu language novel, Nazir Ahmed was born into a landowner's family. He earned his college education in Delhi, and was influenced by the reformist views of Sir Syed Ahmad *Khan and the French enlightenment.

Nazir wrote some of the first Urdu novels: the didactic duo *Mirat al-Urus* (The Bride's Mirror, 1869) and *Binat an-Nash* (Ursa Major, 1872), about the necessity of female education and emancipation of women; *Taubat an-Nasuh* (Nasuh's Repentance, 1877), an apology for traditional family ethics; and *Afsana-i-Mubtala* (The Story of Mubtala, 1885), denouncing polygamy and male despotism in a Muslim family.

In the novel *Ibn al-Waqt* (The Opportunist, 1884), Nazir Ahmed advocates mastering European culture but cautions against blind imitation of the British. His novels laid the basis of enlightenment in Urdu literature of the time.

In his later years, Nazir Ahmed was mainly engaged in translation and compiling commentaries on religious texts. He was awarded the title of *Shams al-Ulema* (The Sun of the Learned), the degree of Doctor of Law from Edinburgh University (1902), and Doctor of Oriental Studies from the Punjab University (1910).

BIBLIOGRAPHY: *A.S. Sukhochev, 'From the Dastan to the Novel', Moscow, 1971 (in Russian); K.K. Khullar, 'Urdu Nawal ka Nigarkhana' (A Gallery of Urdu Novels), Delhi, 1973; E.A. Arshad, 'Nazir Ahmad ki Nawalnigari' (Nazir Ahmad's Novels), Patna, 1984.*

A.S. SUKHOCHEV

Ahrar

(In Arabic: free, independent, liberal) A religio-communal party in Pakistan; (*see also* Majlis-i-Ahrar-i-Islam).

YU.V. GANKOVSKY

Ahson, S.M., Vice-Admiral (1920–90)

Naval Officer. S.M. Ahson was *Aide de Camp* to the Viceroy Lord Mountbatten, then to *Quaid-i-Azam Mohammed Ali *Jinnah. He eventually rose to be commander-in-chief of the Pakistan Navy. He was Governor of *East Pakistan during the 1971 crisis. Contrary to the consideration of his peers, Ahson favoured a political solution, not a military one, to the inter-wing problem that was later to split the country (*see*, Bangladesh-Pakistan Relations). He resigned when his advice was not heeded.

YU.V. GANKOVSKY

Akhund, akhun

A Muslim title for a spiritual leader, teacher, guardian, and trustee.

YU.V. GANKOVSKY

Alghoza

Musical Instrument. A type of double flute used in Pakistan and India. The instrument is constructed with two wooden tubes that are connected to a common mouthpiece. It is used in both solo and ensemble performances. Popular in *Sindh and the *Punjab, the *alghoza* is often used by shepherds.

I. PIRACHA

Ali, Chaudhri Mohammad (1905–80)

Prime Minister of Pakistan from 1955 to 1956. A graduate of the Punjab University in Lahore, he joined the elite Finance Services of *British India. As a senior Finance Ministry official, he guided Liaquat Ali *Khan of the All-India Muslim League.

He became Pakistan's Minister of Finance in 1951, and was elected in 1955 to the second *Constituent Assembly. In August 1955, he became prime minister, leading a coalition government of the *Muslim League and the United Front. Chaudhri Mohammad Ali presented Pakistan's first Constitution in 1956.

Chaudhri Muhammad Ali, Prime Minister of Pakistan (1955–56).

WORKS: *'The Emergence of Pakistan', New York, 1964.*

BIBLIOGRAPHY: *Safdar Mahmud, 'Pakistan: Political Roots and Development', Karachi, 2000.*

YU.V. GANKOVSKY

Ali, Chaudhri Rahmat (1895–1951)

Statesman. The founder and leader of the Pakistan National Movement in 1933. He came from a family of small landowners and graduated from the University of Punjab. Starting in 1915, he published the journal 'The Crescent' for several years.

He received degrees from Cambridge and Dublin Universities. In 1930, Chaudhri proposed to establish an independent Muslim state in the northwest of British India. He named the proposed state 'Pakistan'. He visited Lahore and Karachi in 1948.

WORKS: *'Now or Never: Are We to Live or Perish Forever'? Cambridge, 1933; 'Pakistan, The Fatherland of the Pakistan Nation', Cambridge, 1947.*

BIBLIOGRAPHY: *Yu.V. Gankovsky, 'On the Origin of the Name Pakistan', Toponymy of the East, Moscow, 1969 (in Russian); Khan A. Ahmad, 'The Founder of Pakistan, Through Trial or Triumph', London, 1942; K.K. Aziz (ed.), 'Complete Works of Rahmat Ali', 2 Vols., Islamabad, 1979.*

YU.V. GANKOVSKY

Ali, Malik Barkat (1886–1946)

Statesman. Educated at Forman Christian College, Lahore, and obtaining his LLB (Punjab University) in 1916, Malik Barkat Ali was to become a member of Sir Fazle *Husain's Progressive Muslim League and a delegate to the All Parties Convention in 1928. When the *All-India Muslim League was reorganized, he became its Vice-President.

Malik Barkat Ali was one of only two candidates (along with Raja Ghazanfar Ali Khan) to be returned on the *Muslim League ticket to the Punjab Legislative Assembly, and the only one not to cross benches. He co-drafted the Jinnah-Sikander Pact, but differed sharply with Sir Sikander *Hayat's interpretation of the document. He asked the speaker of the Punjab Assembly to allot him a seat separate from the *Unionist Party benches, since he did not feel that the Unionists and AIML were one party (4 November 1940).

He remained the mainstay of the All-India Muslim League in *Punjab throughout the Unionist term of office. In 1946, he was elected for the Eastern Town Committee, but died soon after.

BIBLIOGRAPHY: *Mohammad Rafique Afzal (ed.), 'Malik Barkat Ali: His Life and Writings', Lahore, 1969; Ashique Husain Batalvi, 'Hamari Qaumi Jidd o Jahad January 1940 Sey December 1942 Tak', Lahore, 1974.*

M.R. KAZIMI

Ali, Muhammad, Maulana (1878–1931)

Statesman/Poet/Writer. Maulana Muhammad Ali studied at Aligarh, and later at the Universities of Allahabad and Oxford. He worked as a civil servant in the states of Rampur and Baroda from 1902 to 1910. He was an active figure in the *Muslim League, founder of the weeklies, 'Comrade' (Calcutta, 1911) and *Hamdard* (Delhi, 1913) and one of the organizers and leaders of the *Khilafat Movement. He participated in the 1930 *Round Table Conference in London.

WORKS: *'Writings and Speeches of Maulana Muhammad Ali', Lahore, s.a.; 'My Life: A Fragment', ed. by Afzal Iqbal, Lahore, 1942.*

BIBLIOGRAPHY: *G. Allana, Our Freedom Fighters, Karachi, 1969.*

YU.V. GANKOVSKY

Ali, Saiyyid Amir (1849–1928)

Historian/Lawyer. Amir Ali belonged to a noble family who had moved to India from Iran at the invitation of Nasiruddin Muhammad Shah (1719-48). He began his education in Calcutta and completed it in London.

From 1883 to 1878, he was a Member of the Bengal Legislative Council and from 1883 to 1885 of the Imperial Legislative Council of India. He served as a Judge of the High Court from 1890 to 1904, and as a Privy Councillor in 1909.

Amir Ali shared the reformist ideas of Sir Syed Ahmad *Khan and supported the modernization of the

Muslim community. The Central National Mohammedan Association, famous for its educational activities, was organized and headed by Amir Ali from 1877 to 1904.

His historical works expounding the humanitarian nature of Islam and Christianity exerted a profound influence, not only on the Muslim intelligentsia of India, Egypt and other eastern countries but on Western European Islamic studies as well. Amir Ali attached particular importance to the study of Islamic ethics, and insisted that Islam contains basic moral values which have been operative throughout the course of history, and are applicable to all nations and eras.

WORKS: *'Memoirs and Other Writings of Sayyid Amir Ali', Lahore, 1968; 'The Spirit of Islam', Calcutta, 1902; 'The Life and Teachings of Muhammad', Lahore, 1891; 'A Short History of Muhammadan Law', Vols. I-II, Calcutta, 1892-94; 'A Short History of the Saracens', London, 1889.*

A. NIYAZI

Ali, Shakir (1916–75)

Artist. A leading figure in the modern art movement in Pakistan, Shakir Ali was born in Rampur. From 1938 to 1944, he attended an art school in Bombay, where he received a diploma in wall painting. He also studied in Britain and worked in France.

Shakir Ali was influenced by Cubism and other modern trends in painting. He taught in Czechoslovakia, where he was greatly affected by Julius Fucik's book *Reportage with a Noose Round the Neck* and by the poetry of the German poet Rilke. In 1952, Shakir Ali headed the National College of Arts in Lahore, a post that permitted him to powerfully influence two generations of young, aspiring artists. His work opened up the epoch of experiments and innovations in the country's painting. His art asserted basic human values. The artist's style took shape by the mid-1960s. He worked a great deal on colour, form and line. He also saw great potential in calligraphy and painted some of his most outstanding works, using it as a structural basis. Decorative elements in his work are frequently linked with calligraphic forms. He executed several monumental panels on various themes e.g., *A Pastoral*, a panel in the Nuclear Energy Centre in the form of illustrated pages of a manuscript. Shakir Ali was awarded the Presidents Medal for the best work of art in 1962, and the *Sitara-i-Imtiaz* (Star of Distinction) in 1971. In 1975, a museum named after him was opened in Lahore; exhibitions of young Pakistani artists are staged there.

Some of Shakir Ali's works are *A Still Life* (1952), *Calligraphy* (1969), and *A Nude* (1970).

BIBLIOGRAPHY: *'Paintings from Pakistan', Islamabad, 1988.*

N.K. KARPOVA

Ali, Shaukat, Maulana (1873–1938)

Statesman. A public figure and politician of *British India, Shaukat Ali was the brother of Maulana Muhammad *Ali. Educated at Aligarh, he served as an Indian Civil Service Officer in the United Provinces from 1896 to 1913. From 1913 to 1914 he was secretary to *Aga Khan III.

Ali participated in the publication of the 'Comrade' and *Hamdard* weeklies. He served as President of the First Khilafat Conference in 1919 and was a delegate to the All-Parties Muslim Conference in Delhi in 1929. He was also chosen as a delegate to the London *Round Table Conference (1930–31) and organized the 1932 World Muslim Conference in Jerusalem. Shaukat Ali was a noted leader of the *All-India Muslim League.

YU.V. GANKOVSKY

Allah Bakhsh, Ustad (1885–1978)

Artist. Allah Bakhsh was an informally trained painter whose first personal exhibition was staged in Lahore in 1903. Between 1904 and 1932, Allah Bakhsh taught and painted. In 1960, he was awarded the *Tamgha-i-Pakistan* (Pakistan Medal). He belongs to the older generation of traditionalist artists, trained in the traditions of the Mughal school of *miniature and ancient Indian wall paintings.

Allah Bakhsh's works depict the history and culture of the peoples of the *Punjab. His trademark is a clearly defined main figure, both in his portraits and his genre scenes, with many figures against the background of a landscape stressing the subject's mood. The way the Ustad positions some figures, as if they are going beyond the frame, gives the impression that the figure is in action. Also characteristic of Allah Bakhsh's works is a richness of colour scheme, always in tune with the nature of the action. Light modelling of faces and the use of deep shadows in his figure painting makes the Ustad's art somewhat similar to wall paintings. He painted portraits in the 'realistic' manner: his male images are monumental, while the female ones (in the best traditions of the miniature) are very feminine and beautiful.

Some of the main works of Allah Bakhsh are *A Poet in the Garden*, *The Blind Singer*, *Ploughing with Oxen*, and *In the Family of Weavers*.

BIBLIOGRAPHY: *'Paintings from Pakistan', Islamabad, 1988.*

N.K. KAZPOVA

Allama

(in Arabic: learned man, sage, erudite) An honorary title Muslims use which precedes a proper name.

YU.V. GANKOVSKY

Alliance for Restoration of Democracy

(ARD) The Alliance for Restoration of Democracy is an opposition group in Pakistan. It was created to campaign for the return to civilian rule after the 1999 military coup by General Pervez *Musharraf. Two main political parties involved are PML-N (Pakistan Muslim League Nawaz Group) and PPPP (*Pakistan People's Party Parliamentarians).

M.R. KAZIMI

All-India Muslim League

(AIML) The most influential political party in the history of Pakistan. It was organized on 30 December 1906. The first session of the League was held in December 1907 in Karachi. The League emerged as a political organization representing the interest of the well-to-do upper and middle strata of the Muslim community in *British India. In 1927 the League had only 1,330 members. At its twenty-seventh annual session in March 1940 the League called for the formation of two independent Muslim states in the northern and eastern part of the South Asian subcontinent (*see* Lahore Resolution, 1940), which helped the League to become a mass organization. In April 1946, in Delhi, the League proclaimed its aim of founding a unified independent Muslim state, Pakistan. It headed the movement for the establishment of Pakistan. In 1947 Pakistan and India were divided. The *Pakistan Muslim League became the leading political party of Pakistan, By 1953, however, the league was divided into various different factions. Currently, PML (Quaid-i-Azam) is in power and PML (Nawaz) is in opposition.

BIBLIOGRAPHY: *L.R. Gordon-Polonskaya, 'Moslem Trends in the Social Life of India and Pakistan', Moscow, 1963 (in Russian); A.G. Belsky, 'Moslem Communalism in India: Origins, Ideology, Policies', Moscow, 1988 (in Russian); 'Foundations of Pakistan—All-India Muslim League Documents: 1906-1947', Vols I-II, Karachi, 1970; Lal Bahadur, 'The Muslim League', Agra, 1954.*

A. NIYAZI

All-Pakistan Federation of Labour

(APFL) Founded in 1955 by Rahmatullah Khan Durrani and headquartered in Peshawar, the Federation enjoys the greatest influence in the *North West Frontier Province. In the late 1980s, it had a membership of some 380,000. The federation united 600 trade unions of the country. It is a member of the International Confederation of Free Trade Unions.

M.YU. MOROZOVA

All-Pakistan Federation of Trade Unions

(APFTU) It emerged in 1963. In 1989, the APFTU united about 600,000 workers and employees in textile factories, oil fields, pharmaceutical factories, machine-building and food industries, mines, etc. Located in Lahore, it has branches in Rawalpindi, Peshawar, Faisalabad, Multan and Karachi. The Federation has a women's and a young people's division. It has no links with political parties and is a member of the International Confederation of Free Trade Unions.

M.YU. MOROZOVA

All-Pakistan Trade Union Organization

(APTUO) Early in 1989, it united 123 trade unions representing workers and employees of the road-building and machine-building industries, as well as state banks and financial organizations. The organization enjoys the greatest support in the *Sindh province. It actively supports general political demands, including the completion of the country's democratization.

D.B. NOVOSYOLOV

All-Pakistan Women's Association

(APWA) One of the oldest organizations for women, the APWA was set up in 1950. Begum Raana Liaquat Ali *Khan (1905-90), the wife of the country's first Prime Minister Liaquat Ali *Khan, was its founder and lifelong Honorary President. Its headquarters are in Karachi; it publishes a monthly, *The APWA Bulletin*. According to its charter, any woman in Pakistan can join it regardless of her religion and race. Its aim is to involve Pakistani women in the country's development; improve women's position by upgrading their legal, political, social, and economic status; contribute to social, educational, and cultural programmes; and promote mutual understanding and cooperation between nations.

The association holds its national conferences once every three years. The 1985 conference adopted a resolution to hold a 'Decade of the Pakistani Woman' (1985-95). The 1988 Conference discussed 'Crimes Against Women' (abuse of women, forced prostitution, women prisoners, abduction of women and so on).

The National Executive Committee (NEC) is the leading body of APWA; the sessions are held annually. The activity is conducted through sections: financial, organizational, informational, cultural and educational, production, agricultural, legal, medical, youth, and international.

The association subsists on membership dues and donations, charity campaigns conducted by the association, government subsidies, and help from international donor organizations.

The association has schools, literacy centres, vocational training courses for women, medical centres, family planning centres, pre-school establishments and folk crafts shops. In 1968, the APWA was awarded the UNESCO bronze medal for its efforts in inculcating literacy among the adult population.

The association has branches in all Pakistani provinces and large cities and also abroad—in London, Washington, and Colombo. It enjoys the consultative status of a non-governmental organization of the second category in the UN and cooperates with ECOSOC and UNICEF. It maintains active relations with women activists abroad, is a member of the International Women Alliance, the International Women's Council, the World Association of Peasant Women and the Universal Federation of Women Clubs.

F.A. ABDRAKHMANOVA

Alvi, Hatim (1898–1976)

Statesman. Regarded as one of the builders of modern Karachi, where he served as mayor from 1938 to 1939, Hatim Alvi joined the *Muslim League and became a confidant of M.A. *Jinnah. He alerted the latter when G.M. *Syed was set to move a no-confidence motion against the Sindh Muslim League Ministry of Sir Ghulam Husayn *Hidayatullah and was appointed a member of the Sindh Muslim League election committee. After independence, he played the role of senior statesman.

BIBLIOGRAPHY: *Suhail Zaheer Lari, 'A History of Sindh', Karachi, 1994.*

M.R. KAZIMI

American Institute of Pakistan Studies

(AIPS) At Villanova University in Pennsylvania, USA. The Institute was inaugurated by Prime Minister Z.A. *Bhutto on 21 September 1973. It is administered by a board of trustees representing thirty-seven US universities and the Pakistan American Foundation. The Pakistan government and the US Education Department provide major financing. The Smithsonian Institute in Washington, DC and others also subsidize the institute. Experts in Pakistan studies plan the AIPS research work (including R. Braibanti, Hafeez *Malik, L. *Ziring, Stanley *Wolpert, Craig *Baxter, J.H. Korson, and Charles *Kennedy). The institute is represented in Pakistan by the Director of the US Education Foundation. It regularly delegates research groups and specialists (including professors from US universities), and conducts field research on current social, economic, political and cultural-linguistic problems. The AIPS cooperates with the leading Pakistani universities and scientific centres and frequently organizes seminars and conferences on Pakistan.

YU.V. GANKOVSKY

American-Pakistan Relations

See, US-Pakistan Relations.

Amin, Nurul (1893–1974)

Statesman. Nurul Amin belonged to Mymensingh and came into political prominence as convener of the Bengal Muslim League Committee, formed to negotiate the modalities and constitutional framework of a united and independent Bengal with Indian National Congress and Hindu Mahasabha members. He became Chief Minister of East Bengal after Sir Khwaja *Nazimuddin was inducted as the Governor-General of Pakistan. Nurul Amin was the Chief Minister when the Bengali Language Movement erupted into riots. He responded with repression, which permitted the Bengali nationalists to gain popularity. He also arrested a number of *Awami League members on the eve of the 1954 elections. This loss of popularity resulted in defeat in his own seat in the elections.

In the 1970 nationwide elections, Nurul Amin was one of only two non-Awami League candidates, who were returned from *East Pakistan. He was briefly designated as prime minister by General Yahya *Khan in 1971. With the secession of East Pakistan, and transfer of power to the PPP, Nurul Amin was designated Vice-President of Pakistan until the *Constitution of 1973 was enacted.

M.R. KAZIMI

Amri

A pre-Harappan or early *Harappan archaeological culture (first half of the 3rd millennium BC), in the *Indus Valley in *Sindh, Pakistan. It gets its name from a multi-level settlement near the village of Amri discovered in 1929 by N. Majumdar on the Indus western bank opposite *Chanhu-Daro. In 1959, a French archaeologist J.M. Casal carried on the diggings. He studied two tells: Tell A (12 metres high) and Tell B (4 metres high), and identified five cultural periods (I-V): I A-D—culture A; II A-B—intermediate mixed level; III A-C—Harappan cultural level; III related to Jhukar culture; IV related to *Jhangar culture; V–historical time. In culture A, dwellings were registered in I B-D period. Rectangular houses (16 x 3 m) were divided into several rooms. The modelled and wheeled pottery had black and red painting on it arranged into geometric patterns and these colours and motifs characterize Amri ware. Implements were made of bone, copper and stone; shell bangles and terra cotta figurines were also found. Faunal remains include bones of domesticated (oxen and goat) and wild (gazelle) animals. Twenty-odd settlements with A pottery were discovered. The characteristic Amri style can sometimes be found in Balochistan; there are analogies with the *Kot Diji culture. Pakistani archaeologists are now making progress in studying A.

BIBLIOGRAPHY: *J.M. Casal, 'Fouilles d'Amri', Vols. 1, 2, Paris, 1961; D.P. Agrawal, 'The Archaeology of India', Scandinavian Institute of Asian Studies monograph series, No. 46, London, 1982; M.R. Mughal, 'The Early Harappan Period in the Greater Indus Valley and Northern Balochistan', A. Arbor, 1970.*

B.A. LITVINSKY

Anglo-Pakistan Relations

Foreign relations between Pakisan and England. Dealings between the UK and Pakistan embrace economic, political, military, cultural, and other spheres. Initiated during colonial times, England inherited predominant positions in Pakistani foreign trade which were retained throughout the 1940s and 1950s. British economic aid was relatively modest; nevertheless, it supplied most of Pakistan's arms, at least until the 1950s.

From 1947 to 1956, Pakistan remained a dominion of the British Commonwealth. In 1956 Pakistan became a republic but remained a member till 1971. In January 1972, Pakistan left the Commonwealth as a protest against Britain's recognition of Bangladesh as an independent state. In July 1973, Zulfikar Ali *Bhutto visited London, and in January 1978, British Prime Minister James Callaghan visited Pakistan. In the 1980s, due to the basically common positions of the two countries regarding the Soviet invasion of Afghanistan, Anglo-Pakistani relations were greatly improved and consolidated. Regular contacts between state leaders resumed and the two countries coordinated their positions in the UN on the Afghan War. In October 1989, Pakistan restored its membership in the Commonwealth under Benazir *Bhutto, the then prime minister. Anglo-Pakistan relations were strained mildly when Pakistan responded to the Indian nuclear tests of 1998, and during the Kargil crisis of 1999. When the military government took over in 1999, relations became almost hostile. In the aftermath of the 11 September 2001 terrorist attacks on the US, relations have thawed somewhat but remain ambiguous.

R.M. MUKIMJANOVA

Anglo-Sikh Wars

A series of wars between the *Sikh State in the *Punjab and the British East-India Company. The First Sikh War (November 1845-March 1846) began with the Battle of Mudki and Firuzpur (eastern Punjab). The Sikh army dealt heavy losses to the British forces but, thanks to the betrayal of Sikh commanders *Sardar* Lal Singh and *Sardar* Tej Singh, who failed to pursue the retreating British army, General Hugh Gough avoided complete defeat. The decisive battle took place on 10 February 1846 near Sabraon. Lal Singh informed the British command about the whereabouts of the Sikh army and in the heat of the battle he defected to the other side. Thus, the Sikh army lost the battle. On 20 February 1846, the British army occupied Lahore. On 9 March, a peace treaty was signed ceding the lands between the rivers *Sutlej and *Beas to the British East-India Company. The Sikh Chieftain was to pay 15 million rupees to the British, reduce his army to 32,000 men and recognize the independence of Maharaja Gulab Singh, the ruler of Jammu, who had helped the British during the war.

The Second Anglo-Sikh war was fought from January to March 1849. In the Battle of Chilianwala (1 January), *Sardar* Sher Singh succeeded in stopping the British army but in the decisive battle of Gujrat (21 February), the Sikh army was defeated. By the treaty of 23 March 1849, the *Punjab was annexed to British rule.

BIBLIOGRAPHY: *V.I. Kochnev, 'The Sikh State and England', Moscow, 1969 (in Russian); J.A. Cunningham, 'History of the Sikhs', Calcutta, 1903; S.S. Thorburn, 'The Punjab in Peace and War', London, 1904.*

YU.V. GANKOVSKY

Anis, Mir Babar Ali (1803–74)

Poet. Anis was an *Urdu language poet, representing the Lucknow school of poetry, who worked in the genre of the Shia elegy—the **marsiya*. He belonged to a famous dynasty of Urdu poets and was the grandson of Mir Husain, as well as a disciple of his father, the poet Khaliq. In Anis's poetry, the *marsiya* themes of the martyrdom of Imam Husain (626-684) in Karbala were canonized as objects for poetic assimilation. Anis made an important contribution to the art of ritual recital of *marsiyas* during the remembrance days of *Ashura* by introducing what is now the accepted method of vocal performance of a *marsiya*. This tradition, once introduced by Anis, has had many followers, including those in *Urdu literature. His followers include his brother Munis; his son Nafis and great grandson, Arif.

WORKS: *'Anis ke Marsie', Vols. 1, 2, Delhi, 1980; 'Ruh-i-Anis', Allahabad, 1951; 'Marasi-i-Anis', ed. Nayab Naqvi, Lahore, 1959.*

BIBLIOGRAPHY: *A.H. Sharar, 'Lucknow: The Last Phase of an Oriental Culture', London, 1975; Jafar Ali Khan Asar, 'Anis ki Marsianigari' (Anis's Elegiac poems), Lucknow, 1951; Shibli Numani, 'Muazana-i-Anis-o-Dabir' (Comparative Study of Anis and Dabir), Delhi, reprint 1982; Fazal-i-Imam, 'Anis Shahsiyat-o-Fan' (The Life and Work of Anis), Jaipur, 1984. 'Mah-i-Nau' Mir Anis Number (ed.) Fazl. Qadeer Karachi, 1972; 'Risai Adab', Mir Anis Number ed. Hilal Naqvi, Karachi, April 1997.*

A.A. SUVOROVA

Arabian Sea

(Ancient name: Erythrean Sea) A semi-closed sea in the Indian Ocean between the two peninsulas—Arabian and Indian. The south-western border passes from Cape Hafoon (Somalia) through Addu atoll, along the western edge of Maldive and Laccadive islands up to the lighthouse Sada-Chivzhad (14°48' N. lat, 74°06' E. long). Its area is about 4,832,000 sq.km., maximum depth—5,803 metres. The two largest bays are Aden (Yemen) and Oman. The Arabian Sea is divided into two large basins—the Arabian (over 5,300 metres deep) and the Somalian in the south-west (up to 4,600 metres deep). The two basins of the Arabian Sea are bordered by two underwater plateaus (less than 1,800 metres deep). The sea is crossed by the oceanic range which is 3,600 metres deep in the rift. The shelf width of the Indian coast is 120 km. and the depth is 90 metres. The shore is low-lying. Near the Indus delta, the shelf is indented with underwater canyons. The solid flow of the *Indus is 435 million tons per year. In the eastern part of the Arabian Sea, the suspension content increases to 0.5-1.2 million particles per litre. On the Makran coast, the shelf narrows to 35 km., and continues to narrow towards the west. The shoreline is steep and rocky, reaching a depth of up to 2,750 metres. The mainland slope is covered with sediments of terrigenous nature, while the hollows are covered with red clay. The sedimentary layer diminishes from 2,500 metres in the northern section of the Arabian basin to 500 metres in its southern section. The bottom relief was formed in the Mesozoic (248-65 million years ago) and Cainozoic (66 million years ago till today) eras. A considerable portion of the bottom was formed during the Pliocene. The climate is tropical monsoon. Precipitation ranges from 25 to 125 mm. in the west up to 3,000 mm. in the east. Minimal temperature of the surface layer is 24-25°C in January and February, the maximum temperature is sometimes over 28°C in June. Salt content during the south-west monsoon is less than 35 per cent and during the north-eastern monsoon it exceeds 36 per cent. The more salty waters of the Red Sea have been observed to intrude into the Arabian Sea at a depth of 200-4,000 metres. In winter (from November till March), the north-eastern monsoon drift flows along the Indian coast and then turns to the south. At 10°N. lat., it turns to the west and continues to flow into the Aden bay and along the Somalian coast. During the south-western summer monsoon season, a strong Somalian current is observed. At 10°N. lat., near the Indian coast, it joins the south-western monsoon drift stream. The tides are uneven for 12-hours up to 5.1 metres. There are oil deposits on the Indian shelf near Gulf of Cambay Khambat, up to the Bombay Region. The Arabian Sea is one of the most productive aquatories of the world. Tuna, sardinella, flying fish, sea-cod, southern herring, reef fish, and shrimp are abundant. The fishing industry is mainly concentrated in the shelf regions. The main ports are Bombay (India), Karachi (Pakistan), and Aden (Yemen).

BIBLIOGRAPHY: *The Indian Ocean, Leningrad, 1982 (in Russian); V.O. Kanayev, Indian Ocean, Moscow, 1975 (in Russian); Oceanographic Encyclopaedia, Leningrad, 1974 (in Russian).*

N.N. ALEXEEVA

Arain

One of the most numerous and influential clans in the province of *Punjab. Before the 12th century, the Arain were an agricultural Hindu caste; during the 12th through 16th centuries, they converted to Islam. They are divided into 80-90 sub-groups. According to Arain legends, they moved to Punjab from the lower reaches of the *Indus (one of the Arain sub-groups in *Bahawalpur call themselves *Sindhi) or from Rajasthan. Some of the sub-groups claim Arabic descent (e.g., Multani), others claim *Rajput origin (Bhaddu, Janjua). For this reason they do not marry members of other sub-groups. The wealthy landowners of the Arain caste also play an active role in Punjab's political life.

BIBLIOGRAPHY: *'A Glossary of the Tribes and Castes of the Punjab and the North West Frontier Province', Vol. II, Lahore, 1978.*

YU.V. GANKOVSKY

Arbab

(Arabic, plural of *rabb*: master, ruler, owner) The clan elder; village headman among *Pashtuns; respectful address to a senior official; landowner.

YU.V. GANKOVSKY

Arif, Iftikhar (1943–)

Poet. An *Urdu language poet, who graduated from Lucknow University with a degree in sociology, before moving to Pakistan in 1965. From 1983 to 1990, Arif lived in London. He is the Honorary Secretary of the Urdu Centre (*Urdu Markaz*). His first collection of poetry was called *Mehr-i-Do Nim* (The Split Sun). He is a great admirer of Faiz Ahmad *Faiz.

The main poetic forms in which Arif writes, are **ghazals* and **nazm*. He was awarded the Pakistan Writers' Guild Prize (1984), the Faiz Ahmad Faiz International Prize (1989) and the Pakistan State Prize (1990). In 1991, he returned to Pakistan. Currently, he is Chairman of the *Pakistan Academy of Letters in Islamabad.

WORKS: *'Mehr-i-Do Nim', London, 1983; 'The Twelfth Player,' London, 1989; 'Harf-i-Baryab', New Delhi, 1996.*

BIBLIOGRAPHY: *A. Suvorova, Iftikhar Arif, 'Inostrannaya Literature', No. 5, 1991; G. Narang, 'Saniha-i-Kerbela Batour Sheri-Istiara', Delhi, 1986; A. Schimmel, 'Preface to The Twelfth Player', London; 1989. 'Jawaz-i-Iftikhar' (ed.) Shima Masjid, Lahore, 2000.*

A.A. SUVOROVA

Arkan

(Arabic: support) Plural of **Rukn*.

Artistic Ceramics

This is one of the most ancient crafts in Pakistan. It was already highly developed at the time of the *Harappan civilization. Vessels ornamented with chasing, stuck-on reliefs, and paintings have been recovered along with ceramic figurines of the mother goddess, of humans and animals, toys, and beads. Unglazed ceramic items are traditionally manufactured in Pakistan for daily use for storing water, oils, groats, and for making some dishes and for ceremonies, festivals, rituals, and weddings. Unornamented vessels are used for everyday occasions. Particularly famous are painted ceramics of *Sindh, characteristically two-colour decor of black and purple ornaments painted on before firing. Especially striking are vessels for sweets that are traditional gifts on festival days. Ornaments in the shape of fish, elephants, and plants are painted on these vessels in bright red, blue, and yellow colours. Glazed ceramics first appeared in the territory of Pakistan in the 13th century. Glazed tiles were widely used to decorate mosques, tombs, and palaces. There is an obvious influence from the art of Muslim countries (Iran, Central Asia, etc.) and the *Kashigar*, or master ceramist, usually belongs to a high Muslim caste.

The technique of making glazed ceramics is as follows: clay is dried in the sun, a white engobe is applied and the object is dipped in glaze then fired. The floor of glaze traditionally combines shades of blue, light blue, and turquoise with white; sometimes brown, green, and yellow colours are added.

Multan was a major centre for manufacturing ceramic tiles for architecture. *Huqqas*, *gulab-pashes* (vessels for sprinkling rose water), and *surahis* (vessels for water) were also made there. The decor of these vessels combines stylized floral motifs with geometrical ones.

O.V. LYSTSOVA

Arts Council of Pakistan

Founded in 1956 in Karachi to promote the development of visual arts, arts and crafts, theatre, and music. It organizes festivals and exhibitions, and promotes research and lectures for the population. It has more than 2,500 members.

YU.V. GANKOVSKY

Aruz (also arud)

A versification system (prosody) in Arabic poetry, widely used in the literature of the Middle East and South Asia. It applies a theory of metrical structures and rhythmic patterns created by certain sequences of long and short syllables. A theory of verse-forming assonances determines the strophic composition of the poem—rhyme (*qafia*) and **radif*.

N.V. GLEBOV

Arya

Self-appellation of a group of nomadic peoples speaking languages of the Indo-European family of languages, who fanned out from their original homelands in the 3rd millennia BC. In due course, they entered Iran, northern India and Europe. Particularly widespread is the hypothesis of their origin from the steppes in the south of Russia (from the Dniester to the River Urals). Archaeologists associate Aryas with the Andronovo culture (Volga Region, Trans-Urals) and to some extent with the *Srub* (timber framework) culture (south-east Europe and elsewhere). Arya as ethnonym underlies such place-names as Eyre (Ireland), Ariana (Afghanistan), and Aryavarta (northern India). Iranians and the so-called Indo-Aryans went their separate ways not later than the beginning of the 2nd millennia BC. The 14th-13th century BC saw the Arya tribes penetrating into South Asia. On the territory of South Asia, the term Arya is not used in the ethnic sense. It came to designate 'noble' or 'free' applied, to people of noble descent, in distinction to those of low social status or slaves. It is believed that the Arya people mixed with the local Australoids, Dravida and Munda peoples, who assimilated their language and came to regard the Aryas' direct descendants as people of higher social status. These notions gave rise to the division of the Varnas into 'twice-born' and 'once-born', and also into Aryas and Malecchas.

The Arya made an important contribution to the establishment and development of subcontinental civilization. They are credited with the writing of the *Rigveda*, the first book of the Indo-European cultures, and the entire *Vedic* literature. Arya mythology formed the basis of the Indian epics *Mahabharata* and *Ramayana*; the Aryas' religion, known as *Vedism*, gave birth to the later version of Hinduism. Sanskrit was developed on the basis of Aryan languages (the literary language of antiquity).

L.B. ALAYEV

In the *Rigveda*, in addition to its original meaning, 'Arya' also designates a social status as opposed to that of the aliens, enemies, and slaves (*dasyu*). In the late Vedic literature of the Arya, three Varnas of the 'twice-born' (Brahmins, Kshatriyas, and Vaishyas) have the right to perform Upanayana and read the *Vedas*, in distinction to Shudras who could not be initiated into Vedic cults. Sometimes the term 'Arya' is only applied to Vaishyas. In the *Arthashastra* and certain other Sanskrit texts, the term 'Arya' is applied to all the Varna Indians, as opposed to Maleccha, i.e., untouchables and slaves. In the Buddhist texts, 'Arya' indicates nobility of spirit and knowledge of Buddha's teaching. In Sanskrit and Pali, the word 'Arya' often means personal freedom, sometimes master, slave-owner. It is uzsed as a respectful form of address, e.g. a wife addressing her husband.

A.A. VIGASIN

Ashraf

(Arabic, plural of '*sharif*': noble; historically—Arabic nobility) Also the descendants of the Prophet Muhammad (PBUH) (the same as *Sayids* or **Sayyids*).

YU.V. GANKOVSKY

Associated Press of Pakistan

(APP) A news agency set up in 1948 modelled on the Karachi department of the Associated Press of India. It functioned for some time as a private agency and later came under government control. APP has its headquarters in Islamabad with a network of offices in all administrative centres of the country. It transmits daily about 50,000-60,000 words to its subscribers in Pakistan and about 5,000 words to subscribers abroad. APP has agreements on exchange of information with news agencies abroad; it is a member of the Pool of News Agencies of the Non-Aligned Countries and Organization of Asian and Pacific News Agencies.

V.A. LAVROV

Athan

A dance of religious students, who sing praises of Allah and the Prophet (PBUH) as they dance. It is possible that this dance may be an influence of the 'whirling dervishes' of Konya, Turkey, who are associated with the *Sufi teachings of Maulana Jalaluddin Rumi (1207-73).

M.R. KAZIMI

Atta-ur-Rehman (1942–)

Scientist/Chairman Higher Education Commission. Educated at Karachi Grammar School he topped the Cambridge Overseas School Certificate. He obtained his MSc in Organic Chemistry securing first position. He did his PhD (1968) and DSc (1987) from the University of Cambridge. Atta-ur-Rehman was appointed lecturer in the University of Karachi in 1964. In 1990 he became Director of the HEJ Institute. Dr Rehman is a UNESCO Science Laureate, Co-ordinator General COMSTECH, and was Pakistan's Minister of Science and Technology from 1999 to 2002.

M.R. KAZIMI

Attock

Attock is a district in the Rawalpindi division and the city is located on a historical crossing point of the *Indus.

The *Shahi* Road and later the Grand Trunk Road used this crossing. There is also a rail bridge here used by the Islamabad-Peshawar track. The main sightseeing attraction is the fort built by Mughal Emperor Akbar, an imposing monument of *Mughal architecture.

YU.V. GANKOVSKY

Aufi, Muhammad Samarkandi (late 12th–early 13th century)

Writer. Aufi (real name: Sadiduddin Muhammad) was a chronicler and Persian-language author, who grew up in an aristocratic family in Bukhara, Kharezm and Khorasan. At the onset of the Mongol invasion, he fled to India, where he compiled one of the first known anthologies—*Tazkire*—of Persian-language poetry: *Lubab al-Albab* (The Heart of the Essence). This study still retains its importance as a reliable source on the work of poets included therein. Aufi also compiled a collection of prose works *Jawam al-Hiqayat wa Lawam ar-Riwayat* (1228), which includes more than 2,000 works: short novellas based on historic plots, didactic and religious sermons, anecdotes, fables, parables, stories and myths about strange animals and other wonders of the world.

WORKS: *'Lubab-al-Albab', ed. E. Browne, London-Leiden, 1903.*

N.V. GLEBOV

Auraq

A quarterly from Lahore, started publication in 1966. Initially edited by Wazir *Agha and Abdul Mateen Arif, it is now edited by Wazir Agha and Sajjad Naqvi. *Auraq* represents the rightwing writers of Pakistan, is known for promoting *Inshaia*, light essays in *Urdu and is devoted to a cultural orientation of literature.

N.V. GLEBOV

Awami League

(AL) Founded in 1949 as the 'Awami Muslim League' and called by that name until 1955. In 1953, the Awami League initiated in *East Pakistan the United Front as an electoral alliance opposed to the *Muslim League. From September 1956 to October 1957, the party's leader H.S. *Suhrawardy headed the government of Pakistan in coalition with the Republican Party. In the summer of 1957, the party's left wing headed by A.H. Bhashani broke away from the AL and joined the *National Awami Party.

In December 1970, the Awami League won Pakistan's first general election, securing 160 seats out of 300. Martial Law President Yahya *Khan's refusal to recognize the election results led to an acute political crisis, which in turn led to the formation of the People's Republic of Bangladesh (1971). After the achievement of independence, the Awami League became the ruling party in Bangladesh.

V.P. BAIDAKOV

Awami National Party

(ANP) Founded in 1986 by several groups of the National Democratic Party, the Pakistan National Party, *Awami Tehrik*, the Workers and Peasants Party, and some other smaller groups.

The party's leadership was in favour of adopting a new constitution. The election programme of 1988 envisaged the building in Pakistan of a society of 'economic and social democracy' in which all citizens would be guaranteed food, housing, clothes, education, health services and employment. The election manifesto bore the imprint of the party founders' left-of-centre positions and dealt mainly with the problems of the NWFP. The authors of the programme promised to be guided by a new economic concept according to which industries using local resources would be given priority. They also promised to eradicate smuggling. Other measures proclaimed were the freeing of the country from foreign influence, achievement of self-sufficiency, mobilization of inner resources for development and reduction of unproductive expenditure.

O.V. PLESHOV
YU.V. GANKOVSKY

Awan

An ethnic group related to the *Punjabi. Awans are *Sunni Muslims. They occupy the area around the *Salt Range, between the *Jhelum and the *Indus, and the western bank of the Indus from Peshawar to Dera Ismail Khan. Awans speak the north-eastern dialects of Punjabi. Remnants of the traditional social organization are still extant. The population is mainly engaged in agriculture. The landowning Awan elite, led by Amir of Kalabagh, play a noticeable role in the political and socio-economic affairs of *Punjab and Pakistan as a whole. Many Awans hold important posts in the army, police, and in the business arena.

BIBLIOGRAPHY: *'Glossary of the Tribes and Castes of Punjab and North West Frontier Province', Vol. II, Lahore, 1978.*

YU.V. GANKOVSKY

Awliya

(Arabic) Plural of **Wali*.

Ayaz, Shaykh Mubarak (1923-97)

Poet. A leading *Sindhi language poet and man of letters, who also wrote in *Urdu. He has published a collection of poems in Urdu and five books in Sindhi and is the author of several non-fiction works. Ayaz was an active participant in the *Pakistan Progressive Writers Association and was persecuted under the Martial Law governments of Ayub *Khan and Ziaul *Haq. He took part in the peace movement and in the movement of Afro-Asian writers. He served as Vice Chancellor of Sindh University prior to his death.

BIBLIOGRAPHY: *S. Gazdar, 'Shaykh Ayaz ke Sath Ek Sham' (An Evening with Shaykh Ayaz), 'Pakistani Adab Magazine', 1974, No. 1; Annemarie Schimmel, 'Sindhi Literature'—A History of Indian Literature', Vol. 73, Wiesbaden, 1974.*

A.S. SUKHOCHEV

Azad Kashmir

(Urdu: Free Kashmir) A state that emerged in the south-western territory of the state of Jammu and *Kashmir in the division of British possessions in South Asia and the formation of independent Pakistan and the Indian Union. Area: 13,297 sq.km. Administrative centre: Muzaffarabad. The native population speaks Pahari, *Punjabi, and Gujuri (a dialect of Rajasthani). After 1947, more than 200,000 *Kashmiri refugees moved to Azad Kashmir from the former state of Jammu and Kashmir. The entire population of Azad Kashmir is Muslim. Administratively, Azad Kashmir is divided into five districts: Bagh, Mirpur, Kotli, Poonch and Muzaffarabad. The formation of Azad Kashmir was preceded by armed raids (encouraged by the state's administration) on the Muslim villages in Jammu. On 24 October 1947, Azad Kashmir was proclaimed in Muzaffarabad; its government was headed by Sardar Muhammad Ibrahim, a native of Poonch.

Azad Kashmir's economy is agriculture, including farming, market gardening, semi-nomadic cattle breeding and logging. A part of the population, notably the Gujars, leads a semi-nomadic life. Traditional home crafts are well developed. Azad Kashmir has a University in Muzaffarabad and a polytechnic institute in Rawalakot.While officially independent, with its own president, parliament, government and courts, Azad Kashmir is heavily controlled by Pakistan. According to the Constitution of Azad Kashmir, the Government of Pakistan issues banknotes, ensures the defence and security of Azad Kashmir and controls its foreign relations. Since the 1970s, many public organizations in Azad Kashmir have advocated its formal incorporation in Pakistan. (*See*, Kashmir).

BIBLIOGRAPHY: *Yu.V. Gankovsky, 'Azad Kashmir, Kratkiye soobshcheniya Instituta narodov Azii AN SSSR', No. 51, Moscow, 1962 (in Russian); J. Korbel, 'Danger in Kashmir', Princeton, 1954.*

YU.V. GANKOVSKY

Azad, Muhammad Hussain (1829–1910)

Poet/Critic. Azad was a critic and poet, writing in *Urdu. Azad was educated at Delhi and became an authority on Persian and Arabic literature. He was commissioned by the British authorities to make a trip to Iran and Central Asia. Working in the education system in Lahore, he had a chance to study *English literature. In 1874, he founded the Punjab Society (*Anjuman-i-Punjab*), which played an important role in the renovation of *Punjabi literature. Azad stood for revising old canons, democratisation of literature, and making literary language more colloquial.

His main works include: *Ab-i-Hayat* (The Water of Life, colloquial: Fountain of Youth), a history of *Urdu poetry with pen portraits of major poets; *Nairang-i-Khayal* (The Magic of the Mind), a collection of allegoric essays; *Darbar-i-Akbari* (Akbar's Court), a historical novel; *Nazm-i-Azad* (Azad's Poems), a collection of poetry; and more. Azad is considered to be one of the finest stylists in *Urdu literature. Together with *Hali, he carried out a reform of Urdu poetry and democratised Urdu poetic canons. Azad is best known for his *Sukhandan-i-Fars*, Urdu's first book on philology, in which he traces the common roots between Indian and Indo-European languages. He suffered from mental illness for the last twenty-five years of his life.

BIBLIOGRAPHY: *A.S. Sukhochev, 'From Dastan to the Novel', Moscow, 1971 (in Russian); A. Farrukhi, 'Muhammad Hussain Azad', Karachi, vols. 1-2, 1965; M. Sadiq, 'A History of Urdu Literature', London, 1964; F.W. Pritchett, 'Nets of Awareness' Karachi, 1995.*

A.S. SUKHOCHEV

Aziz, Abdul, Syed (1885–1948)

Statesman. Syed Abdul Aziz was also known as *Aziz-ul-Millat* to the Muslims of Bihar. He attended Patna College, Bihar National College, and was chairman of the Reception Committee for the 1938 *All-India Muslim League annual session at Patna. This was the first annual session at which Mohammad Ali *Jinnah would be hailed publicly as the *Quaid-i-Azam (Great Leader). A year later, Syed Abdul Aziz hosted an AIML Workers Conference at Darbhanga; Liaquat Ali *Khan, who presided, wrote to Jinnah saying that the people showed great enthusiasm. Syed Abdul Aziz delivered the inaugural address at the All-India Muslim Students Federation at Calcutta on 27 December 1937. He served as Minister for Law and Judiciary in the Nizam's Dominion of Hyderabad. He had been Minister for Education in Bihar between 1934 and 1937. He headed the United Muslim Party before joining the All-India Muslim League.

WORKS: *'Reflections on the Bihar Tragedy', 3 parts, Patna, 25 October 1946 to 28 February 1947.*

BIBLIOGRAPHY: *M. Anis ur Rahman, 'Karnamey: Aziz-ul-Millat', Karachi, 1979.*

Aziz, Khursheed Kamal (1927–)

Historian/Writer. K.K. Aziz obtained his MA degrees in *English Literature and Political Science from Government College, Lahore. He was awarded his PhD from the University of Manchester in 1959. He was Deputy to the Official Historian, Government of Pakistan (1961–63). He was a professor at the University of Khartoum, and subsequently at the Quaid-i-Azam University. He was Chairman, *National Institute on Historical and Cultural Research, Pakistan. He was later visiting professor at the South Asia Institute, Heidelberg, Germany.

K.K. Aziz is a prolific writer and an eminent scholar. He has written and edited a number of books but the best received has been *The Making of Pakistan*, in which the theoretical aspect of Pakistani nationhood has been well interpreted.

WORKS: *'Britain and Muslim India', London, 1963; 'The Making of Pakistan', London, 1967; 'Rahmat Ali: A Biography', Lahore, 1987; 'The Murder of History: A Critique of History Text Books used in Pakistan', Lahore, 1993 etc.*

M.R. KAZIMI

Aziz, Shaukat (1949–)

Prime Minister of Pakistan since 2004. Shaukat Aziz, the twenty-first prime minister of Pakistan, is a former private banker credited with recent reforms of the country's economy. Born in Karachi on 6 March 1949, he received his early education at Saint Patrick's School, Karachi and Abbottabad Public School. He was awarded the Master of Business Administration (MBA) degree in 1969 at the Institute of Business Administration (IBA). He joined Citibank, Karachi in 1969 and served overseas in 1975, holding positions in Philippines, Jordan, Greece, USA, UK, Malaysia, Singapore and Saudi Arabia. He has been a member of the Board of several Citibank owned bodies, including Saudi American Bank and Citi Islamic Bank, as well as several non-profit organisations. He was appointed Executive Vice President of Citibank in 1992 and till he joined the Government of Pakistan as Finance Minister in 1999, had 30 years of experience in global finance and international banking. When former Prime Minister Zafarullah Khan Jamali resigned in June 2004, the ruling party swiftly declared that Aziz would take over. He first had to secure a seat in parliament—a requirement to take up the top post-and did so in August 2004 with victory in two by-elections. Mr Aziz replaced *Pakistan Muslim League leader, Chaudhry Shujaat *Hussain, who had been in temporary charge.

Under his tenure as minister of finance the economy reportedly displayed growth of 6.4% a year. Observers attribute this success largely to debt reduction and the securing of hundreds of millions of dollars in loans and aid in return for support in the US-led war on terror.

On 30 July 2004 a suicide bomber attempted to assassinate Aziz. It was while campaigning for the by-elections that this event occurred in the *Punjab province. Aziz enjoys golf, music and art. He is married with three children.

M.R. KAZIMI

B

Badshahi Masjid

A red limestone monument of Pakistan's seventeenth-century architecture in Lahore. It is one of the largest mosques in the world, and was built by Emperor

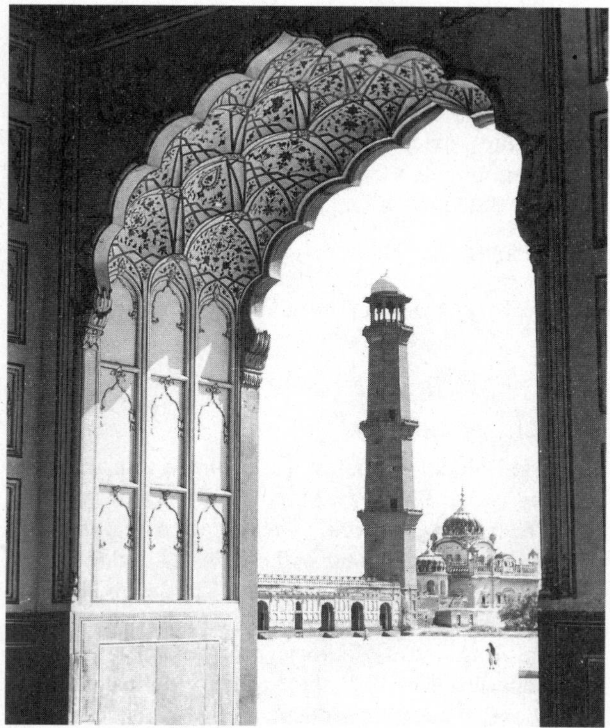

One of the largest and most beautiful mosques in the world.

Aurangzeb Alamgir in 1670. It follows a symmetrical ground plan in the shape of a closed rectangle of walls surrounding an inner court measuring 176 metres by 176 metres, and a prayer hall under three onion-like domes of white marble. At the corners stand octagonal laminates ending in cupola kiosks. The entrance pavilion is set on a high stepped stylobate and lies opposite the entrance to the *Lahore Fort.

A.A. RALLEV

Bahai

From the honorary title Bahaullah or Behaullah, meaning 'the followers of Bahaism'. This is a religious teaching founded in the 1860s in Iraq by Mirza Husayn Ali (1817–82), an exile from Iran. He preached the equality of all humanity and the merger of all religions and states into one. Today Bahaism has evolved into a new religion with followers in many countries of Asia, Western Europe and America. The major centres are in the USA and Germany, with headquarters in Haifa (Israel). In Pakistan the community is led by the National Spiritual Assembly of Bahais of Pakistan.

The Bahai faith is an offshoot of the Babi Religion founded by Ali Muhammad Bab (1820–50); Bahaulla (d. 1892) took over the leadership from Subh-i-Azal in 1866. The Bahais of Pakistan had themselves declared a non-Muslim minority in Pakistan.

YU.V. GANKOVSKY

Bahawalpur

1. Founded in 1748 by Nawab Bahawal Khan, after whom it was named, it was the capital of Bahawalpur princely state until 1955, when the state was abolished. Today it is the administrative centre of the division of the same name and the main town serving the Cholistan Desert. The city is a major trade centre, dealing mainly in the food industry and large-scale light manufacturing. It is also home to a university and several colleges. Bahawalpur is known as a centre for Islamic study and is the location of a theological college, Jamia Abbasia.

2. A former Princely State, now an administrative Division in the southeastern part of the Punjab. In 1951 the area was 45,400 sq.km. with a population of 1,823,000, mostly *Siraikis. The rulers (Nawabs) of Bahawalpur came from the Abbasi-Daudputra dynasty. Originally from Sindh, they claimed to have descended from the Abbasid caliphs who ruled in Baghdad in 749-1258 and in Cairo in 1261-1517. From 1748 to 1802 the Bahawalpur rulers were vassals of the *Durrani kings and since 1833 vassals of the British sovereign. Bahawalpur's rulers actively helped Britain during the first Anglo-Afghan War (1838-42), in the conquest of the Punjab (1847-48), and during the second Anglo-Afghan War (1878-80). Bahawalpur was included as a part of Pakistan on 5 October 1947. The State was abolished in 1955 and amalgamated into *West Pakistan.

3. A Division in the Province of Punjab, consisting of three districts: Bahawalpur, Bahawalnagar and Rahimyar Khan. Area: 45,400 sq.km.; population: 4.7 million (1981).

BIBLIOGRAPHY: *R. Hashmi, 'Brief for Bahawalpur Province', Karachi, 1972; Shahamat Ali, 'History of Bahawalpur', London, 1848.*

YU.V. GANKOVSKY

Bahawalpur Central Library

It was built in 1948 in *Bahawalpur to house about 200,000 books, mainly in English and Urdu, including collections of Oriental manuscripts, geographical maps, newspapers and periodicals that appeared after 1948. The library houses a special children's collection.

Bahawalpur Central Library.

YU.V. GANKOVSKY

Baloch (People)

An Indo-Iranian people inhabiting the historico-geographical area of *Balochistan. Their population is estimated at 6 million (1990). The majority, more than 3 million Balochis, live in the province of Balochistan, about 1.2 million in *Sindh, over 300,000 in *Punjab, 700,000 in the south-west regions of Iran and about 150,000 in south-western Afghanistan. Migrants from Balochistan are found in India and in the Arab states of the Persian Gulf. Serveral thousand Balochis reside in south-eastern Turkmenistan.

The *Balochi language belongs to the north-western sub-group of the Iranian languages. Since the 1940s written literature has been rapidly developing. The majority of Balochis are *Sunni Muslims. In the Makran division (Balochistan province), the Zikri sect includes several tens of thousands.

The Balochi culture began to form in the middle of the first millenia AD. Balochi migration from the Iranian territories of Kirman and Sistan to present day Balochistan province in Pakistan was a major landmark in their ethnic history. There they mixed with the local Iranian, *Indo-Aryan, and *Dravidian ethnic groups and tribes. Balochis have preserved many elements of their time-honoured way of life and traditional social structures, such as tribes—'*tumans*', clans—'*pharas*', families—'phallis'. The largest tribes (groups of tribes), are the following: Marri, Bughti, Jamadini, Leghari, Zehri, Rind, Magsi (Magasi), Dombki, Buledi, Khosa, and Gichki. About fifteen per cent of Balochis still lead a nomadic or semi-nomadic life. The Balochi economy is mainly based on irrigated farming (grain-growing, horticulture), extensive cattle breeding, coastal fishing, and the mining of various minerals in the mountains of northern Balochistan.

BIBLIOGRAPHY: *Yuri Gankovsky, 'The Peoples of Pakistan', Lahore 1972; M. Pikulin, 'Balochi', Moscow, 1959 (in Russian); M. LOngworth Dames, 'The Baloch Race', London, 1904.*

YU.V. GANKOVSKY

Balochi Academy

The first Balochi Academy was founded in Karachi, in 1958 by Akbar Barakzai, Murad Sahir, and Juma Khan Baloch, among others. The Academy publishes collections of poetry and anthologies of Baloch poets and conducts educational activities. The second Balochi Academy was founded in Quetta, to publish books on Balochi linguistics, history, culture and literature. Between 1961 and 1991 the Academy published about 150 books, mainly in Balochi, and also in *Urdu and English, by Balochi researchers, writers, and poets, as well as translations from other languages (including translations from Russian works by Chekhov, Gorky, Chinghiz Aitmatov and others). Works by some Balochi poets have been published in Urdu. The Academy publishes a popular series of pamphlets in Balochi and promotes a better understanding of *Balochi literature.

V.V. MOSHKALO

Balochi (Language)

Balochi is spoken in Pakistan, Iran, Afghanistan, India, the Arab Gulf States, Turkmenistan and East Africa. It is classified as a member of the Iranian group of the Indo-European language family which includes

Kurdish, Persian (Farsi), Pashto, Dari, Tajik, Ossetian. Balochi is closely related to Kurdish and Persian.

There are two main dialects: Eastern and Western. It is difficult to estimate the total number of Balochi speakers, but there are probably around six million, most of whom speak Western Balochi, which is also the dialect that has been most widely used in *Balochi literature. Within the Western dialect are two further dialects, Rakhshani (in the northern areas) and Makrani (in the south). The areas where Eastern Balochi dialects are spoken (the north-eastern areas of Pakistani Balochistan, *Punjab and *Sindh) are in many ways less developed, especially when it comes to education, than other parts of Balochistan, which accounts for why it is little used in the written form.

Although some works in Balochi had appeared before partition, the Balochi literary movement got fully under way only after the creation of Pakistan in 1947.

BIBLIOGRAPHY: *B.A. Baloch, 'The beginning of radio broadcasting in Baluchi: a brief report', Newsletter of Baluchistan Studies (No. 2, Spring 1985), Naples, Italy; Carina Jahani (ed.), 'Lanugage in Society—Eight Sociolinguistic Essays on Balochi', Acta Universitatis Upsaliensis, Uppsala, 2000.*

YU.V. GANKOVSKY

Balochi Literature

The first recorded works of folk literature—epics, romantic ballads, lyrical and heroic poems depicting the legendary history and genealogy of the Balochi tribes—dates back to the sixteenth century. The extant poems include: 'Hani and Shah Murad,' 'Shahdad and Mahnaz,' 'Lallah and Granaz,' 'Bebarg and Granaz,' 'Mast and Sammo.' They reflect the social structure of the traditional *Balochi society, its code of honour, and military skills. The more noteworthy poets of the early period are: Mir Chakar Khan Rind (early sixteenth century), Mir Biwragh Puzh Rind, Gwahram Lashari, Mir Shahdad, Shah Murad Kaheri and Baloch Gargej.

Some rulers of Kalat, such as Abdullah Khan (r. 1715-30) and Khan Khudad Khan (r. 1875-93), patronised literature and the arts. Jam Durrak Dombki, who introduced the **ghazal* into Balochi poetry, worked at the court of Mir Nasir Khan (1750-95). Other notables in eighteenth to nineteenth century Balochi poetry were Mullah Fazil Rind, Mullah Ismail, Izzat Panjguri, Jihand Rind, Muhammad Khan Gishkori, Nur Muhammad Bampushti, Usman Kalamati, Mitha Khan and Haidar Balachani.

In the second half of the nineteenth century and early twentieth century small circles of poets existed at the Khans' courts and tribal leaders' camps. The well-known poets of those days include Huzur Baksh Jatoi, Mast Tawakkali, Jawansal Bugti, Rahim Ali Shaheja, Ismail Pullabadi, and Mullah Ismail Sarbazi.

Balochi prose didn't appear until the beginning of the twentieth century. It consisted mainly of textbooks, commentaries on religious texts, translations from other languages and short stories published in periodicals. Balochi literature made great progress on the eve of, and following, Pakistan's liberation from the colonial yoke, when the poetry expressed strong patriotic sentiments related to the struggle for independence, and for the development of the Balochi language and folk traditions. A number of cultural and literary societies sprang up, such as *Anjuman-i-Islah-i-Balochan* (the Society for Balochi Education) (1946), Balochistan Progressive Writers' Association (1949), *Balochi Sarchmay* (1951) and *Balochi Academy (1961). A number of Balochi periodicals were established: a literary monthly *Uman* (1950), the journals *Naukin daur* (New Times), *Ulus* (1960), *Saugat* (Good News); *Zamana Balochi* (1968), *Sanj, Balochi,* and newspaper *Jad-o-Jihad* (Struggle).

Among the poets, particularly noteworthy are Azad Jamaldini (b. 1918), Sayid Zahur Muhammad Hashmi (1926-85), and Mir Gul Khan Nasir (1914-83). These were innovative poets, who strove to introduce new elements into the imagery and subject matter of Balochi poetry: Muhammad Husain Unqa (b. 1924), Mumin Bazdar (b. 1930), and Ata Shad (b. 1939). Considerable contributions to Balochi poetry have also been made by Muhammad Ishaq Shamim (b. 1923), Qazi Abdurrahim Sabir (b. 1919), Abdul Hakim Haqqu (b. 1912), Murad Sahar (b. 1929), Malik Muhammad Taqi (b. 1921), Ahmad Jigar (b. 1921), and Dost Muhamad Bekas (b. 1916).

Prominent prose writers include Muhammad Husain Unqa, Azad Jamaldini, Mali Muhammad Panah (b. 1913), Muhammad Beg Baloch (b. 1936), and Muhammad Sadiq Azad (b. 1941).

Periodicals occasionally carried translations from foreign authors, including Leo Tolstoy, Chekhov, Gorky, and some Urdu writers such as Krishan Chandar. Despite the achievements of post-partition Balochi literature, its progress has been hampered by the low education level of the Balochi population, lack of stability in the literary journals and few publishing houses.

BIBLIOGRAPHY: *M. Longworth Dames, 'Popular Poetry of the Baloches', Vol. I-II, London, 1907; Hetu Ram, 'Balochi Nama', Lahore, 1881; I.I. Zarubin, 'Balochi Tales', Vol. 1, Leningrad, 1932, Vol. 2, Moscow-Leningrad, 1949 (in Russian); Niamatullah Gichky, 'Balochi Language and its Literature', Newsletter of Balochistan Studies, No. 3, Naples, 1986; Abdullah Jan Jamaldini, 'Balochi Adab men Fikri Irtiqa' (Evolution of Philosophy in Balochi Literature), Irtiqa, Karachi, February 1989.*

A.S. SUKHOCHEV

Balochistan (Physical)

A historico-geographical region in Asia in the south-eastern part of the Iranian Plateau. Area: more than 0.5 million sq.km. Eastern Balochistan (347,000 sq.km.) forms part of Pakistan (Balochistan province), Western Balochistan forms part of Iran. In antiquity Balochistan's territory was populated by the Maka, the Gedrosians and other peoples. In the Middle Ages Balochistan successively formed part of the Arab Caliphate, the *Ghaznavid state, the states of the Seljuqs, the Mongols and the Timurids. Early in the seventeenth century, several feudal principalities emerged in the territory of Balochistan, whose rulers were vassals of the Safavids and Great *Mughals. Nasir Khan Baluch (1750-95), ruler of Kalat (Eastern Balochistan), the most powerful of these principalities, united the whole of Balochistan under his authority, recognising the *Durrani kings as his feudal over-lords.

Early in the 19th century Great Britain began to penetrate into Balochistan. According to the treaties of 1854, 1876, and 1879 imposed on the rulers of Kalat and Kabul, Eastern Balochistan passed under British rule and was divided into the province of British Balochistan and the Federation of Balochi States (Kalat, Kharan, Makran, and *Lasbela). Western Balochistan was incorporated into Iran in 1849-57. In August 1947 British Balochistan was included in Pakistan and in March 1948 the Federation of Balochi States joined Pakistan. The border between Eastern and Western Balochistan was defined by the Pakistan-Iranian Treaty of 29 October 1956.

BIBLIOGRAPHY: *Mir Gul Khan Nasir, 'Tarikh-i-Balochistan', Vols. I-II, Quetta, 1952; Mir Ahmed Yar Khan Baluch, 'Inside Balochistan', Karachi, 1975; Nasser Brohi, 'Studies in Brahuic History', Karachi, 1977.*

YU.V. GANKOVSKY

Balochistan (Political)

A province in south-western Pakistan, bordering on Afghanistan and Iran. Its area is 347,000 sq.km. Its population is 6,511,358 people (1998). The province consists of six divisions: Quetta, Sibi, Kalat, Makran, Nasirabad, Zhob; seventeen districts and two agencies: Kohlu and Dera Bugti. The capital is Quetta (Population 285,000). The indigenous population includes *Balochi, *Brahui, *Pashtun and in the eastern districts also *Punjabi, *Sindhi, and *Muhajir. It is largely desert and is sparsely populated (population density: 12 people per sq.km).

There are no major economic centres. The main occupation of the indigenous population is dry-farming (wheat, sorghum), fruit-growing in oases, apple, (plum, apricot trees, fig palms), and pasture and nomadic cattle-breeding. There is a well-developed mining industry: coal, brimstone, natural gas, oil. There is a major gas deposit in *Sui. Balochistan covers 43.7 per cent of Pakistani territory and had 5.1 per cent of its population, while it accounts for only 2 per cent of its agricultural output and 5 per cent of its industrial production.

YU.V. GANKOVSKY

Baltistan

(also *Tibet-i-Khurd*, or Small Tibet).

1. A historico-geographical area between the Rivers North Shigar and Nubra in the upper reaches of the *Indus in the Greater *Himalayas area. The greater part of the population speaks Balti, a western dialect of Tibetan, and is Muslim.

2. From 1948-71 one of the two political agencies in the Pakistan-controlled Northern Areas of the former state of Jammu and *Kashmir. The administrative structure of the agency changed many times. In 1971 it was divided into the districts of Skardu, Shingar, Randu, Khaplu, and Kharmong.

3. Since 1972, an administrative district of the *Northern Areas. Administrative centre: Skardu.

Bibliography: V.A. Pulyarkin, 'Kashmir', Moscow, 1956 (in Russian); O.H.K. Spate, 'India and Pakistan', London, 1954; A.H. Dani (ed.), 'History of Northern Areas Pakistan', Islamabad, 1989.

YU.V. GANKOVSKY

Bamqa

A dance from Balochistan. It is a mixed dance of boys and girls, perfomed to the beat of the drum and the sonorous sound of the *shehnai* pipe.

R. HUSAIN

Bandung Conference of 1955

The Conference was held on 18-24 April in Indonesia on the initiative of Indonesia, Burma, India, Pakistan, and Ceylon (since 1972, Sri Lanka) and was attended by state, government, and territorial representatives. The Conference took place against the background of de-colonization and the Cold War, in which the Afro-Asian world became a focal field of the East-West confrontation. The documents adopted by the Conference—the Concluding Communique and the Declaration—set down the principles of solidarity, unity of action, and co-operation among Afro-Asian countries despite differences in their economic and political systems.

The declaration on promoting universal peace and co-operation included a clause in support of the principles of respect for basic human rights. Also noted was the support for the goals and principles of the United Nations Charter, the principle of self-determination for peoples and nations, recognition of equality of all races and nations, advice to refrain from exercising external pressure on any country, non-intervention or interference in the internal affairs of other nations, not to promote agreements on collective defence in the interests of any of the great powers, respect for the right of all countries to individual or collective security in accordance with the United Nations Charter, settlement of all international disputes by peaceful means, and respect for justice and international obligations. The Communique appealed to all states to lend their support for disarmament, and proposed a ban on nuclear weapons.

The Bandung Conference acquired importance in the achieving of mutual understanding among the countries of Asia and Africa concerning the process of decolonisation and strengthening of the foundations of peace and security. Its decisions paved the way for the founding and consolidating of the Non-Aligned Movement, and the emergence of the movement for solidarity between the social forces of Asia and Africa.

Pakistan was represented at the Conference by Prime Minister Mohammad Ali *Bogra who had a verbal confrontation with Indian Prime Minister Jawaharlal Nehru. Nehru accused Pakistan of being an American stooge. Bogra retaliated by calling India a Soviet stooge. In the Bandung Conference. M.A. Bogra established a rapport with Zhou EnLai, the Chinese Premier, who conceded that Pakistan's membership of SEATO was not motivated by hostility against China.

PUBLICATION: *'Bandung Conference, 1955, Selected Documents', No. 9, 1955.*

BIBLIOGRAPHY: *Qutbuddin Aziz, 'Exciting Stories to Remember', Karachi 1995.*

M.R. KAZIMI

Bangladesh-Pakistan Relations

These relations began with mutual recognition on 22 February 1974. In the initial stage, relations were tense. The two countries had to overcome the traumatic events of the 1971 war and to start shaping their relations on a new basis of common interests. This task was made difficult by the financial and economic issues involved in the repatriation of Bengalis living in Pakistan and *Biharis living in Bangladesh. The repatriation of Bengalis did not take long, whereas the deportation of several hundred thousand Biharis stretched out over several years. The division of assets remains a lingering issue between the two countries.

The development of Bangladesh-Pakistan relations accelerated as a result of changes in the Bangladeshi leadership after the 15 August 1975 *coup*, in which Shaikh Mujibur *Rahman was killed. The policy of consolidating links with the Muslim world initiated in the mid 1970s by Bangladesh was in line with the desire of Pakistan's leaders, who opted to use Islamic ideology as the political basis for the relations between the two countries. These relations were greatly strengthened in the 1980s. An official visit of S. Yaqub Khan, Pakistan's Foreign Minister, to Bangladesh in August 1983 initiated regular political contact between the leaders of the two countries. There followed a visit of President H.M. Ershad of Bangladesh to Pakistan in June 1986, a meeting between Ershad and the President of Pakistan in Karachi in July 1987, and Benazir *Bhutto's visit to Bangladesh in the autumn of 1989. One of the most important factors which stimulated relations, especially in the political sphere, is the participation in the *South-Asian Association for Regional Cooperation (SAARC). In 2000 Bangladesh sent emissaries to both Pakistan and India seeking to mediate the *Kashmir dispute. Shortly after this the Indian press published excerpts of the Hamood ur Rahman Committee Report which described the atrocities of the Pakistan army against the Bengali population in 1971. When Inamur Raja, Pakistan's Deputy High Commissioner to Bangladesh, asserted during a seminar that the Pakistan Army was only responding to the atrocities committed by *Awami League 'miscreants' relations took a plunge. Although Pakistan had already announced his withdrawal, the Bangladesh government expelled the Deputy High Commissioner.

The victory of the Bangladesh National Party led by Khaleda Zia In October 2001, is expected to improve relations.

On 29 July 2002 President General Pervez *Musharraf, during his visit to Dhaka, publicly expressed his regrets over the excesses committed by the Pakistan Army during the 1970 conflict. The next day President Musharraf and Prime Minister Zia signed cultural and technology exchange agreements. The issues of repatriating stranded refugees and division of assets stay unresolved. Prime Minister Zia visited Pakistan for the SAARC summit of 4 January 2004.

R.M. MUKIMJANOVA

Bannu

1. A mountain valley in the North West Frontier Province. Its area is 4,400 sq.km., with an average height of 240-450 metres above sea level. The River Kurram and its tributaries have braided channels with wide river beds that stay dry most of the year. The soils are predominantly sandy, but along the Kurram the land is covered with silt. The larger part of the territory is occupied by a waste of dry shrub land. Annual precipitation does not exceed 300 mm. Irrigated lands are mainly situated between the Rivers Kurram and Tochi and have to be reclaimed every year, over 50 per cent of the land that is cultivated is sown with wheat, though fodder crops are of great importance. Cattle breeding is well developed, as well as the breeding of sheep, camel, and mules.

M.YU. MOROZOVA

2. A district in the Division of Dera Ismail Khan of the North West Frontier Province. Situated in the mountain valley of the same name, it is located in the valley of the Kurram River. Its population is 711,000 people (1981).

3. A town and administrative centre of the district of the same name. It is the home of a large-scale woolweaving industry, as well as carpet and rug making. It includes a cantonment. Bannu has been known since ancient times. It is referred to as 'Pona' in 404 AD by a Chinese pilgrim Fa-Hien. At that time there was a Buddhist monastery in Bannu housing 3,000 monks. From the middle of the eighteenth century until 1819, it was under the rule of the *Durrani Shahs of the Afghan Empire; then, until 1849, it fell under the *Sikhs. In 1849, Bannu became a part of *British India and was temporarily renamed Edwardesbad. Since August 1947, it has been a part of Pakistan. The town is surrounded by palm trees and mango orchards, and has a crowded market. It is the center of a densely populated well-irrigated and wooded farmland.

4. The town of Bannu is situated in an almost circular basin on the Kurram River, where it leaves the Kohat and Wazir hills, and was originally a trading route between the *Indus Valley and Kabul.

V.YA. BELOKRENITSKY

Barelwi

Barelwi derives its name from the town of Bareily in Uttar-Pradesh, India, when a *Sunni theological college (*dar-ul-ulum*) was established.

Founded at the end of the 19th century by Maulana Ahmad Reza Khan (1865-1921). In addition to the traditional theological disciplines, the *dar-ul-ulum's* curricula included extensive study of *Sufism. Barelwi **ulema* are quite tolerant towards various manifestations of popular Islam, syncretic beliefs and rituals. They take a conservative attitude towards legal and social problems. In India, Barelwi followers have a solid position in Western Bengal, Gujarat, Mysore, and the eastern districts of Uttar-Pradesh. In Pakistan the *ulema* of this school occupy some key positions under the leadership of **Jamiat ul-Ulema-i Pakistan*, founded in 1970 and led by Shah Ahmad *Noorani. Another organisation of the Barelwi sect is the *Sunni Tehreek* whose leader was Saleem Qadri until he was assassinated on 18 May 2001.

YU.V. GANKOVSKY

Barelwi, Syed Ahmed (1786–1831)

Religious leader. A founder and leader of the Movement of *Mujahidin* (see Mujahid) (Holy Warriors), who led an armed insurrection on the western bank of the *Indus against Maharaja Ranjit Singh. He was a disciple (**murid*) of the noted Muslim theologian Shah Abdul Aziz (Delhi, *c.* 1804-86), and the chief imam in the army of Nawab Muhammad Amir Khan, the ruler of the princely state of Tonk in Rajasthan (1810). Subsequently, he became a wandering preacher and made a pilgrimage to Mecca in 1821. In 1826, he came to Peshawar from Bareily through Rajasthan, *Sindh, and *Balochistan. Once there, he called for *jihad* against the *Sikh authorities. Syed was elected **imam* in February 1827 by the population of what are now the districts of Peshawar, Swat and Hazara of the *North West Frontier Province. In 1830 he occupied Peshawar but was betrayed by the local *Pashtun *Khans and was killed in the Battle of Balakot.

BIBLIOGRAPHY: *W.W. Hunter, 'The Indian Mussalmans', London, 1871; Q. Ahmad, 'The Wahabi Movement in India', Patna, 1966; G.R. Mihr, 'Sayyid Ahmad Shahid', Lahore, 1952.*

YU.V. GANKOVSKY

Bari, Abdul, Maulana (1878–1926)

Statesman. A religious and public figure in British India, and one of the leaders of the *Khilafat Movement, Maulana Abdul Bari was educated in the Hijaz where he obtained a degree in *Hadith. He was President of the Muslim Conference in Lucknow (26 January 1919) that formed the Khilafat Committee. He was one of the organisers and the first President of **Jamiat-ul-Ulema-i-Hind* (1919). A number of books on various aspects of Islam and the Muslim community of South Asia were written by him, including an incomplete exegesis of the Quran.

YU.V. GANKOVSKY

Bari Doab

The Bari Doab is the irrigated territory between the *Beas and the *Ravi in the *Punjab. It derives its name from the initial letter of the names of two rivers, the Beas and the Ravi.

YU.V. GANKOVSKY

Baroghil

A mountain pass which crosses the *Hindu Kush in the northern section of *Chitral, *North West Frontier Province. The height is approximately 3,777 metres and it is accessible for pack-saddle transportation for only eight months of the year.

YU.V. GANKOVSKY

Basawan

Artist. Basawan was an Indian miniature painter of the late 16th/early 17th centuries. More than a hundred miniatures with his signature are among the manuscripts of Jami's (1414–1492, full name: Nur oddin 'abdor-Rahman Ibn Ahmad) poems: *Baharistan* (1595, the Bodleian Library, Oxford), *Darab Nama* (1596, the British Museum, London), *Razm Nama* or The Book of Battles (1584-89, the Maharaja's collection in Jaipur), *Akbar Nama* (1599-1600, the Victoria and Albert Museum, London), and others. Basawan was a skilful graphic artist and painter; he also painted masterful portraits and landscapes. An exceptional sense of composition enabled him to convey the images of human beings and animals in a highly expressive manner and to create refined landscapes. Basawan widely used Indian tradition, his knowledge of Indian literature, mythology and his environment. He combined realism with great emotional intensity. His son, Manohar became an outstanding miniature painter in the first quarter of the seventeenth century.

WORKS: *'A Mullah Reproaches a Darwesh for Playing in Torn Clothes' (1595), Manuscript of Baharistan Jami, Bodleian Library, Oxford.*

BIBLIOGRAPHY: *W. Staude, 'Contribution à l'étude de Basawan', Revue des arts Asiatiques, t. VIII, Paris, 1932; W. Staude, 'Les artistes de la court d'Akbar et les illustrations des Dastan-i-Amir Hamza', Arts Asiatiques, t. II, Paris, 1955.*

N.K. KARPOVA

Batik

A fabric ornamented with the aid of a resistant, batik is popular in the countries of South and Southeast Asia. The process of batik painting is lengthy and labour-consuming. First the fabric is cleaned and boiled, then two kinds of wax are mixed and heated to a liquid state. A wax mass is spread on the fabric with a brush, covering the areas that will remain unpainted. When the wax solidifies the fabric is painted by dipping it in a dye. This process is repeated as one dye is replaced by another and the wax is removed from the areas required by the design. A characteristic feature of batik painting is a lattice of curving lines that cover both the background and the picture, caused by the dye penetrating cracks in the wax in the process of painting. This web of lines lends batik its unique character, as does the traditional colour, chiefly deep indigo-blue and brown. At present batik is used both in costumes and for decorative purposes such as in pictures, pillowcases, tablecloths, etc.

O.V. LYSTSOVA

Baxter, Craig

Historian. As an officer of the Foreign Service of the United States from 1956 to 1980, he was posted in Bombay (1958-60), New Delhi (1961-64), Lahore

(1965-68) and Dhaka (1976-78), and served in Washington on South Asian affairs, 1968-71.

Baxter is editor and contributor to Zia's Pakistan: Politics and Stability in a Frontline State (Lahore, 1985) and with Syed Razi Wasti Pakistan: Authoritarianism in the 1980s (Lahore: 1991). He is the co-author with Shahid Javed Burki of 'Pakistan Under the Military: Eleven Years of Ziaul Haq' (Lahore: 1991). He is also the co-author with Yogendra K. Malik, Charles H. Kennedy, and Robert C. Oberst of Government and Politics in South Asia, now in its third edition (Boulder Co: 1993).

YU.V. GANKOVSKY

Bazm-i-Saqafat

(Urdu: Cultural Society) It was set up in April 1961 in Multan to promote national literature, exchange cultural information, and disseminate written works of cultural achievements of Pakistan's region. The society contributes to publications of classical and contemporary literature, the gathering and publication of folklore, printing *Urdu and English translations of the best of national literature, extending financial help to publishing houses, journals and writers, cultural and literary centres, promoting cultural ties with Afro-Asian countries, and organising conferences and symposia. The Society has its own publications in Urdu, *Punjabi, English, *Siraiki, and others.

N.V. GLEBOV

Beames, John (1837–1902)

British Indologist. He was one of the fathers of the study of contemporary Indian languages. From 1859 to 1893 he served in the Indian colonial administration, in the *Punjab, Bihar, Orissa, and *Bengal.

WORKS: *'Outlines of Indian Philoilogy', London, 1868: 'A Comparative Grammar of the Modern Aryan Languages of India', Vols. 1-3, London, 1872-9, New Delhi, 1970; 'Grammar of the Bengali Language'; 'Literary and Colloquial', Oxford, 1894.*

V.P. LIPEROVSKY

Bean, Lee L. (1933–)

American Sociologist. Economist and demographer he has been professor and head of the sociology department at the University of Utah, USA since 1987. From 1967-68 he was an advisor on demography at the Institute of Development Economics in Pakistan. From 1968 to 1972, he served as the Population Council's assistant director for the Middle East in the Demographic Division, New York.

WORKS: *'The Population of Pakistan: 1960-2000', Karachi, 1968.*

YU.V. GANKOVSKY

Beas (also Bias)

(Old Greek: Chyphasis; Sanskrit: Wipasa) One of *Punjab's five rivers, it is the largest tributary of the *Sutlej. It is 460 km. long and has its source in the *Himalayas, from the southern extremity of Pir-Panjal Range near the Rokhtang pass, at an altitude of 4,000 metres. It flows into the Sutlej River 25 km. from the north near the Pakistani border. In the upper reaches the Beas is fed by glaciers and in the plain by rain and underground water. Flooding mainly occurs in summer. Beas waters are used extensively for irrigation. Water available for irrigation from the surface flow is 15.8 cu. metres per second and from the underground flow, 3.3 cusecs. There is a hydro-electric power station near Pong. The use of the Beas flow was, for a long time, a source of conflict between India and Pakistan, because the Beas is one of the main water supplies for the Sutlej. Historically, the Beas is believed to be the farthest point reached by the armies of Alexander of Macedonia in 326 BC.

S.B. ROSTOTSKY

Bedil, Mirza Abdul Qadir (1644–1721)

Poet. A Persian-language poet and thinker, Bedil travelled extensively in India. *Sufism and Vedantic philosophy influenced his philosophical views. Bedil left a rich legacy of prose and poetry. His poetic works—**ghazals, *qasidas, *rubais, *tarkibbands* and **masnawis*—number some 100,000 verses.

In the *masnawis, Talism-i-Hairat* ('A Talisman of Wonder', 1669), *Muhiti Azam* ('The Great Ocean', 1681), *Tur-i-Maarifat* ('The Sinai of Knowledge', 1687), and *Irfan* ('Knowledge', 1712), *Sufi themes exist side by side with descriptions of everyday Indian life and realistic treatments of nature and man. The romantic long poem *Komde-Modan,* included in the *Masnawi Irfan,* develops the traditions of Persian romantic *mathnawi* on Indian material.

His prose works *Chahar Unsur* ('Four Elements', 1685) and *Ruqaat* ('Epistles') are valuable sources on the era and the poet's own life. See also: *Sabk-i-Hindi.*

WORKS: *'Kulliyat -i-Bedil' (Collected Works), Bombay, 1882.*

BIBLIOGRAPHY: *G. Yu. Aliyev, 'Persian-language Literature of India', Moscow, 1968 (in Russian); I. Muminov, 'Bedil's Philosophy', Tashkent, 1957 (in Russian); Khwaja Ibadullah Akhtar, 'Bedil', Lahore, 1952.*

M.M. OSIPOVA

Bedil Rohri (1814–72)

Poet. Bedil Rohri (real name, Faqir Kadir Bakhsh) was a *Sindhi poet, who wrote in both Sindhi and Persian. He had a good command of Arabic, *Urdu, *Hindi, *Siraiki, and probably Sanskrit. *Sufism strongly influenced his work. His three-volume collection of *Sufi poetry includes *Wahdat-Nama* ('The Book of Unity'), *Sarod-Nama* ('The Book of Songs'), and *Faraiz-i-Sufia* ('A Sufi's Duties'), consisting of poems in the genre of **doha* and *bait.*

Bedil Rohri's work is also rich in Sindhi folk poetic forms, such as **wai*, **kafi*, and others. Many of his verses have been set to music and have become popular songs in *Sindh. Bedil Rohri is a follower of Rumi and Sachal *Sarmast.

BIBLIOGRAPHY: *Pir Husamuddin Rashdi, 'Sindhi Adab', (Sindhi Literature), Karachi (undated).*

A.S. SUKHOCHEV

Beg, Farrukh

Artist. Farrukh Beg was a painter of the *Mughal *miniature school of the 16th century. He moved from Shiraz to Kabul, where he lived in 1576-85, then to India, to the courts of Akbar and Jahangir (c. 1601-8), and later to Bijapur, Deccan. His works in the style of Iranian miniatures are remarkable for their picturesque colour scheme, subtle and elegant presentation of colours and careful attention to detail. He painted many portraits, in which he achieved masterful likenesses, a high degree of realism and psychological depth. The main works signed by him and ascribed to him are: *A Portrait of Sultan Ibrahim Adil Shah of Bijapur with a Musical Instrument* (c. 1610-11; the Naprstek Museum, Prague); miniatures in the manuscripts of *Jami-at-Tawarikh* by Rashidaddin (1595, the Shah's library, Tehran); *The Poet in the Garden* (Fine Arts Museum, Boston, USA); and *Saints Against a Landscape Background* (State Hermitage, St. Petersburg).

N.K. KARPOVA

Beg, Mirza Kalich (1853–1929)

Writer. A man of letters and an educator in *Sindh, Mirza Kalich Beg was awarded the title 'The Sun of the Learned' (*Shams al-Ulema*). According to family tradition, his ancestors came from Georgia as prisoners of war during the Iranian war and were converted to Islam during the reign of the *Talpurs. He received his education at Elphinstone College in Bombay. He wrote in Sindhi, Persian, *Urdu, *Hindi, English, and other languages. He became known following his writing the play *Khurshid* ('The Sun', 1885), based on a Gujarati play. In all, he wrote about 350 pieces in various genres. He translated such books as Swift's *Gullivers Travels*, Defoe's *Robinson Crusoe,* and T. Day's *The Story of Sandford and Merton* into Sindhi. He also translated from Arabic.

Mirza Kalich Beg is a founder of the novel in Sindhi literature. His *magnum opus* is the novel *Zinat* (1890) about the need for female education in Muslim society. He devoted much attention to popularising Firdousi's *Shah Nama.* His play *Inspector* is based on Gogol's *Government-Inspector.* He compiled a number of dictionaries, reference books, textbooks, and did much to promote learning. He had a profound influence on the development of an enlightened *Sindhi literature.

BIBLIOGRAPHY: *'Sindh ja Manya' (The Pearls of Sindh), Bombay, 1938 (in Sindhi); L.H. Ajwani, 'History of Sindhi Literature', New Delhi, 1977.*

A.S. SUKHOCHEV

Bek

(Turkic: Beg, Bey) A title designating master, aristocrat, prince. Begler Beg (Turkic: the prince of princes), the title of the rulers of Kalat principality in *Balochistan before 1955.

YU.V. GANKOVSKY

Bekas (1858–82)

Poet. Bekas (real name, Abdul Qadir) was a *Sindhi poet also writing in Persian. He was a follower of Sachal *Sarmast and the son of *Bedil Rohri. He was educated by his father, who emphasised *Sufi traditions.

His poems in the genre of **kafi*, singing the love of God, enjoyed great popularity among the common people. The **diwans* of Bekas and his father Bedil were collected and published by Gidumal Harjani, who also wrote a fundamental study of their work that marked a turning point in the styles of Persian and Sindhi poetry.

A.S. SUKHOCHEV

Bengal

A historico-geographic region in the northeast of South Asia. Bengal occupies the main part of the *Bengali plains–the excessively humid delta of the Rivers Ganges, Brahmaputra, Meghna, and their tributaries. In the areas close to the sea the average height above sea level is as little as 1 to 3 metres; in the north and north-west, 20 to 40 metres. Area: about 230,000 sq.km.; population: over 200 million (1990 estimate). More than 90 per cent of the people speak Bengali.

Bengal is one of the most densely populated areas of the globe. Fertile soils and a favourable climate yield two or three crops a year. The main cultivated plants are rice, wheat, jute and tea.

The first state structures on Bengali territory, Wanga and Pundra, emerged in the middle of the first millennium BC. From the 4th to the 2nd centuries BC, Bengal was ruled by the *Maurya dynasty. After the disintegration of the latter several small independent states (Tamralipta, Suhma, Radha, Samatata, and others) emerged here. Early in the 4th century all of them were incorporated into the *Gupta Empire. In the 6th century, after the fall of the Gupta Empire, a vast state arose in Bengal. This was successively ruled by the dynasties of the Gauda (6th-7th centuries), Pala (8th-11th centuries), and Sena (11th-early 13th centuries). In the 13th century, Bengal was conquered by the generals of the Delhi sultans. This promoted the spread of Islam there. In 1576 Bengal was conquered and added to the Great *Mughal Empire by the Emperor Akbar. After the Battle of Plassey, in 1757, Bengal came under the rule of the British East India Company. In August 1947 during the division of *British India, the greater (eastern) part of Bengal (141,000 sq.km.) was included in Pakistan. Since 1971 this has been the People's Republic of Bangladesh. West Bengal (88,000 sq.km.) became part of India and is known as the State of West Bengal. The largest cities are Calcutta (Kolkatta) in India; Dhaka and Chittagong in Bangladesh.

YU.V. GANKOVSKY

Bengali (Language)

Bengali was, until 1971, the official and national language of *East Pakistan. It belongs to the eastern subgroup of the new *Indo-Aryan languages of the Indo-European family and has its roots in the Middle Indian language of Magadhi. It is also spoken by 200 to 300 thousand Bengalis living in Pakistan. Bengali is traditionally divided into seven dialects or dialect groups: 1. central or standard, 2. western 3. south-western, 4. northern, 5. Rajbangshi, 6. eastern, and 7. south-eastern. As a result of the division of India in 1947, speakers of dialect groups 1, 2 and 3, and most of 4 and 5, remained in India while speakers of dialects 6 and 7, and partly 4 and 5, went to Pakistan.

Modern Bengali exists in two functional styles, the classical (*Shadhubhasha*) and the standard or spoken (*Cholitbhasha*). The difference between them shows both in grammar (those of pronouns and verbs), and in vocabulary (the *Shadhubhasha* vocabulary is more archaic, mostly Sanskrit). The division of functions is also significant. *Shadhubhasha* exists only in written form, where as *Cholitbhasha* is used in both its written and oral varieties and serves as the principal means of interdialect communication.

Three periods can be distinguished in the history of the Bengali language: 1. Old Bengali (10th through 12th centuries), 2. Middle Bengali (13th through 18th centuries), 3. Modern Bengali (from the beginning of the 19th century to the present day). The structural features of Bengali were determined by its early contacts with unrelated languages. These include Munda (Santali and others) and *Dravidian (Malto and Kurukh) in the west, numerous Burmese languages, and Khasi (the Mon-Khmer group) in the north. They influenced not only Bengali vocabulary but also its grammar and phonetics. They also influenced the existence in some of these dialects of semantically relevant tones. Historically the Bengali language, especially its vocabulary, was influenced by those languages which functioned officially in the territory in which it was in use: Persian and Arabic in the thirteenth through 18th centuries and English from the beginning of the 19th century. Bengali was affected by Sanskrit more than any other closely related language, borrowing from it up to 80 per cent of its vocabulary.

BIBLIOGRAPHY: *Ye.M. Bykova, 'The Bengali Language', Moscow, 1966; 'The Bengali Language—Questions of Grammar', Moscow, 1962; 'Questions of Bengali Grammar', Moscow, 1964; L.M. Chevkina, 'On the Role of Social Factors in the Development of Bengali: The People's Republic of Bangladesh', Moscow, 1979; Essays in the Grammar of Bengali, Pt. 1, Moscow, 1968, S.K. Chatterji, The Origin and Development of the Bengali Language, Pts I-III, London,*

1970-2 P.S. Ray, M.A. Hay and L. Ray, Bengali Language Handbook, Washington, 1966.

L.M. CHEVKINA

Bengal, Partition of, 1905–11

The partition of *Bengal was carried out in 1905 by Viceroy Lord Curzon (1859-1925). It proved to be a rehearsal for the partition of India in 1947 and the 1971 emergence of Bangladesh (see Bangladesh-Pakistan Relations). The Viceroy had proposed partition for administrative reasons. With a population of 78 million and with an area of 189,000 square miles, the Province was too large to govern and the eastern districts suffered neglect. Officials in the Viceroy's Secretariat had been formulating proposals for partitioning Bengal since 1902. The partition gave rise to agitation because, although Bengal had an overall Muslim majority, the Hindus were concentrated in the west and the Muslims in the east.

The communal implications of the partition were spelt out by the Maharaja of Kasimbazar in a Calcutta meeting held on 7 August 1905. There was a massive agitation at the Kali temple in Calcutta on 16 October 1905 when the partition went into effect.

The agitation was led by the professional classes of lawyers, doctors and academics, who comprised the politically active sector. The communal complexion of the anti-partition agitation led Muslims to organize themselves politically, first in the *Simla Deputation of 1905 and the foundation of the *All-India Muslim League in 1906 at Dhaka—the capital of the newly created province of East Bengal. The new province would have a Chief Court at Dhaka.

A Dhaka Medical College and Dhaka University would be founded. The jurisdiction and thus the influence and affluence of the (mainly West Bengali and therefore Hindu) professional classes would be reduced. The agitational politics of the Congress and the Hindu parties led to the annulment of partition by the King-Emperor, George V in his 1911 Delhi Durbar proclamation.

BIBLIOGRAPHY: *Sufia Ahmad, 'Muslim Community of Bengal 1884-1912', Dhaka, 1974; K.K. Aziz, 'Britain and Muslim India', London, 1963; P. Hardy, 'The Muslims of British India', Cambridge, 1972; Matiur Rahman, 'From Consultation to Confrontation', London, 1970; Z.H. Zaidi, 'The Partition of Bengal and its Annulment 1905-1911', London University, 1964 [Unpublished Ph.D. Thesis].*

M.R. KAZIMI

Betel

Betel pepper (*piper betle*—Malaysian pepper), a bush of the pepper family. It is cultivated all over tropical Asia. Together with *areca* its leaves are used as a chewing mixture in tropical countries. A chewing mixture widely popular in the countries of South-East Asia. Fresh betel leaves are cut in strips and covered on the inside with quick lime on *orke* to neutralize the acidity in the leaves which have a peppery spicy taste. Pieces of red *areca* fruit are wrapped in betel leaves and chewed for a mild intoxicating effect on the nervous system. The mouth, tongue, and gums become coloured bright red, saliva is profusely secreted, and the teeth become black.

O.A. DRUZHININA

Bewas (1885–1947)

Poet. Bewas (real name, Kishinchand Tirathdas Khatri) was a poet and dramatist writing in *Sindhi. He worked as a schoolteacher and his literary career began with children's verse, which he later published as a collection titled *Shirin Shair* ('Sweet Tunes'). His poetry combines the multiple influences of Indian and Middle East literatures. The narrative poem *Samundi Sipun* ('Sea Shell') is based on Krishnavite motifs. His *Musaddas* was composed according to the rules of Persian poetry. *Gariban ji Jonpri* ('Beggar's Hut') and *Porhiyut* ('Toiler') are noted for their social message. Bewas's language is close to the people's spoken language. He made a wide use of original Sanskrit and Arabic-Persian words that had become part of spoken Sindhi.

Many followed Bewas's attempt to revitalize Sindhi poetry. His influence is particularly evident in the early work of Shaykh Ayaz. Bewas's plays are mainly devoted to Sindhi peasant life.

BIBLIOGRAPHY: *L.H. Ajwani, History of Sindhi Literature, New Delhi, 1977.*

A.S. SUKHOCHEV

Bhangra

A dance originally performed by the men of Gujrat, *Jhelum and Wazirabad districts to celebrate the success of a harvest or at the onset of spring. Now people in all urban areas of the country perform Bhangra at wedding parties and other occasions of happiness with great abandon. Bhangra is performed in villages as well as cities, to large drums, called **dhols*. It is a most energetic dance.

R. HUSAIN

Bharata Natyam

A dance evolved in southern India. The long history of this stylised dance has been well recorded both in visual and textual documents. These dance traditions were the heritage of performers who were part of the courts of kings, or performers who were part of religious traditions. In Pakistan the statuette of the dancing girl of Mohenjo-Daro, with her limbs and hip frozen in a particular pose, evokes those traditions.

It was in the 1930s that pioneers such as Rukmini Devi and Krishna Iyer revived dancing traditions and set the tone for the Bharata Natyam dance of today. It is one of the most developed art forms, that relates to all the aspects of human existence: body, psyche and the soul.

A peculiar style or stance of Bharata Natyam is *arai mandi* or half bent knees position. The dancer combines body movements, eyes, head and neck movements, facial expressions and hand gestures in a repertoire that normally begins by salutations to the gods, the *guru* and the audience. After the first two dance items called *allarippu* and *jatiswaram*, which are purely abstract, are performed the *abhinaya* or *nritya*. This is a part of the dance full of sepression. *Tillana* is the final item in the Bharata Natyam repertoire, and is another excellent example of pure and abstract dance. It is entirely governed by the scintillating musical score and incorporates intricate foot-work and sculpturesque poses.

R. HUSAIN

Bhashani, Abdul Hamid Khan, Maulana (1885–1976)

Politician. Educated in *Deoband, Maulana Bhashani was a leader of the national liberation movement in *British India and later a public and political figure in Pakistan and Bangladesh. Throughout his life he remained a strong proponent of the interests of the peasantry and the rural poor. Before 1947 he was President of the *Muslim League in Assam and publisher of the newspapers *Assam Herald* and *Mujahid*. He participated in the *Khilafat Movement. He became a Member of the Assam Legislative Assembly in 1937. From 1949 to 1957 Bhashani was Chairman of the *Awami League of *East Pakistan. From 1957 to 1967 he was Chairman of the National Awami Party. After the National Awami Party's split he became the Chairman of its so-called 'Pro-China' faction from 1967 to 1974. In 1971 he was a member of the Consultative Political Committee, which coordinated the national liberation struggle in East Bengal. His decision not to contest the 1970 elections gave the Awami League a clear field.

V.P. BAIDAKOV

Bhita

The contemporary name of an archaeological site found 16 km. to the southeast of Allahabad. In ancient times, according to inscriptions on seals, it was called Buru. John *Marshall, head of the Indian Archaeological Survey, studied this site from 1909 to 1912. The site covers 0.26 sq. km. and the diggings reveal 1-1.5 per cent of its surface. The defence wall was 3.4 metres thick and about 12 metres high. The southern gates have also been execrated. The town square was crossed by several parallel streets. One of these, which Marshall called the 'main street', began at the gates and led to the sanctuary in the town's centre. This street was 10 metres wide. There was a narrower parallel street, tentatively called 'the bastion street'. The houses along these two streets were completely identical in layout, but noticeably bigger along the main street.

There were two rows of houses between the two main streets. They had two or three storeys and probably accommodated from ten to twenty people, including servants. A general assessment gives the number of such houses as 940, with a total population of 10,000-20,000.

One of the houses in the main street was built with burnt bricks. Twelve rooms were arranged around a rectangular court and covered an area of 14 x 13.4 metres. It probably had two storeys. Other houses consisted of two parts. The front looking into the 'High Street' comprised three rooms with a staircase leading from the street into the central room. This part was probably used as a shop. The houses formed cells looking into the street and surrounded with back alleys on three sides. The seals found in the site allowed archaeologists to establish the names of some of the house-owners.

Marshall believed that the houses he opened existed for almost a thousand years from the fifth *Maurya period to the 5th century AD.

BIBLIOGRAPHY: *B.A. Litvinsky, A.V. Sedov, 'Tepai-Shah, Kushanic Bactria's Culture and Ties', Moscow, 1983 (in Russian); J. Marshall, Archaeological Exploration in India, 1909-10', IRAS, 1911; J. Marshall, 'Excavations at Bhita-Arasi for 1911-12', Delhi, 1915; D. Schlingloff, 'Das*

Altindische Stadt Eine Verglichende Untersuchung', Wiesbaden, 1970.

B.A. LITVINSKY

Bhitai, Shah Abdul Latif (1689–1751)

Poet. A classical *Sindhi poet and musician, he was a follower of Jalaluddin Rumi (1207-73). Regarded as a major saint, his tomb at Bhit Shah, is a place of pilgrimage. His major work is a collection of mystical and narrative poems *Shah Jo Risalo* ('The Shah's Epistle'), in which the legends and folklore of the *Sindhis, *Punjabis and *Balochis are used as metaphors for the *Sufi concept of heavenly love and the soul's fusion with the Absolute, the soul being represented by the heroine. The text of the Epistle is divided into thirty chapters (*surs*), each of which has a corresponding music scale (**raga*). In the *surs* the lengthy narrative **dastans* are interspersed with short lyrical **wais*. The poet used *aruz* in his *dastans*, while in the *wais* he used Sindhi folklore metres: *boroduho* and *tumberiduho*. He turned to such traditional Indian forms as *barahmasa, chakki-nama* and others. The Epistle reflects everyday life as well as the social and spiritual atmosphere of medieval *Sindh. The poetry of Shah Abdul Latif had an enormous influence on the subsequent development of *Sindhi literature. In Europe the Epistle has been known since 1866, when it was translated by E. Trumpp and published in Leipzig.

WORKS: *'Risalo—Shah Abdul Latif', Karachi, 1961.*

BIBLIOGRAPHY: *A. Dekhtyar, 'On the Composition of the Sindhi Literary Monument 'Shah Jo Risalo'', in: The Collection Literature and the Times, Moscow, 1973 (in Russian); A. Dekhtyar, 'Shah Abdul Latif, the Classical Sindhi Author', in: The Collection Indian Literatures (in Russian); M. Jotwani, 'Shah Abdul Latif, his Life and Work', New Delhi, 1975; J. Parsram; 'Sindh and its Sufis', Madras, 1965; P. Mayne, 'Saints of Sindh', Oxford, 1956; A. Schimmel, 'Pain and Grace', Leiden, 1976; H.T. Sorley, 'Shah Abdul Latif of Bhit: his Poetry, Life and Times', Oxford, 1966; U.M. Daudpota, 'Sindhi Literature', Karachi, 1951.*

A.A. SUVOROVA

Bhopal, Mohammad Hamidullah, Sir, Nawab of (1894–1960)

Statesman. H.H. Sikander Saulat, Nawab Iftikharul-Mulk, Sir Mohammad Hamidullah, Nawab of Bhopal, succeeded to the throne of Bhopal, the second largest Indian princely state ruled by a Muslim, in 1926. He had been educated at the University of Allahabad (BA) and Aligarh Muslim University (LLB).

In 1923 the Nawab of Bhopal was elected to the Standing Committee of the Chamber of Princes. This did not prevent him from demanding Dominion Status for India. He promoted Hindu-Muslim amity and repealed a law that made apostasy from Islam a criminal offence in Bhopal.

Because of his nationalistic views, he had established contact with Congress leaders, but became estranged when the *Nehru Report discarded the Delhi Muslim Proposals. Noticing this, the Congress organized a strike in Bhopal in 1938. In the same year the Quaid-i-Azam paid a visit to Bhopal and close, friendly relations were established between *Jinnah and the Nawab.

In 1944 he was elected Chancellor of the Chamber of Princes. In 1946, after the *Cabinet Mission Plan had floundered, Hamidullah attempted reconciliation between Gandhi and Jinnah, getting the former to sign a formula for communal representation in the Interim Government, but, in a replay of the *Round Table Conference scene, Gandhi retracted the following day. Hamidullah attempted a device of block negotiation of the Chamber of Princes with the Constituent Assembly of India. On 3 June 1947, when the Partition Plan was announced, the Nawab of Bhopal resigned as Chancellor of the Chamber of Princes. On 14 August 1947 Bhopal acceded to the Dominion of India.

BIBLIOGRAPHY: *Ian Coupland, 'The Quaid-i-Azam and the Nawab Chancellor' in: Mushir-ul-Hasan (ed.), Islam: Communities and the Nation, New Delhi, 1998.*

YU.V. GANKOVSKY

Bhutto, Benazir (1953–)

Politician. Twice Prime Minister of Pakistan. She is the daughter of former Prime Minister Z.A. *Bhutto. After completing her early education in Pakistan, she attended Radcliffe College and Oxford University. As well as obtaining a degree in Philosophy, Politics and Economics, she also took a course in International Law and Diplomacy at Oxford.

Benazir Bhutto, first female head of the state of a Muslim country. Prime Minister (1988–90) and 1993–96).

On 2 December 1988 Benazir Bhutto was elected as Prime Minister of Pakistan, becoming the first woman to head the government of an Islamic State.

In the preceding decade of political struggle she was arrested on numerous occasions. In all she spent nearly 6 years either in prison or under detention for her political policies in opposition. She was twice ousted from the office of prime minister first in 1990, and then from 1993 to 1996. Her husband, A.A. Zardari gained a reputation for corruption, and her own dealings with the MQM caused her political career considerable harm. She has been kept out of politics by a decree that no one can be prime minister of Pakistan for more than two terms of office. At the time of writing this entry, she is in exile from Pakistan.

She received the Bruno Kreisky Award for Human Rights in 1988 and the Honorary Phi Beta Kappa Award from Radcliffe in 1989.

WORKS: *'Foreign Policy in Perspective' (1978); 'Daughter of the East' (1988).*

BIBLIOGRAPHY: *Dianne Sansevere–Dreher; 'Benazir Bhutto', New York, 1991; Iqbal Akhund, 'Trial and Error: The Advent and Eclipse of Benazir Bhutto', Karachi, 2000; Muhammad Ali Shaikh, 'Benazir Bhutto', Karachi, 2000.*

M.H. ASKARI

Bhutto, Murtaza, Mir (1954–96)

Politician. The elder son of Z.A. *Bhutto, Mir Murtaza lived in exile after his father's execution. Accused of running the terrorist Al-Zulfikar organization, he became an opposition leader during the term of his sister, Benazir *Bhutto, and founded his own faction of the *Pakistan Peoples Party. He was killed in a police encounter on 20 September 1996.

BIBLIOGRAPHY: *Raja Anwar, 'The Terrorist Prince', Lahore, 1997.*

M.H. ASKARI

Bhutto, Shahnawaz, Sir (1888–1957)

Statesman. Educated at Larkana and Karachi, he won the *Sindh seat of the Imperial Legislative Council in 1919. The same year he was made an OBE was awarded KIH in 1924 and received a knighthood in 1930. In 1925 Sir Shahnawaz Bhutto became President of the Sindh National Mohammedan Association. Sir Shahnawaz, played host to M.A. Jinnah in 1928, and was a delegate to the *Round Table Conferences. He was a member of the Lord Russell Committee, which recommended the separation of Sindh from Bombay Presidency. This was considered the first constitutional victory for Muslims after the annulment of the *Bengal Partition (1911). From 1937 to 1946, Sir Shahnawaz was a member of the Bombay/Sindh Public Service Commission.

In 1946 he was appointed *Dewan* (Premier) of Junagarh state, and in this capacity advised Nawab Sir Mahabat Khanji, the Muslim ruler of the Hindu majority state, to accede to Pakistan at the time of Partition. At his invitation, Sir Zafrullah Khan arrived to draft the Instrument of Accession to Pakistan. He was followed soon by V.P. Menon, who threatened dire consequences if Junagarh did not revoke its accession to Pakistan. Under mounting pressure Nawab Mahabat Khanji left Junagarh at the end of October 1947. Sir Shahnawaz stayed on till 8 November, when a Minister, Captain Harvey Jones, called in the Indian Army. Sir Shahnawaz Bhutto spent the last decade of his life in peaceful retirement. His son, Z.A. *Bhutto, became Prime Minister of Pakistan.

WORKS: *Memoirs [Unpublished].*

BIBLIOGRAPHY: *Husain Shah Rashdi, 'Sir Shahnawaz Bhutto', Karachi, 1998; Muhammad Ali Shaikh, 'Luminaries of the Land', Karachi, 1999.*

M.H. ASKARI

Bhutto, Zulfikar Ali (1928–79)

Zulfikar Ali Bhutto, Prime Minister of Pakistan (1973–77).

Politician/Statesman/Prime Minister of Pakistan from 1973 to 1977. Zulfikar Ali Bhutto was born into a well-to-do family of Larkana in *Sindh. His father, Sir Shahnawaz *Bhutto (1888-1957) had been a minister in the government in Bombay Presidency and, at the time of partition, was the *Dewan* of Junagarh state. Educated in Bombay, California, and Oxford and called to the Bar at Lincoln's Inn (1953), Bhutto was destined to play a prominent role in the politics of Pakistan at a crucial time. He led his own *Pakistan Peoples Party, founded in 1967, breaking the virtual monopoly of the *Muslim League in the governance of the country.

His major achievement, shortly after coming to the helm of the nation, was to negotiate peace with India, which had militarily aided former *East Pakistan in its struggle for independence. At the *Simla Conference, at the end of June 1972, he secured the Indian Prime Minister Indira Gandhi's agreement to the release of some 93,000 Pakistanis, mostly military personnel, whom the Indian army had taken prisoner at the surrender in Dhaka on 16 December 1971. India withdrew from approximately 5,139 square miles of Pakistani territory in the Western wing, which had been occupied during the war.

Another important event of Bhuttos term of office was the promulgation of the *Constitution of 1973. He believed in the concept of Islamic socialism, which implies that there are some common areas in socialism and the Islamic system of thought.

Bhutto's strength as a politician was his skillful handling of Pakistan's foreign relations. Z.A. Bhutto had been Foreign Minister in Ayub *Khan's government from 1963 to 1967 and also later under Yahya *Khan. Apart from the Simla Agreement negotiated with Mrs Gandhi, he secured Soviet Russia's pledge of $ 517.64 million by way of loans for the building of a steel mill in Karachi. However, the project was obstructed at various stages and the mill could not go on stream until after Bhutto's removal. Bhutto tried to mend fences with Afghanistan (see Afghanistan-Pakistan Relations) but with little success. He made a substantial contribution towards the development and strengthening of ties with China. He pulled Pakistan out of the US-sponsored SEATO and CENTO pacts, convened a well-attended summit of Islamic countries in February 1974, and proclaimed the recognition of Bangladesh, managing to persuade Shaikh Mujibur *Rahman to attend the moot.

Bhutto's problems began with his holding of general election in March 1977. His party secured an overwhelming mandate, but several prominent opposition parties, irritated by his autocratic style of governance, subverted the outcome through mass agitation, accusing Bhutto of having rigged the elections. They organised themselves under the banner of *Pakistan National Alliance and held massive street demonstrations, creating a serious law and order problem. Bhutto called upon the army to restore order, but his handpicked Chief of Army Staff, General Ziaul *Haq, who had pledged personal allegiance to him at the time of his appointment in 1976, turned against him and ultimately ousted him through a *coup* on 5 July 1977. Zia, for the sake of his own survival, had Bhutto tried on a charge of conspiracy to murder a political rival and the Supreme Court held him guilty by a controversially divided (four to three) verdict against him. He was hanged on 4 April 1979.

WORKS: *'The Myth of Independence', Karachi, 1969; 'The Great Tragedy', Karachi, 1971; 'If I am Assassinated', New Delhi, 1979.*

BIBLIOGRAPHY: *J.C. Batra, 'The Trial and Execution of Bhutto', Delhi, 1979; Shahid Javed Burki, 'Pakistan Under Bhutto', 2nd ed., London, 1988; Mubashir Hasan, 'The Mirage of Power', Karachi, 2000; S.N. Kaushik, 'Pakistan Under Bhutto's Leadership', New Delhi, 1985; Piloo Mody, 'Zulfi, My Friend', Delhi, 1973; Dilip Mukherji, 'Zulfikar Ali Bhutto: Quest for Power', New Delhi, 1972; Rafi Raza, 'Zulfikar Ali Bhutto and Pakistan', Karachi, 1997; Victoria Schofield, 'Bhutto; Trial and Execution', London, 1979; Anwar Husain Syed, 'The Discourse and Politics of Zulfikar Ali Bhutto', New York, 1992; Salman Taseer, 'Bhutto: A Political Biography', London, 1979; Stanley Wolpert, 'Zulfi Bhutto of Pakistan', New York, 1993.*

M.H. ASKARI

Bihari

Urdu-speaking Muslim immigrants from northern India, who settled mostly in *East Pakistan and also *West Pakistan after 1947. According to the 1961 census, they numbered 311,000, or 0.6 per cent of the East Pakistan population.

R.M. MUKIMJANOVA

Bilgrami, Syed Hasan, Dr. Major (d. 1915)

Syed Hasan Bilgrami was a physician who joined the British Army. He had helped his brother, Nawab Imadul Mulk, to draft the memorandum to Lord Minto at Simla. He was elected Honorary Secretary of the *All-India Muslim League in March 1908. In the same month he sailed for London as a member of the Council of the Secretary of State for India. Bilgrami, more than any other leader, was responsible for the successful campaign for separate electorates for Muslims. This was an issue on which both Lords Minto and Morley had been non-committal. After a very contentious debate, both in India and England, it was included in the Morley-Minto Reforms 1909. Bilgrami retired from politics in 1910 and died five years later.

BIBLIOGRAPHY: *Matiur Rahman, 'From Consultation to Confrontation', London, 1970; 'Liaquat Ali Khan and the Freedom Movement', Karachi, 1997.*

M.R. KAZIMI

Bin

(*murli, pungi*) A variety of bagpipe in which the shell of a pumpkin acts as the air chamber and the elongated part of the pumpkin is used as a mouthpiece. Two bamboo shoots, with differing numbers of apertures, are connected to the air chamber. The instrument is used for both solo (in *Sindh) and ensemble (e.g., with the *sarinda*) performances. One type of bin, called bin *baja*, is often played with a *shahnai* during wedding ceremonies and traditional dances.

I. PIRACHA

Biotechnology

The importance and potential of biotechnology was realized as far back as 1959 when Pakistan's first Commission on Science and Technology emphasised the need for setting up research organisations in areas of vital importance to national development. Biotechnology has since been promoted in practically every science policy document. Pakistan's commitment to this field has been reflected in a separate allocation of the development budget to biotechnology in the Eighth and Ninth five year Plans.

The National Institute of Biotechnology and Genetic Engineering (NIBGE) is the country's major biotech research establishment, concentrating on research into plant, environmental, and medical biotechnology. NIBGE has produced some impressive results in a short time. Most recently scientists at the Institute have found a biotechnology-based solution which may help to eliminate Pakistan's recurring cotton leaf-curl virus (CLCV), which has been a recurring problem

NIBGE undertook a rewarding programme of reclaiming nearly 11 million acres of saline and sodic soils by biological methods. This technology developed by NIBGE has now been exploited by the International Atomic Energy Agency for initiating an integrated model project for eight countries. NIBGE is also researching the use of biotechnology to extract minerals and fossil fuels. It has developed methods to extract copper and uranium using bacteria. This technique has potential applications in the development of the Saindak mines in *Balochistan, Pakistan's biggest copper mining project.

Biotechnology also has environmental applications. NIBGE has helped industry in the area of effluent detoxification and waste management through the use of microbes. Industrial effluent tends to be discharged into sources of potential drinking water. Microbes can be used to clean up textile industry effluents, which have a high concentration of dyes, and which are carcinogenic. Different micro-organisms developed by the Institute not only degrade the dyes, but also make them colourless, allowing them to be recycled.

Biomedical and Genetic Engineering Division

Pakistan has one outstanding organisation devoted to research into human genetics, one of the most costly areas in molecular biology. A group of scientists at the Institute of Molecular Genetics in Islamabad have identified the gene responsible for Retinitis Pigmentosa, a hereditary degenerative disease, which leads to complete loss of sight. More than 3,000 lymphoblastoid cell lines have been prepared from Pakistan and other populations of clinical and anthropological interest. This is the largest collection of human cell lines in the world. Duplicates of these cell lines have been banked at CEPH, Paris, France and the department of Biochemistry at Oxford University, with the financial support of the Wellcome Trust, UK. The descent of various Pakistani and world populations has been examined for genetic relationships using Y-chromosomes (patrilineal) and autosomal microsatellite markers.

The Centre for Advanced Molecular Biology (CAMB) was established in 1981 at Punjab University. During the past ten years the Centre has discovered forty-five new restriction enzymes which interfere with DNA replication. CAMB has also pioneered DNA-based methods for the pre-natal diagnosis of Beta-thalassaemia. Methods for early detection of tuberculosis, hepatitis, and breast cancer have also been developed. In 1988 the status of the Centre was upgraded to a Centre of Excellence in Advanced Molecular Biology. In addition to the above mentioned organisations biotechnology is being taught at general as well as agricultural and medical universities.

T. NAIM

Biryani

A variety of a *pilau* introduced in Indian cuisine during the Muslim rule. Classical *biryani* is cooked with chunks of meat marinated with spices and underdone fried rice with onions and spices. The food is then laid out in a metal sauce pan in layers and cooked to readiness. Today there are vegetarian recipes for *biryani*. It is a dish for festive occasions which is cooked with the best-quality rice.

O.N. BOBYLEVA

Bizenjo, Ghaus Bakhsh Khan, Mir (1917–89)

Politician/Statesman. A prominent political figure of Balochistan, Bizenjo graduated from the Aligarh Muslim University. In the 1940s he served as President of the National Party of the Kalat princely state in Balochistan. He went on to become one of the organisers and leaders of the *National Awami Party. He became Governor of *Balochistan province in 1972. In June 1979 he founded and headed the Pakistan National Party.

YU.V. GANKOVSKY

Bogra, Mohammad Ali of (1900–63)

Prime Minister from 1953 to 1955. Mohammed Ali graduated from Calcutta University in 1930 and worked as a leader of the *Muslim League in *Bengal from 1937 to 1947. In the late 1940s and in the 1950s he was, successively Pakistan's Ambassador to Burma, Canada, USA and Japan. In April 1953 he became Prime Minister of Pakistan following the removal of the government of Khwaja *Nazimuddin by Governor-General Ghulam *Muhammed. He presented the draft 1954 constitutions and signed the SEATO and Baghdad pacts with the USA held this office until August 1955. Mohammad Ali co-sponsored and attended the *Bandung Conference (1955). In 1962–63, he became Minister of Foreign Affairs in the Ayub *Khan government.

Mohammad Ali Bogra, Prime Minister of Pakistan (1953–55).

YU.V. GANKOVSKY

Bohra (also Bohora)

(from the Gujarati '*wohuru*' meaning 'trade, craft')

One of the two main Ismaili sects in South Asia. It is also known as Mustalite after al-Mustali, a Fatimid caliph in Egypt (1094–101), from whom Bohra **imams* trace their origin. The sect appeared in the twelfth century as a result of the work of Bohra missionaries from Egypt and Yemen, and the conversion to Islam of some Hindu Gujaratis from the local trade and money-lending castes. Bohras are divided into several sub-sects. The first is the Daudi, followers of Daud ibn-Ajab Shah, who moved to India from Yemen in 1539 and died in 1589. They inhabit western and northern India, Pakistan and Bangladesh. The seat of the sub-sect's leader, *dai al-mutlaq* (the supreme *dai*) is in the town of Surat (the state of Gujarat, India). At present the **Dai* is Syedna Burhanuddin. The second sub-sect is the Sulaymani, named after its founder, Sulayman ibn-Hasan. They live in Gujarat, Maharashtra and south India. There is also a small sub-sect of *Sunni Bohra (Jafaris), who mainly engage in farming.

YU.V. GANKOVSKY

Bolan Pass

A pass located in the northern part of the Central Brahui Range in Pakistan. It is approximately 1,792 m above sea level. A railroad and highway connect Quetta with the *Indus Valley via the pass.

YU.V. GANKOVSKY

Bolitho, Hector (1898–1974)

Novelist/Historian/Biographer. Hector Bolitho was born in Auckland, New Zealand. He was a reporter on a New Zealand newspaper at seventeen and published his first novel at twenty-five. He travelled widely in Australia, Africa, Canada, America, Europe, and the Middle East.

By 1963 he had published fifty-two books of history, biography, and fiction in barely thirty-eight years. The longest he took to write a book was *Jinnah: Creator of Pakistan*. It took him a little less than three years, including the period consumed by his travels in the subcontinent and interviews and research in England. *Jinnah* was 'his best book for many years', remarked the *Daily Telegraph* (24 November 1954).

His writing is characterised by elegance, and his narrative engaging and absorbing. Above all, his approach is empathic, enabling him 'to get behind the mask' and unravel the intricacies of thought behind his subject's policies decisions and predilections. All these attributes seem tailored to unravelling the human side of the subject under study, and sketch in a convincing portrait.

WORKS: *'Albert The Good', London, 1932; 'Edward VIII. His Life and Reign', London, 1937; Jinnah: Creator of Pakistan, London, 1954.*

SHARIFUL MUJAHID

Brahui (also Braui)

Total population (People) approximately 1.5 million. Brahui are settled in central *Balochistan, south-western *Punjab, and northern *Sindh. Brahui-Balochi mixed settlements can be found in south-east Iran and south-west Afghanistan. The tribal systems among Brahui have been preserved well. The largest tribes are the following: Mambarani, Samalari, Mengal, Bizenjo, Sasoli, Shahwani, Lehri, Langar, Raisani, and the Nichari. Brahui are Sunni Muslims. Their main occupation is agriculture with elements of nomadic cattle-breeding.

BIBLIOGRAPHY: *M.G. Pikulin, 'Brahui', Moscow, 1967 (in Russian), Yuri Gankovsky, 'National-Ethnic Movements in Pakistan', Moscow 1989 (in Russian); A. Rooman, 'the Brahuis of Quetta-Kalat Region', Karachi, 1960; N. Brohi, 'Studies in Brahui History', Karachi, 1977.*

YU.V. GANKOVSKY

Brahui (Language)

Brahui belongs to the north-western group of *Dravidian languages. It is used in Pakistan in the provinces of *Balochistan and *Sindh, southern Afghanistan, and eastern Iran.

Two primary dialects are distinguished: the Jhalawan (north of Kalat) and the Sarawan (south of Kalat).

Regional influences such as Iranian (of *Balochi, *Pashtu and Farsi) and *Indo-Aryan (of *Sindhi and *Lahnda) are especially strong in syntax (the absence of absolute participial and adverbial-participial constructions and the use of postpositive particles in attributive groups). Brahui vocabulary also borrows heavily from Arabic as well as from Iranian and Indo-Aryan languages.

The writing system is based on the Arabic alphabet. The earliest known literary works date back to the eighteenth century (Malik-Dad Gharshin's treatise *Tohfat-ul-Ajaib*).

BIBLIOGRAPHY: *M.G. Pikulin, 'Brahui', Moscow, 1967 (in Russian); D. Bray, 'The Brahui Language', Pts 1-3, Calcutta-Delhi, 1903-34 M.B. Emeneau, 'Brahui and Dravidian Comparative Grammar', Berkeley-Los Angeles, 1962; S.M. Kamil-al-Qadri, 'All about Brahui', IJDL, 1972, Vol. 1, No. 1; D. McAlpin, 'Linguistic Prehistory. The Dravidian Situation', in: Aryan and Non-Aryan in India, Ann Arbor, 1979; M.S. Andronov, 'The Brahui Language', Moscow, 1980.*

N.V. GUROV

Brahui (Literature)

The first extant manuscripts of Brahui are of a didactic nature and date back to the late seventeenth century. At the end of the eighteenth century, the first **diwan* of Muhammad Kalati's religious poetry was compiled. Kalati traditions were developed by Maulana Nabujan. In the first half of the nineteenth century Muhammad Husain Bangalzai introduced **ghazals* into Brahui literature. Abdul Majid Chotwai turned to the genres of *qissa* and **dastan* and enriched the essentially religious poetry with secular motifs.

Ballu Sahir and Shahwar made an important contribution into the formation of Brahui poetry. Faqir Tajal (d. 1945) was another prominent poet who followed *Sufi traditions while at the same time turning to themes from everyday life. His Sufi-spirited verse bears a clear mark of Persian influence, while his poetry on everyday themes is rooted in the folk tradition. In the 1830s the rich Brahui folklore began to be recorded and published. Later, Brahui folk poetry appeared in various collections in English and *Urdu. In the 1940s a group of religious activists in Dadu (*Sindh) started publishing religious literature in Brahui. After independence studies into Brahui folklore appeared—songs, tales, heroic epics, poetry, and stories of a didactic and educational nature.

In 1951 a group of writers established '*Brahui Adabi Diwan*' (Brahui Literary Society). The year 1954 was a turning point in the history of Brahui literature, when a clear change could be seen from the traditional poetry, largely imitating Persian and *Balochi verse, to the poetry which was contemporary in style and subject matter. The major poets of that period include the famous journalist Pir Muhammad Zubairani (b. 1932), who translated into Brahui A.H. *Hali's *Musaddas;* the author of several collections of lyric poetry on nature, Muhammad Ishaq Soz (b. 1948); and Nadir Kambarani, who made an important contribution to the progress of patriotic poetry in Brahui. Ghulam Nabi Rahi is a leading prose writer and dramatist.

In 1966 a group of lecturers from the State College in Quetta founded the Brahui Academy to promote *Brahui language and literature. Its president is Muhammad Khan Raisani and Vice President is Mahmud Aziz Kird. Among the authors who published their work in periodicals and in book form, mention must be made of Nur Muhammad Parwana Brahui (b. 1918). He launched the first newspaper in Brahui and wrote a number of essays on Brahui literature. The critic and novelist Abdur Rahman Brahui (b. 1940) writes in Brahui, Urdu and English. The poet and literary scholar Zafar Ali Mirza (b. 1935) translated Muhammad Iqbal's poetry into Brahui, and Kamal al Qadiri (b. 1932) is a poet and literary critic.

In the *Brahui Adabi* Society, founded in the 1970s in Quetta, and in the journal published by the Television Centre in Quetta, as well as other literary organisations and periodicals, active members include Afzal Miran, Arif Ziya, Jawrah Brahui, Wahid Zubair, Aziz Mengal, Amir-ul-Mulk Mengal, Ali Ahmad Shad, Malik Tahir Shamim and Tahira Ehsan. The first weekly magazine in Brahui, *Eelum* (Brother), has been published since 1960. The Quetta-based magazine *Ulus* (People) carries poetry and short stories in Brahui. Illiteracy and poor printing facilities stand in the way of further development of Brahui literature, particularly prose genres.

BIBLIOGRAPHY: *Kamal al-Qadiri, 'Abdur Rahman Brahui', Balochi, Brahui: Metaaruf-i-Musanifin (Balochi and Brahui: Introducing Writers), Karachi, 1973; Abdur Razzaq Sabir, 'Brahui Adab Men Jadid Rujhanat' (Contemporary Trends in Brahui Literature), Irtiqa (Progress) magazine, Karachi, September 1989.*

A.S. SUKHOCHEV

British India

This comprised several provinces in colonial India, directly controlled by British authorities. It occupied 59.3 per cent of Indian territory and accounted for 77 per cent of the population (1941 census). These provinces were divided into two groups: 1. Governors' Provinces, i.e., those ruled by a Governor, which were Assam, *Bengal, Bihar, Bombay, Central Provinces and Berar, Madras, *North West Frontier Province, Orissa, *Punjab, *Sindh and United Provinces; 2. Chief Commissioners' Provinces, i.e., those ruled by a Chief Commissioner, which were *Balochistan, Delhi, Ajmer-Merwara, Coorg, Panth Piploda, and the Andaman and Nicobar Islands. According to the Government of India Act 1935, these Provinces formed a Federation with the Indian Principalities, whose hereditary Rulers were vassals of the Paramount Power, i.e. the British Sovereign. The Indian principalities enjoyed a nominal autonomy but in fact were controlled by the British Residents, appointed by the Governor-General, later titled the Viceroy.

YU.V. GANKOVSKY

British-Indian Civil Service

The ICS was composed of the top echelon of the British colonial bureaucratic apparatus, which administered the countries of South Asia conquered by Great Britain (modern India, Pakistan, and Bangladesh) before 15 August 1947. It began to evolve in the seventeenth century. In 1784 the British parliament passed the Government of India Act, according to which the British possessions in Madras and Bombay came under the authority of the Governor-General of Fort William in *Bengal. In 1833 the office of Governor-General of India was created; from 1858 to 1947 he was called Viceroy and Governor-General of India. The Governor-General of India was the highest official, supervising the work of the civil service and of all the British armed forces in India.

The principal divisions in the ICS in the 1940s included the political department and the departments for external affairs, home affairs, defence, revenue, finances, transport, communications, agriculture, justice, education, health, land, and others. Until the end of the nineteenth century, only highly paid members of the upper stratum of British society could be servants of the ICS. As a rule they were specially trained at Haileybury College, which opened in England in 1804. Although members of higher Indian society were granted access to the ICS in the course of the eventually reforms of Minto-Morley in 1909, Montagu-Chelmsford in 1919, and successive the Government of India Act of 1935, even as late as 1947 only 549 out of the 1,157 members of the ICS (47.4 per cent) were of Indian origin. After the declaration of independence of India and Pakistan the ICS was reorganised, in India, as the Indian Administrative Service, and in Pakistan, as the *Civil Service of Pakistan.

In the vassal states of India functions similar to that of the ICS were performed by the Indian Political Service, whose members were recruited from British officers of the colonial army, the police, and also from members of the ICS.

BIBLIOGRAPHY: *'Asian Bureaucratic System' (ed.) R. Braibanti, Durham, 1969; E. Blunt, 'The Indian Civil Service', London, 1937.*

YU.V. GANKOVSKY

British-Pakistan Relations

See, Anglo-Pakistan Relations.

Brocade

A fabric with a complex decorative design on a silk base containing metal threads of gold or silver, or imitations of these metals in the weft, more rarely in the warp. Brocade fabrics of the period of the *Mughal empire, manufactured at the court workshops of Lahore were especially magnificent and refined. Brocade was used in the costumes of court aristocracy, in the scarves, shawls, turbans, belts, etc., and also in the manufacture of curtains, canopies, and bedspreads.

Brocade is manufactured through a complex manual process in which the ornament is created by weaving an additional thread in the warp. This thread is woven into the warp with special little shuttles. According to the kind of thread forming the ornament, brocade is called gold, silver, silk, or cotton. True brocade, that is, gold or silver brocade, is called *kimkhab*.

The main centres of brocade manufacture in Pakistan are Lahore, Karachi, and Khairpur. *Saris*, scarves, shawls, and other items are woven here. The ornament is mostly floral and stylised geometrically.

O.V. LYSTSOVA

Bugti, Akbar Shahbaz Khan, Nawab (1926–)

Statesman. The hereditary *nawab, **sardar* and **tumandar* of the *Balochi tribe of Bugti, he graduated from Aitcheson College in Lahore and later received a degree from Oxford University. In the 1940s he was Vice-President of the Tribal Federation of *Balochistan. Bugti became Pakistan's Defence State Minister in 1958 and in 1973 became Governor of Balochistan. He was the founder and leader of the Balochistan National Alliance.

YU.V. GANKOVSKY

Bukhari, Ahmad Shah 'Patras' (1898–1958)

Writer/Statesman. Patras Bukhari was principal, Government College, Lahore; Director-General, All-India Radio; Pakistan's Permanent Representative to the United Nations and thereafter the UN Under-Secretary-General for Information.

Bukhari's claim to fame rests on a slim volume of humorous essays called *Patras Kai Mazameen*. These contain ironically humourous situations, with subtlety brought about through his restrained but sparkling style. His reticence and formality represent high culture among all humorists of the *Urdu language and serve as a model that has never been emulated successfully.

WORKS: *'Patras kai Mazameen', Lahore, 1929.*

BIBLIOGRAPHY: *Mohammad Tufail (ed.) 'Nuqoosh Patras Number', Lahore, 1958.*

YU.V. GANKOVSKY

Bukhari, Farigh (1918–97)

Poet. Real name Sayid Mir Akbar Shah Bukhari was a Pakistani poet writing in *Urdu, *Pashto and *Hindko. He was trained in medicine in Peshawar but also studied *English literature and Pashtu folklore. He wrote poetry from the 1940s, deriving inspiration from the philosophical poetry of *Iqbal, the poems of Josh *Malihabadi and the lyrical verse of Akhtar Shirani. Bukhari edited a number of left-wing newspapers and literary journals in Lahore and Peshawar. His journal *Sang-i-Mil* ('Landmark') was banned for violating censorship rules. In 1970 he was convicted and sentenced to one year's imprisonment in Peshawar.

Farigh Bukhari is particularly noted for his **ghazals*. His work incorporates the chanting folk intonations and folklore rhythms of northern Pakistan. In the 1980s he published the following collections: *Piyase Hath* ('Thirsting Hands'), *ghazals* and long poems reflecting his travel impressions of England, France, Germany, Switzerland, the United States and Mexico (Lahore, 1982); *Songs of Love and Struggle,*—English translations of his poetry (Lahore, 1982); and *Aine Sadaon ke* ('The Echo of Voices'), published in Stockholm in 1985. Farigh also wrote political pamphlets and essays, including *Khunchakan* ('The Bleeding One'); studies of folklore in literature, *Adabiyat-i-Sarhad* ('Literature of the *North West Frontier Province'), *Pashtu Lok Git* ('Pashtun Folk Songs'), *Pashtun Shairi* ('Pashtun Poetry') and *Hindko Adab ki Tarikh* ('History of Hindko Literature'), to name a few.

WORKS: *'Shishe ke Pairahan' (Crystal Clothes), Lahore, 1971; 'Aine Sadaon ke' (The Mirror of Voices), Stockholm, 1985.*

N.V. GLEBOV

Bulleh Shah (1680–1758)

Poet. He was a poet writing in *Punjabi. He was educated at an Islamic school in Lahore and represents the late *Sufi poetry. He used various poetic forms in his work, including **kafi, barahmasah* and **doha*, and brought his poetic language closer to the spoken language. He believed in monotheism and opposed pilgrimages to Mecca. His teaching on religious equality reflected indirectly the eternal dream of social equality. In his religious and philosophic views, he was influenced by the philosophy of Vedanta. His work is well known in Arab countries and Iran.

WORKS: *'Bulhe Shah 50 kaphian', Ed. with introduction and notes by Mohan Singh, Lahore, 1930; 'Jivan te Rachna', Patiala, 1970.*

N.I. TOLSTAYA

Burishki

A genetically isolated language spoken in the mountainous regions of Hunza (Kanjut), Nagar (Nagir) and in Yasin on the outer spurs of the *Karakoram Mountains. The principal dialects are Burushaski proper and Vershik, or Vershiwar (in Yasin). It has no written tradition. At present a written system for the language is being developed on the basis of the Arabic alphabet in the *Urdu version.

The vocabulary is particular to Burishki. Words are derived mainly from *Dardic languages (*Shina and *Khowar), less from Urdu, and only a few from neighbouring Iranian languages. Persian and Arabic words came via intermediate languages.

BIBLIOGRAPHY: *I.I. Zarubin, 'The Wershik Dialect of the Kanjut Language', Leningrad, 1927 (in Russian); G.A. Klimov, D.I. Edelman, 'The Burushaski Language', Moscow, 1970 (in Russian); D.L.R. Lorimer, 'The Burushaski Language', Vols. 1-3, Oslo, 1935-8; id., Werchikwar-English Vocabulary, Oslo, 1962, H. Berger, 'Das Yasin-Burushaski' (Werchikwar), Wiesbaden, 1974.*

N.V. GLEBOV

Buta

An ornamental motif, mostly used on fabrics. It has the form of an elongated bud with a downturned upper end and is sometimes ornamented with leaves and flowers.

N.R. GUSEVA

C

Cabinet Mission Plan

The decision in January 1946 to send a three member Cabinet Mission comprising of Pethick-Lawrence, Stafford *Cripps and A.V. Alexander to India fulfilled the British promise of discussions on the form of a constitution making body following the holding of elections. The issue was not whether power would be transferred but the form of the post-imperial order. The Mission's preferred option was for a united India on strategic grounds, By mid-June it appeared that a plan had been agreed upon for the grouping of provinces into three sections and with a central government confined to control of defence, foreign affairs and communications. The *Muslim League had accepted the scheme because of the autonomy it gave to the six Muslim provinces, although this fell short of a sovereign Pakistan. The Congress wanted a much stronger centre and Nehru's hedging around the future working of the grouping element led the League to withdraw its acceptance on 29 July 1946. The British then went ahead with the establishment of a Congress only 14 member Interim Government. This forced the League into adopting direct action. This course of action following from the failure of the Federal scheme of the Cabinet Mission meant that the Partition of the subcontinent became virtually inevitable.

I. TALBOT

Carpet weaving

A traditional industry that flourished in the epoch of the *Mughals. During Akbar's rule a carpet weaving workshop was established in Lahore, to where Persian weavers were invited. The influence of Iranian art was noticeable in Mughal carpets. The carpets of the Akbar epoch are almost indistinguishable from those of Herat and Khorasan. Their original feature is the colour, either wine red or dark orange. Under Jahangir (r. 1605-27) carpets were woven with a virtuoso technique of execution, including great density of knots, and softness of pile. Flowering plants, the most favoured motif of these carpets, are reminiscent of the best ornaments of Mughal architecture. Fantastic monsters, fights between them, and hunting scenes are the most frequent themes of Mughal carpets.

Carpet weaving in Pakistan.

At present, carpets are produced in Karachi, Hyderabad, Multan, Quetta, Lahore, and Peshawar. They are woven by hand out of wool, often with added silk, with ornamentation in the form of various combinations of floral and stylized geometrical motifs. Another traditional industry is non-pile carpet weaving. *Dari* and *satrangi* carpets are woven out of thick cotton or jute. Their characteristic feature is simple ornamentation in the form of coloured stripes or checks. *Balochis weave *farshi* carpets, without pile, out of camel hair or goat wool, with geometrical ornaments against coloured strips. Felt carpets called *namda* are made out of the wool of sheep, goats, or camels. They are mostly manufactured in *Kashmir, *Balochistan, *Swat and Rawalpindi. They are ornamented with embroidery and appliqué work. Sometimes coloured wool is used against a monochrome background.

Carving

This is popular as a kind of artistic treatment of natural materials in Pakistan. The principal materials with which the engravers work are stone, wood, and ivory.

The earliest specimens of glyptic, the art of engraving on gem stones, are steatite seals of the *Harappa civilisation. The earliest specimens of figurines also belong to the same period. Objects carved of wood have not survived, although wood was the main architectural material in the Vedic period. The monolithic architecture of rock monasteries and temples of the third to first centuries BC are representative of the period. It is clear from these data that a variety of wood was widely used in the architecture of the Vedic period. Wood was used to construct buildings and to craft numerous carved details. Wood varieties used for carving were mostly mahogany and ebony, Himalayan cedar, pine, walnut, and sandal. Hardwood is carved deeply, while soft varieties of wood like sandalwood are covered with fine, detailed patterns. As a rule, carving is on a single plane, with a hollowed out background.

In traditional architecture, carving is used to embellish the details of buildings-doors, windows, orioles, balustrades, and columns. Many carving methods and styles are used in architectural decor: flat and high relief, and fully volumetric sculpture. Especially characteristic are carved shutters on which the jail, or net ornament, is executed, usually of geometrical or floral character, and varying from region to region. Openwork arches and consoles cover carved panels, creating double ornamental spaced planes.

Carving on stone in architecture and sculpture is found mainly from the third century BC. It is just as varied as carving on wood and the techniques of carving in these materials have many common features. Carving on stone retains the one-plane, mostly flat-relief engraving of ornament. The greatest achievements were in the sphere of volumetric carving. Different kinds of stones were used in different areas; their textures became an identifying feature of the famous schools of sculpture of antiquity and the Middle Ages. The main form was complemented with small details of decor and design on carvings representing fabrics, which created an impression of magnificent ornamental 'clothing' of the sculptures.

Over a long period, in antiquity and the early Middle Ages, sculpture was an integral part of temple architecture, especially in rock temples. The Muslim tradition brought a new attitude towards the treatment of stone, shifting the emphasis to the ornament, in which geometrical and floral patterns were mostly used. The treatment of window shutters, bay windows, and balustrades is close to that of wooden architectural details.

Work in semiprecious stone occupies a special place in decorative art. Nephrite, chalcedony, and crystal were used in the hilts of sabres and daggers and in making cups and other objects. The relief on items made of semiprecious stones is not, as a rule, high, and the background is of the 'cushion' type.

Modern carving preserves traditional techniques, imitating the works of old masters. Fashioning models of old architectural structures is very popular nowadays. Small-scale objects predominate and they are mostly intended for the tourist trade.

E.V. GANEVSKAYA

Central Brahui Range

To the south of Zhob and west of the *Sulaiman Range lies a north-south hilly range that has historically presented a barrier between the territories of the Persian and Indo-Gangetic empires. High cliffs in the Brahui Range give way to deep valleys with stony river beds, which remain dry for most of the year. The braiding rivers turn into raging torrents in the flash floods of summer. 'The Bolan Pass' at the northern end of the range has been of importance throughout history.

This famous pass links Quetta to the rest of Pakistan via a main road and railway. The pass itself is approximately 1,792 metres above sea level. In prehistoric times this route was used by nomads and travelers to journey from Central Asia to the sub-continent. It is an easier route than the *Khyber Pass to the north. Officially 96 kilometers long, the western end starts with a dramatic, narrow winding 15 kilometers gorge. Villages dating from 7,000 BC onwards have been excavated beyond the eastern end of the pass at Mehrgarh.

M. STONEY

Central Secretariat Library

Founded in 1950, it remained in Karachi until 1972 when it was moved to Islamabad. It holds about 22,000 volumes of official publications of the central and local governments of Pakistan.

YU.V. GANKOVSKY

Central Treaty Organization (also CENTO)

(until 25 June 1959, the Baghdad Pact) A military-political bloc founded on the initiative of Great Britain and the United States during the Cold War. The first step in its establishment was the signing, in Baghdad, on 24 February 1955 of the Pact of Mutual Co-operation between Iraq and Turkey. It was later joined by the United Kingdom on 4 April 1955, by Pakistan on 23 September 1955, and by Iran on 3 November 1955. Though not formally a member of the bloc, the United States participated in its main committees in 1956 and 1957. In March 1959 Iraq formally relinquished its membership of the organization. On 25 June 1959 the Baghdad Pact was renamed CENTO.

To step up the alliance's activity and to consolidate the links of the three remaining member countries with the West, on 3 March 1959, the United States signed, identical bilateral co-operation agreements against direct or indirect aggression, with Iran, Pakistan, and Turkey. The US then played the determining role in CENTO activity. CENTO members regularly held naval, air, and ground forces manoeuvres.

In the 1960s and early 1970s serious differences arose between CENTO members. In particular, the Asian countries asked for CENTO support in their conflicts with neighbouring states and for greater economic co-operation in the framework of the alliance. After Iran and Pakistan left CENTO in March 1979, the government of Turkey proposed the dissolution of the Pact.

CENTO's principal bodies were the Permanent Council of Ministers, with annually held sessions, the secretariat, and four committees. The united headquarters for military planning, a permanent group of military representatives, and a number of subcommittees and working groups were set up. The headquarters, originally in Baghdad, have been located in Ankara since 1959.

R.M. MUKIMJANOVA

Chagai Range

The Chagai Hills are an east-west montain range lying across the north side of the *Balochistan Plateau. The range marks part of the border of Pakistan and Afghanistan, close to the western tip of Balochistan province. The route from Quetta to Iran runs to the sough of the range. There are several inactive or dormant and extinct volcanoes in the area, the largest of which is *Koh-i-Sultan. Its height is 2,332 metres. It holds deposits of high-quality sulphur.

M. STONEY

Chalma

(Turkish, in Persian: *Dastar*) A turban worn by Muslim men. A long piece of cloth is wrapped several times around a hat, skullcap, or *fez*. The colour and shape of the *chalma* indicate the ethnic, social and religious affiliation of the owner.

YU.V. GANKOVSKY

The Chagai Hills.

Chanhu-Daro

A multi-level settlement of the Bronze Age was found beneath a mound here, 130 km to the southeast of *Moenjodaro in northern *Sindh. It was discovered in 1931 by N.G. Majumdar. E.J.H. Machay worked there in 1935–6. In 1984 G.M. Sher and M. Vidale resumed diggings. The lower levels yielded remains of three periods of settlement of the *Harappan Civilisation. In the 16th-15th centuries BC people of the *Jhukar came to Chanhu-Daro. In about 12th-11th centuries BC people of the Jhangar appeared.

BIBLIOGRAPHY: *G.M. Bongard-Levin, G.F. Ilyin, 'India in Ancient Times', Moscow, 1985 (in Russian); E.J.H. Mackay, 'Chanhu-Daro Excavations 1935-6', New Haven, 1943; G.M. Sher and M. Vidale, 'Surface Evidence of Craft Activity at Chanhu-Daro', March, 1984.*

A.YA. SHCHETENKO

Chaudhury (also Chaudri)

An honorary title used in conjunction with names of elders, chieftains or chiefs mainly in Pakistan and India, especially for land owners.

YU.V. GANKOVSKY

Chenab

(In Sanskrit: *Asikni*; in Greek: *Acesines*; called Rima in the section below its confluence with the *Ravi) This is one of the five major rivers of the *Punjab and the biggest tributary of the *Sutlej, joining it from the west.

The Chenab is 950 km. long and its basin is 138,000 sq. km. in area. The general direction of the flow is from north-east to south-west. It is formed by the confluence of the rivers Bhaga to the west and Chandra from the east. These take their source respectively from the north-west and south-east of the Bara Lacha Pass (4,883 metres) in the Main *Himalayan Range. The two tributaries join near Tandi at about 2,300 metres above sea level. The Chenab breaks its way through a narrow deep gorge across the Pir-Panjal and Siwalik Ranges and enters the arid Punjab Plain in the region of the Indo-Pakistan frontier. In its lower reaches, the river is 1.5 km. wide. The main tributaries are the *Jhelum and Ravi.

In the upper reaches the river is fed primarily with glacier and subsoil waters and in the plain by rainfall. The regimen is determined by the monsoons. Water begins to rise in March with the peak of the flood season occurring in July and August. It is its lowest level between November and February. The average discharge in the region where the river emerges into the plain is 890 cubic m. per sec. During flooding the level of the water rises by up to 4.5 metres. In the lower reaches the Chenab floods to 3-10 km. wide, the loose sandy soils in the territory causing extensive flooding. In its lower and middle course the river is navigable. The waters of the Chenab are extensively used for irrigation. The total area irrigated by the river exceeds 2.5 million hectares. The valley is densely populated.

Chiantar

A valley glacier in the *Hindu Kush on the northern slopes of the *Hinduraj in the *Indus Valley. Its length is 32 km. its area, 260 sq.km. It ends at approximately 3,600 metres above sea level.

YU.V. GANKOVSKY

Chilas petroglyphs

There are large groups of petroglyphs (bas reliefs carved into the native rock) on rocks and stones in the upper reaches of the Pakistan *Indus. The several thousand rock drawings around the village of Chilas on the banks of the Indus were studied by K. Yettmar and A.H. *Dani. Hunters with bows and arrows, and wild goats predominate. There are a few scenes with groups of hunters or large groups of animals. These petroglyphs were made with a stone or a sharp metal object, figures being outlined with deep or shallow points. All of them are covered with a patina to different degrees. Buddhist symbols, (especially stupas) are of interest.

The style, patina and symbols allowed archaeologists to divide the drawings into several age groups: 1. Prehistoric drawings, presumably starting with the Mesolithic and the Bronze Age; 2. A group stylistically close to Scythian-Sarmatian art of the 1st millennium BC; 3. Buddhist drawings of the late 1st millennium BC-early 1st millennium AD; 4. Mediaeval, 5th-13th centuries and later up to recent times. Chilas has the largest group of petroglyphs on the Great Silk Route.

There are also about 2,000 inscriptions in seventeen languages and twenty-four scripts that are often connected with drawings. The majority of them are Indian, in the Kharoshthi and Brahmi scripts. The former are dated from the 1st century AD, the bulk of them belong to the 2nd-3rd centuries. The inscriptions in the Brahmi script are later, up to the 8th century. There are many Buddhist inscriptions among them. Sogdian inscriptions predominate among the Iranian inscriptions. There are also Bactrian, Parthian, and middle Persian inscriptions. The Sogdian inscriptions are mostly names including ethnic names and the place of origin, mentioning areas of Samarkand and Tashkent. There are Chinese inscriptions, one of which is connected with a Chinese embassy to Samarkand.

BIBLIOGRAPHY: *A.H. Dani, 'Chilas: the City of Nanga Parbat' Dyamar, Islamabad, 1983.*

B.A. LITVINSKY
V.A. RANOV

China-Pakistan Relations

See, Sino-Pakistan Relations.

Chinioti Sheikhs

A group of the Punjabi Muslim trading community, called Chinioti Sheikhs, or Chiniotis. They take their name from the town of Chiniot on the *Chenab River. At the time Chinioti Sheikhs owned 190 companies with basic assets in excess of three billion rupees. The 1970s nationalisation did not affect them much and their business activity has grown dramatically since then. Together with certain other *Punjabi business groups, in particular '*Ittefaq* Brothers', whose representative, Mian Nawaz *Sharif, was twice the Prime Minister of Pakistan, the Chinioti Sheikhs have a major stake in the private business sector, occupying key positions in the Karachi business world.

V.YA. BELOKRENITSKY

Chionites

See, Ephtalites.

Chishtiya

A Sufi order (see, Sufi orders), whose founder and eponym, Khwaja Abu Ishaq ash-Shami (d. 941 CE), founded a *Sufi monastery at Chisht near Herat, Afghanistan. In 1193 the Chishti order spread in South Asia as a result of the spiritual work of Khwaja Moinuddin Hasan Chishti (1142-236). The Chishtiya proved to be the most venerated and influential Sufi order in South Asia, many of the most illustrious saints belonged to the order. Moinuddin's spiritual successor Qutbuddin Bakhtiyar Kaki (d. 1235) sojourned in Multan before moving on to Delhi. Bakhtiar Kaki was offered several offices by Sultan Iltutmish, which he refused, and by the time of his death his circle of devotees had greatly increased.

The Chishtiya order gained a firm basis in the *Punjab due to Fariduddin Ganj-i-Shakar who passed on the torch to Nizamuddin Awlia (d. 1325) among whose votaries were the two poets Amir Khusrau (d. 1324) and Amir Hasan Sijzi. Khusrau celebrated his saint in a number of devotional lyrics while Sijzi recorded the sayings of Nizamuddin Awlia under the title *Fawaid-ul-Fawad,* thus setting a trend in *Sufi literature. Nizamuddin Awliya's successor was Naseeruddin Chiragh-i-Dehli (d. 1356). In the late seventeenth and eighteenth centuries Chishtiya was promoted further in the north western areas of present day Pakistan by Shah Kalimullah Jahanabadi (1650–1729) and his successors.

YU.V. GANKOVSKY

Chitral (Physical)

Chitral is a long, isolated valley extending some 320 km, with a population of some 250, 000 people, in the NWFP. A river by the same name, with its source in the *Hindu Kush mountains, flows through the valley. The river is 190 km long. At its source it is called the Yarkhun, then in its upper course it is called *Mastuj. The Mastuj is fed by the Shever-Shur Glacier. During the melting period the level of the water rises by some 12-15 meters and floods the bed of the valley, disrupting transport and communications between the villages and towns along the river. Down to the town of Mastuj, the valley is actually a mountain gorge with steep banks on both sides. Below Mastuj it broadens out and reaches a width of 3 km near the town of Chitral. It crosses the Chitral district and near the village of Arandu, on the Afghan-Pakistan frontier, joins the Kunar, which flows into Afghanistan. The valley is cut off by snow for part of the year, although a small Fokker plane maintains a vital link. The valley is regarded as particularly beautiful with stunning views of Tirich Mir, the tallest peak in the Hindu Kush at 7,708 meters. Although the area is currently governed directly by Pakistan, through the Deputy Commissioner, the Mulk family, with its princes is still important in the valley.

YU.V. GANKOVSKY

Chitral (Political)

1. A princely state in the valley of the Chitral river. In 1951, its area was 14,900 sq.km.; population 106,000, mostly *Khos, and also *Kohistanis. Since 1585 Chitral was ruled by the dynasty founded by Mirza Ayub, a fourth-generation descendant of Timur (1370-1405). From 1747-1819, Chitral was a vassal dependency of the *Durrani kings, and from 1889-1947, a vassal of the British sovereign. Since 18 February 1948 Chitral has been a part of Pakistan. In April 1953, Chitral's constitution was adopted and an Advisory Council set up. In 1955 the state was abolished.

2. A district in the Malakand division of Pakistan's NWFP. Area: 14,850 sq.km.; population 209,000 (1981 data).

YU.V. GANKOVSKY

Choudhury, Fazal Ilahi (1904–82)

Fazal Ilahi Choudhry, President of Pakistan (1973–78).

President of Pakistan from 1973 to 1978. He graduated from the Punjab University in Lahore in 1927 and became a lawyer by profession. From 1944 to 1958, he was a member of the *Muslim League. In 1948, he became Minister for Education and Health in the *Punjab government. Choudhury served as Speaker of the West Pakistan Assembly from 1956 to 1958 and was one of the leading members of the *Pakistan Peoples Party from 1967 to 1977. He became Pakistan's President in 1973 and was at first retained in that office by General Ziaul *Haq when he seized power in July 1977. However, he was also retired from office in 1978, when General Ziaul Haq also assumed the mantle of President.

YU.V. GANKOVSKY

Choudhury, Ghulam Wahid (1926–97)

A Pakistani historian, political scientist and public figure. A graduate of Calcutta University and Columbia University, he was professor at Dhaka University, now in Bangladesh, from 1949-59. He was an advisor to the Pakistan Constitution Committee (1960), Director-General of the Pakistan Ministry for Foreign Affairs (1969), and Minister for Communication of Pakistan (1969-71). After 1971 he lived in England and later moved to the USA.

WORKS: *'Democracy in Pakistan', Dhaka, 1963; 'Pakistan's Relations with India', New York, 1968; 'Constitutional Development in Pakistan', London, 1969; 'The Last Days of United Pakistan', Bloomington, 1974.*

YU.V. GANKOVSKY

Christians

Christians arrived in the territory of present-day Pakistan at the turn of the 17th century, with the first Christian missions in the south of *Sindh. Their numbers grew rapidly: 1901–32,000; 1921–214,000; 1941–421,000; 1961–584,000; 1981–1,311,000 or 1.5 per cent of the country's population. The majority of Christians are concentrated in the *Punjab province (1,061,000 in 1981). Pakistani Christians are predominantly Catholics. Since 1950 they have been headed by the Archbishop of Karachi Evarist Minto. There are Christian schools of all levels, colleges, hospitals and other Christian organisations, including women's, students', professional, charity and political parties. In March 1986 nine Christian parties formed the National Christian Alliance of Pakistan.

YU.V. GANKOVSKY

Chughtai, Abdur Rehman (1894–1975)

Artist. A celebrated exponent of the New Bengal School, was among the leading painters of Lahore at the time of the Partition in 1947. Chughtai began his painting career in 1916 and got early recognition in various parts of India. In keeping with the revivalist spirit of the New Bengal School he sought inspiration from the *Mughal Miniature and the '*Naqsh*' or patterns of the Islamic decorative arts. His themes borrowed from popular folklore, Hindu Mythology and Islamic epics.

Chughtai had a distinctive style of painting. The elongated elegant human figure is always central to his work, which he portrayed in a linear iconography with a soft wash resulting in an ethereal ambience. In soft, clear tones, emerged exquisite details of costume, jewellery, architecture, landscape, flora and fauna.

Chughtai's work echoed the creative sensibilities of his people. In *Muraq-i-Chughtai* and *Amal-i- Chughtai,* his famous illustrations of the verses of *Ghalib and *Iqbal, he gave a contemporary interpretation to the classical tradition of Persian painting.

Chundrigar, Ismail Ibrahim (1897–1960)

I.I. Chundrigar.

Statesman. Chundrigar graduated from Bombay University and went on to practise law. He led the Bombay branch of the *Muslim League from 1940 to 1946 and was a member of the Working Committee of the *All-India Muslim League from 1943 to 1947. He was the first Minister of Commerce, Industry and Works of independent Pakistan. From 1948 to 1950 Chundrigar served as Pakistan's Ambassador to Afghanistan. In 1950 he became

Governor of the *North West Frontier Province and of *Punjab from 1951 to 1953. From 1955 to 1956 he served as Pakistan's Law Minister.

YU.V. GANKOVSKY

Cinema in Pakistan

The Pakistan film industry is one of the biggest in the world and quantitatively, Pakistan ranks among the top ten film-making countries in the world. In spite of remaining in a perpetual state of crisis, the Pakistan film industry continues to release at least 80 films per year. Cinema going is still a favourite pastime of the population. Pakistani films are currently seeing a revival with support from both the electronic and print media. Pakistani film songs are popular among all segments of society and many Pakistani film stars have become household names.

In spite of their popularity inside the country, Pakistani films are largely limited to the local market. They have failed to make any mark outside the country and do not have any standing in the international market.

At the time of independence in 1947 Bombay was the leading film-making centre of the subcontinent. Lahore was a secondary centre with three studios, and a negligible number of films used to be made there mostly utilising the services of stars and directors from the bigger and more glamorous centre of Bombay.

Following the upheaval of partition most of the Hindu and Sikh workers and technicians moved to India, leaving behind a big void. A few veterans such as W.Z. Ahmed, Shaukat Hussain Rizvi, Nazir, Sibtain Fazli, Munshi Dil, Luqman and Ataullah Shah Hashmi opted to migrate to Pakistan and laid anew the foundation of the country's film industry.

Few of the leading stars of the time came to Pakistan. Those who did included top heroine and singer Nur Jehan, who was married to Shaukat Hussain Rizvi, Khurshid, who soon withdrew from the scene, Swarnlata, wife of Nazeer, and Ragni. Pakistan was, however, lucky to get music directors of the calibre of Khursheed Anwar, Ghulam Haider, Feroz Nizami, Rashid Attre, and the legendary Timir Baran.

For several years after independence the distributors and cinema owners of Pakistan were heavily dependent on films produced in Bombay and the other established film centres of India, and Indian films continued to be imported without any restriction. The first indigenous Pakistani film, *Teri Yad,* was released on 2 September 1948. Produced by Deewan Sardari Lal and directed by Daud Chand, the film starred Nasir Khan, younger brother of superstar Dilip Kumar, and a little-known actress Asha Posley. A poor effort, both production-wise and technically, the film flopped miserably.

In 1949 six films were released, five of which failed at the box office. The surprise hit of the year was *Pherey,* a low budget film which was also the first *Punjabi language film of Pakistan. *Pherey,* produced and directed by Nazeer and starring himself and his wife Swarnlata, was a big success and became the first Pakistani film to enjoy a silver jubilee, a continuous run of 25 weeks.

The following year saw another silver jubilee hit, Anwar Kamal Pasha's *Do Aansoo* which introduced a new leading pair, Santosh Kumar and Sabiha, to the viewers. The pair went on to become the superstars of the country and starred in innumerable hit films. Other major hits of the early period include Shaukat Hussain Rizvi's *Punjabi venture, *Chanway,* starring Nur Jehan and Santosh Kumar; Sibtain Fazli's *Dopatta*, with Nur Jehan and Ajay Kumar; *Gulnar* with Nur Jehan and Santosh; *Gumnaam*, directed by Anwar Kamal Pasha and starring Sabiha and Sudhir; and *Qatil* also by Anwar Kamal Pasha, starring Sabiha and Santosh.

A major landmark of that period was *Sassi,* a lavish production by film distributor J.C. Anand, based on Shah Latif *Bhitai's well-known folk tale. The film, starring Sabiha and Sudhir, created a record by becoming the first golden jubilee film of Pakistan - running for an unprecedented fifty weeks. The film also did very well in India, beating some major Bombay productions.

From the beginning producers had been agitating with the government to stop the import of Indian films in order to provide protection to the newly emerging local film industry. Their efforts bore fruit in 1954 when a concerted movement was undertaken to stop the release of the Indian film *Jaal.* The movement was successful and this opened a new phase in the history of Pakistani cinema.

The restriction on Indian films proved to be a double-edged sword. In one way it gave a new impetus to local productions and many excellent films were produced. But conversely it proved harmful, as the lack of competition made producers complacent. It also opened the flood gates for plagiarism of Indian hit films, which became a common practice after the ban. A number of successful films were produced which were blatant copies of Indian hit films such as *Naukar,* a rip-off of *Aulad*, and *Hameeda*, a copy of *Vachan*. The most shameful example of this piracy is *Bedari*, a patriotic film full of noble sentiments about the motherland and uplifting *Qaumi Naghmas* (national songs) which are still played and enjoyed on Pakistan's national days. However the film was a scene for scene copy of an Indian hit *Jagriti*, and the noble and inspiring songs were also lifted entirely with their words and tunes, with the sole difference that *Vande Mataram* had became *Pakistan Zindabad* and references to *Bapu* Gandhi were replaced by references to *Quaid-i-Azam. The same child star Ratan Kumar acted in both versions.

Since no action was taken against these artistically reprehensible acts, other producers were encouraged and stories, dialogues, sequences, and songs featured in Indian films continued to be lifted with impunity.

The effects of having a captive audience were disastrous. Frame by frame plagiarisation should have brought Pakistan's film industry at least to the technical excellence of India but it had the opposite effect. There was a structural fault in the film industry because directors like Zia Sarhady, Nakhshab, and M. Sadiq, who had proved so eminently successful in India, were unable to find their bearings in Pakistan. It was not as the producers tried to explain, that Pakistani cine goers were not appreciative of sophisticated efforts. New Theatres and Bombay Talkies films dating from the 1930s were popular throughout the Pakistan areas.

From time to time the Pakistani film industry would rise above itself. *Ruhi* (1954), an artistic film, was banned because of its socialist slant. *Mutthi Bhar Chawal,* based on Rajinder Singh Bedi's novel, *Ek Chadar Maili Si,* was a classic production by film star Sangita. Such films were few and far between, and when television overtook the cinema in 1964 it was not because of the convenience of home entertainment, it was because of the high standard of the teleplays.

By the end of the first decade after independence the Pakistan film industry was firmly established economically and the future seemed full of promise.

At this time Karachi had also emerged as a film-making centre and a number of new directors and new stars had appeared on the scene, including Mussarat Nazir, Shamim Ara, Nayyar Sultana, Neelo, Zeba, Rani, Darpan, and Mohammad Ali.

Some of the major hits of the second decade included *Waadah, Saat Lakh, Saheli, Kartar Singh,* and *Shaheed.*

In 1966 a film was released which besides being the biggest blockbuster ever, also proved to be a trendsetter for the industry and upset all the old and set ideas about film-making in Pakistan. The film was *Arman*, which gave a new young and fresh look to the film industry and introduced a team of four young men, well educated, enlightened, creative, and brimming with fresh ideas. They were producer and actor Waheed Murad, director Pervez Malik, music director Sohail Rana, and Masroor Anwar, poet and writer. *Arman* went on to celebrate its platinum jubilee, and Waheed Murad, son of a film distributor and an MA in *English literature, became the first superstar of the Pakistan film industry, remaining a cult figure till his death in 1982.

Meanwhile, *East Pakistan had also come into its own as a producer of *Urdu films and had given the industry two of its biggest stars - Shabnam and Nadeem - who continued to rule over the hearts of film goers for several decades. Shabnam was discovered in East Pakistan thanks to her rustic charm, while Nadeem, an aspiring singer, who went to Dhaka from his home city of Karachi, caught the attention of director Ihtesham, and was cast as hero in *Chakori*. After enjoying a long innings as hero Nadeem is still going strong, enjoying top billing as character actor and now as a TV star.

The credit for producing historical films like *Sirajuddaulah* (1967) and *Shaheed Titu Mir* (1969) goes to East Pakistan (Bangladeshi) producers. The art film *Akhri Station* and first colour film *Sangam* were also produced in East Pakistan.

The period from 1967-77 was the most prolific of the Pakistan film industry. The number of films being produced was steadily rising and reached its peak in 1968, when 124 films were produced. A number of hit films were produced during this time, the biggest of all being *Aaina,* starring Shabnam and Nadeem, released in 1977, which created a record by running for 250 weeks in Karachi.

In 1973 the government established the National Film Development Corporation (NAFDEC) with the laudable motive of giving an impetus to the national film industry. But the bureaucratic organisation which took too much into its hands, from the import of foreign films to production of feature films and documentaries, sustained heavy losses and did not do anything tangible to help the film industry. In 2000, after remaining a white elephant for several years, was unceremoniously wound up.

The late 1970s almost proved to be the death knell for Pakistan cinema. This was the period when the VCR had became a household word, and the forbidden fruit of Indian films could now be tasted in every home.

Video shops were full of the latest Amitabh Bachan, Rekha, and Zeenat Aman films and the viewers could not get enough. Communal shows began to be arranged in private homes and entire neighbourhoods turned out to watch. Besides the latest blockbusters, classic Indian films such as *Mughal-e-Azam* and *Pakeezah* became the rage and the Pakistan film industry realised too late the mistake it had committed in 1954 with the restriction of Indian origin films.

The Martial Law period of General Ziaul *Haq heralded the worst period for Pakistani cinema. The developments in the country could not but have an effect on films and film goers. The uncertain law and order situation, the high price of cinema tickets and the difficulty in obtaining transport took their toll, and the elite and educated classes found it easier and more economical to watch films, Indian and English, in the security of their homes rather than go to the cinema. This change in the composition of cinema goers coupled with the new culture of weapons, violence, and drugs introduced by the Afghan war, and the rise of ethnic and sectarian movements in the country, also changed the content of the films. Now instead of family-oriented social dramas, a new genre of films glorifying violence, brutality and revenge became the norm.

As this genre was more suited to Punjabi and *Pashto than Urdu films, the production of Urdu films declined substantially. A new kind of hero, wielding a gun or an axe, who singlehandedly got rid of scores of enemies came in place of the romantic 'chocolate' heroes.

The biggest representative film of this genre was the legendary Punjabi film *Maula Jat,* which created a new record by running continuously for more than five years and became the biggest box-office hit in the history of Pakistani cinema.

Its lead actor, Sultan Rahi, became a cult figure, the biggest superstar of Pakistan, who was named in the Guinness Book of World Records by working in 650 films as the leading man. In most of his films he was paired with leading lady Anjuman and villain Mustafa Qureshi.

Meanwhile in 1979 General Ziaul Haq announced a new film policy and following the wave of moralisation, a new and more strict censorship code was introduced. All the films released earlier had to apply for a fresh censor certificate. These new measures proved to be deadly for quality films which were already suffering due to the prevalence of Indian and international films on video, and a large number of cinema houses had to be closed down.

For a time the producers toyed with co-productions and joint ventures with other South Asian and Far Eastern countries such as Sri Lanka, Nepal, Bangladesh, and Indonesia to find new markets for their products. A number of new faces from these countries and fresh locations attracted cinema goers for a while, but the trend did not last for long.

In the 1990s Urdu cinema saw a revival and many new faces such as Reema, Shaan, Babar Ali, Resham and Meera were introduced. Conscious attempts were made to bring back families and the educated middle class to the cinema and to some extent, with the help of other media, these have been successful.

The turnabout came in 1990 with *Bulandi,* which introduced two newcomers Shaan and Reema in the leading roles. The film was a major success and encouraged other film-makers to lanch romantic films with a new cast. Another superhit of the period was *Jeeva* with Babar Ali and Resham, followed by *Hathi Mera Sathi, Munda Bigri Jai, Chief Sahib, Sargam, Inteha, Jo Dar Gaya Woh Mar Gaya.*

The revival of the Pakistani film industry is in no small part due to the support of television. The age of the satellite has brought into every home a spate of film channels and an onslaught of film-based programmes featuring hit songs and movie stars. Pakistani channels did not lag behind and programs such as *Lollywood, Top 10* and *Yehi to Hai* publicised new films. *Lollywood* played a major part in popularising Pakistani film songs and film stars among the middle class audiences who had for several years forgotten their existence.

The directors of today, who are mostly young and educated, have made a great contribution. Syed Noor, Sajjad Gul, Sangita, and Samina Pirzada are some of the names which have a number of artistic and commercial hits to their credit. For the moment the future looks bright. The need is to expand the market by making Pakistani films strong both aesthetically and creatively, and better able to compete in the international arena.

BIBLIOGRAPHY: *Mushtaq Gazdar, 'The Pakistani Cinema', Karachi, 1997.*

S. KAZI

Civil Service of Pakistan

This elite of the civil bureaucratic apparatus in Pakistan started functioning in 1947. It emerged through a reorganisation of the Indian Civil Service. In December 1948 34 per cent of the CSP were British. Through the 1960s to the 1980s there were between 501 and 550 members of the CSP. CSP officials hold the top posts in practically all state and provincial institutions. The CSP is divided into three services: Federal, All-Pakistan, and Provincial. The CSP trains its recruits at the Civil Service Academy in Lahore. A federal commission on CSP affairs annually holds competitive entrance examinations which are open to university graduates (in 1950-64, 315 persons were selected out of 120,000 applicants). There is a quota system; 50 per cent of the individuals enrolled in the Civil Service Academy must come from *Punjab and the Federal Capital Territory of Islamabad while the Punjab's population is 60 per cent of Pakistan's total population. Despite its numerous reorganizations in 1956, 1962, 1973, etc., the CSP is still elitist in character.

BIBLIOGRAPHY: *'Asian Bureaucratic System' (ed.) R. Braibanti, Durham, 1969; 'Pakistan: A Country Study', Washington, 1984; H. F. Goodnow, 'The Civil Service of Pakistan', New Haven, 1964; R. Braibanti, 'Research on the Bureaucracy in Pakistan', Durham, 1966; Charles Kennedy, 'Bureaucracy in Pakistan', Karachi.*

YU.V. GANKOVSKY

Cohen, Stephen P. (1936–)

Writer. Director of the Programme of Arms Control, Disarmament, and International Security (ACDIS), and Professor of History and Political Science at the University of Illinois. He first visited Pakistan in 1977 and subsequently made numerous return visits.

Dr Cohen has written or edited a total of eight books, including *The Pakistan Army* and *The Indian Army* (revised edition, 1990), and co-authored *Brasstacks and Beyond: Perception and Management of Crisis in South Asia* (1995), which is based on extensive interviews with and first-hand accounts of Pakistanis, Americans, and Indians. His edited books include *Nuclear Proliferation in South Asia* (1990) and *South Asia after the Cold War: International Perspectives* (1993). Other works include a monograph contrasting regional and non-regional perceptions of South Asian security issues *Every Fifth Person: Perception of War and Peace in South Asia,* and a study of the possibility of a 'peace process' for South Asia, *India: Emerging Power* Washington, 2001.

N.P. KOCHERGINA

Communal Award

Issued by the British Prime Minister Ramsay MacDonald (1866-1937) on 16 August 1932, after the Indian delegates to the second *Round Table Conference failed to produce an agreement on the modalities of communal representation in elected bodies. In May 1931 the sole Congress representative, M.K. Gandhi, had admitted his failure to secure a consensus on communal issues and, since he had suggested that the British Prime Minister would have to arbitrate, this course remained the only way out of the impasse.

For the Muslims separate electorates and weightages were both retained in the Communal Award. In Hindu majority provinces Hindus would have the majority of legislative council seats. In the two Muslim-majority Provinces of *Punjab and *Bengal, because of weightage given to minorities, the Muslim representation was reduced. In the Punjab the Muslim population majority was fifty seven per cent but in the Punjab Legislative Assembly it was reduced to forty-nine per cent. In Bengal the Muslim population was fifty-five per cent, which was reduced to forty-eight per cent in the Bengal legislature. Practically, however, Muslim representation in these provinces rose through the special seats reserved for landlord, labour and university constituencies.

Sikhs were also given a weightage beyond their population per centage, to which no serious objection was raised. The small award of separate electorates to low caste Hindus, known as depressed classes, was however deeply resented by M.K. Gandhi, who undertook a fast to death against it on 20 September 1932 and broke it five days later when the Poona Pact was signed by him and Dr Bhimrao Ramji Ambedkar, leader of the depressed classes. The Poona Pact provided for enlarged representation for the depressed classes under joint electorates.

BIBLIOGRAPHY: *'East India (Constitutional Reforms) Communal Decision' Cmd. 4147, London, 1932; K.K. Aziz, 'Britain and Muslim India', London, 1963; K.B. Sayeed, 'Pakistan: The Formative Phase', 2nd. ed., (Karachi, 1969).*

M.R. KAZIMI

Communist Party of Pakistan (CPP)

Founded in February 1948 at the first Congress in Calcutta, where a Central Committee headed by Sajjad *Zaheer was elected. In July 1950 the CPP published a draft programme of the party called 'Pakistan's Way to Freedom and Democracy'. The party consolidated its position in such mass organisations as the Railwaymen's Trade Union and the Democratic Students Federation. After 1951 the CPP was subjected to reprisals and split into two virtually independent organisations working in *West and *East Pakistan respectively. On 5 July 1954 the CPP was banned in East Pakistan and on 24 July in West Pakistan. From 1965 to 1975 a Maoist group operated within the CPP. In August 1972, after Z.A. *Bhutto's government came to power, the work of the CPP was legalised. From 1977 to 1978, under Ziaul *Haq, the CPP was again subjected to reprisals and went underground. During the 1988 general elections it formed the Democratic Front together with five other left-wing parties. In 1989 a group of CPP members set up the People's Revolutionary Party.

O.V. PLESHOV

Constituent Assembly of Pakistan, the first

In accordance with the Indian Independence Act of 1947, its responsibility was to draft Pakistan's Constitution, while it also functioned as the federal legislative body. The first session was opened on 10 August 1947. On 11 August 1947 Quaid-i-Azam M.A. *Jinnah was elected Chairman of the Constituent Assembly. The Constituent Assembly of Pakistan consisted of members of the Constituent Assembly of India who were from the territories which formed Pakistan. Indirect elections to the Constituent Assembly of India were held in June 1946, when the members were elected by members of the provincial legislative assemblies, one deputy representing one million voters. The elections were held separately for religious communities.

Representatives of the princely states were appointed by their rulers. Eight deputies of the Constituent Assembly gave up their mandates, as the vacancies were filled by members representing refugees. Four additional seats were reserved for the princely states. Forty-four members represented the province of *East Bengal, twenty-two the province of *Punjab, five and the province of *Sindh, three. The *North West Frontier Province, the province of *Balochistan, the Balochistan States Union, *Bahawalpur, Khairpur and the princely states of the NWFP were represented by one member each.

Non-Muslims were represented by fifteen members, thirteen from East Bengal, one from Punjab and one from Sindh. There were forty-nine members of the *Muslim League in 1947 and sixty in 1953. The League was also supported by two members from the Scheduled Castes Federation, one representative of the *Parsis, and two women representatives.The opposition was represented by members of the National Congress of Pakistan, sixteen in 1947 and eleven in 1953, and, since 1950, by members of the *Azad* Pakistan (Free Pakistan) Party. In 1953 there were twenty-seven landowners in the Constituent Assembly, nine businessmen, thirty -one lawyers, and twelve persons from different professions.

The Constituent Assembly was dissolved by a decree of Pakistan's Governor-General on 24 October 1954, because of a political crisis in the wake of the defeat of the Muslim League in the elections of East Bengal (spring of 1954). (See also Constituent Assembly of Pakistan, the second)

BIBLIOGRAPHY: *'Constituent Assembly of Pakistan: Debates', Vols. I-VIII, Lahore, Karachi, 1947-1955; K. Callard, 'Pakistan. A Political Study', London, 1957; Yuri Gankovsky, V.N. Moskalenko, 'The Three Constitutions of Pakistan', Lahore, 1978.*

YU.V. GANKOVSKY

Constituent Assembly of Pakistan, the second

Formed by indirect elections on 21 June 1955, it's members were elected by members of provincial legislative assemblies and also by members of the urban municipalities of Karachi and Quetta. The Constituent Assembly consisted of eighty members; forty members from each of the two parts of Pakistan, West and East. Of these, twenty-eight were landowners; twenty-three lawyers; fourteen retired civil servants; seven businessmen; eight *ulema*, journalists, etc. Most members represented the coalition of the *Muslim League (twenty-five members) and the United Front of *East Pakistan (sixteen members). The opposition was represented by the **Awami* League (the People's League), *Azad* Pakistan (Free Pakistan), *Ganatantri Dal* (Democratic Party), United Progressive Party, the National Congress of Pakistan, and the Scheduled Castes Federation. On 9 January 1956, a draft constitution was tabled before the Constituent Assembly, worked out by a Committee consisting of members of the ruling coalition. On 29 February 1956 the draft was adopted by 52 members representing the ruling coalition as well as members who broke away from the *Awami* League and the Scheduled Castes Federation. On 2 March 1956 the draft was approved by the Governor-General of Pakistan.

BIBLIOGRAPHY: *Mushtaq Ahmad, 'Government and Politics in Pakistan', Karachi, 1963; G.W. Choudhury, 'Constitutional Development in Pakistan', London, 1969.*

YU.V. GANKOVSKY

Constitution of Pakistan, 1973

Adopted by the National Assembly in April, the Constitution came into force on 14 August 1973. It was suspended during Ziaul *Haq's military regime from 5 July 1977 to 30 December 1985. After the abolition of Martial Law and changes in the Constitution, known as the Eighth Amendment, which was passed in October 1985, the Constitution was brought into force again.The Eighth Amendment involved dozens of the Constitution's articles and paragraphs. The President's legislative, executive, and judicial powers were significantly extended. Along with parliament, the President became part of the legislative authority and was granted the right of suspensory veto, was declared head of the executive branch of government (previously, the Prime Minister was the head of executive authority), and commander-in-chief of the armed forces. The President was less bound by the Prime Minister's recommendations than before. The sphere of exclusive rights of the head of state was very wide; in some cases he could dissolve the lower chamber of parliament, the National Assembly, hold new elections, form an interim government, conduct referendums and make appointments to the highest posts in the state and the army. The President received the right to appoint the Prime Minister and the cabinet and was granted considerable influence in the matter of their resignation. Similarly, the rights of Governors were extended at the expense of the provincial legislative assemblies and the cabinets of ministers. In accordance with the Eighth Amendment to the Constitution, all decrees and orders of the President and of the military administration promulgated after the introduction of the military regime acquired the force of law. To consolidate these changes the passing of new amendments was made more difficult. To amend the constitution, it was now necessary for a vote of no less than two-thirds of both houses of parliament.

Just as in all previous constitutions, the 1973 Constitution embodies the Objectives Resolution passed by the first *Constituent Assembly of Pakistan in 1949. It declares that the sovereignty over the entire universe belongs to Almighty Allah alone, and claims 'the authority to be exercised by the people of Pakistan within the limits prescribed by Him through the chosen representatives of the people'. The Objectives Resolution also proclaims the principles of democracy, freedom, equality, tolerance, and social justice, as envisaged by Islam. It is stated that while 'the Muslims shall be enabled to order their lives in the individual and collective spheres in accordance with the teaching of Islam as set in the Holy Quran and Sunnah', religious minorities are granted the right of professing their religion and developing their culture.

The Constitution includes seven appendices or schedules: 1. the laws which are not covered by the articles of the Constitution relating to the basic human rights; 2. the procedure for Presidential elections; 3. the texts of oaths taken by the President elect, the Prime Minister, and other top officials on taking office; 4. the powers in the jurisdiction of the Central government or concurrent powers of the Centre and the provinces; 5. the conditions of service of the members of the High Court and of the Supreme Court; 6. a list of important laws not subject to change, amendment, or abolition without the President's sanction; 7. nine Presidential decrees from the period of the military regime which became law and, moreover, now require a procedure accepted in the passing of constitutional amendments, which include the decrees on the establishment of the International Islamic University, the institution of the post of ombudsman or *wafaqi muhtasib*.

Article 3 declares the objective of the state to be 'the elimination of all forms of exploitation and the gradual fulfilment of the fundamental principle, from each according to his ability, to each according to his work'. It is declared that all citizens of Pakistan are under the protection of law (Article 4). Abrogation or attempt at abrogation of the Constitution by 'unconstitutional means' is regarded as high treason (Article 6). The Constitution declares the basic civil rights, including inviolability of the person, freedom of movement, of speech, of association and organization, freedom of faith, and inviolability of the home (Articles 9, 15, 16, 17, 19, 20). These rights are subject to qualifications. Thus, freedom of speech and of the press are 'subject to any reasonable restrictions imposed by law in the interest of the glory of Islam or the integrity, security, or defence of Pakistan or any part thereof, friendly relations with foreign states, public order, decency or morality...' (Article 19). Equality of all citizens before the law is declared regardless of race, religion, caste, or sex; slavery and forced labour are banned, as is the employment of children under the age of 14 in industries which may impair their health (Articles 11, 25, 26, 27). Violation of law is subject to punishment envisaged by criminal law; some types of crime, such as theft, adultery, consumption of alcoholic drinks, and perjury incur traditional Muslim punishments. Any citizen of Pakistan subjected to arrest must be taken to court within 24 hours of arrest and cannot be held in custody without the court's sanction after that period. However, preventive detention up to a month can be used as a measure against persons acting to the detriment of Pakistan's integrity, security, defence, political position, or public order (Article 10). The third amendment to the Constitution, passed in February 1975, extended that term to three months.

The Constitution stipulates the right of all citizens of Pakistan to acquire, possess, and dispose of property (Article 23). The possibility to nationalize any kind of property is envisaged, with compensation (Articles 24 and 2). A law relating to the nationalization of any kind of property must stipulate either the size of the compensation or the principles according to which it must be determined, and also the mode of its payment (Article 24, point 4); no law relating to nationalization can be challenged (Article 24, point 4). The state may take control of any property acquired by unfair means or in any manner contrary to law; property may also be taken if the state feels it is necessary for the development of education, health services, benefits for the homeless and the unemployed, for construction of housing, or for other public needs (Article 24, point 3).

The provision of the Constitution that all laws incompatible with the basic civil rights are invalid is not applicable to the laws listed in the first appendix (Articles 8 and 3). These include laws passed under Z.A. *Bhutto, which relate to important socio-economic problems; for example, those on land reform, the liquidation of the managing agencies, etc. A special section of the Constitution is devoted to principles of state policy by which all officials and state bodies must be guided. These include participation of women in all spheres of society's life, elimination of illiteracy and introduction of obligatory free secondary education, guarantees for the well-being of all citizens regardless of sex, race, caste, or convictions, improvement of living standards, prevention of concentration of wealth and means of production in the hands of the few, just regulation of relations between industrialists and workers, between landowners and tenants; the right to work, to rest, and social welfare benefits; and reduction of the gap in incomes (Articles 32-39).

The basic principles of foreign policy are 'to preserve and strengthen fraternal relations among Muslim countries based on Islamic unity, support the common interests of the peoples of Asia, Africa, and Latin America, promote international peace and security, foster goodwill and friendly relations among all nations and encourage the settlement of international disputes by peaceful means' (Article 40). The Constitution includes some Islamic provisions; apart from those mentioned above, there is Article 2 which declares Islam a state religion. Among the other principles of state policy is the requirement that the state should make it possible for Muslims 'to order their lives in accordance with the fundamental principles and basic concepts of Islam' (Article 31, and 1). For Muslims, the study of the Holy Quran is compulsory (Article 31, and 2). Only Muslims can hold the offices of President and Prime Minister. The Muslim population must pay the traditional taxes, the **zakat* and *ushr*. The Constitution envisages the formation of the Council of Islamic Ideology and of the Federal Shariat Court. They aim to order legislation in accordance with the requirements of Islam (Articles 227, 228, 229, 230).

Electoral system: The Constitution of Pakistan envisages general secret direct elections of the legislative organs of power. All citizens of Pakistan 21 years of age and older, who are not mentally ill, have the right to vote. A citizen who has attained the age of 25 can be elected to the lower house of parliament and to the provincial legislative assemblies; for the upper house, the age requirement is 30 (Article 62). Any citizen of Pakistan can be elected to these bodies if they are not mentally ill or insolvent, have not lost Pakistan citizenship, have not held a paid post in the administrative organs apart from those permitted by law, have not been disqualified by a special act of parliament, have not been discharged from public service for misconduct, have not been guilty of corruption, illegal activity, false witnessing and other crimes of 'shameful nature', have not engaged in propaganda or acted to the detriment of Pakistan's ideology, its sovereignty, integrity and security, public order, and morality. A candidate must be of 'good character, sagacious, righteous and nonprofligate, and honest and of good moral reputation'. A representative of the Muslim part of the electorate must also have 'adequate knowledge of Islamic teachings' and practice 'obligatory duties prescribed by Islam' (Articles 62, 63). Double membership, that is, membership in several legislative organs, is forbidden (Article 223).

The system of elections in Pakistan is based on religious membership; non-Muslims vote separately. During parliamentary elections and elections to the provincial legislative assemblies, election districts are set up with approximately equal numbers of voters. One deputy is elected from each district; the number of electoral districts thus equals the number of seats in a given legislative organ. Elections are held on the relative majority system. To win an election, a candidate must win more votes than each of his opponents. If only one candidate is nominated in a district, he is declared without voting. The President is the head of state and the symbol of its unity, head of the executive power, a part of the legislative authority, and the supreme commander-in-chief of the country's armed forces. The President has the right of pardon and the right to cancel or mitigate sentences by any court (Article 45). The President is elected by the majority of the college of electors consisting of deputies of both houses of parliament and provincial legislative assemblies (Article 41, and 3). The term of office is five years. The same person cannot be elected for more than two terms (Article 44). To remove the President from power, the proposal for impeachment must be put forward by no less than half the deputies of one house, to be followed by a vote of no less than two thirds at a joint session of the two houses (Article 47). The President makes appointments to many of the highest state posts: those of Prime Minister and members of the government, governors of the provinces, members of the Supreme Court of Pakistan and the High Courts of the provinces, Chairman of the Federal Public Service Commission, Chief Commissioner of the Election Commission and members of the Election Commission, Chairman of the Joint Chiefs-of-Staff Committee and the three services chiefs. The President summons the sessions of both houses of parliament and their joint sessions and may interrupt such sessions; the President addresses the highest legislative body at the first annual joint session of the houses and at the first session after elections (Articles 54 and 56). All bills passed by parliament are sanctioned by the President who may withhold such a sanction, the bill is then returned to parliament; if it is again approved by the majority of deputies at a joint session of both houses of parliament, the President must sign such a bill, which then becomes law (Articles 75 and 2). The President's veto is not applicable to financial bills. Between the sessions of the National Assembly, the President may promulgate decrees which have the force of law and are effective over a period of four months; if the parliament approves such a decree, it becomes law (Article 89).The President has the right to dissolve the National Assembly and may do so both on the advice of the Prime Minister, or of their own accord, in those cases where the head of government received a vote of no confidence and no member of the National Assembly has the support of the majority. The President may also do so if a situation has arisen in which the government cannot act in accordance with the Constitution, and there is a need to appeal to the electorate (Article 58).

Fresh elections must be held during a ninety-day period from the dissolution of the National Assembly; in that period, an interim government appointed by the President may act in a caretaker capacity. The President may hold a referendum on issues of state significance on the recommendation of the Prime Minister or of their his own accord (Article 48).The President may impose a state of emergency if Pakistan's security is threatened by war, external aggression, or internal disorder (Articles 232 and 2A). The Central government may give orders to any province concerning the means in which executive authority should be implemented. The Central government may assume, or impose on the province's Governor, all or some of the functions of the given province or of any other state body with the exception of the legislative assembly and the High Court. Finally, the federal government may suspend some provision of the Constitution in relation to any organ of provincial authorities, except of the High Court (Articles 232 and 2).

During an emergency situation the President has the authority to suspend the basic civil rights or, otherwise, may forcibly implement them by order of the courts throughout the territory of Pakistan or any part thereof (Article 233). After the introduction of the state of emergency, the President is obliged to summon, within thirty days of the proclamation of the state of emergency, a joint session of both chambers of parliament. If parliament does not approve the Presidential decree on the state of emergency, the decree becomes invalid two months after its proclamation. If it is so approved, the state of emergency is maintained until it is lifted by the decision of a joint session of the two houses of parliament (Articles 232 and 7). In case of failure of the constitutional machinery in a province, the President may issue a decree on the incapacity of the constitutional mechanism in some province for a term of up to six months. In this case, the President may assume, or hand over to the Governor, the fulfilment of all or some functions of the provincial government; and may also redistribute the powers of a provincial legislative assembly to the country's parliament. The parliament may hand such powers back to the President. The head of state may suspend some provisions of the Constitution in relation to any organ of power in any province, except for the Supreme Court (Articles 232 and 1). Finally, the President may issue a decree declaring a state of financial emergency. When such a decree, which cannot last more than six months, is in force, the Central government may issue directives on the finances of a province (Articles 235 and 1). Apart from the sphere of exclusive competence, within which 'the President acts at his own discretion, on all other occasions he must be guided by advice and recommendations of the cabinet of ministers and its head.' But the President may demand that the cabinet, or the Prime Minister, revise their recommendations. It is noted that the original text of the Constitution rigidly stipulated that the Prime Minister's advice is obligatory for the President; no revision of the recommendation was provided for. The President's decrees had to be signed by the head of the cabinet. All these original provisions were cancelled by the Eighth Amendment to the Constitution.

Parliament: The highest legislative organ, or parliament, consists of two chambers; the lower house, the National Assembly; and the upper house, the Senate. The Provinces, the Federal Capital Territory of Islamabad, and the *Federally Administered Tribal Areas are represented in the National Assembly in proportion to the size of their population. In the Senate, all the provinces are equally represented. The National Assembly consists of 237 deputies, 207 of which are elected by the Muslim electorate, 10 of which come from the religious minorities list, and 20 of which are reserved for women. The National Assembly is elected for five years (Article 51). The law provides for the following representation in the lower house: 115 seats for *Punjab, forty-six for *Sindh, twenty-six for the *NWFP, eleven for *Balochistan, one for Islamabad, and eight for the *Federally Administered Tribal Areas. Non-Muslim representatives are elected only in the provinces. Of the ten candidates, four are Christians, four are Hindus, one each is from the *Sikh, Buddhist, and *Parsi Communities, and one from the *Ahmadiya sect. Representatives of the provinces included candidates to fill the 20 women's seats, who were elected by members of the National Assembly, divided into four groups in accordance with their provincial membership. In 1990 the provision for special representation of women was invalidated. Thus now the total membership of the National Assembly is 217.

The Senate consists of eighty-seven members: fifty-six senators are elected by the deputies of the provincial legislative assemblies and there are fourteen senators from each province. In the same way, the provinces elect five senators each to represent Muslim theologians (Ulema), technocrats, and other professional groups. The deputies of the National Assembly elect eight senators from the FATA, and three from Islamabad. The Senate is elected for six years, half the members are reelected at three-year intervals. Since each province sends an uneven number of senators representing professional groups, two senators are re-elected after the first three years, and three after the next three-year period. The same principle applies to representatives of Islamabad; one senator is elected and after the three-year period two more senators are chosen from the capital district. At the first session after the elections, the National Assembly elects the speaker and the deputy. The speaker supervises the functioning of the chamber, summoning its sessions at the request of no less than one fourth of the deputies. The Speaker does not take part in the voting except for those cases when the votes are evenly divided (Articles 55 and 1).

Each year, no less than three sessions of the National Assembly must be held; the interval between the sessions must not exceed 120 days; the deputies of the lower house must put in no less than 160 working days per year (Articles 54 and 2). One-fourth of the total number of the house's membership represents the necessary quorum (Articles 55 and 2). The Chairman of the Senate and the deputy are elected for three years at the first session of the Senate after its 50 per cent re-election. The functions of the Chairman and Deputy Chairman of the upper house are similar to those of the Speaker and Deputy Speaker of the lower house. In case of the President's death, illness, or temporary absence, the duties are performed by the Senate Chairman, with the speaker of the National Assembly next in line (Article 49). The schedule of the Senate's work, its convocation, necessary quorum, and the procedure of the passage of a bill, is the same as in the National Assembly (Article 61).

All bills, except those of financial nature, are introduced in one of the chambers of parliament. After discussion and acceptance by a majority vote, a bill is passed on to the other house. If it is rejected by the latter, the issue is taken to a joint session of the two chambers and is decided by a simple majority (Article 70). A bill on financial issues is introduced in the National Assembly and, being adopted by this chamber, is handed over to be signed by the President (Articles 73 and 1).

The Government: The government's primary task is 'to aid and advise the President in the exercise of his functions' (Articles 91 and 1). The President appoints one of the members of the National Assembly, who must be a Muslim, as Prime Minister, if convinced that the deputy has the confidence of most members of the National Assembly. On the Prime Minister's advice, the President appoints members of the government; these may be chosen from the deputies of the National Assembly or senators, or they may come from outside the parliament. After this, the government must win a vote of confidence in the National Assembly. The number of ministers who are simultaneously senators must not exceed one-fourth of the total membership of the cabinet. Any minister not a member of the National Assembly must seek to be elected to that chamber within six months of appointment, otherwise they cease to be a member of the government. The government is collectively responsible to the National Assembly (Articles 91 and 4). The President dismisses ministers on the advice of the head of government. He also has the right to dismiss the Prime Minister if the latter does not have the confidence of the majority of the National Assembly. To decide the issue, the President summons a session of the lower house (Articles 91 and 5). The members of the National Assembly may remove the Prime Minister. The removal must be supported by no less than a fifth of the Assembly's deputies, after which the question is put to a session of the chamber (Article 95).

In accordance with the Eighth Amendment to the Constitution, the Prime Minister is obliged to present to the President information on the work of the government, its decisions, and proposed legislative initiatives. The President may demand that the cabinet should discuss any decision by its head or by any minister, if that decision was not already discussed by the cabinet (Article 46). The government's executive powers extend to all issues on which parliament may pass laws (Article 97). The cabinet of ministers may instruct a provincial government to perform certain functions in some areas to which the federation's executive authority extends (Article 146). The cabinet has considerable power during emergency situations (Article 232).

The Prime Minister heads, ex officio, a number of important state institutions, such as the National Economic Council, the country's highest economic organ which works out the plans for economic development (Article 156). The Prime Minister may head the Council of Common Interests established to co-ordinate the interests of the Centre and the provinces, and interprovincial interests (Article 153).

The Government of Pakistan consists of federal ministers, state ministers, advisors, special assistants of the Prime Minister having the rank of federal ministers, and assistants of the Prime Minister having the rank of state ministers. Federal ministers form the nucleus of the government or the ministerial cabinet. State ministers are ranked lower than federal ministers. The Attorney-General, appointed by the President, is also a member of the government. The official principal duty of the Attorney-General is to advise the government on the legal aspects of its activities (Article 100). As there is no Deputy Prime Minister in Pakistan's government, these duties are fulfilled by the senior minister, when the Prime Minister is unable to perform them. The seniority of the members of government is determined by its head, the Prime Minister.

The principal Federal ministries in order of seniority, as of 2005, are as follows:

Ministry of Defence; Commerce; communications; Culture, sports and Youth Affairs; Defence production; Education; Environment; Food, Agriculture and Livestock; Foreign Affairs; Health; Housing and Works; Industries and Production & Special Initiatives; Information and Broadcasting; Information Technology; Interior; Kashmir Affairs and Northern Areas; Labour, Manpower and Overseas Pakistanis; Law, Justice and Human Rights; Local Government and Rural Development; Textile Industry; Tourism; Narcotics Control; Parliamentary Affairs; Petroleum and Natural Resources; Population Welfare; Ports and Shipping; Privatisation and Investment; Railways; Religious Affairs & Zakat and Ushr; Science and Technology; Social Welfare and Special Education; States and Frontier Regions; and Water and Power. The ministries consist of departments and sectors; the staff of a ministry is headed by a Secretary or Chief Secretary.

Matters of prime importance for the state come within the exclusive jurisdiction of central government. Examples of such matters concern defence, external relations, currency circulation, foreign trade, revenue, planning and co-ordination, communications, and interprovincial trade. If an act of a provincial assembly contravenes some law passed by parliament within its competence, exclusive or concurrent with the provinces, this act is regarded as null and void (Article 143). To regulate the relations between of central government and the provinces and the relations among the provinces, the Council of Common Interests has been established. It consists of Chief Ministers of the provinces and an equal number of members of the central government who are appointed by the Prime Minister; if the latter is a member of the council they its Chairman; in other cases the council is headed by one of the members of the central government (Article 153). Decisions of the Council of Common Interests are made by a majority vote. If the federal or any of the provincial governments are not satisfied with the Council's decision, the disputed issue is considered by a joint session of the two houses of parliament whose decision is final (Article 154, S 2,5). All the provinces of Pakistan are equally represented in the National Economic Council; with one representative from each province recommended by the Governor (see Article 156). The National Economic Council, which offers recommendations on the division of revenues from taxes between of central government and the provinces, on federal subsidies to the provinces, etc., consists of the Finance Minister of the federal government, the ministers of finances of the provinces, and persons appointed by the President after consultation with the Governors of provinces (Article 160).

PUBLICATIONS: *'The Constitution of the Islamic Republic of Pakistan', Lahore, 1989.*

BIBLIOGRAPHY: *Yuri Gankovsky, V.N. Moskalenko, 'The Three Constitutions of Pakistan', Lahore, 1978.*

V.N. MOSCALENKO

Cornelius, A.R., Justice (1920–94)

Statesman. Chief Justice A.R. Cornelius sat on the bench of the Federal Court of Pakistan. He held that the Constituent Assembly, which was dismissed by Governor-General Ghulam *Mohammad, was the supreme body of the state and refused to uphold its dissolution. From 1960 to 1968 he served as Chief Justice of Pakistan. He was law minister from 1969 to 1971. He was in favour of Islamic punishments for criminals.

BIBLIOGRAPHY: *Ralph Braibanti, 'Chief Justice Cornelius of Pakistan'*, Oxford, Karachi, 1999.

YU.V. GANKOVSKY

Cripps Mission

Sir Stafford Cripps, the Leader of the House of Commons was sent by Churchill to India in March 1942. The background to his mission was the growing Japanese threat following the fall of Singapore and the need to demonstrate good faith to the Americans who were now war-time allies, but had traditionally voiced anti-Imperialist sentiment. Cripps promised India dominion status at the end of the war. In the short term all that was on offer, however, was an expansion of the Ciceroy's Executive Council. Crucially there was to be no Indian control over defence. The Cripps Offer held out for the *Muslim League support in theory for the Pakistan demand in that it included a proviso that no part of India could be forced to join the post-war arrangements. The Mission failed to the relief of Chruchill because of Gandhi's opposition within the Congress. Its rejection led to the British repression of the ensuing Quit India movement. Many of the Congress leaders spent the final three years of the war in jail. Jinnah was able to take advantage of this in consolidating the Muslim League's position.

I. TALBOT

Crocodiles in Pakistan

Until the 1950s, the Mugger of March Crocodile (*Crododiles palustris*) was widespread throughout the province of *Sindh. Exploitation of its skin to make decorative shoes, handbags and luggage led to its virtual disappearance by the 1980s. Only a small remnant population survived in the seeping lakes of Sanghar District. Fortunately, the Sindh Wildlife Management Board designated part of this area as a sanctuary for the Mugger and there is now a healthy population surviving within the sanctuary area. There is also a thriving colony of captive snub-nosed crocodiles attached to the tomb of a local *Sufi saint at Mangho Pir, near Karachi, reputed to have special healing powers for skin problems.

The fish eating Ghavial Crocodile (*Gavialis gangeticus*), however, has become virtually extinct in Pakistan. It was always confined to the main river system and the construction of irrigation barrages, as well as persecution by fishing tribes resident on the *Indus had reduced its numbers severely. A captive breeding programme that has led to a partial recovery currently exists in Pakistan.

T.J. ROBERTS

Cunningham, Alexander Sir (1814–93)

Archeologist. Arrived in India in 1931 and became a lieutenant of the Royal Engineers in 1833. Between 1861-65 and 1871-85 he served in the Archaeological Department in northern India. He studied archaeological and architectural landmarks in northern India, as well as epigraphics, numismatics and historical geography.

He also initiated a unified system of registering monuments.

WORKS: *'The Bhilsa Topes', 1854; 'Ancient Geography of India: Buddhist Period', Varanasi, 1871; 'Inscriptions of Ashoka', Calcutta, 1873; 'Stupa of Bharhut', 1879; 'Book of Indian Eras with Tables for Calculating Indian Dates', Calcutta, Thacker, Spink, 1883.*

BIBLIOGRAPHY: *N.P. Chakravarti, 'The Story of Indian Archaeology,' in: Archaeology of India, Delhi, 1950; S. Roy, 'The Story of Indian Archaeology, 1784-1947', New Delhi, 1961; Abu Imam, 'Sir Alexander Cunningham and the Beginning of Indian Archaeology', Dhaka, 1966.*

N.P. KOCHERGINA.

D

Daf

(Arabic) A large one-sided drum played with one hand. Metal discs are sometimes fastened to the frame. The *daf* usually accompanies women's singing.

I. PIRACHA

Dakhini

See, Urdu.

Damru

A small wooden two-sided drum shaped like an hourglass with a rope tied around the middle. As the performer twists the drum rapidly, the knotted ends of the rope strike the membranes producing a distinctive clicking sound. The instrument is used in Pakistan and India to accompany performances by itinerant actors, jugglers, snake charmers, animal trainers, etc.

I. PIRACHA

Dandia

Dandia has gained popularity as a special dance in celebration of a wedding particularly in Karachi. It originates from the Gujarati speaking Hindu and Muslim communities of India from where dances such as *Raas, Garba*, etc. have also originated. The *dandiyaas* or two short sticks are held in each hand of all the dancers. Ideally, two circles, one formed by men and one by women move in clockwise and anti-clockwise directions. Romantic songs are sung on the occasion. *Raas* is very energetic, colourful and playful, providing opportunity for acting and exchanging messages through eye contact. Many romances are said to bloom during these performances and these dances are particularly popular among the younger generation.

I. PIRACHA

Dani, Ahmad Hasan (1920–)

Historian Archeologist. A specialist in the ancient and medieval history of South and Central Asia. He served as professor at several universities, including Dhaka (Bangladesh), 1950-62; Peshawar, 1962-71; and Islamabad, 1972-80 and has been a visiting professor at universities in America and Australia. He has been Director of the Centre for the Study of the Civilization of Central Asia (Pakistan) since 1980, and was Vice-President of the International Association for the Study of the Cultures of Central Asia.

WORKS: *'Dhaka, A Record of Its Changing Fortunes', Dhaka, 1962; 'Indus Civilization', Islamabad, 1981; 'The Historical City of Taxila', Tokyo, 1986; 'Recent Archaeological Discoveries in Pakistan', Tokyo, 1988.*

YU.V. GANKOVSKY

Danish, Ahsan (1914–82)

Poet. Ahsan-ul-Haq (his real name) was an Urdu language poet. From a poor family, Ahsan Danish did not receive a formal education. He visited many Indian cities in search of employment, and worked as a porter, day labourer, gardener, printer and street vendor. He first published his verse in the early 1930s. Shortly before 1947 he moved from Delhi to Lahore, where he started his own business—*'Muktaba-i-Danish'*. His poetry depicted the everyday life of workers and his emotional verse expressed strong social protest, similar to the work of poet Nazir Akbarabadi. Danish was influenced by the poetry of Josh *Malihabadi and Muhammad *Iqbal. He has ten collections of verse to his name: *Hadis-i-Adab* ('Literary *Hadis*'), *Chiraghan* ('Illumination'), *Jada-i-Nau* ('New Way'), *Nafir-i-Fitrat* ('The Trumpets of Nature'), *Nawa-i-Kargar* ('The Voice of the Toiler'). His poetry includes **ghazals, *rubai, *masnawi* and both rhymed and unrhymed **nazms*. He published his autobiography, *Jehan-i-Danish,* in 1973 in Lahore.

BIBLIOGRAPHY: *N. Glebov, A. Sukhochev, 'Urdu Literature', Moscow, 1965; Abdul Wahid, 'Jadid Shuara-i-Urdu', Karachi (s.a.); 'Jam-i-Nau', Ahsan Danish Number, ed. Mazhar Khairi, Karachi, November 1974.*

N.V. GLEBOV

Darbar

(Persian: the ruler's residence or court; also, audience, reception) In the Muslim states of medieval South Asia and in more recent times, a gala reception of the senior officials of the court and the vassals held by the suzerain. Under the Great *Mughals the coronation *darbars* were to be attended by all courtiers. Apart from the ceremonial functions, *darbars* were often used to perform judicial functions. In the British period *darbar* meant an assembly in Delhi of vassal rulers for the demonstration of Royalty to the British crown. At the first *darbar* on 1 January 1877, Queen Victoria (r. 1837–1901) was proclaimed Queen-Empress of India. At the second *darbar* on 1 January 1903, King Edward VII (r. 1901–10) was proclaimed King-Emperor; and at the third *darbar* on 12 December 1911, the announcement was made by King George V in person. L.B. Alayev concerning the transfer of British India's capital from Calcutta to Delhi and the cancellation of the partition of Bengal.

L.B. ALAYEV

Dard, Khwaja Mir (1721–85)

Poet. A *Sufi poet and preacher, known as one of the 'four pillars' of *Urdu poetry, Mir Dard wrote in Urdu and Persian. A *Naqshbandi Sufi, he was a follower of his father, Muhammad Nasir Andalib, who preached *Tariqa-i-Muhammadiya* ('The Way of Muhammad' (PBUH)), demanding complete annihilation of the mystic's being in devotion to the Prophet (*Fana fi al-Rasul*). Dard wrote two Sufi compositions in Persian: *Ilm al-Kitab* ('Knowledge of the Book') and *Chahar Risala* ('Four Treatises') and made his name with a small **diwan* of his Urdu poems. He was the first to introduce the practice of singing Urdu **ghazals* at poetic symposia. Dard enjoyed great popularity among the followers of the Urdu tradition.

WORKS: *'Mir Dard, Chahar Risala', Delhi (undated); 'Intikhab-i-Kalam-i-Dard' (Selected Works), Patna (undated); 'Dewan-i-Dard', Delhi, n.d.*

BIBLIOGRAPHY: *A. Schimmel, 'Pain and Grace', Leiden, 1976.*

A.A. SUVOROVA

Dardic Languages

A group of Indo-Iranian languages descending from a branch of Indian (*Indo-Aryan) languages. On typological grounds, Nuristian languages are sometimes also included in this group. Proper Dardic languages are spoken in the mountainous regions of Afghanistan, Pakistan, and India by approximately four million people. They are subdivided into two subgroups: eastern (including *Kashmiri, *Shina, *Phalura, Garwi, Torwali, Mayan and others) and central (subdivided into the northern subgroup, including *Khowar and *Kalasha); and southern, (comprising Gawar, Shumashti, Katarqalai, Glangali, Tirahi, Dameli, and the Pashai group of dialects or languages). The borrowed elements mostly come from *Urdu, *Pashtu, Persian, Kashmiri, and also from Sanskrit and English. Arabic lexical items are borrowed through mediating languages and from books. Only Kashmiri has a long written tradition. Traditional writing is based on the systems of Sharada and Nagari. The speakers of the Kashtawari Kashmiri dialect used a variety of Takari. Modern Kashmiri, and also Khowar, Mayan, Shina, and Pashai, which have recently acquired systems of writing, use various modifications of the Arabic alphabet.

BIBLIOGRAPHY: *D.I. Edelman, 'Dardic Languages', Moscow, 1965 (in Russian); id., 'Dardic Languages', in: Languages of Asia and Africa, Book 2, Moscow, 1978 (in Russian); A.L. Gryunberg, 'An Essay in the Linguistic Mapping of Nuristan, The Countries and Peoples of the East', Moscow, 1971, No. 10 (in Russian); G.A. Grierson, 'Linguistic Survey of India', Vol. 1, Pt. 1, Calcutta, 1927; G. Fussman, 'Atlas Linguistique des Parleurs Dardes et Kafirs', t.1-2, Paris, 1972; G. Morgenstierne, Irano-Dardica, Wiesbaden, 1973; id., 'Languages of Nuristan and Surrounding Regions', in: Cultures of the Hindukush, Heidelberg, 1974; G. Buddruss, 'Nochmals zur Stellung der Nuristan Sprachen des Afghanistan Hindukusch', Münchener Studien zur Sprach-wissenschaft, 1977, Bd. 36; D.I. Edelman, 'The Dardic and Nuristani Languages', Moscow, 1983.*

D.I. EDELMAN

Darkot

A mountain pass in the *Hinduraj Range in northern Pakistan. It is approximately 4,575 metres above sea level and is situated in an almost inaccessible glacier-clad region where there are snowstorms in both winter and summer. The footpath through the pass connects the valleys of the Yasin and the Yarkhun rivers. The path is only passable for draught animals from the middle of June to the middle of September.

M.YU. MOROZOVA

Dar-ul-Ulum

(Arabic: The house of knowledge) A higher Muslim theological school or a religious academy. Each *dar-ul-ulum* has its own distinctive traditions and curricula. In this way, each *dar-ul-ulum* represents its own **madhab*. They also differ according to their traditional public and political trends.

M.R. KAZIMI

Dastan

In the literatures of South Asia, this is a narrative genre in prose (*Urdu) or in poetry (*Sindhi). *Dastan* is usually epic and romantic in spirit and is reminiscent of imitation early epic poetry. *Dastan,* as a genre, originated in Iran and was disseminated by folk storytellers. It was assimilated by individual authors. *Dastan's* plots are based both on folklore and classical literary subjects. *Dastan* was particularly popular in *Urdu literature, typologically close to other narrative genres in Eastern literatures, such as Persian **masnawi*, *Punjabi *qissa*, *Sindhi *waqayati bait*, etc, and also reminiscent of the European novel. The oldest known Urdu *dastans* are *Dastan-i-Amir Hamza,* recorded in the early seventeenth century, and the extinct *Bustan-i-Khayal* ('The Garden of Imagination' or 'The Garden of *Khayal*') by Mir Taqi Khayal (d. 1760). Most of the narrative *dastans* were recorded in the early nineteenth century, representing contaminations of 'wandering', motifs borrowed from the folklore of the Middle East, central Asia and northern India. These include *Bagh-o-Bahar* ('The Garden and Spring') by Mir Amman, *Mazhab-i-Ishq* (The Religion of Love) by Nihalchand Lahori, *Araish-i-Mahfil* ('The Adornment of the Assembly') by Hyderbakhsh Hyderi, *Gulzar-i-Chin* ('The Flower Bed of Chin') by Khalil Ali Khan Ashq, and the smaller *dastans*.

The category of Urdu *dastan* sometimes includes literary treatments of Sanskrit novels, e.g. *Indian Virtue* by Husayni, *Parrot's Tales* by Hyder, and also certain original works, such as *Rani Ketki ki Kahani* ('The Story of Rani Ketki') by Insha, and *The Story of Miracles* by Surur. Dastans are written in rhymed (*saj*) or metred (*murassa*) prose with verse inclusions. *Dastan* has always been considered a low genre and was not included in the genre hierarchy of standard poetry. *Dastan* represents a typical medieval poetic form abounding in standard turns of phrases, repetitions, figurative cliches and stereotyped introductions and endings. The style of the *dastan* is characterized by rich embellishments, euphemism, abundance of parallelisms, and attention to detail of everyday life. The style relies on a combination of fantasy and adventure with naive realism. *Dastan* provided a good foundation for the genre of the novel in Urdu literature. Several smaller *dastans* have been translated into European languages, including Russian.

WORKS: *'Dastan-i-Amir Hamza', Lucknow, 1960; 'Talism-i-Hoshruba (The Magic that is Enchanting the Mind), Karachi, 1967.*

BIBLIOGRAPHY: *A.S. Sukhochev, 'From Dastan to the Novel', Moscow, 1971 (in Russian); A.A. Dekhtyar, 'Poetics of the Dastan Urdu', Moscow, 1979 (in Russian); Wakar Azim, 'Hamari Dastanen' (Our Dastans), Rampur, 1968; Jain Gyanchand, 'Urdu ki Nasri Dastanen' (Dastan Urdu in Prose), Karachi, 1954; F. Pritchett, 'Marvellous Encounters: Folk Romance in Urdu and Hindi', Chicago, 1985.*

A.A. SUVOROVA

Daud Khel

Lying south of the old town of Kalabagh and close to the Jinnah Barrage, the town has chemical, pharmaceutical, fertilizer and cement industries. In the 1970s it was called Iskandarabad, in honour of President Iskandar *Mirza.

M. STONEY

Daultana, Mumtaz Muhammad Khan, Mian (1916-95)

Statesman. Daultana was born into a large, land-owning family. He graduated from the Punjab University in Lahore and later received a degree from Oxford. A lawyer by profession, he became Deputy to the Punjab Legislative Assembly as a representative from the *Muslim League (1943–47). He served as a Member of the first *Constituent Assembly of Pakistan (1947 to 1954), Chief Minister of *Punjab province (1951 to 1953) and Defence Minister of Pakistan (1957). A victim of Ayub *Khan's notorious EBDO (Electoral Bodies Disqualification Order), Daultana is noted also as among the organizers of the Council of the Muslim League that opposed the Ayub government. He was a Member of the National Assembly (1970–72) and was appointed Ambassador to the United Kingdom in 1972.

YU.V. GANKOVSKY

Dawn

A daily newspaper, published in English and *Gujarati founded by Mohammad Ali *Jinnah. In 1942, *Dawn* appeared in Delhi. From 1947 the paper was published in Karachi and a second printing plant was started in Lahore. The newspaper belongs to the Haroon family, and between 1947 and 1957 it served as a non-official organ of the Pakistan *Muslim League. In the 1960s and early 1970s its policy became more liberal with Mazhar Ali Khan as its editor. Today Dawn is published in English from Karachi, Lahore and Islamabad. It also has an Internet Edition. Dawn Gujarati ceased publication in 1997.

SHAHNAWAZ

Dayaram, Gidumal (1857–1927)

Writer/Statesman. Dayaram was a *Sindhi poet, writer and public figure. A graduate of Bombay University, his work is permeated with ideas of enlightenment and represent a synthesis of *Sufism, Vedanta, and Sikhism. His work covers a broad range of socially significant themes, such as the spreading of enlightenment, the campaign for women's emancipation and the democratisation of the literary language. The novelty of form in Dayaram's works had a great influence on the development of *Sindhi literature. His main works include didactic dialogues *Satta Saheliun* ('Seven Friends'), a collection of philosophical poems *Mana-ja-Chabuk* ('The Curse of the Mind', 1923-26) the first *vers libre* in Sindhi literature, a number of literary studies of Sindhi classics, and translations of philosophical-ethical compositions from Sanskrit and medieval Hindi.

BIBLIOGRAPHY: *L.H. Ajwani, 'History of Sindhi Literature', New Delhi, 1977.*

A.S. SUKHOCHEV

Dehlawi, Amir Khusrau (1253–1325)

Poet. Born in Delhi to a family of Central Asian Turkic origin, Amir Khusrau was a scholar, a court historian, a musician, an author of treatises on music and a poet writing in both Persian and in the *Hindavi language, immediate ancestor of both *Urdu and Hindi, then emerging in the environs of Delhi. Dehlawi was in fact the first to write poetry in Hindavi. He lived at the court of the Delhi Sultan Alauddin Khilji (1286-1316) and was a member of the Chishtiya *Sufi Order. His in the lyrical **qasidas*, **ghazals*, and **rubais* Persian language have been compiled in five collections (**diwans)*. His poetry reveals the influence of Sa'di, Khakani, and Anwari. Khusrau was the first Persian poet to write a response to Nizam's *Khamse*, imitating its style. Stylistic perfection conveying the *Chishtiyas' religious, philosophical, and ethical views distinguish Khusrau's poems and **masnawais*.

Khusrau is responsible for five poems devoted to historic events in India of which he was a witness. These include the poem *Masnawi 'Dowal-rani Khizr Khan'*, in which the tragic love of Sultan Khizr Khan and his Hindu concubine is interpreted as an allegory of Hindu-Muslim unity, and the idea of spiritual rapprochement and mutual enrichment of the two cultures is promoted. The poem reveals a new trend in the development of Persian language literature (*masnawi* and **dastan*) and the use of Indian sources in the plot. Khusrau incorporates local dialects into his work. The five-volume prose work *Ijaz-i-Khusrawi* ('The Wonders of Khusrau') reflects the author's broad knowledge of different disciplines, including history, philosophy and music theory.

Khusrau is considered one of the founders of Indo-Pakistan classical music. His musical compositions unite Indian and Arab-Muslim elements, resulting in a new variety of vocal and instrumental expressiveness. He collected and classified a large number of the **ragas* that are the basis of Indo-Pakistan classical music. He established some of the functions of the basic instruments—the **sitar* and **tabla*. Legend credits him with being the inventor of these two instruments. The genre of **qawwali* is of particular importance in the creative work of Khusrau. His musical compositions are often performed during folk festivals and are widely popular in India and Pakistan. Khusrau's treatises on music look at the key questions of music theory and practice of his time, such as harmony formation and types of harmonies, rhythmic organization, music forms and genres, musical instruments, and performing methods. In his treatment of questions of music theory, he follows the traditions of Arab-Iranian music e.g. relying on sound acoustic characteristics of the string instruments. Of particular interest are descriptions of contests of court musicians—*majlis*.

WORKS: *'Kulliyat-i-ghazaliyat' (Complete collection of ghazals), Rawalpindi, 1972-74, vols 1-3; 'Dowal-rani Khizr Khan', Aligarh, 1917; 'Hasht Behesht' (Eight Heavenly Gardens), Aligarh, 1918; 'Jawahir-i-Khusrawi' (The Treasures of Khusraw), Aligarh, 1918; 'Ijaz-i-Khusrawi' (The Wonders of Khusraw), Lucknow, 1876.*

BIBLIOGRAPHY: *G.Yu. Aliev, 'Persian Language Literature of India', Moscow, 1968 (in Russian); Mumtaz Husain, 'Amir Khusraw Dehlawi', Karachi, 1986; Zoe Ansari, 'Khusraw ka Zahni Safar', New Delhi, 1977 and 1988.*

A.S. ALPATOVA
M.M. OSINOVA

Delhi Sultanate

An imperial state in northern India during the 13th to the 15th centuries, which appeared as a result of the conquests of Shahabuddin Muhammad Ghuri and his Turkic and Afghan generals. The Delhi Sultanate was only loosely connected territorially, with ever changing borders and considerable political instability. The real power of the Delhi Sultans was only recognised in the central regions of northern India. The Delhi Sultans' vassals, particularly those in the south and in Bengal, did little more than pay formal tribute and supply soldiers to the Sultan's army. The continuous power struggles led to frequent changes of ruling dynasties. The Delhi throne passed from one dynasty to another: including the Turki Sultans (so-called 'Slave Dynasty'), Khiljis, Tughluqs, *Sayyids, and Lodis. The Delhi Sultanate's territory was divided into *khalisas*, paying taxes to finance inspectors, and **iqta* or lands conditionally granted to officials. The holders of large *iqtas* (known as *muqtas*) spent part of the collected taxes on keeping their own military detachments that they made available to the Sultan when commanded. Part of the lands belonged to individual feudal lords (**milk*, **inam*), some to Indian princes and **zamindars* who had been accepted as vassals of the Delhi Sultans. The state treasury was mainly replenished through **kharaj*, trade, travelling taxes, taxes on urban crafts and **jiziya* or poll tax. The Delhi Sultans' attempts to consolidate the state, e.g. the reforms of Alauddin Khilji (1296-1316), fell through. By the end of the 14th century, centrifugal tendencies prevailed.

In 1389 Timur destroyed Delhi. After Timur's invasion the Delhi Sultanate remained little more than a local kingdom and the ruling families of the Sayyids and Lodis had to make do with only remnants of the Sultanate's former power and extent of domain. Their authority was limited to the capital territory and parts of the *Punjab. On the ruins of the Delhi Sultanate appeared the Bahmani, Jaunpur and Gujarati Sultanates and the Malwa and Rajputana Principalities. In 1526 Kabul's Mughal ruler, Babur, defeated the armies of the Delhi Sultan, Ibrahim Shah Lodi, in the battle of Panipat and laid the base of the *Mughal Empire.

The era of the Delhi Sultanate was characterized by the development of agriculture, facilitated by the building of irrigation canals under Feroz Shah Tughluq (1351-88). New cities were built, such as Ferozabad, Jaunpur, Dawlatabad, Hissar, Burhanpur, as well as new fortresses. The textile industry became highly developed. Between the 14th and the 16th centuries firearms were introduced to India. India's trade relations with the countries of central Asia, the Middle East, East Africa and South East Asia developed successfully. Interpenetration of traditional cultures and mutual cultural enrichment between Indians and the newcomers from Iran and Central Asia played an important role in the Delhi Sultanate's development. This synthesis was reflected in literature, architecture, music and lexicography. It was a period of intellectual and spiritual enquiry. *Sufism began to spread and various sects sprang up within Islam. The Bhakti movement took shape among Hindus. The era of the Delhi Sultanate coincided with the activities of some major *Sufi preachers, such as Nizamuddin Awliya, Sharafuddin Ahmad Maneri, Fariduddin Ganj-e Shakar, and some of the most celebrated poets and preachers of the Bhakti movement, such as Ramanand, Kabir, Namdev, Ravidas and, of course, Nanak, the founder and first Guru of the *Sikh religion.

The 'Slave' Sultans of Delhi: Qutb ad-Din Aybak (r. 1206-10), Aram Shah (r. 1210-11), Shams ad-Din Iltutmysh (r. 1211-36), Rukn ad-Din Firuz Shah (r. 1236), Jalalat ad-Din Radiya Begum Sultana (r. 1236-40), Muiz ad-Din Bahram Shah (r. 1240-2), Ala ad-Din Masud Shah (r. 1242-6), Nasir ad-Din Mahmud Shah I (r. 1246-66), Ghiyaz ad-Din Balban (r. 1266-87), Muiz ad-Din Kay Qubad (r. 1287-90), Shams ad-Din Kay Umars (r. 1290);

The Khilji dynasty: Jalal ad-Din Firuz Shah II (r. 1290-6), Rukn ad-Din Ibrahim Shah I (r. 1296), Ala ad-Din Muhammad Shah I (r. 1296-1316), Shihab ad-Din Umar Shah (r. 1316), Qutb ad-Din Mubarak Shah (r. 1316-20), Nasir ad-Din Khusraw Shah (r. 1320);

The Tughlaq dynasty: Ghiyaz ad-Din Tughlaq Shah I (r. 1320-25), Muhammad Shah II (r. 1325-51), Mahmud (r. 1351), Firuz Shah III (r. 1351-88), Ghiyas ad-Din Tughlaq Shah (r. 1388-9), Abu Bakr Shah (r. 1389-90), Nasr ad-Din Muhammad Shah III (r. 1390-93), Ala ad-Din Sikandar Shah I (r. 1393), Nasir ad-Din Mahmud Shah II (r. 1393-5), Nusrat Shah (r. 1395-9), Mahmud Shah II (second term: 1399-1414), Daulat Khan Lodi (r. 1413-4);

The Sayyid dynasty: Khidr Khan (r. 1414-21), Muiz ad-Din Mubarak Shah II (r. 1421-35), Muhammad Shah IV (r. 1435-46), Ala ad-Din Alam Shah (r. 1446-51);

The Lodi dynasty: Bahlul Lodi (r. 1451-89), Nizam Khan Sikandar II (r. 1489-1517), Ibrahim II (r. 1517-26);

The Sur dynasty: Sher Shah Suri (r. 1540-45), Islam Shah (r. 1545-54), Muhammad V Adil Shah (r. 1554), Ibrahim III (r. 1554-5), Ahmad Khan Sikandar Shah III (r. 1555).

BIBLIOGRAPHY: *K.Z. Ashrafyan, 'The Delhi Sultanate', Moscow, 1960 (in Russian); I.H. Qureshi, 'The Administration of the Sultanate of Delhi', Karachi, 1958.*

YU.V. GANKOVSKY

Democratic Women's Association of Pakistan (also *Anjuman-i-Jumhuriatpasand Khawatin*, AJK)

The Association was set up in 1950. Between 1953 and 1963 it was banned. Its headquarters are in Lahore and it has branches throughout the country. The organization was set up by Tahira Mazhar Ali, a prominent public figure. It is administered by its executive committee. Until 1977 the AJK regularly convened its congresses. In the early 1970s the Association actively promoted women's constitutional rights, more democratic laws on the family and marriage, and women's greater involvement in the country's national reconstruction. It called on women to campaign for free education accessible to all citizens. Under military regimes it has demanded radical democratic changes and the abolition of Martial Law. In 1968 it became a member of the Women's International Democratic Organization. It maintains an active relationship with the latter and takes part in all its initiatives. In 1988 it campaigned widely to collect signatures in support of the Geneva Agreements on Afghanistan (*see*, Afghanistan-Pakistan Relations). For a number of years now, as a member of the *Women's Action Forum, it has been actively campaigning against the Hudood Ordinance and the Law of Evidence passed in the time of General Ziaul *Haq, which it sees as directly aimed against women, and the *Qisas* and *Diyat* Ordinance. Its programme envisages co-operation with the democratic women's organizations in other countries and peace movements.

YU.V. GANKOVSKY

Deoband

A *Sunni **dar-ul-ulum* or religious academy, one of the most prestigious theological centres in South Asia. It was based on the ideology of Shah Waliullah. It was founded on 30 May 1867 by Maulana Fazlur Rahman and Maulvi Zulfikar Ali, but was established on a firm footing by Maulana Muhammad Qasim Nanotavi and Maulana Rashid Ahmad Gangohi. In their attitude towards religious and legal questions, Deoband theologians follow the principle of **Taqlid*, i.e., reference to a precedent in the medieval legal practice, the legal norms of the *Hanafi **madhab*. The curriculum stresses Muslim jurisprudence (*fiqh*), and the Quranic commentaries (*tafsir* and *ahadith*). The Deoband school became more widely known during the early 20th century under the rectorship of Maulana Mahmud al-Hasan (1851–1920), when many of its teachers took an active part in the *Khilafat Movement. Students from south-east Asia, Iran, Afghanistan, and South Africa were attracted to the school both for its theological traditions and its anti-colonial orientation. Deoband *ulema* played an important role in establishing **Jamiat ul-ulema-i-Hind* in India and **Jamiat ul-ulema-i-Islam* in Pakistan. Deoband never accepted any grant from the British government and its *ulema* played a leading role in the struggle for independence. The Deoband persuasion is regarded as puritan or austere in its religious attitude.

A. NIYAZI

Dera Ghazi Khan

The town is the administrative centre of a division of the same name. It was founded in the fifteenth century by Mir Ghazi Khan, the **Sardar* of the *Balochi tribe of Rind. It was originally in Balochistan but boundary changes made by the British, for administrative and strategic reasons, tranferred it into the *Punjab. Following the flood of 1910-11, when the banks of the *Indus were breached with disastrous results, the present-day town was rebuilt, 9 kms. further upstream, on more organized lines. The town is a trading and industrial centre. It is also known for rope-weaving handicrafts of lacquer, wood and leather. It also produces date palm baskets, and textiles. The town is a well-known Muslim religious centre.

M. STONEY

Derajat

This is the name of the trans-*Indus plain between the the *Sulaiman Montains to the west and the Indus to the east, in the territories of the *Punjab and *North West Frontier Province. It has an area of some 40,000 square kms, three quarters of which is unproductive waste land. It consists of an elevated treeless area called Daman, a barren plain with clay soils unsuitable for farming. This barren region is criss-crossed by streams flowing off the mountains. On its eastern side, near the Indus, there is swampland. The area is, for all practical purposes, cut off from the more developed and densely populated east bank of the Indus. The population practices dry-farming (wheat, millet), but the area under cultivation is not large. Nomadic cattle-breeding is poorly developed.

M.YU. MOROZOVA

Derwish (also Darwish)

(Meaning 'mendicant, beggar' in Persian; '*faqir*' in Arabic) A member of a *Sufi order; a sufi; a begging ascetic-mystic who has pledged voluntary poverty. Some Derwishes live permanently or temporarily in monasteries (in Persian—*Khanaqa*; Arabic—*ribat*, or *zawiya*) under the guidance of a *Sheikh, or instructor. Others are wandering Derwishes. (In Persian—*darbedar*, i.e., wandering from door to door). Among the wandering Derwishes, the most numerous were those from the Qalandariya order, a branch of *Naqshbandiya Order.

YU.V. GANKOVSKY

Dhammaal (also Julli, Athan)

Dances associated with mysticism. Pakistan is a land of mystics and shrines. People flock to these shrines in large numbers. The *Sufi saints and poets who lie in their graves in these shrines are revered throughout Pakistan, and devotees go bare footed, dancing and twirling, singing spiritual songs. In particular the death anniversaries, or *urs,* of these men are celebrated with fervour each year. Drums are beaten, soul-inspiring music is played, and onlookers dance in ecstasy. The *Dhammaal* is similar to the **Bhangra*. Holy men, or **pirs*, who generally dance in their hermitages or *khangahs* perform **Julli*. Sometimes they dance around a saint's grave. Normally the dancer wears black.

R. HUSAIN

Dhol (also Dholak)

This is the most widely used musical instrument in Pakistan. It is a two-sided wooden drum of cylindrical form. Flour paste containing metal filings is applied to one of the membranes, producing a lower sound. The *dhol* accompanies certain types of traditional singing and dancing. The *dhol* is played together with wind instruments at wedding ceremonies.

I. PIRACHA

Dhrupad

A genre of classical vocal music in the *Hindustani tradition that is known for its monumental composition and a complex system of fixed patterns. *Dhrupad* embodies a unique balance between rational correctness of all the elements of the sound structure and intense concentration of psycho-emotional energy, which explains, in particular, the high artistic standard of the **ragas* of this genre. The central element of the *dhrupad* expressive system is the sound, in slow time and usually with a bass voice regarded as a special means of intuitive contact with the world. The correctness of the performance of each tone determines the fullness of the philosophical-mystical perception of the truth embedded in the word sung. The main stress in teaching the art of *dhrupad* is on breathing techniques, through which the mastery of the vocal apparatus is brought to the peak of perfection. Traditionally, *dhrupad* performances use medieval text in Braj with considerable intrusions of Sanskrit. Muslim singers add to this the *Sufi perception of the world.

Structurally, the *dhrupad* form has gone through a long evolution. To achieve continuity and the energy intensity of the sound, the *jugalbandi* principle is often used in *dhrupads*, that is to say, the melody line is distributed between two performers, typically close relatives. *Dhrupad* flourished at the time of the *Mughal empire, reaching its peak of popularity and becoming the favourite form for musicians of different religions. In the eighteenth century *dhrupad* began to give way to **khiyal* and **thumri*, which were performed with greater freedom on the emotional planes.

The name *dhrupad* is derived from the Sanskrit word *Dhrur* which means the Pole Star, a symbol of constancy. The *raga* in *dhrupad* ascends and descends very gradually. It is devotional in origin, therefore resting inflections are not allowed. The *dhrupad* is structured in four parts: *Asthai*, *Antara*, *Sanchari*, and *Abhoga*. *Dhrupad* is sung accompanying the *mirdang*, an ancient drum instrument. *Dhrupad* had already moved from temple devotional into the vernacular by the time of Amir Khusrau Dehlawi. *Dhrupad* has four styles known as *bânîs*: i. *Gobahar* or *Shudh bani* ii. *Dagar bani* iii. *Khandar bani* and iv. *Nauhar bani*. *Dhrupad* has receded before *khiyal* ore creative music since the reign of Sultan Husain Shah Sharqi (1457-83) of Jawnpur, but until the twentieth century, *dhrupad* singing had been preserved and promoted by the Talwandi **Gharana*, represented before independence by Mian Maula Bakhsh Khan Khanderay (d. 1930), then in Pakistan by Khan Sahib Mehr Ali Khan Khanderay (d. 1976) and his two sons M. Afzal Khan Khanderay (b. 1933) and M. Hafiz Khan Khanderay.

M.R. KAZIMI

Din-i Ilahi

(Arabic: holy faith) A syncretic religion established in 1581 by the *Mughal emperor, Akbar. In 1579 the *ulema* at Akbar's court, including Sheikh Mubarak,

Abul Fazl, and Abd un-Nabi, signed a **fatwa* proclaiming the Emperor a **mujtahid*. *Din-i Ilahi* incorporated *Sufi, Mahdavi and *Shia ideas, and also some pantheistic views typical of Hinduism and Zoroastrianism. Akbar emphasized the undying significance of religious ethics in private and public relationships. The followers of the religion were supposed to be tolerant towards other faiths. Frugal, patient, pious and devout, they were never to resort to violence. They were to cultivate nobility of heart and mercy, and were to stay away from falsehood, greed and spite. S.M. Ikram in his *Rud-i-Kausar* asserts that this name was not known in Akbar's own time. Only Mirza Jani Khan the Governor of Thatta has mentioned '*Din-i-Ilahi* of the Akbar Shahi' which Ikram holds was a sycophantic expression. This term occurs for the first time in *Dabistan-i-Mazahib* sixty to seventy years after Akbar's death.

A. NIYAZI

Dir

1. A *Pashtun princely state situated in the valley of the Panjkora, and inhabited by the Pashtun tribe of the Yusufzai. 10,400 sq.km.; with an area of and a population: 767,000. Founded in the late eighteenth century by Qasim Khan, descendant of Akhund Ilyas. In 1895 Muhammad Sharif Khan (1884-1907), ruler of Dir, recognized the suzerainty of Great Britain. In 1897 he received the title of *Nawab for aiding the British authorities in suppressing the uprising of Pashtun tribes on the northwestern frontier of *British India. In the 1930s Dir was the scene of a massive peasant anti-feudal movement, which was suppressed with the aid of British troops. On 8 February 1948 Dir became part of Pakistan. In 1955, when the united province of *West Pakistan was established, the state of Dir was abolished and its territory included in the Peshawar Division.

2. A district in the Malakand division of the *North West Frontier Province of Pakistan. Area 10,400 sq.km., population 767,000 (1981 data).

BIBLIOGRAPHY: *I.M. Reisner, 'The Development of Feudalism and the Formation of the State among the Afghans', Moscow, 1954 (in Russian); V.A. Romodin, 'Dir and Swat', in: Countries and Peoples of the East, No. 1, Moscow, 1959 (in Russian); L. Temirkhanov, 'The Eastern Pashtuns', Moscow, 1987 (in Russian).*

YU.V. GANKOVSKY

Diwan

(in Arabic: to record in a book) A collection of poems by one author, compiled according to a certain canon. The poems were placed in the following order (genre-wise): **qasida*, **ghazal*, **marsiya*, **kita'a*, **rubai*, followed by other strophic forms. Within one genre, the verses are arranged alphabetically, according to the last letter of the rhyme (**radif*). Sometimes the initial letters are used as an organizing principle. The term *diwan* is used in the literatures of the Middle East, Central and South Asia.

In the Middle Ages and in today's Muslim countries of the Middle East, Central and South Asia, *diwan* is also a chancellory, a department; assembly, conference of high officials; court, tribunal.

N.V. GLEBOV

Diwani

Related to government or state, (from the Arabic: *dawwana*–to write down, to take accounts). 1. State-owned lands in the Muslim countries of South Asia; 2. A system of government introduced by the British East-India Company in 1765 in the conquered territories of north-east India. The company collected taxes whilst law and order were the responsibility of the local authorities.

BIBLIOGRAPHY: *K.Z. Ashrafyan, 'The Agrarian System of North India', Moscow, 1965; 'Feudalism in India', Moscow, 1977 (in Russian).*

E.YU. VANINA

Doha

This is the most popular metre in medieval poetry in the languages of Apabhramsha, Rajasthani, Gujarati, Braj, Awadhi, Bhojpuri and others. *Doha* belongs to the Hindu metric system (*matra* meaning measures). *Doha* is a rhymed distich. The lines have the same rhythmic organization and each is divided by caesura into two parts (*charana*) with thirteen and eleven matras, further subdivided into groups. Naturally, in the work of different poets there are deviations from the norm. They are particularly typical of the work of Kabir and other Sant poets, and of the **Sufis*.

Doha is an independent small poem mostly belonging to the didactic, aphoristic and similar genres and is an important component of a number of complex poetic strophes. Kabir's poems consist of several lines in the *chaupai* metre and conclude in a *doha*.

In Rajasthani poetry, *doha* also means ballad, legend, eg, *Dhola Maru ra Duha* (Ballad of the Love of Dhola and Marwani). The earliest version of the ballad (twelfth century) is written in the *doha* metre, while the later ones are a combination of *chaupai* and *doha*, and also *chaupai*, *doha* and prose. Doha was a very popular genre with Amir Khusrau Dehlawi who used it to compose verses in a strange melange of Persian and *Urdu. *Dohas* of Khusrau are sung by leading Pakistani singers and form part of the faith culture today. The genre of *doha* remains popular among contemporary and past Pakistani poets. The main Pakistani practitioners are Jamiluddin Aali, Jamil Azimabad and Ilyas Ishaqi.

N.V. GLEBOV

Dravidians

A collective term for a number of ethnic groups comprising Telugu, Tamil, Malayali, Kannada, Tulu, Kurgi, Gond, and Brahui to name a few. They mainly inhabit India, Pakistan, Sri Lanka, and South-East Asia. They speak *Dravidian languages that belong to the Nostratic sub-family of languages. The more widespread of the Dravidian languages, Tamil, Malayalam, Telugu, and Kannada have independent well-developed scripts and a rich literary tradition. The languages of ethnic minorities, e.g., Irula, have no written versions and have thus far been little studied. Dravidians are one of the oldest races to inhabit South Asia, arriving even before the Aryans. Anthropologically, Dravidians are a blend of at least three different racial types: Dravidoid, South-Europeoid, and Veddoid. Their original birth place is not known, but they are certainly not indigenous to South Asia. The fact of Dravidian southward migration from the north-west has been deduced from the Dravidian origin of proto-Indian inscriptions on some archaeological finds in Mohenjo Daro and Harappa (3-2 millennia BC), and is also supported by the *Regvada* hymns. In all probability, they reached the south of the subcontinent by the middle of the first millennium BC. The study of the Dravidian ethnogenesis is made difficult by the lack of source material.

BIBLIOGRAPHY: *(in Russian): M.F. Albedil, B.Ya. Volchok, Yu.V. Knorozov, 'The Study of proto-Indian Inscriptions. Forgotten Scripts', Moscow, 1982; 'Types of Proto-Indian Inscriptions. Ethnic Semiotics, Ancient Scripts', Moscow, 1985; M.S. Andorran, 'Comparative Grammar of the Dravidian Languages', Moscow, 1978; G.M. Bongard-Levin, N.V. Gurow, 'The Genesis of the Dravidian Culture', in: USSR Academy of Sciences Vestnik, No. 10, 1985; Yu.V. Knorozov, 'Proto-Indian Inscriptions: Problems of Decyphering', in: Soviet Ethnography No. 5, 1981; 'Ethnic Minorities of South Asia', Moscow, 1978. (In English): B. and R. Allchin, 'The Rise of Civilization in India and Pakistan', Cambridge, 1982; H.S. David, 'The Original Home of the Dravidians. Their Wanderings in Pre-historic Times (BC 4500-1500). Tamil Culture', 1954, Vol. 3, No. 1; Y.V. Knorozov, M.F. Albedil, B.Y. Volchok, Proto-Indica, 1979, 'Report on the Investigation of the Proto-Indian Texts', Moscow, 1981.*

M.F. ALBEDIL
N. R. KRASNODEMBSKAYA

Dravidian Languages

The Dravidian family of languages includes approximately 26 languages that are mainly spoken in southern India and Sri Lanka, as well as certain areas in Pakistan, Nepal, and eastern and central India. Dravidian languages appear to be unrelated to languages of other known families. Some scholars include the Dravidian languages in a larger Elamo-Dravidian language family, which includes the ancient Elamite language of what is now southwestern Iran.

The existence of the Dravidian language family was first suggested in 1816 by Alexander D. Campbell in his Grammar of the *Teloogoo* Language, in which he and Francis W. Ellis argued that Tamil and Telugu were descended from a common, non-Indo-European ancestor. However, it was not until 1856 that Robert Caldwell published his comparative grammar of the Dravidian or South-Indian family of languages, which considerably expanded the Dravidian umbrella and established it as one of the major language groups of the world. Caldwell coined the term 'Dravidian' from the Sanskrit *drāvida*, meaning 'south'.

D.I. EDELMAN

Dupatta

A long wide scarf worn in India and Pakistan, it is one of the oldest articles of costume. It was particularly popular in the Kushan epoch, when it was worn by both men and women. Today the *dupatta* is mostly worn by Pakistani women over the shoulders with its ends thrown from front to back. The *dupatta* can be made of silk, transparent muslin, or cotton. It is often embroidered, decorated with printed patterns, or dyed by tie and dye methods.

BIBLIOGRAPHY: *S.N. Dar, 'Costumes of India and Pakistan', Bombay, 1982.*

O.V. LYSTSOVA

Durand Line

So named after Sir Mortimer Durand, Secretary for Foreign Affairs of the British colonial administration in

*British India, who signed the treaty on 12 November 1893, in Kabul with Amir Abdurrahman Khan (1880-1901) establishing the state border between Afghanistan and the British colonial possessions in South Asia at that time stretching from Iran to China. The treaty was confirmed by the Anglo-Afghan treaties of 8 August 1919 and 22 November 1921. In July 1949 Afghanistan declared that it did not recognize the Durand Line Treaty.

BIBLIOGRAPHY: *C.U. Aitchison, 'A Collection of Treaties, Engagements and Sanads Relating to India and Neighbouring Countries', Vol. XI, Calcutta, 1909; 'A History of Afghanistan', Moscow, 1982.*

YU.V. GANKOVSKY

Durrani Empire

This was the first state formation (1747-1819) to unite the lands populated by *Pashtuns, and had its capital at Kandahar (1747-76) and thereafter (1776 to 1819) at Kabul. The leading position in the Durrani Empire belonged to the *Khans of the tribe of Ahmad Shah Abdali (1747-73), the Khan of the Abdalis, who became the first ruler of the Durrani Empire. In order to emphasize the privileged position of the Abdali tribe, Ahmad Shah named it 'Durrani', meaning 'Pearl'. The downfall of the united Iranian state after the assassination of Iran's *padishah*, Nadir Shah Afshar (1736–47), the collapse of the *Mughal empire in India and the feudal internecine strife in Central Asia, all contributed to creating favourable conditions for the spread of Ahmad Shah's power into the territories of northwest India, eastern Iran, and southern Turkistan. Ahmed Shah carried out numerous expeditions deep into the subcontinent, sacking both Lahore and Multan his birthplace. He marched on Dehli and defeated the armies of the dominant *Rajputs on the historic battlefield of Panipat. In the 1760s the area occupied by the Durrani Empire exceeded two million sq. km. By the end of the 18th century the Empire was on the decline as a result of the mutinies of various Pashtun Khans and the uprisings of the subjugated peoples including *Punjabi *Sikhs and Uzbeks of south Turkistan. In 1819 the empire fell apart.

Rulers: Ahmad Khan Durrani (1747-73), Timur Shah (1773-93), Zaman Shah (1793-1801), Mahmud Shah (1801-3), Shah Shuja (1803-9), Mahmud (the second term: 1809-18), Sultan Ali Shah (1818), Ayub Shah (1819).

BIBLIOGRAPHY: *Yuri Gankovsky, 'The Durrani Empire', Moscow, 1958 (in Russian); Mir Ghulam Muhammad Ghubar, 'Ahmad Shah Baba-i Afghan', Kabul, 1422.*

YU.V. GANKOVSKY

Dymshits, Zalman Movshevich (1921–90)

He was a specialist in the grammatical structure of Hindi and *Urdu. After graduating from the Moscow Institute of Oriental Studies (1950), he obtained a DSc (Philology), and became a professor. He later served in the Soviet Army (1940-46), and fought in the Second World War (1941-45). He was a lecturer at the Moscow Institute of Oriental Studies (1951-54); assistant professor and professor of the Moscow Institute of International Relations at the USSR Foreign Ministry (since 1954); and author of linguistic studies, textbooks, and dictionaries. He translated the works of Premchand from Hindi into Russian.

WORKS: *'The Language of Urdu', Moscow, 1962; 'Textbook of Hindi', Moscow, 1953-7; 'Pocket-book Hindi-Russian Dictionary', Moscow, 1958; 'Essays on Hindi Grammar', Delhi, 1966 (in Hindi); 'Textbook of Hindi', Moscow, 1969-70.*

A.S. SUKHOCHEV

E

East Bengal

See, East Pakistan.

East Pakistan

Between August 1947 and March 1956, the Province of *East Bengal in the Dominion of Pakistan. According to the 1956 and 1962 Constitutions, East Pakistan was one of the two provinces of the Federal Islamic Republic of Pakistan. Area: 141,000 sq.km. East Pakistan was divided into four administrative Divisions, viz. Dacca, Khulna, Rangpur and Chittagong. The provincial capital was at Dhaka, which was also intended under the 1962 Constitution, to be the principal seat of the Federal Parliament. Executive authority was headed by a Governor, appointed by the President. The Governor appointed the Chief Minister and the members of the provincial government. The legislative authority was in the hands of the Legislative Assembly elected for five years. In 1971 the independent People's Republic of Bangladesh (see Bangladesh-Pakistan Relations) was formed on the territory of the province.

BIBLIOGRAPHY: *Yuri Gankovsky, V.N. Moskalenko, 'The Three Constitutions of Pakistan', Lahore, 1978.*

YU.V. GANKOVSKY

Economic Co-operation Organization (also ECO, Regional Co-operation for Development until 1985)

Founded in 1964, its members are Iran, Pakistan, and Turkey, and since February of 1992 also include, Afghanistan, Azerbaijan, Kyrgyzstan, Tajikistan, Turkmenistan, and Uzbekistan. ECO's principal aim is the development of regional co-operation in economic relations, expansion of trade links, and the improvement of standards of living of the member countries. ECO's governing body is the Council of Ministers, which functions at the level of deputy foreign ministers and meets twice a year. ECO's influential Council for Regional Planning (CRP) consists of representatives of the planning institutions of the member countries. There are also working committees for the specific spheres of co-operation and a secretariat consisting of the general secretary, his three deputies, and six directors. ECO has supported more than thirty joint projects in Pakistan, Iran, and Turkey. They included chemical plants, pharmaceutical factories, metal-working plants, a number of motorways, and railways. Agreements have been concluded on air and maritime communications, also on postal, telegraph and telecommunications, tourism, and the development of cultural links. A joint insurance centre and a commercial-industrial chamber are functioning. Considerable attention is paid to avoiding double taxes in foreign trade and to the liberalization of foreign trade links.

S.N. KAMENEV

Edhi, Abdus Sattar (1946–)

Philanthropist. An outstanding social worker with a nationwide network of dispensaries, kitchens, orphanages, and ambulances, Edhi started with a small dispensary in Mithadar, Karachi. In 1975 he was a candidate for the National Assembly, but lost. Since then, he has devoted himself to social work.

WORKS: *'A Mirror to the Blind' as narrated to Tehmina Durrani, Islamabad, 1996.*

V.YA. BELOKRENITSKY

Embroidery

This has been practised by the people of Pakistan since antiquity. Needles for embroidery were found in the *Mohenjo-Daro and *Harappa excavations. Descriptions of embroidery often occur in old epic literature.The embroideries produced at the court workshops of the *Mughals were distinguished for their excellent quality and artistic merit. One of the best-known workshops was in Lahore. The embroideries embellished numerous curtains, canopies, and drapes. Extremely fine silk embroideries were made on a cotton base. The ornament of these objects, including branches, flowering plants, and cypresses, is reminiscent of the architectural ornament of the epoch. Embroideries decorated court costumes: belts, shawls, and turbans. In the *Punjab and *Swat, women create embroideries in the ancient *phulkari* style (Farsi for flowerwork; *phulkari* is a corruption of the original Farsi *Golkari*). These are usually curtains, canopies, shawls, and pillowcases intended for brides' dowries and also for religious festivals. *Phulkaris* are mostly executed on large rectangular pieces of cloth of coarse homespun of orange, deep red, or dark-blue. The whole surface of the fabric is covered with embroidery in untwisted fibre of raw cotton in darning satin-stitch. The darning stitches create geometrical designs, such as rhomboids, triangles, and strips. *Phulkaris* with figures of human beings and animals are rare. Embroidery ornaments are often linked with ritual ideas and are looked upon as protection against evil forces. For example, the mirch or pepper ornament embroidered on a bride's veil protects her against the evil eye.

The embroideries of *Balochistan and *Sindh are well known. There are a great number of designs and each tribe has a favourite set of ornaments. There are embellished costumes, caps, tablecloths, napkins, and bags in which the Quran and amulets are kept. Silk, gold, and silver thread, as well as shells and mirrors, are used in the embroideries of these regions of Pakistan. *Kashida* type embroideries are common to the Swat region. As a rule, these embroideries are executed in untwisted silk in bright colours-dark pink, dark red, green and white, and orange-against a black background. Embroidery in braid enhances the *chogha*, long woollen costumes. Embroidery on leather is traditional in Pakistan. It decorates various leather items like the harness of camels and horses, also shoes and bags. The embroidery is done with a special hooked needle.

O.V. LYSTSOVA

Emeneau, Murray Barnson (1904–)

Philologist. An American philologist, he was one of the authors of the etymological dictionary of the *Dravidian languages. Emeneau studied in Canada and the USA and became a Doctor of Philosophy (Yale, 1931). He taught at Yale University, conducted field research in India (1935-38), became a lecturer, then Professor of the University of California (Berkeley). Emeneau was a member of the American Philosophical Society, the American Oriental Society (President), the American Linguistic Society (President in 1949), the American Folklore Society, New York Linguistic Circle, and others. Emeneau was also a recipient of the Guggenheim Prize (1949-50, 1956-57).

WORKS: *'Kota Texts', Berkeley, Vols. I-IV, 194446; 'Studies in Vietnamese (Annamese) Grammar', Berkeley, 1951; 'Kolami: A Dravidian Language', Berkeley, 1955 (with T. Barrow); 'A Dravidian Etymological Dictionary', Vols. I-II, 1961; 'Brahui and Dravidian Comparative Grammar', Berkeley, 1962 (with T. Burrow); 'Dravidian Borrowings from Indo-Aryan', Berkeley, 1962; Kalidasa's Shakuntala, (Translator) Berkeley, 1962; 'Language and Linguistic Area': Essay, Stanford, Cal., 1980.*

I.A. MURAVYEVA

Enamels

Enamelling is believed to have appeared in South Asia under the influence of the countries of the Muslim Orient and flourished at the time of the *Mughals. Trays, dishes, caskets, jewellery, and weapons were ornamented in the workshops of Lahore and Multan. In terms of technique, enamels were of the *champlevé* type. Cuts on metal surfaces were filled with powder consisting of ground metal oxides mixed with glass, the object was then fired. Enamels were applied to gold and silver. The reverse side of almost all Mughal ornaments was covered with enamel embellished with extremely fine patterns reminiscent of those on the best specimens of Mughal architecture.

In modern Pakistan, the main centres of production of enamels on silver are Multan, Karachi, and Lahore. Enamels on copper are popular in the *Punjab.

O.V. LYSTSOVA

English Literature

The tradition of using English for literary purposes goes back to the 18th century and pre-dates the Raj, but with the advent of British rule, English replaced Persian as the instrument of government. English medium schools were established and some South Asians started to write a rather derivative English poetry and fiction, but did not develop original creative work until the twentieth century. English also became the language of political debate and played a pivotal role in the independence struggle and the Pakistan Movement. After partition, English remained Pakistan's official language, alongside *Urdu. The English language press thrived. But Pakistani English poetry, fiction and drama was largely regarded as an elitist, colonial hangover and had a limited, if faithful audience. A body of good English poetry developed before prose, however, and the dialogue on the use of English by Pakistanis as a creative medium included critical writings and anthologies by Shahid Hosain and Yunus Said. In 1991 Tariq Rahman wrote *A History of Pakistani Literature in English,* but in the 1980's the electronic revolution, the global domination of English, the assertion of strong South Asian communities in the West and the increasing interest in new English literatures, gave

English poetry, fiction and drama new impetus in Pakistan.

In 1947 Pakistan already had a few writers of English fiction, poetry and drama. The most eminent were H. Shahid *Suhrawardy (1890–1965) and Ahmed Ali (1908–1994). Suhrawardy's *Essays in Verse* (1937) had established his reputation as the first modern poet of undivided India. The bilingual Ahmed Ali had published South Asia's first major Muslim novel in English, *Twilight in Delhi* (1940). Other early writers include Mumtaz Shahnawaz (1912–48) and Zaibunissa Hamidullah (1921–2000). The towering presence in Pakistani English poetry, however, was Taufiq Rafat (1927–98). He was the first to successfully introduce a Pakistani 'idiom' into his verse that reflected responses to history, heritage, culture and environment. He also developed the narrative poem. His two collections *The Arrival Of The Monsoon* (1984) and *Taufiq Rafat: A Selection* (1997), reveal the quality and sophistication of his writing. He also acted as guide, mentor and critic to younger poets, including Waqas Ahmed Khwaja, Shuja Nawaz, Kaleem Omar and Athar Tahir. The 1970's saw much English poetry activity in Pakistan, including workshops, broadcasts, multi-media and multi-lingual events, and the publication of anthologies. This included the excellent *Wordfall: Three Pakistani Poets* edited by Kaleem Omar, which confirmed the expertise of Rafat, the rich, visual language of Omar and established Maki Kureishi (1927–96) as Pakistan's first woman poet in English to rank among the best. Her posthumous collection *The Far Thing* (1997) consolidated her reputation further and reveals the quiet precision and the discipline of her writing. Kureishi believed that her English poetry should express the East-West duality of her world, not suppress it, in search of a culture-specific idiom. Adrian A. Hussain, winner of the Guinness Prize for poetry, shared this view. His classical and academic background is evident in his collection *Desert Album* (1997). Cultural duality is central to the work of Salman Tarik Kureshi. His collection, *The Landscapes of The Mind* (1997) is remarkable for its use of language and imagery. In Peshawer, Daud Kamal (1935–87) forged his own distinct voice, building up sparse poems with brief visual images. His several volumes of poetry include *Before the Carnations Wither: Collected Poems* (1995). Waqas Ahmad Khwaja's book of poetry include narrative poems in *Miriam's Lament* (1992) re-constructing Biblical lore and a *Punjabi folk legend. Rhodes scholar Athar Tahir published a first collection of short stories and brought out three poetry collections including *The Yielding Years* (2001). These bring together his best work, including his mystical poems. G.F. Riaz won the Patras Bokhari Award for his first collection *Shade in Passing* (1989). The much travelled Alamgir Hashmi published several volumes, including his collected works *The Poems of Alamgir Hashmi (1992)*. This work is permeated with the poetry of exile and weaves in memories of other countries, giving texture to uncluttered verse. More recently, Hina Raza published her remarkable first collection, *Memory Stains* (2000), which experiments with language, words, rhythm and space.

Among expatriate poets, the polished sophisticated verse of Zulfikar Ghose stands in a class of its own. His five poetry volumes include *Selected Poems* (1991). In Britain, Moniza Alvi is among the few Asian women to forge a place for herself in mainstream writing. Her three lyrical collections *The Country At My Shoulder* (1993), *A Bowl of Warm Air* (1997) and *Carrying My Wife* (2000) weld her dual culture. She has won the 1991 Poetry Business Prize, been shortlisted for the T.S. Eliot and Whitbread prizes and selected for the New Generation Poets promotion. In Manchester, Tariq Latif's promising collections *Skimming the Soul* (1991) and *The Minister's Garden* (1996) reclaim both rural Pakistan and immigrant life in Britain.

The tradition of English drama in Pakistan is minimal and no original script has been published. Significantly, the few Pakistani English dramatists or screenwriters to establish themselves, including Rukhsana Ahmad, Tariq Ali Shahurkh Hussain, Ayub Khan-Din and Hanif Kureishi, have all done so in Britain. In 1967 Zulfikar Ghose published *The Murder of Aziz Khan*, the first cohesive Pakistani novel written in modern English and Ghose's only novel set in his homeland. He lives in Texas, has published over ten novels and a collection of short stories. He won great acclaim for his historical trilogy, *The Incredible Brazilian* (1972–9) and writes extensively about South America but his theme remains alienation. His novel, *The Triple Mirror Of The Self* (1992), is a complex exploration of exile and exclusion across three continents.

In 1980 Bapsi Sidhwa became the first Pakistani English writer living in Pakistan to receive international recognition since Ahmed Ali. The ribaldry of Sidhwa's first novel *The Crow Eaters* (1978) was rare for South Asian fiction. It was also the first major novel about the *Parsi community, to which she belongs. She went on to write *The Bride* (1982) and *The American Brat*

(1994) and is the recipient of Pakistan's Patras Bokhari Award, Germany's 1991 Literature Prize, and the 1993 Reader's Digest's Lila Wallace Award. Her third novel, *Ice Candy Man* (1988) is her most powerful and haunting work. Linguistically, it was important because it was the first to successfully employ a narrative written in Pakistani English. It remains the only Pakistani English novel to focus upon the partition riots.

In Britain, Adam Zamenzad, won the 1987 David Higham Award for his Karachi novel, *The Thirteenth House* (1987). His other novels include the enchanting *My Friend Matt and Henna The Whore* (1988), about famine in Africa and his most ambitious work, *Cyrus, Cyrus* (1990), a bawdy, gargantuan book revolving around a man's search for dignity and salvation across four continents. The short story writer Aamer Hussein has brought together a myriad of cultures in his three collections: *A Mirror To The Sun* (1993), *This Other Salt* (1999), and *Cactus Town* (2002). As a Pakistani-born Londoner, he perceives much of his fiction as an imaginary discussion on issues of history, migration, gender and text.

Several Pakistani English writers are translators of Urdu or other indigenous literature, including Ahmed Ali, Daud Kamal, Shuja Nawaz, Taufiq Rafat, Tariq Rahman and Athar Tahir. But to an ex patriae, translation and the writing of English fiction is a process of reclamation and the search for an identity. This is true of the Pakistani-born Rukhsana Ahmad, Aamer Hussein, his screenwriter sister Shahrukh Hussain, Tahira Naqvi and Javed Qazi. The diminishing of linguistic boundaries is evident in the work of Aamer Hussein and Naqvi's stories. *Attar of Roses* (1997). Now the distinguished Urdu novelist, Abdullah Hussein in Britain has written an English novel, *Émigré Journeys* (2002).

The feminist consciousness permeates the work of poet Hina Faisal Imam and almost all women discussed here. In *Bitter Gourd and Other Stories* (2001), Talat Abbasi's sensitive story deals with poverty, gender and displacement while playwright and novelist Rukhsana Ahmad has a strong political commitment as an Asian woman and an Asian Briton. Runner up for the Writers Guild and CRE awards, her radio and stage plays include *Song For A Sanctuary* about battered women (1993). Her novel *The Hope Chest* (1996) focuses on relationship between mothers and daughters.

All Pakistani English writers live between East and West, literally or intellectually, and express this through their work. Those living in foreign lands have also been irrefutably shaped by their Pakistani heritage. This is evident in the work of the British born, Hanif Kureishi. His writing largely makes a comment on contemporary British society and the exclusion, overt and covert that Asian Britons battle against. He won the 1981 George Devine Award for his play, Outskirts, an Oscar nomination for the screenplay *My Beautiful Launderette* (1986) and a Whitbread Award for his first novel *The Buddha of Suburbia* (1990). He has written many successful scripts since, as well as two collections of short stories and two more novels, *Black Album* (1995) *Intimacy* (1998) and *Gabriel's Gift* (2001).

Many Pakistani English writers, such as Tariq Ali, perceive themselves in universal terms, yet identify with Pakistan. Ali's work includes stage and television plays, two novels *Redemption* (1990) and *Fear of Mirrors* (1998) about post-Communist Europe, and a forthcoming historical quintet, exploring Islamic history, of which three have been published so far. The first, *Shadows of the Pomegranate Tree,* about the fall of Granada, won Spain's Archbishop San Clements del Institute Rosalia de Castro prize for the best translation. Sara Suleri forged new dimensions for Pakistani English writing with the quality of her prose and her creative memoir, *Meatless Days* (1989), a collage about love, memory and loss, which is divided into chapters according to metaphor.

Meanwhile a new generation is taking the Pakistani English novel to new horizons. Zeeba Sadiq's autobiographical first novel, *38 Bahadurabad* (1996), is a rich tapestry of interlocking stories. Nadeem Aslam's poetic first novel, *Season of the Rainbirds* (1991), about the loss of innocence in a small Punjab town, won the Betty Trask and Author's Club awards-and was shortlisted the Whitbread and John Rhys Llewellyn prizes. The accomplished *Moth Smoke* by Mohsin Hamid (2000) set in Lahore, looks at justice and social iniquity in a drug-and-kalashnikov culture. He won the 2001 Betty Trask Award and was shortlisted for the Commonwealth and PEN/Hemingway awards. Kamila Shamsie's first novel, *City By The Sea* (1998), which welded politics and the magic of childhood, was shortlisted for the 1999 Mail on Sunday/John Llewellyn Rhys Award. Her second, *Salt and Saffron*, (2000), about a family scarred by its myths and divided by class and by Partition, was selected for the Orange Futures promotion of 21 young women writers of the 21st century. It also won Pakistan Academy Letters, Prime Minister's Award for 1999. Her third *Kartography*

(2002) is a lovesong to her native Karachi. Uzma Aslam Khan's incisive and satirical first novel *The Story of Noble Rot* (2001) tells the story of child labour, exploitation, loss and longing. Other promising writers with published full length works include novelists Maniza Naqvi, Bina Shah, and poet Harris Khalique.

There are some excellent books of Pakistani English non-fiction with a literary quality by distinguished journalists and columnists, including Mazhar Ali Khan (1917-93), Razia Bhatti (1944-96), I.H. Burney, Khalid Hassan, Omar Kureishi and Anwer Mooraj. Their essays provide the historical, political, cultural and social context to Pakistan, and to Pakistani literature in English.

M. SHAMSIE

Ephtalites

(Greek: Hephthalite, also: Abdali, Heital, *Chionite, *Yue-Chi, *White Huns) A confederation of East Iranian, and Turkic (proto-Turkic) tribes that appeared in the beginning of the 4th century AD near the north-eastern frontiers of Sassanid Iran. In *c.* 460 the Ephtalites seized and sacked Gandhara. At the end of the 5th century AD the armies of the Ephthalite leader Toramana subjugated Punjab, Sindh, Rajasthan and the area of the Ganges-Jumna interfluve. In 533 Mihiragula, another Ephthalite military leader, and ruler of northwest India, was defeated by the local chiefs. The final blow was dealt by Sassanid Iran and the West-Turkish Khakans. About the year 567 the confederation of the Ephtalites fell apart. Their descendants in the subcontinent today may include such peoples as the Rajputs.

BIBLIOGRAPHY: *Yuri Gankovsky, 'The Peoples of Pakistan', Lahore, 1972; A. Biswas, 'The Political History of the Huns of Hephtalites', in: East and West, Vol. VI, No. 3, 1955; R. Ghirshman, 'Les Chionites-Hephtalites', Le Caire, 1948.*

YU.V. GANKOVSKY

F

Fairservis, Walter A. (1925–)

Archeologist. An American historian and archaeologist, associate of the department of anthropology at the American Museum of Natural History (New York), and writer for archaeological journals. Specializing in the archaeology of South Asia and the Near and Middle East, he has conducted field research in northern Africa, Pakistan, Afghanistan, and India. Fairservis is the author of a series of books on the origins of the Oriental civilization, the history and culture of Egypt and Nubia, and the archaeology of eastern Iran, Afghanistan, and Pakistan. He wrote a definitive history of ancient India.

WORKS: *'Preliminary Report on the Prehistoric Archaeology of the Afghani-Balochi Areas', in: American Museum Novitates, No. 1587, New York, 1952; 'Excavations in the Quetta Valley, West Pakistan', in: Anthropological Papers of the American Museum of Natural History, Vol. 45, Part 2, New York, 1956; 'Archaeological Surveys in the Zhob and Loralai Districts, West Pakistan', Anthropological Papers of the American Museum of Natural History, Vol. 47, Part 2, New York, 1959; 'Archaeological Studies in the Seistan Basin of South-western Afghanistan and Eastern Iran', in: Anthropological Papers of the American Museum of Natural History, Vol. 8, Part I, New York, 1961; 'The Ancient Kingdoms of the Nile and the Doomed Monuments of Nubia', New York, 1962; 'The Origin, Character and Decline of an Early Civilization', in: American Museum Novitates, No. 2302, New York, 1967; 'The Roots of Ancient India', New York, 1971.*

A.YA. SHCHETENKO

Faiz, Faiz Ahmad (1911–84)

Poet. Born in Sialkot, Faiz was an *Urdu poet, arguably one of the greatest of his time. He was also a journalist, critic and public figure. He attended various colleges in Lahore and lectured and wrote for the press. Faiz was editor-in-chief of the literary journal *Adab-i-Latif* (1938-41) and the newspapers *Pakistan Times* and *Imroze*. He was repeatedly arrested (1951-55, 1958) for his left wing opinions and activities. Faiz was a member of the World Peace Council and one of the leaders of the Movement of Afro-Asian Writers. He chaired the Arts Council under the first PPP administration and published the political and literary journal, *Lail-o-Nahar* ('Days and Nights').

Famous Poet, Faiz Ahmad Faiz.

After 1977 he lived in exile in Lebanon for a few years, before accepting the position of editor-in-chief of the magazine *Lotus* in 1979. From 1935 he was a member of a Communist study group. His early poems of 1927-35, which made up the first part of his collection *Naqsh-i-Faryadi* ('The Features of the Supplicant'), 1941, are written in a semi traditional manner and reflect Faiz's romantic nature. His collections *Dast-i-Saba* ('The Hands of the Wind'), 1952, and *Zindan Nama* ('Prison Verse'), 1956, intensified the revolutionary sentiments in *Urdu literature, widening the gap between progressive writers and followers of traditional literature. The theme of national and spiritual liberation occupies an important place in Faiz's work, e.g., *Mere Dil Mere Musafir* ('My Heart My Wanderer'), 1982. The poetry of his later years is marked by reflections about the fate of man: *Sar-i-Wadi-i-Sina* ('At the Edge of the Sinai Valley'), 1971. Problems of literature and culture are discussed in his articles and essays: *Mizan* ('Scale'), 1963, *Mata-i-Loh-o-Qalam* ('Pen and Paper'), 1973, his book *Hamari Qaumi Saqafat* ('Our National Culture'), 1976, *Maqalat-i-Faiz* ed. Sheema Majid, Lahore, 1990. Faiz won a number of literary prizes. He was awarded the Lenin Peace Prize in 1962 and posthumously awarded *Nishan-i-Imtiaz* in1988. Exceptionally popular in Pakistan, he was also widely acclaimed abroad.

WORKS: *Dast-i-Tah-i-Sang (The Hand Arrested by the Stone), 1965; 'Sham-i-Shahr-i-Yaran' (Evening in the City of my Beloved), 1978; 'Nuskhaha-i-Wafa' (Poems of Fidelity), Lahore, 1984; 'Sare Sukhan Hamare' (All My Verse), London, 1983; 'Mah-o-Sal-i-Ashnai' (Months and Years of Acquaintance), 1982.*

BIBLIOGRAPHY: *N. Glebov, A. Sukhochev, 'Urdu Literature', Moscow, 1967; Ashfaq Husain, 'Faiz: Ek Jaiza' (Faiz: a Study), Karachi, 1977; Sibte Hasan, 'Sukhan dar Sukhan' (Word within Word), Karachi, 1985; 'Afkar Faiz No'., (ed.)*

Sahba Lucknowi, Karachi 1965; Mirza Zafrul Hasan, 'Khoon-i-Dil ki Kasheed', Karachi, 1983; Aftab Ahmad, Faiz Ahmad Faiz, Shair aur Shakhsh, Karachi, 1999; Nazr-i-Fazi, ed. Aizaz Afzal and Asaduz Zaman, Calcutta, 1980.

L.A. VASILYEVA

Faizi, Shaykh Abul Faiz (1547–95)

Poet. A Persian-language poet of India and a scholar who has to his credit works on philosophy, religion, philology, medicine, mathematics and astrology. Faizi promoted the synthesis of all the religious communities in India on the basis of their spiritual legacy. He headed the translation projects at the court of Akbar, including his translation of a poetic text on mathematics from Sanskrit into Farsi, and edited the Persian translation of Mahabharata, Ramayana, and Atharvaveda. Faizi wrote the commentary of the Quran, *Mawarid al-Qalam* ('Foundations of Theology'), and *Sawati al-Ilham* ('The Splendour of Inspiration'). Faizi's poems have been collected in a **diwan*; among them are **qasidas*, **ghazals*, and **rubai* that were composed in the traditions of classical Persian poetry. His *ghazals* betray the influence of Hafiz and Jami. From the 'Quintuple' in response to *Khamse* by Nizami and Amir Khusrau *Dehlawi, Faizi managed to complete only two poems, including the **masnawi*, *Nal wa Daman*—a creative interpretation of the poem *Nal* and *Damayanti*, a component of the Mahabharata. Faizi's poem is one of the first examples of a plot for a *masnawi* being borrowed from traditional Indian literature by a Persian-language poet of India. (See also: *Sabk-i-Hindi*).

WORKS: *Nal wa Daman, 'Diwan-i-Faizi', Lucknow, 1834.*

M.M. OSIPOVA

Faqir

Arabic: beggar, mendicant.

Farangi Mahal

A *Sunni **dar-ul-ulum*, a major theological centre in India that was founded in the late 17th century in Lucknow (Uttar-Pradesh) by Muhammad Sahalwai with money donated by the Emperor Aurangzeb. In the 18th century Mulla Nizamuddin (d. 1747) worked out a teaching system known as *Dars-i Nizamiya* (perfect or systematic learning), which is still used in many *madrasah* and *dar-ul-ulums* of India, Pakistan, and Bangladesh. Originally his curriculum, consisting of sixteen different disciplines, aimed at a balanced study of 'rational' sciences (*Maqulat*) and confessional literature (*Manqulat*). Subsequently, other theological disciplines prevailed. Theologians of *Farangi Mahal* adhere to conservative principles in solving social and legal problems. They strictly follow *taqlid*. In India some of the *ulema* of this school took part in establishing **Jamiat ul-ulema-i Hind*.

A. NIYAZI

Fatwa (also Fetwa)

(from Arabic: *afta*, to pass judgement, explain, give advice) A ruling on some legal questions. It is also a decision passed by a Muslim theologian—a **mujtahid*, a **mufti* or a **qadi*—on the permissibility of some action or deed; a decision or sentence (according to the *Shariat). A *fatwa* is passed in oral or written form.

YU.V. GANKOVSKY

Federally Administered Tribal Areas

An administrative division in north-western Pakistan, along the Pakistan-Afghan border. It is approximately 27,200 sq.km. subject to population in area 3,138,000 (1998). Administratively, it comes under the central government and consists of seven political agencies (Bajaur, Mohmand, Khyber, Kurram, Orakzai, North and South Waziristan), and four frontier regions. The indigenous population is *Pashtun. In 1893, the area was acceded to *British India.

M.YU. MOROZOVA

Federation of Balochi Princely States

See, Balochistan.

Feldman, Herbert

Feldman came to the subcontinent as a soldier during the Second World War and decided to remain after the hostilities ceased. A business executive by profession, Herbert Feldman was a keen observer of political events, and kept a diary. His early years in Pakistan, once the partition upheaval was over, were quite unremarkable. Initially he had great hopes for the military coup of 1958 and wrote a laudatory account of it in *Revolution in Pakistan* (London 1967) which reads like a publicity manual. He revised his opinion when political malaise set in in Pakistan and wrote *From Crisis to Crisis* (London, 1972), and finally the *End and the Beginning 1969–1971,* concerning the *East Bengal crisis.

WORKS: *'The Herbert Feldman Omnibus', Karachi, OUP, 2001.*

V.N. MOSKALENKO

Filmi Songs

Filmi is a term used to describe Indian and Pakistani popular music, with specific characteristics arising from its use in film soundtracks. Most pop stars sing in some form of *filmi* music, which has multiple subgenres including *filmi-ghazal* and **ghazal*-song. *Filmi* is often said to have begun in 1931, with the release of Ardeshir M. Irani's 'Alam Ara' and its popular soundtrack. Music is an essential component of Pakistani cinema, perhaps because of South Asian linguistic diversity, which means that much of the audience could not understand the dialogue no matter what language it is in. Thus, music, not being tied to any one language, can express the feelings of the characters even to those who do not speak the language. Some notable personalities attached with filmi music are: Mala, Mujib Alam, Ahmad Rushki, Noor Jehan, Mehdi Hassan and Nayyara Noor.

I. PIRACHA

Folk Art Museum

(Lok Virsa Museum) Located in Islamabad it was founded in 1974 and linked to the National Institute of Folk and Traditional Heritage, also in Islamabad. Lok Virsa Museum has religious departments, and since 1981 has held annual autumn festivals of art and fairs to exhibit Lok Virsa products Museum. The museum also collects and preserves works of folk art in Pakistan. It has permanent exhibitions as well as exhibitions of foreign works. The museum collects and records folk songs and music. It is also engaged in publishing. It has a specialized library of books and journals, and also of audio and video films freely accessible to the public. It co-ordinates and plans the work of craftsmen, supporting and developing various kinds of crafts. The museum endeavours to discover master craftsmen and organizes public presentations for them. Since 1993 the president of Pakistan has awarded medals to outstanding masters for the best works of art. In the 1970s construction began on the museum's new building. An adjoining park was restored in which an open-air museum was installed. The museum's annual publication is 'Folk Festival of Pakistan'.

BIBLIOGRAPHY: *'Folk Festival of Pakistan', 1988.*

N.K. KARPOVA

Fourteen Points

These were the proposals presented by M.A. *Jinnah at the session of the *All-India Muslim League Council at Delhi on 28 March 1929, to be incorporated in the future Constitution of India. The Fourteen Points represented a reunification of Muslim politicians–particularly the All-India Muslim League, which had split over co-operating with the *Simon Commission. The break had not been merely communal or even loyalist. Sir Mohammad *Shafi, President of the All-India Muslim League, was joined by Allama *Iqbal as Honorary Secretary and Maulana Hasrat Mohani as Associate Secretary in their resolve to co-operate with the Simon Commission. M.A. Jinnah, Sir Mohammad Yaqub and Dr Saifuddin *Kitchlew had formed another AIML to boycott the Simon Commission. The *Nehru Report, which resiled from the *Delhi Muslim Proposals of 20 March 1929, vindicated the Shafi League and underlined the necessity of separate electorates. M.A. Jinnah had at that time written a history of the Fourteen Points in which he plainly characterized the Nehru Report as Hindu counter proposals to the Delhi Muslim Proposals. The Delhi Muslim Proposals had been formulated as an alternative to Separate Electorates. With their experience of the accepted Delhi Proposals subsequently being rejected, the Fourteen Points incorporated both the Delhi Proposals and Separate Electorates these were:

1. The form of the future Constitution shall be federal, with the residuary powers vested in the provinces.

2. A uniform measure of autonomy shall be granted to all provinces.

3. All legislatures in the country and other elected bodies shall be constituted on the definite principle of adequate and effective representation of minorities in every province without reducing the majority in any province to a minority or even equality.

4. In the Central Legislature, *Mussalman* representation shall not be less than one-third.

5. Representation of communal groups shall continue to be by means of separate electorates as at present, provided it shall be open to any community, at any time, to abandon its separate electorate in favour of joint electorate.

6. Any territorial re-distribution that might at any time be necessary shall not in any way affect the Muslim majority in the *Punjab, *Bengal and NWF Province.

7. Full religious liberty i.e., liberty of belief, worship and observance, propaganda, association and education, shall be guaranteed to all communities.

8. No bill or resolution or any part thereof shall be passed in any legislature or any other elected body if three-fourths of the members of any community in that particular body oppose such a bill, resolution or part thereof on the ground that it would be injurious to the interests of that community or in the alternative, such other method is devised as may be found feasible and practicable to deal with such cases.

9. *Sindh should be separated from the Bombay Presidency.

10. Reforms should be introduced in the NWF Province and *Balochistan on the same footing as in other provinces.

11. Provision should be made in the Constitution, giving Muslims an adequate share along with the other Indians in all the services of the State and in local self-governing bodies, having due regard to the requirements of efficiency.

12. The Constitution should embody adequate safeguards for the protection of Muslim culture and for the protection and promotion of Muslim education, language, religion, personal laws and Muslim charitable institutions and for their due share in the grants-in-aid given by the State and by local self-governing bodies.

13. No Cabinet, either Central or Provincial, should be formed without a proportion of at least one-third Muslim ministers.

14. No change shall be made in the Constitution by the Central Legislature except with the concurrence of the States constituting the Indian Federation.

BIBLIOGRAPHY: *S.M. Burke and S.A.D. Quraishi, 'Quaid-e-Azam Mohammad Ali Jinnah: His Personality and his Politics', Karachi, 1997; Durga Das, 'India From Curzon to Nehru and After', 2nd ed., New Delhi, 1977; Dwarkadas Kanji, 'India's Fight For Freedom 1913–1937'—Bombay, 1966; Saad R. Khairi, 'Jinnah Reinterpreted, Karachi, 1996; Stanley Wolpert, 'Jinnah of Pakistan', Karachi, 1989.*

M.R. KAZIMI

Franco-Pakistan Relations

These relations have developed best in the economic sphere, such as trading links and France's economic aid. Joint participation in SEATO stimulated the development of Franco-Pakistan relations in the military sphere. The leaders of the two countries regularly maintain contact with each other on vital international issues. Co-ordinating its position with that of France, Pakistan refused to commit its forces or finances to aid the United States in its war in Vietnam despite SEATO decisions on this issue. This problem was discussed, among others, during the official visit of President Ayub *Khan to Paris in October 1967.

During the 1970s-80s a significant strengthening of cooperation took place in the military sphere. France offered Pakistan military equipment, which included warplanes and ships. It helped Pakistan to build an aviation repair plant in the *Punjab, as well as other projects, including a nuclear agreement which was concluded in 1976. This agreement was aborted under US pressure (see US-Pakistan Relations). Relations were normal until the Kargil crisis in 1999, when France asked Pakistan to vacate its position.

R.M. MUKIMJANOVA

Funoon

A quarterly published from Lahore since 1963, initially edited by Ahmad Nadeem Qasimi and Habib Ash'ar, it is now edited by Qasimi and Mansoora Ahmad. This is essentially a left wing journal which gives precedence to classical literature. One landmark issue was the *Jadeed Ghazal* Number of 1969-70 in two volumes.

A. NIYAZI

G

Gandhara

1. A historico-cultural area in the northwest of modern-day Pakistan, in the lower reaches of the river *Kabul. The name probably derives from the Gandhari tribe mentioned in *Rigveda*. At the end of the 6th century BC, Gandhara was a satrapy of the Persian state of the *Achaemenids.

2. The Gandhara state is mentioned in Buddhist sources as one of the sixteen great states of ancient India, existing in the 6th century BC. Mention of Gandhara also occurs in the *Puranas*, among the *Janapads* (states), with its centre in Pushkalavati (present-day Charsadda). According to the Buddhist tradition, as far back as the 6th century BC, Gandhara was an independent state with its capital at *Taxila. The Gandharan King Pukusati was a contemporary of the Magadha ruler Bimbisara and of Buddha. Chandragupta *Maurya*, the founder of the *Maurya* dynasty, whose capital was at Magadha, is said to have been a native of Taxila in Gandhara. According to the fifth Asokan inscription, in the 3rd century BC Gandhara was an eminent part of the Mauryan empire. From here the Buddhist missions to Central and East Asia are said to have gone out. In the 2nd century BC, under King Menander, Gandhara found itself included in the Graeco-Bactrian kingdom. In the middle of the 1st century BC it was acceded by one of the Indo-Sakan states, and by the end of the 1st century BC/early 1st century AD, it was joined to the Indo-Parthian Kingdom. In the 1st to 3rd centuries AD Gandhara was in the vassalage of the Kushan Empire. Buddhism came to Gandhara early. Many Buddhist relics of the past, such as Buddhist sculpture visibly influenced by Hellenism including one of the earliest representations of Buddha, have been preserved in Gandhara.

BIBLIOGRAPHY: *W.W. Tarn, 'The Greeks in Baktria and India', Cambridge, 1951; A.K. Narain, 'The Indo-Greeks', Oxford, 1957.*

YU.V. GANKOVSKY

Gandhara Culture

This major ancient culture and civilization flourished in *Gandhara, on the territory of present-day Pakistan. Represented by various artistic forms, its architecture

Gandhara Culture.

and town planning was a blend of the Indian and Hellenistic principles. The culture is typified by the fortified settlements of Sirkap and Sirsukh in *Taxila and Charsadda in Peshawar district. Protected by powerful walls, these ancient towns had a regular layout, comprising dwelling quarters, and special palace and religious zones. Numerous monastery complexes that comprised sanctuaries, stupas and monks' quarters testify to the predominance of Buddhism. A large number of monasteries were found in Taxila, *Takht-i-Bahi near Peshawar and Butkara in the *Swat valley. Their architectural forms display Indian influence, although Hellenistic elements can be found in some of the details. They were constructed in the Graeco-Bactrian and Sako-Parthian periods. Ionic and Corinthianized capitals and profiles can be easily identified. Sculpture and high relief are two important decorative elements of Buddhist architecture where stone was normally used. A unique Gandhara school of sculpture took shape. The Buddhist iconographic canons took their form under the Mahayana influence, starting with an image of Buddha not found in earlier Buddhist art. There is an opinion that he resembled the classical Apollo in nose and head-dress, with pronounced Indian features such as the shape of his face and eyes, and a mole over the nose bridge.

Three canonical positions of the deity were adopted, the seated and meditating Buddha, the walking and preaching Buddha and the Buddha reclining in the *Mahaparinirvana* position. The *Bodhisattva* images, though equally canonized, allowed a freer interpretation. An entire typological cycle of Buddhist mythology was formed—saints, monks and secular characters. Graphic stereotypes gradually evolved. The compositions on the subjects of the Jatakas and lives of Gautama-Buddha that comprise many scenes from everyday life are executed in a freer style. Some of the scenes and images are obviously influenced by the Graeco-Roman tradition such as 'the Athena from Lahore', a Vajrapani that resembles in many details Heracles, 'Cupids with garlands' and Atlases. All of them are, however, dominated by the purely Indian ideal of male and female beauty as well as illustrating Indian regalia, architecture and everyday scenes. The scenes with musicians give an idea of the range of musical instruments used at that time: flute, drum, lute and harp played mainly by women. Ceroplastics or wax moulding was the most important of all minor arts with the range stretching from the traditional figurines of mother-goddess to those also of the Hellenic and later Roman and forms figurines of the local type. Chased and embossed metal work and jewellery included vessels, bangles, necklaces and silver and gold figurines of the Aphrodite, Hypocratus and Silenus type (Taxila).

This was a syncretic culture, taking whatever it regarded as best from each religion, with an Indic substratum permeated by Greek, Sako-Parthian, Bactrian-Kushanic and Roman influences that combined produced a new style. In the first half of the 1st millennia AD, during the *Kushan and *Gupta empires, the images and subjects of Gandhara architecture and especially sculpture spread to Nagarahara, Tokharistan and further on to China.

BIBLIOGRAPHY: *G.A. Pugachenkova, 'The Art of Gandhara', Moscow, 1972 (in Russian); A. Foucher 'L'art Greco-Bouddhique du Gandhara', Vols. 1-4, Paris, 1905-51; G. Ingholt, 'Gandharan Art in Pakistan', New York, 1947; D. Faccenna, 'Butkara. Sculptures from the Sacred Area of Butkara I', Rome, 1962.*

G.A. PUGACHENKOVA

Ganeriwala

A large ancient settlement in the Cholistan desert. M.R. Mughal studied it between 1974 and 1977. It is a multi-layer tell with clearly identifiable citadel and the lower town covering some 81.5 hectares. The remains of an early settlement scattered over an area of 27.3 hectares belong to the earlier stages of the *Harappan civilization (middle of the 3rd millennium Buddhism); the upper levels belong to the developed and later stages of the same culture (17th-16th centuries BC). Intensive diggings on the site are going on.

BIBLIOGRAPHY: *M.R. Mughal, 'Recent Archaeological Research in the Cholistan Desert'. In: (ed.) G.L. Possehl, Harappan Civilization: A Contemporary Perspective, Delhi, Oxford and IBN Publishing Co., 1982; M.R. Mughal, 'Archaeological Exploration in Cholistan', Islamabad, Lok Virsa and Department of Archaeology and Museums, 1989.*

A.YA. SHCHETENKO

Gankovsky, Yuri V. (1921–2001)

Historian. A historian of the East, with a DSc (History) he who graduated from the History Department of Moscow University (1942), saw action in the Second World War (1942-45), and was decorated with orders and medals. He taught at the Military School of Foreign Languages (Moscow, 1945-7), and was arrested by the KGB in May 1947 and released in June 1956. He was a research associate, Learned Secretary, and a department head at the Institute of Oriental Studies of the USSR (from 1956). Gankovsky was a lecturer at the

Moscow Institute of International Relations (1959-61); co-chairman of the USSR-Afghanistan Society of Historians (1985-88); President of the Association of Afghan Studies (from 1989); and, in 1966, Vice-President, and later, President of the USSR-Pakistan Society (Association of the Friends of Pakistan).

WORKS: *'The Durrani Empire, Moscow', 1958 (Pashto translation, Kabul, 1972, 1979); 'Political Situation in Pakistan' (jointly with V. Moskalenko), Moscow, 1960 (in Russian); 'History of Pakistan' (jointly with L. Polonskaya), Moscow, 1961 (in Russian) (English translation, Washington, 1966; Lahore, 1972; Pashto translation, Kabul, 1987); 'The Peoples of Pakistan. The Main Stages of Ethnic History', Moscow, 1964 (English translation, Lahore, 1972); 'The National Question and the National Movement in Pakistan', Moscow, 1967 (in Russian); 'Three Constitutions of Pakistan' (jointly with V. Moskalenko), Moscow, 1975 (in Russian) (English translation, Lahore, 1978); 'The National-Ethnic Movement in Pakistan', Moscow, 1989 (in Russian); Editor: 'History of Afghanistan', Moscow, 1982 (in Russian); Afghanistan: Economics, Politics, History, Moscow, 1984 (in Russian); 'Afghanistan: History, Economics, Culture, Moscow, 1989 (in Russian); 'Russia and Afghanistan', Moscow, 1989 (in Russian); 'The People's Republic of Bangladesh', Handbook, Moscow, 1974 (in Russian); 'The People's Republic of Bangladesh: Economics, History, Culture', Moscow, 1979 (in Russian); 'Pakistan. Handbook', Moscow, 1966; 'Pakistan Today: Economics, History, Culture', Moscow, 1976 (in Russian); 'Pakistan—Essays on History, Economics and Culture', Tashkent, 1977 (in Russian); 'Pakistan: Political and Economic Problems', Moscow, 1978 (in Russian); 'Pakistan: History and Economics', Moscow, 1980 (in Russian); 'Pakistan Society: Economic Development and Social Structure'; Moscow, 1987 (in Russian); 'Soviet Scholars View South Asia, Lahore, 1975.*

V.N. MOSKALENKO

Gazdar, Mohammad Hashim (1893–1968)

Statesman. Mohammad Hashim Gazdar was educated in the *Sindh *Madrasah* Karachi, D.J. Science College, and thereafter Engineering College, Poona. From 1934 to 1943 he was a member of the Karachi Municipal Corporation. Gazdar was an elected member of the Sindh Legislature Assembly when it was established in 1937. He was Mayor of Karachi in 1941-42 and Home Minister Sindh in 1942-45. He represented Pakistan at the International Trade and Employment Conference Havana (1947) and attended the Inter-parliamentary Conference in Rome in 1948.

M.R. KAZIMI

Geneva Agreements on Afghan political settlement

These were initiated in June 1982 and were signed on 14 April 1988, as a result of indirect negotiations between Afghanistan and Pakistan through the mediation of the personal representative of the UN Secretary-General. The Agreements include the bilateral agreement which states the principles of non-interference and non-intervention in mutual relations; provides for the voluntary return of refugees; the international guarantees signed by representatives of the USSR and the United States; the agreement on the withdrawal of Soviet troops from Afghanistan, which was signed by Afghanistan and Pakistan and was countersigned by the guarantors, the USSR and the United States. In addition to the latter, a Memorandum of Understanding was adopted relating to the modalities and logistics for the work of the UN Goodwill Mission in Afghanistan and Pakistan. The Geneva Agreements came into effect on 15 May 1988.

R.M. MUKIMJANOVA

German–Pakistan Relations

Diplomatic relations between Pakistan and the Federal Republic of Germany (FDR) were established five years after the establishment of Pakistan in 1951. Incredibly the state of war between Pakistan, a dominion of the British Commonwealth, and Germany ended only in 1952. The political relations between Pakistan and Germany have been trouble free except during the 1971 crisis, when FDR supported the secession of *East Pakistan, and in 1998 when Pakistan went nuclear. Pakistan had been subject to the Hallstein Doctrine, which prevented states with the pro-west FDR from recognizing the pro-Soviet German Democratic Republic, GDR. Only in the aftermath of its own dismemberment, Pakistan recognized the GDR. After its re-unification, Germany imposed sanctions on Pakistan following the 1998 nuclear tests, but these sanctions were lifted on 1 July 2003.

To maintain cordial relations, the leaders of both countries have visited each other repeatedly. In 1961 and 1965 President Ayub *Khan paid a visit to the FDR. Prime Minister Zulfikar Ali *Bhutto visited in 1976, General Ziaul *Haq paid a visit in 1980, Prime Minister Muhammad Khan *Junejo in 1986. In 2004 President Pervez *Musharraf and Chancellor Gerhard Schroeder exchanged visits. The previous German leaders to visit

Pakistan were President Heinrich Lubke (GDR) in 1962 and Dr. Helmut Kohl (FDR) in 1984.

Germany has emerged as the third largest donor of economic aid to Pakistan after the US and Japan since the early 1950s and the second most important trading partner in Europe after the United Kingdom and the sixth largest trading partner in the world. German assistance for Pakistan is made available by way of funds, soft term loans, commercial loans and technical assistance. German investment in Pakistan is in the form of direct equity participation, supplies of credit and transfer of technology. Its investments in Pakistan have mainly been in the electro–chemical, pharmaceutical and machine-building industries and in the banking sector. German funds have been given in essential fields such as the building of the infrastructure in energy resources, irrigation, transportation, telecommunications, and commodity supply like raw materials and spare parts for industry. In 1972 the Government of FDR agreed to provide grant assistance to the Government of Pakistan for financing 13 projects under an umbrella agreement for technical cooperation. Besides this, the following bilateral agreements are in force between the two countries: Air Transport Agreement, Investment Promotion Agreement, Double Taxation Agreement and Framework Agreement on Technical cooperation. Germany has also offered technical assistance to improve the investment climate in Pakistan and the quality of Pakistani products, also to promote the marketing of goods to the European Markets. Presently over 32 joint venture projects are operating successfully. These provide jobs for more than 4,000 qualified Pakistani citizens.

German military officials have been offered training facilities in Pakistan's Staff and Command College and the National Defence College. Germany is providing technical assistance as grant-in-aid for projects in different fields such as basic education, basic health services, development of hydel energy, promoting agriculture, rural development, vocational training, power generation, environmental protection, promotion of small and medium sized enterprises and telecommunications. Germany is also co-financing the Ghazi Barotha Hydro-Power plant and Kot Abhu Gas Turbine power station. The Pakistan-German Development cooperation began in 1961, and Germany has provided over DM five billion for joint development activities in Pakistan in the social sector, NGOs and environmental areas. Trade relations between West Germany and Pakistan were established in 1955. A trade agreement granting each other Most Favoured Nation (MFN) status was concluded in 1957 and a Pakistan-German Trade Committee was set up in 1973. The main German imports from Pakistan are garments, textiles, leather products, carpets, hosiery and knitwear items, food items, surgical instruments and spectacle frames. The main imports from Germany are machinery, engineering goods, chemicals and chemical products, iron and iron products, electrical and non-electrical goods, optical goods and vehicles. Close relations began when a German team of mountaineers visited Pakistan in 1950 to scale cultural the mountain K2. The German Pakistan Forum (GPF) was established in 1957. It has been working towards improving human, cultural, commercial and political relations between the two countries. In northern Pakistan, Germany shaped two institutionalized projects: the Pakistan-German Study Group, which had been researching and documenting the rock inscriptions along the *Karakorum Highway, and a cultural-cum-scientific project named Cultural Area Karakorum (CAM) in which cultural changes in Pakistan's mountainous regions have been investigated.

From the late fifties onwards the DAAD (Deutscher Akademischer Austauschdienst) has been providing scholarships together with the reputed Alexander Von Humboldt Foundation. Some other non-governmental organizations and associations include the Pakistan-German Cultural Association, Pakistan- German Forum, the Hans Seidel Foundation, and the Friedrich Ebert Stiftung are developing closer cultural and academic cooperation between the two countries. Germany is also keen to promote its language. In Pakistan there are two branches operating, in Karachi and Lahore, by the name of Goethe Institute. The institute, besides holding language classes, presents film evenings, talks, theatrical performances and exhibitions of the works of German writers translated into *Urdu. Sir Muhammad *Iqbal, poet philosopher of Pakistan received his doctorate from Heidelberg, leading scholars from both countries to establish cultural relations. The most prominent german scholar was Annemarie *Schimmel and, from Pakistan, M. Ikram *Chughtai and Saeed Akhtar Durrani.

BIBLIOGRAPHY: *A.A. Kadeer, Naveed Ahmad Tahir (eds.) 'Pakistan-Europe Ties', Karachi, 1988.*

T. SULTANA

Gesudaraz, Sayid Muhammad Husain Bandanawaz (1318–1421)

Poet. A mystic poet, preacher and *Shaykh of the *Sufi order of *Chishtiya who wrote in Farsi and *Dakhini* (South Indian *Urdu). He was a disciple of Shaykh Nasiruddin Chiraghi Dehlvi and went through all the stages of Sufi initiation. His pupils later compiled a collection of his utterances (*malfuzat*), entitled *Jawami al-kalim*. Gesudaraz was a major authority on *Sufism in the Bahmanid Sultanate, the Khalifa of the Chishtiya Order in Deccan, translator and commentator of *Mashariq al Anwar* by Raziuddin Hasan ibn Muhammad Saghani, and *Al-Fiqh al Akbar* by Abu Hanifa. He is believed to be the author of the first prose work in Urdu—*Miraj al-Ashiqin* ('The Ascension of the Lovers'). Gesudaraz's tomb in Gulbarga is an attraction for pilgrims.

BIBLIOGRAPHY: *A.N. Shamatov, 'Classical Dakhini', Moscow, 1974 (in Russian); Hashimi Nasiruddin, 'Dakkan Mein Urdu, New Delhi, 1985.*

A.A. SUVOROVA

Ghalib, Mirza Asadullah Khan (1797–1869)

Poet. Frequently considered the greatest poet in the *Urdu language, in his own time Ghalib was perhaps better known for his works in Persian. He composed his poetry under the poetic pen name of Asad and later of Ghalib. He was orphaned early and brought up by his uncle in Agra. At the age of thirteen, on the decision of his relatives, he married Umrao Begum, daughter of poet Ilahi Baksh Marufi. He moved to Delhi in 1810, where he lived on a meagre pension granted to his uncle by the British Government. After the defeat of the Indian peoples' uprising in 1858, he visited the Nawab of Rampur, who granted him a stipend of Rs 100 a month.

His creative work was influenced by Mirza Abdul Qadir *Bedil (d. 1721) and the traditional school of Persian poetry. At the age of twenty-three Ghalib compiled the first collection of his Urdu poetry, and for the next thirty years continued to write poetry in Persian. In 1828 he published a selection of his Persian and Urdu verse, *Guli-Rana*. In 1837 he published *Kulliayat-i-Nazm-i-Farsi,* a collection of his poetry in Farsi. In 1868-69 a collection of his letters, *Ud-i-Hindi*, and then *Urdu-i-Mualla*, a larger collection of letters, were published.

BIBLIOGRAPHY: *N. Glebov, A Sukhochev, 'Urdu Literature', Moscow, 1967 (in Russian); Ralph Russel, Khurshidul Islam, 'Ghalib: Life and Letters' (Delhi, Oxford University Press, 1994; 'Zoe Ansari Ghalib Shanasi', 2 Vols., New Delhi, 1969; 'Nuqoosh, Ghalib Number' 3 Vols., (ed.) M. Tufail, Lahore, 1969; Abdul Latif, 'Ghalib', Hyderabad (Dn.), 1924; Natalia Prigarina, 'Mirza Ghalib: A. Creative Biography, Moscow', 1986.*

N.V. GLEBOV

Gharana

Gharana literally means household, but in music it means a specialized school of music having particular nuances. A *gharana* is the most important institution in the musical culture of Pakistan and India ensuring the viability of the musical tradition, from the Sanskrit expression for 'transmission of knowledge from teacher to disciple'. The roots of *gharana* go back into antiquity. *Gharana* retained its importance throughout the historical development of the countries of the region. *Gharana* acquired special significance in the classical *Hindustani music of the seventeenth to twentieth centuries, contributing to stylistic diversity of performance. There are four major *gharanas* represented in Pakistan: 1. *Kirana*, by Roshan Ara Begum, 2. *Sham Chaurasi*, by Salamat Ali and Nazakat Ali Khan, 3. *Pitala*, by Hamid Ali Khan and Asad Amanat Ali Khan, and 4. *Talwindi*, by *dhrupad* singers Muhammad Afzal Khan and Muhammad Hafiz Khan.

I. PIRACHA

Ghazal

(in Arabic: lyrical poem, ode) A variety of lyrical verse, usually consisting of twelve to seventeen *baits* (verses) in a monorhyme. In the first *bait* (*matla*) two hemistiches (*misra*) are rhymed according to the pattern; ba, ca, da...The concluding *bait* (*maqta*) usually mentions the poet's *takhallus* (poetic name). *Ghazal* took its final shape in the thirteenth to fourteenth century. As this genre developed *ghazals* turned more and more towards Eastern mysticism, the ideas of Sufism, philosophy and morality, in addition to the usual love themes. In contemporary poetry *ghazal* also looks at political and social themes. This genre is widespread in the poetry of the Middle East and South Asia.

BIBLIOGRAPHY: *A.M. Mirzoyev, 'Rudaqi and the Evolution of Ghazal in the 10th-15th Centuries', Dushanbe, 1958 (in Russian); M.L. Reisner, 'The Evolution of the Classical*

Ghazal in Farsi. 10th-15th centuries.', Moscow, 1989 (in Russian).

N.V. GLEBOV

Ghaznavids (Also: Ghaznawi)

The ruling dynasty of the Ghaznavid Empire (963-1186). The capital, until 1151, was at Ghazni in southeast Afghanistan and from 1151-86 at Lahore. The first independent ruler was Aleptegin. The empire saw its heyday under Sultan Mahmud Ghaznavi (998-1030), who controlled the territories of modern Afghanistan, eastern Iran, northern Pakistan and a considerable part of Central Asia.

Ghaznavid Rulers: Alptegin (r. 963), Nasir ad-Dawlah Sebuktegin (r. 977), Ismail (r. 997-8), Yamin ad-Dawlah Mahmud (r. 998-1030) Jalal ad-Dawlah Muhammad (r. 1030-31), Shihab ad-Dawlah Masud (r. 1031-41), Muhammad (r. 1041), Shihab ad-Dawlah Mawdud (r. 1041-50), Masud II (r. 1050), Baha ad-Dawlah Ali (r. 1050), Izz ad-Dawlah Abd ar-Rashid (r. 1050-3), Jamal ad-Dawlah Farrukhzad (r. 1053-9), Zahir ad-Dawlah Ibrahim (r. 1059-99), Ala ad-Dawlah Masud III (r. 1099-1115), Kamal ad-Dawlah Shirzad (r. 1115), Sultan ad-Dawlah Arslan Shah (r. 1115-8), Jamin ad-Dawlah Bahram Shah (r. 1118-52), Muizz ad-Dawlah Khusraw Shah (r. 1152-60), Taj ad-Dawlah Khusraw Malik (r. 1160-86).

YU.V. GANKOVSKY

Ghungru

A set of hollow bronze bells containing iron balls. The bells are connected to each other by rope and are tied to a dancer's ankles, wrists, or waist. The *ghungru* chimes during each movement of the dancer. Wearing ghungru symbolizes a performer's membership in the dancers' group. The *ghungru* has been widely used since the earliest times in numerous rituals and by shaman to drive away evil spirits.

I. PIRACHA

Ghurids

A ruling dynasty on the territory of present-day Afghanistan, Pakistan and northwest India (*c*. 1000–1215), which laid the foundations of the *Delhi Sultanate.

The Rulers: Muhammad ibn Suri, Abu Ali, Shis, Abbas, Muhammad, Qutb ad Din Hasan (the dates of the rule of the first six Ghurid rulers have not been established with any degree of certainty), Izz ad-Din Husayn (r. 1100-46), Saif ad-Din Suri (r. 1146-9), Baha ad-Din Sam I (r. 1149), Ala ad-Din Husain (r. 1149-61), Sayf ad-Din Muhammad (r. 1161-3), Ghiyas ad-Din Muhammad (r. 1163-73), Shihab ad-Din (Muiz ad-Din) Muhammad (r. 1173-1206), Ghiyas ad-Din Mahmud (r. 1206-12), Baha ad-Din Sam II (r. 1212-3), Ala ad-Din Atsiz (r. 1213), Ala ad-Din (Diya ad-Din) Muhammad (r. 1214-5).

YU.V. GANKOVSKY

Gidda

*Punjab's most famous folk dance for women. It can be danced by as few as two dancers. Women enact verses called *bolis* and folk poetry. The subject matter of these *bolis* include a wide range, from arguments with the father-in-law to political affairs. The dance rhythm is set by the **dhols* or drums and the distinctive hand claps of the dancers.

R. HUSAIN

Gilgit

1. A river in the north-western region of the former princely state of Jammu and *Kashmir (currently *Northern Areas controlled by Pakistan). It flows through the foothills of the *Hindu Kush and *Karakoram mountains. A tributary of the *Indus, the Gilgit is formed by the confluence of the Yasin and Hunza rivers. Its length is about 450 km., its surface area, 26,000 sq.km.

2. The Gilgit Valley. From 1948 to 1971, one of the two political agencies in the Pakistan-controlled Northern Territories of the princely state of Jammu and *Kashmir. The administrative structure of the agency was changed a number of times. In 1971 it was divided into the districts of Gilgit, Astor Chilas, and Darel-Tanghir; the political districts of Punial, Yasin, *Koh-i-Ghizar, Ishkuman; and into the princely states of Hunza and Nagar.

3. Since 1972 Gilgit is an administrative district in the Northern Territories. Its capital is also named Gilgit.

BIBLIOGRAPHY: *O.H.K. Spate, 'India and Pakistan', London, 1954; (ed.) A.H. Dani, 'History of Northern Areas of Pakistan', Islamabad, 1989.*

YU.V. GANKOVSKY

Graeco-Bactrian Kingdom

This appeared in *c*. 250 BC on the eastern outskirts of the empire created by Alexander of Macedonia (356-23 BC). Spreading to India, it lasted until the year 140 or 130 BC. The lands on the north of modern-day

The beauty of Gilgit.

Afghanistan and the south of central Asia were the territorial nucleus of the kingdom. In its heyday it also embraced the whole of Afghanistan and a considerable part of the *Indus Valley, conquered in *c.* 190-180 BC by King Demetrios. The most powerful of the rulers was Menander (middle of the 2nd century BC). After the latter's death, the Graeco-Bactrian Kingdom fell apart into numerous small states.

YU. V. GANKOVSKY

Gujarati (Language)

It belongs to the *Indo-Aryan group of the Indo-European family of languages and is the official language of the state of Gujarat (West India). About 42.35 million (1987) Gujarati speakers also live in Pakistan. Bhili and Kandeshi, spoken in the areas of Rajasthan and Maharashtra which border on Gujarat, may be regarded as dialect forms of Gujarati. The Gujarati language began to evolve in the twelfth century on the basis of two Late Middle Indian languages, Gurjara and Nagara Apabhransha. Originally Gujarati had close affinity with Rajasthani dialects. Towards the middle of the fourteenth century the two forms of the language were finally differentiated. The history of Gujarati proper dates back to the fifteenth century. The present-day literary standard language began to evolve in the second half of the nineteenth century. The structure of Gujarati is intermediate between Hindi and Marathi, but differs from both languages.

BIBLIOGRAPHY: *I.V. Savelyeva, 'The Gujarati Language', Moscow, 1965 (in Russian); G. Cardona, 'A Gujarati Reference Grammar', Philadelphia, 1965; H.M. Lambert, 'Gujarati Language Course', Cambridge, 1971; N.B. Divetiya, 'Gujarati Bhasa ane Sahitya', Mumbai, 1964; K.K. Shastry, 'Gujarati Vyakaran Sastra', Mumbai, 1963.*

L.V. SAVELYEVA

Gujarati (People)

A people inhabiting India and Pakistan. Their population is approximately 40 million people, out of which one million live in Pakistan and the rest in India. Gujaratis belong to the Indo-Mediterranean race of the larger

Europeoid race. Their native tongue is *Gujarati. The overwhelming majority practice Hinduism, but there is a significant number of Muslims and Jains.

The ancestors of present-day Gujaratis (Gujar or Gujara tribes) are believed to have come to Gujarat in the beginning of the first millennia AD and were partly assimilated by the local tribes of Bhil and *Indo-Aryans. In the Middle Ages the Gujaratis reached a high level of ethnic consolidation. They constituted the bulk of the population in the states of Valabha, Chalukya, and Gujarati sultanate. During the colonial period Gujarati principalities formed part of the Bombay Presidency. Their traditional occupations include ploughed farming (*jowar, bajra,* wheat, corn, peanut, rice in irrigated areas), and cattle breeding (buffalo, zebu, sheep, goat). Also well-developed are silk and cotton weaving (brocade-*kamkhab*, *chundari*), pottery painting, wood and stone carving, embossing, and jewellery making. The traditional urban architecture is of the western Indian type. The houses are built of brick and stone with covered galleries and inner yards. Gates, windows, and doors are often decorated with rich carvings.

Gujarati villages are usually large, often with more than 1,000 inhabitants. A traditional village dwelling is a single or two-room adobe or stone house, in some places gypsum is used, with a tiled roof. Traditional clothes for men consists of wide pants gathered at the shins and narrowing below the knee, shirts with gathers from under the neckband, narrow long sleeves, *dhoti*, and long shirts. In town, men wear European clothing. Women dress in wide solid coloured skirts, embroidered along the hem, with embroidered blouses and shawls that cover the head and shoulders. In towns they often wear *saris* with the upper end thrown over the shoulders from the back to the front. Wearing jewellery is common. The staple diet—in accordance with consists of flat bread, called *chapati*, with peas and vegetables, rice, fish, poultry and goat meat. Families are monogamous and patriarchal. Gujaratis are famous for their arts including literature, music, dancing, drama, architecture, and particularly the Gujarati school of miniature painting.

BIBLIOGRAPHY: *'Ethnic Processes in South Asian Countries', Moscow, 1976 (in Russian); Hasmukhal D. Sankalia, 'Studies in the Historical and Cultural Geography and Ethnography of Gujarat', Poona, 1949; N. Shah, 'Some Facets of Industrial Development of Gujarat', Bombay, 1979.*

N.R. GUSEVA

Gumal/Gomal

(Ancient Indian: Gomati) A river that flows through Afghanistan, where its upper reaches are about 100 km. long, and continues in Pakistan where the middle and lower reaches are about 250 km. long. It flows in a general west to east direction, through South Waziristan and the district of Dera Ismail Khan (*North West Frontier Province). The confluence with the *Indus is to the south of Dera Ismail Khan.

S.B. ROSTOTSKY

Gumla

A settlement of the Neolithic, Bronze and Early Iron Age in northern *Balochistan (Pakistan) is to be found in the Gumal valley to the north-west of Dera Ismail Khan. Since 1971 it has been studied by an expedition of the University of Peshawar headed by A.H. *Dani. He has identified six chronological periods. Period I (3300-100 BC) has not yielded any pottery and is the earliest period. Large pits with ashes, bones, stone microliths, grain grinders and mortars belong to this period. Period II (3100-2700 BC) is characterized by pits with high-quality wheel manufactured painted ware. There is some similarity with the pottery of the Quetta culture in Balochistan (Kili-Ghul-Muhammad III-IV) and the Mundigak III5-IV1 settlement in Afghanistan. Clay figurines, stone and bronze implements were found. Period III (2700-400 BC) is genetically connected with the first two periods. The percentage of ornamentation styles has changed. Its pottery relates it to the lower levels in *Amri and *Kot Diji.

Solid brick constructions belong to Period IV (2400-2000 BC). This material is typical of the classical development stage of the *Harappan Civilization. Period V of the later Harappa (first half of the 2nd millennium BC) yielded five cremation burials in which vessels of the Late Harappan type were found side by side with the *Gandhara culture or *Swat culture ware. Several burials were dug in Period VI that have been dated to the Early Iron Age. These studies shed light on the origins and decline of the Harappa civilization and *Indo-Aryan penetration into South Asia.

BIBLIOGRAPHY: *A.H. Dani, 'Excavations in the Gomal Valley', AP, V, 1970-1; Allchin Brigget and Raymond, 'The Rise of Civilization in India and Pakistan', Cambridge, 1982.*

A.YA. SHCHETENKO

Guptas

A state and dynasty in northern India of the 4th-5th centuries. Its original territory was located in the area of Magadha. The Gupta rise began with Chandragupta I, who assumed the title of 'the Great King, the King of Kings'. The beginning of the Gupta era is associated with his coronation. The state was further strengthened thanks to the union with the Lichhavi, consolidated by Chandragupta's marriage to Kumaradevi from the influential Lichhavi clan of Nepal. The most extensive conquests were achieved by their son Samudragupta. The most flourishing period coincided with the rule of Chandragupta II, who awarded himself with the title of Vikramaditya. Following the relatively peaceful rule of Kumaragupta I (414-55), under Skandagupta (455-67) the Gupta Empire was attacked by the *Ephtalites. Despite victory over the invaders at the end of the 5th–early 6th century, the Gupta Empire began to fall apart. In the period of its greatest power the Guptas ruled over the entire Gangetic Plain, the *Punjab, Malwa, Gujarat, and Kathiawar. However, many regions of this huge empire were sufficiently autonomous to be ruled by the local dynasties. On the basis of extant inscriptions on buildings it has been established that lands were assigned to monasteries, temples, and Brahmins on a regular basis. The Gupta Era is characterized by a large-scale colonization of previously ill-developed territories and by growing ties with South-East Asia. The Gupta Empire was visited by Fa-hsien, a Chinese Buddhist pilgrim. The Guptas encouraged the spread of Hinduism (Vishnuism, Shivaism), and Mahayana Buddhism. According to tradition, some of the more illustrious names among the literati and scholars in ancient India are associated with the Gupta. Among them are the poet Kalidasa, lexicographer Amarasinha, mathematician Aryabhata. The Gupta style in art influenced artists of later eras.

BIBLIOGRAPHY: *G.M. Bongard-Levin, G.F. Ilyin, 'Ancient India', Moscow, 1985 (in Russian); D.R. Bhandarkar, 'Inscriptions of the Early Gupta', Corpus Inscriptionum Indicarym, Vol. III, Delhi, 1981; H. Chakraborti, 'India as Reflected in the Inscriptions of Gupta Period', Delhi, 1978; P.L. Gupta, 'The Imperial Guptas', Vol. 1-2, Varanasi, 1974-80; (ed.) B.L. Smith, 'Essays on Gupta Culture', Delhi, 1983.*

A.A. VIGASIN

Gur

A home-made brown sugar used in South Asia. A variety made out of palm sap is known as *jaggery*. It is produced out of sugar cane by boiling the syrup until it thickens. Gur is 65 per cent sucrose. The sugarcane is shredded and boiled in open cauldrons. When the syrup cools and solidifies, it is chopped into pieces. The losses in the home-made production of *gur* are 25 per cent more than in factory production. It generally takes a team of four people to prepare *gur*. There is no exact data on its production because it is both produced and consumed within the peasant household. The estimated amount produced is 800-100,000 tons a year. In industrial areas and areas adjacent to sugar factories, over a third of farms growing sugarcane specialize in *gur* production. The main centres of *gur*-making are Faisalabad, Sheikhupura, Sahiwal, Sargodha (*Punjab), and Nawabshah (*Sindh).

M.YU. MOROZOVA

H

Hadith

(in Arabic: message, tale, tradition; also: quotation) A tale or tradition about the deeds and pronouncements of the Prophet Muhammad (PBUH). Hadith consists of narration of tales or tradition (*isnad*—support). Also the contents of the story (*matn*—text).

YU.V. GANKOVSKY

Haj (also hajj)

(Arabic: pilgrimage) One of the five pillars of Islam (**rukn*). At least once during their lifetime, Muslims are required to make a pilgrimage to the holy city of Mecca and visit the mosque of *Kaaba* (Kabah).

YU.V. GANKOVSKY

Hali, Altaf Husain (1837–1914)

Poet/Critic. Poet-enlightener, reformer, and founder of scholarly criticism in *Urdu literature, Hali descended from an impoverished aristocratic clan. He received a traditional Muslim education, with literary instruction from Sheafta and Mirza *Ghalib. At the beginning of his literary career, Hali mainly wrote traditional **ghazals*. By the mid 1870s, he became close to the Aligarh movement and was also introduced to European literature and Western thinking, which led him to conclude that traditional literature was in need of modernization. His poems written for the Lahore *mushaira* of 1874 marked the beginning of new poetry (*Nai Shairi*) in his creative work. His poems touched on issues of that time, homeland and patriotism: *Barkharut* ('Rainy Season'), *Hubb-i-Watan* ('The Patriot'); East-West relations, democracy, and despotism: *Munazira-i-Rahm-o-Insaf* ('Dialogue of Compassion and Justice'). These were the first attempts at civic-spirited verse. Hali's *magnum opus* is the poem *Madd-o-Jazr-i-Islam* ('The Ebb and Flow of Islam'), 1879, otherwise known as *Musaddas Hali*. The poem sums up Hali's reflections on the fate of the Muslims and the reasons behind the crisis experienced by the Muslim community in India. He sets himself to the task of awakening the people. He was the first to write biographies in *Urdu: *Hayat-i-Saadi* ('The Life of Saadi'), 1876; and *Yadgar-i-Ghalib* ('The Memoirs of Ghalib'), 1897. In his *Muqaddama-i-Sher-i-Shairi* ('Introduction to Poetry'), 1893, Hali formulated the aims, principles, and methods of poetic reforms and expounded his ideas about the two-way influence between literature and society. He introduced the concept of 'historicism in literature'. While paying tribute to the best samples of classical poetry, he submitted court poetry to harsh criticism seeing it as the main obstacle in the way of literary progress. Hali's poetic reforms opened new vistas for the development of Urdu poetry in modern times.

WORKS: *'Majmua-i-Nazm-u-Hali', 1880; 'Diwan-i-Hali', 1893; 'Hayat-i-Jawed, a biography', 1901; 'Chup ki Dad' (A Tribute to Silence), 1906.*

BIBLIOGRAPHY: *L. Vassilyeva, 'Altaf Husain Hali', in: Collection of Indian Literatures, Moscow, 1988 (in Russian); L. Vassilyeva, 'Hali-Muhammad Iqbal's Predecessor', in: The Work of Muhammad Iqbal, Moscow, 1982 (in Russian); N. Glebov, A. Sukhochev, 'Urdu Literature', Moscow, 1967 (in Russian); Muin Ehsan Jazbi, 'Hali ka Siyasi Shaur' (Hali's Political Views), Lucknow, 1959; Saliha Abid Husain, 'Yadgar-i-Hali' (The Memoirs of Hali), Allahabad, 1959; Khurshid ul-Islam, 'Hali', Aligarh, 1958; Shujat Sandelwi, 'Hali ba Heisiyat-i-Shair' (Hali as a Poet), Lucknow, 1960; 'Hali key Sheri Nazariat, Karachi, 1988.*

L.A. VASILYEVA

Halqa-i-Aadab-i-Zawq

(Circle of Connoisseurs of Art) It was founded in 1939 in Lahore by the famous poets N.M. *Rashid and Miraji (1912-49) as an alternative to the All-India Progressive Writers Association (PWA) (1936). The group calls itself 'a circle' in order to emphasize the modesty of their aims and unpretentious nature of their activities that included promoting creative and artistic fiction in *Urdu literature. The circle engages in literary experiments in imitation of the Western avant-garde. The poets favoured *vers libre* and blank verse to open new possibilities for artistic self-expression. The circle became an artistic centre attracting such poets as Muhammad Din Tasir (1902-50), Yusuf Zafar (b. 1914), Qayum Nazar (b. 1914) and Akhtar al-Iman (b. 1915). In literary criticism, the most consistent follower of the 'Connoisseurs of Art' was Muhammad Hasan Askari. Later, some prose writers joined the circle: Sadat Hasan *Manto, Aziz *Ahmad, Mumtaz Shirin, Hajra *Masrur,

Khadija *Mastur. The circle has always been open for literary discussions, particularly after the PPWA *Pakistan Progressive Writers Association had been banned. At that time, the contradictions between the 'Connoisseurs of Art' and 'Progressive Writers' became increasingly less acute. Today both these trends complement one another within a broader movement—*Jadid Adab* ('Contemporary Literature').

BIBLIOGRAPHY: *Glebov, A. Sukhochev, 'Urdu Literature', Moscow, 1967 (in Russian); Muhammad Sadiq, 'A History of Urdu Literature', London, 1964, Ibadat Barewlwi, 'Jadid Shairi', Aligarh, 1983.*

A. NIYAZI

Hamdard Foundation

Was founded in 1953 in Karachi by Hakim Muhammed *Said for the purpose of organizing national and international conferences to discuss problems in medicine, humanities, science, and Islamic studies. The Foundation has branched out into Lahore, Rawalpindi, and Peshawar, since 1953. The Hamdard Foundation publishes the quarterly journal, *Hamdard Islamics and Hamdard Medicus*.

Hakim Muhammad Said, Founder of the Hamdard Foundation.

YU.V. GANKOVSKY

Hamdard Foundation Pakistan Library

Founded in 1954 in Karachi it has more than 100,000 volumes including collections on Oriental medicine, homeopathy, and Islamic studies as well as periodicals and Oriental manuscripts.

YU.V. GANKOVSKY

Hanafi

They are the followers of the Hanafi **madhab* (religion). The founder and eponym was Abu Hanifah (*c.* 696-767). Hanafi *madhab* was popular in the Abbasid Era and became the state religion of the Ottoman Empire. The rulers of the *Delhi sultanate, and most of the rulers of the states which sprang up after its disintegration, as well as the kings of the Great *Mughal dynasty, were Hanafi. The founders of the Muslim theological school in *Deoband (1867) were Hanafi. Currently, the majority of *Sunni Muslims in Pakistan and South Asia follow Hanafi *madhab*.

YU.V. GANKOVSKY

Haq, Abdul Kassem Fazlul, Moulvi (1873–1962)

Statesman. Called *Sher-i-Bangla* (Tiger of Bengal), A.K. Fazlul Haq was one of the earliest Muslim politicians of Bengal with a rural base and representative of the vernacular classes. He graduated in Arts and Law from the University of Calcutta in 1896. He was President of the *All-India Muslim League intermittently. In 1927, he founded the *Krishak Proja* Party (later named the *Krishak Sramik* Party), representing the peasantry. After the elections of 1937, after some initial flirtation with the Congress, Huq formed a coalition government in Bengal province with the *Muslim League. He went on to move the famous *Lahore Resolution of 1940. His relationship with the Muslim League remained erratic and he split from the Party in 1943.

After the creation of Pakistan, A.K. Fazlul Haq was first Advocate-General for East Bengal but, following the overwhelming victory of the Jugto Front in the 1954 provincial assembly elections, he became Chief Minister of East Bengal. His controversial remarks, questioning the *raison d'étre* of Pakistan during a visit to Calcutta, led to a number of protest meetings in East Bengal, and one, according to H.S. *Suhrawardy, presided over by Maulana Abdul Hamid Khan *Bhashani. This incident strained Fazlul Haq-Suhrawardy relations and, on the latter's crossing over to the opposition, Fazlul Haq joined the Central cabinet as Law Minister in August 1955 and stayed until March 1956. From 1956 to 1958, he was Governor of *East Pakistan. After the military takeover of 1958, Fazlul Haq led a life of political retirement.

WORKS: *'Muslim Sufferings under Congress Rule', Calcutta, 1939.*

BIBLIOGRAPHY: *Humera Momen, 'Muslim Politics in Bengal. A Study of the Krishak Praja Party and the Elections of 1937', Dhaka, 1972.*

M.R. KAZIMI

Haq, Abdul, Maulvi (1870–1961)

Linguistic Scholar. Best known by the title *Baba-i-Urdu* ('Father of the *Urdu Language'). Maulvi Abdul Haq was a linguist, enlightener, publisher and an Urdu literary scholar. Abdul Haq enrolled at Aligarh University in 1888 and received his BA in 1896. His creative principles and worldview were strongly influenced by Sir Syed Ahmad *Khan, Altaf Hussain *Hali and Shibli *Nomani. In 1921, he headed the Society for the Development of Urdu (*Anjuman-i-Taraqqi-i-Urdu*). Under the auspices of this Society, some fundamental journals that influenced the scholarly and public thought of several generations of intellectuals were published: *Hamari Zaban* ('Our Language', 1939), *Urdu* (1921), *Maashiyat* ('The Economy'), and *Science* (1928-47). He was in charge of the Society's publishing and translation activities. Abdul Haq wrote introductions and commentaries for a number of books published in Hyderabad (Deccan), and later in Aurangabad, Delhi, and Karachi. He is responsible for the publication of manuscripts of some early Urdu writers and poets and for the translation of classics of antiquity and major epic works from Sanskrit, Arabic, and Persian. He published several world literary classics and studies in Urdu, reflecting the contemporary state of Western scholarship. Abdul Haq was one of the organizers of the present-day system of education and personally helped establish Osmania University in Hyderabad, Deccan. He acquired private libraries and collections that laid the basis of public libraries in Hyderabad, Delhi and Karachi. After the partition in 1947, Abdul Haq moved to Pakistan. He contributed to the setting up of the Urdu College in Karachi and *Anjuman-i-Taraqqi-i-Urdu Pakistan* (1948). On his initiative, several journals, especially *Qaumi Zaban* ('The Language of the Nation'), and *Urdu* were circulated in Karachi. He authored important scholarly works on linguistics and literary criticism, Urdu grammar, textbooks, and dictionaries. He published studies on the life and work of Wajahi, Ali Adil Shah, Amir Khusrau *Dehlawi, Syed Ahmad Khan, *Mir Taqi Mir, Altaf Hussain Hali, and others.

WORKS: *'Sayyid Ahmad Khan, Hayat-o-Afkar', Karachi, 1976; 'Lugat-e-Kabir', in 2 vols, Karachi, 1976.*

BIBLIOGRAPHY: *Shahabuddin Saqib, 'Baba-i-Urdu; Maulvi Abdul Haq', Karachi, 1988.*

M.R. KAZIMI

Haq, Mahbubul, Dr (1934–98)

Statesman. Mahbubul Haq was an economist who graduated from Government College in Lahore and earned his doctorate from Yale University (USA). In 1957, he joined the Pakistan Planning Commission and helped to draw up the country's Second and Third Five-Year plans. His work, *The Strategy of Economic Planning* (1963), brought him fame. However, by the late 1960s, Dr. Haq was highlighting the excessive concentration of wealth in the country by showing that 'twenty two families' controlled the bulk of the country's industrial and financial resources. This became a prime political issue in the late 1960s and early 1970s, driving the populistic slogans and governmental measures of the time. In the 1970s, Dr. Mahbubul Haq worked with the World Bank. In the early 1980s, he became Minister of Planning and Minister of Finance in the Pakistan Cabinet.

WORKS: *'The Strategy of Economic Planning', Karachi, 1963; 'Behind the Poverty Curtain: A Choice Before the Third World', Karachi, 1976.*

V.YA. BELOKRENITSKY

Haq, Muhammad Ziaul, General (1924–88)

President of Pakistan from 13 September 1978 to 17 August 1988. Ziaul Haq's career as a Military Officer began in 1945. He served for a decade in the armoured units, from 1964 to 1974. In 1975, he was appointed Corps Commander and in 1976 was promoted to the rank of General, and appointed Chief of Staff of the Pakistan Army. After the military *coup* of 5 July 1977, he became the Chief Martial Law Administrator. His death in an air crash in 1988 marked the end of his Presidency. His period in office was noted for the trial and execution of former Prime Minister Zulfikar Ali *Bhutto and for Pakistan's successful campaigns, alongside the USA, against the Soviet occupation of

Military Ruler of Pakistan Ziaul Haq (1978–88).

Afghanistan. It is also noteworthy for its plethora of 'Islamic' legislation, some of which is regarded as primitive and unfair to women and to minorities, the spread of addiction to hard drugs, the growth of ethnic and sectarian tensions and the breakdown of law and order owing to easy availability of armaments.

YU.V. GANKOVSKY

Harappa

Central *Punjab is the location of this, one of the main centres of the Harappan (*Indus Valley) civilization. Harappa is a multi-level settlement of the Bronze Age; 27 km. to the south-west from Sahiwal (Pakistan). It was studied by R.B. Sahni (1921), M.S. Vats, K.N. Sastri, R.E.M. Wheeler and M.R. Mughal. The western tell was a rectangular citadel (Eight hectares), the eastern tell–the lower town (58.1 hectares). Two burials were investigated; the first (R-37) yielded burials of the Harappan culture, the second (H) consisted of two periods: the early one (cremation in graves) and later (fragmented burials in urns). All of them differ in anthropological material, which is an evidence of a mixed population and the long time of settlement. Harappa existed from the 3rd millennium BC to the 17th-16th centuries BC; burial ground 'H' was used in the 12th-11th centuries BC.

BIBLIOGRAPHY: *See Bibliography to Harappan Civilization.*

A.YA. SHCHETENKO

Harappan Civilization (also Indus Valley Civilization)

Contemporary with Sumer and ancient Egypt, the Indus Valley was home to a well developed urban culture that appeared approximately in the middle of the 3rd millennium BC in the west of Pakistan. It covered an area from Sutkagen-Dor in southern *Balochistan in the west to Alamgirpur in Uttar-Pradesh (India) in the east and from Mandi in *Kashmir in the north to Daimabad in Mahatashta (India) in the south. With about 2 million sq. km. it was twice as large as the Egyptian and Mesopotamian civilization combined. It was discovered in 1921; the first studies were conducted by Indian (R.B. Sahni and R.D. Banerji) and British (J. *Marshall, E.J.H. *Mackay, and R.E.M. Wheeler) archaeologists. The Archaeological Service of India conducted diggings after 1947 (B.B. Lal, S.R. Rao, B.K. Thapar, S.A. Sali, R.S. Bisht, S. Bhan, J.P. Joshi, U.M. Chitalwala), the Department of Archaeology and Museums of Pakistan (F.A. Khan, A.H. *Dani, F.A. Durrani, M.R. Mughal) and archaeologists from other countries (J.M. Casal, W.A. *Fairservis, G.F. Dales, J.F. Jarrige, G.L. Possel) carried out their investigations. Diggings were carried out in *Harappa, *Mohenjo-Daro, *Chanhu-Daro, Allahdino, Balakot, *Ganeriwala, *Mehargarh in Pakistan; and–Lothal, Rangpur, Kalibangan, Surkotada, Banawali and Mandi in India. More than 700 settlements were discovered.

Harappa and Mohenjo-Daro cover over 50 hectares, other sites are smaller. They are represented by fortified outposts, centres of handicrafts and trade, ports (from 2 to 12 hectares) and smaller settlements (up to 1 hectare). They can be divided into several types by their layouts: 1. Settlements divided into parts—the so-called citadel and the lower city. The rectangular citadel with its longer north-southern axis orientated towards the river occupied the western tell. The lower city was in the east. 2. Settlements with two equal parts divided with a wall into nearly square parts (Surkotada, Banawali, Balakot). 3. Rectangular settlements with a square citadel in the southwestern corner (Lothal). All of them stood on platforms (418 x 195 x 15 metres in Harappa, 119 x 127 x 7 metres in Lothal); there were walls with counterforces and corner towers (in Harappa they were 13 metres thick at the foundation, in Surkotada 3.6-4 metres). 4. Non-fortified settlements without platforms and walls (Allahdino). Different construction materials were used in different geographical zones: burnt and adobe bricks in the Indus valley, adobe bricks and stone with pebbles in Kathiawar, adobe bricks in Hariana and stone blocks in Ali-Murad. All of them had regular layouts. In *Mohenjo-Daro, the main street (9 metres wide) divided the city into rectangular parts (363 x 242 metres), divided with smaller streets into living quarters. Sewerage pipes made of burnt bricks ran along the streets; houses and other buildings were made of these bricks as well. A house generally had a central court with a well around it, where living rooms, a kitchen, a room of ablutions and a toilet were arranged. A smaller house in Mohenjo-Daro had two to four rooms and a court; on the average, however, a house had eight or nine rooms with 355 sq. m. of floor space. A house of nine rooms was discovered in Surkotada. In the lower city the houses had five rooms. In Allahdino the houses of five or six rooms covered an area of 80 to 140 sq. metres, while industrial complexes were from 375 to 780 sq. m. The former were discovered in the dig's southern part, the latter were found in the northern part where a furnace, grain storage, a stone paved road that led to a pool, and some smaller storage rooms were

Statue of The King Priest Unearthed at Taxila.

found. Household and industrial constructions were found in Harappa to the north of the citadel: round platforms for making flour, houses of craftsmen and a large granary with a floor space of more than 800 sq. m.

In Mohenjo-Daro there were some public houses in the citadel: an ablution pool (11.7 x 7 metres and 2.4 metres deep) surrounded with a colonnade and rooms for dressing, a building (81 x 23 metres) with the central court, several rooms and two stairs, a granary, and a square hall with columns. In Lothal, a granary was found in the citadel with a pool nearby (214 x 37 metres, 4.5 metres deep). In the lower city, archaeologists discovered a shop that specialized in ceramic beads; the kiln was found nearby. A similar shop was discovered in Balakot; kilns for firing pottery and bricks and smelting metals were found in Alamgirpur, Harappa, Mohenjo-Daro, *Chanhu-Daro, and Kalibangan. Fireplaces plastered with clay (probably of cultic nature) were found in Kalibangan. They belonged both to the citadel and the houses of the lower city. The Harappan burials were placed outside the settlements (Harappa, Lothal, Kalibangan, Surkotada). The burial rite differed from place to place: 1. supine placing of the body, orientated to the north, in a rectangular grave the walls of which were faced with adobe bricks. Remnants of a wooden coffin were found in one of the graves. There are also double burials (of a man and a woman); 2. burials in a vessel placed in a grave (in one case it was covered with a stone slab); 3. pottery alone was placed in the grave. Grave goods comprised from fifteen to twenty vessels; ornaments such as bangles, necklaces, beads, rings and earrings were rare.

Crafts and applied art reached a high level. There were copper and bronze tools (knife blades, sickles, chisels, fishing hooks, saws, blades and other similar objects, arrowheads, short swords, spears and other weapon types). Clay ware was varied and richly ornamented. It was made on fast wheels and burnt in special kilns. The art of stone sculpture ('King Priest') and ceroplastics (figurines of people and animals) were widely known. They also made stone seals with carved animals, men and deities in them. Trade was widespread—weights and measuring rods made of ivory are an evidence of this. Cylinder seals and imported Indian objects found in western Asia illustrate the wide-flung international trade. Sea routes were probably used together with the caravan routes. The possibility of sea trade is supported with seals from the Persian Gulf found in Lothal and also a pool used probably as a dock, drawings of ships on one of the seals and on a shard from Mohenjo-Daro. The economy was based on agriculture. High yields of wheat, barley, millet, and peas (rice at the later stages), melons and banana were possible thanks to the rich alluvial soils, numerous rivers and the mild climate (much more favourable than now). People were breeding buffalos, sheep and pigs; they had already domesticated dogs, cats and, probably, elephants and camels. There is evidence that they used oxen and camels as draught animals. In Kalibangan people knew how to till land; cotton was grown. People dressed in *dhoti* and shawls; bronze, silver and gold jewellery with semi-precious stones was popular; as also necklaces, earrings, rings, belts and bangles.

The anthropological composition was varied. Mediterranean, Alpine and Negro-Australoid racial types have been identified. We have some general ideas about the Harappan population's religious beliefs: they worshipped trees, animals, the Mother-Goddess (female figurines), fire (altars), water (pools) and practiced the fertility cult. Some archaeologists believe that the 'horned god' seen on seals is a prototype of Shiva. The calendar had been already invented. The Harappan civilization's chronological frames are determined by the seals found in Mesopotamia (Ur, Kish, Tell Asmar) related to the period between Sargon of Akkad to the end of the Isin Larsa period (*c*. 2370 BC to 1900 BC and later). At this time the Harappan civilization had already reached its peak. The radiocarbon dates place it *c*. 2500-1700 BC; there is a lot of discussion about its origins. The pre-Harappa or early Harappa complexes of *Amri, *Kot Diji, Kalibangan, Harappa demonstrate the origins and development of the Harappan civilization's main elements first in the Indus Valley (4th-3rd millennium BC) and *c*. 2000 BC (at the later states): a shift of Harappan migrants to the east, into the valley of the Saraswati and Drisadwati rivers (*Punjab and Hariana) and to the south (Kathiawar peninsula and the Deccan). Probably, the people came into motion because of an ecological crisis in the Indus Valley (aridity, salinization and bogging of soils and devastating floods), relative overpopulation, epidemics; probably an internal social crisis was one of the reasons. The recent studies have failed to support a popular hypothesis of an *Aryan invasion as a cause of destruction of the Harappan cities. There is a temporal gap between these two events; the stratigraphic sequences of Lothal, Rangpur, Daimabad (in central India) and the evidence from Banawali and Bhagvanpur (in eastern India) testify that complexes of the late Harappa civilization existed synchronously with a wide range of the culture of the Late Bronze Age and their co-operation in the genesis of the early historical cultures of the contemporary peoples of India and Pakistan.

Until the inscriptions are deciphered, it is hard to tell what the civilization's social and political system was like. If one surmises that it had some common features with Sumerian society (where important economic archives have been found), one can admit to an early class system in the Harappan civilization. Social inequality was quite noticeable and, obviously, slave labour was used. The poor lived in small houses while the rich occupied two and three-storey homes.

The economic structure rested on efficient land tilling that used irrigation: in Lothal, archaeologists discovered a canal 2.5 km. long. Land yielded two crops a year. Even one crop allowed people of Mohenjo-Daro to build up state grain reserves.

One can imagine that the political organization resembled that in other countries of the Ancient East. Not only rulers but also the clergy enjoyed real power. Attempts to decipher the written language related to the proto-*Dravidian language continue

BIBLIOGRAPHY: *G.M. Bongard-Levin, G.F. Ilyin, 'India in Ancient Times', Moscow, 1985 (in Russian); V.M. Masson, The Earliest Civilizations', Leningrad, 1989 (in Russian); J. Marshall, 'Mohenjo-Daro and the Indus Civilization', Vols. 1-3 London, 1931; M.S. Vats, 'Excavations at Harappa', Vols. 1-2, Delhi, 1940; E.J.H. Mackay, 'Further Excavations at Mohenjo-Daro', Vols. 1-2, Delhi, 1937–38; 'Chanhu-Daro Excavations 1935-6', New Haven, 1943: R.E.M. Wheeler, 'The Indus Civilization', Cambridge, 1968; S.A. Sali, 'Daimabad 1976-9', New Delhi, 1986; A.H. Dani, 'Recent Archaeological Discoveries in Pakistan', Tokyo, 1988; F.A. Durrani, 'Excavations in the Gomal Valley: Rehman Dheri Excavations Report No. 1' 'Ancient Pakistan', in: Vol. 6, 1988; M.R. Mughal 'Archaeological Explorations in Cholistan', Islamabad, 1989.*

A.YA. SHCHETENKO

Harmonium

The harmonium is a small, manually-pumped reed. There are two main types of harmonium: a foot-pumped version that resembles a small organ, and a hand-pumped portable version that folds up for easy transport. The harmonium was invented in Europe in Paris in 1842 by Alexandre Debain. During the mid 19th century missionaries brought hand-pumped harmonium to India, where it quickly became popular due to its portability and its low price. Its popularity has stayed intact to the present day, and the harmonium remains an important instrument in many genres of sub-continental music, as well as being commonly found in the homes of music lovers.

I. PIRACHA

Haroon, Abdullah, Sir (1872–1942)

Statesman. Abdullah Haroon was orphaned at the age of four. He was admitted to a *Gujarati vernacular school in Karachi but had to discontinue his studies. It was only after he had begun supporting his family financially that he took admission to the *Sindh Madrassatul-Islam in 1887 but again had to leave in 1888. Joining the office of his brother-in-law in 1887, by 1896, he was able to start his own business. By 1932 he was one of India's leading business magnates. The same year, he was nominated as a delegate to the Imperial Economic Conference at Ottawa and was knighted. Sir Abdullah Haroon entered public life in 1913, when he was elected to the Karachi Municipal Committee. In 1917, he joined both the Indian National Congress and the *All-India Muslim League, which were then allies. By 1918, he was in the thick of the Khilafat Movement, becoming in 1919 President of the Sindh Provincial *Khilafat Committee. In 1920, he launched the Sindh journal *Alwaheed*. He remained President of the Sindh Khilafat Committee up until 1924. In 1927, he became President of the Central Khilafat Committee.

In 1923, Sir Abdullah Haroon was elected to the Bombay Legislative Council and in 1926 he was elected to the Indian Legislative Council. He took an active part in the All-India Muslim Conference, becoming its President in 1929 and in 1935. Sir Abdullah Haroon consistently advocated the separation of Sindh from Bombay. Sir Abdullah Haroon's most important political role came in October 1938, when he organized and presided over the Sindh Muslim League Conference at Karachi, at which the entire All-India Muslim League leadership, including M.A. *Jinnah, were present. Sir Abdullah proposed the division of India between Hindu and Muslim Federations. The Karachi Resolution formed the basis of the *Lahore Resolution. In 1939, Sir Abdullah Haroon became the President of the Sindh Muslim League and organized a large number of branches in the province.

BIBLIOGRAPHY: *Muhammad Ali Shaikh, 'Luminaries of the Land', Karachi, 1999.*

N. AFZAL

Hasan, Fatema (1953–)

Poet. Anis Fatema Zaidi (her real name) obtained her M.A. in Journalism from the University of Karachi in 1976. She works for the provincial government of Sindh. She is a widely respected poet who demonstrated a unique skill and artistry in her second collection. The themes of separation that permeated her first collection have lessened with the passage of time. She now peels layer after layer from her literary topics, exposing the kernel to sensitive yet critical inquiry. Hasan's literary thought stands independent of the conventional. She is courageously outspoken. Hasan does not feel it necessary to conform to popular guidelines.

WORKS: *'Behtay Huway Phool', Karachi, 1997; 'Dastak Se Dar Ka Fasla', Karachi, 1993; 'Kahanian Gum Ho Jati Hain, Karachi, 2000.*

E. DRYLAND

Hasan, Khwaja Sarwar (1902–73)

Statesman. Khwaja Sarwar Hasan was educated at Aligarh and Cambridge and was called to the bar at the Middle Temple. He practised law at Aligarh and later became Professor of Law at Delhi University. He participated in the Pakistan Movement. He became Secretary of the Indian Institute of International Affairs in Delhi in 1944. At the time of partition he shifted the Institute to Karachi with all its movable assets, including its library of rare books. In August 1947, it was established as the Pakistan Institute of International Affairs (PIIA) in Karachi. In 1948 Sarwar Hasan was advisor to the Hyderabad Delegation to the Security Council. In 1955 he became joint secretary of the historic Bandung Conference. He represented Pakistan several times at the United Nations General Assembly and the Security Council. He was advisor to the Constitution Commission in 1961 and Visiting Professor of Government at Columbia University in 1963. On account of his expertise in international affairs, foreign policy, and international law his advice was widely sought in official and academic circles and he represented Pakistan on these issues in conferences and conventions throughout the world. As the founder Secretary of the PIIA he edited the *Pakistan Horizon* for twenty-five years.

WORKS: *'Introducing Pakistan', Karachi, 1948; 'The Genesis of Pakistan', Karachi, 1950; 'Pakistan and the Commonwealth', Karachi, 1950; 'The Strategic Interests of Pakistan', Karachi, 1954; 'Pakistan and the United Nations', New York, 1960.*

M.R. KAZIMI

Hasan, Mahmud-ul, Maulana, Shaykh al-Hind (1850–1920)

Political Activist. A graduate from the **Dar ul-Ulum* in *Deoband, Mahmud-ul Hasan served as its principal from 1888 to 1920. He was the founder of the Muslim organization *Jamiat al-Ansar* in 1909 and helped establish several theological schools in the northwestern region of present-day Pakistan. The *maulana* established contact with the leaders of the Young Turks; in 1915 he met Enver Pasha in Hijaz. He was the leader of the '*Silk Letter Conspiracy' and was arrested in Malta in 1917. The *maulana* was also one of the leaders of the *Khilafat Movement. In 1920, he became the first President of *Jamia Millia Islamia*.

BIBLIOGRAPHY: *Aziz Ahmad, Islam in India, Edinburgh, 1969.*

YU.V. GANKOVSKY

Hasan, Mir Ghulam (1727–87)

Poet. An *Urdu-language poet who belonged to an aristocratic clan that also produced other major poets, e.g., Mir Anis. He was one of the 'four pillars of Urdu poetry' in his time. He held the post of poet laureate and chronicler at the court of the Oudh Nawab. He has to his credit a *Sufi composition *Rumuz-i-Arifin* ('Mysteries of the Initiated'), *Tazkira-i-Shuara-i-Urdu* ('Anthology of Urdu Poetry'), **ghazals*, **qasidas*, **rubai*, and other works. His *magnum opus* is the *masnawi Sehr al-Bayan* ('The Magic of Eloquence'), 1785, which is believed to be a classic in this genre of Urdu poetry and which inspired many imitations and interpretations.

WORKS: *'Sehr al-Bayan', Lahore, 1966; 'Masnawi Sehr al-Bayan, modern edition' Delhi, 1984; Mathnawiyat-i-Mir Hasan, Lahore, 1966.*

BIBLIOGRAPHY: *Wahid Qureshi, 'Mir Hasan aur Unka Zamana', Lahore, 1959; Mahmud Faruqi, 'Mir Hasan aur Khandan ke Dusre Shuara' (Mir Hasan and Other Poets of his Family), Lahore, 1953; R. Russel, 'Khurshid ul-Islam, Three Moghal Poets', Cambridge, 1968.*

A.A. SUVOROVA

Hasan, Shahida (1953–)

Poet. Shahida Hasan's *Urdu poetry has strong lyrical overtones but basically she is a poet with a vision and an undefined ideal. The operative sense of her poetry is visual. Her poetry is fresh but not juvenile. Her short poems drew inspiration from a happy childhood. It is only later that bitter political allusions crept into her poems; otherwise her themes have been more cosmic and her concerns more widespread. Shahida Hasan is an outstanding literary critic as well. She has visited the United States and China and has been the guest of the Virginia Centre for the Creative Artist. She was awarded the 1993 Fani Prize for Urdu Poetry at the World Urdu Conference, New Delhi. She has published one volume of poetry, *Ek Tara hai Sirhane Mere* ('A Star On My Bedstead', Lahore, 1995).

F. MUSHTAQ

Hasan, Syed Sibte (1916–86)

Writer. Sibte Hasan was a writer and social commentator, mostly in the *Urdu language. He was a publicist and an active participant in the Movement of Progressive Writers of India and Pakistan. In the 1940s, Hasan was a correspondent for the *Crossroads* newspaper (organ of the Communist Party of India) in the USA. He was the first to translate the Communist Manifesto into Urdu. In the nineteen fifties and sixties, he was repeatedly arrested for his outspokenly left-wing views. Between 1972 and 1977, he was President of the Pakistan-USSR Friendship Society. He published several literary magazines including *Pakistan Adab* in the seventies. His other publications include *Mazike-ke-mazar,* 1969; *Sukhan dar sukhan,* 1987; his reminiscences about Faiz Ahmad *Faiz; *Musa-se-Marx-tak,* 1976, a historical survey of socialist teachings; *Pakistan-men Tahzib-ka Irtiaq,* and others.

BIBLIOGRAPHY: *'Tulu-i-Afkar journal', April 1988 (a special issue dedicated to Syed Sibte Hasan).*

YU.V. GANKOVSKY

Hasan, Wazir, Justice Syed Sir (1872–1947)

Politician Lawyer. Syed Wazir Hasan belonged to Jaunpur. He was educated at Aligarh and thereafter at Muir College, Allahabad. After graduating in Law, he set up his practice and joined the AIML (*All-India Muslim League) in 1907. He was appointed Joint Secretary, became acting Honorary Secretary on the demise of Aziz Mirza when he moved for changes in the creed and constitution of the AIML. In the December 1912 Annual Session, he was elected Honorary Secretary despite strong opposition from the old Party faction. He changed the creed of the AIML from being a loyalist to an anti-Imperialist party. He played a prominent part in bringing about the *Lucknow Pact. After resigning his Party position, he was elevated to the Bench as puisne judge Oudh Chief Court and retired in 1936 as Chief Justice. In 1936, he presided over the Annual Session of the AIML but, shortly after, joined the Congress. This led to his expulsion from the AIML by the member he had himself inducted, M.A. *Jinnah. Lady Wazir Hasan contested on the Congress ticket in 1937. Ten years later, Sir Wazir Hasan died.

BIBLIOGRAPHY: *Matiur Rahman, 'From Consultation to Confrontation'; M. Saleem Ahmad, 'The All-India Muslim League from the late Nineteenth Century to 1917', Bahawalpur, 1988.*

YU.V. GANKOVSKY

Hashim, Abul (1905–74)

Political Activist. Abul Hashim was born in Burdwan and educated at Calcutta University. He was member of the Bengal Legislative Assembly and member AIML (*All-India Muslim League) since 1937. Abul Hashim became President of the Burdwan Muslim League in 1942; the same year he became Secretary of the Bengal Muslim League, and remained so until independence in 1947. His political creed included a form of Islamic Socialism. When his president (of the Bengal Muslim League and Chief Minister) Husein Shaheed *Suhrawardy moved an amendment to the Lahore Resolution at the AIML Delhi Convention 1946, changing the word from states to state, Abul Hashim lodged a strong protest with *Jinnah, stressing his support for two Muslim majority states. Later, he supported the move for a united and independent Bengal.

WORKS: *'In Restrospection', Dhaka, 1974.*

BIBLIOGRAPHY: *'Draft Constitution of United and Independent Bengal' in: Z.H. Zaidi (ed.), Jinnah Papers, First Series Vol. II; Raghib Ahsan, 'H.S. Suhrawardy and the Inner History of the United Bengal Scheme', Karachi, 1951.*

YU.V. GANKOVSKY

Hashmi, Sayyid Zahur Shah (1926–85)

Poet/Writer. A *Balochi writer, poet, scholar and public figure. Hashmi's work is an important contribution to the development of contemporary *Balochi literature and the Balochi literary language. Particularly noteworthy is his short novel *Nazuk*. In 1983, the Sayyid Hashmi Academy was set up in Karachi. Its president was Ghulam Rasul Mulla, a Balochi poet and literary critic. The Academy is responsible for publishing the Balochi literature of Hashmi and other authors. The Academy is preparing a large dictionary for publication: *Khizana-i-Sayyid* ('Sayyid's Treasures').

WORKS: *'Nazuk', Karachi (s.a).*

V.V. MOSHKALO

Hayat, Sikandar, Sardar Sir (1892–1942)

Statesman. A political figure in *British India and a graduate of the Aligarh and London universities, Sir Sikandar was a major land-owner of northern *Punjab. From 1935 to 1936, he served as Deputy Governor, Reserve Bank of India, and was a member of the Boards of eleven major commercial and industrial companies. Between 1935 and 1942, he served as President of the Punjab National Unionist Party. After signing the Liaquat-Sikandar pact in 1937, under which Muslim members of the Unionist Party could also enjoy membership of the *Muslim League, he was also simultaneously a member of the *All-India Muslim League. From 1937 to 1940, he served as Chief Minister of Punjab. Elevated as Governor Punjab, he died in office in 1942.

BIBLIOGRAPHY: *Lajpat Rai Nair, 'Sir Sikandar Hayat Khan: The Soldier-Statesman of the Punjab', Lahore, 1943.*

YU.V. GANKOVSKY

Heavy Mechanical Complex

The Heavy Mechanical Complex is Pakistan's leading engineering enterprise and forms a unit of the State Engineering Corporation, a holding corporation under the Ministry of Production. The engineering and manufacturing complex comprises two main production units: Mechanical Works, Foundry and Forge Works. Mechanical Works began commercial production in 1971 and Foundry and Forge Works started commercial production in 1978. The major facilities of this integrated complex include design and engineering, fabrication, machine shops, steel foundry, forging, heat treatment, pattern shop, galvanising shop, assembly and tool room and a comprehensive quality assurance set-up in addition to other infrastructure facilities. HMC is manufacturing cement plants, sugar plants, chemical petro-chemical plants, oil and gas processing plants, industrial steam boilers, thermal and hydel power plants, road construction machinery, railway equipment, overhead travelling cranes, chassis for trucks/buses, and general steel structures. The capacity of this complex is however, still underutilized.

T. KHALID

Hidayatullah, Ghulam Husain, Sir (1879–1948)

Statesman. Sir Ghulam Husain was born in Shikarpur and had his early education from Shikarpur High School and then went on to the Sindh Madrasah. He graduated from D.J. College, Karachi in 1901and took his LLB from Government Law School, Bombay, in 1903. In 1904, He was elected Vice-President of the Hyderabad Municipality and was the first non-official President of the Hyderabad Local Board. As a member of the Bombay Legislative Council (1912–20), he gave evidence before the Royal Commission on Public Services.

Sir Ghulam Husain Hidayatullah was nominated to the Bombay Legislative Council in 1923 and was a member of the Governor's Executive Council from 1928, later its Vice-President. He was made Knight Commander of the Star of India in 1933. As a delegate to the *Round Table Conference, he strongly pleaded for the separation of *Sindh from Bombay. Sir Ghulam Husain was nominated member of the Council of State (June to December 1934) and in 1935 he became a member of the Independent Party led by M.A. *Jinnah, at which time he was a member of the Indian Legislative Council.

After the 1937 provincial elections, Sir Ghulam Husain became the first Chief Minister of Sindh but soon his government was defeated by a combination of G.M. *Syed, Khan Bahadur Allah Bux Soomro and Congress Legislators. Sir Ghulam Husain Hidayatullah rejoined the AIML in 1938 and attended the October 1938 Sindh Muslim League Session held at the Eidgah Maidan, Karachi.

After endorsing the Sindh Muslim League Resolution on the division of India, he left the AIML the next year to join the cabinet of Allah Bux Soomro and denounced the 23 March 1940 Resolution. Sir Ghulam Husain rejoined the AIML in 1942, forming a new cabinet on 22 October and in 1943, he supported the resolution tabled by G.M. Syed that upheld the principles of the *Lahore Resolution. In 1945, he was a delegate to the *Simla Conference.

At the advent of the 1945-46 elections, the differences between Sir Ghulam Husain Hidayatullah as Chief Minister of Sindh and G.M. Syed as President Sindh Muslim League ultimately led to the expulsion of the latter from the AIML. After the foundation of Pakistan, he was appointed Governor of Sindh. He was in office when he died.

BIBLIOGRAPHY: *D.A. Pirzada, 'Growth of Muslim Nationalism in Sindh. Interview Ghazanfar Hidayatullah', Quaid-i-Azam Papers, Islamabad.*

YU.V. GANKOVSKY

Himalayas

(Himalayan Mountains; in Sanskrit: 'the snow abode') The world's highest mountain range, it divides central Asia from South Asia. Its borders are the Indus-Ganges Plain in the south and the Tibet Plateau in the north. The Himalayas are shaped like a bow stretching towards the south for more than 2,500 km. They cross the territories of Pakistan, India, Nepal, Bhutan, and China. The Nanga Parbat Range (8,126 metres), is considered to be the western extremity of the Himalayas, while the eastern extremity is the mount of Namchabarva (7,765 metres). The two great Asian rivers, the *Indus in the west and the Brahmaputra in the east, are the natural borders of the Himalayas.

Geologically, the Himalayas are a complex fold-mountain system that formed in the southern outskirts of the ancient ocean Tethys, in the epoch of the Alpine orogenesis. The rock composition includes pre-Cambrian metamorphoida: gneisses, crystalline schists. The northern slopes are composed of sedimentary rocks of later eras. In the foothills, and partly in the lower sections of the mountains, these rocks are covered with sedimentary deposits.

The Himalayas have a terraced structure. Three parallel belts of mountain ranges of differing heights can be identified. They all have steep southern slopes and a relatively gentle slope northward, and are known as the Cis-Himalayas, the Small Himalayas, and the Great Himalayas. The *Karakoram Range is often seen as the fourth belt. In Pakistani territory, we find the Cis-Himalayas and individual foothills of the Small Himalayas.

The Great Himalayas are the highest belt, approximately 50 to 90 km. wide, with an average height of about 6,000 metres. The ten highest Himalayan peaks, all exceeding 8,000 metres, including Jomolungma and Mount Everest, the world's highest peak, are in this belt. The entire area under ice is more than 33,000 sq.km., with glaciers stretching up to 32 km.

The Smaller Himalayas, the next range towards the south, are approximately 80 to 95 km. wide and of medium height; from 2,500 to 4,000 metres such as Pir-Panjal, Dhaoladhar, Mahabharat and Daury.

The Cis-Himalayas occupy the southern edge of the Himalayas and are a widely scattered foothill zone approximately 30 to 50 km. wide with peaks higher than 1,200 metres. Included in the Cis-Himalayas are the *Salt Range, *Potwar Plateau, Siwalik Range, Dundva Range, and Churiag-Khati.

The Himalayas form a natural barrier preventing the equatorial monsoons of South Asia reading the highland Tibetan deserts. The mean monthly temperatures, on the southern slopes up to 3,000 metres high, remain above zero centigrade all year round. The daily temperatures vary greatly, sometimes rising up to 45°C. The snowline ranges from 4,500 metres in the east to 5,300 metres in the west. Precipitation diminishes from 2,500-5,500 mm annually in the east to 1,000 mm in the west). The northern slopes have a cold, dry climate with an average of 100 mm precipitation annually, characteristic of mountain deserts. The daily temperatures vary greatly, sometimes ranging up to 45ºC. The eternal snow line lies at 5,500-6000 metres.

All the largest South Asian rivers, such as the Indus, the Ganges, the Brahmaptura, and the *Sutlej flow from the northern slopes of the Himalayas, cutting through the entire system. The rivers are mostly fed by melting snow and glaciers. They flood in the summer spate. The rich power potential is, to date, under-utilised.

Almost all the highland landscape flora varieties are represented; evergreen sub-equatorial and oak woods, coniferous forests, stunted forests, and alpine meadows. Foothills and mountain valleys are intensively cultivated and many areas are terraced. Timber cutting is extensive. Copper, bauxites, gold, chromites, and sapphires are among other minerals that are mined.

S.B. ROSTOTSKY

Hindi (also Hindavi/Hindustani)

Hindi belongs to the *Indo-Aryan group of languages, a subset of the Indo-European family. It has been influenced and enriched by Persian, Turkish, Farsi, Arabic, Portuguese, and English. Hindi is broadly identical with *Urdu, the official language of Pakistan, and is closely related to Bengali, *Punjabi and *Gujarati. The script, Devanagari, is extremely logical and therefore straightforward and easy to learn. The general appearance of the Devanagari script is that of letters 'hanging from a line'. This 'line', also found in many other South Asian scripts, is actually a part of most of the letters and is drawn as the writing proceeds. The script has no capital letters.

Hindi is the official language of the Republic of India, and the common second language of Mauritius, Fiji, Trinidad, Guyana and Surinam.

BIBLIOGRAPHY: *G.H. Fairbanks, B.G. Misra, 'Spoken and Written Hindi' 1966; A. Rai, 'A House Divided: The Origin and Development of Hindi-Hindavi', 1985.*

G.A. ZOGRAF

Hindu Kush

This is the westernmost of the three major mountain systems in northern Pakistan, forming a barrier between the Indus and the Amu-Darya Valleys. The Hindi Kush is approximately 800 km. long from the west-south-west to the east-north-east. The system, at its widest, ranges from 50 to 350 km. The average height of the mountains is 4,500 meters above sea level. The highest peak, Trichmir, is 7,690 meters.

The name, which translates into 'Hindu Killer', is believed to derive from the fact that many Indians used to perish here on their perilious journey from southern Asia to Central Asia. According to another version it comes from the Persian meaning 'Indian Mountain'. The principal ranges are Baba, Pagman, and the Hindu Kush proper, as well as the *Hinduraj. The latter is divided into the western, central and eastern Hindu Kush by the valleys of the Surkhab and the Kokcha rivers. Formerly the Parapamiz Mountains, the western branch of the Hindu Kush, were also considered part of the Hindu Kush and in ancient times the name Parapamiz was applied to the entire Hindu Kush mountain system.

The high alpine-desert plateaus to the east, with their typical alpine relief with characteristic sharp peaks, and deep longitudinal and lattitudinal faults and valleys, give way to more moderate, round-topped mountains towards the west. The main mountain passes are Shibar (3,260 meters) and Salang (4,075 meters). The lowest mountain pass in the high desert area is Baroghil Mountain at approximately 3,777 metres above sea level. The Baroghil Pass is accessible for pack-saddle transport for only eight months of the year. The snow line lies at 5,000 metres. Glaciers and ice cover some 6,200 sq.km.

The Hindu Kush massif is a complex system of block mountains, called horst-anticlinarium in geological terms, that formed in the era of alpine building. Predominant in the rock composition are pre-Cambrian and Palaeozoic metamorphides, and Mesocainozoic sedimentary rocks. The Hindu Kush is a highly seismic area, rich in coal, high-quality iron and ores containing a variety of metals. There are occasional deposits of gold, lazurite, brimstone, graphite and other minerals.

The climate of the Hindu Kush is subtropical. The windward north-western slopes receive 400-800 mm. precipitation annually. At an altitude of 1,800 metres the dry steppes of the foothills are replaced with a belt of forest-steppe. Above 2,500 metres there are pine or mixed forests. Still higher there are alpine meadows and an eternal snow zone. The leeward south-eastern slopes are very dry with less than 300 mm. precipitation annually.

The vegetation consists of semi-desert plants and prickly shrubbery. The fauna is represented by various central Asian and mountain Indo-Himalayan species.

S.B. ROSTOTSKY

Hinduraj Range

This range in the *Hindu Kush system lies in the extreme north of Pakistan, between the valleys of the Rivers *Mastuj (Yarkhun) and *Swat. The length of the range from north-east to south-west is about 400 km., with an average height of 6,500-7,000 metres. Southwards the average height drops to 5,000-6,900 metres. On the northern and southern slopes there are a number of high glaciers, for example Chiantar. The longest, at 33 km., descends into the valley of the Yarkhun to an altitude of 3,800 metres. The lower northern slopes are covered with grass, and occasional copses of pistachio trees on grey soils. On the damp western slopes there are deciduous woods to height of approximately 2,500 meters above sea level. Evergreen woods extend up to 3,300 meters and above these coniferous or mixed forests extend up to 3,700 meters. At higher elevations, sub-alpine vegetation is to be found. The Darkot pass through the range is approximately 4,575 meters above sea level and is situated in an often inaccessible glacier-clad region where there are snowstorms in both the winter and the summer. The footpath through the pass connects the valleys of the Yasin and the Yarkhun rivers leading eventually to *Chitral. The path is only passable for draught animals from the mid-June to mid-September.

M.YU. MOROZOVA

Hindustani

Musical tradition along with Karnataka it is one of the most important players in the musical culture of South Asia. It is a classical tradition in the music of north India, Pakistan, and Bangladesh. Its separation from the south Indian (Karnataka) tradition in the twelfth-thirteenth centuries was largely prepared by development and links with the musical traditions of the Near and Middle East, and later also by the Hindu-Muslim cultural synthesis. The early period in the development of classical Hindustani art was linked with the name of the outstanding poet and musician Amir Khusro *Dehlawi (thirteenth century). A new type of sound-musical expression evolved in his work, the main musical genres developed, and the functions of the musical instruments in the Hindustani tradition became established. A great contribution to the process of the formation of Hindustani music was made by the remarkable musicians Baiju Bawra, Subhan Khan, Swami Haridas, and Mian Tan Sen (sixteenth century). These musicians actually gave birth to the genre system in the Hindustani tradition.

Until the eighteenth century, the classical Hindustani tradition was primarily represented by vocal music (the **dhrupad* and **khiyal* genres); in the eighteenth and nineteenth centuries, instrumental music began to develop. In this period, a new, semi-classical or light-classical type of Hindustani music evolved; it generated a great many styles and genre varieties: **thumri*, *dadra*, *tappa*, **ghazal*, etc., which spread in various parts of South Asia, and some of them beyond its boundaries-in Southeast Asia, in the Near and Middle East, and in central Asia. In the twentieth century, after a long period of isolated development of the Hindustani and Karnataka traditions as two largely different directions in the musical culture of South Asia, a tendency became apparent towards increasing mutual interest, intersection, and interaction. This was expressed, in the first place, in the fairly active exchange of information between the two schools and forms of concert practice, partly conditioned by their involvement in the system of world musical art.

I. PIRACHA

Hookah (also Huqqa)

A smoking device, a variety of a *nargileh*, popular in South Asia. The smoke passes through water whereby it is partially purified. A *hookah* consists of a water container, tobacco box, and two pipes. One of the pipes connects both containers and is immersed in the water, the other is stuck into the water-container without reaching the water. Its free end has a mouth-piece. *Hookahs* differ in size and shape. The two main types resemble a hand held smoking pipe and a free standing pipe. The latter has a solid bell-shaped support which serves as a water container. There is a short neck in the upper part of the support-container into which both pipes are inserted. The inhaling pipe is connected to a flexible tube. The *hookah* is a favourite object of decoration for various artists and craftsmen. *Hookahs* are mainly made of metal. In Lahore, leather *hookahs* are made and decorated with stylish designs. The aristocracy uses *hookahs* made of precious metals such as silver studded with precious stones, and sometimes transparent glass. The main decorative pieces are supports and mouthpieces often shaped as small sculptures. *Hookahs* sometimes feature medieval miniature paintings and are a typical object of everyday life.

E.V. GANEVSKAYA

Howar (also Khowar)

A group of related languages dating back to the Old Indian language; together with Dardic and Iranian languages, they are descendants of the Indo-Iranian language community which is part of the Indo-European family of languages.

Indian languages are spoken in northern and central India (Hindi, *Urdu, *Bengali, *Punjabi, Marathi, *Gujarati, Oriya, Assami, *Sindhi and others), Pakistan (Urdu, Punjabi, Sindhi), Bangladesh (Bengali), Sri Lanka (Sinhala, in the south of the island), Maldive Republic (Divehi), Nepal (Nepali), Gypsy and Parya (a dialect spoken in the Gissar Valley of Tajikistan). In all, approximately 770 million people speak *Indo-Aryan languages. In the west and north-west, Indian languages border or Iranian (*Balochi, *Pushtu) and Dardic languages; in the north and north-east, with Tibetan and *Himalayan languages; in the east, with a number of Tibetan-Burmese and Mon-Khmer languages; in the south, with *Dravidian languages (Telugu, Kannada). In India, a few islands of other linguistic groups (Munda, Mon-Khmer, Dravidian and other languages) exist surrounded by the Indian languages.The oldest period in the development of Indo-Aryan languages is represented by the Vedic language that functioned since the early twelfth century BC and several literary varieties of Sanskrit (the epic variety of the third and second centuries BC, the epigraphic variety of the first centuries of the new era, and classical Sanskrit which flourished in the fourth and fifth centuries of the new era). A few Indo-Aryan words from a dialect different from the Vedic (names of gods and kings and a few terms from horse-breeding) are recorded since the sixteenth century BC in what is known as Mittanian *Aryan in documents from Asia Minor and Near Asia.The Middle Indian period, in the development of Indo-Aryan languages, was represented by numerous languages and dialects used in spoken and later, written forms in the middle of the first millennium BC. The most archaic of these was Pali (the language of the Buddhist Canon), followed by the Prakrits (the Prakrits of inscriptions are the more archaic ones) and Apabhransha (the dialects that evolved from the first millennium AD through the development of the Prakrits); they are a transitional stage of modern Indian languages.

BIBLIOGRAPY: *G.A. Zograph, 'Languages of South Asia', Moscow, 1990 (in Russian); id., 'The Morphological Structure of New Indo-Aryan Languages', Moscow, 1976 (in Russian); T.Ya. Yelizarenkova, 'Studies in the Diachronic Phonology of Indo-Aryan Languages', Moscow, 1974 (in Russian); 'Languages of Asia and Africa', Vol. I. Indo-Aryan Languages, Moscow, 1976 (in Russian); J. Beames, 'A Comparative Grammar of the Modern Aryan Languages of India: to Wit, Hindi, Punjabi, Sindhi. Gujarati, Marathi, Oriya and Bengali', Vols. 1-3, London, 1872-9; R. Hoernle, 'A Comparative Grammar of the Gaudian Languages', London, 1880; G.A. Grierson, 'Linguistic Survey of India', Vols. 1-11, Calcutta, 1903-28; T.G. Bailey, 'Studies in North Indian Languages', London, 1938; J. Baloch, 'Indo-Aryan from the Vedas to Modern Times', Paris, 1965; R.L. Turner, 'A Comparative Dictionary of the Indo-Aryan Languages', London, 1962-9.*

T.YA. YELIZARENKOVA

Hub River

(In antique sources: Arbis or Arbios) This river has its source in the north-south lying Kirtha Range to the north of Karachi. The river is 400 km. long. In its lower reaches it crosses the eastern end of the *Lasbela district. A barrage almost five kilometers long contains the water of the Hub, from where the river provides part of the water supply for the city of Karachi. The shallow lake behind the dam is a haven for wildlife, especially migratory birds. What is left of the river below the dam flows into the Arabian Sea to the west of Karachi.

YU.V. GANKOVSKY

Hur

(Arabic: *hurr*—free, independent) A Muslim sect founded in the 1820s in northern *Sindh by Sayyid Ahmad Barelwi (1786–1831). The sect was ruled by the Pir Pagaros (Turbaned *Pirs). The ideas of social equality and the anticolonial struggle attracted thousands of peasants and craftsmen into the sect. The activities of the sect were kept in strict secrecy, and were based on severe discipline and self-sacrifice. *Hurs* staged uprisings against the British rule in 1883, 1896-1908, 1930-1, 1941-3, in an attempt to establish an independent Sindh state. In 1965, the *Hurs* took an active part in the armed conflict between India and Pakistan.

YU.V. GANKOVSKY

Husain, Altaf (1953–)

Political activist from Karachi. He first founded the All Pakistan Muhajir Students Association (APMSO) at the University of Karachi Campus in 1986.

This was in the background of a discriminatory legislation against **Muhajirs* (Migrants from India) which constricted theirs entries to professional educational institutes offering engineering and medical education courses as well as a rural/urban employment recruitment formula which was peculiar to only *Sindh province.

There was ethnic violence in Karachi between the Pathan transporters and *Muhajir* passengers specially in the wake of the Bushra Zaidi case in 1983. Simultaneously there had been sectarian riots in Karachi, during which stressing the ethnic rather than the sectarian identity. The *Muhajir Qaumi* Movement (see, *Muttahida Qaumi* Movement) was formed on 18 March 1984. Thereafter, whenever the MQM stood for elections in the urban areas of Sindh, it won by a wide margin displacing the otherwise popular religious parties.

On 1 January 1992 Altaf Husain left for Jeddah enroute to London where he now permanently resides. On 19 June 1992, the first army operation against the MQM was launched in the wake of which a parallel organisation was formed. He converted the MQM from *Muhajir Qaumi* Movement to *Muttahida Qaumi* Movement, to accommodate members from other ethnic groups. He still holds considerable political influence and power despite his self-exile.

M.R. KAZIMI

Husain, Fazle, Mian Sir (1877–1936)

Politician. With a Masters degree from Cambridge University, Sir Fazle Husain was called to the Bar at Gray's Inn. Returning to India, he worked as Professor and Principal, Islamia College, Lahore (1907–8) and then as Syndic, University of the Punjab (1912–21). He was President of the All-India Mohammedan Educational Conference in 1922. Entering politics, he was elected to the Punjab Legislative Council in 1920 and became Minister for Education, *Punjab, in 1921. He served as Member (for Education) Viceroy's Executive Council, Member Indian delegation to League of Nations, delegate to *Round Table Conferences and Vice-President Governor-General's Council (1934).

Sir Fazle Husain started a party called the *Muslim League in 1905. Later, it came to be known as the 'Progressive' Muslim League. In 1923, he co-founded with Sir Chotu Ram the Punjab National Unionist Party, later to be called simply the Unionist Party. The creed of Sir Fazle Husain was loyalty to the British, to strive for the statutory majority of Muslims in the Punjab, provincial autonomy and promotion of the feudal class. All these considerations led him to organise the Unionist Party on intercommunal lines, along with Hindus and *Sikhs. This cooperation enabled him to counteract moneylenders and re-inforce the protective Land Alienation Act 1900 as well as to keep all-India Parties like the Congress and the Muslim League out of Punjab.

Sir Fazle Husain's simultaneous opposition to weightage and support to separate electorates led him to adopt an equivocal attitude to the *Lucknow Pact and of hostility to the *Delhi Muslim Proposals. In 1931, however, he was prepared to consider joint electorates, provided that the Muslim majority in Punjab and *Bengal was guaranteed. He co-founded with Sir Mohammad *Shafi the All-India Muslim Conference, which favoured cooperation with the Simon Commission. The All-India Muslim Conference co-sponsored the *Fourteen Points but preferred an intercommunal Unionist party and rebuffed the efforts of M.A. *Jinnah to form a parliamentary party of the AIML in the Punjab. This led to the defeat of the AIML in the Punjab provincial elections of 1937.

WORKS: *'Our Political Programme', Lahore, 1930; (ed.) Waheed Ahmad, 'Letters of Mian Fazle-Husain', Lahore, 1967; Id. 'Diary and Notes of Mian Fazle-Husain, Lahore, 1976; Mian Sir Fazle-Husain Papers', I.O.L. MSSEUR-E352, London.*

BIBLIOGRAPHY: *Sayyid Nur Ahmad, 'Mian Fazle-Husain', Lahore, 1935; Azim Husain, 'Fazle-Husain', Lahore, 1946.*

YU.V. GANKOVSKY

Husain, Intizar (1925–)

Writer. Intizar Husain is a novelist and short story writer in the *Urdu language. Born near Bulandshahar in Uttar Pradesh, he was educated in Meerut, India, before migrating to Lahore, Pakistan, in 1947.

His earlier collections of stories *Gali-Koche* ('Streets and Alleyways', 1951) and *Kankri* ('Pebbles', 1955) are marked with nostalgia for the split country. His later works included the novels *Basti* ('Little Town', 1980) and *Tazkire* ('Lies', 1987), and collections of stories *Akhiri Adami* ('The Last Man', 1967), *Shahr-i-Afsos* ('Wretched Town', 1972), and *Kachhwe* ('Turtles', 1981). Mythological elements, parable-like plots, rich symbolism, allusions and allegories make his work difficult. Yet the writer had considerable influence on the younger generation of Urdu writers and contributed to the renovation of contemporary Urdu prose. Intizar Husain also has a collection of literary criticism to his credit: *Alamat ka Zawal*, 1983 ('The Decline of Symbols').

BIBLIOGRAPHY: *R.A. Elizarova, A.S. Sukhochev, 'Pakistan's Progressive Writers', Tashkent, 1978 (in Russian); 'Urdu Afsana Riwayat aur Masail' (Urdu Short Story, Traditions and Problems), Compiled by N. Narang, Delhi, 1981; 'Naya Urdu Afsana' (The New Urdu Short Story), Compiled by G. Narang, Delhi, 1988.*

A.S. SUKHOCHEV

Husain, Mahmood, Dr. (1907–75)

Scholar/Statesman. He was a historian, an educationist, a public figure and a state official of Pakistan. His brother, Zakir Husain, became President of India. Mahmood Husain studied at the universities of Aligarh and Delhi, and received his Doctorate from Heidelberg University (Germany) in 1932. He taught modern history and the history of international relations at the University of Dhaka (1933-48) and was elected to the first *Constituent Assembly (1946). He held several government positions: Deputy Minister for Defence and for the States and Frontier Regions of Pakistan (1949); Deputy Minister for Foreign Affairs and Commonwealth Relations, for Finance and for Economic Affairs and also for Kashmir (1950-53). He was Dean of the Faculty of History (1953-74) and Vice-Chancellor of the University of Karachi (1974-75). He launched and edited the multivolume *History of the Freedom Movement* (Karachi, 1957-70).

YU.V. GANKOVSKY

Hussain, Shujaat, Chaudry (1945–)

Statesman. Son of the well-known political figure Chaudry Zahur Ilahi (assassinated in 1981), Chaudry Shujaat Hussain graduated from the Forman Christian College, Lahore, and pursued post-graduate studies at Government College, Lahore. Thereafter, he went to Britain and obtained a Diploma in Industrial Management from Watford College of Technology, London.

In 1977, he took charge of his family business and initiated his political career. He was a candidate for election to the Provincial Assembly of the *Punjab in 1977 but, since his party, the *Pakistan National Alliance (PNA), decided to boycott the elections, he withdrew. Chaudry Shujaat served in Ziaul *Haq's nominated *Majlis-e-Shoora* in 1982. He was elected as member of the National Assembly from Gujrat in the 1985, 1990, 1997 and 2002 general elections. In 1993, he was elected as a Senator.

From January to December 1986, he served as Minister of Information and Broadcasting; from June 1986 he served (at first concurrently with above) as Minister for Industries until December 1988. He again held the Industries portfolio from August to November 1990.

Chaudry Shujaat Hussain was elected President of the *Pakistan Muslim League, Quaid-e-Azam Group (Q) on 16 November 2002. Following the resignation of Mir Zafarullah Jamali, Chaudry Shujaat Hussain was sworn in as the nineteenth Prime Minister of Pakistan on 30 June 2004. As per prior arrangement, he surrendered the office of Prime Minister three months later to Mr Shaukat *Aziz.

RAFIUDDIN

Hussein, Akmal, Dr. (1951–)

Economist. Dr. Akmal Hussain is a Pakistani economist who defended his doctorate thesis in Cambridge (Britain). He is Director of UN/ILO on South Asian Social Challenge and lecturer at the University of the *Punjab as well as the author of many works.

WORKS: *'Strategic Issues in Pakistan's Economic Policy', Lahore, 1988.*

V.YA. BELOKRENITSKY

Hyder, Qurratulain (1927–)

Writer. An *Urdu novelist and short story writer and a public figure, is the daughter of the famous writer Sajjad Hyder Yaldram. She graduated from Lucknow University and in 1947 moved to Pakistan, then lived in England before returning to India in 1951. She has been writing since she was 11 years old. Her main theme is the intellectual's role in the fast-moving modern world. Her early work is dominated by romantic tendencies: *Sitaron ke Age* ('Beyond the Stars'), 1947, a collection of stories; the novels *Mere bhi Sanamkhane* ('My Temples Too'), 1949 and *Safina-i-Gham-i-Dil* ('Boat of Heartache'), 1952. Hyder's later work leaned towards realism. Her work is noted for a wide range of original themes and intonations, marked by Muslim aristocratism and refinement: the novel *Aag ka Daryaa* ('River of Fire', 1959); *Patjar ki Awaz* ('The Voice of Autumn', 1965); *Roushni ki Raftar* ('The Speed of Light', 1982); the short novel *Chae ke Bagh* ('Tea Plantations', 1965); and the family chronicle *Kare Jahan Daraz He* ('The World's Travails are Long'). Her work represents an Indo-Muslim cultural synthesis with elements of Western aesthetics. She is the winner of several literary prizes, including the *Bharatiya Gnanpith*

(1989), India's highest literary award, for her book *River of Fire*.

BIBLIOGRAPHY: *Tulu-i-Afkar, ed. Husain Anjum, Karachi, 1988.*

L.A. VASILYEVA

Hyder, Sajjad (1920–2000)

Statesman. A career diplomat, Sajjad Hyder served as Pakistan's Ambassador to Iraq, Egypt, West Germany, the Netherlands and was the High Commissioner to India. From June 1975 until November 1978, he served as Ambassador to the Soviet Union. He became President of the Pakistan-Soviet Friendship Society in 1990.

WORKS: *'The Foreign Policy of Pakistan', Lahore, 1987.*

YU.V. GANKOVSKY

I

Ibrahim, Mirza Muhammad (1910–)

Political Activist. A trade union activist and political figure in *British India and Pakistan, Mirza Ibrahim was a railroad engineer by training and worked in the railroad shops in Moghalpura. From 1941 to 1947 and from 1948 to 1979, he headed the Trade Union of North-West Railroad Workers, and was a member of the Communist Party of *Pakistan from 1948 to 1954. He became President of the Pakistan Trade Union Federation and was elected President of the Pakistan Workers' Party at the Lahore Conference on 9 October 1972. Mirza Ibrahim was repeatedly arrested and in 1951 he was arrested in connection with the Rawalpindi Conspiracy case.

YU.V. GANKOVSKY

Iftikharuddin, Muhammad, Mian (1908–62)

Politician. Mian Iftikharuddin graduated from the Punjab University in Lahore and later received a degree from Oxford. In 1937, he was elected to the Punjab Legislative Assembly as a member of the Indian National Congress. He was a founder member of the Congress Socialist Party in 1938. In 1945, he joined the *Muslim League. Mian Sahib served as a Member of the *Constituent Assembly from 1947 to 1954 and from 1955–56. From 1947 to 1948, he was Minister for Refugee Rehabilitation in the *Punjab government. He was also founder and leader of the Azad Pakistan Party from 1950 to 1956 and one of the founders and leaders of the National Awami Party of Pakistan from 1956 to 1958.

YU.V. GANKOVSKY

Ijma

(from Arabic: *ajmaa* 'to decide together') A joint unanimous decision of a group of authoritative Muslim theologians (called **mujtahids*) on disputed issues of Muslim law and also of social or religious life.

YU.V. GANKOVSKY

Ijtihad

(from Arabic: 'Zeal', from *jahada* 'to show zeal') The study of higher theological knowledge and the ability to put it into practice. *Ijtihad* is also the passing of a decision or judgement by an authoritative theologian (see **mujtahid*), or group of theologicans, on debatable issues of Muslim law or social or religious life, on the basis of the Quran, comments on the Quran (*Tafsirs*), and other sources of law. (See also **Ijma*).

YU.V. GANKOVSKY

Imam

(Arabic: 'forerunner', 'precursor') A person conducting the daily Muslim prayers; a keeper of a mosque. It is the term for leader or head of a Musim community (**umma*) (see, *Imamat).

YU.V. GANKOVSKY

Imam, Syed Husain (1897–1985)

Statesman. Syed Husain Imam was born in Gaya and was educated at the Imperial College of Science and Technology, London. On his return home, he entered politics by becoming a member of the Gaya Municipal Corporation. In 1930, he was elected to the Council of State. In 1932, he became the leader of the *All-India Muslim League in the Council and the leader of the opposition. He was a member of the AIML Working Committee after the retirement of Syed Abdul *Aziz. After the creation of Pakistan, he became Chairman of the House Building Finance Corporation (1954–59). For years he was regarded as an elder statesman of Pakistan.

YU.V. GANKOVSKY

Imamat

(Arabic: 'the place where the Imam is', the title and obligations of the Imam') The supreme authority and leadership in a Muslim community or Muslim state. Among *Sunni Muslims, the *Imamat* is ideally implemented by an elected individual who has both secular and religious authority. Among *Shia Muslims, the *Imamat* is a divine institution handed down from generation to generation to the descendants of Ali, the cousin and son-in-law of the Prophet Muhammad (PBUH), husband of his daughter Fatima.

The Quran (XI: 124) mentions *Imamat* being granted to Abraham. According to XVII: 71, all people will be summoned on the Day (of Judgement) with their Imams. Thus, the *Imamat* has a spiritual connotation, not merely leadership of the community.

YU.V. GANKOVSKY

Imami (also Imaimya)

(Arabic: Imam; also: *Ithna Ashriya*) The Imami is one of the basic sects in *Shia Islam. The term also applies to followers of the Twelve *Imams, and the **madhab* of the sixth Shia Imam Jafar ibn-Muhammad as-Sadiq (*c*.700-65), or the Jafarite *madhab*, as well as *Fiqh-i Jafariah*. It has been the official religion in Iran since the 16th century. In Pakistan, Imami is the largest active Shia sect to take part in the country's political life.

YU.V. GANKOVSKY

Imroz

An *Urdu newspaper with a circulation of 50,000 which is published in Pakistan. It began operating in 1948 in Lahore; in 1964 a second publication was opened in Multan. The newspaper, founded by Mian Iftikharuddin, had as its first editor-in-chief *Faiz Ahmad Faiz (1948-51), who was followed by Ahmad Nadim *Qasmi (1951-58). Following the 1958 *coup d'état* the newspaper was largely controlled by the military administration. Mujibur Rahman Shami was installed as the paper's editor-in-chief. It went bankrupt and was shut down in early 1991.

SHAHNAWAZ

Inam

(Arabic: a gift or award) A form of land ownership in medieval South Asia; the lands allotted to religious and charitable institutions, religious activists, and also as an award to military commanders and government officials. *Inam*-owner, *inamdar,* did not pay government taxes and his lands were crossed out from state tax registers. In the colonial times, most of the *inams* were abolished and their owners were made to pay taxes on land.

BIBLIOGRAPHY: *K.Z. Ashrafyan, The Delhi Sultanate, Moscow, 1960 (in Russian); Irfan Habib, The Agrarian System of Mughal India, Aligarh, 1963.*

L.B. ALAYEV

Inayatullah, Attiya (1936–)

Statesperson. Attiya Inayatullah is a veteran member of Pakistan's Central Legislature. In recognition of her prominence as a social worker, she was appointed Adviser (1981–85) to the President of Pakistan for population welfare and women's affairs. In 1985, she was made minister of state in the same Ministry from 1985 to 1986. During 2000–02, she was appointed Minister for Women's Development, Social Welfare and Special Education. From 1982 to 2000 she attended numerous international conferences dealing with family planning, status of women, child survival and environmental issues. To honour her contribution, the UNESCO elected her chairperson for 1994–95; and since 1999 she has been a member of UNESCO's Executive Board. She has received numerous awards from Pakistani and international organizations including the Rotary International, the United Nations and Human Rights Society of Pakistan.

H. MALIK

Incrustation or inlaid work

This is mostly connected with the Muslim tradition in South Asia. Incrustation flourished during the *Mughal empire. In architecture, inlays in marble on red sandstone were first made in the *Delhi Sultanate period (thirteenth-fourteenth centuries). Under Akbar, inlays in semiprecious stones on marble became widespread. The best works in this style were created under Shah Jahan. Inlaid ornaments are characteristic of Muslim culture: arabesques, panels with pictures of trees and birds, geometrical, and floral designs. Shellac was used as reinforcement in inlays. The surface was carefully polished. A cheaper kind of inlay existed in the Mughal period; namely, mosaics of mirrors and coloured glass on walls covered with plaster.

The most common type of inlays found in decorative applied art were ivory incrustations in wood, and in coloured varieties of wood and brass wire. Pieces of furniture and various household objects were inlaid, especially boxes and caskets, as well as musical instruments. The objects were made of heavy varieties of hardwood, mahogany, and ebony. Inlays in particoloured varieties of wood are reminiscent of marquetry. The best works in this technique are manufactured in the *Punjab. At the beginning of the nineteenth century a new technique came from Iran of inlays on ivory, painted horn and wood, combined with carved panels and ivory plates.

Legend links inlaid metalwork or *koftgari* with the name of the well-known *Sufi, Haji Muinuddin Chishti (1326-1411). Inlaid metalwork declined in popularity during the Mughal period. Especially difficult was incrustation on steel objects, including damask steel of which weapons and armour were made. Steel was inlaid with gold. The surface of the object was polished with agate and cleaned with lemon juice. The main centres of the manufacture of these objects were Delhi and Lahore. All these types of inlays are still practised.

E.V. GANEVSKAYA

Indo-Aryans

See, Arya.

Indo-Aryan Writing Systems

The name for an extensive group of South and South-east Asian writing systems linked by a community of origin and a uniform (phonetic) principle of alphabet structure. Apart from their native country India, variations of Indian writing systems were, and still are, widespread in neighbouring areas such as Tibet and Central Asia as far as Mongolia in the north, and Sri Lanka, Myanmar, on the peninsula of Indo-China, Indonesia and the Philippines in the south-east. Indian writing systems spread to neighbouring countries in the first and early second millennium largely due to the spreading of Buddhism and associated literature and writings.

Writing systems in South Asia are approximately five thousand years old. The oldest type of writing system is represented by the hieroglyphic inscriptions of the *Harappan civilization (third millennium BC). The Kharoshthi or Indo-Bactrian writing system emerged in India at this time, surviving until the third century AD. Kharosh was written right to left and can be traced back to Aramaeic script. Simultaneously, the Brahmi syllabic system functioned in India. Brahmi was of local origin and served as the source of all later proper Indian writing systems. Like Kharoshthi, it was written left to right. Even the earliest monuments in Brahim (third century BC to fifth century AD) show signs of differences between its local styles. On this basis, two main branches of Indian writing systems evolved, northern and southern. The latter gave rise to a third, the south-eastern. The following principal kinds of writing are singled out in the northern branch. Their alphabets are marked by angular shapes of letters with straight vertical and horizontal strokes: 1. Siddhamatrika, known from monuments of the sixth and seventh centuries in the territory of modern Bihar; 2. Vertical and slanting Central Asian Brahmi (also called *Gupta Script), used to record texts in Sanskrit, Saka, Kuchean and other languages; from the sixth to the tenth century in Central Asia; 3. Tibetan writing, evolved in the seventh century and is still used in several varieties, including the canonical *dwo-can* and the cursive (*dwu-med*); 4. The Nagari script, which developed in the seventh and eighth centuries (the monumental type) and was first recorded in MSS in the tenth and eleventh centuries; 5. A later derived script from of Nagari called Devanagari, which now occupies a central place among the alphabets of North India and is used for Hindi, Marathi, and some other languages of South Asia and their dialects, as well as for recording and publication of Sanskrit texts; 6. Sharada, which has been in use in *Kashmir since the eighth century, 7. Nevari has been used since the twelfth century and is a Nepali writing system, now giving way to Devanagari; 8. Bengali script, used for Bengali and Assamese languages, as well as for Sanskrit, which evolved in the fifteenth century, though its early 'proto-Bengali' form were first recorded in the eleventh century; 9. The Oriya script; its distinctive feature is that its letters are inscribed within an arc corresponding to the upper horizontal line in the letters of other alphabets; 10. The *Gujarati script, which developed from a cursive variety of Nagari known as Kaithi; its distinguishing mark is the absence of an upper horizontal stroke in the letters; 11. Gurmukhi, a *Punjabi script introduced in the sixteenth century by *Sikhs. Apart from these, there are a great number of MS and cursive forms used in private correspondence, and commercial and business records. Distinct local variations include Kaithi (throughout the area in which Hindi is spoken), Mahajani (in Rajasthan and among tradesmen who come from this state), *Lahnda (in the Punjab and *Sindh, where the printed form of this writing has also evolved), Modi (in Maharashtra), Takri (in the foothills of the Himalayas), Manipuri (in Manipur), and others.

BIBLIOGRAPHY: *G. Bühler, 'Indische Palaeography', Strasbourg, 1986; 'Contemporary Indian Printed Alphabets: The Short Literary Encyclopaedia', Vol. 3, Columns 141-2 (in Russian); 'The Great Soviet Encyclopaedia', 3rd ed., Vol. 10 (in Russian).*

G.A. ZOGRAF

Indo-Gangetic Plain

This is one of the world's largest alluvial plains, embracing the valleys of the *Indus, the Ganges, and the Brahmaputra. It occupies the northern part of India and the greater part of Pakistan and Bangladesh. In the north-east it is bordered by the *Himalayas, in the north-west by the *Sulaiman Mountains, in the south by the Deccan tableland. It has the shape of an arc, convex towards the north. It stretches about 3,000 km. from west to east and 250-300 km. from north to south. It was formed when the deep-pre-Himalayan 'cave-in' was filled up with sedimentary materials, brought down by in-flowing rivers and therefore the soils are predominantly of alluvial origin. The relief of the Indo-Gangetic Plain is characterised by gentle slopes, disrupted only by crystalline remnants of rocks in the west and the ledges of ancient alluvial terraces, marking the changes in location of the beds of the rivers. The mean slope is 17-20 cm./km. In watershed areas, the slope is about 35 cm./km. and in the lowest-lying parts, 10 cm./km.

Climatically, the Indo-Gangetic Plain is divided into two parts. The western or *Indus Valley, primarily in Pakistan, is characterised by a dry tropical climate, the annual precipitation being 100-200 mm. The valleys of the Ganges and the Brahmaputra, in the eastern part, by contrast have a tropical monsoon climate. In both parts the mean air temperature is high. In the larger part of the plain the mean temperature for January is 15-20ºC. In the eastern part, there is a summer season of heavy rainfall usually up to 90 per cent of the total annual precipitation. The south-western extremity of the plain is occupied by the *Thar Desert.

All three rivers and their tributaries have great seasonal fluctuations of their discharge. The waters of the rivers are extensively used for irrigation, without which agriculture is practically impossible in the valley of the Indus. The fertile alluvial soils of the Indo-Gangetic Plain are believed to have been the birthplace of ancient agricultural civilisation. The main crops cultivated in Pakistan are wheat, cotton, rice and millet.

S.B. ROSTOTSKY

Indo-Greek Kingdom

A state that sprang up in northwest India after the fall of the *Mauryan empire and as a result of the Graeco-Bactrians' Indian conquests (*see* Graeco-Bactrian Kingdom). Menander, the most famous ruler of the Indo-Greek Kingdom (2nd century BC), served as a prototype of king Milinda in the Buddhist epos '*Milinda-panha*'. The capital was the city of Sagala, known today as Sialkot. Coins and literary sources testify to an active interpenetration of Indian and Hellenic cultures in the Indo-Greek Kingdom. In the 1st century BC, the kingdom was overcome by the Sakas, who founded a number of their own kingdoms.

BIBLIOGRAPHY: *A.K. Naraian, 'The Indo-Greeks', Oxford, 1962; W.W. Tarn, 'The Greeks in Baktria and India', Cambridge, 1951.*

A.A. VIGASIN

India–Pakistan relations

These occupy an extremely important place in the system of Pakistan's foreign relations, in the political, economic, social, religious, and other areas. They are of vast significance for Pakistan's external security and also make a great impact on its domestic politics.The division of *British India entailed numerous disputes between Pakistan and India on territorial, financial, and property issues, which created an atmosphere of tension, anxiety, and mutual mistrust, which in turn slowed down the resolution of the conflicts. In the late 1940s, bilateral disputes arose related to the division of the currency and gold reserves, the property of state institutions and private individuals, the refugees, and the stocks of military equipment. Only some were settled; most simply ceased to be as acute as before. Nevertheless, the tension in relations continued to increase over the long, drawn-out dispute over Jammu and *Kashmir. This dispute, which has not been resolved to this day, resulted in the armed conflicts of 1947-48 and 1965 between Pakistan and India (see *Kashmir Dispute). The conflict in September of 1965 remained confined to the south-western sector of the border between India and Pakistan. While the 1965 war was settled by an agreement reached in Tashkent in January 1966, some of its articles were never fulfilled, hostile propaganda never ceased, mutual accusations and suspicions were voiced both by official representatives and the mass media.

During the constitutional crisis of 1971 the confederal six points of the *Awami League, the elected party, came into conflict with the military regime's Legal Framework Order, guaranteeing the territorial integrity of Pakistan (See Bangladesh-Pakistan Relations). Awami League volunteers began an armed struggle by attacking the non-Bengali settlers. India and the Soviet Union took the joint position that any reprisal against *Mukti Bahinis* (the militant wing of the Awami League) would be treated as an act of war. The Indo-Soviet Friendship Treaty which was signed when China and the US were unable to stabilize their relations, worked to the advantage of India. On 25 March 1971 the military reprisal by the Pakistan Army precipitated the crisis. On 26 March 1971, Awami League leaders who had escaped to India proclaimed an independent Bangladesh and on 17 April formed a government in exile on Indian soil. Pakistan's Deputy High Commissioner was arrested by Indian authorities. This triggered a flood of refugees to India which resulted in a sharp deterioration of relations between the two countries. In the summer of 1971, Pakistani and Indian troops on the eastern border met in dangerous confrontation. Early in the winter, the crisis entered a phase of armed conflict both in the east and west, and along the ceasefire line in Jammu and Kashmir. On 16 December 1971, the East Pakistani army capitulated. Hostilities on the western front ceased on 17 December 1971. As a result, Pakistan occupied about 50 square miles in the Chamb sector which controlled the communications of the state of Jammu and Kashmir with the rest of Indian territory. These communication facilities were the main target of strikes by the Pakistani army, just as they were during the 1965 armed conflict. Pakistan also seized control over Indian territory in the state of *Punjab. Indian troops seized about 50 Pakistani posts north and west of the ceasefire line in Kashmir and some territories of Pakistan in the Punjab and *Sindh.

Realizing the need to solve disputes by political means, Z.A. *Bhutto proposed, in January 1972, to begin negotiations with the Government of India. In late June-early July 1972, a meeting took place in Simla between President Z.A. Bhutto of Pakistan and Prime Minister Indira Gandhi of India. At the end of the talks, an agreement was signed in which the two sides assumed the obligation to achieve normal relations and to consolidate peace and security in South Asia (see Simla Agreement. The restoration of diplomatic relations between India and Pakistan in July 1976, and the resumption of air travel between them signified the conclusion of an unfortunate stage in their relations and the overcoming of the negative consequences of the 1971 armed conflict.

At the end of the 1970s and especially in the early 1980s, the development of these relations slowed down. Serious differences and contradictions emerged, not only on a number of issues of bilateral relations but also on regional issues relating to the Soviet intervention in Afghanistan. The growing scale of US-Pakistan cooperation in military and political spheres evoked a negative reaction from India.

In the 1980s and early 1990s there was a growing danger from the Kashmir problem to the stability of the relations between India and Pakistan. The Kashmir dispute was complicated by new conflicting territorial claims on the Siachen glacier (length 85 km., width 5 to 10 km.) in the *Karakoram Mountains. Since the spring of 1984, the Siachen glacier repeatedly became the scene of armed conflict between the two armies' special units. In the second half of the 1980s, several rounds of Indo-Pakistan negotiations were held on the Siachen question; these talks revealed the fundamental difference of the political position between the two countries. In the same period, their differences over the nuclear problem deepened.

Subsequently the two states made efforts to settle their disputes and to normalize their relations. Rejecting the January 1980 proposal made by Prime Minister Indira Gandhi to conclude a non-aggression pact which would contain the two countries' obligation to reject aggression and use of force in their mutual relations, the Government of Pakistan proposed, in the autumn of 1981, to begin bilateral agreements aimed at concluding a treaty on mutual guarantees of non-aggression and non-use of force. Early in 1982, the Indian government proposed to Islamabad a treaty of peace, friendship, and cooperation. It was assumed that the treaty would state the obligation not to permit foreign bases on their territory, settling all issues between the two nations without reference to any third party. From 1982 to 1989, Delhi and Islamabad continued to meet on this issue, but failed in the end to conclude any agreement. The unstable relations between India and Pakistan were repeatedly discussed during high-level meetings of representatives of the two countries; these became regular, especially in connection with the annual conferences of the heads of states and governments of the *South Asian Association for Regional Cooperation (SAARC). One important diplomatic event in the relations was the arrival of Rajiv Gandhi in Islamabad in December 1988 for the Fourth SAARC summit conference. His talks with Benazir *Bhutto resulted in the signing of several agreements, including the obligation not to attack each other's nuclear sites. The top-level contacts between them continued during Rajiv Gandhi's brief visit to Islamabad in July 1989. Intense negotiations on various levels at the end of the 1980s and in the early 1990s resulted in agreements on such issues as joint actions to combat drug smuggling, measures to strengthen the Pakistan-Indian border (to stop illegal crossings), easier contacts between the citizens of the two countries, and easier access for tourists. Having proposed, as early as the mid 1970s, the idea of transforming South Asia into a nuclear-free zone, Pakistan continued to search for ways to its implementation. In June 1991, Prime Minister Nawaz *Sharif of Pakistan called for mediation of the United States, the Soviet Union, and China on the issue of non-proliferation of nuclear weapons in South Asia. Pakistan also proposed to conclude bilateral agreements or a common agreement by the South Asian nations to ban all weapons of mass destruction. Pakistan also proposed measures for mutual balanced reduction of conventional armed forces in South Asia in accordance with the principle of equal and guaranteed security.

Relations between the two countries worsened when the BJP, a fundamentalist Hindu party, formed the government in India in 1998. The threatening posture of the Indian Prime Minister Atal Bihari Vajpayee was followed by nuclear tests on 11 and 12 May 1998. After waiting to judge the intensity of world reaction to the Indian tests, Pakistan conducted its own nuclear tests on 28 and 30 May 1998. This stand-off gave rise to a temporary thaw during which Atal Bihari Vajpayee visited Lahore on a goodwill visit inaugurating a bus service between Lahore and Delhi. However, from March 1999 a major crisis erupted when *Kashmiri volunteers aided by Pakistani irregulars captured the Kargil heights on the Line of Control. Following intense international pressure, Pakistan withdrew from Kargil. The military takeover of 12 October 1999 worsened relations. The attack by militants on the Indian Parliament (13 December 2001) brought the two countries to the brink of war. The SAARC summit in Kathmandu on 6 January 2002, saw the Pakistan President making a personal initiative but it has not resulted in the relaxation of tension. The Almaty Conference of 4 June 2002 had also failed. As against the Pakistan proposal for neutral monitoring of the LoC, Vajpayee offered joint Indo-Pakistan monitoring which was unacceptable to Pakistan as it would penetrate the security system of the country and would render it open to Indian propaganda. One 23 August 2002, Pakistan repulsed an Indian attack on the Gultari sector. On 8 February 2003 India expelled the acting Pakistan High Commissioner. There was a change for the better on 18 April 2003 when Atal Bihari Vajpayee offered to hold talks with Pakistan Prime Minister Mir Zafrullah Khan Jamali. On 29 October 2003, India proposed 12 Confidence Building Measures (CBMs) mostly dealing with the resumption of air, train, road and sea routes including the revival of the Khokhrapar-Munabao rail links which had since the 1965 war, opening of a bus route between Lahore and Amritsar, and a Srinagar-Muzaffarabad bus service linking both sides of Kashmir. In view of the disputed nature of the territory, Pakistan initially wanted UN monitoring on this route, but does not insist on it anymore it. The same evening Pakistan responded with 13 CBMs mostly in acceptance of Indian CBMs. The thirteenth measure was the offer of a 100 scholarships in Pakistan technical institutes to Kashmiris from Indian held areas. On 24 September 2003, Prime Minister Jamali announced unilateral cease-fire on LoC and Siachen. On 30 November, Pakistan allowed over-flight rights to India. On 17 December, President *Musharraf expressed his willingness to set aside UNSC resolution on Kashmir, a development welcomed by India. Pervez Musharraf said that accepting LoC as an International border was not acceptable. Following a meeting on the sidelines of the SAARC summit in Islamabad, Pervez Musharraf and Atal Bihari Vajpayee issued a joint statement on 6 January 2004. Both sides hoped to consolidate the CBMs earlier proposed. President Musharraf undertook not to allow any territory under Pakistan control to be used for terrorism in any form. Both leaders looked forward to 'composite' dialogues between the two countries, which would include the resolution of the Kashmir dispute. Foreign Ministers talks are scheduled for 13 and 14 September 2004.

M.R. KAZIMI

Indo-Scythians

See, 'Shakas'.

Indus Basin, Agreement on the

India and Pakistan have generally implemented the Indus Water Treaty and Indus Basin Development Fund Agreement, which was signed on 19 September 1960 in Karachi. India received the right to use the waters of three eastern rivers; the *Ravi, the *Beas, and the *Sutlej (80 per cent of the water resources of the Indus basin). Pakistan was to utilize the resources of the three western rivers; the *Indus, the *Jhelum, and the *Chenab. To compensate Pakistan's loss of the eastern tributaries of the Indus, the construction of a complex of hydropower plant and irrigation project at the cost of ten billion rupees, and the setting up of the Indus Basin Development Fund were envisaged in the treaty. The project was financed and built by a consortium of several countries under the supervision of the International Bank for Reconstruction and Development (IBRD).

Tarbela Dam on the Indus basin.

The bulk of the work envisaged by the 1960 agreement was concluded in 1965-67, including the construction or reconstruction of seven connecting canals (which were to move 17 thousand million cubic metres of water from the western rivers of the basin to the eastern rivers), five dams, and the Mangla water reservoir and hydro-electric plant on the Jhelum. The last project, the Indus-Jhelum canal, was completed in 1973. In April 1964, the Consortium and Pakistan concluded an additional agreement worth $315 million to finance the Tarbela dam on the Indus.

BIBLIOGRAPHY: *G. Mueen-ud-Din, 'Indus Waters Treaty Negotiations', Indus (Lahore: Vol. 1 No. 9 October 1960); 'Soviet-Pakistan Relations and Post-Soviet Dynamics', London: Macmillan Publishing Co., 1995.*

R.M. MUKIMJANOVA

Indus Plain (also Sindh Plain)

The valley of the River *Indus, a large geographical subdivision of Pakistan, the western part of the Indo-Gangetic Plain. It is bordered on the west by the Iranian Plateau (the *Sulaiman Mountains, the Kirthar Range), on the north by the *Salt Range, and on the east by the *Thar Desert. The length of the valley along the course of the Indus is about 1,000 km., the width in *Punjab is about 350 km., and in lower *Sindh it is 200 km. It is subdivided into the trans-Indus Plain (Derajat), the right bank of the Indus, the Thal Desert in between the water beds of the Indus and the *Jhelum, the Punjab Plain, and the Sindh Lowlands.

M.YU. MOROZOVA

Indus Valley Culture

(Indus Valley Civilization) *See*, Harappan Civilization.

Indus

(From the Sanskrit, '*Sindhu*'—'river', called by other geographers *Sinthos*, in Pushtu, *Abba-Sin*—'The father of rivers', *Darya*—'river'—the local name within Sindh province) The Indus is one of the biggest rivers in Asia, with a length of 2,900 km. and a basin of some 960,000 sq. km. The mean discharge of water at Hyderabad is 33,850 cu.metres per sec. The Indus has its source in China, on the slope of the Kailas Range in the Tibetan Plateau, at an altitude of 5,300 metres above sea level. The upper reaches lie mainly in *Kashmir, the middle and lower reaches in the *Punjab and *Sindh. The river flows into the Arabian Sea, forming a delta of 8,000 sq.km. The chief tributary, flowing into the Indus from the north east, is the Panjnad, formed by the confluence of the Punjab's five rivers the *Jhelum, *Chenab, *Ravi, *Beas, and *Sutlej. Other major tributaries are the Shinghar, *Gilgit, and Kabul from the north west. In its upper third, the Indus flows almost due north-west along the bottom of a deep tectonic valley between the *Himalayas and the *Karakoram Ranges. Below the confluence with the Gilgit the Indus rushes through a number of narrow mountain gorges. It then turns to the south-east at Jalkot. Near Abbottabad the gigantic Tarbela Dam makes use of the flow to provide hydro-power. At the western extremity of the Salt Range (33°N. lat.), the river enters the Indo-Gangetic Plain. This sector of the Indus lies at the western border of the Himalaya. From its source to the plain has descended from a height of 5,100 metres the river.

About 28 per cent of the river's drainage basin, or 270,000 sq. km to below 200m above sea level is in mountainous regions above the town of Attock. No other river on the subcontinent has such a vast drainage area in the mountains. In the upper and middle reaches there are many rapids, and in the stretches where the river is squeezed into a sequence of narrow gorges 20 to 50 metres wide, the velocity of the stream rises. Navigation here is not possible.

The speed of the current falls sharply in the lowlands, where the river spreads to 1-6 km. wide. In the lowlands the slow flowing Indus divides into braided channels. At Attock 1,600km from the sea, its width is 100-375 metres, its depth is 14-40 metres and the velocity of the current is 9.20 km per hr. Above the confluence with the Panjnad the river is 500 metres wide and 4 metres deep and the velocity of the current is 8 km. per hr. Downstream the width increases to 1-2 km. reaching, at times of maximum water, a width of 5.7 km. Near the town of Dera Ismail Khan the river can be 20-22 km. wide.

In its lower reaches the Indus flows along the western borders of the sand deserts *Thal and *Thar. Here the river meanders and often changes its course. There are numerous sandbanks, islands, and old abandoned river beds. Near Thatta where the delta reaches the ocean, the river divides into several channels.

In its upper course the Indus is mainly fed glaciers, in the middle course by underground waters, and in the plain by rainfall. Floods occur mainly in the summer or monsoon season. On average about 68 per cent of the discharge falls in the three months of the rainy season July to September. The total volume of the discharge in the basin is 220 cu.km., of which only 94 cu.km. reaches the mouth of the river. In drought years the waters of the Indus may not reach the ocean at all. This is partly accounted for by high evaporation, the losses from which, during flooding alone, sometimes reach 28 cu.km. However, the main reason is the large consumption of water for irrigation, which amounts to 70 per cent of the discharge. In this, as well as in the size of the irrigated areas, which are more than 12 million hectares, the Indus tops the list of the world's rivers. The sediments carried by the river amount to 450 million tons a year. The *Indus Valley is one of the most ancient centres of agriculture. In recent years the intensive development of irrigated farming in the plains sector of the river has caused water logging which has led to salinity of the irrigated fields and rendered them unusable.

S.B. ROSTOTSKY

Insha, Ibne (1926–78)

Writer. A satirical author writing in *Urdu who was educated in Lahore and Karachi. His poems express the dreams of common people (the collection *Chandnagar*—'Lunar Town'). He made an important contribution to the renovation and aesthetic perfection of verse. His satirical bent was expressed with particular force in his numerous *Safar-name* ('Travel Books'): *Ibn Batuta ke Taaqub men* ('Chasing Ibn Batuta', 1974), *Dunya Gol he* ('The Earth is Round', 1972), *Awaragard ki Diari* ('Diary of a Tramp'), and in his book of humorous sketches: *Urdu ki Akhri Kitab* ('The Last Book of Urdu'). An accomplished stylist, Ibne Insha exerted a telling influence on many contemporary Urdu writers.

BIBLIOGRAPHY: *Ibadat Barelwi, 'Jadid Shairi' (Contemporary Poetry), Karachi-Lahore, 1961; Riaz Ahmad Riaz, 'Ibn-e-Insha Ahwàl o Asar', Karachi, 1986.*

A.S. SUKHOCHEV

Insha, Inshallah Khan (1766–1818)

Poet. Insha was an *Urdu language poet. The son of a court physician, he served at the courts of several **nawabs* of Oudh and, as a person of great wit, he set the tastes at the court. He had to his credit **diwans* in Urdu and Farsi, humorous verses and riddles and a treatise on grammar and rhetoric entitled *Darya-i-Latafat* ('The Sea of Elegance', 1807, in co-authorship with Mirza Qatil). Insha was engaged in formal literary experiments: his narrative *Kahani Rani Ketki aur Kunwar Udaibhan ki* ('Tale of Princess Ketki and Prince Udaibhan') is written without a single Arabic-Persian borrowing despite the rules of the 'lofty style' in *Urdu literature. He was one of the first to work in the style of **rekhti* poetry, i.e., written in the name of a woman and in the *Zanana* idiom, the language of the female part of the house. The history of Urdu literature has recorded many instances of Insha's competitiveness with Mushafi.

WORKS: *'Kulliayat-i-Insha', Lahore, 1969; 'Kalam-i-Insha', Allababad, 1952; 'Insha, Dariya-i-Latafat', Aurangabad, 1935.*

BIBLIOGRAPHY: *Abdul Ali Barlas, 'Hayat-i-Insha', Lahore, 1959; Aslam Parwez, 'Inshallah-Khan Insha, ahd aur fan', Delhi, 1961; (ed.) Ahmed Ali, 'The Golden Tradition. An Anthology of Urdu Poetry', New York, 1973; Abid Peshawari, 'Inshallah Khan Insha', Lucknow, 1985.*

A.A. SUVOROVA

Institute of Sindhology

It was founded in 1962 in Jamshoro (*Sindh). Between 1962 and 1964 it was known as the *Sindhi Academy. Its task is to study Sindhi history and culture, and to translate into foreign languages literary masterpieces and historical sources. The institute collects and publishes Sindhi folklore, historical sources, official documents, and works of art. It also maintains a specialized library.

The Institute publishes the *Sindhi Adab* journal in Sindhi and *Sindhological Studies* in English (twice a year).

YU.V. GANKOVSKY

International Committee for Balochistan Studies (ICBS)

It was established on 10 April 1983 at the *Instituto Universitario Orientale*, Naples, Italy. The *Seminario di Studi Asiaticci* of the *Universitario Orientale* houses its secretariat in Naples. Its central tasks are: publication of monographs on *Balochi problems, compilation of a complete bibliography of *Balochistan, and organization of international conferences and seminars. Scholars from Italy, France, USA, Russia, Germany, Canada, Iran, and Pakistan comprise its membership. The committee publishes the *Newsletter of Balochistan Studies*.

V.V. MOHSKALO

Ipi, Mirza Ali Khan, Faquir of (1890–1960)

Political Activist. A mercurial personality, Mirza Ali Khan was leader of the congregation of the mosque of Ipi near *Bannu. He gained prominence following an incident involving a Hindu lady, Chand Bibi, who was abducted by a Waziri Pathan and underwent a marriage ceremony with him. The Hindu husband claimed conjugal rights, which the court restored. This re-conversion of the lady to Hinduism created communal tension that the Faquir of Ipi whipped up into to a high frenzy. From 1936 to 1939, the Faquir was in armed opposition to the British authorities. His militant personality provided an emotional counterbalance to the Congress influence in the NWFP. At the time of the Referendum in the NWFP, the Faquir put his full weight behind the Pakistan Movement, which proved very valuable. After the Referendum, the Congress tried to enlist him to the Pakhtunistan demand and in 1950 he joined the Pakhtunistan Movement.

BIBLIOGRAPHY: *Alan Warren, 'Waziristan, The Faqir of Ipi and the Indian Army', Karachi, 1997.*

M.R. KAZIMI

Iqbal Academy

It was founded in 1951 in Karachi. The Academy houses a library and museum entirely devoted to Muhammad *Iqbal's life, poetry, philosophical ideas, and political work. The Academy conducts annual conferences, and publishes research into Pakistani literature, and the quarterly, *Iqbal Review,* in English.

YU. V. GANKOVSKY

Iqbal Society (*Bazm-i-Iqbal*)

It was founded in 1950 in Lahore, to publish and promote the philosophical heritage of Muhammad *Iqbal. The Society regularly reprints Iqbal's philosophical works and publishes new research into his life and work in *Urdu and English. Since 1952, the society has published a quarterly scholarly journal, *Iqbal,* in Urdu and English.

N.V. GLEBOV

Iqbal, Javid (1924–)

Literary scholar. He earned his Bachelor's degree with honours in 1944 from Government College, Lahore. In 1947, he earned a Master's Degree in *English Literature and a year later another Master's Degree in Philosophy for which he was awarded a gold medal as a Distinguished Student.

Subsequently, he earned a PhD in Political Science at Cambridge University in 1954 and two years later became a Barrister at Law from Lincoln's Inn in London. In 1989, Villanova University in Pennysylvania awarded him an honorary doctorate of Humane Letters. A year later Seljuk University in Konya, Turkey, awarded him an honorary Doctorate of Literature and Science.

After his return from Britain to Pakistan, Dr Iqbal became an advocate (from 1956-70) at the Lahore High Court. He was made Judge of the Lahore High Court (1971-82). The Government of Pakistan then appointed him Judge at the Supreme Court of Pakistan from 1986-89 and from that position he retired in 1989. Five years later in March 1994, Dr Iqbal was elected to the Senate of Pakistan for a term of six years.

In addition to holding these positions in law and politics, Dr Iqbal has been active in scholarship. He has authored seven books in English and in *Urdu. He wrote a biography of his late father, Dr Mohammad *Iqbal, in Urdu, *Zinda Rood* (The Living Stream), in three volumes. These three volumes are considered to be the definitive biographical information on the life of his distinguished father.

YU.V. GANKOVSKY

Iqbal, Mohammed, Allama Doctor Sir (1877–1938)

Philosopher/Poet/Political leader. Sir Muhammad Iqbal was born at Sialkot. He was educated at Sialkot and thereafter at Government College, Lahore, where he completed his Masters in Philosophy in 1899. He initially taught at Oriental College and then at Government College, Lahore. He began to be noticed as a poet when he read out his poem *Nala-e-Yateem* ('Wails of an Orphan') at the annual function of *Anjuman-e-Himayat-e-Islam* at Lahore in 1900 and, shortly after, published *Himala* published in the literary periodical *Makhzan*. In 1905, he travelled to England for higher studies and then proceeded to Germany, where he completed his PhD at Munich University, Germany (Thesis: Development of Metaphysics in Persia). While a Professor of Arabic at London University, he appeared for the Bar in 1908. The same year, he returned to India and established his Law practice at Lahore while also working as a part-time Professor of Philosophy and *English Literature. Over the next few years, he published *Shikwa* ('The Plaint') in 1911, *Jawab-e-Shikwa* ('Reply to the Plaint') in 1912, 'History of India' in 1913, *Asrar-e-Khudi* ('Secrets of the Self' in 1915) and *Rumuz-e-Bekhudi* ('Mysteries of Selflessness' in 1918). In 1920, he visited *Kashmir and presented his famous poem *Saqi Nama* at Srinagar. He was awarded knighthood at Lahore in 1923. *Payam-e-Mashriq* ('The Message of the East' appeared that year and *Bang-e-Dara* ('Call of the Caravan') in 1924.

Allama Mohammad Iqbal, National Poet.

Alllama Iqbal entered politics in 1926 and was elected to Punjab Legislative Council, Lahore (1926-1929). In 1930, he became President of the *All-India Muslim League. Initially a supporter of Hindu-Muslim unity in a single Indian state, he later became the foremost advocate of Pakistani independence. Allama Iqbal came to feel that Muslims throughout the world had detached themselves from the Qur'an as a guiding principle and a living force. After the disaster following the Balkan War of 1912, the fall of the caliphate in Turkey and many anti-Muslim incessant provocations in India, Iqbal suggested that a separate state should be given to the Muslims of the Indian subcontinent. In his famous 1930 Presidential speech delivered to the annual session of *Muslim League at Allahabad, Allama Iqbal demanded 'the formation of a consolidated Muslim state in the best interests of India and Islam. For India, it means security and peace... for Islam, an opportunity to rid itself of the stamp that Arabian imperialism was forced to give it, to mobilize its laws, its education, its culture, and to bring them into closer contact with its own original spirit and with the spirit of modern times.'

Iqbal participated in the Second *Round Table Conference in 1931. In addition to his political activism, Iqbal was considered the foremost Muslim thinker of his day. His poetry and philosophy, written in *Urdu and Persian, stress redemption through self-development, moral integrity, and individual freedom. In 1931, he published 'Reconstruction of Religious Thought in Islam'. *Javed Namah* appeared in 1932 and, after a visit to Spain in 1933, the poems *Dua* ('Supplication') and *Masjid-e-Qurtuba* ('The Mosque of Cordoba'). His further publications included *Musafir* ('The Traveller') in 1934, *Bal-e-Jibril* in 1935, *Zarab-e-Kalim* and *Pas Che Bayad Kard* in 1936. A further collection of poems *Armughan-e-Hijaz* was published posthumously.

Allama Iqbal died at Lahore on 21 April 1938. Although he did not live to see the creation of an independent Pakistan in 1947, he is nevertheless regarded as the symbolic Father of the Nation.

S.T. KUREISHI

Iqbal, Nasira (1940–)

Lawyer. Educated at Queen Mary's College and Kinnaird College, Lahore, she earned in 1975 a Bachelor of Laws degree from the Punjab University. In 1986, she earned a Master of Laws (LLM) degree with distinction from Harvard University Law School. Nasira Iqbal practiced law from 1978-94 initially before the Lahore District Courts and then the Lahore High Court and the Supreme Court of Pakistan. She was invited twice to serve as a Judge of the Lahore High Court during 1994-96 and 2001-02. She served as legal advisor and vice-chairperson of the *Punjab branch of *All-Pakistan Women's Association, an organization devoted to the promotion and protection of Pakistani women's rights, and, from 1990-2001, she functioned as the convener of the Fatima Memorial Legal Aid Centre. She has travelled extensively and lectured on women's rights and development in China, Australia, Europe, the Middle East and the United States. Also, she is a member of several international interfaith dialogue groups.

H. MALIK

Iqta

(Arabic: partition, separation) A form of land ownership and government in South Asia at the time of the *Delhi Sultanate. A military officer was given the right to collect state taxes from a certain area in his own name. In return, he was to maintain law and order in that territory and to supply armed cavalry forces to the Sultan on his order, for parades in the case of war, in quantities in accordance with the *iqta* size. Originally, *iqta* was a temporary ownership, but during the decline of central power the *iqta* came to be inherited. The *iqta*-owner was called *iqtadar*.

BIBLIOGRAPHY: *K.S. Ashrafyan, 'The Delhi Sultanate', Moscow, 1960 (in Russian); I.H. Qureshi, 'The Administration of the Sultanate of Delhi', Karachi, 1958.*

L.B. ALAYEV

Iqtadar

(Persian; in Arabic: *muqta*) The *iqta* owner in South Asia at the time of the *Delhi Sultanate. All *iqtadars* received their *iqtas* directly from the Sultan; each could sublet their land to their subjects.

L.B. ALAYEV

Iranian Plateau

This plateau stretches for 2,500 km. Its territory is 2,700 sq.km., about 70 per cent of which lies beyond the Iranian border. Some border regions reach between Iraq and southern Turhmenia. The eastern region lies in Pakistan, where parts of it are called the *Zhob Plateau. The highest peak is at 5,604 metres called the volcano Demavend in the Elburz Mountains of Iran. The inner plateaus are approximately 500 to 2,000 metres above sea level and are fringed with mountains such as the Elburz, Kopetdag, *Hindu Kush, *Sulaiman Mountains, *Makran, and Zagros. There are many depressions with no outlet into the sea, semi-deserts and deserts, and salt lakes and freshwater lakes that dry up in summer. The rivers carry an insignificant amount of water.

YU.V. GANKOVSKY

Iran-Pakistan Relations

On the whole friendly, the two countries have extensive ties in political, economic, and military areas. From 1955-80, Pakistan, together with Iran and Turkey, was a member of CENTO; since 1964, of the Regional Cooperation for Development; and since 1985, of the Economic Cooperation Organization. Topping this, Iran gave Pakistan strong support in the 1965 war.

In the 1970s, the relations between Iran and Pakistan strengthened. Pakistan counted on the support of its neighbour and CENTO partner in the solution of some important foreign and domestic problems. Iran was one of the first countries visited by Z.A. *Bhutto in his capacity as head of state in January 1972. Cooperation between Iran and Pakistan in the military-political area grew significantly. In the 1970s, their economic ties noticeably increased as in 1974-76, Iran agreed to grant Pakistan two loans, one for $580 million and another for $150 million, and several loans for the construction of industrial and other projects, primarily in *Balochistan.

After the fall of the Shah's regime in Iran in 1979, Islamabad was the first country to recognize the new Iranian provisional government. Pakistan was strictly neutral in the Iran-Iraq military conflict. In the mid-1980s, after a brief period of cool relations, the ties were noticeably strengthened. The late 1980s saw an expansion of Pakistan-Iranian links in the military field; Pakistan helped Iran to train its military personnel, supplied spare parts for the Iranian army's military equipment and machines, etc. Highly placed statesmen of the two countries maintained active contact.

Iran did not supply oil to Pakistan in the late 1970s, but in the 1980s and early 1990s it became a major exporter of liquid fuel to this country. Iran also became a major consumer of Pakistan's exports, such as foodstuffs and textiles. The Pakistan-Iranian agreement signed in November 1987 envisaged expansion of bilateral trade to $400 million a year.

Relations came under a strain after sectarian strife increased in Pakistan. The Multan branch of the Iranian Cultural Centre came under attack, and its director, M.A. Rahimi was killed on 20 February 1997. Iranian engineers constructing the Clifton Bridge in Karachi were shot dead in February 1998, delaying the completion of the project. More serious than sectarian trouble was Pakistan's recognition of the Taliban regime in Afghanistan. The Taliban attack on Herat and Mazar-i-Sharif, where large number of Shiites (see Shia) reside, had led to the beginning of alienation. However, the struggle between the Reformists under President Khatami and Conservatives under Ayatollah Khamenei had provided a respite. Even after Pakistan's withdrawal of support to the Taliban in September 2001, differences remained. Pakistan favoured cooperation with the US but not with the Northern Alliance, Iran's stance was completely the opposite. Afghanistan remained a source of discord. The Irani government asked Pakistan on 3 September 2002 to prevent Al-Qaeda elements, the militant body led by Osama bin Laden, the Saudi exile, from crossing over to Iran from Pakistan.

On 22 December 2002 President Muhammad al Khatami of Iran arrived on a three day visit. Presidents Khatami and *Musharraf called for de-escalation of focus on the Indo-Pakistan border. On 21 October 2003 Prime Minister Mir Zafarullah Jamali visited Iran and called for greater interaction between the two neighbors. Pakistan proposed agreements on issues of double taxation, cultural exchanges, customs, science and technology, livestock and defense. President Khatami assured Prime Minister Jamali that the growing Indo-Irani relations could not affect Pakistan-Iran relations. On 2 January 2004 the two countries signed a memorandum of understanding (MoU) for the development of Compressed Natural Gas (CNG). In the latest development on 13 January 2004 both countries undertook to increase trade relations and general economic interaction.

R.M. MUKIMJANOVA

Iron Age

This engulfed Pakistan in the late 2nd and early 1st millennia BC. The culture of cairn-burials was discovered in the valleys of the rivers Zhob and Loralai in *Balochistan. Around 1,000 burials have been found so far with a large number of iron arrowheads, swords, knives and hooks. The pottery is modelled. The settlement of Pirak in the valley of the Kachni River in Balochistan is unique. It existed between the 15th and 18th centuries BC. Iron implements appeared side by side with the old bronze ones at the second development stage (13th-12th centuries BC) that continued into a later period. In Pirak, the shift from the Bronze Age (phase I) to the Early Iron Age was smooth—there are no changes in pottery, the adobe houses became smaller. Phase III of Pirak is characterized with wheeled grey burnished pottery with grooved patterns. It can be compared with the *Jhangar ware dated to the first half of the 1st millennium BC. Jhangar, a culture of the Early Iron Age, can be traced in *Sindh over a limited territory (settlements of *Amri, *Chanhu-Daro). The burials and settlements of the later period of the *Swat culture (dated between the 8th and 4th centuries BC) are related to the Early Iron Age of the northwest of Pakistan. There are spears, arrowheads, knives and parts of harness. There are analogies with the Iron Age II in Iran, that iron metallurgy may have penetrated the northwest of Pakistan from Iran.

BIBLIOGRAPHY: *N.R. Banerjee, 'Iron Age in India', Delhi, 1965; D.P. Agrawal, 'The Archaeology of India', Copenhagen, 1982.*

N.M. VINOGRADOVA

Isa, Qazi Mohammad (1914–76)

Statesman. Qazi Mohammad Isa was the mainstay of AIML politics and the Pakistan Movement in the province of *Balochistan. He first became President of the Balochistan Muslim League and later a member of the *All-India Muslim League (AIML) Working Committee. In 1943, he was appointed member of the AIML Committee of Action. The hallmark of his achievements was the Muslim League Conference held at Quetta between 26 and 29 August 1940. Liaquat Ali *Khan, who presided, was ecstatic in describing the enthusiasm of the masses and attributed the phenomenal rise of AIML popularity to Qazi Mohammad Isa's 'untiring zeal and enthusiasm'.

In 1946, apprehending that he may be sidelined, he wrote to Liaquat Ali Khan that he would not countenance any office-holder in Balochistan appointed while by-passing him. In 1947, Qazi Isa did not favour the *Shahi Jirga* as the Electoral College to determine accession to Pakistan. He suggested giving this role to the Balochistan Muslim League or, failing that, holding a limited plebiscite based on adult franchise.

After independence, Qazi Mohammad Isa became General Secretary of the *Pakistan Muslim League. He was appointed Pakistan's Ambassador to Brazil (1951–53) and a member of the Pakistan delegation to the UN in 1950, 1954, and 1974.

YU.V. GANKOVSKY

Ishan

(Persian: they) A respectful address; a Muslim theologian.

YU.V. GANKOVSKY

Islam, Nazrul (1899–1976)

Poet. Nazrul Islam was a Bengali language poet of peasant origin with twenty-five collections of poetry and three novels to his name. He began publishing during his military service in Karachi and Mesopotamia, in the journals *Shobuj Potro* ('Green Leaves') and *Muslim Bharat* ('Muslim India'). From the 1920 to the 1930s, he took part in the revolutionary movement in Bengal. He viewed his creative work as a contribution to the struggle to restore rights to the downtrodden. He made his name with the collection of verse *Ogni Bina* ('Fiery Guilt'), published in 1919. In order to disseminate his revolutionary ideas, he started publishing the literary magazine *Dhumketu* ('The Comet') and in 1923 he published a long poem of the same title in the magazine. The comet that destroyed the outdated order symbolized the inevitability of historical change. The issue of the magazine carrying this poem was banned and Nazrul Islam was arrested by the British government. Themes of mass patriotic movement and universal brotherhood occupy much space in the poet's work, including *Bidrohi* ('The Rebel'), 1922; *Kandari, Hyshiyar* ('Beware, the Helmsman'), 1924; and *Shorbohara* ('The Proletarian'), 1926. Nazrul Islam was the first Bengali poet who directly addressed workers, peasants, fishermen and *rickshawallas*. He had great admiration for the poetry of Rabindranath Tagore but never shared his views on the elitist role of poetry and poets. He devoted much of his time to love lyrics. His collections of poetry include *Chokher Chatok* ('The Bird of My Eyes'), 1929; and *Nuton Chand* ('The Young Moon'), 1942. Nazrul Islam translated famous *rubais* of Hafiz into Bengali (1937). His distinguishing features are a combination of oratory with poetic speech, dynamic hyperbolized imagery and scenes, and wide use of *vers libre*.

BIBLIOGRAPHY: *G. Aliev, 'Persian-language Literature of India', Moscow, 1968 (in Russian); Shanti Ranjan Bhattacharia, 'Iqbal, Tagore and Nazrul', Calcutta, 1978; M. Abdullah, 'Qazi Nazrul Islam' Dhaka. (n.d.); 'Maghribibengal Baghi Shair Nazrul Islam', (ed). S.K. Sen-Gupta, Calcutta, 1980.*

E.K. BROSALINA

Islamic Democratic Alliance (IDA, or *Islami Jamhuri Ittehad*, IJI)

Opposition party to Benazir *Bhutto's *Pakistan Peoples Party during the 1988 general elections. The principal parties united in the IDA were the *Pakistan Muslim League, **Jamaat-i-Islami* and the National Pakistan People's Party of G.M. *Jatoi. The IDA was joined by the **Jamiat-ul-Ulema-i-Islam* (A. Darkhwasti's group) and several parties mostly influential in the *Punjab: *Jamiat-i-Ahl-i-Hadith* (the Lakhvi group), *Jamiat-i-Mashaiykh* (led by Sajjada Nashin), *Hizb-i-Jihad* (led by A.M. Puya), the *Azad* group (led by Fakhr Imam), and **Khaksar Tehrik*. The IDA's election manifesto promised to defend the rights and interests of the working people through merging all projects for the improvement of the people's living standards in one single agenda whose realization would make education, health services and old-age pensions accessible to everyone. The manifesto did not define the methods and means for the realization of these ideas. In the National Assembly, the IDA opposed Benazir Bhutto's government, actively supporting the political course of the Ziaul *Haq regime. In October 1990, the IDA won the elections to parliament.

O.V. PLESHOV

Ismaili

Ismailis are followers of a *Shia sect founded in the 18th century and named after Ismail (d. 762), the elder son of the sixth Shia *Imam, Jafar as-Sadiq. The Ismailis established the Fatimid Caliphate, first in Rakkada, North Africa in 909, and in Egypt in 969. The Ismailis believed in *Batini* or esoteric doctrines by which the Imam was authorized to interpret dogma. At the turn of the 9th century, the Ismailis broke into several branches. One of them, *Karmatiya*, seized Multan in the early 10th century; they created their own state that was eliminated by Sultan Mahmud Ghaznavi (see Ghaznavid) in 1010. Following the death of the Fatimid caliph al-Mustansir in 1094, Ismailiya divided into Nizari (see 'Khoja' and 'Aga Khan') and Mustalites (see 'Bohra'). Ismailiya appeared in South Asia at the turn of the 9th century.

YU.V. GANKOVSKY

Ispahani, Mirza Abul Hasan (1902–81)

Politician/Businessman. Mirza Abul Hasan Ispahani belonged to a business family that played a major role in industrializing the eastern part of *Bengal. He was born in Madras and educated at St. John's College, Cambridge, from where he obtained his MA and LLB degrees and was called to the Bar from the Inner Temple. His political career began when he founded the United Muslim Party in Bengal in the mid 1930s. However, when the 1937 elections were approaching, he was persuaded to join the *All-India Muslim League. He corresponded with and became a confidant of M.A. *Jinnah and, along with the Raja of *Mahmudabad; he contributed to the party funds. From 1941 to 1947, he was a member of the AIML Working Committee. He helped set up Orient Airways and **Dawn* newspaper. He was thereafter elected to the Pakistan *Constituent Assembly. M.A.H. Ispahani was sent as Ambassador to the United States immediately after Independence in 1947 and, during his tenure until 1952, he largely bore the expenses for running the embassy himself. He was Ambassador at the initial and crucial stage of Pakistan-American relations when the Cold War had just begun. Thereafter, M.A.H. Ispahani was High Commissioner to the United Kingdom (1952–54). He became Minister of Commerce and Industry in 1954.

WORKS: *'The Case of Muslim India', New York, 1946; 'Quaid-i-Azam Mohammad Ali Jinnah As I knew him', Karachi, 1966; (ed.) Zawar Hasan Zaidi, 'M.A. Jinnah—Ispahani Correspondence', Karachi, 1970.*

M.R. KAZIMI

Italo-Pakistan Relations

The initial relations between Italy and Pakistan were adverse. Italy pursued a policy of colonialism in 1947 and Pakistan's representative to the UN, Zafrullah *Khan opposed vehemently in the UNGA First Committee that Libya's independence from Italy be deferred by ten years. He opposed a similar move regarding Italy's occupation of Somaliland. In both cases, Pakistan's views were upheld. Pakistan and Italy established diplomatic relations in 1950. Apart from an attempt to pursue a colonial policy, Italy adopted a low diplomatic profile. Its policy towards Pakistan followed the general trend of Western Europe; a benign attitude towards Pakistan, keeping in sight Indian susceptibilities. The diplomat who founded the Pakistani Legation in Rome, Sultan M. Khan, felt that there was no need for it in view of monetary constraints: 'Italy was not then an influential country on the European scene, hardly any trade existed and there were no significant issues between the two countries.'

Later the diplomatic profile increased when Begum Raana Liaquat *Khan, the widow of the slain first Prime Minister of Pakistan was appointed Ambassador to Italy.

Politically the two countries never entered into remarkable relations, yet cordial relations unmarred by conflict enabled them to develop mutually beneficial ties to the extent that Italy became Pakistan's fourth European trade partner, sixth world partner in the 1980s and the biggest buyer of Pakistani leather and leather goods. Apart from commerce, both countries have cooperated in the field of industry, technology and culture. In culture the emphasis has been on archaeology. The first visit to Italy by a Pakistani head of state took place between 17 to 20 January 1982, when President M. Ziaul *Haq paid a state visit, and, it was during the 1980s Afghanistan crisis that relations received an impetus. Pakistan received generous Italian support during the period of the Soviet occupation of Afghanistan. Italy insisted on Soviet withdrawal from Afghanistan, and the restoration of that country's non-aligned status. Italy rendered financial assistance to the refugees. It consistently voted in favour UN resolutions calling for the withdrawal of Soviet troops.

In the 1990s, the Italian government appreciated Pakistan's privatization and liberation policy. In 1995, Foreign Minister Sardar Assef Ahmad Ali paid a three day official visit to Italy. Here the Foreign Minister stressed that the already existing cordial political relations be enhanced in economic fields. Pakistan urged Italy to condemn the human rights violations taking place in Indian held *Kashmir. Political support was not visible but Pakistani exports increased from $185 million in 1993-94, to $238 million in 1994-95, and imports from Italy also increased from $206 million to $542 million during the some period. In the 1990s major Italian companies contributed in Quetta Power Projects, the construction of a bypass on the Indus River, and Ghazi Brotha Power Projects. In July 1997, Italy and Pakistan signed on agreement for promoting and protecting bilateral investment and enhancing economic cooperation. According to the agreement, 'Most Favoured Nation Treatment will be granted to all investments of the respective countries'. The agreement was enforced for an initial period of ten years and thereafter would continue to be in force for a period of five years.

Subsequently in 2000, the Italian government donated 15,000 metric tons of wheat worth $2.3 million to Pakistan. In March 2000, Italy showed appreciation of the steps taken by Pakistan to keep peace in the region. It was also appreciative of Pakistan's role following the 9/11 tragedy. In November 2000, the Italian Government signed a Memorandum of Understanding (MOU) for the establishment of an Enterprise Development Centre in Pakistan. This involved Italian assistance ranging between $10 million to $20 million.

In November 2001, Italy offered military help to Pakistan in the war against terrorism. In March 2002, the Italian government converted $85 million loan into a social action grant. It also provided $7 million for small and medium projects. Technological collaboration in the textile industry and electronic industry has continued.

The Iraq War of 2003 showed a difference of perception. While Italy favoured the invasion of Iraq, Pakistan opposed it. Italian presence in Pakistan is significant in the cultural sector as well. An Italian Language Learning facility has been opened at the University of Karachi. Italian Scholars led by Allesandro Bausani have projected *Urdu and Pakistani literature in Italy. Greater activity was witnessed in the fields of archaeology and anthropology for over five decades. Italians have worked on archaeological sites in *Swat and the *Gandhara region generally.

R. HASAN

Ithna Ashariya

(Arabic: twelver) The main branch of *Shia Islam, who follow twelve imams (*see,* 'Shia').

YU.V. GANKOVSKY

Ivory-work

One of the most ancient crafts practised by the peoples of South Asia. Tusks of local elephants were used as were tusks imported from Africa, *narwhal* tusks, and 'fish teeth' (most likely the tusks of mammoths). Various methods of ivory-work were practised in the territory of Pakistan, including carving-openwork or tracery-polishing, tooling on a lathe, engraving, painting, and etching. Ivory is also used as finishing material in inlays on wood. The tools used are saws, drills, and chisels. To make work easier, ivory is softened through storage in a wet cloth.

The most ancient objects made of ivory belonged to the *Harappa civilization. Combs, hairpins, sticks for painting eyelids, batons, seals, and other objects of everyday use were found there. These objects continued to be made of ivory in the centuries that followed. The most ancient ivory sculpture dates from the second century BC.

Ivory tooling was particularly widespread in the *Kushan empire. The world's largest find of ivory objects from the first-second century AD was made in Bagram, Afghanistan: among other objects, some 6,000 plaquettes were found bearing reliefs for decorating furniture. Plates with engraved drawings were also discovered there.

In the *Mughal empire, ivory was fashionable, but mostly objects of everyday use were produced: dagger hilts, powder flasks, and dice, for example. Floral and geometrical ornaments were predominant. Ivory inlays on wood were also known in that period.

In the nineteenth century, the character of ivory objects changed under European influence. Sculptures with a likeness to the original became valued, as did accuracy in the representation of ethnic types, their costumes and animals, all of which seem exotic to the European eye.

E.V. GANEVSKAYA

J

Jafri, Ada (1924–)

Poet. Her real name is Aziza Jahan Begum. She writes under the pen-names Ada, Ada Jafri and Ada Badayuni. Born in Uttar Pradesh, India, she grew up in the family of a government official and received a traditional domestic education. She was tutored in poetic craftsmanship by such well-known traditionalist poets as Akhtar *Shirani and Asar Lakhnawi. In 1941, she published her poems in the magazine *Ruman* (Romance).

After 1947, Ada Jafri settled in Pakistan. Her first collection of poems *Men saz dhundhti pahti* (In Search of Harmony) was published in 1950. In 1967, she published another collection of her verse, *Shehr-e-dard* (The City of Pain).

Her verse often appears today in various Pakistani magazines. *Ajkal* (Nowadays) has been publishing her poetry since 1950.

Jafri experiments with various formal devices, uses free and unrhymed verse. Her lyrical **ghazals* are permeated with a deep melancholy feeling. She looks for solace in communion with nature and she is known for confronting acute contemporary problems. (*see* Urdu Literature)

WORKS: *'Shehr-i-dard' (The City of Pain), 1967, Karachi, Lahore, Dhaka.*

BIBLIOGRAPHY: *Abdul Wahid, 'Jadid Shuara-i-Urdu' (Anthology of Contemporary Urdu Poetry), Lahore, Karachi.*

N.V. GLEBOV

Jagir

(Persian: holding a place) A form of land ownership and administration in South Asia under the Mughals. A **jagirdar* (*jagir* holder) received his *jagir* directly from the *padshah*. *Jagir* could be taken away or replaced at any time. With the weakening of the *Mughal Empire, many *jagirs* became hereditary. During the British rule (*see* British India) most of the *jagirs* were abolished or confiscated. (*see* Jagirdar)

BIBLIOGRAPHY: *I.H. Qureshi, 'The Administration of the Mughal Empire', Karachi, 1966.*

L.B. ALAYEV

Jagirdar

**Jagir* holder in South Asia under the Great Mughals. A government employee (*mansabdar*) with a military rank could be paid with a *jagir* from the state treasury, instead of a salary. The tax rate applied depended on the *jagirdar's* rank.

A *jagirdar* was supposed to keep his land allotment in perfect order and also keep a cavalry detachment in accordance with his rank.

Under Akbar (*see* Mughal Empire), ranks were abolished and came to be reflected in the number of persons a *jagirdar* was obliged to support: from ten to five hundred, which determined his place in the social hierarchy. Besides, each *jagirdar* was supposed to supply a required number of horsemen (*sawars*) to the state.

During the British rule (*see* British India) and the subsequent tax settlement, the majority of *jagirdars* lost their land allotments.

L.B. ALAYEV

Jahangir, Asma (1952–)

Lawyer/Human rights activist. A human rights activist, lawyer, author and defender of freedoms, especially of minorities and women. Married to fellow lawyer Shezad Jahangir, Asma Jahangir was a founding member of the Human Rights Commission of Pakistan (HRCP) in 1986, and in 1995 received the Ramon Magsaysay award for 'greatness of spirit shown in service of the people'.

She was only twenty, and not yet a lawyer, when she first filed a constitutional petition in the Supreme Court (*See* Judicial System in Pakistan) challenging the arrest of her father, Malik Ghulam Jilani. She earned a degree in Law in 1978, and in 1981 she and her sister, Hina Jilani established their own law firm. They were founding members of the *Women's Action Forum (WAF), a campaigning pressure group for women's rights.

In 1986, they set up AGHS Legal Aid, the first free legal aid centre in Pakistan.

In 1982, Asma Jahangir earned the nickname 'little heroine' after leading a protest march in Islamabad against a decision by the then President Ziaul *Haq to enforce religious laws that were perceived to be detrimental to the rights of women and minorities. She managed in the mid-1980s to overturn a death sentence against a blind woman who was gang-raped and then charged with adultery. Since then, she and I.A. Rehman, director of the Human Rights Commission, have defended thousands of cases.

In 1998, United Nations Secretary-General Kofi Annan appointed her as the UN Special Rapporteur of the Commission on Human Rights on extra judicial, summary or arbitrary executions. Since her appointment, Jahangir has visited Albania, Macedonia, Mexico, East Timor, Nepal, Turkey and Honduras responding to the keenness of governments to improve the situation, while also documenting human rights abuses.

In 2001, Asma Jahangir and Hina Jilani were awarded the Millennium Peace Prize.

S.T. KUREISHI

Jalal, Ayesha

Historian. Ayesha Jalal graduated as a double major in history and political science from Wellesley College in 1978. Her doctoral research at the University of Cambridge focused on the most important event in modern South Asian history—the partition of India at the moment of decolonization in 1947.

Her first book, on Mohammad Ali *Jinnah and partition, put forward the view that Jinnah had not really wanted Pakistan, but was forced to accept it because of Congress manoeuvres. This is also known as the Revisionist theory of partition.

WORKS: *'The Sole Spokesman: Jinnah, the Muslim League and the demand for Pakistan', Cambridge, 1985; 'The State of Martial Rule', Cambridge, 1990; 'Democracy and Authoritarianism in South Asia', Cambridge, 1995; 'Self and Sovereignty: Individual and Community in Islam, since 1850s, Lahore, 2001.*

YU.V. GANKOVSKY

Jalaliya

A *Shia *Sufi order of the 'wandering derwishes'. Its founder was Sheikh Jalaluddin Surkh Bukhari (1307–83).

It sprang up as a Shia branch of the *Suhrawardiya order in the town of Uch-Sharif (district Bahawalpur, *Punjab province, Pakistan).

YU.V. GANKOVSKY

Jalibi, Jameel, Dr. (1928–)

Lirerary Critic. Jameel Jalibi obtained his MA, LLB and PhD degrees from the University of Karachi. He joined the Central Superior Services, eventually retiring in 1983 as Commissioner of Income Tax. The same year, he was appointed Vice-Chancellor of Karachi University, a position he retained until 1987, when he was appointed Chairman National Language Authority.

He received the Daud Prize for critical literature four times. He was awarded the *Sitara-i-Imtiaz* and *Hilal-i-Imtiaz*.

Dr Jameel Jalibi was a scholar and critic, equally at home with the most ancient and most modern tracts of *Urdu literature. His critical acumen and erudition have made him an outstanding historian of Urdu literature.

WORKS: *'Pakistani Culture', Karachi, 1964; 'Tanquid-o-Tajruba', Karachi; 'Tarikh-i-Adabi-Urdu' 3 Vols., Lahore, 1975–82; Muasir Adab, Karachi, 1991, (ed.) Kadam Rao, Padam Rao, Karachi, 1972; 'Dewan-i-Hasan Shauqui', Karachi, 1971.*

BIBLIOGRAPHY: *'Dr. Jameel Jalibi Ek Mutalia', Delhi, 1991; 'Armaghan', (ed.) Musharraf Ahmad, Karachi, 1996; Nasim Fatima, 'Swanhi Kitabiat', Islamabad, 1988.*

M.R. KAZIMI

Jallandhari, Hafeez (1900–82)

Poet. Muhammad Hafeez (his real name) was an *Urdu-language poet who is best known as the author of the national anthem. He grew up in an orthodox Muslim family. Upon graduation from a college in Jallandhar, he set up a modest publishing house in Lahore, and worked for a pittance as editor of many literary journals. According to his short autobiography, Hafeez underwent great hardship, sometimes working as a manual labourer.

During the Second World War, Hafeez worked for the War Publicity Department in Delhi, editing and publishing a number of newspapers and magazines. In 1947, he moved to Pakistan, where he lived in Karachi and Lahore.

His creative thinking was influenced by Muhammad Iqbal, which explains his interest in social and political problems. In 1925, he published his first collection of lyrical verse, *Naghma-Zar* (Melancholy Melodies); he later published other collections of poetry: *Soz-o-Saz* (Joy and Sorrow), and *Talkhaba-i-Shirin* (The Sweetness of Grief). His *Shah Nama-i-Islam* (Great Poem of Islam) is particularly popular in Pakistan. While exploiting the possibilities of prosody and the figurative style of Urdu poetry, Hafeez tried to revive and modernize Islamic chronicles.

He experimented with many forms in his poems, making them more akin to *geet* or songs. His poems and lyrics had great freshness and vitality as he broke away from the Persian mould of Urdu poetry and inclined towards Bhasha. He wrote stanzas containing short lines, sometimes evocative in nature, sometimes reflective, but always unaffected and captivating. His poems and lyrics have been used in music, thus adding to his popularity. He is the winner of a number of prestigious literary prizes.

BIBLIOGRAPHY: *Abdul Wahid, 'Jadid Shuara-i-Urdu' Anthology of Contemporary Urdu Poetry, Lahore-Karachi, undated; 'Afkar-Hafiz Jullundhri Number', (ed.) Sahba Lucknowi, Karachi, 1963; (ed.) Habib Ahmad Siddiqui, Guldasta, Gorakhpur, 1942.*

N.V. GLEBOV

Jam Nizamuddin Tomb

A monument of medieval architecture in Pakistan. The tomb is in cubic form, built of red sandstone with an unfinished dome. It stands on Makli Hill in Thatta, in a necropolis (1509).

On the entrance side, the facade has a decorative stone balcony of a complex configuration whose elements (consoles, columns, belts, little arches, etc.) are covered with carpet-like ornamentation reminiscent of wood-carving techniques.

A.B. RALLEV

Jamaat-i-Islami

(Islamic Society) A religious-communal party founded on 25 August 1941 in Lahore. Its founder and leader from 1941 to 1972 was Maulana Abul Ala *Maududi, considered one of the outstanding Islamic scholars of his time.

Prior to 1947, *Jamaat-i-Islami* opposed the formation of Pakistan. At the 1948 Conference in Allahabad, it was divided into *Jamaat-i-Islami-Hind* (which operates in India) and *Jamaat-i-Islami* Pakistan (which functions in Pakistan); in 1972, *Jamaat-i-Islami* Bangladesh separated from the latter.

From 1947 to 1977, the party was in opposition to all the regimes that came to power in Pakistan. However, it joined the regime of General Ziaul *Haq for a time. It called for the transformation of Pakistan into a theocratic state, based solely on Islamic principles.

It was banned from October 1958 to June 1962 and from January to August 1964.

The party is most active in the *Punjab province and in the southern districts of *Sindh. In 1953, it was one of the principal organizers of the anti-*Ahmadiya riots (*see* Ahmadiya). In January 1977, it was a member of the *Pakistan National Alliance, opposing Z.A. *Bhutto's government. In October 1988, it became been a member of the *Islamic Democratic Alliance, or **Islami Jamhuri Ittehad.*

Since 2002, it has been one of the dominant parties in the Muttahida Majlis-i-Amal (MMA), an alliance of religiously oriented political parties that leads the opposition to the government of General Parvez *Musharraf. The MMA has a dominant position in the NWFP Provincial Assembly and has formed the government in that province. It is part of the governing coalition in Balochistan as well.

The party consists of full members (or **rukn*, some 1,200), persons holding the same views as the party (*muttafiqin*), sympathizers (*hamdard*), and those influenced by the party (*mutassir*). The party's leader (*Amir-i-Ala)* presides over a consultative council (*Majlis-i-Shura),* consisting of 50 members elected for three years by party members, and appoints an executive committee.

BIBLIOGRAPHY: *R.I. Sherkovina, 'Political Parties and Political Struggle in Pakistan', Moscow, 1983 (in Russian); Kalim Bahadur, 'The Jamaat-i-Islami of Pakistan: Political Thought and Action', Lahore, 1978; L. Binder, 'Religion and Politics in Pakistan', Los Angeles, 1961.*

N.G. PRUSSAKOVA

Jamaldini, Abdul Wahid Azad (1918–1980)

Poet. A *Balochi language poet, Azad was the head of the Balochistan Progressive Writers' Association and, in 1955-56, he published the journal *Balochi.* Azad also published a collection of his verse with parallel *Urdu translations in 1952. Most of his poetry has been published only in periodicals. Azad Jamaldini made an important contribution to the renovation of Balochi poetry and democratisation of *Balochi literature, retrieving it from medieval canons.

His poetry is inspired by the revival of the Balochi people, language, and culture.

BIBLIOGRAPHY: *Baloch, 'Brahui ma Faaruf-i-Musanifin', Karachi, 1973.*

A.S. SUKHOCHEV

Jamiat ul-Ulema-i-Hind

(Society of Indian Ulema) Founded in 1919 by a group of patriotically-minded **Ulema* (religious leaders) of *Deoband, *Nadwat ul-Ulema* and **Farangi-Mahal*, led by Maulana Mahmud Al-Hasan. Took an active part in the *Khilafat movement.

In the 1930s, broke into two practically independent factions. One was influenced by the ideas of Maulana Abul Kalam *Azad and opposed the formation of an independent Muslim state in *British India. The other, led by Shabbir Ahmad Usmani (1885–1949), supported the movement for the formation of Pakistan.

YU.V. GANKOVSKY

Jamiat ul-Ulema-i-Islam

(Society of Muslim Theologians) One of the more influential organizations of Pakistani **Ulema*. Founded on 29 October 1945 at Calcutta by a group of Muslim theologians. They supported the appeal of the *Muslim League to set up independent Muslim states in *British India, on the territories where the majority of the population were Muslims. They were led by Maulana Shabbir Ahmad Usmani (1885-1949).

JUI was mainly composed of the followers of the **Dar-ul-Ulum* of *Deoband. JUI had a certain influence on the elaboration of principles underlying all the Constitutions of Pakistan. Members of JUI engage in religious propaganda as well as charity work.

After 1947, the JUI formed several factions. The leaders of the right-wing factions as a rule, often lead campaigns against progressive and democratic forces. Moderate leaders tend to avoid confrontation with the government.

JUI stands for the consistent Islamization of the social and political life of Pakistan. It joined the Movement for the Restoration of Democracy (MRD) and is, at the time of writing, the largest single party within the MMA (*Muttahida Majlis-i-Amal*), an alliance of religiously oriented political parties that leads the opposition to the government of General Parvez *Musharraf. Its president is Maulana Fazlur Rahman, being the Leader of the Opposition.

JUI's supreme body is a council– *Majlis-i-Shura*, which elects the leader–*Amir-i-Ala*–and his deputies. The largest number of followers is in the southern regions of the *North West Frontier Province.

BIBLIOGRAPHY: *R.I. Sherkovina, 'Political Parties and Political Struggles in Pakistan', Moscow, 1983 (in Russian), S.A.S. Pirzada, 'The Politics of the Jamiat Ulema-i-Islam', Karachi, 2000.*

A.SH. NIYAZI

Jamiat-ul-Ulema-i-Pakistan

(Society of Pakistan's *Ulema*) One of the more influential organizations of Muslim theologians in Pakistan. Founded in 1948 in Multan by a group of orthodox *Sunni **Ulema* led by Sayid Muhammad Ahmad Qadri, it aims at the complete Islamization of Pakistan.

Ideologically, it is based on the Barelwi School. The party's vote bank is mostly concentrated in the cities of *Sindh. The supreme body is the Council *(Shura)*, electing the leaders. The party is a component of the MMA (*Mutahida Majlis-i-Amal*), its late president Maulana Shah Ahmad Noorani being the head of the MMA prior to his death. There are several factions.

BIBLIOGRAPHY: *R.I. Sherkovina, 'Political Parties and Political Struggles in Pakistan', Moscow, 1983 (in Russian).*

A. NIYAZI

Jang Group

A newspaper and publishing group owned by Khalilur Rahman, a successful businessman. The Jang Group owns the *Urdu newspaper *Jang* (published in Karachi, Lahore, Rawalpindi, Quetta, and London), the evening newspaper Daily News (in English), the weeklies *Akhbar-i-Jahan* (in Urdu), and Mag (in English).

In 1989 their readership reached one million, to a large extent thanks to computerized typesetting in Urdu.

V.A. LAVROV

Jat

A large agrarian caste in the *Punjab, Haryana, Rajasthan, and in the Indian state of Uttar Pradesh.

Jats speak *Punjabi and Western Hindi dialects. They profess Hinduism, Sikhism, and Islam. Instead of endogamous subdivisions and subcastes, they have many exogamous subdivisions and subcastes called 'got' or 'gotra', and bear proper names.

The Jats originally came from the western trans-Indus regions following the Muslim conquest of northern India.

L.B. ALAYEV

Jatoi

A large influential clan in *Sindh. In the mid-18th century, the Jatoi clan moved to Sindh from East *Balochistan. They mainly settled in the Nawabshah district, Sukkur Division. The *Sindhi Jatoi clan is ethnically related to the *Balochi Jatoi tribe, inhabiting the Kachhi district in Sibi Division, Balochistan.

The senior members of the clan cooperated with the British colonial authorities from 1849–1947, and were rewarded with considerable land allotments and honorary titles. After the formation of Pakistan in 1947, the Jatoi clan took an active part in the country's political life.

YU.V. GANKOVSKY

Jatoi, Ghulam Mustafa (1931–)

Prime Minister of Pakistan (August 1990–October 1990). Born to a wealthy land-owning family, Mustafa Jatoi has a degree from Cambridge and is a lawyer by profession. He was a Member of the Provincial Assembly of *West Pakistan in 1956 and the National Assembly of *Pakistan in 1965, 1970, and 1977. He joined the Pakistan People's Party in 1969.

From 1972 to 1973, he served as Minister for Communications and Natural Resources in the Central government and, from 1974 to 1977, as the Chief Minister of the *Sindh provincial government. In 1986, he organized and led the National People's Party. On 6 August 1990, following the dissolution of the National Assembly and the dismissal of Benazir *Bhutto from the post of prime minister, G.M. Jatoi was installed as interim prime minister. He remained in the post until 6 October 1990, when he was replaced by Mian Nawaz *Sharif.

YU.V. GANKOVSKY

Jatoi, Hyder Bakhsh (1901–71)

Civil Rights Activist/Poet. Also known as *Baba-i Sindh* (Father of *Sindh), Hyder Bakhsh Jatoi was both a public figure and poet. He graduated from Bombay University in 1923. From 1927 to 1945, he was a member of the Indian Civil Service. In 1930, he helped organize the Sindh *Hari* Committee (Committee of the *Sindhi Sharecroppers) and, from 1946–70, served as its president.

From 1948 to 1969, he actively participated in the Sindhi movement and was repeatedly arrested. His well-known works include the long poems *Shikwah* (Complaint, 1929),and *Azadi-i Qaum* (National Freedom, 1946), both of which were devoted to the national liberation struggle.

WORKS: *'Shall Sindhi Remain in Karachi or Not'?, Hyderabad, 1957.*

YU.V. GANKOVSKY

Jewellery making in Pakistan

It was practised as an art as far back as the *Harappan civilization; its centres, *Mohenjo-Daro and Harappa. Beads made of semiprecious stones, ceramics, and metal, as well as bracelets, earrings, and other pieces of jewellery for both men and women have been found in digs.

At the time of the Mughals, magnificent ornaments were made of gold with precious stones and enamels. The stones were not faceted: their natural beauty and glitter were underlined.

In modern Pakistan, jewellery is made in all regions; in rural areas, silver ornaments are traditionally worn. The jewellery of *Sindh, *Balochistan, and the *Punjab is particularly famous.

In Sindh, *kundan* necklaces of unfaceted stones or glass with coloured backgrounds are made. In *Chitral, *Kohat, and *Swat, heavy necklaces are manufactured consisting of beads and coins, often with a large central pendant with a blue stone. The ornaments often act as amulets or protection against the 'evil eye' and generally against evil forces; they also help to achieve, according to local beliefs happiness and prosperity.

O.V. LYSTSOVA

Jhangar

An archaeological culture of the first half of the 1st millennia BC was discovered in Sindh in the 1930s, on Lake Manchhar. In *Sindh, this culture can be observed at several sites (*Amri, *Chanhu-Daro); this culture is best identifiable in Chanhu-Daro.

No dwelling remnants have been found at Jhangar. Pottery is made mostly of grey clay with grooved triangles, herring-bone and chevrons as ornaments. Kernoses and stylised anthropomorphic figurines with grooved ornaments were also found. The pottery is similar to Pirak culture (III period) in *Balochistan. Some believe that this culture belonged to the *Aryans.

BIBLIOGRAPHY: *Mackey E., 'Chanhu-Daro Excavation 1935-6', New Haven, 1943.*

N.M. VINOGRADOVA

Jhech Doab (also Chaj Doab)

A territory between the *Jhelum and *Chenab in *Punjab Derives its name from the initial letters of the rivers Jhelum and Chenab. Doab means a tract of land between two rivers.

YU.V. GANKOVSKY

Jhelum (also Jhelam)

(In Kashmir; *Veth*; ancient name, *Hidaspes*, *Bidaspes*, and in Sanskrit *Witasta-tasta*) This river lies to the east of the *Indus and west of the *Chenab, of which it is the largest tributary. It is approximately 810 km. long. The basin area is 55,300 sq. km.

Its source is to be found in the northern slope of the Pir-Panjal range in the *Himalayas, 20 km. to the south-east of Banihal, at an altitude of about 3,000 metres.

The Jhelum is mainly fed by glacier and subterranean waters. In its upper reaches it flows though Vular Lake, thus becoming navigable for about 110 km.

Rushing through Pir-Panjal, it pass through a deep gorge, Baramula, which has almost vertical sides and is 2,100 metres deep in parts. Crossing the *Salt Range in the vicinity of the town of Jhelum, the river flows onto the Indus-Ganges Plain and becomes navigable again for about 320 km. In its lower reaches, it borders the western edge of the *Thal Desert.

Its largest tributaries are the Kishanganga from the west and the Punch from the east. On the plain, its water supply comes from rain. It floods in the summer. The mean water discharge is 930 cu. meters/sec. The Jhelum is rich in fish.

Its waters are widely used for irrigation. There is a reservoir and hydro-power station near Mangla. The largest cities near the Jhelum river are Sargodha and Jhelum.

S.B. ROSTOTSKY

Jhoomar (also Ghoomar)

(literally spinning or going around) This is the name given to two different kinds of dances. One is a dance from *Balochistan whereas the other is from the *Punjab. This dance is very much part of Punjab's folk heritage. It is a graceful dance based on a *Jhoomar* rhythm. Dancers circle around the drummer and sing graceful lyrics as they dance.

In Multan, Muzaffargarh and *Bahawalpur, women perform the *Jhoomar*. It is a romantic dance, beginning with a circle, but breaking and forming patterns as it progresses–much like the patterns in a kaleidoscope. In *Jhelum, men perform it, but it is quite different from the women's dance.

R. HUSAIN

Jhukar

A late *Harappan culture of the first half of the 2nd millennium BC has been found at Jhukar in *Sindh. N.G. Majumdar discovered it in 1925, 20 km. to the west of Mohenjo-Daro. It consists of two tells 'A' and 'B', 5 metres and 21 metres high.

Majumdar identified three periods: the lower prehistoric, with Harappan ware, the upper pre-historic with the 'D' type ware and the later Indo-Sassanid.

Culture 'D' is a local culture that can be identified over a limited territory. It can be found in multi-level sites of *Amri and *Chanhu-Daro; there is no chronological gap between the Harappan levels of the classical period and 'D' on these sites.

In culture 'D' the Harappan pottery ornamentation changes into the new style in which the patterns are executed in two colours, black and red. The vessel shapes also change. This is a trace of *Balochi ware (see *Kulli culture).

Round and square seals made of stone that differ from similar objects from Harappa; bronze socketed axes, bronze dress pins with double-spiral heads are especially interesting. Some archaeologists identify the people of 'D' culture with Indo-Aryans. Recent studies on the sites of the Harappa culture allow one to surmise that 'D' culture is a later Harappa variant on Sindh territory.

BIBLIOGRAPHY: *N.G. Majumdar, 'Excavation at Juhar', AKASI 1927-8; 1929; Brigget and Raymond Allchin, 'The Rise of Civilization in India and Pakistan', Cambridge, 1982; Mackay Ernest, 'Chanhu-Daro Excavation 1935-6', New Haven, 1948.*

N.M. VINOGRADOVA

Jihad

(from the Arabic *jahada*—to devote all of one's strength, to fight) A holy war against infidels; a struggle for a righteous cause.

YU.V. GANKOVSKY

Jinnah, Fatima (1893–1967)

Political Activist. Popularly referred to as *Madar-i Millat* (Mother of the Nation), the younger sister of *Quaid-i-Azam* Mohammad Ali *Jinnah received her higher education in Bombay and Calcutta and had a degree in Dentistry. From 1923 to 1929, she practiced as a surgeon. Fatima Jinnah took an active part in the movement for the formation of Pakistan.

Fatima Jinnah, sister of Quaid-i-Azam, Muhammad Ali Jinnah.

In September 1964, the Combined Opposition Parties (COP) selected her as presidential candidate to run against President Ayub *Khan. In the presidential elections of 2 January 1965, she received 36.3 per cent of the votes (Ayub Khan received 63.3 per cent).

Fatima Jinnah was a consistent fighter for the restoration of democracy, for direct elections of the president, parliament, provincial legislative assemblies and for the parliamentary system of government.

WORKS: *'My Brother', Karachi, 1987.*

YU.V. GANKOVSKY

Jinnah, Muhammad Ali (1876–1948)

Founder of Pakistan. Born in Karachi on 25 December 1876, Muhammad Ali Jinnah died in the same city on 11 September 1948 as the founder and the first Governor-General of Pakistan. Known to the nation as *Quaid-i-Azam* (Greatest Leader), it can be truly said about Jinnah, as about very few other statesmen, that he actually changed the map of the world. His father, Mr. Jinnah Poonja, was a businessman.

Muhammad Ali Jinnah, Founder of Pakistan.

Young Muhammad Ali received his primary education from *Sindh Mudrasatul-Islam* in Karachi. He worked for a while in a trading company with which his father did business and then left for England, where he studied Law. He was called to the Bar at Lincoln's Inn in 1896.

Returning to India, he helped his father overcome a financial crisis. He moved to Bombay (now Mumbai) and commenced his own law practice in partnership with Kanji Dwarkadas. He actively practiced Law well through the 1930s.

Jinnah married Ruttie, the daughter of the wealthy businessman, Sir Dinshaw Petit, in 1918. Their daughter Dina was born in 1919. After Ruttie's death from cancer in 1919, Jinnah never remarried.

As an admirer of the great Liberal theorist John Bright, with whom he maintained a correspondence for many years after his return to India, Jinnah held firmly the ideals of democracy, tolerance, constitutionalism and national self-determination. Jinnah's political career can be divided into two broad phases: 1906-37 and 1937-47.

In the first phase, Jinnah was a staunch Indian nationalist and a member of the Indian National Congress. He called himself 'an Indian first, and a Muslim afterwards.' It was through his efforts that *Muslim League and Congress Party agreed to a political settlement in 1916. This agreement is known as the '*Lucknow Pact', according to which Congress for the first time recognized a separate position of the Muslims and accepted the Muslim demand for a separate electorate. Jinnah's disillusionment with the Congress began to manifest itself when the party turned away from constitutional struggle to embrace the agitational methods advocated by Mohandas Gandhi, simultaneously launching the Civil Disobedience Movement and *Khilafat Movement in 1920. In due course, Jinnah left the Congress and devoted his energies towards the welfare of the Muslims of the subcontinent.

In 1928, Motilal Nehru put forward the *Nehru Report, which rejected the proposition that Muslims are a separate nation within India. Jinnah responded with his *Fourteen Points in 1929, in which it is clearly stated that there are two big nations in India, Muslims and Hindus. Jinnah's Fourteen Points also included demands for constitutional reforms.

In 1934, Jinnah took over the control of the Muslim League and began the process of developing it into a strong and organized party. Jinnah's policies became progressively opposed to his previous positions. He was especially angered by the Congress Party's ultimatum to the Muslim League to merge with the National Congress in order to participate in provincial governments in 1937. Furthermore, during the period of Congress provincial governments, the principle of majority rule was exercised to the neglect and even the detriment of the Muslims. All this convinced Jinnah that the Congress was determined to establish the majority Hindu rule in a united India. Following this and many other political developments, Jinnah finally got Pakistan. He chose Karachi as the capital, established an independent currency, and the State Bank.

Jinnah died on 11 September 1948 after suffering from Tuberculosis. He is buried in Karachi.

H. MALIK

Jinnah, Ruttie (1900–29)

Wife of M.A. *Jinnah. Ruttie Jinnah was the daughter of Sir Dinshaw Petit. She was born into a *Parsi family but converted to Islam the day before her marriage to Mohammad Ali Jinnah on 19 April 1918 in Bombay (now Mumbai).

On 11 December 1918, she joined her husband in braving police brutality during a demonstration organized against Lord Willingdon, the Governor of Bombay.

Ruttie Jinnah made her only public speech in May 1919, from the platform of the first All-India Trade Union Congress, held to protest the deportation of B.G. Horniman, editor of the *Bombay Chronicle*.

She was an ardent nationalist and very outspoken. She had close relations with Jinnah's political associates, notably Mrs Annie Besant and Mrs Sarojini Naidu. M.K. Gandhi tried to influence Jinnah through her to adopt his programme of boycotting foreign goods, but Mrs Jinnah plainly told Gandhi that his programme was impractical.

Her marriage, involving estrangement from her family, was not a lasting success. Jinnah had resigned from the Orient Club where he played billiards and chess, but his preoccupation with law and politics gave him little time for family life. One daughter, Dina Wadia, was born to them in August 1919 in London.

Ruttie Jinnah was interested in theosophy and was a champion of animal rights. She died, after a protracted illness, on her birthday, 20 February 1929.

BIBLIOGRAPHY: *Kanji Dwarkadas, 'Ruttie Jinnah: The Story of a Great Friendship', Bombay, 1963.*

M.R. KAZIMI

Jirga

(In Farsi and Pashtu, circle) Originally, the *Jirga* was the council of a gens, a clan, or tribe among the *Pashtuns. *Ahl-i jirga* is a council or meeting of all the men belonging to the given gens, clan, or tribe. *Jirga-i malikan* is the council of elders. In a broader sense, a *jirga* is a conference, a council of common law experts (*Jirgamar*) authorized by disputants to hear a case.

YU.V. GANKOVSKY

Jiziyah

(Arabic: *Jaza*, to compensate, to replace, to recover) Originally meant 'poll tax' that had to be paid by non-Muslims in Muslim states (*Ahl az-dhimma*–protected persons).

In the *Mughal empire, *Jiziyah* was abolished first by the *Padshah* Akbar and then by Shah Alam Bahadur Shah I (1707–12).

BIBLIOGRAPHY: *H.G. Keene, 'The Turks in India', London, 1879; I.H. Qureshi, 'The Administration of the Mughal Empire', Karachi, 1966.*

YU.V. GANKOVSKY

Judicial System of Pakistan

The judicial system is headed by the Supreme Court. Its decisions are binding for all the legal bodies of the country. The Supreme Court is located in Islamabad, with divisions in Lahore and Karachi. The Chief Justice of Pakistan and judges of the Supreme Court are appointed by the president. Junior judges are appointed by the president after consultation with the chief justice. Supreme Court judges may serve until they are 65. Only misconduct or incapacity to serve may be grounds for removal of a Supreme Court judge.

The Supreme Court has original jurisdiction in any dispute between the federal and provincial governments, and also between provincial governments. The Supreme Court acts as an appeal court in considering decisions of the High Court cases involving essential legal issues connected with interpretations of the constitution, which involve a death or life sentence.

The Supreme Court also functions as a consultative body, formulating its conclusions on issues of law on which the president seeks its opinion. One of the most important functions of the Supreme Court is supervision over the observance of the fundamental rights of citizens. Of extreme importance are the Supreme Court's decisions on the constitutionality of certain actions of state agencies and on the broader issue of their legitimacy.

In the provinces, the top legal bodies are the High Courts. The Chief Justice and the members of a High Court are appointed by the president. The Chief Justice of a High Court is appointed after consultations between the president, the Chief Justice of Pakistan, and the governor of the province in question. High Court judges must leave office at the age of 62. The High Court guides and controls the work of all other legal bodies of the province. It considers their decisions and hears appeals. A death sentence must be confirmed by the High Court even if there is no appeal in the case. The High Court supervises the activities of the administrative bodies and the observance of civil rights embodied in the constitution. The Supreme Court develops procedures regulating the work of the members of the Supreme Court and of the High Courts. The Attorney-General of Pakistan and the Advocates-General of the provinces, appointed by the governors, help the federal and provincial governments in dealing with legal issues.

The president appoints a Federal Ombudsman for the term of five years, whose duty it is to control the work of the federal administrative bodies and to consider complaints about violations of established norms and procedures, cases of corruption, misconduct, etc. The ombudsman's powers do not extend to the armed forces or to defence offices and enterprises.

The lower courts are established at the district level and are divided into criminal and civil branches. In each of these categories there are several levels; the lowest, concerned with minor matters; the district, concerned with important cases. Criminal cases, depending on their gravity, are considered in magistrate courts of various classes and at courts of sessions, the highest legal bodies dealing with criminal cases in the districts. Courts of sessions have the right to pass any sentence, including the death penalty. Legal bodies concerned with civil matters are headed by district courts.

District courts and courts of sessions are the highest level courts in a district as well as the highest appeal courts. They are appointed by the governors in consultation with the provinces' chief justices. Administrative courts and tribunals, which hear cases against civil servants, may be set up under proper legislation. The final decisions on criminal cases in which traditional Islamic punishments are levelled are passed by the Federal Shariat Court. It also determines how laws correspond to the principles of Islam.

V.N. MOSKALENKO

Junejo, Mohammed Khan (1932–92)

Prime Minister of Pakistan from 1985 to 1988. He belonged to a land-owning family. Having begun his college education in Karachi, he later studied in England. He was a disciple (*murid*) of Pir Pagaro.

Mohammad Khan Junejo, Prime Minister of Pakistan.

Junejo was a member of the West Pakistan Assembly from 1962 to 1969 and was a member of the provincial government as a Minister for Communications, Health, Local Bodies and Railways. In 1978, he became Minister for Communications of Pakistan.

YU.V. GANKOVSKY

K

Kabaddi

A traditional sport in Pakistan. It is played by two teams consisting of twelve players each, seven players on the field and five in reserve. The field is 13 x 10 metres, divided into two equal parts with special marks. The team that begins the game sends one of its players into the competitor's section of the field. As soon as the player crosses the central line, he is to keep repeating the word '*Kabaddi*' in one breath, quickly and loudly, and at the same time try to tag one or more players. The object of the game is to cross, at least once, the defence line, 3.5 metres from the control line.

The player then returns to his own section. The tagged players leave the field and the player's team gets a point.

The game consists of two, twenty minute sets. The team that scores more points wins. The rules of the game were unified in 1944. The game is also popular in Burma, India, Sri Lanka and China.

Since 1982, it has been presented as a demonstration sport in the Asian Games.

BIBLIOGRAPHY: *R.G. Goel, 'Encyclopaedia of Sports and Games', New Delhi, 1984.*

YU.V. GANKOVSKY

Kabul River

Referred to as *Kophen* by authors of antiquity, and as *Kubha* in old Indian sources. This is a river flowing through Pakistan and Afghanistan. It is 460 km. long and has a basin of approximately 75,000 sq.km. Its source is found in the *Hindu Kush Mountains and it joins the *Indus near the town of Attock.

Its waters are used for irrigating the *Peshawar Valley. The narrow gorge of the Kabul River forms the route of the famous *Khyber Pass. The river cuts through the Safedkoh (*Koh-i-Safed*, Spinghar) Mountains between Pakistan and Afghanistan, 17 km. from Peshawar. The pass is 53 km. long and 305 km. wide. The highest elevation is 1,072 meters and it is in the territory of Pakistan, at a distance of 10 km. from the border with Afghanistan.

The walls of the gorge, composed mainly of slate and limestone, rise sharply over the passage. Their height ranges from 430 to 1,000 meters. The gorge has a deserted appearance, arid climate, and practically no trees. The highest temperature is 47.8C.

In 1879, the British authorities built a road leading from Peshawar to Kabul along the Khyber Pass, and in the 1920's, a railroad was built in Pakistani territory reaching the Afghan border.

The Khyber Pass has always had considerable strategic importance as the most convenient route from Afghanistan to India. In the broader sections of the pass, there are villages, and old fortifications have been partly preserved.

YU.V. GANKOVSKY

Kafi

This is a brief lyrical poem of mystical nature in *Punjabi, *Sindhi and *Gujarati literatures. It is intended to be sung with musical accompaniment in fixed **raga* and *ragini*. The theme of exalted love is rendered in *kafi* through imagery of sensualily.

Kafi appeared for the first time in the work of Punjabi poet Shaykh Farid Ganj-i-Shakar (1173-1266), but it became particularly well developed in Sindhi literature of the seventeenth to eighteenth centuries.

A.S. SUKHOCHEV

Kafirs, Dances of the

Danced by the residents of the Kalash Valleys of Rumbur, Bunboret and Birir that lie within *Chitral in

Kalash dances at a ceremony.

the *North West Frontier Province. These valleys are the home of a primitive pagan tribe–the Kafirs. They wear black robes and elaborate headdresses as well as colourful bead and silver jewellery.

The Kafirs have a religion and culture of their own. There is much dancing in the celebration of all their festivals and special occasions, whereby the elders chant legends to drums and the women dance arm-in-arm in a circle.

R. HUSAIN

Kaikobad (1857–1951)

Poet. Muhammad Kazim al-Qureshi (his real name) was a Bengali poet, who attended St. Gregory School and Madrasah in Dhaka. He became head of the post office in his native village.

His early verse was published in a collection *Biroh-Bilap* (Lament in Separation, 1870). His later collection *Oshru-Mala* (A Garland of Tears, 1895) was very popular and his *magnum opus* is the long poem *Mohan Shoshan* (The Great Burning of the Dead, 1904), an epic portrayal of the Third Battle of Panipat and the downfall of the Maratha Confederacy.

Kaikobad's work reflected the spiritual yearnings of Bengali Muslims at the turn of the century; it was a search for identity and historic roots in conditions of modernization and the onslaught of alien cultures. At the end of his life, he took Pakistani citizenship.

S.D. SEREBRYANY

Kakar

A *Pashtun tribe belonging to the Ghurghusht group of tribes. The main clans are the Babi, Sardar-Khel, Hamazai, Mando-Khel, Saragzhai, Nagra, Dawi, Bayanzai, Khojazia, and the Kibzai. The estimated total population is more than 200,000.

The majority of Kakars live in the north-eastern districts of the Pakistani province of Balochistan and in individual *khels* in south-western Afghanistan.

BIBLIOGRAPHY: *Muhammad Hayat Khan, 'Hayat-i Afghan', Lahore, 1867 (in Urdu); L. Temirkhanov, 'Eastern Pashtuns and the New Times (Ethno-Social Characteristics)', Moscow, 1984 (in Russian); 'Eastern Pashtuns: Main Issues of Modern History', Moscow, 1987 (in Russian).*

YU.V. GANKOVSKY

Kalabagh, Amir Mohammad Khan, Malik, Nawab of (1900–70)

Statesman. The Nawab of Kalabagh belonged to the Punjab Unionist Party before independence. During the Ayub *Khan era, he first became Chairman of the West Pakistan Industrial Development Corporation, and then Governor of West Pakistan (1960–66). He had the reputation of being autocratic.

M.R. KAZIMI

Kalamkari

(from Arabic and Farsi: *kalam,* brush and *kar,* work)

A kind of hand-painting of fabrics, it is also the name for the fabrics decorated in this way.

Kalamkari painting is conducted in several stages. First, a thick cotton fabric, which will serve as the base for painting, is treated with mordants to make threads capable of absorbing the desired dye. The mordants are laid on with the aid of a brush or dye. Traditionally, natural dyes are used.

The succulent and bright colours of *kalamkari* fabrics, as well as the fact that they are sunproof and hold up to frequent washing, brought them well deserved fame.

Nowadays large decorative fabrics are manufactured, inspired by traditional kalamkari fabrics, as are textile products in everyday use-saris, kerchiefs, tablecloths, etc.

O.V. LYSTSOVA

Kalasha

Language it belongs to the *Dardic group of *Indo-Aryan languages, to the northern group of the central sub-group. The language is spoken in Kalashdesh in South *Chitral. On phonetic, morphological, and lexical criteria, the northern and southern groups of dialects are distinguished.

There are no old monuments which portray writing. Traces are observed of the influence on this language of the pre-Indo European substratum, especially in phonology.

The vocabulary is basically primordial, not borrowed from any other language. There are many loan words from the Persian language (and through it, from Arabic), some of which came through the mediation of *Urdu. Some of the loan words are from neighbouring Dardic languages.

BIBLIOGRAPHY: *D.I. Edelman, 'Dardic Languages', Moscow, 1965 (in Russian); id., 'The Dardic and Nuristani Languages', Moscow, 1983, G.A. Grierson, 'Linguistic Survey of India', Vol. VIII, pt. II, Calcutta, 1919; G. Morgenstierne, 'Indo-Iranian' Frontier Languages, in: Vol. IV, The Kalash Language, Oslo, 197; I.J. Afghani, 'The Kalash Society of Chitral', Peshawar, 1973.*

D.I. EDELMAN

Kalat Plateau

This plateau lies in the eastern part of *Balochistan, to the south-west of Quetta, between the Kirthar and *Chagai Ranges. The average elevation is 2,100-2,400 metres and it covers an area of approximately 15,000 sq. km.

It consists of hard limestone, with deposits of manganese, copper, chromium, and lead ores.

YU.V. GANKOVSKY

Kalat

1. A princely state in *Balochistan. Area: 80,100 sq.km. consisting of mostly *Brahuis, but also *Balochis, *Pashtuns, and *Sindhis.

Kalat emerged in the middle of the seventeenth century. Its ruler, Beglerbeg Nasir Khan I (1750-95), who came from the Brahui dynasty of the Ahmadzai or Kambarani, united under his authority the whole of Balochistan; he recognized the sovereignty of the *Durrani Shahs.

In April 1839, Kalat was seized by British troops and its ruler, Mehrab Khan (1817-39), was killed. According to the treaties of 1854, 1876 and 1879, Kalat ceded to Britain a considerable part of its territory (Quetta, Nushki, Nasirabad) and came under British supervision, implemented by the political agent whose seat was in the city of Kalat and who represented the Governor-General and Viceroy of India.

On 15 August 1947, the Kalat ruler Mir Ahmad Yar Khan (1902-77; reigned in 1933-55) briefly declared the state's independence. Kalat state was included in Pakistan on 31st March 1948 and abolished as a state entity in 1955.

2. A division in the province of Balochistan. It has four districts: Kalat, Kharan, Khuzdar, and *Lasbela. Area: 138,700 sq.km. Administrative centre: city of Kalat (11,000 inhabitants in 1981).

BIBLIOGRAPHY: *See Balochistan.*

YU.V. GANKOVSKY

Kalhora

A ruling dynasty in *Sindh from 1707–84. From 1750, the Kalhora were vassals of the Afghan *padishahs* Ahmad Shah Durrani (1747–73) and Timur Shah (1773–93). They were dethroned by the **sardars* of the *Balochi tribe of the *Talpurs (see: Talpur).

BIBLIOGRAPHY: *Khudadad Khan, 'Lub-i Tarikh-i Sindh', Karachi-Hyderabad, 1958.*

YU.V. GANKOVSKY

Karakoram Mountains

A range of mountains that lie to the north and west of the *Himalayan ranges. These form a vertical barrier some, 150 km. wide, with nearly 100 of its peaks rising to over 7,000 meters, including K-2 (also Godwin Austin), the second highest peak in the world, at 8,616 meters.

Unlike the alpine peaks of the south, these are massifs rising straight out of the valley floor, creating a spectacular landscape. The ranges, however, present a barrier to the monsoon and only the highest peaks receive any precipitation.

The land is largely vertical desert with an average rainfall of only 200 mm. per annum. Small areas of uncultivated flat land are covered with rolling dunes and the mountains are barren, giving rise to the nickname of 'Little Tibet' for the region.

M. STONEY

Kardar, Abdul Hafeez (1925–96)

Cricket Player. Kardar is one of the few players to have represented United India before partition in two Test matches. Kardar was the first Test captain of Pakistan.

Pakistan achieved victory in Karachi in 1951 under his captaincy to gain ICC membership. He won the first match (Karachi, 1956) against Australia and against New Zealand in 1955–56 and retired after playing against the West Indies in 1957–58.

Kardar was a left-arm batsman and scored 847 runs in 23 Tests with an average of 24.91 runs. His highest score was 93 against India at Karachi during the 1954–55 series.

As a left-arm leg spinner he took 21 wickets, average 45.42 runs per wicket. His best bowling figures were 3 for 35 against New Zealand in 1955–56.

As a captain he won six out of twenty-three Test matches and lost five. He was head of the Board of Control of Cricket Pakistan (BCCP). He was also

Member of the Punjab Assembly 1970–77, Minister for Education, *Punjab, and Ambassador to Switzerland.

S. ZAKIUDDIN

Kashmir

A historico-geographical area in the northwest of South Asia in the upper reaches of the *Indus. The historical nucleus of the area is the Kashmir valley. The bulk of the population are *Kashmiri speaking. The first states, run by Hindu *rajas*, emerged here at about the beginning of the new era. In the 7th century, the rulers of Kashmir, having consolidated their power, seized a considerable portion of *Punjab and lands on the right bank of the Indus. In 1015 and 1021, Mahmud Ghaznavi (998-1030) made an unsuccessful attempt to seize Kashmir. In 1335, a Muslim dynasty became established in Kashmir, whose founder was Shah Mirza Swati (1335-46), during whose reign the majority of the population embraced Islam. In 1586, Kashmir was conquered by the Mughal Emperor Akbar (see Mughal Empire). Between 1752 and 1819, Kashmir came under the domination of Afghan kings of the Durrani dynasty, to be conquered by Maharaja Ranjit Singh, ruler of Punjab, in 1819. In 1849-1947, Kashmir was a vassal princely state of *British India. Since 1947, north and northwest Kashmir have been under Pakistan's control (see Kashmir Dispute, Simla Agreement) and are known as '*Azad Kashmir' while the valley proper and other areas are occupied by India. (see Azad Kashmir)

BIBLIOGRAPHY: *P.N.K. Bamzai, 'History of Kashmir', Delhi, 1962; P.N. Bazaz, 'The History of Struggle for Freedom in Kashmir', New Delhi, 1954; G.M.S. Sufi, 'Kashmir', Vols. 1-2, Lahore, 1948.*

YU.V. GANKOVSKY

Kashmir dispute

This dispute arose after the partition of India and Pakistan in 1947. The Independence Act of India gave rulers of princely states the right to join one of the dominions or to remain independent. *Kashmir's Hindu ruler did not join either country. The situation was complicated in October 1947 by the invasion of a *Pashtun force from the tribal areas of the *North West Frontier Province of Pakistan. Kashmir's ruler appealed to India for help, and was advised to join the Indian Union. In October 1947, the ruler acceded to India, but Pakistan refused to recognize his accession just as India has refused to recognize the accession of Junagadh state's Muslim ruler to Pakistan. These developments led to an armed conflict in 1947-48 between India and Pakistan.

The ceasefire line, established on 1 January 1949, and confirmed by the Indo-Pakistan Agreement (see Indo-Pakistan Relations) of 29 July 1949, divided the princely state into the territories controlled by Pakistan (see Azad Kashmir, Northern Areas) and those controlled by India. The latter retained about 60 per cent of Jammu and Kashmir. The Indian controlled part was later declared a state with a special status, which was confirmed by the Indian Constitution (Article 370).

When war broke out in Kashmir, India brought the matter before the UN Security Council in January 1948, accusing Pakistan of assisting the tribesmen in violating the territorial integrity of Kashmir.

During 1948-49 the UN Security Council passed several resolutions about the settlement of Kashmir, including 1. the resolutions of 17 and 20 January 1948, which recognized the need 'to find some common ground on which the structure of a settlement may be built'. Also, a three-member commission was created with the task 'to proceed to the spot' in order to investigate the facts. The second resolution of 20 January established a mediatory commission which eventually came to be known as the United Nations Commission on India and Pakistan (UNCIP); 2. the Resolution of 21 April 1948 became the principal term of reference for all subsequent UN efforts for the settlement between India and Pakistan over Kashmir. The resolution recommended that Pakistan should secure the withdrawal of tribals and Pakistani nationals from Kashmir; India should undertake a subsequent and progressive withdrawal of the Indian forces to the minimum strength required for maintenance of law and order; a coalition government in Kashmir, representing all major political groups should be formed; and a plebiscite administrator in Kashmir should be appointed to ascertain the preference of the people.

The Security Council did not condemn Pakistan, as demanded by India, nor did it deal with the legal aspects of Kashmir's accession to India. Subsequently, relying upon Soviet diplomatic support in general, and its veto in the UN Security Council in particular, India thwarted all attempts at organizing a UN-supervised plebiscite in Kashmir; 3. the UNCIP visited the area of conflict in Kashmir, held consultations there and passed two resolutions on 13 August 1948 and 5 January 1949. Both resolutions were accepted by India and Pakistan, and were endorsed by the UN Security Council. These resolutions provided for a ceasefire and the demarcation of the ceasefire line, the demilitarization of the state, and a free and impartial plebiscite to be conducted by the United Nations. The ceasefire was soon enforced, but the withdrawal of Indian and Pakistani troops from Kashmir proved to be an insoluble problem. Since the withdrawal of forces could not be attained, a plebiscite could not be held.

Following these developments, the UN Security Council attempted to resolve these issues through mediatory roles of UN representatives, including Sir Owen Dixon, Dr Frank Graham, and Gunnar Jaring, by discussing these issues at the Security Council, and by encouraging bilateral discussions between India and Pakistan.

In 1953-54, when Pakistan agreed to accept the US military assistance, Jawaharlal Nehru, Prime Minister of India, rejected the already promised plebiscite in Kashmir. From then on, it was Pakistan who repeatedly brought the Kashmir problem to the UN Security Council's attention. In 1957 the Security Council discussed the Kashmir issue in response to Pakistan's complaint that India had annexed the state with the help of the Constituent Assembly of Kashmir, which declared in November 1956 that 'the State of Jammu and Kashmir is and shall be an integral part of the Union of India'. The Security Council met in January 1957 and not only reaffirmed its earlier resolutions, but also resolved that this development was in conflict with the accepted principle of a plebiscite.

Since then, despite all bilateral negotiations, and the UN exhortations, India has not agreed to hold a plebiscite in Kashmir, and the deadlock has remained across the ceasefire line in the state.

Another armed conflict occurred between Pakistan and India in September 1965. The hostilities involved major army units, airplanes, and tanks not only in Kashmir but also in the border regions of both countries.

As a result of efforts by the United States and the Soviet Union, and also through coordinated actions of the UN Security Council members, India and Pakistan agreed to

1. Cease hostilities on the night of 23 September 1965; 2. Restore the ceasefire line in Jammu and Kashmir as it existed before 5 August 1965; 3. and move their troops back from the border. On 4 September 1965, the government of the Soviet Union expressed its readiness to offer India and Pakistan its 'good offices' in settling the armed conflict. The Soviet offer was accepted by both sides. From 4 January to 11 January 1966, talks were held in Tashkent (Uzbekistan) between India's Prime Minister Lal Bahadur Shastri and Pakistan President M. Ayub *Khan, in which A.N. Kosygin, Chairman of the USSR Council of Ministers, also took part. On 10 January, Shastri and Ayub Khan signed a document which is known to history as the Tashkent Declaration. Nine articles defined in this focused on the urgent measures to restore the situation in the subcontinent which existed before the armed conflict, and to withdraw troops to the positions that they held before 5 August 1965.

Pakistan and India fulfilled most of the Tashkent Declaration's provisions on the normalization of the situation; before March 1966, full diplomatic relations were restored, the troops were withdrawn on both sides, prisoners of war and interned civilians were exchanged.

After the 1971 military conflict, the demarcation line changed somewhat in favour of India; it was thereafter called the Line of Control LoC (as it existed on 17 December 1971). This deprived the group of United Nations observers of their legal status, but they still stayed on in Kashmir for more than fifteen years and were only recalled at the request of India.

In 1998 the Hindu fundamentalist party, the BJP, came to power in India and immediately called on Pakistan to cede *Azad Kashmir. Tensions were heightened when after its 11 and 12 May 1998 nuclear tests the Indian Prime Minister repeated the demand. When Pakistan conducted its own nuclear tests on 28 and 30 May, the situation somewhat stabilized. A.B. Vajpayee the then Prime Minister led a goodwill mission to Lahore, but the Kashmir crisis had in no measure abated. Kargil was a strategic location on Pakistan's side which oversaw access to Srinagar uptil 1971. The fall of Kargil to India was responsible for the outbreak of the 1965 war. Kargil was on the side of Pakistan till the 1971 war. In 1999 Pakistan's occupation of Kargil for the same strategic concern started of a major crisis. On 17 December 2004, President Pervez *Musharraf stated that he was prepared to leave behind the UNSC resolutions on Kashmir, a statement welcomed with alacrity by the United States of America, India and the United Nations. The SAARC (*South* Asian Association for Regional Cooperation) summit held from 4 to 6 January 2004 in Islamabad and attended by Indian Prime Minister Atal Bihari Vajpayee has led to prospects of a 'composite' dialogue between India and Pakistan, including Kashmir on the agenda.

On 26 January 2004, President Musharraf proposed a midway compromise solution definitely ruling out recognising the LoC as a permanent border.

BIBLIOGRAPHY: *P.N.K. Bamzai, 'A History of Kashmir', Delhi, 1962; P.N.B. Bazaz, 'The History of Struggle for Freedom in Kashmir', Delhi, 1954; J. Korbel, 'Danger in Kashmir', London, 1954; (ed.) K. Sarwar Hasan, 'The Kashmir Question: Documents', Karachi, 1966; G.W. Choudhury, 'Pakistan's Relations with India', London, 1969; 'White Paper on Jammu and Kashmir Dispute', Ministry of Foreign Affairs of Pakistan, 1977.*

I.V. KHALEVINSKY
R.M. MUKIMJANOVA

Kashmir shawls

These are manufactured by *Kashmiri craftsmen from fine woollen fabrics woven out of the wool of mountain goats, brought from Tibet or Ladakh. *Padshah* Akbar is believed to have introduced Kashmiri shawls. In the Mughal period (see Mughal Empire) , Kashmir shawls were regarded as the most precious of gifts and were given to foreign ambassadors.

The technique of weaving was extremely labour-consuming, as the whole of the ornament was woven by hand on a small horizontal loom without a shuttle, with the aid of wooden spools only. It sometimes took more than a year to make one shawl.

Kashmir shawls are very light and warm; the best specimens are so fine that they can be pulled through a ring. The only remaining fragment of an early Kashmir shawl dates from the seventeenth century (Ahmedabad, the Textile Museum). This shawl is ornamented with an edge of a woven floral pattern characteristic of the Mughal period. Ornaments in the form of a vase with a magnificent bouquet of flowers predominate on shawls made in the beginning and middle of the 18th century. At the end of the 18th century, *buta* became the most widespread motif in Kashmir shawl decorations. This is a motif in the form of a bud or almond tapering toward the upper part and filled with floral ornament. In the middle of the 19th century the ornamental compositions became more complicated: nearly the whole of the field became filled with patterns, the **buta* increased in size and assumed quaint shapes. Architectural motifs like arches, columns, and pavilions are also widely used on shawls.

Refined decor, filigree ornamental work, and intense colours were characteristic of Kashmir shawls at all stages of development.

At the beginning of the 19th century, Kashmir shawls became popular in Europe. It is believed that the fashion for these was introduced by Josèphine, wife of Napoleon. Since Kashmir shawls were very expensive, therefore imitations were made in Europe and Russia. Deprived of the European market, production of Kashmir shawls began to die out. At present, attempts are being made to revive the weaving of Kashmir shawls (mostly embroidered ones); today they are mainly exported or purchased by tourists.

O.V. LYSTSOVA

Kashmiri (People)

A people inhabiting South Asia. They are Indo-Mediterranean belonging to the larger Europeoid race. Their native tongue is Kashmiri, the *Dardic sub-group of the Indo-European family.

Today the majority of the Kashmiris are *Sunni Muslims. In ancient times Kashmir was an area dominated by Hinduism. In the 14th to 18th centuries, majority of Kashmiris converted to Islam.

Their main occupations include ploughed farming (rice, corn, wheat, barley, cotton, saffron, oil-seeds, fruit, vegetables, flowers), and cattle-breeding (sheep and goat producing the famous Kashmiri wool). Traditional crafts include woollen shawls (see Kashmir Shawls), carpets, embroidered felt rugs, papier-mache artifacts, brass ornaments, enamels, and wood-carvings. A traditional Kashmiri dwelling is a two or three storey house, made of stone, brick, or wood. The ground floor is reserved for cattle and is used as a storage for household objects, the first floor is living quarters. The roof is high and covered with tiles, straw, or shingle. Kashmiris wear *burqas*, long shirts, buttonless phiren coats and pants (men's pants are called *paijama*, women's pants are called *shalwar*). Men wear skullcaps, women wear round-shaped caps or shawls, or cover their heads with the loose end of their scarf. Female clothes are decorated with embroidery.

BIBLIOGRAPHY: '*Ethnic Processes in South Asian Countries*', Moscow, 1976 (in Russian); A.E. Snesarev, '*Ethnographic India*', Moscow, 1981 (in Russian).

N.R. GUSEVA

Kashmiri (Language)

Belongs to Eastern subgroup of *Dardic group of Indo-Aryan languages. The language is spoken in the *Kashmir valley and neighbouring regions. The dialects of Kashmiri are Kashmiri proper, Kashtawari, Siraji, Poguli and Rambani. Literature in Kashmiri proper dates back to the 13th or 14th centuries; at present there are works of fiction, readers, anthologies, and textbooks in this language. The traditional writing system is based on the *Sharada* and *Nagari* scripts. The modern system of writing is based on an Urdu modification of the Arabic script.

Kashmiri is used in radio broadcasting and teaching.

BIBLIOGRAPHY: *B.A. Zakharyin, D.I. Edelman, 'Kashmiri Language', Moscow, 1971 (in Russian); B.A. Zakharyin, 'The Structure and Typology of Kashmiri', Moscow, 1981 (in Russian); G.A. Grierson, 'Essays on the Kashmiri Grammar', London-Calcutta, 1899; id., 'A Manual of the Kashmiri Language', Vols. I-II, Oxford, 1911 (reprinted as Standard Manual of the Kashmiri Language, vols. I—II, Rohtak, Jammu, Lucknow, 1973); id., 'A Dictionary of the Kashmiri Language', Vols. I—IV, Calcutta, 1915-32.*

D.I. EDELMAN

Kashmiri, Zahir (1919–95)

A poet, literary critic and public figure. Zahir wrote in *Urdu and in *Punjabi. He graduated from the Amritsar College. He edited the Lahore-based newspaper *Musawwat* (Equality) and the literary magazine *Sawera* (Sunrise). He was an active member in the *Pakistan Progressive Writers' Association and was arrested on several occasions for his political activities.

Literary essayism takes an important place in his work. Zahir compiled several anthologies of contemporary Urdu poetry. In his collection of essays *Adab ke maadi nazariye*, ('Materialistic Theory of Literature, 1950'), he expounded a Marxist understanding of the literary process. He has several collections of poetry to his credit, including *Azmat-i-Adam* ('The Greatness of Man, 1965') that won him the Adamji Prize.

BIBLIOGRAPHY: *I. Barelwi, 'Jadid Shairi' (Contemporary Poetry), Lahore, 1961.*

A.S. SUKHOCHEV

Kathak

A dance that traces its origins to the nomadic bards of ancient northern India, known as *Kathaks*, or storytellers. These bards, performing in village squares and temple courtyards, mostly specialised in recounting mythological and moral tales. Their recitals were embellished with hand gestures and facial expressions. With the advent of the Mughul (see Mughal Empire) rule in India (11th-18th centuries), Kathak was transformed and became a court dance performed for entertainment. The Mughul emperors patronised it and refined its different aspects. It is known for its sparkling footwork, swift whirling movements and understated *abhinaya* or mime.

After the power of the Mughal Empire declined, Kathak was patronised by minor princely states. Wajid Ali Shah, the Nawab of Oudh, founded the famed Lucknow **Gharana* or Lucknow School. Lucknow, Banaras and Jaipur are recognised as the three schools where this art was nurtured and refined.

Kathak footwork is matched by the accompanying percussion instruments such as *tabla* and *pakhawaj*, and *jugalbandi* or a friendly competition, a sort of rhythmic wizardry, between the dancer and percussionists. It is often a source of delightful entertainment.

The dance movements include numerous pirouettes executed at lightning speed and ending in statuesque poses.

Kathak can be danced with a wide variety of music, such as classical songs, e.g. **Thumri, Dadra, Kajri, Hori* and *Darbari* and **Ghazals* or Urdu love poetry that includes themes of admiration, infatuation, and separation. Dance dramas based on Hindu mythological epics or any musical composition or film song based on **ragas* can blend with a Kathak performance.

It is believed that Kathak and Flamenco, a Spanish dance, have common traditional roots. Gypsies from India carried the tradition to the Middle East and Europe. In the Andalusia region of Southern Spain, it blended with other cultural influences, evolving into the emotional and highly dramatic dance known today as Flamenco.

In Pakistan, Maharaj Ghulam Husain Kathak–the grand old man of Kathak, who danced in the Lucknow *Gharana* style and dedicated his life to this art form, taught until his death in Lahore a few years ago.

Madam Azurie (d. 1998) (owned a dance school in Karachi. She arrived from Bombay where she had worked in the movies), Rafi Anwar (recieved his training in India. After migrating to Pakistan, the Kathak dancer became a popular 'peacock dance' performer, but he also taught Kathak for several years until he passed away), Zareen Suleman (popularly known as *Panna*), and Amy Minwala, are other dancers who popularised Kathak on stage and in films.

R. HUSAIN

Kennedy, Charles (1951–)

Historian. Charles Kennedy was Assistant Professor of Politics in the Wake Forest University, USA. He has been President of the American Institute of Pakistan Studies University of Villanova, Pennsylvania. He wrote an analysis of 'Zulfikar Ali *Bhutto's Administrative Reforms' for Duke University.

Dr Charles Kennedy made a number of trips to Pakistan in the 1970s and has written authoritatively on a subject central to the study of Pakistan.

YU.V. GANKOVSKY

Kermani, Sheema

Dancer. As a teenager, she had started learning dance with the Ghanshyams. She then earned a degree at the Croydon College of Arts in London and gained prominence and popularity in the **Bharata Natyam* and *Odissi* styles of dance. Later, she pursued dance in India with Leela Samson, Mayadhar Raut, and Aloka Pannikar.

Sheema Kermani.

Kermani has extended the classical dance genre into theatre productions under the banner of *Tehrik-e-Niswan* (Women's Movement), which was established in 1980. Amjad Ansari, Sadia Khan and Mani Chau are some of Kermani's outstanding students, who now perform, choreograph and teach on their own.

R. HUSAIN

Khairpur

1. A princely state in northeastern *Sindh. Area: 15,700 sq.km. The state emerged in the 1780s as a part of the confederation ruling arrangement set up by the *Talpur Mirs, after the fall of the *Kalhora dynasty that had ruled Sindh until then. The first ruler of Khairpur was Mir Sohrab Khan from the Talpurs.

The state was included in Pakistan on 5 October 1947 and merged into the province of Sindh in 1955.

2. A district in the Sukkur division of the Sindh Province in Pakistan. Area: 15,700 sq.km.

YU.V. GANKOVSKY

Khaksar Tehrik

(Movement of the Obedient (to Allah)) A Muslim religio-communal organization in *British India and Pakistan. Founded in the early 1930s in the *Punjab by Inayat Allah Khan Mashriqi, the members of the KT wore brown uniforms and were inspired by the Nazi party's discipline under Hitler. From 1940 to 1942 the party was banned.

In 1943, it organized an unsuccessful attempt to assassinate M.A. *Jinnah. In 1947, the movement opposed the partition of British India. In May 1959, the party was outlawed by the provincial government of *West Pakistan for organizing the assassination of Dr Khan *Sahib, former Chief Minister of the province. After Mashriqi's death, the organization split into several factions.

BIBLIOGRAPHY: *Yuri Gankovsky, L.R. Gordon-Polonskaya, 'A History of Pakistan', Lahore, 1972; W.C. Smith, 'Modern Islam in India', London, 1946;*

YU.V. GANKOVSKY

Khaksar

(Urdu: dustlike, submissive) Member of a Muslim organization in *British India and Pakistan called **Khaksar Tehrik* (the *Khaksar* Movement).

YU.V. GANKOVSKY

Khalid-bin-Sayeed (1926–)

Historian/Political Scientist. He was educated in the universities of Madras and London. He got his doctorate from McGill University, Montreal (Canada), and was professor of political science at Queen's University (Kingston, Ontario, Canada). He also taught in the universities of Dhaka (1951-53), New Brunswick, Duke, McGill, Harvard, and London. In 1970-71 he was a UN consultant in Iran.

WORKS: *'Pakistan—the Formative Phase: 1857-1948', Karachi, 1960 (2nd ed. Bristol, 1968); 'The Political System of Pakistan', Boston, 1967; 'Politics in Pakistan. The Direction of Change', New York, 1980; 'Western Dominance and Political Islam', Karachi, 1997.*

YU.V. GANKOVSKY

Khalif

(Arabic, the politically correct form: *khalifah*, plural: *khulafa*—governor, deputy heir, successor, from *khalafa*—to deputize for, to follow someone) 1. The head of a Muslim community (**umma*), a deputy of the Prophet Muhammad (PBUH), the Messenger of Allah.

The first four *khalifs* highly revered, *al-khulafa al-rashidun* (the rightly guided Caliphs). These four *khalifs* are: Abu Bakr (r. 632–4), Umar or Omar (r. 634–44), Usman or Osman (644–56), and Ali ibn Abi Talib (r. 656–61).

After Ali's death, the rulers of the Omayyad dynasty (661–750) became *khalifs*. They were succeeded in turn by the rulers of the Abbasid dynasty (750–1517), who were also called *khulafa*.

From 1517 to 1924, Turkish Sultans of the Ottoman dynasty were *khalifs*.

In Sufi and other fraternities, *khalifs* are the deputies of the *sheikhs* and *pirs*, the chiefs of Sufi orders.

BIBLIOGRAPHY: *Sir Thomas Arnold, 'The Caliphate', Oxford, 1924; Sir William Muir, 'The Caliphate, Its Rise, Decline and Fall', Edinburgh, 1924.*

YU.V. GANKOVSKY

Khalisa

(from Arabic: pure, free) A form of category of state feudal land ownership in medieval India, in the 13th–18th centuries. They were under the jurisdiction of a special state fiscal department (*divan-i wazarat*, or *diwan-i khalisa*).

Until the 17th century, *khalisa* lands were not usually separated from the ruler's domain and were the hereditary property of peasant commoners. *Khalisa* tax or rent funded the army, the state bureaucracy, and the courts. The lands granted as **jagir, suyurghal, *iqta, wakf* were excluded from *khalisa*.

YU.V. GANKOVSKY

Khalsa

(pure; plural of the Arabic '*khalis*'—pure, genuine, real; also: sincere, simple-hearted) A military-religious order founded in 1699 by the last *Sikh *guru* Gobind Singh. The **Khalsa* order became the backbone of the Sikh army fighting against the Mughals and the Durrani kings. Admittance into the army followed a special ritual upon which the name 'Singh' (lion) was added to the given name of the initiated one.

Khalsa members were supposed to strictly observe all Sikh rules. Smoking, alcohol, and eating the meat of animals killed by Muslims were forbidden. *Khalsa* structure was based on democratic principles. Questions of mutual interest were discussed at annual general meetings where each member, regardless of his position, had one vote and equal rights and duties. Questions of local importance were solved at the general meetings of local *Khalsa* organizations.

Currently, *Khalsa* implies an orthodox Sikh community observing all the religious postulates and rules. It opposes other sects and movements with different rituals and rules. *Khalsa* ruling bodies are elected democratically i.e., committee for *Gurdwara* administration. In the first half of the 19th century, the army and the state of the Maharaja Ranjit Singh was also called *Khalsa*.

B.I. KLYNEV

Khan

(Turkic: Mongolian for ruler, prince) An honorary title. A ruler of a princely state; head of a clan or tribe.

YU.V. GANKOVSKY

Khan, Abdul Ghaffar (1890–1988)

Political activist. A major figure in the independence movement against the British Raj and, in independent Pakistan, a prominent participant in pro-democracy movements and a promoter of *Pashtun causes. Ghaffar Khan also participated in the *Khilafat Movement. He organized and led the *Anjuman-i-Islahi Afghania* (Society for the Enlightenment of the Afghans) in 1921, the Pashtun Conference (*Pakhtun *Jirga*) in 1926 and the volunteer Red Shirts detachments (**Khudai Khidmatgars)* in 1929.

A staunch nationalist during the freedom struggle, Khan was known as the 'Frontier Gandhi' and locally as '*Baacha* Khan'. After the formation of Pakistan, he became the leader of the People's Party (or People's Organization of Pakistan) in 1948.

In 1956, on his initiative, the National Party was formed to unite the opposition organizations of *West Pakistan. Khan was one of the organizers and leaders of the *National Awami Party. Throughout his life, he was repeatedly arrested by both the British and the Pakistani authorities. He was the younger brother of Dr *Khan Sahib, Chief Minister of NWFP in the Congress-led government of 1946-47 and of the 'One Unit' West Pakistan province in 1954-55. He was the father of Mr Abdul Wali *Khan, himself a prominent leader of the National *Awami Party and later the Awami National Party.

Abdul Ghaffar Khan is buried in Jalalabad (Afghanistan).

WORKS: *'My Life and Struggle, New Delhi, 1969.*

BIBLIOGRAPHY: *F. Bukhari, Bacha Khan, Peshawar, 1971; M.S. Korejo, The Frontier Gandhi, Karachi, 1993.*

YU.V. GANKOVSKY

Khan, Khan Abdul Ghani (1915–1996)

Poet/Writer. A poet in the Pashtu language and writer in English. He is the son of Abdul Ghaffar Khan, who was a leader of the *Pashtun national movement. Ghani studied in England, the United States and India. He was a member of the Indian Parliament but, after the formation of Pakistan, he retired from political activity.

Ghani's poetry is distinguished by its rich thematic range, including the glorification of man, love, life and death, and the Pashtuns' code of honour. In his fables he conveys his political views and critical attitudes towards reality. His work is mainly noted for its humanism. It is rich in original imagery and combines the artistic achievements of both national and Western poetry.

WORKS: *'Da Panjare Chigha', Peshawar, 1956; 'Palwashe' (Rays), 1960; 'Kulliyat' (Collected Poems), Kabul, 1985; 'Pathans', Peshawar, 1958 (in English).*

BIBLIOGRAPHY: *G.F. Girs, 'Literature of the Undefeated People', Moscow, 1966 (in Russian).*

A.S. GERASIMOVA

Khan, Abdul Qadeer (1935–)

Scientist. Abdul Qadeer Khan graduated from D.J. Science College, Karachi, after which he was appointed Inspector of Weights and Measures. He did his MSc in Metallurgy from Technical University, Delfat. His PhD came from the University of Leon (Belgium) in 1972. He was appointed an expert in the Physical Dynamics Research Laboratory in Amsterdam, as well as the Urenco Enrichment Plant, Holland.

Abdul Qadeer Khan, father of Pakistan's Nuclear programme.

His speciality is strengthening of metallurgy for centrifuges required for making nuclear fuel. He established the Advanced Nuclear Enrichment Plant at Kahuta in 1976. This was renamed after him in 1981. Abdul Qadeer Khan was awarded the *Hilal-i-Imtiaz* on 23 March 1990.

He is one of the main architects of Pakistan's nuclear programme and successful testing in 1998. In January 2004, A.Q. Khan accepted having been involved in an international network of nuclear prosiferation from Pakistan to Iran, and North Korea. On 5 February 2004, President Pervez *Musharraf announced that he had pardoned Dr Khan.

T. NAIM

Khan, Abdul Qaiyum (1901–81)

Statesman. He graduated from the Aligarh Muslim University and later studied in England. A lawyer by profession, he participated for a time in the Red Shirts movement of Abdul Ghaffar *Khan. He became a member of the *Muslim League and, from 1947 to 1953, served as the the Chief Minister of the NWFP.

In 1953–54, he was Minister for Industries of Pakistan. In 1957, he became president of the Muslim League and was prominent in the movement agitating for the conduct of national elections–a movement that was terminated by Ayub *Khan's seizure of power in 1958 and the arrest of Qaiyum Khan.

Khan organized and led the Quaid-i-Azam Muslim League in March 1969 (January 1970 onwards known as the *All-Pakistan Muslim League). From 1972 to 1977, he was Minister of Home, Kashmir Affairs, and Frontier Regions in the PPP-led government of Zulfiqar Ali *Bhutto.

WORKS: *'Gold and Guns on the Pathan Frontier', Bombay, 1945.*

YU.V. GANKOVSKY

Khan, Abdul Wali (1917–)

A Pakistani politician, son of Abdul Ghaffar Khan. Abdul Wali Khan was educated in Dehra Dun (India) and was an active nationalist, participating alongside his father and uncle in the Red Shirts movement and later in the Pashtun movement.

From 1968 to 1975, he was Chairman of the *National Awami Party of Pakistan. He was the leader of the National Democratic Party from 1975-86 and has been the *Awami National Party leader since 1986.

WORKS: *'Facts are Facts', New Delhi, 1987.*

YU.V. GANKOVSKY

Khan, Agha Muhammad Yahya, General (1917–80)

Military President of Pakistan (1969-71). Yahya Khan graduated from the Punjab University in Lahore. In 1938, he entered the armed forces and saw action in Egypt, Libya, and Italy during World War II. In 1946, he studied at Staff College in Quetta. He was appointed Commander-in-Chief of the Pakistan Army in September 1966 and was promoted to the rank of General.

In March 1969, Yahya Khan assumed presidential authority, which had been passed on to him by Field Marshal Ayub *Khan. He presided over the conduct of Pakistan's first general elections in 1970, in which the *Awami League of Sheikh Mujibur *Rahman swept the then *East Pakistan (now Bangladesh), securing an absolute majority in the new National Assembly. The *Pakistan People's Party of Zulfiqar Ali *Bhutto performed strongly in the provinces of the former *West Pakistan. Yahya Khan successfully played off the ambitions of the one against the other. However, the consequence of this was the breaking out of violent separatist agitation in the eastern wing. Yahya ordered brutal military reprisals to quell the agitation. The resulting civil war between the army and the East Wing separatists led, in due course, to armed intervention by India, the military defeat of the Pakistan army and the successful secession of the eastern wing from Pakistan as Bangladesh.

Yahya was forced by his military colleagues to resign and hand over power to Zulfiqar Ali Bhutto in December 1971.

M.R. KAZIMI

Khan, Ahmad Yar, Khan of Kalat (1904–77)

Statesman. The Khan was educated traditionally and privately. He succeeded to the Khanate in September 1933. With an area of 73,378 sq. miles, the Khanate of Kalat is the largest in *Balochistan and the most strategically located. As his further title of *Khan-i-Khanan* implies, he was Liege Lord to most of the *Balochi and *Brahui chieftains, who were bound to him as vassals.

After announcement of the *Third June Plan, he was warm to the idea of acceding to Pakistan. He corresponded with and invited M.A. *Jinnah to *Kalat. On the advice of Sir Walter Monckton, that he need not accede immediately, he waited till 1948 before finally signing the instrument of accession.

Ten years later, there were disturbances in Balochistan and President Iskander *Mirza took exception to the Khan flying his personal flag. On 5 October 1957, army detachments surrounded Kalat State. The Khan was arrested and deposed in favour of his son Daud Khan. He was later reinstated and came into prominence again during the first PPP government, when he served as the Governor of Balochistan from January 1974 to July 1977.

BIBLIOGRAPHY: *S. Matheson, 'The Tigers of Baluchistan', Karachi, 1997; S. Khan Mazari, 'A Journey to Disillusionment', Karachi, 1999.*

M.R. KAZIMI

Khan, Azam, Lieutenant General (1908–94)

Statesman. Azam Khan was the first person to function as a Martial Law Administrator in Pakistan, although under civilian dispensation and for a particular area, *Punjab. This was from 6 March to 14 May 1953 in the wake of the anti-Ahmadi riots.

He was one of the main leaders of the Ayub *Khan's October 1958 military *coup*. Lt. General M. Azam Khan proved to be a very efficient Minister for Rehabilitation and was responsible for the swift completion of small housing colonies in Karachi and Dhaka for migrants from India who had been without proper shelter for more than a decade. Between 1960 and 1962, Azam Khan was Governor of *East Pakistan. As governor, his popularity was extraordinary. He is said to have identified himself with the people and to have always shown exceptional fairness and justice. His successor Abdul Monem Khan (1899–1971), although a native Bengali unlike Azam Khan, proved unpopular and was the cause of accelerating disaffection against President Ayub Khan.

M.R. KAZIMI

Khan, Colonel Mohammad (1920–99)

Writer. Mohammad Khan was a career Army officer who retired as a colonel. He wrote an account of his life in the army, beginning with his recruitment and early training and going on to cover his foreign postings.

His first book *Bajang Amad* does not appear to be ostensibly humorous, but it became an overnight success. Two other books followed, sustaining his popularity. All his books have elements of autobiography. He writes in a languid manner and the humour of his writings is more cumulative rather than being frequently intrusive. He is vivid and graphic in his descriptions and his style is graceful throughout.

WORKS: *'Bajang Amad', 1966; 'Ba Salaamat Ravi', 1975; 'Bazm Araian', 1980.*

BIBLIOGRAPHY: *Brigadier Ismail, 'Urdu Zarafat ka General Rommel', Islamabad, 1999; (ed.) Sultan Rashk, 'Urdu Punch', Mohammad Khan edition, Rawalpindi.*

YU.V. GANKOVSKY

Khan, Ghulam Ishaq (1915–)

The President of Pakistan from 1988 to 1993. He was formerly employed by the Civil Service of India since 1940. In 1961, he was appointed Director of the Water and Power Development Authority in Pakistan and in 1967 became Minister of Finance. From 1971 to 1975, Ghulam Ishaq Khan was the Governor of the State Bank of Pakistan. In 1976, he was appointed Minister of Defence and, in July 1978, Minister of Finance, Planning and Provincial Coordination. In 1985, he was elected to the senate and later became Senate Chairman. He became President of Pakistan after the death of General Ziaul *Haq in 1988. He resigned in 1993.

Ghulam Ishaq Khan, President of Pakistan from 1988–93.

BIBLIOGRAPHY: *R. Khan, 'Pakistan: A Dream Gone Sour', Karachi, 1997.*

YU.V. GANKOVSKY

Khan, Hashim (1916–)

Squash player. Born in Navakili near Peshawar. Hashim Khan became the first Pakistani to win the British Open Squash Tournament, the world championship at that time. From 1951 to 1958 he won the championship seven times, a record broken later by Geoff Hunt. He currently resides in Denver, Colorado, USA.

S. ZAKIUDDIN

Khan, Imran (1952–)

Cricketer/Statesman. Born 25 November 1952 in Lahore, Imran began his career in first class cricket in 1969, Test career in 1971 and one-day cricket in 1974. His peak period was between 1978 and 1992, during which he played against every international cricket team. He is the first Pakistani bowler to take 200 and then 300 wickets. Apart from Ian Botham he is the only player to have scored a century and taken ten wickets in a single match (117 runs and 11 wickets against India at Faisalabad 1982–83). In the same series he took the highest number of wickets 40, in six Test matches and scored more than 300 runs. He took 14 wickets against Sri Lanka at Lahore in 1981–82. He was the first Pakistani player to score a century (102 not out) against Sri Lanka at Leeds in 1983.

Imran Khan, outstanding Cricket player. Now in politics.

As captain he led Pakistan to victory against many teams but his crowning achievement was winning the World Cup in 1992 against Australia.

Imran Khan has played 88 Test matches and taken 362 wickets with an average of 22.81. His best bowling figures were 8 for 58 runs against Sri Lanka in 1983. He has scored 3,807 runs with an average of 37.69 including six centuries. In one-day internationals, out of 175 played, he has scored 3,709 runs with an average of 33.41. He has taken 182 wickets with an average of 26.61. In 1992, he retired from cricket and moved into Pakistan politics. In 1996 he launched the Pakistan *Tehreek-i-Insaaf* (Pakistan Movement for Justice). Although it failed to win even a single seat in the 1997 elections, it became successful in the October 2002 elections.

S. ZAKIUDDIN

Khan, Jahangir (1963–)

Squash player. Son of Roshan Khan, himself a world champion. In technical skill and in statistical records Jahangir Khan is the greatest player Squash has yet seen. When he retired in 1993, he had a record of winning ten British Open Squash Championships, six World Open titles, two North American Championships, and two WPSA titles.

Jahangir Khan, the greatest player Squash has ever seen.

S. ZAKIUDDIN

Khan, Jansher (1969–)

Squash Player. Jansher Khan became World Junior Champion in 1986 and in 1987 won the World Open Championship. Jansher Khan has won the World Open

Championship eight times and British Open Championship six times.

S. ZAKIUDDIN

Khan, Liaquat Ali, Nawabzada (1896–1951)

Statesman. First Prime Minister of Pakistan from 1947 to 1951. The son of Nawab Rustom Ali Khan, Liaquat Ali Khan was born in Karnal, eastern *Punjab. He was educated at Aligarh and Oxford, achieving an MA in Jurisprudence. In 1922, he was called to the Bar from the Inner Temple. He returned the same year to India and was immediately involved in politics, as a Hindu-Muslim riot in Karnal required his services as peacemaker.

Liaquat Ali Khan, first Prime Minister of Pakistan from 1947–51.

Liaquat Ali Khan joined the *All-India Muslim League (AIML) in 1923. It was as an AIML delegate to the 1928 All-Parties Conference at Calcutta that he established close contact with Mohammad Ali *Jinnah. From 1926 to 1940, Liaquat Ali Khan was Member of the Utter Pardesh Legislative Council/Assembly. In 1933 he was elected Deputy President. Here, he formed the Democratic Party, which had both Hindu and Muslim members. During this phase, although Liaquat was still an ardent advocate of the interests of the feudal classes, he had a good head for figures, and could speak incisively on budgets and finance bills. It was only later, when he was in the vanguard of the Pakistan Movement, that he turned towards socialism.

He gained public prominence in 1931 when he became a member of a Board of Inquiry to investigate the causes and fix the responsibility for the Kanpur Riots. In 1933, shortly after his second marriage to Raana Liaquat (see Khan, Raana Liaquat), he called on Jinnah at Hampstead and urged him to return to India. Jinnah returned in 1935 and the AIML was re-organized in April 1936 when Liaquat was first elected Honorary Secretary.

After the breakdown of the Congress-League electoral understanding, Liaquat became engaged in organizational work.

Liaquat became Finance Member and leader of the AIML bloc in the Interim Government formed under the *Cabinet Mission Plan (5 October 1946). He presented the 1947 budget that, because of taxing the rich heavily and providing succour to the lower classes, was hailed as the 'Poor Man's Budget'. Liaquat's proposals were directed mainly against British interests, but the incidental effect was to tax all profits exceeding Rs 100,000, which hurt the plutocrats financing the Congress.

Liaquat's role in the Interim Government had enabled the *Muslim League to transit as the successor authority in Pakistan.

After independence, he was sworn in as the first Prime Minister of Pakistan. Liaquat Ali Khan though Prime Minister was not Chief Executive till 12 September 1948. He framed the first constitution, the Objectives Resolution of 1 March 1949, which was promising and proved to be a resilient constitutional document in Pakistan. The Rawalpindi Conspiracy, uncovered in 1951, was a plot between certain army officers and members of the Communist Party to stage a *coup d'etat* against Liaquat Ali Khan.

Liaquat's stance on the Korean War, which broke out during his stay in America, was supportive of the West. However, he overruled his cabinet, which wanted to commit troops, and confined his support to equipment and supplies. Relations with India, already strained by *Kashmir, worsened when communal riots broke out in both countries. Liaquat went to Delhi and signed a pact with his Indian counterpart, Jawaharlal Nehru, on 8 April 1950 that guaranteed the human rights of minorities in both countries. Liaquat met the Indian military threat in July 1951 with resolve and mobilized world opinion to de-escalate the crisis.

Liaquat Ali Khan's assassination by an Afghan national, Said Akbar, on 16 October 1951, while addressing a public meeting in Rawalpindi, brought to an end the stability Pakistan had enjoyed in an era it had not even been expected to survive.

WORKS: *'Pakistan: The Heart of Asia', Harvard, 1951; (ed.) M. Rafique Afzal, 'Speeches and Statements of Quaid-i-Millat Liaquat Ali Khan', Lahore, 1967.*

BIBLIOGRAPHY: *Z. Ahmad, 'Liaquat Ali Khan', Karachi, 1970; M.R. Kazimi, 'Liaquat Ali Khan and the Freedom Movement', Karachi, 1997.*

M.R. KAZIMI

Khan, Mazhar Ali (1918–93)

Politician. Mazhar Ali Khan graduated from the Punjab University in Lahore in 1939 and was the leader of student movements from 1935 to 1940. From 1942 to 1945, he served in the Second World War in North Africa and Italy on the side of the Allies. Mazhar was one of the leaders of the peace movement in Pakistan and, since 1974, was a member of the World Peace Council. He was repeatedly arrested by the government. He served as the editor-in-chief of the newspapers *Pakistan Times* from 1951 to 1959, *Dawn* in 1972, and the journal *Viewpoint* since 1976.

WORKS: *'Pakistan: The Barren Years', Karachi, 1998.*

YU.V. GANKOVSKY

Khan, Mohammad Ismail, Nawab (1886–1958)

Politician. The Nawab was the scion of a noted aristocratic and literary family, being the grandson of the celebrated 19th-century critic and poet, Nawab Mustafa Khan Shefta. Nawab Ismail was educated at the Aligarh Muslim University and Cambridge and was called to the Bar from the Inner Temple. Originally a member of the Indian National Congress, for strategic reasons he was asked by his party leadership to contest in 1937 for a Utter Pradesh Legislative Assembly seat on the AIML ticket. Once elected on the AIML (*All-India Muslim League) ticket, he remained loyal to the league, refusing the offer of a provincial ministry in return for winding up the AIML as an assembly party. Nawab Ismail became a member of the AIML Working Committee and in 1943 was made Chairman of the AIML Committee of Action. On his own request, he was not inducted in the interim government. At partition, he remained behind in India as member of the Indian Constituent Assembly and lok sabha from 1946 to 1952. He was Vice-Chancellor of the Aligarh Muslim University from 1947 to 1948.

BIBLIOGRAPHY: *A.K. Azad, 'India Wins Freedom: The Complete Version', Lahore, 1989; C. Khaliquzzaman, 'Pathway to Pakistan', Lahore, 1961.*

M.R. KAZIMI

Khan, Muhammad Asghar, Air Marshal (1921–)

Statesman. He received his military training in Dehra Dun. As a career Air Force officer, he achieved the rank of Air Marshal, serving as Commander-in-Chief of the Pakistan Air Force from 1957 to 1965. From 1965 to 1968, he was President of Pakistan International Airlines, Pakistan's national flag carrier. Retiring from the Airline, Asghar Khan entered politics.

In March 1969, Asghar Khan organized and headed the Justice Party, known as *Tehrik-i Istiqlal*, from March 1970. Prominent in the 1977 PNA (Pakistan National Alliance agitation) against Zulfiqar Ali *Bhutto's election rigging, Asghar Khan is perceived as consistently advocating pro-democracy and anti-establishment political positions.

WORKS: *'The First Round', New Delhi, 1979; 'Generals in Politics', New Delhi, 1983. We've Learnt Nothing From History, Oxford, 2005.*

YU.V. GANKOVSKY

Khan, Muhammad Ayub, Field Marshal (1907–74)

President of Pakistan from 1960–69.

President of Pakistan from 1960 to 1969. Ayub Khan graduated from the Aligarh Muslim University and received military training in Sandhurst, England. He commanded a battalion on the Burma Front during the Second World War. In January 1951, he was appointed Commander-in-Chief of the Pakistani army, and in 1954–55 became Minister of Defence. He was appointed Chief Martial Law Administrator on 7 October 1958, after the *coup* perpetrated by Iskander *Mirza thereafter staging a further *coup* against Mirza on 27 October and seizing the office of president for himself. Ayub Khan ruled under martial law in 1962 and subsequently under his own tailor-made constitution until 1969. In 1959, he awarded himself the title of field marshal and in 1960 was confirmed as president of Pakistan by means of a referendum.

Ayub Khan initiated reforms in the fields of agriculture, education and law, including family law. He oversaw the rapid industrialization of Pakistan, bringing stability and prosperity. Uneven distribution of wealth caused complaints, especially in the East Wing. Although his foreign policy was initially pro-west, it began to move towards a better balance later, when he developed close ties with China and became the first head of state to visit the USSR (1964). He was re-elected for a second term in 1965 under a system of indirect elections known as 'Basic Democracy'. However, the widespread public enthusiasm shown to the candidate of the Combined Opposition Parties

(COP)–no less a personage than Fatima *Jinnah, sister and close confidante of the Quaid-i-Azam–shook the confidence of the Ayub regime.

The *Rann of Kutch and *Kashmir Wars took place during his term (1965). He signed the *Tashkent Declaration (1966), after which his popularity declined. Major demonstrations against the Ayub Khan government began across a widening spectrum of groups in different regions in 1968. The vociferous public demands for democratic political institutions, social justice and regional autonomy unnerved Ayub Khan.

In March 1969, the office of the president was passed on to General A.M. Yahya *Khan.

WORKS: *'Friends not Masters, A Political Autobiography', London, 1967.*

BIBLIOGRAPHY: *H. Feldman, 'Revolution in Pakistan', London, 1967; A. Gauhar, 'Ayub Khan', Lahore, 1993.*

YU.V. GANKOVSKY

Khan, Munir Ahmed (1926–99)

Scientist. Educated at Government College, Lahore and the Engineering College, Lahore. Munir Ahmad Khan thereafter took his MS in Electrical Engineering from North Carolina State University in 1952. He completed postgraduate studies at the Illinois Institute of Technology. He served on the International Atomic Energy Commission from 1958 to 1972. In 1972 he was appointed Chairman of the *Pakistan Atomic Energy Commission in succession to Dr I.H. Usmani. He also personally headed the Reactor Division. Munir Ahmad Khan made a significant contribution towards the development of nuclear power and research reactor utilization. Munir Ahmad Khan held the post of Minister of State under the second PPP regime from 1988 to 1989. He left the PAEC in 1991 and settled in Europe.

Munir Ahmed Khan.

YU.V. GANKOVSKY

Khan, Nur, Air Marshal (1927–)

Statesman. Nur Khan was the second Commander-in-Chief of the Pakistan Air Force and led the Air Force during the 1965 War. He was chief of the Pakistan International Airlines (PIA). During the Yahya *Khan government, he became Minister of Health, Education and Social Welfare. His report, popularly called the 'Nur Khan Report', advocated nationalization of education (This was later implemented by the PPP government in 1972).

After being minister, Nur Khan became Governor of *West Pakistan but resigned in 1971 to join the Council *Muslim League. In 1973, he again became head of PIA. He was elected to the National Assembly in 1977, and in 1988 on the ticket of the *Pakistan Peoples Party.

M.R. KAZIMI

Khan, Raana Liaquat Ali (1905–91)

Statesperson. Begum Raana Liaquat was born at Almora, UP (United Provinces or Uttar Pardesh), Lucknow. She obtained her BT from the University of Calcutta. She was appointed lecturer in economics at the Indraprastha College, Delhi, and taught there until her marriage to Nawabzada Liaquat Ali *Khan. She accompanied her husband to Hampstead to persuade M.A. *Jinnah to return to India.

During her husband's tenure as Prime Minister of Pakistan, she founded the *All-Pakistan Women's Association (APWA), the pioneering social work institution in Pakistan, in 1949. After her husband's assassination in 1951, she continued her contribution to public life. She was appointed Pakistan's ambassador to the Netherlands (1954 to 1961) and to Italy with concurrent accreditation to Tunisia (1961–66). She served as Governor of Sindh (1973–76) and was concurrently chancellor of all the universities in Sindh.

She was awarded the Woman of Achievement Medal (USA, 1950), the *Nishan-i-Imtiaz* (Pakistan, 1959), *Grande Cross of Orange-Nassau* (Netherlands, 1961), *Caraliera di Gran Croce* (Italy, 1966) among many other decorations.

WORKS: *'Woman Labour in Agriculture in the United Provinces', Lucknow; 'Challenge and Change', Karachi, 1980.*

BIBLIOGRAPHY: *K. Miles, 'The Dynamo in Silk', Karachi, 1963; M.N. Mastoor, 'Ra'ana Liaquat Ali Khan', Karachi, 1980; Begum S.A. Khan, 'Yeh Qaum Ki Hain Betian', Karachi, 1981.*

M.R. KAZIMI

Khan Sahib, Dr. (1882–1958)

Statesman. A politician in British India and Pakistan, he was the elder brother of Abdul Ghaffar *Khan. A doctor by profession, he studied in Peshawar and London. In 1930, he left the medical profession to take part in the Red Shirts (see **khudai khidmatgars*) movement founded by his brother.

He served as Chief Minister of the *North West Frontier Province from 1937 to 1939 and from 1945 to 1947. He became a minister in the Government of Pakistan from 1954 to 1955 and Chief Minister of *West Pakistan province from 1955 to 1958.

Khan was one of the founders and leaders of the Republican Party. He was murdered by an angry employee in the Department of Irrigation.

YU.V. GANKOVSKY

Khan, Saleemullah, Nawab of Dacca (1884–1915)

Political activist. Saleemullah Khan was given the title of Nawab Bahadur in 1903. He formed the Mohammedan Provincial Union to project the benefits to Muslims of the 1905 Partition of Bengal (see Bengal, the partition of). The *All-India Muslim League (AIML) was formed at Dacca (now Dhaka) on 30 December 1906 by a resolution moved by him. He presided over the March 1912 Calcutta session of the AIML to protest revocation of the Bengal partition.

BIBLIOGRAPHY: *K.K. Aziz, 'Britain and Muslim India', London, 1963; M. Matiur Rahman, 'From Consultation to Confrontation', London, 1970.*

YU.V. GANKOVSKY

Khan, Syed Ahmad, Sir (1817–98)

Political activist/Writer. From 1838 to 1858, Syed was an employee of the British East India Company in Delhi, Agra, and Bijnore. From 1859 to 1876, he served in the British administration in Muradabad and Aligarh. From 1869 to 1970, he studied the European educational system in England.

On his initiative and under his control, the Scientific Society, in 1864, and the Aligarh Mohammedan College, in 1875 were initiated. He began to publish the journals, *Aligarh Institute Gazette* in 1866, and *Tahdhib-i Akhlaq* ('Inculcating Morality') in 1870. He was awarded the Order Star of India in 1888.

WORKS: *'Maqalat' (Collected Works), Vols. 1-12, Lahore, 1962-1965; 'Causes of the Indian Revolt', Benares, 1873; 'Asar-us-Sanadid'.*

BIBLIOGRAPHY: *A.H. Hali, 'Hayat-i Jawid (Eternal Life), Delhi, 1982; H. Malik, 'Sir Sayyid Ahmad Khan and Muslim Modernization in India and Pakistan', New York, 1980; 'Political Profile of Sir Sayyid Ahmad Khan, A Documentary Record', (ed.) H. Malik, Islamabad, 1982.*

YU.V. GANKOVSKY

Khan, Tamizuddin, Maulvi (1889–1963)

Statesman. Born in Faridpur, East Bengal, Tamizuddin Khan was educated at Calcutta. He passed his BA (Hons) in English from the Presidency College in 1911, his MA in 1913 and LLB in 1914. He joined the Faridpur Bar and the *All-India Muslim League (AIML) in 1915. In 1921, he joined the Indian National Congress. In 1922, he was jailed and publicly flogged for participating in the *Khilafat and Non-Cooperation Movement.

In 1923, he was released and in the elections of 1926, 1930, and 1937, he was returned to the Bengal Legislative Assembly. From 1937 to 1947, he was Minister for Health, Agriculture, and Industry in the Bengal Government.

On the establishment of Pakistan, Tamizuddin Khan was elected Deputy-President of the *Constituent Assembly. Unanimously elected president on the death of the Quaid-i-Azam in 1948, he faced his first crisis in 1953 when Governor-General Ghulam *Mohammad dismissed Prime Minister Khwaja *Nazimuddin. On 24 October 1954, when the draft of a new constitution was ready, the governor general dissolved the constituent assembly. Tamizuddin Khan filed a writ on 7 November 1954, challenging the action of the governor general. His plea was upheld by the Sindh Chief Court but the government went in appeal to the Federal Court, which, with the solitary dissent of Justice *Cornelius and following the lead of Justice M. Munir, overturned the decision of the Sindh Chief Court in 1955.

In 1962, when President M. Ayub *Khan promulgated the 1962 Constitution (the country's second), Tamizuddin Khan was elected speaker. He died while in office and was widely mourned.

WORKS: *'The Test of Time', Dhaka, 1989.*

BIBLIOGRAPHY: *A. McGrath, 'The Destruction of Democracy in Pakistan', Karachi, 1998.*

M.R. KAZIMI

Khan, Tikka, General (1917–2002)

Statesman. Hailing from the *Jhelum district of the *Punjab, General Tikka Khan came into the public eye when he was called upon to quell insurgency in *Bengal in the Ayub *Khan era. He was appointed Governor of *East Pakistan on 4 March 1971. When the Chief Justice refused to swear him in, he assumed charge on 9 March by presidential fiat. General Tikka Khan carried out the controversial military action at midnight on 25 March 1971. Under his command the military carried out an assault on Dhaka University, the centre of other places, which left thousands of *East Pakistan's dead. He scandalized the country by stating that 'only' thirty thousand Bengalis had been killed.

On 2 September, General Tikka Khan was recalled and replaced as Governor of East Pakistan by Dr Abdul Malik and as General Officer Commanding by Lt. Gen. A.A.K. Niazi.

General Tikka Khan was appointed Chief of Army Staff by President Zulfikar Ali *Bhutto in 1972 and retained his command until 1976. After retirement, he joined the ruling *Pakistan Peoples Party, in due course becoming its secretary-general. He was appointed Governor of the Punjab (1988–90). General Tikka Khan died in Rawalpindi and was laid to rest with full military honours.

M.R. KAZIMI

Khan, Yaqub, Lieutenant-General Sahibzada (1920–)

Statesman. A Pakistani diplomat and a member of the Nawab Rampur family, Sahibzada Yaqub graduated from the Military College of Dehra Dun (India) in 1940, continued his military training in England and France, and served in the Second World War. From 1946 to 1947, he was *aide-de-camp* to the Indian Viceroy, Lord Mountbatten, and in 1948 commanded the bodyguard of the first Governor General of Pakistan, Mohammad Ali *Jinnah.

From 1949 to 1971, Yaqub Khan served in the Pakistan armed forces in various posts, including Chief of General Staff. From August 1969 to March 1971, he was the Martial Law Administrator in *East Pakistan. He retired from the military on 7 March 1971 and joined the diplomatic ranks. From 1972 to 1973, he served as Pakistan's Ambassador to France and simultaneously to Ireland. From December 1973 to January 1979, he was Ambassador to the USA and, from February 1979 to February 1982, Ambassador to the USSR. From 1982 to 1985 he served as Minister for Foreign Affairs of Pakistan.

YU.V. GANKOVSKY

Khan, Zafar Ali, Maulana (1873–1956)

Poet/Journalist/Statesman. Hailing from the *Punjab, he graduated from the Mohammedan Anglo-Oriental College, Aligarh. Thereafter, he joined the service of the Nizam of Hyderabad, Deccan. He rose to be secretary to Nawab *Mohsinul Mulk. Maulana Zafar Ali Khan was a founding member of the *All-India Muslim League. He first edited the *Deccan Review* from Hyderabad in 1903. He later made Lahore his centre, from where he published his widely circulated and influential Urdu newspaper *Zamindar*. This journal carried a number of famous patriotic poems including those by *Iqbal and himself.

BIBLIOGRAPHY: *S.N.H. Zaidi, 'Moulana Zafar Ali Khan', Karachi, 1986.*

M.R. KAZIMI

Khan, Zafrullah, Choudhury Sir (1893–1985)

Statesman. Zafrullah Khan studied at the Punjab University in Lahore and later at London University, majoring in Law. He belonged to the *Ahmadiya community and was publisher of the journal, *Indian Cases*, from 1916 to 1932. From 1930 to 1932, he was a delegate to the *Round Table Conference in London; from 1935 to 1941, a member of the viceroy and Governor-General of India's Executive Council in *British India. He was a member of the Punjab Legislative Assembly from 1926 to 1935. In 1931, he became President of the *All-India Muslim League. After independence, he served as Pakistan's first Minister for Foreign Affairs and Commonwealth Relations until 1954. He then became a judge, vice-president and president of the International Court of Justice at The Hague.

YU.V. GANKOVSKY

Khandsari (or Khanda)

Raw sugar manufactured by traditional methods in the countries of South Asia. It is made by open boiling sugarcane without vacuum devices as in modern factories. It is 85 per cent sucrose. The sugar output of home-made *khandsari* is half that of factory production.

In Pakistan, the main centres of *khandsari* and *gur*-making are in the north-west (*Peshawar Valley) and central *Punjab (Faisalabad, Sheikhupura, Sahiwal). It is mainly manufactured in rural areas that lack sugar factories.

Up to 90 per cent of *khandsari* is sold locally or in the neighbouring villages, while a small amount is exported to other provinces. Since the mid-1960s, the manufacturing of raw sugar has declined due to the growing demand for refined sugar. When there is overproduction of refined sugar in the domestic market, 70 per cent of sugarcane is processed into *khandsari* and **gur*.

M.YU. MOROZOVA

Khans

A leading, big business group in Bangladesh. Until 1972, it was listed in the thirty largest monopolistic business groups in Pakistan. Traditionally, they specialized in the jute and cotton industries.

A.M. SCHEGLOVA

Kharaj

(Arabic, *kharaja*: to leave, to lead from) Land revenue. According to Muslim law, *kharaj* is one of five kinds of state revenue. It was paid in kind in the form of a share of the produce (*kharaj-i muqasama*) or in a set sum of money per unit of land area (*kharaj-i misaha*). Originally (until the 18th century), *kharaj* was paid by non-Muslims only.

BIBLIOGRAPHY: *I.P. Petrushevsky, 'Islam in Iran', Leningrad, 1966 (in Russian); F. Lokkegaard, 'Islamic Taxation in the Classic Period', Copenhagen, 1950.*

YU.V. GANKOVSKY

Kharan (Political)

A historical and geographical division of Pakistan, in the *Balochistan province, it includes a number of palaya lakes, the largest being *Hamun-i-Mashkel*, a shallow lake turned into a swamp that changes shape from year to year. The feeding rivers are shallow and do not reach the lake in summer.

The indigenous population, the *Baloch, are mainly engaged in breeding.

M.YU. MOROZOVA

Kharan (Physical)

This region of *Balochistan, approximately 48,000 sq. km. in extent, lies between the *Chagai range and the Siahan Range at the south westerly tip of the province. Drainage from the surrunding hills flows into the central basin which contains numerous intermittent lakes or *playa*, the largest of which is called *Hamun-i-Mashkel*. This shallow lake turns into a swamp after heavy rain and changes its shape each year. During the summer the rivers flowing into this lake dry up.

S.B. ROSTOTSKY

Khatri

A trading community (caste) in *Punjab (Pakistan) and northwest India that claims *Kshatriya* origin. The community includes a large number of territorial divisions, the largest of which are Multani, Peshawariya, Lahoriya, Sirhindiya, Delhiwala and Agrawala. Each of these consist of several sub-divisions or *gotras*. Many leading businessmen of Pakistan's top industries belong to this community, e.g., the *Saigols.

BIBLIOGRAPY: *D. Ibbetson, 'A Glossary of the Tribes and Castes of the Punjab and North-West Frontier Province', Lahore, 1978.*

YU.V. GANKOVSKY

Khattak (Dance)

The most popular of the dances from the *North-West Frontier Province. The Pathan men, known for their warrior like nature, perform this dance by holding either big handkerchiefs or swords. There are many variations of the dance, as each tribe has its own style. In Hazara, the *Khattak* is performed to the accompaniment of wooden clappers, much like the Spanish *castanets*. Wearing embroidered waistcoats with the traditional *shalwar kameez* costume, the dancers normally dance in a circle, which becomes bigger when more men join in when the tempo of the drum increases.

Khattak (People)

A *Pashtun tribe belonging to the Kerlarni group of tribes. It falls into two branches: Tari, or Tarai (the clans of Ano-khel, Ismail-Khel, Mire-Khel), and Bulak or Bolak (the clans of Lundkhor, or Lundkhwar, Marozai, Shabar-Khel). Khattaks reside in the southern area of the *Peshawar district. Khattak settlements are also found in the Kohat district of *North West Frontier Province. Their total population is approximately 300,000.

BIBLIOGRAPHY: *M.H. Khan, 'Hayat-i Afghan', Lahore, 1964; I.M. Reisner, 'The Progress of Feudalism and the Formation of Afghan States', Moscow, 1954 (in Russian).*

YU.V. GANKOVSKY

Khattak, Khushal Khan (1613–89)

Poet. Khushal Khan is the most widely known and perhaps greatest poet of the *Pashto language, the most versatile and with the most vigorous and individual style. His command over all classical forms of poetry, such as the **masnavi* and **qasida*, as well as all types of poetry, revolutionary, devotional, romantic, and didactic, has caused him to be emulated by poets beyond the boundaries of regional *Pashto literature.

Khushal Khan Khattak, Warrior Poet.

His most celebrated admirer was Allama *Iqbal, who is said to have adopted from Khushal Khan the symbol of the falcon.

Khushal Khan's poetry was by no means confined to the traditional romantic and courtly themes, ranging over a wide range of issues, including religious questionings, poems of his people, expression of the places he moved in or visited, and poems of political protest. Khushal Khan is known for his defiance of Mughal authority; he had to endure five years imprisonment under Aurangzeb. On his release, he resumed his struggle. Not content with representing the falcon in his poetry, Khushal Khan wrote a veterinary treatise on the diseases and remedies of the bird. He also wrote on medicine, as well as on social topics notably in his *Dastarnameh*. He translated a work of jurisprudence into Pashto.

M.R. KAZIMI

Khattak, Muhammad Ajmal (1926–)

Poet. Ajmal Khattak is a poet, writer, political and public figure, who writes in *Pashto. He is a descendant of an aristocratic *Pashtun family. Khattak graduated from the Punjab University and worked as a schoolteacher. He launched his literary career in the early 1940s. He was editor and publisher of several newspapers published in the NWFP and an active participant in the left-wing factions of several political movements. In 1972-73, he was general secretary of the *National Awami Party (NAP). In 1973, he migrated to Kabul. His poetry is socially and politically motivated and looks at such themes as liberation struggle, social justice, humanism and the toiling man. He has also written didactic stories and historical essays.

In 2000, he was expelled from the ANP (*Awami National Party) and revived the NAP, but less radical and secessionist than the original NAP.

WORKS: *'Collections of verse: Da Jwand Shpelay' (The Reed Pipe of Life); 'Da Ghairat Chigha' (The Voice of Courage), Peshawar, 1958; 'Ghuluna Takaluna' (Roses and Aspirations), Kabul, 1983; 'Gul-i-Parhar' (Wounded Rose), Kabul, 1985; collections of stories: 'Tikrai' (Shawl), Kachkol (The Mendicant's Bowl), Peshawar, 1960.*

BIBLIOGRAPHY: *G.F. Girs, 'Literature of the Undefeated People', Moscow, 1966 (in Russian); Abdurrauf Benawa, 'Osani Likwal' (Contemporary Writers), Vol. 1, Kabul, 1961.*

A.S. GERASIMOVA

Khel

In *Pashtun, *Khel* means family, clan, tribal branch, sometimes tribe itself (also *qabila, taifa, qam, qaum, pata, pha*). Khel often forms part of the names of tribes and clans (e.g., the clans of Darwesh Khel of the Waziri; Adam Khel of the lowland *Afridi; Khan Khel—the Khan clan of the Pashtuns) and of names of places. *Khel khana* means 'dynasty'.

YU.V. GANKOVSKY

Khilafat Movement (1918–24)

The Khilafat Movement was the first mass movement of Indian Muslims to be directed against the British rule in India. As soon as it became apparent that Germany, along with its ally the Turkish Ottoman Empire, would lose the First World War, Indian Muslims became apprehensive about the fate of the Sultan of Turkey who was also the Caliph (*Khalifa*)—the spiritual head of the Muslims. The agitation became pronounced with the imposition of the Treaty of Sevres (1920), which was harsh and was rejected by Turkey. Ever since Indian Muslims had been deprived of political power, the *Khilafat* had served as a symbolic reminder of past greatness and its survival was a matter of deep sentimental concern.

The Maharaja of Mahmudabad and Mohammad Ali *Jinnah, two prominent leaders of the *Muslim League, initially opposed deliberating the crisis in the *All-India Mulsim League (AIML) Council, a stand that made them unpopular. M.K. Gandhi, the Home rule/Congress leader, who had until recently adopted a loyalist stance towards the British and had omitted to present Muslim grievances to the viceroy as scheduled, now turned hostile and started his Non-Cooperation Movement because he could now carry the Muslims with him. Gandhi disregarded M.A. Jinnah's plea that the religious sentiments of the people should not be aroused. In consequence, Jinnah and the Muslim League were cast into the shade and Gandhi became the leader of both Hindus and Muslims. In the exuberance of this fraternal sentiment, Muslim politicians like Dr Saifuddin *Kitchlew (d. 1963) took the lead in asking for the abolition of the *Lucknow Pact, 1916.

The Muslim League gave way to the Khilafat Conference, formed in September 1919. The guiding spirit and financer of this Movement was Mian Mohammad Haji Jan Mohammad Chotani (1873-1932); but the political leaders were Maulana Shaukat Ali, Maulana Muhammad *Ali, Maulana Abul Kalam *Azad, Maulana Hasrat Mohani, Dr Saifuddin Kitchlew and Sheikh Ubaidullah Sindhi. The Congress and the Muslim League officially supported the movement in 1921.

After the Turkish victory and the treaty of Laussane in 1923, presentiments about the independence of Turkey receded but apprehensions regarding the fate of the Caliphate remained. The Khilafat Movement received a setback when M.K. Gandhi called off the Non-Cooperation Movement on 11 February 1928. It became a completely lost cause when Mustafa Kemal Ataturk abolished the Caliphate in 1924. One of the Khilafat leaders, Maulana Abul Kalam Azad (d. 1958) issued a religious decree supporting the action of Ataturk, which the new Turkish government distributed in the form of leaflets.

Politically, the Khilafat Movement was a setback to the Muslim League, since it eroded the Lucknow Pact, until then the solitary political gain of the Muslims. It also brought religious sentiments into politics—the avowed aim of Gandhi. However, it also gave the Muslims an advantage that perhaps outweighed the disadvantages. It created a cadre of political workers tempered and trained in the art of agitation, calling of strikes, holding public meetings, leading processions and filling jails. This venture into mass politics benefited the future Pakistan Movement.

BIBLIOGRAPHY: *K.K. Aziz, 'The Indian Khilafat Movement 1915-1937. A Documentary Record', Karachi, 1972; P.C. Bamford, 'Histories of the Non-cooperation and Khilafat Movements', Delhi, 1925; Gail Minault 'The Khilafat Movement' (New Delhi, 1999).*

M.R. KAZIMI

Khilnani, Kaudomal Chandanmal (1844–1916)

Writer. A *Sindhi author who studied in Karachi, Kaudomal headed a teacher-training college, where he wrote many textbooks. He was one of the founders of Sindhi literature. Considered an enlightener, he was particularly known for his didactic work *Pako Pahu* (Strict Oath, 1862) that addressed the subject of female education. He translated from Sanskrit, English, and Bengali, respectively, the following three major works: Harshi's play *Ratnawali* (1888); a collection of famous women's lives (1905); and some works by Bankim Chandar Chattarjee. He collected poems of the Sindhi classical poet *Sami, accompanied by a serious study of his work (Vol. 1, 1890, Vol. 2, 1898, Vol. 3, 1914).

A.S. SUKHROCHEV

Khiyal (also *khayal*)

From Arabic: delusion, imagination, inspiration) One of the dominant genres of vocal classical music in South Asia, it is distinguished by its romantic ecstatic manner of enunciation combined with allegorical-mystical poetics. *Khiyal* has a highly developed grammatical system based on the principles of **raga* and **tal* and includes varied devices of virtuoso concert performance. It emerged in the eleventh-thirteenth centuries (it is said to have been developed by Amir Khusro *Dehlawi. It is more likely that *khiyal* was developed by Sultan Husain Shah Sharqi (1457-83), the last king of Jaunpur.

It is derived from **dhrupad*, but retains only the first two stages *Asthai* and *Antara*, dropping *Sanchari* and *Abhog*. While *dhrupad* was devotional, *khiyal* was secular depicting love themes and fantasies, though also carrying *Sufi overtones. It was performed mostly in Braj.

Khiyal has *tâns*, a vocal line advancing upwards in an uninterrupted breath stream, allowing for inflections in quick succession.

The normative composition of the *khiyal* includes the greater *khiyal* and the lesser *khiyal*, each of which is based on the development of an original musical-poetic model. The structural model and principles of musical unfolding of *khiyals* are widely used in instrumental music.

The principal *gharanas* are those of Gwalior, Agra, Delhi, the *Punjab, Jaipur, etc. The most famous *khiyal* performers were, in the eighteenth century, Niyamat Khan of Sadarang and Firuz Khan of Adarang; in the twentieth century, Abdul Karim Khan, Bade Ghulam Ali Khan, Amir Khan, Malik Arjun Khan, the female singers Kishori Amonkar, Hirabai Barodekar. The younger generation includes Muhammad Dilshad Khan and Parwin Sultan. To Pakistan belonged Roshan Ara, Nazakat Ali, Salamat Ali, Fateh Ali and Amanat Ali and A. Hamid Ali Khan and Asad Amanat Ali.

M.I. KARATYGINA

Kho (also Chitrali)

A people in northern Pakistan (see Northern Areas) mainly inhabiting the district of *Chitral in Malakand division (see Malakan Pass), *North West Frontier Province. Their native tongue is *Khowar, which belongs to the central group of *Dardic languages. Their religion is Islam (considerable number are *Ismailis). The main occupations are farming in the river basins of northern Chitral, horticulture, bee-keeping, and cattle-breeding. Local industries include metal-working and smithery.

BIBLIOGRAPHY: *U.A. Rustamov, 'Hindu Kush Principalities in Northern India at the Turn of the 20th Century', Tashkent, 1956 (in Russian); A.H. Dani, 'History of Northern Areas of Pakistan', Islamabad, 1989.*

YU.V. GANKOVSKY

Khoja

(Persian *Khwaja*: master, chief, primarily an ethnic term) One of the two main *Ismaili sects in South Asia. Khojas are also known as Nizari, after Nizar, the son of al-Mustansir, a Fatimid caliph of Egypt (1036–94). Khoja sect appeared in the 12th century as a result of the missionary activities of some Ismaili preachers from Iran, who came to western India and converted the local trade and money-lending castes to Islam. The hereditary religious leader (**imam*) bears the title *Aga Khan. At present, Khoja communities exist in many Asian countries, including Central Asia, as well as in East Africa, America and Western Europe. The members pay 10 to 12 per cent of their annual income to Aga Khan. In Pakistan, the majority of Nizari Khoja live in the north-western region and in the south of *Sindh. They number nearly one million (estimate). They are ruled by His Highness Prince Aga Khan's Ismailia Federal Council for Pakistan. Nizari Khojas have numerous public organizations (students, women's, charity), educational establishments of all levels, banks, etc. Some of the richest businessmen in Pakistan, such as A. A. Fancy, G.A. Allana, S. Hoodbhoy, Y. Chinoy and others, belong to the Khoja sect. Some Khojas belong to **Ithna Ashari* sect.

M.R. KAZIMI

Khowar

Khowar, the language of the *Kho people, is the name used by its speakers. Neighbouring people call it *Chitrali, Chatrari, or Chatrori, after the name of its locality, *Chitral. In literature, the language is also referred to as Arniya and Owar, an inaccurate reading of Khowar. The language belongs to *Dardic group of *Indo-Aryan languages, the northern group of the central subgroup. There are isolated groups of Khowar speakers in Afghanistan, and a few speakers, originally from Chitral, in the Pamir. There are no discernible dialect subdivisions and no written tradition. In recent years, some publications have appeared in the *Urdu version of the Arabic script. The language is used in radio broadcasting.

BIBLIOGRAPHY: *D.I. Edelman, 'Dardic languages', Moscow, 1965 (in Russian); D.I. Edelman, 'The Dardic and Nuristani Languages', Moscow, 1983; G.A. Grierson, 'Linguistic Survey of India', Vol. III, pt. II, Calcutta, 1919; G. Morgensterne, 'Iranian Elements in Khowar', BSOAS, Vol. VIII, 1936; id., 'Some Features of Khowar Morphology', Norsk Tidsskrift for Sprogvidenskap, BD XIV, Oslo, 1947; M.I. Soloan, 'Khowar—English Dictionary', Peshawar, 1981.*

D.I. EDELMAN

Khuhro, Mohammad Ayub (1901–80)

Statesman. He came from a wealthy land owning family, and in the 1930s Ayub Khuhro took an active part in the movement for the separation of *Sindh from the Bombay Presidency. He was a member of the first *Constituent Assembly of Pakistan from 1947 to 1954. He was president of the *Muslim League's Sindh branch in 1948. He became Chief Minister of Sindh from 1947 to 1948, again in 1951 and still again from 1954 to 1955. He was Pakistan's Minister of Defence in 1956 and was one of the leaders of the Council Muslim League in 1967.

BIBLIOGRAPHY: *H. Khuhro, Mohammad Ayub Khuhro, Lahore, 1998.*

YU.V. GANKOVSKY

Khuhro

A land-owning clan in *Sindh. They gained importance in the eighteenth century, when they moved to Larkana. Before that time, the Khuhros owned lands in Khairpur. Representatives of the clan's top brass, such as Muhammad Ayub *Khuhro, Shah Muhammad Pasha Khuhro, Rashida Khuhro, Hamida Khuhro, Nisar Khuhro, Mahmud Khuhro and others, have always played a major role in the political, social, and economic life of Sindh. In the 1920s and 1930s, they took an active part in the movement for the recession of Sindh from the Bombay Presidency; in the 1930s and 1940s, in the movement for the formation of Pakistan; and in the 1960s through 1980s, in the Sindhi movement.

YU.V. GANKOVSKY

Khyber Pass

A pass in the Safedkoh (*Koh-i-Safed*, Spinghar) Mountains between Pakistan and Afghanistan, 17 km. from Peshawar and 16 km. from the unapproachable gorge of the *Kabul River. The pass is 53 km. long and 305 metres wide at its narrowest point. For a length of 8 km., the pass is approximately 180 metres wide. The highest elevation is 1,072 metres (Landi Kotal Fort) and it is in the territory of Pakistan, at a distance of 10 km. from the border with Afghanistan. The walls of the gorge, composed mainly of slate and limestone, rise sheerly over the passage. Their height ranges from 430 to 1,000 metres. The gorge has a deserted appearance, arid climate, and practically no trees. The highest temperature is 47.8ºC. In 1879, the British authorities built a road from Peshawar to Kabul along the *Khyber Pass, and in the 1920s a railroad was built in Pakistani territory reaching the Afghan border. The Khyber Pass has always had considerable strategic importance as the most convenient route from Afghanistan to India. In the broader sectors of the pass, there are villages. Old fortifications have been partly preserved.

Khyber Pass.

S.B. ROSTOTSKY

Kikli

A dance of young girls performed in pairs. The dancers face each other, cross their arms, and hold each other's hands, whirling around and singing folk songs. The girls stretch themselves backwards and forwards and whirl in a circle. Sometimes four girls join hands to perform this dance. Often the songs are devoted to theme of relationship with the in-laws.

R. HUSAIN

Kili-Ghul-Muhammad

This was a multi-level settlement (0.5 hectares) of settled agricultural tribes in the vicinity of Quetta (northern *Balochistan). W.A. *Fairservis studied it in the fifties. He identified four stages (Kili I-IV) of a neolithic culture (4th-3rd millennia BC) marked by adobe houses, flint and bone implements, bones of domesticated ox, sheep and goat. Modelled pottery was typical for the beginning of Kili II; towards the end of the period it was supplanted with wheeled painted ware. During Kili III (first copper implements) and Kili IV, modelled pottery gave place to wheeled painted pottery; ornamentation was gradually becoming more complex; vessels painted in two colours appeared. A similar situation can be observed in the neighbouring Loralai valley on the Rana-Ghundai settlement that suggests an influence (and probable infiltration) of western Asian tribes in the mid-3rd millennium BC.

BIBLIOGRAPHY: *W.A. Fairservis, 'Excavation in the Quetta Valley', New York, 1956.*

A.YA. SHCHETENKO

Kingri

A two-string musical instrument of the *wina* type.

A.S. ALPATOVA

Kirthar Mountains

This north-south Mountain range is 560 km. long. At an altitude of between 1,000 and 1,500 metres. The highest peak, Zardak, is 2,237 metres high. The Kirthar is located in the south-east of the Iraian Plateau near the *Indus Valley, and forms the natural western border of the *Sindh province. The southern part of the Kirthar

Kirthar National Park, set up in 1974.

Range is also known as Sindh *Kohistan. It is largely formed of limestone and sandstone. It features mountainous semi-deserts and deserts and patches of brushwood and space woods. In the southern part of the range, the Kirthar National Park, (*see*, image) covering an area of 3,000 sq. km., was set up in 1974.

YU.V. GANKOVSKY

Kit'a

(in Arabic: section, part) 1. A poem on a lyrical, philosophical or didactic subject; a genre form in the poetry of the Middle East and South Asia. Similar to **ghazal*, **kit'a* is a monorhyme, but in the first *bait* the double rhyming is absent.
2. An excerpt from a poem (either *ghazal* or **qasida*).

N.V. GLEBOV

Kitchlew, Dr Saifuddin (1888–1963)

Politician. Saifuddin Kitchlew was born in Amritsar and educated at Cambridge. In 1915, he was externed from Bengal for sedition. He led the Anti-Rowlatt Act agitations in Amritsar (This act gave extra-judicial powers to the police in order to suppress *pulshi* dissent) in the fateful year of 1919, which climaxed in the infamous Jallianwala Bagh massacre and the declaration of martial law in *Punjab. In April 1919, he was deported from Lahore (in which an army officer opened fire on unarmed protesters, killing, it is said, over a there and people) by the martial law authorities. He was sentenced at Karachi for inciting Indian soldiers to revolt.

In 1922, Kitchlew was Honorary Secretary of the Central Khilafat Committee and became its president in 1924. In the same year, he was elected Secretary of the Indian National Congress. In 1926 he was honorary secretary of the *All-India Muslim League (AIML).

Kitchlew launched his Muslim *Tanzim* Movement to counteract the Hindu *Shuddhi* and *Sanghatan* movements. It was in this phase that he struck a strident communal note, threatening Hindus with an invasion from Afghanistan. Dr Kitchlew was honorary secretary of the AIML when he split with President Sir Mohammad *Shafi when the latter wished to cooperate with the *Simon Commission. He transferred his office to the non-cooperating faction headed by M.A. *Jinnah.

Following the reconciliation between Sir Mohammad Shafi and M.A. Jinnah, he resigned from the AIML. Soon after he formed the India Peace Council. In 1933, he was elected president of the Indian National Congress. He died thirty years later in his native Amritsar in penury.

BIBLIOGRAPHY: *(ed.) K.K. Aziz, 'The Indian Khilafat Movement: A Documentary Record', Karachi, 1972; (ed.) M. Hasan, 'Muslims and the Congress', New Delhi, 1979.*

M.R. KAZIMI

Kohat Pass

It is situated in the *North West Frontier Province of Pakistan and lies in the Kohat Mountains. The mean elevation is approximately 1,000-1,500 metres. The Kohat Pass connects the Peshawar Valley with the *Kohat Plain, which lies to the south.

YU.V. GANKOVSKY

Kohat Plain

A plain in the *North West Frontier Province, to the west of the *Indus. The mean elevation is approximately 500 metres. It is composed of alluvial material and is intersected with latitudinal limestone ridges. The limestone hills are rich in spring wells. Subsoil waters remain at a high level. The clayey sections are very fertile.

YU.V. GANKOVSKY

Kohistan

A historical and geographical region in northern Pakistan (see Northern Areas). It consists of mountainous territory between the rivers *Gilgit and *Swat.

It consists of an area of apprximately 7,600 sq km. of mountainous territory. Administratively, it forms part of Hazara, NWFP.

M. STONEY

Kohistani (Language)

The generic name for a number of languages and dialects belonging to the eastern subgroup of *Dardic languages. They are mostly spoken in the hilly region of northern Pakistan. The term 'Kohistani' is applied to a group of languages and dialects in the mountainous regions through which the rivers Panjkora, *Swat and *Indus flow. The principal languages are Bashkarik (Garwi), Torwali, Mayan. 'Kohistani' also applies to the Mayan language spoken in the valley of the Indus and its neighbouring regions (the term 'Mayan' is used by the speakers of this language, the term 'Kohistani' by the surrounding population) and to one of the dialects of *Shina spoken in the same area, which does not belong to the Kohistani group.

The principal features of the Kohistani languages, except Shina, are as follows. In morphology, there is no category of person in most finite forms of the verb (including the copula); person and number are present. Transitive verbs in the past tense are used in sentences with regulative structure.

The languages have no writing systems.

BIBLIOGRAPHY: *D.I. Edelman, 'Dardic Languages', Moscow, 1965 (in Russian); 'Linguistic survey of India', (ed.) G.A. Grierson, Vol. 8, top. 2, Calcutta, 1919; G.A. Grierson, 'Torwali, An Account of a Dardic Language of the Swat Kohistan', London, 1929; G. Buddruss, 'Kanyawali. Probe eines maiya-Dialektes aus Tangir' Hindukusch, M¸nchen, 1959.*

D.I. EDELMAN

Kohistani (People)

Inhabitants of *Kohistan and its adjacent territories in the northern mountains, the valleys of the *Indus, *Swat, and the Panjkora. They speak the *Dardic languages of Bashkarik, Garwi, Torwali, Mayan (some linguists regard the above languages as one, or view them as one group of dialects of the *Kohistani language) and *Shina. Their religion is Islam (mostly *Shia). Their main occupations include pasture cattle breeding, ploughed and terraced farming, and horticulture.

YU.V. GANKOVSKY

Koh-i-Sultan

An extinct volcano in the *Chagai Mountains in the northern part of the Chagai District of the *Balochistan province. Its height is 2,332 metres. It holds deposits of high-quality sulphur.

YU.V. GANKOVSKY

Koroson, J. Henri (d. 1995)

Sociologist. He was an American sociologist and professor of sociology at the University of Massachusetts in Amherst. He earned his PhD at Yale University, lectured at the University of New York, was a sociology professor at the University of Karachi (1964-65), and served as a consultant for a government-sponsored family planning programme in Pakistan. He was treasurer of the American Institute of Pakistan Studies (1974-75), and edited collective publications on modern Pakistan.

WORKS: *'Modernization and Social Changes in the Family in Pakistan', New York, 1974; (ed.) 'Contemporary Problems of Pakistan', Leiden, 1974.*

YU.V. GANKOVSKY

Kot Diji

A pre-Harappan or early *Harappan archaeological culture of the first half of the 3rd millennium BC. Kot Diji settlement is located 40 km. to the east of *Mohenjo-Daro. The lower levels here belong to the Kot Diji culture. F.A. Khan excavated it in 1955–57, 1965 and 1981. The site consists of two 'tells': 'A' citadel and 'B', the lower town. It covers an area of 214 x 122 metres. F.A. Khan relates the upper levels of tell 'A' (levels 1-3) to the Harappan civilization, the lower levels (4-16) to the cultural complex Kot Diji. Brick houses on stone foundations are typical for the Kot Diji culture; fireplaces and stoves were also found. The settlement was protected by a high wall, placed on a stone foundation 1.5 metres wide. Stone and bone labour implements and weapons were found in addition to sickles, knives, arrowheads, whorls, terra cotta figurines, beads and clay bangles. Ornamentations were made in black, red and sometimes white paint; pottery was modelled and wheeled. The ware of the Kot Diji culture can be found in northern *Balochistan and central *Punjab. There are similarities with the *Amri, *Nal, and Sothi cultures.

BIBLIOGRAPHY: *F.A. Khan, 'Excavations at Kot Diji', PA, 2, 1965; F.A. Khan, 'Kot Diji Culture–Its Greatness'; 'Indus Civilization. New Perspectives', Islamabad, 1981; W.A. Fairservis, 'The Roots of Ancient India', Chicago-London, 1975.*

N.M. VINOGRADOVA

Kulli-Mehi

The settlements of Kulli and Mehi are the better-known sites of this archaeological culture in southern

*Balochistan and have given their names to the culture. There are also important settlements at Edith Sahr (complex A), Nindowari, and Sutkagen-Dor (the lower town). Ancient brick houses on stone foundations were found here, the settlements' cultural layer containing burials with cremations in urns and burial goods (bronze axes, pendants and terra cotta figurines). The urns and female clay figurines have direct analogies to the *Zhob culture. The pottery has black or sometimes red ornamentations against the vessels' own background; ornamental friezes formed by stylised elongated animals or plants are also typical.

Two development stages have been identified with this civilization: the earlier one is synchronous with Mundigak IV, Damb Saadat II-III (the Quetta culture) and the pre-Harappan sites of Balochistan; the later stage related to the developed Harappan culture. The settlements of Kulli (360 x 300 metres) and Mehi (330 x 300 metres) were discovered and studied by A. Stein.

BIBLIOGRAPHY: *A. Stein, 'An Archaeological Tour in Gedrosia. Memoirs of the Archaeological Survey of India', 43, 1931; W.A. Fairservis, 'The Roots of Ancient India', Chicago-London, 1975.*

N.M. VINOGRADOVA

Kulliyat

These is the collected works of one poet compiled according to prescribed rules. A *kulliyat* usually opens with an introduction carrying the author's name, the compiler's name, the poet's biography and an expression of appreciation of his work. The order of the works in the *kulliyat* are as follows: **ghazals*, compositional strophes (*mukhamas, *musaddas, tarkibband, *tarjiband*, etc.) **qasidas, *kit'a, *rubai, *marsia, *masnavi,* and other poems (**nazm*). Within each section the poems are arranged alphabetically, according to the last letter of rhyme, or **radif.*

N.V. GLEBOV

Kurram Valley

A river valley in Pakistan, 260 km. long, with its source on the southern slopes of the *Koh-i-Safed* Range. It flows in a south-eastern direction, through the valley, which covers an area of some 4,400 sq.km. at an average height of 2,400 meters above sea level, and joins the Indus to the north of Kalabagh.

The Kurram Valley floor is composed of alluvium and glacial debris. The River Kurram and its tributaries flow in braided channels with wide river beds that stay dry most of the year, until the melt-water spate in spring. The soils are predominantly sandy, but along the banks of the Kurram the land is covered with silt. As a result the riparian land, partivularly in the Kurram-Tochi interfluve to the south of the town of *Bannu, is highly fertile.

A large part of the remaining territory is occupied by dry shrub wasteland. About 50 per cent of the riverside land is under cultivation at any one time whilst a considerable area is left to lie fallow every year. Annual percipitaton does not exceed 300 mm, making irrigation a necessary part of farming. Irrigated lands are mainly situated between the Rivers Kurram and Tochi and have to be reclaimed every year. Over half of the cultivated land is sown with wheat, though fodder crops are of great importance. Cattle breeding is of importance, as well as the breeding of sheep, camel and mules.

YU.V. GANKOVSKY

Kurta

A knee-length shirt with long sleeves. The *kurta* was originally worn by urban aristocracy, high-ranking military officers and courtiers. *Kurta* and other types of jackets have been popular in South Asia since the time of the Great Mughals (*see*, Mughal Empire).

BIBLIOGRAPHY: *S.N. Dar, 'Costumes of India and Pakistan', Bombay, 1982.*

O.V. LYSTSOVA

L

Lacquers

These are made in several centres in Pakistan. In *Sindh lacquer is applied to wooden objects by rotating them on a lathe at great speed over a fixed piece of lacquer, which is heated by friction and sticks to the surface. Using lacquers of different colours, the craftsmen make coloured stripes on the object. Chairs, legs of bedsteads, and mortars are decorated in this technique. Engraved patterns are sometimes filled with coloured lacquer on objects of bone and antler. Highly popular are striped boxes and caskets for *betel. This type of lacquered object is produced by rubbing a lacquer stick against the surface of an object rotated on a lathe. The ornament is mostly geometrical or highly stylized floral designs. In *Azad Kashmir various caskets, trays, vessels, cups, kalamdans or pencil cases, book bindings, and bracelets are made of papier-mache, painted and covered with transparent lacquer. To make papier-mâché, paper pulp is fragmented, mixed with rice paste, and applied layer by layer to a brass or ceramic mould. The mould is removed after the product is sliced in two, then it is glued together and a glue, with gypsum and white clay primer is applied before the object is polished with a stone (mostly agate), painted with a fine hair brush, and lacquered after drying. Sometimes very fine silver or gold foil is applied together with dyed paint which lends the details of the painting a special shimmering effect. Floral motifs as well as scenes from the life of the Mughal court (*see,* Mughal Empire), hunting scenes, and conventional ornamental compositions similar to shawl designs, dominate the decorative style. Lacquers are manufactured mostly by Muslim craftsmen. The origin of *Kashmir lacquers is unknown, but they have a stylistic affinity to the lacquers of Iran and central Asia is obvious.

O.V. LYSTSOVA

Lahnda (also Lahndi)

Also known as Western *Punjabi, Lahnda includes a number of Western Punjabi dialects belonging to the north-western group of *Indo-Aryan languages. It is sometimes known by the names of the individual dialects, such as Jatki or Multani. Lahnda is also sometimes regarded as a modern Indo-Aryan language with territorial dialects. In this broader meaning, it is called *Siraiki (Seraiki).

Lahnda dialects are spoken in northern Pakistan, mostly in the *Punjab Province. In the north, they border on the *Dardic languages, in the east, on Punjabi, and in the south, on *Sindhi. In the south-east, they are contiguous to Rajasthani, in the west, to the Iranian languages, *Balochi and *Pashtu. The point of confluence of the rivers *Jhelum and *Chenab may be taken as the geographical centre of the area in which Lahnda dialects are spoken. Within this area, starting from Peshawar and moving clockwise, the following cities lie along the perimeter: Peshawar, Attock, Haripur, Muzaffarabad, Rawalpindi, Jhelum, Gujrat, Gujranwala, Sahiwal, Khairpur, *Bahawalpur, Alipur, Dera Ghazi Khan, Dera Ismail Khan, Mianwali, *Kohat. Lahnda dialects are divided into two distinct groups: 1. southern, spoken on the plains, and 2. northern, spoken in the hills. The conventional boundary between these two groups lies along the southern spurs of the *Salt Range. Each of the groups has phonetic, grammatical and lexical features of its own. Lahnda dialects serve as the basis for the formation of several languages. Potohari, Hindko and Siraiki are examples of such languages. The former two evolve on the basis of northern dialects, and latter, on the basis of the southern. Official Pakistani publications refer to Siraiki, which is vigorously coming into literary use, and Hindko and Punjabi as the country's principal languages.

Most Lahnda speakers are Muslims, who use a modified Arabic script. Hindu speakers of Lahnda use a variety of the Lahnda alphabet, which is related to the Mahajani writing system and the *Kashmiri script called Sharada. *Sikh speakers of Lahnda often write texts in the Gurmukhi script.

BIBLIOGRAPHY: *'The East Outside the Borders. Language Situation and Language Policy. A Reference Book', Moscow, 1986 (in Russian); G.A. Zograf, 'New Indo-Aryan languages', Vol. I, Moscow, 1976 (in Russian); G.A. Zograf, 'The Languages of India', Pakistan, Ceylon and Nepal, Moscow, 1960 (in Russian); G.A. Zograf, 'The Languages of South Asia', Moscow, 1990 (in Russian); Yu.A. Smirnov, 'Lahndi Language', Moscow, 1970 (in Russian); G.A. Grierson, 'Linguistic Survey of India', Vol. 8, pt. 1, Calcutta, 1919; C.*

Shackle, 'The Siraiki Language of Central Pakistan: A Reference Grammar', London, 1976; Yu.A. Smirnov, 'The Lahndi Language', Moscow, 1975; G.A. Zograf, 'Languages of South Asia', London, 1982.

YU.V. ARESHKO
V.P. LIPEROVSKY

Lahore Fort

A monument of Pakistan's defensive architecture, a fortified residence of the Mughals in the 16th-18th centuries (see Mughal Empire). The walls of the fort

Lahore Fort, a momentous defence architecture of the Mughal era.

are built of brick and enclose an area of some twelve hectares on which stand magnificent mansions, a mosque, audience chambers, gardens, and pavilions. The palace of Jahangir was built there in 1617. South of the palace lies the *Diwan-i-Am* (hall of public audience, 1631-32, later rebuilt) with an arcade of forty marble pillars; the small *Moti Masjid* (Pearl Mosque, 1645) of white marble; the Shah Jahan palace complex (1631-32), *Shish Mahal* (Mirror Palace) magnificently decorated with marble panels and openwork railings and with inlays of pieces of mirror; the finely carved *Naulakha* pavilion, with a copper-covered curvilinear roof of the Bengal type, and the *Hathi Pol* gates (elephant gates). In the 1570s the fort was surrounded by powerful brick walls with gates (rebuilt in 1673-74), of which the Hazuribagh and Alamgiri gates stand out, with massive ribbed towers on either side of the entrance leading into the *Badshahi Mosque's court.

A. RALLEV

Lahore Museum

The oldest museum in Pakistan, it was founded in 1864 as the Punjab Industrial Art Museum. It owns collections on the history of the culture of Pakistan from antiquity to the present day, and also monuments of the artistic culture of India, Nepal, Tibet, Southeast Asia, the Arab countries, and Iran. The museum has twenty galleries plus storerooms, workshops, restoration laboratories, and photographic studios. The main sections of the museum contain manuscripts and miniatures, also *Gandhara objects of art, coins, weapons, and modern paintings, including a gallery of *Sadequain's works. Exhibited in the general gallery are Chinese porcelain, ivory objects, metalwork, embroideries from various countries, and Russian porcelain. Private collections from many countries of Asia and Africa are prominently displayed. The archaeological digs in *Taxila yielded a stream of new exhibits. The library has over 35,000 volumes. The Museum has published the Lahore Museum Bulletin since 1988.

BIBLIOGRAPHY: *S.R. Dar, 'Lahore Museum Treasures', Lahore, 1988; B.A. Qureshi, 'Lahore Museum Then and Now', in: Lahore Museum Bulletin, Vol. I, 1988, No. 2.*

N.K. KARPOVA

Lahore Resolution of 23 March 1940

This Resolution was moved by Abul Kasem Fazlul *Haq, the premier of Bengal, and seconded by Chaudhri Khaliq-uz-Zaman. The Resolution was grounded on the basic principle that: Geographically contiguous units are demarcated into regions which should be so constituted with such territorial readjustments as may be necessary that the areas in which the Muslims are numerically in a majority, as in the north-western and eastern zones of India, should be grouped to constitute independent States in which the constituent units shall be autonomous and sovereign.

The Resolution is not very precisely worded and does not contain the word 'Pakistan'. It was preceded by the Sindh Muslim League Resolution of 10 October 1938, moved by Sir Abdullah *Haroon, who called for the division of India into two federations, Muslim and Hindu respectively. On 25 March 1939, at Meerut, Liaquat Ali *Khan, the AIML Secretary, voiced his preference for division. The main importance of the Lahore Resolution is that the AIML forsook its role of seeking guarantees for Muslims as minorities, but asserted their right as a separate nation. In constitutional terms, this meant that the Muslims would not be subject to law of the land but to international law where, despite territorial and demographical disparities, Hindus and Muslims would be regarded as equally sovereign entities. This resolution became the basis of the Pakistan movement.

BIBLIOGRAPHY: *(ed.) L.A. Sherwani, 'Pakistan Resolution to Pakistan', (Karachi, 1969).*

M.R. KAZIMI

Lakhtai

A dance from the frontier province, but unlike the *Khattak, *Lakhtai* can sometimes be performed solo.

R. HUSAIN

Lamb, Harry Alastair (1930–)

Writer. Alastair Lamb (born in China) was educated at Harrow and Cambridge, from where he obtained his PhD. He has devoted his life to studies pertaining to the Orient, especially South Asia.

WORKS: *'The China–India War', RIIA London, 1964; 'Crisis in Kashmir 1947 to 1996', London, 1996; 'Kashmir: A Disputed Legacy 1946–1990', London, 1991; 'Incomplete Partition', London, 1997.*

YU.V. GANKOVSKY

Landscape Gardens

A type of landscaping used by the Mughals. It is rooted in the Muslim gardens associated in Islam with paradise. Gardens were part of palace halls that were open to the outdoors. The planning of the gardens followed the *charbagh* or 'four gardens' square principle. The square ground plan is divided into four smaller ones with the aid of paths, plants, and narrow ditches filled with water. In the centre of the squares are ornamental ponds with fountains feeding water into the system. Peacocks lived in the gardens and birds sang in gilded cages. Despite the unity of composition, the gardens varied in their appearance and size. Landscape gardening reached the peak of its development in the Mughal epoch. Especially striking are the Shalimar Gardens laid out in 1640 by Emperor Shah Jahan in Lahore, the gardens of the palaces of Agra, Fatehpur-Sikri (16th century) and Shahjahanabad (17th century) in India, which are deemed to be among the highest achievements of landscape gardening.

Shah Jahan Mosque, an example of Landscape gardens.

Landscapes made a direct impact on the planning of palace ensembles and major mosques.

S.S. OZHEGOV

LaPorte Jr., Robert (1940–)

Political Scientist. His PhD in Political Science was completed at Syracuse University in 1967. LaPorte's career has combined research, university teaching, and international consulting. Most of these activities have been related to Pakistan.

As a South Asia Fellow at the Maxwell School of Citizenship and Public Affairs, he began his career-long study of Pakistan in 1963. His first research work on Pakistan resulted in a management case study of the West Pakistan Water and Power Development Authority (WAPDA) as part of his PhD dissertation.

Early on in his career he concentrated on the public administrative system of Pakistan and on the Civil Service as a political institution. Over the past three decades he has examined the changes in governance and politics in Pakistan and written about them. He has written or co-authored numerous books, chapters in various books, and articles on Pakistan.

YU.V. GANKOVSKY

Lasbela

1. A princely state in the southeastern part of *Balochistan, in the valley and delta of the Porali. In 1951 the area was 18,300 sq.km., with a population of 76,000, mostly *Sindhis. The ruler, or *Jam*, of Lasbela was a vassal of the *Khan of *Kalat. Under British rule (see British India) the administration of Lasbela was actually controlled by the political agent representing the Viceroy and Governor-General of India in the city of Kalat. The princely state was incorporated into Pakistan on 17 March 1948 and abolished as a State entity in 1955.

2. A district in the Kalat division of the province of Balochistan in Pakistan. Area: 12,574 sq.km.; population 188,000 (1981 data).

YU.V. GANKOVSKY

Lawni

Vocal compositions, along with *qawwalis*, that reflect attempts to combine Hindu religious singing called *bhajan* with Persian musical forms. *Lawnis* are close to *qawwalis*, but simpler in terms of performance technique.

I. PIRACHA

Leghari, Farooq Ahmad (1941–)

Farooq Ahmad Khan Leghari, President of Pakistan (1993–97).

President of Pakistan from 1993 to 1997. Educated at Aitchison College Lahore and St. Catherine's College, Oxford, Farooq Leghari qualified for entering the *Civil Service of Pakistan in 1964. He resigned at the behest of Zulfikar Ali *Bhutto. Winning elections to the National Assembly in 1970, 1977 and 1988 on the PPP ticket, he served as Minister for Water and Power in 1989 and acting Foreign Minister in the 1993 caretaker cabinet. On 4 December 1993 Farooq Leghari was elected the eighth President of Pakistan. On 5 November 1996 he dismissed the PPP government of Benazir *Bhutto and dissolved the National Assembly. He subsequently attempted to dismiss the PML government of Mian Mohammad Nawaz *Sharif by temporarily suspending the repeal of the Eighth Amendment. He resigned as President in December 1997. He formed the Millat Party, which he now heads.

M.R. KAZIMI

Leva

A dance supposed to be of African origin. In Karachi's Lyari area, one can see *Leva* performed by the people living there. These are the people whose forefathers migrated from African countries. They introduced *Leva* to the *Baloch community, who have been settled in Karachi for a long time. *Leva* is danced with a wild swagger and fast movements of the dancers, to the rhythmic beat of the drums, and is unique in its style. While *Leva* is given the status of an 'outsider's dance' by the Baloch, *Latti* and *Hambo* are dances of the ancient indigenous people of *Balochistan.

R. HUSAIN

Local Government Institutions (or Local Self-government Bodies)

These institutions are established through general elections, for a term of four years. The lower link in self-government in rural areas is a council of five to ten persons elected by, and operating in the territory of, an historically established community. Each member of the given council is elected by 1,000-1,500 voters. The rural population also elects district councils, each member of which represents between 20,000 and 25,000 voters. In small towns and townships, municipal corporations are elected and consist of 15 to 17 members. In towns with population under 500,000, town committees of twenty to forty members are elected. Larger cities have municipal committees with fifty to sixty members. All the local self-government bodies are concerned with the economic development of the corresponding territorial unit, construction of roads and bridges, the building of small-scale irrigation projects, water supply, public transport, and various public utilities. Local self-government bodies have funds consisting of government subsidies and a share of local taxes.

In the late 1980s and early 1990s the following self-government bodies operated in the rural areas: 4,270 union councils, 93 district councils, and 13 municipal corporations. In the towns and cities there were 298 town committees and 129 municipal committees. In some towns, mostly in the *Punjab and the NWFP, the local self-government bodies were called cantonment boards of which there were 39. In the *Federally Administered Tribal Areas various issues of local character are discussed and decided at a **jirga*. *Khans, **sardars*, and **maliks* of the tribes play significant roles in these matters.

V.N. MOSKALENKO

Lohana

A Hindu trading and money-lending caste in *Sindh. Their origin is traced to Lohanpur (Multan division, *Punjab Province), where they are thought to have specialized in the caravan salt trade. Prior to 1947 the Lohana were the largest Hindu caste in Sindh (460,000 in 1931). After 1947 a majority of them moved to India. Some present-day Muslim castes, such as Memon, are ethnically related to Lohana.

BIBLIOGRAPHY: *V.R. Russel, 'The Tribes and Castes of the Central Provinces of India', Vol. 2, London, 1916; Thakur, 'Sindhi Culture', Bombay, 1916.*

YU.V. GANKOVSKY

Lucknow Pact, 1916

This was a pact signed between Ambica Charan Mazumdar, President of the Indian National Congress, and Mohammad Ali *Jinnah, President AIML, on 30 December 1916. The Pact provided for a joint struggle against British rule (see British India) and for the attainment of representative government in India. In the words of Mazumdar, Jinnah stated that Hindu-Muslim 'Co-operation in the cause of our motherland should be our guiding principle'. Congress conceded separate electorates and weightage in legislative representation, already enacted in the Morley-Minto Reforms of 1909, to the Muslims. The annulment of the partition of *Bengal (1905), through the Delhi Durbar proclamation of 1911, had disillusioned the Muslims against the British, without satisfying the political aspirations of the Hindus. In such circumstances, loyalist Muslim leaders had to yield place to nationalist leaders like M.A. Jinnah and Syed Wazir Hasan. The Lucknow Pact of 1916 was the highest point of communal harmony, Jinnah playing the role of 'Ambassador of Hindu-Muslim' amity, as Congress leader Gopal Krishna Gokhale had earlier termed him. M.K. Gandhi was present at the Lucknow Conference but played no active role. Some leaders of the *Khilafat Movement, both Muslims and Hindus, sought to abrogate the Lucknow Pact, which was temporarily replaced by the *Delhi Muslim Proposals 1927, but ultimately superseded by the *Nehru Report and the *Fourteen Points (1929). This signalled the end of communal unity in the freedom struggle.

BIBLIOGRAPHY: *S. Sharifuddin Pirzada (ed.), 'Foundations of Pakistan', Vol. I, Karachi, 1969; S.K. Mazumdar, 'Jinnah and Gandhi', Calcutta, 1966; M.R. Jaykar, 'The Story of My Life', Bombay, 1958.*

M.R. KAZIMI

Ludab al-Albab

(The Heart of the Essence; in Arabic *lubab*: essence, core) It is one of the earliest anthologies of Persian poetry, compiled by Muhammad Aufi Samarkandi in India in c. 1220. The anthology contains unique information about poets, analyses of their work, and samples of early classical Persian poetry. *Lubab al-albab* is a prototype of *tazkira*, the basis of medieval literary criticism in Persian literature, and later in *Urdu literature.

BIBLIOGRAPHY: *'Lubab al-Albab', (ed.) E. Browne, London-Leiden, 1903.*

N.V. GLEBOV

Luddi

A dance for both men and women, but not together. It is a victory dance where the dancers perform special movements of their heads. It is usually danced when the fields have been prepared for sowing. The costume worn by the dancers is a simple loose shirt with a *lacha* or sarong. The dancers put one hand on their backs and the other hand in front of their faces. The body movement is sinuous and snake-like. There is a drummer in the centre of the dance. *Luddi* may or may not be accompanied by songs.

R. HUSAIN

M

Mackay, Earnest (1880–1943)

Archeologist. He was a British historian and archaeologist. In 1935 he headed the excavation of *Mohenjo-Daro and *Chanhu-Daro, the two most important sites of the *Harappan civilization, conducted jointly by the American School of Indian and Iranian Studies and the Boston Museum of Fine Arts.

WORKS: *'Further Excavations at Mohenjo-Daro, 1927-31', Vols. 1-2, New Delhi, 1938; 'Chanhu-Daro Excavations 1935-6', American Oriental Society, No. 20, New Haven, 1943; 'Early Indus Civilization', London, 1948.*

A. YA. SHCHETENKO

Madhab

(Arabic: way, mode of action, conduct; from *dahaba*: to go, to set off) A theological (religio-legal) doctrine, theory, school, or direction. The main *madhabs* evolved in the 8th and 9th centuries AD. They include the four *Sunni *madhabs*: 1. Hanafiya (Hanifites), which prevailed among the Sunni Muslims of Pakistan and other countries of South Asia and was founded by Numan Abu Hanifa (*c.* 696–767); 2. Malikiya (Malikites), founded by Malik ibn Anas (713–95); 2. Shafiiya (Shafiites), founded by Muhammad ibn Idris al-Shafii (d. 830); and 4. al-Hanbaliya (Hanbalites) founded by Ahmad ibn Hanbal (d. 855). There is also the *Shia *madhab* 'of the twelve imams' or al-Jafariya (Jafarites), whose founder is believed to be Jafar ibn Muhammad al-Sadiq (700–65), the sixth Imam of the Imamite Shias. Since the beginning of the 16th century, this has been the madhab of the state of Iran.

YU.V. GANKOVSKY

Maharaja

(Sanskrit: Great Raja) 1. A title of the ruler of a princely state in India and elsewhere in south-east Asia, in the Middle Ages and in recent times. In India it was preserved as an honorary title after the princely states were abolished in 1948–9. In ancient and medieval India there was a royal title of *Maharajadhiraja–maharaja* over *rajas*. 2. In *British India, *Maharaja* is the title second in importance, after *Maharaja Bahadur*, awarded by the government to Hindu aristocrats (a similar title awarded to Muslim aristocrats was **Nawab*).

T.N. ZAGORODNIKOVA
YU.V. GANKOVSKY

Mahdi

(Arabic: guided by God) A messiah, a renovator of Islam, precursor to the end of the world. A loosely described figure in *Sunni eschatology or doctrine of the last days, identified with Muhammad, son of Hasan Askari, the Twelfth **Imam* in *Shia eschatology.

BIBLIOGRAPH: *Jassim M. Hussain, 'The Occultation of the Twelfth Imam', London, 1982; A.A. Sachedina, 'Islamic Messianism', Albany, 1981; Said Amir Arjomand, 'The Shadow of God and the Hidden Imam', Chicago, 1984.*

YU.V. GANKOVSKY

Mahdism

(*Mahdawi*, *Mahdawiya*) A messianic teaching of Islam, which believes in the coming of the Mahdi. The largest Mahdi movement in medieval India was led by Sayyid Muhammad Jaunpuri (1443–1505). Upon return from his Haj in Mecca in 1495, Sayyid Muhammad announced in Ahmadabad, in 1499, the imminent end of the world and called upon the people to restore the original purity of Islam.

In his sermons, he preached brotherhood and mutual assistance among the Muslims. He rejected the necessity of concentrating political power in the hands of Mahdi, considering himself only a precursor of peace and justice. The movement enjoyed the support of the urban traders and craftsmen, and part of *Gujarati aristocracy. However, it was severely persecuted by Muslim theologians, because the doctrines were considered heterodox. They were mainly: 1. The Holy Prophet preached the literal meaning of the Quran, Mahdi interpreted it (*Tawil*) 2. Muhammad is the last Prophet and Sayyid Muhammad is the last Mahdi, 3. A new profession of faith (*Kalima*) included Muhammad Mahdi as a Messenger, 4. *Zikr*, repeating the names of God, should be substituted for salat or prayers. 5. The fast of *Ramazan should be replaced with seven days fasting every month. 6. *Ushr* should replace *Zakat (*See* Zikri and Rowshaniya).

A. NIYAZI

Mahmood, Fazal (1927–2005)

Cricket player. First came into the international limelight as the Oval Hero who took 12 wickets against MCC in 1954. He began his career in first class cricket in 1943, in Test cricket in 1952; and played his last Test match in 1962. In 34 Test matches he took 139 wickets with an average of 24.70 runs. His best bowling figures were against India at Lucknow: 7 wickets for 42 runs. As a batsman he scored 620 runs with an average of 14.09 runs. His best batting performance was 60 runs against the West Indies at Port of Spain. He was captain for ten Test matches; he won two, lost two, and the rest were draws. He passed away in Lahore on 30 May 2005 due to heart problems.

Fazal Mahmood, well known Cricket player.

WORKS: *'From Dusk to Dawn,' Oxford, 2003.*

S. ZAKIUDDIN

Mahmudabad, Amir Ahmad Khan, Raja of (1914–73)

Statesman. Amir Ahmad Khan and the son of *Maharaja* Sir Ali Mohammad Khan of Mahmudabad (d. 1931). The elder *Maharaja* was a former President of the Muslim League and a patron of the Aligarh and Benares universities, and at one time was put under house arrest for boycotting the *Simon Commission. He was the most prominent Muslim leader to sign the *Nehru Report. Amir Ahmad Khan, the son was something of a radical. He hung a portrait of Bhagat Singh in his room, was partial to Subhash Chandra Bose (leader of the Indian National Army) throughout the freedom struggle and wore homespun clothes. Amir Ahmad Khan formally succeeded to his father's title in 1936. He was inducted into the *Muslim League directly by M.A. *Jinnah. The same year the Muslim League was re-organized and the Raja of Mahmudabad was appointed to the newly created post of Treasurer, a responsibility he fulfilled until Independence. He was also the President of the *All-India Muslim Students Federation (1936–46) and initially also President of the Muslim National Guard.

In 1945 the *Raja* wrote to Jinnah seeking his formal sanction for contesting the elections to the Indian Legislative Assembly. During the campaign he abandoned his own constituency to canvass for Jinnah in the latter's Bombay constituency. Both candidates won. In 1946 he visited Iraq but he was forced to come back in the wake of the August communal riots. He survived three assassination attempts while escorting his sisters to safety in Pakistan. He was in Hyderabad, Sindh, on the morning of 14 August 1947 but refused to proceed to Karachi for the Independence ceremonies. He later explained that, with the achievement of Pakistan, the Muslim League had become redundant. The Raja of Mahmudabad also thwarted Sarojini Naidu's attempt to rehabilitate him in Indian politics, and left for Iraq. Before his departure, he had arranged for his estate in India to be converted into a co-operative farm with the farmers as shareholders, but the land reforms in India overtook his plans.

The Raja of Mahmudabad lived in Iraq for a decade subsisting on small-scale business. In late 1956 he came to Pakistan.

He rejected the offer of President Mohammad Ayub *Khan, to head the official Muslim League. He also declined the offer of a Cabinet post made by President Yahya *Khan. In 1968 he left for London, where he became Director of the Islamic Cultural Centre.

WORKS: *'Some Memories' in: 'C.H. Philips and M.D. Wainright (eds.), The Partition of India: Policies and Perspectives, Aberdeen, 1970; S. Ishtiaq Husain (ed.), 'Khutbat-i-Raja Sahib Mahmudabad' (Urdu Speeches), Karachi, 1997.*

BIBLIOGRAPHY: *Syed Ishtiaq Husain (ed.), 'The Life and Times of the Raja Saheb Mahmudabad', 2 Vols., Karachi, 1993 and 1998; Syed Asghar Ali Shadani (ed.), 'Sawanh-i-Hyat Raja Saheb Mahmudabad'; Husain Anjum (ed.), 'Tulu-i-Afkar Raja Saheb Mahmudabad Number', Karachi, July 1976; M. Qasim Ejaz, 'Raja Saheb Mahmudabad Par Ek Nazar', Karachi, 1997.*

M.R. KAZIMI

Majeed, Amjad (1914–74)

Poet. Amjad Majeed was an *Urdu language poet who was born at Jhang. His earliest poems were published in the *Kaleem* (Delhi), edited by Josh *Malihabadi. Amjad Majeed was a nature poet of rare sensibility and his tree imagery has been the subject of deep critical discussion. The insignificant place of man in this world was one of his most famous themes and his pathos was attuned to the abstraction of his **nazm* poetry. His poetry invites introspection and retrospection despite his wide visual canvas. Three collections, *Shabi-Rafta* ('The Past Night'), *Shab-i-Rafta Ke Ba'ad* ('After the Past Night'), and *Ae Khuda Me'rey Dil* ('O God, My Heart') were published the last, posthumously.

M.N. KHAN

Majlis-i-Ahrar-i-Islam

(Islamic Independent Organization, the *Ahrars*) An orthodox *Sunni religio-communal Party, founded in 1930 in *Punjab by Maulana Ataullah Shah Bukhari. In 1930-32, the organization took part in the Civil Disobedience Campaign led by the Indian National Congress against the British authorities. In 1939 the party opposed India's involvement in the Second World War. In 1944 it declined M.A. *Jinnah's invitation to join the Muslim League and refused to take part in the movement for the formation of Pakistan. In the spring of 1953 it was one of the organizers and activists of the anti-*Ahmadiya riots in *West Pakistan. In the 1960s and 1970s the Party's influence declined. In 1970, 1977 and 1988, it took part in the general elections, the last time as a member of the bloc of forty-seven parties called the Pakistan *Qaumi Jamhuri Ittehad* (PQJI) or Pakistan National Democratic Alliance, but did not win a single seat either in Pakistan's parliament or in the legislative assemblies of the Provinces.

BIBLIOGRAPHY: *Yuri Gankovsky, L.R. Gordon-Polonskaya, 'A History of Pakistan', Lahore, 1972; W.C. Smith, 'Modern Islam in India, London', 1946.*

YU.V. GANKOVSKY

Majlis-i-Taraqqi-i-Adab

(Society for the Development of Literature) It was founded in 1950 in Lahore to publish *Urdu classics and to encourage translations into Urdu of world classics. The society publishes a quarterly journal, *Sahifa* (The Book), and has established a prestigious literary prize for outstanding literary criticism.

N.V. GLEBOV

Makran (also Mekran, Macuran)

Derives its name from Maka, a tribe inhabiting this territory in ancient times: 1. It is a historical-geographical area in south-eastern Iran and south-western Pakistan, on the shore of Oman Bay in the Arabian Sea. It extends from west to east for approximately 1,000 km. and is characterized by a hilly landscape. Mountain ranges, running parallel to the shore, rise 1,500-2,000 metres (Makran Coast Range, Central Makran Range Siahan Range). They line up with the Iranian Plateau from the south and are mainly made up of limestone and sandstone. There is an active seismic zone and the foothills abound in mud volcanoes. The climate is arid subtropical. Most of the rivers dry up in summer. Vegetation is of desert and semi-desert variety. The coastal waters are rich in fish. The population consists mainly of *Balochi who are engaged in cattle, sheep and camel breeding, and irrigation farming (wheat, barley, jowar). By virtue of its position along the main travel routes from Asia Minor to India, Makran was often attacked by various invaders. 2. A former princely state in the south-western part of Pakistan, *Balochistan province. Its territory covered 60,000 sq. km. Its population was approximately 139,000 in 1951. Makran joined Pakistan on 17 March 1948. It was abolished in 1955. 3. A division in Balochistan province. It consists of three districts: Panjgur, Kech, Gawadar. Its area is 54,000 sq. km. Its population was 816,217 in 1998. The capital is Turbat.

S.B. ROSTOTSKY

Malakand Pass

It is situated in the *North West Frontier Province of Pakistan. The Pass crosses the Malakand Range, the mean height of which is 1,500-1,900 metres, and connects the *Swat Valley with the *Peshawar Valley.

YU.V. GANKOVSKY

Malhi, Gobind (1921–)

Writer. Malhi is a *Sindhi language writer, living in Bombay, who has some forty books to his credit. His realistic works are devoted to people's everyday lives and carry important social messages. His more famous novels include: *Ansu* ('Tears', 1952); *Pakziyara Walar Khan Bichhudia* ('Birds that Strayed from the Flock', 1953), about the refugees after India's partition in 1947; *Zindagi je Rah Te* ('The Roads of Life'), about the Indian creative intelligentsia; *Chanchal Nigahun* ('Naughty Looks', 1954); *Pyar ji Pyas* ('A Thirst for Love', 1972), about city slums; and *Dese sen Kanjan* ('Marriage to a Fellow Countrywoman', 1958), about Sindhi fishermen's everyday lives and problems. He has several collections of short stories to his credit and some one-act plays. He has been the winner of several prestigious awards and his stories have been translated into other Indian languages.

BIBLIOGRAPHY: *L.H. Ajwani, 'History of Sindhi Literature', New Delhi, 1977.*

A.A. SUKHOCHEV

Malihabadi, Josh (1898–1982)

Poet. L. Shabbir Hasan Khan (his real name) was one of the most famous lyrical poets writing in *Urdu. He was born into the family of a landowner, although both his father and grandfather were also poets. Josh was keenly interested in classical Farsi and Urdu poetry from childhood. He had his secondary education in Lucknow and went on to St. Peter's College in Agra. In 1924 he took a job at Osmania University (Hyderabad, Deccan) but he was exiled from the Nizam's state in 1934 for lack of loyalty towards the authorities. In Delhi he took an active part in establishing the All-India Progressive Writers Association. He founded the journal *Kaleem* ('The Speaker') and from 1948 edited the journal, *Ajkàl* ('Nowadays'). In 1955 he moved to Pakistan.

As a novice, he had written poetry under the guidance of the lyrical poet Aziz Lakhnawi. His work was, however, deeply influenced by *Ghalib, and particularly by *Iqbal. In his first collection of poetry, *Ruh-i-Adab* ('The Soul of Literature', 1921), he presented a cycle of social verse. Josh's poetry between the 1920s and 1940s is characterized by a romantic perception of reality and an appeal to do away with obsolete traditions. Examples are *Watan* ('Homeland'), *Shikast-i-Zindan ka Khwab* ('Dreams of Defeating the Prison'), *Husn aur Mazduri* ('Beauty and Labour'). His poems were recited at meetings and young people called him 'The Poet of the Revolution' (*Shair-i-Inqilab*). During the Second World War he wrote poetry calling for India's freedom and a secular, democratic order.

He published several collections of his poems in Pakistan, compiled a dictionary of poetic terminology and published a collection of critical essays, *Isharat* (Delhi, 1942). In the 1970s and 1980s, he studied the philosophical works of Iqbal and Rumi and reflected on the problems of the origin of the world and man *(Harf-i-Akhir*—'The Final Word'). Josh was a poet of great themes and movements. He published approximately twenty poetic collections—**rubai, *ghazals, *nazm, *masnawi*, sonnets, ballads, and **marsiya*. Josh was also an excellent prose writer. His best-known prose work is the voluminous *Yadon Ki Barat*, his controversial autobiography, that was particularly shocking to Urdu readers since he portrayed himself as libertine and aberrant.

BIBLIOGRAPHY: *'Afkar, Josh Number', (ed.) Sahba Lucknowi, 1961, Karachi; 'Nuqoosh-i-Josh' Karachi, 1995; 'Risai Adab', (ed.) Hilal Naqvi, Karachi, 1996.*

S.D. SEREBRYANY

Malik

(Arabic for ruler, monarch) An honorary title given to the elder or ruler of a clan or tribe.

YU.V. GANKOVSKI

Malik, Hafeez (1930–)

Hafeez Malik, noted historian and scholar.

Historian/Political Scientist. He is currently Professor of Political Science at Villanova University, Pennsylvania, USA. In 1953 he moved from Pakistan to the US. He earned his PhD degree at Syracuse University in 1960. For several years, he served as a correspondent for leading Pakistani newspapers. Prof Malik taught at the Foreign Service Institute of the US State Department (1961-63; 1966-80). He was also director of the *American Institute of Pakistan Studies (1974–90), President of the Pakistan Council of the Asian Society, USA (1971–74), and President of the Pakistan-American Foundation. He has published and edited the *Journal of South Asian and Middle Eastern Studies* since 1977.

WORKS: *'Muslim Nationalism in India and Pakistan', Washington, 1963; 'Sir Sayyid's History of the Bijnore Rebellion', East Lansing, 1967; (ed.) 'Iqbal: Poet—Philosopher of Pakistan', New York, 1971; 'Sir Sayyid Ahmad Khan and Muslim Modernization in India and Pakistan', New York, 1980; 'Political Profile of Sir Sayyid Ahmad Khan. A Documentary Record', Islamabad, 1982; (ed.) 'International Security in South-West Asia', New York, 1984; 'Soviet-American Relations with Pakistan, Iran and Afghanistan', London and New York, 1987.*

YU.V. GANKOVSKY

Mamdot, Iftikhar Husain, Nawab (1905–69)

Statesman. A politician and statesman in *British India and Pakistan from a wealthy land-owning family of

*Punjab, Nawab Mamdot was a participant in the movement for the formation of Pakistan and the President of the *Muslim League in the Punjab from 1946 to 1947. He served as a Member of the first and second *Constituent Assemblies of Pakistan and was Chief Minister of the Punjab Province from 1947 to 1949. He was Governor of *Sindh Province from 1954 to 1955.

YU.V. GANKOVSKY

Manchhar (also Manchar)

The biggest freshwater lake in Pakistan, lying in central Dadu in *Sindh province. It is fed by streams coming down from the Kirthar Hills to the west, as well as by flood waters from the *Indus during the monsoon period. It is connected with the river Indus by the Dunister canal. At its lowest, the area of the lake is about 40 sq.km., but at its high water it stretches over 500 sq.km. The lake is an important wildlife preserve, with a wide variety of waterfowl, especially during the winter period when it forms part of the 'Indus Flyway' for migrating birds. The Mohanas, or Mirbars, an aboriginal tribe of fisherfolk, live in wooden houseboats on the lake and in colonies along the nearby canals. They use traditional fishing methods and also a unique form of trapping edible birds. They place a stuffed egret on their heads as a decoy and wade out neck deep to catch their unwary prey.

YU.V. GANKOVSKY

Mandal, Jogendra Nath (1897–1962)

Statesman. A lawyer belonging to the scheduled castes of Bengal, he came into prominence as Law Minister in the Bengal Muslim League Government. When the AIML was not allowed the exclusive right to nominate Muslims to the interim government, Jogendra Nath Mandal was inducted as Law Member. This appointment was not universally hailed in All-India Muslim League circles; Mandal's nomination was termed as an injustice to Bengal by H.S. *Suhrawardy.

Jogendra Nath Mandal chaired the inaugural session of the Pakistan *Constituent Assembly. He was a member of the first Cabinet of Pakistan. Dropped from the Cabinet by Prime Minister Mohammad Ali of *Bogra in 1950, Mandal migrated to India without formally resigning as member of the Constituent Assembly of Pakistan. He pursued no political career in India.

YU.V. GANKOVSKY

Manipuri

A dance style that comes from the state of Manipur in the northeast region of India. Its lyrical movements boast of a tradition beginning as early as 154 AD. Pakistani dancers who perform **Bharata Natyam*, also perform the **Odissi* and *Manipuri*, but it is rare that other styles, e.g. the *Kuchipudi*, *Mohini Attam* or the highly theatrical dance from the southern state of Kerala in India, called **Kathakali*, is ever learnt or performed here.

R. HUSAIN

Manki Sharif, Muhammad Amin al-Hasanat, Pir Sahib (1923–60)

Religious/Public/Political Activist. Pir Manki Sharif came into prominence when a *Sikh girl was forced to marry the murderer of her husband. She recanted and was given shelter by the Chief Minister, Dr Khan *Sahib, whose residence the Pir caused to be besieged. The siege was unsuccessful but the incident recalled a similar incident that had brought the Faquir of *Ipi to prominence. Pir Manki Sharif was a member of the *Muslim League from 1945 to 1949 and an activist from 1946 to 1947 in the movement for the addition of the *North West Frontier Province to Pakistan.

YU.V. GANKOVSKY

Mansabdar

A holder of a military rank (**mansab*) in the *Mughal empire beginning with the reign of Akbar. A *mansabdar* was to keep a cavalry platoon of the size in accordance with his *mansab*. For this he was given a **jagir*. Under Akbar's successors, a *mansabdar* could get a considerably larger profit from his *jagir* than he spent on the upkeep of his platoon. The rank and platoon equation could not be maintained for long and *zat* and *sawar* were titles to denote the rank and size of platoon separately.

K.A. ANTNOVA

Manto, Saadat Hasan (1912–55)

Writer. Manto was an *Urdu-language short story writer, who attended Aligarh University (1934-35) and lived in Bombay and Delhi prior to independence, working as script writer for various film companies and editor on a number of periodicals and on All-India Radio. In 1948, he migrated to Pakistan and settled in Lahore. Manto came to be regarded as an outstanding master of the short story with his gift for story telling,

Manto, popular Urdu language author, with wife.

fast moving narratives and unexpected innuendoes, reminiscent of Guy de Maupassant and Anton Chekhov. He followed Chekhov in combining the tragic with the comic. Maxim Gorky's early heroes, independent from society and its morals, fascinated him. Manto's positive hero is very unusual for *Urdu literature, performing his good deeds, not from any sense of duty, but as an inner compulsion of his human nature. Both Indian and Pakistani critics considered Manto's work an important stage in the development of the contemporary short story: *Manto's Short Stories,* 1940; *Dhuan* ('Smoke'), 1941; *Chugad* ('Fool'), 1948; *Siyah Hashiya* ('Black Margins'), 1948. Some modernist influence can be traced in his work. His stories *Sarak ke Kinare* ('On the Roadside'), *Phundne* ('Brushes'), etc. were precursors of the trend known as *Nai Kahani*—the New Story—in Urdu literature.

WORKS: *'Kali Shalwar' (Black Pants), Lahore, 1941; 'Lazzat-i-Sang' (The Taste of Stone), Lahore, 1947; 'Parde ke Pichhe' (Behind the Curtain), Delhi, 1953.*

BIBLIOGRAPHY: *B. Premi, 'Saadat Hasan Manto: Life and Work', Srinagar, 1986 (in Urdu); L.A. Fleming, 'Another Lonely Voice. The Urdu Short Stories of Saadat Hasan Manto', Berkeley, 1979; 'Nuqoosh Manto Number', (ed.) M. Tufail, Lahore, 1956; 'Manto Ek Kitab', (ed.) Sahba Lakhnavi, Karachi, 1995.*

A. NIYAZI

Maqta

See, Ghazal.

Marker, Jamsheed Keikobad Ardeshir (1922–)

Statesman. A Pakistani diplomat and a member of the Parsi family of Marker Dinshaw, who have occupied leading positions in Pakistan's business community. Marker graduated from Forman Christian College in Lahore and served in the Pakistan Navy. From 1965 to 1967 he was High Commissioner of Pakistan in Ghana; from July 1967 to October 1969, Ambassador to Romania and Bulgaria, and, from October 1969 to March 1972, Ambassador to the USSR and simultaneously to Finland. Between 1972 and 1989 he served as Ambassador to Canada, USA, and elsewhere.

YU.V. GANKOVSKY

Marshal, Marshall John Hubert (Herbert) (1876–1958)

Archeologist. A British specialist on India who wrote on archaeology, history, art, and architecture. He was educated at the Dulwich Royal College Dulwich Cambridge. Between 1902 and 1931 he was General Director of the Archaeological Survey of India; in 1906 he was the government epigraphist. He headed the efforts to protect ancient Indian monuments, developed museums, and extended the Archaeological Survey of India considerably by inviting prominent scholars to become involved. Marshal radically changed the nature of Indian archaeology by extending it to embrace material culture of all ages. Archaeological studies became historical and cultural studies. He made a considerable personal contribution to field research and made some significant discoveries. He organized excavations of the *Harappan civilization and worked for many years in *Mohenjo-Daro, the most important of the Harappan sites, which yielded the first ever glimpse of the urban culture of pre-Vedic India. The three-volume report (1931) was in a class of its own. He spent many years digging sites at *Taxila where he illustrated the dynamics of urban development and its culture covering a period of more than a millennium. The results were summarized in a model monograph (1951). His excavations set a standard of methodology, devoting much attention to stratigraphy and chronology. He is the founder of the new, scholarly period of Indian archaeology.

Marshal set up numerous museums and archaeological surveys; he also organized the Central Archaeological Library in India. He edited and contributed to the Archaeological Department's annual reports and a new series, *Materials of the Archaeological Survey of India*. Marshal retired in 1931 and wrote a number of monographs.

WORKS: *'Mohenjo-Daro and the Indus Civilization', Vols. 1-3, London, 1931; 'The Monuments of Sanchi', Vols. 1-3, London, 1940 (jointly with A. Foucher); 'Taxila', Vols. 1-3, Cambridge, 1951.*

BIBLIOGRAPHY: *N.P. Chakravarti, 'The Story of Indian Archaeology,' in: Archaeology of India, Delhi, 1950; S. Roy, 'Indian Archaeology from Jones to Marshal. 1784-1902', AI, 1953, No. 9; S. Roy, 'The Story of Indian Archaeology. 1784-1947', New Delhi, 1961.*

N.P. KOCHERGINA

Marsiya

(Arabic: *risa*—elegy) An elegiac poem, the *marsiya* allows different rhyming sequences: including monorhyme and double rhyme, and different strophic structure: *bait, quatrian, **musaddas, *tarjiband,* and **tarkibband*. This genre originated from ritual laments for fallen warriors, and dates as far back as pre-Islamic culture. The popularity of *marsiya* grew with the development of court literature. In Persian poetry this genre was introduced in the 10th century by Rudaki. In *Urdu literature the first samples of *marsiya* were produced by the poets of the Deccan school in the 16th to 17th centuries. The genre was practiced at the court of the Oudh *Nawabs in the 19th century. Elegiac themes of the death of Imam Husain and other Islamic martyrs in Karbala were widely used in *Shia *marsiyas* that were annually enacted in the streets and squares of Lucknow during the month of *Muharram*. Particularly successful in the use of *marsiya* were the poets Mir *Anis and Mirza Dabir (1803-1975). Their poems described rich palaces, sumptuous feasts and elaborate ceremonies during Husain's time. They glorified the heavily-armed fighters of Imam Husain, duels on horseback and on foot, and they lamented the untimely deaths of heroes. In style and content, they equalled the best examples of epic poetry. *Marsiya* is widely used today in the literatures of the Middle East and South Asia.

In Pakistan, the *marsiya* was used for political and social comment. Josh *Malihabadi, Ali Reza (d.1978) Nasim Amrohivi (d. 1982) were immigrants from India who gave classical grounding to the genre. The second genre was led by Saba Akbarabadi, Shahid Naqvi, Ummid Fazli and Sardar Naqvi. The generation that is currently in the forefront is led by Hilal Naqvi (b. 1950).

BIBLIOGRAPHY: *S.G. Imam, 'Anis and Shakespeare: A Comparison', Lucknow, 1950; S. Numani, 'Muazana-i-Anis-o-Dabir' (Anis and Dabir: Comparative Analysis), Delhi, 1982; H. Glebov, A. Sukhochev, 'Urdu Literature', Moscow, 1967 (in Russian), 'Jadid Urdu Marsia', Karachi, 1981.*

N.V. GLEBOV

Mashriqi, Inayatullah Khan, Allama (1888–1963)

Political Activist. A political figure in *British India and Pakistan, Mashriqi was a mathematics scholar who earned his educational degrees at Punjab University and Cambridge. He also studied in France. In 1915 he became Principal of the Islamia College in Peshawar. From 1916 to 1919 he served as First Under-Secretary at the Ministry of Education, British India. In 1926, he took part in the Motamar *Khilafat Conference in Cairo discussing the restoration of Khilafat. In 1930 Mashriqi was Pakistan's delegate to the International Congress of Orientalists in Leiden. An admirer of Mussolini, in the earlier part of the 1930s, he founded and led the *Khaksar Movement, a militant Islamist organization. He was arrested in 1939 and was interned in Madras from 1940 to 1943. He was repeatedly arrested by Pakistani authorities for organizing anti-government protests in 1950–52, 1957 and 1958.

WORKS: *'Isharat' (Signals), Lahore, undated (in Urdu).*

YU.V. GANKOVSKY

Masjid

(Arabic: a place of worship) A mosque, a building for prayer. The back wall of the *masjid* (*qibla*) always faces Mecca and has a niche, a *mihrab*, which indicates the direction of prayer (*namaz, salat*). To the right of the *mihrab* is a lecturn (*minbar*) from which sermons (*khutba*) are delivered. *Masjids* have one or several towers (minarets, or *minars*) from which *muazzins* call Muslims to prayer by proclaiming *azan*.

YU.V. GANKOVSKY

Masnawi

(in Arabic: doubled, prolonged) 1. Poem rhymed by distiches; or 2. A genre of heroic poem with a didactic and philosophical meaning. In the epic *masnawi* specific *aruz* metre is used, mainly *mutaqarib*. The rhymes are double: aa, bb, cc, etc. *Masnawi* was composed in Turkic literature of the Middle East, in Persian literature and in *Urdu literature.

In Persian poetry, *Shah-nama* composed by Firdousi (11th century) is the most noteworthy example of the heroic *masnawi* poem. Firdousi's patron was Sultan Mahmud of Ghazni. *Khamse* by Nizami (12th century) is a classical narrative poem of romantic love with philosophic-didactic connotations. The ideas, plots, and metres of *Khamse* became an object of numerous imitations. The most outstanding Persian masters of *nazira* are Sa'di, Jami, Jalaluddin Rumi, and Amir Khusrow Dehlawi. In Urdu literature the following *masnawi* are well known: *Sayf al-Mulk wa Badi al-Jamal* by Ghawwasi (1625), *Gulshan-i-Ishq* ('The Flower-bed of Love') by Muhammad Nusrati (17th century), *Qutb-i-Mushtari* by Mullah Wajahi (17th century), *Sahar al-Bayan* ('Wonders of Eloquence') by Mir Hasan (d. 1786), and *Gulzar-i-Nasim* ('Nasim's Garden') by Nasim (d. 1843). Important contributions to the development of romantic and philosophic-lyrical poetry were made by the poets Mir Taqi *Mir, Altaf Husain *Hali, and Muhammad *Iqbal.

BIBLIOGRAPHY: *M.I. Zand, 'Six Centuries of Glory', Moscow, 1964 (in Russian); In. Glebov, A. Sukhochev, 'Urdu Literature', Moscow, 1967 (in Russian); A.A. Suvorova, 'Masnavi'. Karachi, 2000.*

N.V. GLEBOV

Masrur, Hajra (1929–)

Writer. Hajra Masrur is a Pakistani *Urdu writer who was educated in Lucknow. Her main themes relate to the difficult social situation of women in Muslim society, and Hindu-Muslim relations. Her language illustrates the spoken language of Oudh with its poetic folk imagery. Other features of her style include a naturalistic portrayal of everyday life and a mild didacticism. Her main works are collections of stories *Haye, Allah!* ('Oh, God!') and *Tisri Manzil* ('The Third Floor'), and a collection of one-act plays *Ham Log* ('We People').

BIBLIOGRAPHY: *R.A. Elizarova, A.S. Sukhochev, 'Pakistan's Progressive Writers', Tashkent, 1978 (in Russian).*

A.S. SUKHOCHEV

Mastuj

A river in the extreme north of Pakistan (see Northern Areas), flowing through the valley that divides the ranges of the eastern *Hindu Kush from the *Hinduraj Range. In its upper reaches, up to the town of Mastuj, the river is called the Yarkhun; lower down, after the town of *Chitral, it is called, the Chitral. Below the town of Aranduit it is called the Kunar. The Mastuj is fed by the Chiantar Glacier. During the melting period, the level of the water rises by some 12-15 metres and floods the bed of the valley, disrupting transport and communications between the villages and towns along the river. Up to the town of Mastuj, the valley is actually a mountain gorge with steep banks on both sides. Below Mastuj, it broadens out and reaches a width of 3 km. near the town of Chitral.

M.U. MOROZOVA

Mastur, Khadija (1927–84)

Writer. Khadija Mastur wrote in *Urdu. She began publishing in 1942. She received her education in Lucknow and in 1947 moved to Lahore, where she was active with the *Pakistan Progressive Writers' Association and the *Pakistan Writers' Guild. She was influenced in her work by Ahmad Nadeem Qasmi, as was her sister Hajra *Masrur. Khadija Mastur has several collections of short stories to her credit: *Khel* ('The Game'), *Bouchhar* ('Rain'), *Chand Roz Aur* ('A Few More Days'), and *Thaka Hara* ('The Tired One'), devoted to the hard life of the Muslim women. In the novel *Angan* ('The Backyard', 1962), which was awarded the Adamjee Prize, Mastur portrayed the attitudes of various social strata towards the national liberation movement of the 1940s.

BIBLIOGRAPHY: *R.A. Elizarova, A.S. Sukhochev, 'Pakistan's Progressive Writers', Tashkent, 1978; 'Cool, Sweet Water', Tahira Naqvi (translator), Karachi, 2000.*

A.S. SUKHOCHEV

Matla

See, Ghazal.

Maudoodi, Abul Ala, Maulana (1903–79)

Religious Scholar/Political activist. A politician in *British India and Pakistan and regarded as an outstanding Islamic scholar, Maudoodi published the monthly *Tarjuman al-Quran* in Hyderabad (India) from 1933 to 1937. In 1937 he moved to Lahore. There he founded the **Jamaat-i-Islami* Party and served as its leader until 1972. He opposed the formation of Pakistan and was often detained (1964, 1967, etc.) for anti-government activities. Maudoodi is buried at Lahore.

WORKS: *'Jamaat-i Islami', Lahore, 1952; 'The Message of Jamaat-i Islami', Lahore, 1955; 'The Qadiani', Karachi, 1956; 'Capitalism, Socialism and Islam', Lahore, 1977.*

BIBLIOGRAPHY: *S.V.R. Nasr, 'Mawdudi and the Making of Islamic Revivalism', New York, 1996.*

YU.V. GANKOVSKY

Maulana

(Persian: our lord) An honorific title of a Muslim theologian.

YU.V. GANKOVSKY

Maurya

A dynasty and state in ancient India (*c.* 317-180 BC) founded by Chandragupta Maurya. In *c.* 317 BC, as a result of a long and fierce struggle, he overthrew the Nanda dynasty of Magadha in northeast India. Chandragupta's military and diplomatic activities won him all the Indian territories earlier conquered by Alexander of Macedonia. Chandragupta's son Bindusara (*c.* 293-68 BC) subjugated vast territories in west and south India. There is evidence of his diplomatic relations with Hellenic monarchs–the Seleukids and the Ptolemies. Bindusara's son, King Asoka (see picture) (*c.* 268-31 BC) succeeded in extending his kingdom to an extent subsequently only exceeded by the *Mughal Empire and the British Raj at their respective heights. Asokan inscriptions are found in northern India and the Deccan. In the northwest, King Asoka subjugated Kabul and Kandahar. On the Hindustan Peninsula, only some of the southernmost regions remained independent.

King Ashoka, the last of the great Mauryan kings.

The Mauryan Empire was varied in its ethnic composition and socio-economic development. Magadha was its nucleus and officially Asoka called himself King of Magadha. The largest provinces were: the northwest territory, with its capital at *Taxila; West India, with its capital at Ujaini; and the southern regions, centred around Suvarnagiri.

Governors of the provinces had princely titles—Kumara, Aryaputra—and often were closely related to the supreme ruler, the King of Magadha. Kalinga country, reconquered under Asoka, was given a special status. Once every five years, a special ambassador was sent to audit the activities of the local authorities in various Kalingan towns. Similar inspections were undertaken by the governors of Taxila and Ujaini in their provinces every three years.

The Mauryan administrative system was highly liberal, allowing considerable self-government. In some areas, local dynasties or oligarchic unions remained in power. In the vast territories of the Mauryan Empire, people lived in tribal systems and any representatives of state power had to deal with tribal chiefs, often engaging them in government service. The ruler had to share his power with the royal councils (*parishad*), which consisted of courtiers, councillors, and the king's relatives. Patronage of various religions allowed the spread of Buddhism, Jainism and the teaching of the Ajiviks.

In the last years of Asoka's life, the central government started losing its power. The Puranas list about a dozen successors to Asoka; some of them must have reigned simultaneously. The last Mauryan king was killed in the capital Pataliputra in *c.* 180 BC by his general Pushyamitra, who founded the Sunga dynasty. The epoch of imperial unity was amply reflected in Indian historical traditions and legends about Chandragupta and Asoka. The inscriptions on stone, sculpture, and architecture of the Mauryan epoch reflects active borrowings from the *Achaemenid heritage and Hellenic cultural influences. The first all-India Empire played an important role in speeding up economic, social, and political progress in many Indian territories. It was conducive to the unification of Indian culture and the latter's influence on the cultures of the neighbouring countries.

BIBLIOGRAPHY: *G.M. Bongard-Levin, 'India in the Maurya era', Moscow, 1973 (in Russian); H. Alahokoon, 'The Later Mauryas' (232-180 bc), Delhi, 1980.*

A.A. VISAGIN

Mawlawi (also Maulvi)

(Arabic) A learned man, an expert on Muslim law, a teacher. Also: *mawlawiya*—A *Sufi *Sunni order (fraternity) founded by the Iranian mystic and poet, Jelaluddin Rumi (1207-73).

YU.V. GANKOVSKY

Mazar

A burial tomb of a saint, a holy place for Muslim pilgrims.

M.R. KAZIMI

Megalithic Sites

In Pakistan, these comprise a large number of burials related to various chronological periods, from the Bronze Age to the early historic period. The earliest of them belong to the *Swat culture. The best known are cairn burials in *Balochistan and Makran (Periano Ghundai, Moghul Ghundai and Damba Koh). Stone piles, round or rectangular, sometimes with stone rings, mark their locations at the surface. Cremation and partial inhumation burials are found under the stones in small burial pits. The grave goods consist of vessels or fragments of wheel manufactured or modelled pottery, iron, bronze and silver objects (swords, knives, spearheads and arrowheads, fishing hooks, etc.), ornamentations and some glass objects. Sometimes settlements can be found side by side with the burial grounds. The stone and clay houses were built on the surface. The earliest groups of cairn burials are dated to about 900 BC on the strength of comparison with Sialk VI; the later ones are dated to the 1st century BC by the Parthian coins found in them.

Archaeologists differ about the origins of the Megalithic sites in Pakistan and India. Some believe they belonged to the ancestors of the *Dravidian-speaking populations of the *Indus Valley civilization, others think they were left by the later Indo-European speaking invaders, such as the *Aryans (Asko Parpola and N.R. Banerji) or the Scytho-Iranians (S.S. Sarkar and P. Gupta). Some believe that they originate from the Mediterranean.

N.M. VINOGRADOVA

Mehrab (or Mihrab)

Is a niche in the wall of mosques that face the *Qibla*, i.e. the Kaaba towards which all Muslims must face during prayers (**salat*). *Mehrabs* usually blend with the overall architecture of the mosque but in Pakistan they originated with round arches supported by pillars. Quranic inscriptions in the *Kufi* script began adorning the *mehrab* from the Ribat of Ali bin Karmakh. A honey combed *mehrab* with pointed arch came into vogue in the *Dehli Sultanate period. In contemporary mosque architecture the *mehrab* is usually unadorned but smoothly finished.

YU.V. GANKOVSKY

Mehrgarh

A Neolithic settlement (*see*, Neolithic).

Memon (also meman)

A Muslim trading community in Pakistan and western India (the states of Bombay and Gujarat). Ethnically, they are related to the *Gujarati population of Kachi. They adhere to *Sunni Islam, to which they converted in the eleventh-twelfth centuries (*see* Lohana). They are divided into several sub groups (Kachi, Halai, etc.). They have their own public, business, and charitable organizations. The top members of the Memon *baradari* (brotherhood) took an active part in the movement for the formation of Pakistan such as Haroon, Adamjee, Dada, Dawood, Rangoonwala, Bawani, and Hashim.

BIBLIOGRAPHY: *S. Levin, 'The Formation of Pakistan Big Bourgeoisie', Moscow, 1970 (in Russian); Yuri Gankovsky, 'Peoples of Pakistan', Lahore, 1972.*

YU.V. GANKOVSKY

Mian

(in Urdu: master, honourable, reverend) An honorary title in South Asia.

YU.V. GANKOVSKY

Miandad, Javed (1957–)

Cricket Player. Javed Miandad began his first class career in 1973, and Test career in 1976 which he started with a century (163 runs against New Zealand at Lahore 1976–77), and one-day internationals with the 1975 World Cup events. Javed Miandad is the youngest player to score a double century (206 runs against New Zealand in the same 1976–77 series), and holds the third-wicket world record (with Mudassir Nazar) of 451 runs against India in Hyderabad 1982–83. The second Pakistani batsman after Hanif *Muhammad to score a century in each innings of a Test Series (against New Zealand at Hyderabad 1984–85), Javed Miandad is also the youngest player to score a triple century in first class cricket (311 for Karachi Whites against National Bank, Karachi 1974–75). He has played in 124 Test matches and scored 8,832 runs with an average of 52.55. He has scored 23 centuries. His best innings was 280 not out against India at Hyderabad (1982–83). He has taken 17 wickets with an average of 40.11. In one–day internationals, he played 233 matches, made 7381 runs, with an average of 41.70, and scored eight centuries. His most spectacular six was the match-winning stroke against India in the Sharjah Cup final in 1986. He was captain in 34 matches with a win rate of 41.7.

Well known Cricket player, Javed Miandad.

WORKS: *'Cutting Edge', Oxford University Press, Karachi, 2003.*

SHAHNAWAZ

Milk

(also: Mulk, from the Arabic: *malaka*–to own, possess) One of the forms (categories) of private feudal ownership on the land in medieval India of the 14th-18th centuries. *Milk* ownership was not tied up with any military or other government duties, neither did it require any state taxes; a *milk*-owner had alienable hereditary rights on the *milk* property. In official documents in Persian, *milk* often denoted hereditary plots of land belonging to peasants of village communities.

BIBLIOGRAPHY: *K.Z. Ashrafyan, 'Agrarian System of North India. 13th to mid-18th Centuries', Moscow, 1965 (in Russian); I. Habib, 'The Agrarian System of Mughal India', Aligarh, 1963.*

YU.V. GANKOVSKY

Minar

Minaret literally means small *minars*; but *minars* are called minarets in English regardless of their size.

Minarets are associated with mosque (see Masjid) architecture, although they did not appear in the earliest mosques in Islamic history. The first minarets are the four of the grand Mosque of Damascus, which had been watch towers in the Byzantine period. The mosque was built by Khalid bin Walid, in whose reign the conquest of *Sindh took place. The minaret was a Muslim importation into South Asian architecture, and was unknown in Hindu architecture. The towers of the Damascus mosque became a regular feature in other mosques since it was found invaluable for the *azan*, the call to prayer. The second important minaret to be constructed was a single one in the grand Mosque of Qairawan (724–7), juxtaposed in front of the main mosque structure which was square based, had three tiers with a cupola crowning the top. The single minaret theme, similarly positioned, is the spiral minaret at Samarra in Iraq. Closer to South Asia and its history is that of Sultan Masud III (1099-115), a minaret at Ghazni. Built on a circular foundation, this tower had hexagonal walls capped by a conical roof. The Ghorid Sultan, Ghiasuddin Muhammad Ghori (1116-1203), built the *Jam* minaret which now stands alone at the entrance of a gorge. This has two storeys and served as the model for the *Qutub Minar* built by Sultan Qutubuddin Aibak (r 1206-10) and Altutmish (r 1211-35). J. Fergusson calls the *Qutub Minar* the most perfect example of a tower any where in the world. At first imposing structures, minarets in the Mughal period (see Mughal Empire) became slender and decorative. They were symmetrical to the mosque but subordinate, rarely towering above them. In Pakistan, the re-inforced Concrete structures have not generally brought about a radical change. Pre-cast minarets are being used in local mosques. At the Faisal Mosque in Islamabad the Ottoman influence is deliberate, whereas in the futuristic Tooba Mosque in Karachi, the minaret is shaped like a rocket.

BIBLIOGRAPHY: *K.A.C. Creswell, 'Early Muslim Architecture', Harmondsworth, 1958; D.T.R. 'Islamic Art and Architecture', London, 1962.*

YU.V. GANKOVSKY

Minault, Gail

Historian. Professor of History at the University of Texas, Austin in the United States since 1972. She earned her PhD in South Asia Regional Studies at the

University of Pennsylvania in 1972. Prof Minault's area of expertise is 19th and 20th century Indian history, with an emphasis on Islam and Muslims in India. Her more recent work includes the intellectual and social history of South Asia, as well as Muslim women's movements for self-expression and justice. Her analysis of women's education and political participation in India and Pakistan, women's rights and Muslim identity are especially insightful. Prof Minault is the author of two books and numerous articles and book reviews. She has also edited several books.

WORKS: *'The Khilafat Movement: Religious Symbolism and Political Mobilization in India', 1982 and 'Secluded Scholars: Women's Education and Muslim Reform in Colonial India', 1998.*

R. SYMONDS

Miniature painting

The Mughal (see Mughal Empire) school of miniature painting originated around the middle of the 16th century when Emperor Humayun brought two Iranian artists-Mir Sayyid Ali Tabrizi and Abd as-Samad Shirazi to Delhi. They taught Mughal princes and local artists drawing and painting techniques. The school's style developed on the basis of local traditions that were influenced by the miniatures of Iran and central Asia and by European art. Artists often copied European engravings and illustrated books, borrowing some of their technique. One of the first significant works of the Mughal school of miniature painting executed in the court workshop was a set of miniatures for *Hamza Nama* (1759). Over fifteen years some 1,400 miniatures were painted on cloth, of which only a tenth still exist. Only some of them bear traces of the influence of Iranian miniaturists. This includes simple compositions conveying symmetry and static postures. On the whole, the paintings are marked by a different vision of the world. These are identifiable by the use of realistic representation, carefully detailed ornament, with depictions of architecture and clothes, use of chiaroscuro, and a warm colour palette. Illustrations of *Babur Nama*, some five hundred miniatures from thirteen copies, scattered in many museums and private collections of the world, belong to the period of the well established Mughal school of miniature painting. The best known copies of *Babur Nama* are in the National Museum in Delhi, the British Museum in London, and the State Museum of Oriental Peoples' Art in Moscow. They were made in the late 16th and early 17th centuries. Characteristic of these miniatures are close following of the text, a documentary quality, and an interest in the individual. Action-packed compositions of many figures show conventional landscapes in the background. Gradually, miniature painting became an easel art. In the first quarter of the 17th century portraiture became its principal genre. Typically in these portraits, the ruler sits on a throne or stands at full height in full dress with all the attributes of power. The setting is usually an open white terrace, over a smooth grey or blue background (as in the portrait of Akbar at the State Museum of Oriental Peoples' Art in Moscow).

Of special interest are portraits executed in the *siyahi kalam* technique: in black Indian ink, with an extra fine brush. The whole portrait is drawn with a single smooth line and the face of the subject thoroughly drawn. Some details were drawn in the chiaroscuro technique. Group portraits are usually **darbar* scenes or compositions of many figures with the Mughal emperor in the centre. As a rule, most portraits were a good likeness to the original; in other words, court artists or *darbaris* had to keep a kind of chronicle of the life of the Mughal court. Portrayals of women appeared as early as the 16th century. The figures of women were always more stylized than those of men. In the early 17th century, women's portraits conveyed not so much individual features as an idealized type according to the contemporary notions of beauty.

In the first half of the 17th century, scenes of religious disputes and conversations, visits of holy men, readings of religious works, as well as portraits of the prophets, appeared on the miniatures of the Mughal school, which reflected the spread of *Sufism. In the second half of the 17th century, the genre of animal painting began to develop: miniatures of plants, animals, and birds were true to life. In the middle of the 17th century considerable changes occurred in the Mughal school of miniatures. Under Aurangzeb many court workshops were closed. The artists, forced to look for other patrons, went to the courts of *Rajput rulers, to Rajasthan or the Punjab, or to the Deccan. The Mughal school of miniatures merged with other schools of Indian miniature. In the 18th century it did not produce anything fundamentally new, although the subjects of the miniatures changed slightly: court scenes, portraits of court beauties, and scenes of hunting and fighting were portrayed. Human images were distinctly idealized and the proportions of figures were somewhat elongated, which lent them an air of refinement.

N.K. KARPOVA

Mir, Mir Taqi (1723–1810)

Poet. Mir Taqi Mir grew up in the family of a *Sufi preacher. He received a traditional Muslim education and was well versed in Sufi theory and practices. In the mid-1740s, he moved to the capital, took part in the Delhi **mushaira* and was made *Urdu poet laureate. In the 1750s and 1760s he took part in some military campaigns and witnessed the invasion of Afghan and Maratha armies into Delhi. In 1783 he moved to Lucknow, the cultural centre of Muslim India at that time.

His works in Urdu (**kulliyat*) made up six **diwans* comprising **ghazals*, **masnawi*, **nazm*, **marsia*, **rubai* and **qasida*. The most famous *masnawi* include: *Darya-i-Ishq* ('The River of Love'), *Shola-i-Ishq* ('The Flame of Love'), and *Khwab-o-Khayal-i-Mir* ('The Dreams of Mir'). He wrote his prose in Persian, including his autobiography *Zikr-i-Mir*, and biographical sketches of poets *Nukat ash-Shuara* ('Notes on the Poets'). In his *ghazals*, alongside traditional Muslim motifs, he expresses regret on the loss of independence of his homeland and the decline of the Great *Mughal Empire. Central to his later work is the theme of destruction, homelessness and loss of ideals. The style of his *ghazals* also underwent considerable changes: his language became closer the to natural Urdu idiom, and new images were added to the traditional ones. This violation of the artistic and religious syncretism laid the basis for the development of the new Urdu *ghazal*. Mir's lyrics represent great pathos and sensibility.

WORKS: *'Kulliyat-i-Mir', Karachi-Lahore, 1958; 'Zikr-i-Mir', Delhi, 1957; 'Nukat ash-Shuara' (Notes on the Poets).*

BIBLIOGRAPHY: *R. Russel, Kh. Islam, 'Three Mughal Poets', Cambridge, 1968; K.A. Faruqi, 'Mir Taqi Mir: Hayat aur Shairi' (Mir Taqi Mir: Life and Work), Aligarh, 1954; 'Nuqoosh Mir Number' (ed.) M. Tufia, Lahore 3 Vols. 1980; Q.A. Husain, 'Mir ki Sheri Lisaniyat', Delhi, 1983; J. Jalibi, 'Mohammad Taqi Mir', Karachi, 1981; M. Arfi, 'Mir Taqi Mir aur Aj ka Zauq-i-Sheri', Karachi, 1989.*

I.V. ZOTOVA

Mirasdar

Owner of the hereditary right (*mirasi*) on a share in communal land, on certain services of community artisans or an official position in the community. Often all the lands belonged to one or more *mirasdars* who were petty landowners, but some of them could be peasants enjoying respect of the community which entitled them to artisans' services. After the introduction in 1818-23 of the *ryotwari* system in *British India, *mirasdar* was turned into a tax-paying land-owner.

K.A. ANTONOVA

Mirza, Iskander, Major General (1899–1969)

Iskander Mirza, President of Pakistan, (1955–58).

President of Pakistan from 1955 to 1958. Sahibzada Iskander Ali Mirza (his full name) received his military training at Sandhurst, England. In the 1930s and early 1940s Mirza occupied important posts in the colonial administration of Orissa and the *North West Frontier Province in *British India. From 1948 to 1952 he served as Secretary, and from 1952 to 1954 he was promoted to the rank of Major General. In 1954 he was appointed Governor of East Pakistan and from 1954 to 1955 he was Minister for the Interior. He was the last Governor-General, September 1955 to March 1956, and the first President of Pakistan, from March 1956 to 27 October 1958. As President, he abrogated the 1956 Constitution and proclaimed martial law on 7 October 1958, to be deposed in turn by General Muhammad Ayub *Khan on 27 October. Mirza was sent into exile. From November 1958 to November 1969 he lived in London. He is buried in Tehran, Iran.

YU.V. GANKOVSKY

Mirza, Mohammad Aziz (1865–1912)

Statesman. His real name was Mirza Mustafa Beg. Aziz Mirza was in the first batch of Aligarh students. He entered the service of the Hyderabad State and was Home Secretary. He organized relief work during the outbreak of plague in Bir and when the Musa rivulet overflowed. For these efforts he was awarded the *Kaiser-i-Hind* Gold Medal. He was appointed Honorary Secretary of the *All-India Muslim League in 1910. He single-handedly reorganized the Secretariat, which had been re-located from Aligarh to Lucknow. Apart from organizational work, he actively worked to bring about a Hindu-Muslim conciliation, especially in Bengal (see Bengal, the partition of) where the partition issue had created bitterness. A literary man, he co-founded the *Anjuman Tarraqi-i-Urdu*.

WORKS: *'Seerat al Mahmud', Hyderabad, Dn., 1892; 'Khyatat-i-Aziz, Kanpur, 1912.*

BIBLIOGRAPHY: *D. Lelyveld, 'Aligarh's First Generation', Princeton, 1977; Q.A. Badayuni, 'Mehfil-i-Aziz', Hyderabad Dn., 1962; M.A.A. Beg, 'Mohammad Aziz Mirza', Hyderabad Dn., 1987.*

M.R. KAZIMI

Mirzai

See, Ahmadiya.

Misra

See, Ghazal.

Mohenjo-Daro (also Moenjodaro)

The remains of Mohenjo-Daro are located in the modern district of Larkana, *Sindh province. It is the most prominent urban centre of the *Indus Valley Civilization. It is generally dated from 3000-1500 BC.

The discovery of the Indus civilisation first came about in 1926 when Charles Mason, under the pseudonym of James Lewis, was hiding out from the British army and came across a large city of bricks in the *Punjab. He wrote about it later in a much romanticised account. In 1931 Alexander Burns, posing as an American engineer, was scouting the area for possible commercial and strategic potential and remarked on the remains. In 1953, when Punjab had come under British control (see British India), Sir Alexander Conningham followed up the information from Mason and Burns and found large ruins, but his interest in Buddhist remains led him to ignore this important site until 1856. At this time the name of *Harappa was given, after a nearby village 6 miles from the modern bank of the *Ravi river. In 1865 the Karachi-Lahore railroad was built and 100 miles of the track was laid on crushed brick from Harappa, thus destroying large parts of the remains. Conningham did, however, recover many of the steatite seals now on display in the museum. In 1914 Sir John *Marshall made a formal survey of Harapppa, but further excavations ceased until after the war in Europe. In 19119 R.D. Banerjee discovered a site 350 miles south of Harappa which was named Moenjo-daro (place or hill of the dead). In 1921 a trail dig produced coins from the 2nd century, seals and other remains. In 1924 the publication of illustrations of the seals was seen by Ernest *Mackay, an American working on excavations in Mesopotamia. He had found identical seals under the foundations of a temple dated to 2,300 BC.

An authority for the preservation of Moenjo-Daro was set up in 1972 but was disbanded in 1997. The site had been a UNESCO World Heritage site since 1980.

Mohenjo-Daro is dominated towards the west by a citadel of 366x183 sq.m. and a height ranging from 6 to 15 metres. The inhabitants had an advanced sense of town planning. Geometrical patterns were adopted and an elaborate system of water and sewage lines was established. The main street is 9 metres wide, dividing the city into rectangular parts of 363x242 metres.

In addition to the baked bricks employed throughout the city, the walls were plastered with mud. The citadel includes a large bath (11.7x7 metres and 2.4 metres deep) with a colonnade and buildings that may have been either hostels or colleges and a large granary. Arches are rare, only corbel arches were used.

The houses also follow a uniform pattern. According to A. Sarchina, most of the houses were of the same approximate size and plan, having two main designs. One consisted of a courtyard at one corner, flanked by rooms on two sides, and the second having a courtyard in the centre and rooms on three sides. From this, Robert J. Wenke concludes that the distribution of wealth was equitable and a primitive form of socialism was practiced. Seventy-seven per cent of the small structures are houses, the rest are probably small shops. In keeping with the fabric of the buildings, a terracotta industry, producing figures of female (human) dolls and bulls has been excarated. The incidence of geometrical patterns and the contrasting use of black and red also point to a well-developed concept of art. The characteristic steatite seals are the most distinctive artistic remnants of this civilization. They depict a variety of subjects, including animals found in wetter climates, such as tigers, rhinoceri, elephants and crocodiles. They are quite small, suggesting that remarkable control over craftsmanship and intricacy, rather than size, was the artistic aim. A number of bronze figures have also been found, showing expertise in this medium as well. These seals and figurines are an indication of the religion followed by the inhabitants. A seal representing a figure like Shiva suggests that this particular deity may have been adopted by Hinduism from the more ancient beliefs of the Indus Valley people. A small bearded figure, it has been speculated, was that of a priest.

Stuart Piggot had deduced from the similarities of the stratifications that the civilization did not evolve gradually at this site but that its main features had already evolved before the establishment of this settlement. Likewise, the theory that the Mohenjo-Daro city was destroyed due to an invasion has been challenged. J.M. Kenoyer states that there is no evidence for a new population displacing the original inhabitants. The decline was the result of complex factors, such as the drying up of major rivers and the rise of new religious communities.

A.YA. SHCHETENKO

Mohsinul Mulk, Nawab (1837–1907)

Statesman. Nawab Mohsinul Mulk's real name was Syed Mehdi Ali. His early career was in the *Kachahri,* a government complex of the revenue and judicial departments at the district level. He then went to Hyderabad and rose to become Political and Financial Secretary of the Nizam's domain. In 1899 he was elected Honorary Secretary of the Aligarh College. Mohsinul Mulk was the secretary of the *Simla Deputation. When the *All-India Muslim League was formed, he was appointed Joint Honorary Secretary, together with Nawab *Viqarul Mulk of the new body. He died before the constitution of the AIML was finalized. (*see*, also Viqarul Mulk, Nawab).

WORKS: *'Ayat-i-Bayyanat a work of Sectarian polemics'.*

BIBLIOGRAPHY: *Dr S. Mehmud, 'Nawab Mohsin-ul-Mulk', in: M. Tufail (ed.), Nuqoosh Shakhsiyat Number, Lahore, 1955.*

YU.V. GANKOVSKY

Momand (also Mohmand)

A *Pashtun tribe belonging to the group of Sarbani tribes in the *North West Frontier Province. They are divided into highlanders, or *Bar*-Momand, and lowlanders, or *Kuz*-Momand. The *Bar*-Momand mostly dwell in the political agency of Mohmand and also in Bajaur. The clans are Tarakzai, Baezai, Halimzai, Khwaezai. The *Kuz*-Momand reside in the southern part of the *Peshawar Valley. The main clans are Mayarzai, Musazai, Dewazai, Sarghani, and Matani. The total population is estimated at 650,000, 500,000 in Pakistan and 150,000 in Afghanistan.

BIBLIOGRAPHY: *Temirkhanow, 'Eastern Pashtuns: Main Issues of Modern History', Moscow, 1987 (in Russian); A.S. Ahmed, 'Pukhtun Economy and Society', London, 1980.*

YU.V. GANKOVSKY

Moon, Sir Edward Penderel (1904–87)

Statesman. Sir Penderel Moon attended school at Winchester and graduated from New College, Oxford with distinction. He was appointed to the Indian Civil Service (ICS) in 1929. Because of his dissatisfaction with the workings of the Raj (see British india) and his sympathy with Indian demands for independence, he resigned from the ICS in 1943. He was recalled to India after the Cabinet Delegation returned to England. His key appointments included that of Chief Commissioner of Himachal Pardesh and Revenue Minister in *Bahawalpur in Pakistan. Sir Penderel Moon witnessed riots during partition and the political processes of the independence of India and the creation of Pakistan. He dedicated the last several years of his life writing *The British Conquest and Dominion of India,* a long history of the rise and fall of British rule over India.

WORKS: *'Strangers in India', London, 1944; 'Divide and Quit', London, 1961; (ed.) Wavell, The Viceroy's Journals, London, 1973.*

R. SYMONDS

Mosque

See, masjid.

Moulvi

See, Mawlawi.

Movement for Restoration of Democracy (MRD)

An alliance founded on 6 February 1981, to Ziaul *Haq's military regime. The movement united the *Pakistan Peoples Party, the National Democratic Party, the Pakistan in opposition Democratic Party and a number of smaller political entities in a common four-point programme that envisaged 1. abolition of Martial Law and the handing over of power to a civilian government; 2. elections in accordance with the *constitution of 1973; 3. abolition of censorship and freedom for political prisoners; 4. defence of the rights of the people and of the federal units of Pakistan.

Mass action organized by the MRD were accompanied by arrests of the demonstrators and reprisals against members of opposition parties. The 1983 actions against martial law were most widespread in *Sindh. These actions forced Ziaul Haq to conduct the 1984 referendum and the 1985 elections.

After 1984 the scale of actions organized by the MRD diminished and in 1988, in the run-up to the elections to the national and provincial assemblies, the MRD announced its self-liquidation.

O.V. PLESHOV

Mubarakmand, Samar (1942–)

Scientist. Chairman, National Engineering and Scientific Commission, (NESCOM) Islamabad, and formerly Director-General of the National Defence Complex. He was awarded DPhil in Experimental Nuclear Physics from the University of Oxford in 1966. Samar Mubarakmand led a *Pakistan Atomic Energy Commission (PAEC) team to *Chagai to clear a tunnel. As Member (Technical) of the PAEC', Samar Mubarakmand was head of the three-member committee formed to respond to India's nuclear tests of May 1998. He had previously prepared the test site and conducted successful cold tests. After the successful completion of nuclear tests Mubarakmand was inducted into the missile development programme for Shaheen I and II. He also supervised non-defence nuclear endeavours, notably the enhancement of cotton production in Pakistan.

T. NAIM

Mufti

(Arabic: the one who gives the **fatwa*) A judge who formulates a decision or passes judgement (*fatwa*) on debated or complicated juridical, legal and religious issues on the basis of precedent and principles of Muslim law.

YU.V. GANKOVSKY

Mughal Empire

One of history's most brilliant Empires, this was founded by the Timurid ruler of Ferghana in Central Asia, Zahiruddin Babur. Babur (see image) was driven out of Samarkand and Ferghana by the Uzbeks and came to rule Kabul in 1504. During his Indian campaigns, he defeated the armies of the Delhi Sultan Ibrahim Lodi in the Battle of Panipat in 1526 and founded the Mughal Empire. Babur's son Humayun, who was defeated by Sher Shah Suri, fled to Iran in 1540. In 1555 he returned at the head of an Iranian army and recaptured Delhi. In 1556 Humayun was succeeded by his son Akbar (1556–1605), commonly regarded as one of history's most outstanding monarchs. Akbar enlarged the Empire to encompass the territory from the *Himalayas to the river Narbada. He introduced a number of administrative, land-taxation, military and other reforms. The tax on land was reduced to one-third of the harvest, internal customs duties were also reduced. During his reign Roads and caravanserais were built, a unified weight and measure system was introduced. Akbar's son Jahangir (1605–27), who as Prince Salim, had been known primarily for his romantic escapades, presided over a period of great cultural and intellectual excellence and considerable stability, during which the Mughul Empire continued its expansion. He was assisted from behind the scenes by his wife the Empress Nur Jahan. It was during Jahangir's reign that Europeans began to enter India to set up trading stations. In the succession scramble following Jahangir's death, Prince Khurram was successful in securing the throne and adopted the name Shah Jahan. This period (1627–58) is often considered the apogee of the Mughul reign, with relative stability prevailing across the vast Empire and the pursuit of excellence continuing and reaching its climax in some of the most exquisite architectural achievements of all time, such as the Taj Mahal.

Zahiruddin Babar, founder of the Mughal Empire.

In 1658 Shah Jahan fell ill and fears of his imminent death triggered off a bitter and bloody succession struggle between his sons. In due course, Aurangzeb emerged triumphant over the bodies of his brothers and climbed the Imperial throne. The aging Emperor, Shah Jahan, was held captive by him until he died in 1666.

During the reign of Aurangzeb (1658–1707) the Mughal Empire reached its maximum extent with the conquest of the Deccan. While Aurangzeb's own personality was powerful enough to hold together this vast and heterogeneous entity, his divisive methods and beliefs contributed to the eventual weakening of the bonds holding the Empire together. After Aurangzeb's death, in 1707, the Mughal Empire rapidly declined. In 1739 the *Padishah* of Iran Nadir Shah Afshar waged a war against India and annexed all the Mughal territories to the west of the *Indus and northwest *Punjab. Provinces began to break away from Delhi's suzerainty and became independent kingdoms. Notable among these were Hyderabad, Oudh, Bengal with Bihar and Orissa. The confederation of Maratha principalities grew stronger, ruling much of Western India and effectively exercising control over Delhi itself. In the middle of the 18th century the Afghan ruler, Ahmad Shah Durrani, annexed the Punjab, *Sindh, *Kashmir and Sirhind. The later Mughals, Ahmad Shah (1748–54) and Alamgir II (1754–9), ruled only Delhi and its environs. Shah Alam II (1759–1806), together with the Nawab of Oudh and Bengal, Mir Qasim, tried to resist the British East-India Company but they were defeated in 1764 in the Battle of Buxar. The Emperor ended his days living on a pension from the British authorities. His successors, Akbar Shah (1806–37) and Bahadur Shah II (1837–58), also lived on a British pension. During the Indian uprising of 1857-9 Bahadur Shah II was declared India's King by the rebels. The victorious British army seized Delhi and killed Bahadur Shah's sons. He was exiled to Rangoon, where he continued to write exquisite and heart-broken poetry until he died in 1862.

BIBLIOGRAPHY: *S.A. Azimjanova, 'Babur's State in Kabul and in India', Moscow, 1977 (in Russian); S.H. Edwardes, H.L.O. Garrett, 'Mughal Rule in India', New Delhi, 1979; I.H. Qureshi, 'The Administration of the Mughul Empire', Karachi, 1966.*

K.A. ANTONOVA

Mughal

A corporate group of Muslims in Pakistan and other South Asian countries. They are presumed descendants from Turkish and Irano-Tajik nobility of the Great *Mughal Empire. The ethnic origin of the Mughals is evident from the names of their sub-divisions: Chughtai, Barlas, Uzbek, Tajik, and Qizilbash. The top strata of some *Punjabi clans, such as Gakkhars and Jat, also claim Mughal origin. Mughals can be distinguished from other Muslims by such elements in their proper names as Mirza, *Khoja, *Agha, and *Beg, indicating their Mughal descent. In Pakistan, Mughals mostly live in the Punjab and the *North West Frontier Province.

S.F. LEVIN

Muhajir

1. The Prophet Muhammad's fellow immigrants, who went with him to Medina, on 20 September AD 622.
2. An immigrant or refugee.
3. In Pakistan, *Muhajirs* are Muslim refugees from northern and western India and their descendants who started coming into the country after the establishment of Pakistan in August 1947. The *Muhajirs*' native tongue is *Urdu. Most of them settled in Karachi, Hyderabad (*Sindh) and other big cities. They now make up 24 per cent of Pakistan's urban population. In Bangladesh, *Muhajirin* are called 'Bihari'.

YU.V. GANKOVSKY

Muhammad, Ghulam (1895–1956)

Governor-General of Pakistan from 1951 to 1955. Ghulam Muhammad received MA and LLB degrees from the Aligarh Muslim University. He joined the Indian Audit and Accounts Service in the Government of India. He was the Finance Minister of the State of Hyderabad from 1942 to 1947. From 1947 to 1951 he served as Pakistan's Finance Minister.

Ghulam Muhammad, Governor-General of Pakistan (1951–55).

He became Chairman of the International Muslim Economic Organization in 1949, and in 1950 became the Chairman of the Economic Conference of Muslim Countries. He succeeded Khwaja *Nazimuddin as Governor-General of Pakistan, when the latter became Prime Minister in 1951 following the assassination of Liaquat Ali *Khan. He dismissed Prime Minister Khwaja Nazimuddin on 16 April 1953 and dissolved the *Constituent Assembly on 24 October 1954. The dissolution was successfully challenged in the Sindh High Court by the Speaker Maulvi Tamizuddin *Khan but was upheld on appeal to the Federal Court.

YU.V. GANKOVSKY

Muhammad, Hanif (1934–)

Cricket Player. Born in Junagarh, called the Little Master for his youthfulness. Hanif Muhammad's first class career began in 1951, when he was just 17, and his test career in 1952. He played his last test match in 1969 at Karachi, in which his two brothers Mushtaq Muhammad and Sadiq Muhammad also played. He scored 3,915 runs in 55 matches with an average of 43.98. His best innings were against the West Indies (337 runs). He was the first Pakistani batsman to score a century in each innings, against the MCC in Dhaka in 1960–61). His score of 499, in 1959 against Bahawalpur was for long the highest in first class cricket and stood until beaten by Brian Lara's 502 in 1994. He was captain for twelve Test matches, winning two and losing two.

Hanif Muhammad, well known Cricket player.

S. ZAKIUDDIN

Mujahid, Mujahed

(Arabic: one who makes an effort, tries hard; a fighter for his faith, a fighter for a true cause) A warrior, a participant in **jihad*. One who fights in the struggle for Islam.

YU.V. GANKOVSKY

Mujtahid

(Arabic: the one who has attained, from *jahada* 'to endeavour') A theologian and law expert (*faqih*). The representative of the top stratum of Muslim theologians (*see* Ulema) who has the right to pass judgements on questions of the **Shariah*. All the other Muslims, rank-and-file theologians included, are obliged to follow these decisions (*see* *Taqlid). In *Shia Islam, only **mujtahids* have the right to answer questions or pass judgements (*see* fatwa) relating to the Muslim law.

YU.V. GANKOVSKY

Mukimjanova, Railya Mukshinovna (1927–)

Historian. A historian, specializing in Oriental Studies, she graduated from the Central Asian University in Tashkent (1949), and is a research member of the Institute of Oriental Studies of the USSR (1958).

WORKS: *'US Politics in Pakistan', Moscow, 1961; 'Pakistan, South Asia and the US Policy (the 60s—Early 70s)', Moscow, 1974; 'Pakistan and the Imperialist Powers: the 70s—Early 80s', Moscow, 1984 (all in Russian).*

YU.V. GANKOVSKY

Mulla (also Mullah)

(Arabic) A Muslim theologian, an educated person.

YU.V. GANKOVSKY

Murid

(Arabic: *rada*—to seek, to study) One who seeks; a disciple; a follower of a Muslim spiritual leader, **murshid*, **sheikh*, or **pir*.

YU.V. GANKOVSKY

Murshid

(Arabic: *rashada*—to follow the right path; to guide) A guide, an instructor, the head of a Muslim order.

YU.V. GANKOVSKY

Musaddas

(Arabic: six-distriche verse) A strophic poem popular in the poetry of the Middle East and South Asia. Each strophe—*band*—consists of three verses (**baits*), or six distiche *misra*, with different rhyme patterns: aaaaaa, bbbbaa, ccccaa, or: aaaabb, ccccbb, dddddd; or: aaaabb, ccccdd, ccccff, etc. *Musaddas* is used in large-scale works of philosophical nature. In *Urdu literature, *musaddas* was finally introduced in the nineteenth century, and was particularly preferred by Mir *Anis and Mirza Dabir (**marsiya*). *Madd-o-Jazr-i-Islam* ('The Tidal Waves of Islam') by Altaf Husain *Hali, also known as Six-disticjes of Hali, is particularly loved and admired. A variant (aaba, cc), introduced by the Indian poet Jameel Mazhari, found followers in Pakistan.

N.V. GLEBOV

Museums in Pakistan

Pakistan's largest museums are under the auspices of the Department of Archaeology of Pakistan. In 1949 the Pakistan Museum Association was established in Karachi. The Association publishes Museums Journal of Pakistan (two issues a year), and Museum Studies. It maintains close contact with universities, educational, and service institutions.

The oldest museum of Pakistan, the Central Museum in Lahore, was opened in 1864. The largest museums of Pakistan are Lahore Museum, Peshawar Museum, *Lahore Fort Museum, and the National Museum of Pakistan in Karachi. Allama* Iqbal Museums are maintained in Lahore and Sialkot. There are archaeological museums in *Mohenjo-Daro, *Taxila, Bhambore, Saidu-Sharif, and Umarkot. Museums of Regional Studies have been established in Hyderabad and Quetta. The *Folk Art Museum and *National Art Gallery are in Islamabad. The Geological Museum is in Quetta, the Military Museum in Rawalpindi, the Industrial and Commercial Museum in Lahore, and the Museum of Agriculture in Faisalabad. The Government College in Lahore and the Islamia College in Peshawar both have small zoological and anatomical museums organized and supported by enthusiasts. In the 1980s and the beginning of the 1990s about 2.5 million people visited the museums of Pakistan annually.

A.V. ZABOLOTSKY

Mushafi, Ghulam Hamadani (1750–1824)

Poet. Mushafi was an *Urdu poet who came to Delhi in 1776, where he won acclaim for his poetry. In 1787 he moved to Lucknow where he became very popular. He has eight *diwans* to his credit, three of them in Farsi. He is also responsible for *Tazkira-i-Hindigoyan* ('Anthology of Urdu Poetry', 1794) and the long poem *Behr al-Muhabbat* ('The Sea of Love', 1824). Mushafi's creative work was strongly influenced by the poetry of Mir Taqi *Mir and Mirza *Sauda. Mushafi had many disciples to whom he either gave or sold his poems. There is a record of his poetic rivalry with Insha Allah *Khan.

WORKS: *'Kulliyat, Delhi', 1967; 'Intekhab-i-Diwan-i-Mushafi', Kanpur, undated; 'Behr al-Muhabbat', Delhi, 1982.*

BIBLIOGRAPHY: *S. Abullais, 'Mushafi aur Unka Kalam' (Mushafi and his Work), Lahore, undated; D. Matthews, C. Shackle (ed.), 'An Anthology of Classical Urdu Love Lyrics', London, 1972.*

A.A. SUVOROVA

Mushaira

A public contest of poets in the Middle East and South Asia, where literature is based on the Arabic and Persian poetics. These contests originated in the Middle Ages as a platform for an aesthetic-critical appreciation of verbal arts and played an important role in the development of poetry. In South Asia a strict ritual was worked out of the conduct of these contests, beginning with a preliminary selection of a model (*tarah*) to be followed by the participants in composing their *ghazals*. There was a strict order of performance—from the less famous to the established poets. The audience's appreciation was expressed in set phrases. In 1974 the reformers of *Urdu literature, Muhammad Husain *Azad and Altaf Husain *Hali, suggested including thematic poems (*nazm*) as well. There were two ways of reciting poems—chanting (mainly *ghazals*) and declaiming (mainly *nazm*). Poetic contests are still very popular in Pakistan and other Eastern countries, and wherever there are Eastern communities.

A.S. SUKHOCHEV

Musharraf, Pervez, President General (1943–)

President of Pakistan (1999–). President General Pervez Musharraf was educated at St. Patrick's High School, Karachi, Forman Christian College, Lahore, and the Pakistan Military Academy, Kakul. As a career army officer, he held various positions, rising to Chief of Army Staff in 1998 and Chairman Joint Chiefs of Staff in 1999. On 12 October 1999, he dismissed the second PML Government of Mian Mohammad Nawaz *Sharif and assumed governmental authority, initially with the title of 'Chief Executive', President Rafiq *Tarrar continuing in the President's office. President General Pervez Musharraf is the first military ruler of Pakistan who has not declared martial law. The Supreme Court of Pakistan gave him a three-year time frame for the restoration of democracy and constitutional rule. Elections to local bodies, under the new scheme of devolution, were held in March 2001. On 20 June 2001 Pervez Musharraf became President on the basis of a nation-wide referendum whose legitimacy, however, remains controversial. Parliamentary elections were held in 2002, within the Supreme Court's stipulated time frame. While the *Pakistan People's Party gained the single largest number of votes, the *Pakistan Muslim League (Quaid Group), which supported President Musharraf, gained the most seats and, with the support of allied smaller parties, controls the Federal government and the governments of *Punjab and *Sindh. The recently formed Muttahida Majlis-i-Amal (MMA), an alliance of nine right-wing religious parties, emerged strongly in *North West Frontier Province and *Balochistan, and has formed the government in those two provinces. To the time of writing, the positive achievements of President General Pervez Musharraf's regime have included stabilisation of the economy and overall improvement in Pakistan's relations with other countries–notably with the USA, with whom Pakistan is allied in the 'War against Terror', and with India.

S. WOLPERT

Muslim League

This name refers to 1. *All-India Muslim League (AIML); 2. *Pakistan Muslim League; 3. Bangladesh Muslim League.

Muslim (Newspaper)

An English daily newspaper with a circulation of 20,000, that was launched in 1979 in Islamabad. Its motto is 'The nation and its press rise and fall together'. It belongs to Agha Murtaza Pooya, a prominent public figure. Pooya is also the head of the political party '*Islamic Jihad*', which contested the 1990 election in coalition with the Islami Jamhuri Ittehad. A.T. Chaudhri was its first editor (1979-85), he was succeeded by Mushahid Husain Sayyid. In 1988 Dr Maliha Lodi became the first woman editor in Pakistan. She liberalized the newspaper, and was succeeded by Altaf Gauhar. It has since ceased publication.

SHAHNAWAZ

Muttahida Qaumi Movement

(MQM, originally called the *Muhajir Qaumi* Movement, Urdu for *Muhajir* National Movement) A Party formed in 1984, based on the All-Pakistan *Muhajir* Students Organization, and led by its charismatic '*Quaid-i-Tehrik*' Altaf Hussain. The nucleus of the Party were groups of **Muhajirs* who, in 1977, opposed Z.A. *Bhutto's *Pakistan Peoples Party and were on the side of the *Pakistan National Alliance. The MQM has a strong following in *Sindh's major cities, Karachi, Hyderabad, Sukkur, and Mirpurkhas, where its electoral performances have been consistently outstanding. Initially a Party demanding abolition of the regional quota system in government employment, which was felt to favour ethnic groups in the rural areas against the cities, and demanding that *Muhajirs* be declared as Pakistan's fifth nationality, the MQM has, throughout its existence, been surrounded by controversy and subjected to intense criticism by its opponents. The MQM has been part of the governing coalitions of both Benazir *Bhutto and Nawaz *Sharif and is also a part of the governing coalition of President General Pervez *Musharraf. The MQM changed its name to *Muttahida Qaumi* Movement, but a break-away faction has retained the original, ethnically oriented name.

O.V. PLESHOV

Muttahida Qaumi Movement Labour Wing

(MQMLW; Labour Wing of the *Muttahida* National Movement, formerly Muhajir Qaumi Movement) Founded in 1986, with divisions in Karachi, Hyderabad, and Sukkur. In 1989 the Trade Union centres connected with the MQMLW occupied leading positions in most major enterprises of Karachi including the *Pakistan Steel Mill, Karachi Electric Supply Corporation, Karachi Municipal Corporation, and others.

D.B. NOVOSELOV

N

Nadwatul-Ulema

(Arabic: a congregation of the learned ones) A *Sunni **dar-ul-ulum* in Lucknow (Uttar-Pradesh, India) founded in 1894 by the prominent religious and public leaders Abdul Ghafur, Abdul Haqq Haqqani, and Shibli Numani. They adhered to non-traditionalist principles, taking a position between the modernist Aligarh College (later, Aligarh Muslim University) and traditionalist *Deoband. They recognized the right for **ijtihad* for **ulema* but not for rank-and-file Muslims. In distinction from the *darul-ulum,* which follow the classical theological system of education, *Nadwatul-Ulema* teaches non-traditionalist disciplines, such as the English language, history, and comparative religious studies. The theologians of the school concentrate on missionary and educational work. They insist on reforms in the Muslim community of India. The *Darul Musannifin* in the town of Azamgarh (Uttar-Pradesh, India) is affiliated to the *Nadwatul-Musannifin*.

M.R. KAZIMI

Naheed, Kishwar (1940–)

Poet. Pioneer woman poet and feminist activist of Pakistan, Kishwar Naheed has had a long and fruitful literary career. Serving with the government of Pakistan, she edited the literary *Urdu monthly *Mah-i-Nau* of the Ministry of Information and turned it into a highly respected journal. She has represented Pakistan in many international literary gatherings. She also introduced the form of the prose poem in *Urdu literature. She was the Chairperson of the National Arts Council of Pakistan and now runs a women's organization *Hawwa*.

Besides poetry, Kishwar has published an adaptation of *The Second Sex* by Simone de Beauvoir. Her autobiography *Buri Aurat Ki Katha* ('Tale of a Bad Woman'), created a sensation, as it was the first candid and uninhibited personal life-story written by a woman in Pakistan. Kishwar has published several volumes of poetry.

She won the Nelson Mandela Award in 1997 and in 2000 she was decorated by the Government of Pakistan with the *Sitara-e-Imtiaz*.

WORKS: *'Lab-i-Goya', Lahore; 'Benam Musafat', Lahore; 'Main Pehle Janam Mein Raat Thee', Lahore; (English translation) 'The Distance of a Shout', Karachi, 2000.*

F. RIAZ

Nal

This is the name given to an archaeological culture in central and southern *Balochistan. Evidence of its existence is found in the Hingol, Porali and Hab (or Hub), valleys. H. Hargreaves was the first to identify it in the Sohr Dam settlement. It gets its name from the Nal settlement 320 km. to the south of Quetta. The tell where remains were excavated is 12 metres high and cover an area of about 300 metres 170 metres. Adobe houses with floors paved in pebbles stood on stone foundations. There are typical pottery groups: unornamented, dark burnished, painted in black against red and polychrome. The patterns are either geometrical or zoomorphic using animal forms such as an ox, goat, gazelle, lion and fish. Copper objects were found in abundance including chisels, axes, daggers, knives and seals. There are traces of local lead working. Other objects include stone grain grinders, steatite seals, agate and coral beads and shells. Burials of three types were found: 1. Complete inhumation in a pit walled with bricks without a gravestone with two child skeletons and one adult placed on its left side in contracted position; 2. The third type has its analogies in the Sohr Dam settlement. Its painted ware has analogies in Iran at Tepe Yahya. No radio-carbon dates have been established. W. *Fairservis dates the culture to 2500-2000 BC.

BIBLIOGRAPHY: *H. Hargreaves, 'Excavation in Balochistan: 1925', Calcutta, 1929; W.A. Fairservis, 'The Roots of Ancient India', Chicago-London, 1975; D.P. Agrawal, 'The Archaeology of India', Scandinavian Institute of Asian Studies, Monograph series, No. 46, London, 1982.*

N.M. VINOGRADOVA

Namaz

(Persian for 'prayer') *See,* Salat.

Naqoosh

A quarterly from Lahore that has been published since 1948. The first ten issues were edited by Ahmad

Nadeem *Qasimi and Hajra *Masrur, the next five by Viqar Azeem and subsequently by Mohammad Tufail until his death on 5 July 1986. *Naqoosh* was edited is noted for giving primacy to classical literature and creative writers who became legendary in their lifetime. It published special numbers devoted to classical poets such as *Mir, *Ghalib, *Anis, *Iqbal, and contemporaries Saadat Hasan *Manto and Patras *Bokhari. Also then on themes of humour and satire, literary feuds etc. A twelve volume *Rasool* number marked its apogee. After the death of M. Tufail it has come out intermittently. The latest issue (2004) is a four-volume publication on the Quran.

M.R. KAZIMI

Naqqara

These are clay and metal barrel-like drums of various sizes played with wooden sticks. At present the *naqqara* is used both as a single piece (the larger drum) and two piece (*naqqara* proper) instrument, mostly in combination with the **shahnai* and its varieties in Pakistan and India.

I. PIRACHA

Naqshbandiya

A *sufi order named after Sheikh Bahauddin Naqshband (1318, Bukhara—89), the son of an engraver. Naqshbandiya have *Sunni and *Shia branched. They do not recognize hermitage and asceticism. The famous poets, Abdur Rahman Jami (1414-92) and Ali Sher Nawai (1441-501), belonged to this order. In South Asia, Naqshbandiya have existed since the early 16th century. One of its leaders in north India, Sheikh Ahmad al-Faruqi Sirhindi (*c.* 1563-626), actively opposed the eclectism of Emperor Akbar (1556-605). He founded a new branch of Naqshbandiya, named Mujaddidiya after the honorary name given to Ahmad Sirhindi—*Mujadid-i Alf-i Sani*, meaning, in Arabic, 'the reformer of Islam of the second millennia'. The branch is active in the countries of the Middle East and South Asia, and has noticeable influence on the Muslim communities in these regions.

YU.V. GANKOVSKY

Nasir, Mir Gul Khan (1914–83)

Poet. A poet, historian and public figure who wrote in *Balochi, *Urdu, and *Brahui. After 1947 he wrote only only in Balochi. He had no more than a secondary education and was employed in the Civil Service of the *Kalat principality. From 1970 to 1973 he served as Minister of Education of Balochistan. He was author of three collections of poetry, a two-volume 'History of Balochistan' (*Tarikh-i-Balochistan*) and several treatments of folk **dastans*, such as *Dostin-i-Shirin, Hammal wa jenid*. He took an active part in the country's political life. Nasir's work is an important contribution to the revival of Balochi poetry. He introduced elements of Urdu and English (see English Literature) verse forms into it, and made the poetic language more accessible to the public.

BIBLIOGRAPHY: *Balochi, 'Brahui ma Taaruf-i-Musanifin', Karachi, 1973.*

A.S. SUKHOCHEV

National Archives of Pakistan

Established in 1951, the Archives are a collection of 5,000 rare publications and manuscripts documenting the history of the people of Pakistan. The National Archives were first stored in Karachi in 1951, but were moved in the 1970s to Islamabad. The archives of the *Muslim League, the minutes of the *Round Table Conference, minutes of the meetings of the Provincial Assemblies of Pakistan, and documents outlining the life and work of M.A. *Jinnah are among the items in the collection.

YU.V. GANKOVSKY

National Art Gallery, The

The Gallery based in Islamabad and has been part of the National Arts Centre of Pakistan (*Idara Saqafat-i-Pakistan*) since 1970. It has a permanent exhibition representing the work of Pakistan's major artists and mounts exhibitions in the country and abroad. It is.

BIBLIOGRAPHY: *K.S. Butt, 'Pakistan through Canvas', Islamabad, 1987; 'Paintings from Pakistan', Islamabad, 1988.*

N.K. KARPOVA

National Awami Party

(NAP) was founded in July 1957 in Dhaka, at a conference of leaders of left-wing and democratic parties of Pakistan. These included the left wing of the *Awami League, the Democratic Party (*Ganatantri Dal*) of *East Pakistan, the Sindh Hari Committee, Sindh Awami Mahaz, the Azad Pakistan Party, the *Red Shirts, the Pashtun Brotherhood *(Wror Pashtun)* of Balochistan and the Party of the Masses *(Ustoman Gall)* of *Balochistan. The NAP proposed a programme of wide-ranging democratic reforms. From 1958 to 1962 it was banned but resumed its activity in August 1963. From 1964 to 1971 the main areas in which the NAP was active were East Pakistan, the party's provincial division being led by A.H. *Bhashani, the *North West Frontier Province, Balochistan, and Karachi. The National Awami Party was in favour of the restoration of the parliamentary form of government. It was also in favour of partition of the unified province of *West Pakistan, broad socio-economic reforms, and Pakistan's departure from CENTO and SEATO. From 1966 to 1967 factional strife led to the splitting of the NAP into two independent parties, one of which was headed by A.H. Bhashani and the other by Abdul Wali *Khan. The party took part in the 1970 general elections, winning six seats in the National Assembly. From March 1972 to February 1973 NAP representatives held the posts of governors in the North West Frontier Province (Arbab Sikander Khan Khalil) and Balochistan (Ghaus Bux Bizenjo). In March 1973 the NAP joined the United Democratic Front opposed to the government of Z.A. *Bhutto. On 10 February 1975 the NAP was banned. In the autumn of 1975 many prominent politicians and activists of the banned NAP joined the National Democratic Party, founded on 7 November 1975 by Sardar Sherbaz Khan Mazari.

BIBLIOGRAPHY: *R.I. Sherkovina, 'Political Parties and Political Struggle in Pakistan', Moscow, 1983 (in Russian).*

YU.V. GANKOVSKY

National Institute of Electronics

The National Institute of Electronics (NIE) is dedicated to the design, development, and implementation of projects related to electronics, computers, and telecommunications. NIE has developed ten processes, including sine wave uninterruptable power supply system (on-line), emergency tube light controller, traffic controller and fan regulator controller, hearing aids, and hair driers, etc.

T. NAIM

National Institute of Historical and Cultural Research

Founded in 1973 in Islamabad, the Institute studies the history and culture of South Asian Muslims and the impact the Muslim public and political movements have had on the formation of Pakistan. The Institute publishes research, handbooks, and bibliographies, as well as a biannual, *Pakistan Journal on History and Culture*. The Institute also maintains a specialized library.

YU.V. GANKOVSKY

National Library of Pakistan

Under the jurisdiction of the government Directorate of Archives and Libraries, it was founded in 1987 in Islamabad. It holds about 1 million books, 600 periodicals, and 75 newspapers (in the languages of the people of Pakistan. As a matter of regulation, copies of all books and pamphlets published in the country are stored here. The National Library is a member of the International Federation of Libraries.

YU.V. GANKOVSKY

National Museum of Pakistan

It opened in 1851 as the Victoria Museum, in Karachi. In 1950 the State Department of Archaeology of Pakistan transformed it into the National Museum of Pakistan. The museum holds collections of material ranging from the *Palaeolithic (*Soan) to the 6th century AD (*Gandhara), and important collections of coins with more than 10,000 rare coins from central and South Asia. The displays also include manuscripts, sculptures, and materials on ethnology and on the history of the independence struggle.

BIBLIOGRAPHY: *'Museums Journal of Pakistan', Karachi; 'Museum Studies', Karachi (both from 1950); S.R. Dar, Museums in Pakistan, in: Museology and Museum Problems in Pakistan, Lahore, 1981.*

N.K. KARPOVA

National Press Trust

(NPT) A newspaper and publishing amalgamation established in March 1964 with backing from major investors and the government-controlled National Bank of Pakistan and taken over by the Government in 1972. The Board of Trustees headed by a government-appointed chairman is. The Trust owns the newspapers *Morning News*, *Mashriq,* and the women's weekly *Akhbar-i-Khawatin,* published in *Urdu in Karachi. The Trust also operates the Lahore-based Progressive Papers Ltd., which is largely financially autonomous and owns the newspapers *Pakistan Times* and *Imroz.* The Trust was set up to impose government policy on mass media and to control it. This policy is affected through centralized distribution of advertisements of government agencies and companies, and import licences for newsprint. In Pakistan publishers depend on advertisements for their financial success. Government agencies and companies are the largest and most reliable advertisers. The bulk of newsprint is imported and distributed through official channels according to the officially recognized circulation. This allows the authorities to support the unprofitable but politically reliable publications and to exercise strict control over undesirable periodicals.

V.A. LAVRO

Nawab

(Also *Nawwab*, Arabic: plural of *Naib*–governor, deputy, assistant In European literature often spelled as Nabob) In the *Mughal empire, the deputy of **Subadar* (governor of a region); sometimes denotes the governor himself. In *British India, it was an honorary title of the rulers of Balasinor, Cambay, Junagadrh, Palanpur, Rampur, Sachin, Tonk and others. In Pakistan until 1955, this title belonged to the rulers of *Bahawalpur, *Makran, Kharan, and Amb.

YU.V. GANKOVSKY

Nazimuddin, Khwaja (1894–1964)

Governor-General of Pakistan from 1948 to 1951. Khwaja Nazimuddin hailed from Dhaka. He graduated from the Aligarh Muslim University and later received a degree from Cambridge. From 1929 to 1934 he was Minister of Education of Bengal and the Minister for the Interior of Bengal from 1937 to 1941. He was a member of a Working Committee of the *All-India Muslim League. He served as Chief Minister of East Pakistan from 1947 to 1948, when he succeeded M.A. *Jinnah as Governor-General of Pakistan. He held this office until September 1951, when he became Prime Minister of Pakistan. His dismissal from this office in April 1953 by the Governor-General precipitated political crises in Pakistan.

Khwaja Nazimuddin, Governor-General of Pakistan after M.A. Jinnah (1948–51)

YU.V. GANKOVSKY

Nazira

(Arabic: similar) A poetic genre, a form of literary competition, a response to the work of another poet. *Nazira* was to be written in a prescribed poetic key, presupposing imitation of some component in the original poem, that inspired the poem-response. It was to adopt the same system of tropes, metre, rhyme, or **radif*, strophe composition, etc. Already in the 11th century, *nazira* became a channel of literary struggle among rivalling court poets. The term is used in the literatures of the Middle East and South Asia.

N.V. GLEBOV

Nazm

(in Arabic: arrangement, order, poetry) This is the general term for poetic work with the exception of **ghazal*. The term is used in the literatures of the Middle East and South Asia. In Urdu literature, *nazm* also denotes a genre form of a thematic poem a style that had developed by the end of the nineteenth century. *Nazm-i-tawil* is a large-scale poetic work and *nazm-i-azad* is free verse.

N.V. GLEBOV

Nehru Report

This report is named after Pandit Motilal Nehru, who headed a committee appointed by the Congress in its December 1927 Madras Session, which had the task of framing a *Swaraj* or national constitution. The Committee was authorized to co-opt other political organizations and seek their co-operation in producing a constitution.

The Secretary of State for India, Lord Birkenhead, had not included any Indian in the *Simon Commission to frame a new Constitution to replace the Govt. of India Act, 1919. When faced with criticism over this decision, Lord Birkenhead had challenged the Indians on 24 November 1927, to themselves produce a Constitution for India. It was to meet this challenge that the Nehru Committee was set up. Simultaneously with boycotting the Simon Commission, Congress had at the same session ratified the *Delhi Muslim Proposals. Congress was confident that, since it had already arrived at a new constitutional agreement with the *All-India Muslim League, it would need only to fill in the details. The Congress Working Committee extended invitations to twenty-nine political parties, which culminated in an All-Parties Conference held at on 18 February 1928 and presided over by Dr Mukhtar Ahmad Ansari. Two successive sessions, held on 8 March and 19 May, saw the communal harmony of the earlier meetings eroded, as the Hindu *Mahasabha* and *Sikh politicians became insistent that Congress and the Nehru Committee repudiate the Delhi Muslim Proposals. This pressure, although it exposed Congress to the taunts and jibes of Lord Birkenhead, was not resisted.

Pandit Motilal Nehru presented the report of his Committee at Lucknow in August 1928. It thereafter came up for final consideration at the All-Parties Convention at Calcutta (now Kolkata) on 22 December 1928. In its recommendations the Committee opted for Dominion status, which would keep India in the British Commonwealth, as the next immediate step towards reform. The Centre would have a bi-cameral legislature, the lower Chamber of 500 members to be called the House of Representatives and the upper Chamber of 200 members, the Senate. Specific numbers of seats would be allotted to Provinces on the basis of population. The Provinces would have uni-cameral legislatures. All powers not specifically assigned to the Provinces would be vested in the Centre. On 28 December M.A. *Jinnah appeared before the All-Parties Convention and proposed a number of amendments that in effect meant the *reinstatement* in the Report of the Delhi Muslim Proposals. The delegates turned down all the amendments, except for the separation of *Sindh from Bombay and reforms in NWFP and *Balochistan. Shorn of the autonomy enshrined in the Delhi Muslim Proposals, this did not prove to be a palliative. The Nehru Report also rejected the statutory protection of the Muslim majority status in Punjab and Bengal. The Muslims had pressed for this provision because the slight majority they had would be more than counter balanced by their educational and economic backwardness in these provinces. The delegates also refused to provide one-third representation for Muslims in the Central legislature, as the Muslims numbered less than one-fourth of the population of India. Weightages in provincial legislatures and separate electorates were of course not countenanced. M.A. Jinnah's amendments were also rejected because the delegates complained that he had no representative status. The All-India Muslim League, it was felt, had been cast aside by the Muslims in the wake of the *Khilafat Movement. Thereafter, Jinnah caused a split by siding with Congress in boycotting the Simon Commission. His co-operation with Congress eight years after he had resigned from that body cost him dearly. To both Lord Birkenhead and Sir Mohammad *Shafi, President of the *Muslim League in 1928, Mohammad Ali Jinnah appeared a most vulnerable politician. This political and psychological reality eventually proved to be a myopic reading of the situation. The Nehru Report lost its representative status and became a moribund document. The publication of the Nehru Report proved to be a watershed in the political careers of many leaders. Abul Kalam *Azad, Mohammad Ali Currim Chagla and Tassaduq Ahmad Sherwani finally severed their connection with the AIML and went over to Congress. The Maharaja of Mahmudabad, friendly to both Motilal and Jinnah, signed the Report. Shoaib Quraishi wrote a note of dissent to the Nehru Report, on the grounds that it had gone back on the ratified Delhi Muslim Proposals, and he came over to the Muslim League. This situation remained unchanged despite the *Round Table Conferences held in London in 1932.

BIBLIOGRAPHY: *C.F. Andrews, 'India and the Simon Report', London, 1930; K.K. Aziz, 'All-India Muslim Conference', Karachi, 1972; Kanji Dwarkadas, 'India's Fight for Freedom', Bombay, 1966; Peter Hardy, 'The Muslims of British India', Cambridge; 1972, R.J. Moore, 'The Crisis of Indian Unity 1917-1940', Oxford, 1974; K.M. Pannikar and A. Pershad, (eds.), 'The Voice of Freedom: Selected Speeches of Pandit Motilal Nehru', London, 1971.*

M.R. KAZIMI

Neolithic

In Pakistan, several Neolithic settlements have produced evidence from archaeological digs of their own unique material cultures and economic foundations: 1. The Northwestern Neolithic province appears to be the first where a proto-urban civilization appeared. While neighbouring regions were still populated by hunters and gatherers. It seems that the early Neolithic cultures of land tillers (7th-6th millennia BC) appeared under the influence of a major Near Eastern centre, where plants and animals were domesticated at an early stage. Mehrgarh, a multi-level Neolithic settlement on the river Bolan in the *Indus Valley in Pakistan, is one of the most interesting sites. As early as in the pre-ceramic era, Neolithic people lived in houses built of adobe bricks according to a planned layout. It was a period of early land tilling and possibly domestication of cattle. The stone tools carried on the Mesolithic traditions. 2. The Northern Neolithic Province had a very specific general character and material culture. It is best studied at the Burzahom settlement (*Kashmir). The earliest levels are dated to 2400-2200 BC. The walls and floors in the pit-dwellings were plastered with clay. Canine and wolf bones are found together with human skeletons. Tools were made of fragments, small and large flakes predominating. Polished and clay polished implements are also seen, including axes. Knives and stone sickles form a special group, as well as bone harpoons used for fishing. The black and grey modelled semi ware was extremely coarse. In Qufrkala, there is evidence of grain cultivation (wheat, barley and leguminous plants) and domestication of animals (sheep and goats). Ties with Chinese areas are possible.

V.A. RANOV

Nishtar, Abdur Rab, Sardar (1899–1958)

Statesman. A politician and statesman of India and Pakistan and a *Pashtun from the *Kakar tribe, Nishtar was a lawyer by profession. He graduated from the Punjab University in Lahore in 1923 and received an advanced degree from the Aligarh Muslim University in 1925. He participated in the *Khilafat Movement and from 1927 to 1931 was a leader of the Indian National Congress branch in the *North West Frontier Province. Nishtar was also a member of the Muslim League Council in 1936; a member of the NWFP Legislative Assembly from 1937 to 1945; Minister of Finance in the NWFP government from 1943 to 1945; and a member of the Working Committee of the *All-India Muslim League from 1944–47. From 1946 to 1947 he served as Member for Communications in the interim Indian government; as Deputy Premier and Communications Minister in the first Pakistani government from 1947 to 1949; as Governor of the *Punjab from 1949 to 1951; and as Minister for Industries of Pakistan from 1951 to 1953. He served as President of the *Muslim League of Pakistan from 1956 until his death.

YU.V. GANKOVSKY

Nomani, Shibli, Allama (1857–1914)

Poet/Literary Critic. Allama Shibli was a Muslim enlightener and public figure, poet, literary critic, and essayist, who wrote in *Urdu and also in Persian. Shibli received a traditional Muslim education and in 1879 he travelled to Makkah to perform Hajj. For two years he was employed in the Indian Civil Service but, from 1882 to 1898, he taught Arabic at the Aligarh College. He was a close associate of Sir Syed Ahmad *Khan. In 1892 he visited Turkey, Syria and Egypt. A proponent and ideologist of the modernization of Islam and Muslim society, he became one of the founders and the first secretary of the *Anjuman Tarraqqi-i-Urdu* in 1903. He was also a founder (1894) and leader (1904-13) of the religious school, *Nadwat al-Ulema,* in Lucknow and an organizer of the Writers' Society, *Dar al-Musanifin,* in Azamgarh. The Society has survived to this day. Shibli was also a founder of the genre of historical prose in *Urdu literature. He made a comparative analysis of Eastern and Western philosophies, viewing them in the light of Muslim philosophy. He has to his credit a fundamental biography of the Prophet Muhammad (PBUH), *Sirat an-Nabi*, which was completed by his pupil Sayyid Sulaiman Nadvi, and a five-volume history of Persian poetry: *Sher al-Ajam.*

WORKS: *'Sher al-Ajam', Kanpur, 1920-23.*

BIBLIOGRAPHY: *S.S. Nadvi, 'Hayat-i-Shibli', Azamgarh, 1943; S.M. Ikram, 'Yadgar-i-Shibli', Lahore, 1971; M.A. Murad, 'Intellectual Modernism of Shibli Nomani', Lahore, 1976.*

A.A. SUVOROVA

Noon, Firoz Khan, Malik Sir (1893–1970)

Sir Malik Firoz Khan Noon, Prime Minister of Pakistan (1957–58).

Prime Minister of Pakistan from 1957 to 1958. A political figure in British India and Pakistan, Sir Firoz Khan Noon was born into a wealthy land-owning family. Graduating from the Punjab University and later receiving a degree from Oxford, he was called to the Bar at the Inner Temple. He served as an advocate at the Lahore High Court from 1917 to 1926, and became a member of the Punjab Legislative Council (1921-36) and Viceroy's Executive Council of India from 1941 to 1945. He was selected as the Indian delegate to the first United Nations meeting in San Francisco in 1945. Noon would later serve Pakistan in various capacities, including Member of the *Constituent Assembly of Pakistan from 1947 to 1956, Governor of *East Pakistan (East Bengal) 1950 to 1953, Chief Minister of the Punjab provincial government from 1953 to 1955, Minister for Foreign Affairs of Pakistan from 1956 to 1957 and finally as Prime Minister of Pakistan from December 1957 to October 1958. He was decorated several times the awards included the Order of the Indian Empire, Star of India, and Officer of the Order of St. John of Jerusalem.

WORKS: *'From Memory', Lahore, 1966.*

YU.V. GANKOVSKY

Noon (also Nun)

An influential land-owning clan in north-west *Punjab (Pakistan). They are *Rajputs by origin. They migrated to the Punjab from Rajasthan in the 15th century, when they were converted to Islam by the Muslim *sufi preacher, Baba Farid. In the 1840s the Noons assisted the British in conquering the Punjab, and were rewarded with extensive **Jagirs* or estates, by the British authorities. The Noons took an active part in the political life of *British India and Pakistan, usually in conservative political positions. The most prominent Noon was Sir Feroz Khan *Noon, Prime Minister of Pakistan, 1957-8.

BIBLIOGRAPHY: *'Chiefs and Families of Note in the Punjab', Vol. II, Lahore, 1940; 'A Glossary of the Tribes and Castes of the Punjab and NWFP', Lahore 1978.*

YU.V. GANKOVSKY

Noorani, Shah Ahmad, Maulana (1926–2003)

Political activist/Religious leader. A political and religious leader of Pakistan, Noorani graduated from Aligarh Muslim University in India and began missionary work in eastern Africa until he moved to Pakistan in 1949. Noorani served as the Honorary General Secretary of the World Ulema Organization from 1953 to 1964; Member of the National Assembly of Pakistan from 1970 to 1975 and again from 2002 to 2004; a member of the Senate from 1975 to 1977; and the President of **Jamiat-i Ulema-i Pakistan* from 1973 to 1981. In 1988, together with Mohammed Khan *Junejo and M. Asghar *Khan, Noorani co-chaired the *Pakistan Awami Ittehad* (Pakistan's People Union). In 2001, he helped form the *Muttahida Majlis-i-Amal* (MMA), an alliance of nine right-wing religious parties that emerged strongly during the 2002 elections. He was President of the MMA to the time of his death.

YU.V. GANKOVSKY

North West Frontier Province (also NWFP)

A province in north-west Pakistan bordering Afghanistan. Its area is 106,200 sq.km. Its population was 17,555,000 in 1998. It consists of six divisions: Malakand, Hazara, Peshawar, Dera Ismail Khan, Mardan, *Kohat, fifteen districts, and the agency of Malakand. Approximately 85 per cent of the population are *Pashtun. Others include *Punjabis, Urdu-speaking settlers from northern India and their descendants and *Dardic tribes, such as *Kho, *Shina, *Kohistani. The capital is Peshawar, predominantly mountainous landscape. In the north, there are the northern ranges of the *Hindu Kush and the western foothills of the *Himalayas. In the west, there are low hills and a desert plateau. Agricultural areas consist of only 1.4 million hectares being cultivated, mainly in the Peshawar valley. The crops include wheat, rice, cotton, corn, and also vegetables and fruit. Cattle breeding is widespread. NWFP accounts for 9.3 per cent of the Pakistani territory, 13.2 per cent of the population. It produces 8 per cent of sugar cane, 5 per cent of the entire industrial output—mainly coal mining and limestone, food industry (sugar), cotton industry, cottage industries, such as pottery and handicraft.

NWFP was detached from *Punjab province of British India in 1901, and in 1947 joined Pakistan as a result of the referendum of 6-16 July 1947.

BIBLIOGRAPHY: *T.D. Djaborov, 'North West Frontier Province of Pakistan', Moscow, 1977 (in Russian); Yuri Gankovsky, 'Social Structure of the North West Frontier Province of Pakistan', in: 'Narody Azii i Afriki', 1979, No. 6 (in Russian), 1981 Census Report of North West Frontier Province, Islamabad, 1984.*

M.YU. MOROZOVA

Northern Areas

The northern parts of the former princely state of Jammu and *Kashmir are under Pakistan's control since autumn 1947. The areas lie between longitude 71-75 degrees east and latitude 32-37 degrees north and are run by a Commissioner whose residence is at *Gilgit. He is appointed and supervised by the Ministry of Kashmir Affairs and Northern Areas Affairs of the Pakistan government. Until 1972, these areas were officially called the Northern Areas of Gilgit and *Baltistan. Area: 72,500 sq.km.; population: 573,700 (1981 data). The territorial-administrative structure of the Northern Areas changed many times. In the course of the 1972-74 reforms, the princely states of Hunza, Nagar, Punial, Yasin, Ishkuman, Ghizar, *Chilas and Gupis were abolished. Simultaneously the **Jagirdari* system was also abolished and forced labour (**begar*) was banned in 1953. In 1991, the Northern Areas were divided into five districts: Gilgit (administrative centre, Gilgit), Baltistan (administrative centre, Skardu), Diamar (administrative centre, Chilas), Ghanchee (administrative centre, Khaplu) and Ghizar (administrative centre, Gahkuch). The administration of the districts is headed by Deputy Commissioners.

Nanga Parbat peak in the Northern Areas.

The economy of the Northern Areas is farming (mostly without irrigation) and gardening. Some 40,000 hectares are cultivated (of these, only 2,700 hectares are irrigated); the main cultivated crops are wheat, maize, and barley. Handicrafts (woodwork, stonework, leather-tooling, and metalwork) are well developed. There are five colleges and 461 schools (of all types), seventeen hospitals (with 437 beds), and 153 medical institutions of other types. A majority of the indigenous population speak *Shina, Burushaski, and Balti; in the Gilgit district, some 3,000 migrants from northwestern Afghanistan speak Wakhi (a language of the Pamir group of the Iranian languages). *Urdu is used as an official language and that of interethnic communication. The overwhelming majority of the population are Muslims (both Sunni and Shia); in Hunza, *Ismailis predominate. A small fraction of the population in Baltistan are Buddhists. In the 1970s and 1980s, the public organizations of the Northern Areas repeatedly called for their formal incorporation into Pakistan.

BIBLIOGRAPHY: *J.H. Tode, 'Hunza, Adventures in a Land of Paradise', Emmaus (PA), 1960; A.H. Dani, 'History of Northern Areas of Pakistan', Islamabad, 1989.*

YU.V. GANKOVSKY

Ocean research

With a 540-mile coastline facing the *Arabian Sea, Pakistan is ideally placed to benefit from its extensive sea-based resources. Several organizations are carrying out research in this area. Established in 1981, the National Institute of Oceanography (NIO) is Pakistan's premier ocean research establishment and considered to be a local 'Centre of Excellence'. NIO provides advisory and management strategy services to private companies, donor missions, and the Pakistan Navy. The Institute has been working towards developing a low-cost technology package for coastal aquaculture of commercially important seaweed, oysters, mussels, cockles, lobsters, shrimps, and fish. One of the NIO's more high profile achievements includes an expedition to Antarctica in January 1991, where team members established the *Jinnah Antarctic Research Automatic Weather Observatory. A second expedition was undertaken in December 1992, when a second research station, the Iqbal Observatory, was established. In 1985 a government-sponsored National Commission on Oceanography was constituted to promote investigations with a view to learning more about the nature and resources of Pakistan's maritime area and to co-ordinate ocean research, as well as how best to utilize the results of this research. Scientists at the NIO are a unique and multi-disciplinary combination of marine biologists, chemists, physicists, marine engineers, and aquaculturists giving it the capability of conducting marine ecological surveys, oceanographic data collection, coastal hydrographic and marine environmental studies.

T. NAIM

Odissi

A style of dance that came into existence in the state of Orissa in India. The style emerged from a confluence of scholars, teachers of traditional dance, and musicians.

R. HUSAIN

Orakzai

A *Pashtun tribe belonging to the Kerlarni tribal group. They fall into several branches: Ismailzai, Lashkarzai, Daulatzai, and Muhammad-Khel. They mainly live in the political agency of Orakzai, a strip in north-western Pakistan inhabited by Pashtun tribes. Some **khels* can also be found in the political agency of Kurram. The Orakzai from Alizai and Muhammad-Khel are *Shia. The total population is estimated at 350,000.

BIBLIOGRAPHY: *L. Temirkhanov, 'Eastern Pashtuns: Main Issues of Modern History', Moscow, 1987 (in Russian); L. White King, 'The Orakzai Country and Clans', Lahore, 1984.*

YU.V. GANKOVSKY

Organization of Agricultural Labourers of Pakistan (Pakistan *Dehati Mazdur Tanzim*)

It acted jointly with the *Mazdur Kisan Party* (MKP) against landlords' arbitrary rule, large-scale evictions of leaseholders, and tax increases. They demanded the release of repressed peasants and agricultural labourers. There are other peasant organizations in Pakistan including the Organization of Evicted Leaseholders (*Anjuman-i-Bedakhl Muzarain*) and the Allied Organization of Landtillers (*Anjuman-i-Ittehad-i-Kashtkaran*).

S.I. TANSYKBAEVA

Organization of Islamic Conference (also OIC)

Founded in 1969, its headquarters are in Jeddah, Saudi Arabia. It includes fifty-five Muslim countries and the Palestine Liberation Organization (PLO). According to its Charter, the OIC works towards the consolidation of Islamic solidarity and co-operation among its member countries. Pakistan attended a meeting of the heads of state and government of the Muslim countries held in Rabat, Morocco 1969, which set up the OIC. Pakistan played a more active role in the international Islamic movement in the mid 1970s. On 22-24 February 1974 a second conference of heads of Muslim states and governments was held in Lahore. In the 1980s the focus of Pakistan's activity in OIC was on the Afghan problem, although it continued to support the struggle of the Arab people of Palestine for their inalienable right to establish a state of their own, and for the liberation of Israeli-occupied territories both in the OIC and in the United Nations.

BIBLIOGRAPHY: *N.A. Baba, 'OIC Theory and Practice of Pan Islamic Co-operation Karachi', 1994; S.S. Khan, 'Reasserting International Islam', Karachi, 2001.*

R.M. MUKIMJANOVA

Ormuri

An Iranian language mostly spoken in Pakistan, where it is represented by the Kaniguram (obsolete Bargista) dialect in the Kaniguram region in southern Waziristan. This is the most archaic form of Ormuri. The second dialect of the Ormuri language, Logar (an obsolete name, Baraki), is spoken in Afghanistan and is near extinction. Ormuri language has no written system. It is a language of intra-ethnic communication. Opinions differ as to the place of the Ormuri language in the Iranian language group. However, according to linguistic data, the Ormuri language must be included. The forefathers of modern Ormuris, like those of *Balochis in Afghanistan and Pakistan, migrated many centuries ago to the south-eastern part of the Iranian-speaking territory, from areas bordering on the southern coast of the Caspian Sea. The Ormuri language has many features of phonetic and lexical characteristics of eastern Iranian languages such as the *Pashto and Pamir languages, and of non-Iranian languages such the *Dardic and Nuristani, because of long contact with these languages.

BIBLIOGRAPHY: *V.A. Yefimov, 'The Ormuri Language in the Synchronic and Diachronic Light', Moscow, 1986 (in Russian); G.A. Grierson, 'The Ormuri or Bargista language', Memories of the Asiatic Society of Bengal, Vol. 7, No. 1, Calcutta, 1918; id., 'Ormuri or Bargista', Linguistic Survey of India, Vol. 10, Calcutta, 1921; G. Morgensterne, 'Indo-Iranian Frontier Languages', vol. 1, Oslo, 1929 (2nd ed., 1972); id., 'Supplementary Notes on Ormuri', NTS, BD. 5, Oslo, 1932; id., 'Report on a Linguistic Mission to Afghanistan', Oslo, 1926.*

V.A. YEFIMOV

P

Pagaro, Ali Mardan Shah, Pir (1928–)

Political activist. A political leader of Pakistan, and the **Pir* of the **Hurs* sect. Ali Mardan Shah's father, Pir Pagaro Sibgatullah Shah II (1908–43), was the leader of the anti-British uprising of the *Hurs* and was sent to the gallows by the British authorities. Ali Mardan Shah was educated in England. In 1969 he supported the *Awami League and in 1970 the *Muslim League. From May 1975 to December 1976 he was President of the United Democratic Front, in opposition to the government of Zulfikar Ali *Bhutto. In 1977 he supported the Pakistan National Alliance and, since the 1980s, has assumed leadership of his own faction of the Muslim League.

YU.V. GANKOVSKY

Page, David (1944–)

Historian/Researcher. In the early 1960s David Page taught at King Edward's College, Peshawar. It was here that he developed a deep interest in Pakistan Studies which led him to write a doctoral dissertation devoted to South Asian Muslim politics prior to the Government of India 1935 Act. He joined the BBC and for over twenty years was editor of programmes broadcast to South Asia and Afghanistan. Later he was Training Co-ordinator for the European Union's Media Programme. He also lectured on South Asian politics at the universities of Oxford and London.

WORKS: *'Prelude To Partition', Karachi, 1983; 'Satellites over South Asia with William Crawley', Karachi, 2001.*

YU.V. GANKOVSKY

Paijama (also pajama)

Loose pants worn in India and Pakistan. They are gathered at the ankles by sewn-on strips and at the waist by a cord. Sometimes each leg is pleated and gathered at the ankle with an ornamental band. As a rule, the **pajama* is worn by men. **Pajamas* are usually made of cotton, but can also be of silk and sometimes of wool.

BIBLIOGRAPHY: *S.N. Dar, 'Constumes of India and Pakistan', Bombay, 1982.*

O.V. LUSTSOVA

Pakhawaj

A barrel-like two-sided wooden drum. The pitch is regulated with small wooden bars inserted between leather thongs that stretch the membranes. A parchment plate is fixed on the right membrane, and flour paste is applied on the left membrane before a performance. The instrument is used to accompany singing in the classical music of Pakistan and India, especially of the **dhrupad* genre, and in some kinds of traditional singing and dancing.

I. PIRACHA

Pakhtun Conference

(or Pakhtun League, Pakhtun Jirga) A *Pashtu national liberation organization founded in 1926 by Khan Abdul Ghaffar *Khan in the *North West Frontier Province (NWFP) of *British India. The ultimate goal of the Conference was the overthrow of British domination. The Conference strove to unite all *Pashtun lands of British India in a single Province and to implement socio-economic reforms. It conducted an active propaganda campaign and organized volunteer units (see Red Shirts). Early in 1937 the Conference won the election to the Legislative Assembly of the NWFP, forming the provincial government in coalition with the Indian National Congress. It was headed by one of its leaders, Dr Khan *Sahib (1883-1958), the older brother of Khan Abdul Ghaffar Khan. The Conference government (1937-39) abolished certain privileged forms of land ownership and forced labour (**begar*), reduced rents and built more schools. In 1942 the organization took part in the Congress-led 'Quit India!' campaign. In 1939-45 the Pakhtun Conference was forbidden to operate legally. In 1946 it again won the elections in the NWFP and formed a government jointly with the Congress, headed by Dr Khan Sahib. In July 1947, during the referendum on the incorporation of the NWFP in Pakistan, the Conference called for a boycott of the referendum. In May 1948 the Pakhtun Conference merged with the Azad Pakistan Party, to later further merge into the *National Awami Party.

BIBLIOGRAPHY: *Yuri Gankovsky, 'The National Question and National Movements in Pakistan', Moscow, 1967 (in Russian); Mohammad Yunus, 'Frontier Speaks', Bombay, 1947; Abdul*

Qaiyum, 'Gold and Guns on the Pathan Frontier', Bombay, 1945.

YU.V. GANKOVSKY

Pakistan Academy of Letters

Was founded in 1976 in Islamabad to promote Pakistani literature, and to organize and provide financing of literary research. The Academy holds national and international seminars and conferences. It has a translation department and publishes the quarterly journal, *Adabiat* (Literature), in *Urdu, and a monthly, *Academy,* in English.

YU.V.GANKOVSKY

Pakistan Academy of Sciences

Was founded in 1953 in Karachi to co-ordinate theoretical and applied research in the natural sciences. In the late 1960s the Academy, which is financed by the Ministry of Education, was relocated to Islamabad.

YU.V. GANKOVSKY

Pakistan Agricultural Research Council

Following concerns that Pakistan's disparate agriculture research activities needed a central co-ordinating body, the government established the Agricultural Research Council in 1964. This was upgraded in 1978 and renamed the Pakistan Agricultural Research Council (PARC), which became the main agriculture policy-making body. On the basis of a report prepared jointly by the World Bank, USAID, and its Canadian counterpart, CIDA, PARC was again re-constituted in 1980 and given a wider mandate to co-ordinate research across all of Pakistan's four provinces. PARC manages six organizations in various parts of the country: the National Agricultural Research Centre in Islamabad, the Arid Zone Research Institute in Quetta, the Crop Disease Research Institute in Islamabad, the National Tea Research Institute in Mansehra, the Karakoram Agricultural Research Institute for Northern Areas in Gilgit, and the Himalayan Agricultural Research Institute in Kaghan. In terms of successes, PARC, in close collaboration with national, international, and provincial agricultural research institutions, has developed fifty-one varieties of cereals, twenty-eight varieties of legumes, twenty-one varieties of oilseeds, and fifteen varieties of fodder crops. Pakistan is not normally associated with producing tea, but PARC has recently introduced tea cultivation and established a tea nursery in Mansehra, in the north of the country, with 15 million plants. Bee-keeping has also developed, following PARC's initiative to introduce the European honeybee in 1980. At present more than 10,0000 colonies exist, which produce over 1,400 tons of honey per annum. As a result, Pakistan is now not only self-sufficient in honey but has a surplus for export worth US$ 220-250 million.

The lack of available disease- and virus-free potato seed was a serious constraint in Pakistan for many years. PARC has helped to solve this problem through tissue culture and biotechnology. Microbial biotechnology has been used for bio-fertilizer production of chickpea, groundnut, and other legumes. PARC has also made inroads into the field of animal sciences. Livestock reproduction capacity has been increased from one to four offspring, using embryo-transfer technology. Production technology of hydro-pericardium vaccine has been developed and has been transferred to the private sector for commercial-scale production. Agricultural research has also contributed greatly to the development of poultry, which is an important source of protein for the population. Considerable progress has been achieved in developing a fish farming industry in the country.

Over a period of fifteen years PARC has signed many contracts with private sector firms for the commercialization of a variety of new technologies in seed, farm machinery, vaccines, and livestock feed production. The organization has also established a National Agricultural Information System and audio-visual communication facility to pass on research results to farmers. PARC has also been actively involved in training and education. The Pakistan Agricultural Services Academy (PASA) has trained 6,000 students under its various training programmes related to agricultural development. Under its manpower development programme, PARC has funded the training of 400 PhDs and 170 MScs in national and international universities on subjects related to agriculture. Recently, in collaboration with the University of Arid Agriculture, Rawalpindi PARC has initiated joint postgraduate degree programmes with an emphasis on PhD-level training.

PARC has had many successes, but it has not all been plain sailing. Apart from the obvious dearth of research funding for important projects, one of the major areas where PARC has failed to make inroads is that of agriculture extension services. With a few exceptions, disease-free varieties of crops developed in the laboratory have failed to find their way into the farmer's warehouse. External observers suggest that

PARC has not been able to develop adequate channels of communication between scientists and the agricultural community.

YU.V. GANKOVSKY

Pakistan and the Sovereign States of Central Asia

The relations of friendship and co-operation with these states has become an important priority in Pakistan's foreign policy. These relations are perceived to be a source of prosperity and security. Pakistan recognized the independence of all the republics of Central Asia (Kazakhstan, Kirghizstan, Tajikistan, Turkmenistan, and Uzbekistan) in the middle of December 1991. The independence of Azerbaijan, which became a member of the *Organization of Islamic Conference, was recognized earlier. Even before the official recognition of their sovereignty, Pakistan took steps to establish contact with them. In the autumn of 1991 Prime Minister Nawaz *Sharif invited the republics' highest leaders to visit Pakistan. The invitations were accepted.

In 1991 a trade delegation headed by the then Minister for Economic Affairs visited all the republics of Central Asia. A number of initiatives were discussed, some involving co-operation on a trilateral basis. Pakistan expressed an interest in the use of commercial and energy resources. A permanent working group was set up in Kazakhstan for the promotion of trade. Discussions were held with Uzbekistan regarding air and land transport links. Agreements were reached with Turkmenistan regarding the purchase of gas and possible construction of a gas supply pipeline across Iran or Afghanistan. A declarations was signed with Kirghizstan regarding economic and cultural links. Among the subjects discussed with all the Central Asian Republics was the possibility of using Pakitan's communications network, including Karachi port, for transit trade. In 1992 further detail regarding the principles of co-operation in the fields of economy, trade, science and technology, culture, sports and tourism were set out between Pakistan and Kazakhstan. In the same year the joint Pakistan-Uzbek Air Asia airline was set up. Relations with the Cental Asian Republics cooled considerably when, in May 1997, Pakistan officially recognized the Taliban regime in Afghanistan.

With the reports of a Russo-Indian threat to move against militants in Afghanistan the states of Turkmenistan, Uzbekistan and Tajikistan, all having borders with Afghanistan, became alarmed and relations with Pakistan softened.

Even the war against terror in Afghanistan in the aftermath of 9/11, the reversal of Pakistan's policy towards the Taliban, and the dismantling of the Taliban regime did not make a material difference in Central Asia-Pakistan relations. Terrorist pockets have not been obliterated and the suspicion that they find refuge in the Pakistan border area remains a determining factor. Pakistan's strategic location and its warm water ports are also of importance.

Within this framework, due to the membership of some Central Asian States of the ECO Further developments have taken place. In 1996 five Central Asian States signed pacts reducing their armed forces along what used to be the Sino-Soviet border. In the same year, the Shanghai Co-operation Organization (SCO) was set up, consisting of China, Russia, Kazakhastan, Kirgizstan, Tajikistan and Uzbekistan. The May 1998 Nuclear blasts, first by India and then by Pakistan, caused the Foreign Minister of Russia and the presidents of China, Kazakhastan, Kirghistan and Tajikistan to collectively voice their concern. Another neighour which had distanced itself from Pakistan was Iran, and keeping their concerns in mind, Pakistan started scaling down its pro-Taliban policy. On 25 January 2001 Pakistan signed an Extradition Accord with Uzbekistan. On 30 May 2002 Pakistan and Turkeministan signed a pact to supply gas from Daulatabad field to Gwadar port. On June 2002 a Sixteen nation Conference on Interaction and Confidence-building signed an accord against terrorists and seccessionists at Almaty, Kazakhastan. On 20 June 2002 President Pervez *Musharraf signed agreements on economic co-operation with Tajikistan President, Emomali Rakhmonov, at Dushanbe. Big power rivalry resurfaced when the United States set up military bases at Manas in Kirghistan, and Khanabad in Uzbekistan, in 2001 initially with Russian support. Russia opened an airbase at Kant, thirty-five miles from the US base on 25 October 2003. The Russian Defence Minister Sergei Ivanov publicly demanded that the United States pull out from its Central Asia bases within two years. This was prompted by interest shown by the United States in Caspian oil. This afforded Pakistan a rare opportunity to modify its policies. Russian-American attitude against Islamic militants would have the potential of severely constricting Pakistan's options. On 23 September 2003 at Beijing, China joined Russia and the four Central Asian States; in a resolution to set up a base in Uzbekistan.

R.M. MUKIMJANOVA

Pakistan Association for the Advancement of Science (PAAS)

This was established in 1947, at the University of Punjab in Lahore, to promote theoretical and applied research in the natural sciences. The Association has more than 1,500 members and publishes the *Pakistan Journal of Science* and the *Pakistan Journal of Scientific Research*. It is financed by the government of Pakistan. PAAS has, since the inception of Pakistan, aimed at popularising science through meetings to discuss topics of national importance and to stimulate public interest in science. The PAAS has, since 1949 regularly organized the All Pakistan Annual Conferences. Each year scientists from all over the country participate in these conferences where problems of national interest are discussed. These include such topics as Food Technology and Nutrition, Land Utilization, Post-graduate Medical Education and Research, Pollution and Environment, Popularization of Science Energy and Economic Development of Pakistan, and Science Policy and Planning in Pakistan. In addition to these, PAAS also publishes monographs on specialized topics such as a study of the economics of land and water use in land reclamation.

YU.V. GANKOVSKY

Pakistan Association of Scientists and Scientific Professionals (PASSP)

The objectives of PASSP are to promote and safeguard the legitimate interests of its members, and to further the application of science and technology for the socio-economic uplift of the nation. It was the first NGO to organize science fairs on a regular basis and award prizes for the best inventions and exhibits.

T. NAIM

Pakistan Atomic Energy Commission (PAEC)

The Commission was established in 1946 to co-ordinate nuclear research. There were initially two reactors in Pakistan, one for research purposes at Chashma, near Rawalpindi and one for energy located at Kanupp, near Karachi. A further plant was built at Chashma, with Chinese assistance, and was connected to the grid in June 2000. The Kanupp plant was closed for refurbishment in December 2002, after a 30-year design life. Nuclear power represents about 2.6% of total electric power production in Pakistan. The Pakistan Atomic Energy Commission is also in important and often underestimated source of agricultural research. PAEC operates three agricultural research centers, at Tanjodam, at Faisalabad and at Peshawar. The Nuclear Institute for Agriculture and Biology at Faislabad has been the discovery of a new variety of cotton, NIAB-78, which helped to produce a sequence of bumper crops increasing cotton production from 2.1 million bales per annum in the 1970s to 10 million bales in 1995. The Atomic Energy Agricultural Research Centre at Tandojam developed a high yield improved fibre variety 'Chandi-95'. They have also developed new varieties of wheat, a staple food crop in Pakistan.

BIBLIOGRAPHY: *A. Ali, 'Pakistan's Nuclear Dilemma', Karachi, 1984.*

V.A. POGADAEV

Pakistan Central Cotton Committee

With cotton the backbone of Pakistan's economy, Pakistan quickly established a cotton policy-making body under an Act of Parliament in 1949. This authority was named the Pakistan Central Cotton Committee (PCCC). In addition to policy co-ordination, the Committee also manages a number of research institutes, including the Institute of Cotton Research and Technology, Karachi, and the Cotton Research Institutes at Multan and Sakrand. The Multan Institute is internationally known for its innovation in developing new varieties of cotton through genetic engineering.

YU.V. GANKOVSKY

Pakistan Central Federation of Trade Unions (PCFTU)

Organized in 1970, The Federation was originally active only in Karachi. In the 1980s it extended its influence to the working class movement. In 1989 it linked fifty-four trade unions with a collective membership of 36,000 textile and public utilities workers.

D.B. NOVOSELOV

Pakistan Council for Scientific and Industrial Research (PCSIR)

The Pakistan Council for Scientific and Industrial Research is the premier research and development (R&D) organization for scientific and industrial research, and has been involved in multi-disciplinary activities for nearly half a century. The organization was created in 1949, two years after independence, as the Department of Scientific and Industrial Research attached to the Ministry of Industry. PCSIR was reconstituted as an autonomous Council in 1953. After the Ministry of Science and Technology was created in 1972, PCSIR was placed under its administrative control. The main function of the Council is to undertake efforts directed towards the utilization of indigenous resources for industrial development and import substitution leading to self-reliance. PCSIR has established multi-disciplinary laboratories in various parts of the country. Since 1953 PCSIR scientists have developed 648 processes, registered 299 patents, and published over 2,500 papers in the fields of minerals, glass and ceramics, pharmaceuticals, electronics and instrumentation, agro-technology, food technology, industrial and fine chemicals, leather, fuel, oils, and fats. PCSIR now has the capability of setting up various small- and medium-scale units for production. However the organization has had limited success in its role of transferring research methods and processes to industry. So far only 250 processes have been leased out to various private and public sector organizations, with an annual turnover of Rs150 million.

In order to bridge the gap between national R&D organizations and end users of research in industry, health, education, and agriculture, the government established the Scientific and Technological Development Corporation of Pakistan (STEDEC) in 1987. A board of directors, half of whom are from the private sector, manages this. The objective of STEDEC is to introduce and commercialize the processes and products developed by PCSIR.

Most of the industry in Pakistan operates through small production units, which, on the whole, tend to require little research and development. Large private and public sector industries are structured for production and use imported technology. Innovation tends to be tailored to adapting imported machinery to local conditions. According to a recent report by the World Bank, Pakistan's larger enterprises are aware of the capacity of PCSIR, but, for a variety of reasons, are reluctant to become involved in contract research partnerships or to pay commercial rates for the services of PCSIR.

Seven PCSIR laboratories are currently located in Karachi, Lahore, Peshawar, Hyderabad, and Quetta. Their activities include work on industrial chemicals, pharmaceuticals, leather technology, coal preparation and carbonization, food technology, minerals and metallurgy, glass and ceramics, water purification, drugs, rural technologies, solar energy plants, fruits, and marine food. Other major organizations involved in research and development in industry-related fields are the Cement Industry Research Centre, the Metal Industry Research and Development Centre, the Scrap Monitoring Centre, and the Preventive Maintenance Centre, all of which are in Lahore. In Karachi there are r&d centres in the textiles industry, plastic technology, synthetic fibre, and the steel industry.

YU.V. GANKOVSKY

Pakistan Department of the Institute of Oriental Studies of the USSR Academy of Sciences (Moscow)

The Department was established in 1956 to unite specialists on Pakistan. The department was headed by Professor L.R. Polonskaya (1956-59); Professor A.M. Dyakov, Professor Yu.V. Gankovsky (1964-78), and Professor V.N. Moskalenko. The department is engaged in the complex studies of Pakistan, its society, history, social and economic problems, evolution of the state, its administrative and political structure, domestic and foreign policy, sociology, ideology, religion and other subjects. It maintains contacts with similar centres abroad engaged in Pakistan studies and participates in joint publications, symposiums and seminars.

BIBLIOGRAPHY: *Imroz, Lahore, 30 July 1972; 28 December 1975; Pakistan Times, Lahore, 24 September 1966; 2 December 1969; 1 October 1972; 1 August 1975; 15 December 1978; Dawn, Karachi, 11 August 1975; Daily News, Karachi, 30 September 1974; Viewpoint, Vol. 4, Nos. 41, 42; Lahore, 20, 27 May 1979; Trade and Industry, Vol. 20, No. 6, Karachi, 6, 1976; Far Eastern Economic Review, Vol. 46, No. 12, Hong Kong, 17 December 1964; International Studies, Vol. 19, No. 1, New Delhi, 1980; Economic and Political Weekly, New Delhi, 13 February 1982; Central Asian Review, Vol. 8, No. 2, London, 1960; Vol. 11, No. 1, 1963; Vol. 15, Nos. 2, 4, 1967; Journal of Asian Studies, Vol. 26, No. 2, Ann Arbor, 1967; Vol. 32, No. 2, 1973.*

V.N. MOSKALENKO

Pakistan's Federal Shariat Court

Established in May 1980, the court consists of a Chief Justice, four members with the status of judges of the higher courts, (see Judicial system of Pakistan), and three ulema. Justices are appointed by the country's

President for a term of three years. The Court hears criminal cases for which traditional Islamic punishments are required Such criminal cases involve theft, unlawful sexual intercourse, false imputation, and consumption of alcohol. The Court also decides whether laws in force or legislation being adopted correspond to the principles of Islam. Through the government, the decisions of the Federal Shariat Court are introduced in parliament in order to facilitate the necessary changes in existing laws or bills within the period stipulated in the decisions. From 1982 to 1991 the Federal Shariat Court studied 1,511 laws that were in force in Pakistan. 267 were described as totally or partially contradicting Islam.

YU. V. GANKOVSKY

Pakistan Herald Publications Ltd.

A newspaper and publishing amalgamation that belongs to the Haroon family. It publishes the newspaper *Dawn* (in English), the evening newspaper *Star* (in English) and the monthly journal *Herald* (in English). *Watan* (in Gujarati), and *Dawn Overseas Weekly*. *It also used to publish + which have ceased publication now. They are published mainly from Karachi, and since 1986 Dawn has also been published in Lahore.

V.A. LAVROV

Pakistan Historical Society

It was established in 1951 with the aim of studying the history of countries and nations of South Asia and Islam. The Society maintains a specialized library and publishes a quarterly journal.

BIBLIOGRAPHY: *'A History of the Freedom Movement', Vols. 1-4, Karachi, 1957-70; S. Moinul Haq, 'The Great Revolution of 1857', and others.*

YU.V. GANKOVSKY

Pakistan in the United Nations Organization

Pakistan became a member of the United Nations on 30 September 1947, after the Security Council acceded to its request for United Nations membership on 18 August 1947. From 1947-57 Pakistan held permanent or temporary membership in thirty committees, commissions, and other United Nations organs. Its active role in the United Nations was one of the most important aspects of Pakistan's foreign policy. In the late 1940s and early 1950s Pakistan actively supported the movement for the liquidation of colonialism, especially the national liberation struggle of the peoples of North Africa and Indonesia. This was a form of assertion of its independent role in the international arena. It also increased links with the recently established states of Asia and Africa, and consolidated its position in international politics.

Pakistan was one of the authors of the declaration on granting independence to colonial countries and peoples, adopted by the 15th session of the UN General Assembly. Subsequently, Pakistan was active in the implementation of that declaration, condemning the apartheid regime in South Africa and supporting, by political and diplomatic means, the struggle for self-determination and independence of the peoples of Zimbabwe and Nambia. Pakistan took an active part in working toward settling the situation in the Middle East. Since the 1940s Pakistan has called for the withdrawal of Israeli troops from the occupied Arab territories and for the restoration of the former status of Jerusalem. It recognized the Palestine Liberation Organization as the only representative of the Arab people of Palestine, who had the right to establish an independent state. Pakistan's policy in the United Nations was to participate, along with other newly independent countries, in the solution of urgent international problems. This included the strengthening of peace and security, the relaxation of international tension, and the democratization of international economic links. In the 1970s and 1980s Pakistan also took active part in the economic decisions made by the United Nations.

Pakistan has consistently supported the People's Republic of China's claim to representation in UN bodies, especially the Security Council. Pakistani envoys such as A.S. Bokhari, who became undersecretary-general for information, Prince Aly Khan, and Ambassador Iqbal Akhund became prominent figures in the UN headquarters. After India took the *Kashmir issue to the UN in 1948, Pakistan has been able to secure favourable resolutions on the Kashmir dispute. Pakistan is opposed to India acquiring a permanent seat in the security council until and unless the Kashmir dispute is resolved according to UN resolutions. Relations with the UN were strained after military takeover of 12 October 1999. On 14 October UN Secretary General Kofi Annan called for Pakistan to return to civilian rule. On 10 March 2001 Kofi Annan visited Pakistan to discuss both its conflicts with India and with Afghanistan. On 26 September 2001 Pakistan rejected the request of the UN to reopen its borders with

Afghanistan. On 10 November 2001 President Pervez *Musharraf visited the UNHQ in the wake of the 9/11 tragedy. After 13 December 2001, when Indo-Pakistan relations deteriorated, the UN was involved in peace-keeping moves. The initial reaction of Kofi Annan was to blame the crisis on Pakistan. On 7 February 2002 he visited Islamabad, as part of a tour of South Asia to promote peace. On 23 May 2002, Pakistan officially asked for UN intervention to restrain India. Munir Akram, Pakistan's Permanent Representative, opposed the US attack on Iraq, saying that it would give India an opportunity to attack Pakistan. Two days later President Pervez Musharraf addressed the UNGA and urged the international community to help restore peace and normalcy in South Asia. On 27 September 2002 Pakistan was elected as a member of the security council for a two year term beginning 1 January 2003. When, on 17 December 2003, President Musharraf said he was willing to set aside UNSC resolutions on Kashmir, the possibility for a solution to the Kashmir problem improved.

BIBLIOGRAPHY: *K. Sarwar Hasan, 'Pakistan and the United Nations', New York, 1960.*

I.V. KHALEVINSKY

Pakistan Institute of Development Economics

It was founded in 1956, and until 1972 it was located in Karachi. It is now located in Islamabad. The Institute has a vast specialized library and a collection of theses on the economics of Pakistan. Since 1961 it has been publishing the quarterly *Pakistan Development Review*

YU. V. GANKOVSKY

Pakistan Institute of International Affairs

Established in 1947 in Karachi to study Pakistan's international relations and foreign policy and the problems of world economy and international law. The Institute maintains a library, releases its own publications, including the *Pakistan Horizon Journal*, and organizes lectures.

YU.V. GANKOVSKY

Pakistan Medical Research Council

In 1962 the Pakistan Medical Research Council (PMRC) was created on the recommendation of the Medical Reform Commission. It is an autonomous organization attached to the Ministry of Health. In 1972 it was transferred to the administrative control of the Ministry of Science and Technology. In 1996 it was again transferred back to the Ministry of Health. In 1985 the Council was reorganized and made more autonomous to enhance its effectiveness. PMRC operates nineteen research centres in hospitals, which are affiliated to medical colleges. Under the guidance and support of the World Health Organization (WHO), the PMRC together with the Council for Health Research for Development, Geneva, (COHRED) are working towards establishing effective linkages between health policy-makers, health-care providers, and health researchers. PMRC has also established national health research structures, which include representatives of the government, leading NGOs, and international donor agencies working in health-related fields. At the provincial level PMRC has also established provincial co-ordinating bodies. The structures are meant to arrange, co-ordinate, supervise, and utilize the research results at their respective levels.

Besides the PMRC, the *Pakistan Atomic Energy Commission (PAEC) has established research centres in the field of nuclear medicine. Ten centres exist and are affiliated with major teaching/research hospitals. Their two centres, Nuclear Medicine Oncology nad Radiotheragy Institute NORI, Islamabad, and Institute of Nuclear Medicine and Ocology INMOL, Lahore, are particularly known for their services in radiotherapy for treating cancer. Collectively these centres treat over 250,000 patients per year. The PAEC has established a centralized national facility at Pakistan Institute of Nuclear Science and Technology (PINSTECH) (see image) for the production of high-quality radio pharmaceutical kits, which are used by the medical centres of PAEC. At INMOL a highly successful programme for the local production of RIA kits for thyroid-related hormones from imported bulk reagents has resulted in a ten-fold reduction in the cost of the kit. The *Pakistan Council for Scientific and Industrial Research also carries out research into medicinal plants. The Sheikh Zayed Medical Institute and Postgraduate Medical Institute, both in Lahore, are also involved in medical research. In order to improve their operation, the Cabinet Committee, which, recommended the merger of these two institutes in 1992.

Set up with assistance from the United States, the National Institute of Malaria Research and Training made an extremely good start. Malaria was virtually eradicated from many parts of the country by the large-scale use of the chemical DDT. However, some years later, the malaria carrying mosquito developed resistance to this chemical and the disease has returned. In the meantime, the National Institute of Malaria Research and Training, which suffered funding cuts when US aid stopped, is unable to carry out its role.

The National Institute of Reproductive Physiology is one of Pakistan's major family planning research organizations. The National Institute of Health (NIH) was established in 1960 to promote research into immunization and drug development. Its main areas of research and activities include the production and quality control of vaccine and sera, quality control of drugs, research into indigenous systems of medicine, nutritional research, and research into communicable diseases, as well as an expanded programme of immunization. The NIH has developed the capability of manufacturing most vaccines locally. Its expanded immunization programmes have covered almost 70 per cent of the population.

A.V. ZABOLOTSKY

Pakistan Muslim League (PML)

A political party that was founded in August 1947 by uniting the provincial organizations of the *All-India Muslim League. From August 1947 to September 1956 it was the ruling party in coalition with the United Front from August 1955 to September 1956). It also ruled briefly from October to December 1957as a part of I.I. *Chundrigar's coalition government. From September 1962 to March 1969, during the Ayub *Khan government, it was the ruling Party, although popularly referred to as the 'Conventionist Muslim League'. During the latter part of the Ziaul *Haq rule, in the period 1985-88, it was again the ruling Party of the Mohammed Khan *Junejo government. As the dominant component of the *Islamic Democratic Alliance, or IDA it won the elections of 1990 and formed the government under the Prime Ministership of Nawaz *Sharif. Defeated in 1993, the Party was again re-elected with a massive majority in 1995, when Nawaz Sharif again became Prime Minister.

The League has generally expressed and defended the interests of the upper strata of Pakistan's society. The struggle for power among PML leaders from various territorial and ethnic subdivisions has repeatedly led to numerous splits within the Party. In 1949 a group split away from the PML to form the *Awami Muslim League (see Awami League). In October 1962 the opposition *Muslim League (Council Muslim League) was formed which opposed President M. Ayub Khan's regime. In the first general election of 1970 the PML suffered a massive defeat, winning only two seats in the National Assembly and eight in the Provincial Assemblies of the *Punjab and the NWFP. From 1972 to 1977 a Muslim League faction headed by Abdul Qaiyum *Khan supported the government of Z.A. *Bhutto. Through the years, there have been numerous other factions at different times, of varying size and significance, usually revolving around specific personalities.

At the time of writing, the Pakistan Muslim League is the dominant Party in the governing coalition supporting the regime of General Pervez *Musharraf. This is the faction headed by Chaudhri Shujaat *Hussain. However, one of the principal opposition parties to the present regime is the Pakistan Muslim League faction headed by Nawaz Sharif.

BIBLIOGRAPHY: *Yuri Gankovsky, L.R. Gordon-Polonskaya, 'A History of Pakistan', Lahore, 1972; V.N. Moskalenko, 'Problems of Modern Pakistan', Moscow, 1970 (in Russian); R.I. Sherkovina, 'Political Parties and Political Struggle in Pakistan', Moscow, 1983 (in Russian); A.B. Rajput, 'Muslim League Yesterday and Today', Lahore, 1948; K. Gallard, 'Pakistan. A Political Study', London, 1957.*

YU.V. GANKOVSKY

Pakistan National Alliance (PNA)

Founded in January 1977 in the run-up to the general elections, by the opposition parties of the United Democratic Front. The Alliance was also joined by the *Tehrik-i-Istiqlal* and the National Democratic Party. It fielded a single list of candidates. PNA's election manifesto accused Z.A. *Bhutto's government of violating the constitution and civil rights, and of departure from Islamic principles. It called for asserting an Islamic social order in the country, banning family planning, introducing a system of Islamic taxes, and favourable conditions for private capital investments. It spearheaded the agitations of 1977 against the *Pakistan People's Party, which led to the seizure of power by General Ziaul *Haq.

O.V. PLESHOV

Pakistan National Congress (PNC)

The members of the Pakistan *Constituent Assembly and the East Bengal Provincial Assembly who had belonged to the Indian National Congress renamed themselves Pakistan National Congress. It functioned as the official opposition in the Constituent Assembly. Its aims and objectives were the establishment of a democratic socialist republic in Pakistan. It promoted handloom spinning. The leader of the Pakistan National Congress was S.C. Chattopadyaya. The PNC opposed the Objectives Resolution of 1949, the Islamic provisions of the Basic Principles Committee Report of 1953, and the Islamic clauses of the Constitution Bill of 1956, against which they staged a walkout. The well-knit pre-partition organization survived. They won twenty-four seats in the East Pakistan legislative assembly in alliance with the United Front in the 1954 provincial elections, but left the United Front soon after. In the National Assembly, Pakistan National Congress joined the Treasury benches under Feroz Khan *Noon. After the 1958 military coup they did not re-group.

M.R. KAZIMI

Pakistan National Federation of Trade Unions (PNFTU)

Founded in 1962, the Federation united some 250,000 workers in 218 trada unions (1989 data) of Karachi, Hyderabad, Lahore. The Federation is a member of the International Confederation of Free Trade Unions, actively co-operating with its Asian division in Singapore.

M.YU. MOROZOVA

Pakistan National Labour Federation (PNLF)

Founded in 1968, the Federation unites 197 trade unions with 100,000 members (1989 data) of workers and employees of textile factories, machine-building plants, public utilities enterprises of Karachi, Lahore, Rawalpindi, Hyderabad, Multan and Faisalabad. Until the late 1980s the Federation played a leading role in the trads unions of the major state-run industrial enterprises such as Karachi Port, Electric Supply Corporations in Karachi and Lahore, *Pakistan Steel Mill, and others. In the early 1990s the position of the Federation in Karachi weakened. The Federation works in close contact with the *Pakistan National Federation of Trade Unions. The Federation is a member of the International Confederation of Free Trade Unions.

D.B. NOVOSELOV

Pakistan Peoples Party (PPP)

Founded in 1967 by Z.A. *Bhutto, the party's 1970 election manifesto, regarded as its programme, defined its political line in terms of three slogans: 'Islam is our faith; Democracy is our policy; Socialism is our economy.' The manifesto proclaimed its objective of building a classless society in Pakistan based on social justice. It proposed to liquidate monopolies, to nationalise the principal branches of industry, banks, insurance companies, and transport, to do away with feudal survivals in agrarian relations, to develop the co-operative movement in rural areas, and to improve the living and working conditions of the working class. In foreign policy, the emphasis was on extending relations with Muslim countries and condemning military blocs.

PPP's victory at the 1970 general elections in which the party won eighty-one out of 138 seats in the National Assembly, brought it to power in December 1971, following the fall of General A.M. Yahya *Khan's military regime. During the period in which it was in power, December 1971–June 1977, the Party implemented a series of socio-economic reforms envisaged in the Party documents. But many of the measures were in the nature of compromises and did not bring the expected results. These halfway measures included the land reforms and the new policy in labour relations, supposed to lighten the working people's economic hardships. Between 1972 and 1975 many leading figures of the Party left it, including J.A. Rahim and M.A. Kasuri, two of the founders.

The PPP won a controversial majority at the 1977 general elections, both in the National Assembly and in the provincial legislative assemblies. However, the military *coup* of General Ziaul *Haq on 5 July 1977 removed it from power. This marked the beginning of eleven years in opposition for the PPP. In 1979 Z.A. Bhutto was executed, after being accused of complicity in a political assassination. In 1981 the PPP formed a coalition with other opposition parties—the *Movement for Restoration of Democracy—but its participation in this movement, especially in the years before the 1988 election, was only nominal.The resumption of the democratic process after Ziaul Haq's death in the summer of 1988 opened up the prospect of the PPP returning to power. Although several groups broke away from it, the PPP won a relative majority in the National Assembly in the November 1988 general elections. Supported by the *Muhajir National Movement and some independent deputies, it formed a government headed by Benazir *Bhutto.

The PPP election platform, which was in effect its new programme, did not include any radical slogans or the word socialism. The wording of the programme was more moderate. The party promised the voters worker participation in production, management, and the setting up of a special fund to achieve the objective; reorganization of trade unions; extension of labour legislation to cover hired labour in agriculture; encouragement of businessmen to create new workplaces; encouragement of internal capital accumulation; a more rational procedure for exemption from taxes; implementation of land reforms proposed in the 1970s; allocation of 4.5 per cent of GNP for education and introduction of universal secondary education; a rise in electric power production to 40,000 MW; and the construction of 500,000 houses for the homeless per year. PPP leaders declared that they aimed at a Western-type social democracy.

On 6 August 1990 President Ghulam Ishaq *Khan issued a decree to dissolve parliament and remove the PPP government led by Benazir Bhutto from power. Ms Bhutto returned to power again in the elections of 1993, to be again ousted by the President, this time the Party's own nominee Farouq Ahmed Khan *Leghari. During the elections of 2002 the Pakistan People's Party secured a large number of votes and is the single largest Party in the opposition to the regime of General Pervez *Musharraf.

O.V. PLESHOV

Pakistan Press International (PPI)

A news agency that split from the *Associated Press of Pakistan in 1957 and for ten years was called the Pakistan Press Association (PPA). It is a private joint-stock company with headquarters in Karachi and with a network of offices in all major Pakistani cities. The agency co-operates with similar agencies abroad.

V.A. LAVROV

Pakistan Press

The press in Pakistan consisted of several provincial and local newspapers, *Pakistan Times, *Jang, *Dawn,* and *Nawa-i-Waqt* (started in 1945). The *Civil and Military Gazette* (Karachi, publication was discontinued in 1953, in Lahore in 1963), *Sindh Observer* (discontinued in 1952), *Times of Karachi* (1953-61), and *Pakistan Standard*, an official organ of the *Muslim League (published in 1955), were all instrumental in shaping published writing in Pakistan. There were 1,442 periodicals in Pakistan in the early 1990s, 1,097 of which appeared in *Urdu. The polls testify that 97 per cent of those who can read and write, read in Urdu. Two hundred and sixty-six periodicals appear in English. Eighty-nine newspapers and magazines are published in local languages: sixty-seven in *Sindhi, seven in *Pashto, seven in *Gujarati, two in *Punjabi, three in *Balochi, one in *Brahui, and two in *Siraiki. All of the local languages are served by literary and educational weeklies with circulations of 50,000 to 300,000.

Lahore and Karachi are two major publishing centres. The largest nationwide newspapers are: in English—*Dawn* (Karachi, Lahore), *Times* (Lahore, Rawalpindi), **Muslim* (Islamabad), *The Nation* (Lahore), *Business Recorder*, *Daily Times* (Lahore and Karachi) and *Mag* (weekly, Karachi); in Urdu—*Jang* (Karachi, Lahore, Rawalpindi, Quetta), *Nawa-i-Waqt* (Lahore, Karachi, Peshawar, Quetta), *Akhbar-i-Jahan* (Karachi), **Imroz* (Lahore and Multan); in Sindhi—*Hilal-i-Pakistan* (Karachi), *Mehran* (Karachi); and in Gujarati—*Dawn* and *Millat* (both in Karachi). The most important regional publications are: in English *The Frontier Post* (Peshawar), in Urdu *Amn* (Karachi), *Maghribi Pakistan* (Multan, Faisalabad, Lahore, Bahawalpur), and *Hyder* (Rawalpindi).

Normally newspapers and magazines are privately owned by individuals or groups. Pakistan has several newspaper and publishing associations: The *National Press Trust, *Pakistan Herald Publications Ltd., the Jang Group, Nawa-i-Waqt Ltd., and others, and two news agencies (see Associated Press of Pakistan and Pakistan Press International). In the publishing industry, the All-Pakistan Newspapers Society unites owners and publishers and is concerned mainly with their commercial interests. Editors and staff members of periodicals and press agencies are members of the Council of Pakistan Newspaper Editors. Others engaged in journalism and publishing are entitled to join the Pakistan Federal Union of Journalists. There are independent journalists unions in Karachi, Lahore, Rawalpindi, Peshawar, Quetta, Multan, and Hyderabad. These press clubs are run by elected bodies. Article 19 of the Pakistan *Constitution of 1973 proclaims freedom of the press that can, however, be contained within 'reasonable restrictions' by special laws protecting 'the glory of Islam', Pakistan's integrity, security, and defence. The constitution refers the press and publishing to the competence of the provincial organs of power. The decrees of 11 September 1963 and 29 November 1964 regulate the relationships of the authorities and the press.

As a result of lengthy discussions between the authorities and journalists in 1963-64 the Press Code of Ethics was adopted in July 1964 by the Council of

Newspaper Editors of Pakistan. In March 1980 the Council and the Ministry of Information and Broadcasting reached an agreement on a new Code of Ethics for journalists. It warns journalists against using their profession in anti-social and anti-state aims and also against taking money from foreign states. Journalists have the right not to disclose sources of information. The Court of Honour is entrusted with controlling how the Code is observed. The Court's Chairman is appointed from among retired members of Pakistan's High Court while its six members are elected by the journalists from among editors of newspapers and magazines.

In April 1986 the government approved a new system of wages and salaries in the press. According to its direction, all organs and agencies were divided into two main categories: 1. the newspapers published in Karachi, Lahore, and Rawalpindi with circulation of no less than 10,000 or an annual income of Rs 2.5 million, and press agencies with an annual income of no less than Rs 2 million, 2. regional newspapers published in Hyderabad, Multan, Faisalabad, Peshawar, and Quetta, and all others. Salaries and bonuses depend on the periodical's category. Journalists employed by newspapers of the first category receive the highest wages. All journalists and other people employed by the press are divided into nine categories depending on their position, skills, and work record. Degree course in journalism are run by the Punjab, Karachi, Sindh, and Gomal universities although the majority of Pakistani journalists have no special training.

V. A. LAVROV

Pakistan Progressive Writers' Association

(PPWA, *Anjuman-i-Taraqqipasand Musanifin-i-Pakistan*) A literary organization uniting socialist and democratic-minded writers and poets. It was established in 1949 at the Lahore conference as an offshoot of the All-India Progressive Writers' Association. The General Secretary was Ahmad Nadim *Qasmi, who was reelected in 1952. The ideological and aesthetic platform of the PPWA was formulated in the manifesto adopted at the first conference of the PPWA. It includes the aim of giving a truthful portrayal of the country's changing reality, all around promotion of socialist world views, and the preservation of the cultural heritage. Progressive writers set themselves the aim of bringing literature closer to the people. The manifesto also contained some sectarian propositions, a characteristic of the left-wing writers. At the second conference in Karachi in 1952 these were deleted. A special resolution was adopted, proclaiming PPWA a non-political organization. However, in 1954 PPWA was banned. There were attempts to restore PPWA under different names, such as Association of Free-Thinking Authors (*Azad Khayal Musanifin*), but they were unsuccessful. Despite the absence of a leading centre, the local branches of the PPWA continued to function, often under different names. They followed the socialist and democratic principles formulated at the PPWA conferences. From February 1973 regular PPWA conferences were resumed. However in 1977 the martial law put an end to them. The *Sindhi branches of the PPWA–*Sindhi Adabi Sangat* (Sindhi Literary Union) and *Awami Adabi Anjuman* (People's Literary Association) were Particularly active. In March 1986 a conference was held in Karachi dedicated to the fiftieth anniversary of the progressive writers' movement of India and Pakistan. The conference confirmed the writers' adherence to the ideals of the movement. The work of the conference enjoyed wide press coverage. However, no decision was made on resuming its activities or electing governing bodies. The ideas of the progressive writers' movement were supported by the World Conference of Punjabi Writers held in Lahore in April 1986. About three hundred *Punjabi authors, residents of Pakistan and other countries (except India), took part. PPWA united most of the Pakistani authors, published it own periodicals, and had an enormous influence on the literary life of the country.

BIBLIOGRAPHY: *R.A. Elizarova, A.S. Sukhochev, 'Pakistan's Progressive Writers', Tashkent, 1978 (in Russian); 'Taraqqipasand Adab—Dastawizat' (Progressive Literature-Documents), Karachi, 1986; 'Taraqqipasand Adab Pachas Sala Safar' (Progressive Literature. A 50-Year Journey), (ed.) S. Ashur Kazmi and Qamar Rais, London, 1987; Mazhar Jamil, 'Guftgu' (Conversation), Karachi, 1986.*

A.S. SUKHOCHEV

Pakistan Scientific and Technological Information Centre (PASTIC)

It was founded in Islamabad in 1956 and reorganized in 1974. It operates under the Pakistan Science Foundation with branches in Karachi, Lahore, Peshawar, and Quetta. PASTIC has a special library of abstracts and publishes six periodicals and information publications.

YU.V. GANKOVSKY

Pakistan Steel Mill, Karachi.

Pakistan Steel Mill

Among the other major engineering research projects is the production of steel by Pakistan Steel Mill, Karachi. Since its establishment the production of steel has increased to 1.1 million tons. Pakistan Steel produces iron, pig iron, billets, hot rolled coils/sheets, formed sections such as channel angles, and galvanized sheets. Since the demand for iron and steel products in Pakistan is growing at an average rate of 7 per cent per annum, Pakistan Steel plans to cope with the expand the existing capacity to 3 million tons. Other major R&D organizations working in this field are: Metal Industry Research and Development Centre, Heavy Mechanical Complex and Heavy Industries at Taxila, Heavy Electrical Complex at Hattar, Karachi Shipyard and Engineering Works, and Pakistan Machine Tool Factory, Karachi. Pakistan's surgical instrument industry, which contributes 60 per cent of engineering goods for export is, however, losing its competitive edge. The government, through the Ministry of Science and Technology and Commerce, is now helping the surgical instrument industry to achieve ISO-9000 standards. Pakistan's engineering capacity remains inadequate. However, because of a lack of encouragement to engineering industries, a shortage of highly skilled manpower, limited availability of design and engineering facilities, lack of modern technology, the relative absence of quality control, and preference of the private sector to import turnkey plants.

YU.V. GANKOVSKY

Pakistan Times

A Pakistan daily newspaper in English that was launched in 1946 in Lahore. In 1964 it was introduced in Rawalpindi. The newspaper has a circulation of 80,000. Its founder, Mian Iftikharuddin, was the opposition leader in Pakistan's First Constituent Assembly that determined the newspaper's orientation until October 1958. After the *coup* of 1958 Pakistan's military administration determined the paper's official orientation. Its editors-in-chief have included Faiz Ahmad *Faiz (until 1951), Mazhar Ali Khan, Z.A. Suleri, A.T. Choudhuri, and I.A Rahman.

SHAHNAWAZ

Pakistan Trade Union Federation

A trade union centre in Pakistan founded in 1947 on the initiative of Mirza Muhammad Ibrahim, a trade union leader. The Federation primarily unites trade unions of railwaymen and textile workers. In the mid 1970s, it had more than 200,000 members in 227 trade unions. It has divisions in Lahore, Karachi, Multan, Faisalabad, and Peshawar. It calls for bringing together trade unions of all orientations for a united trade union movement in Pakistan. The Federation's main division is the Trade Union of Railwaymen. It maintains links with the Socialist Party of Pakistan. The Federation is a member of the World Federation of Trade Unions.

BIBLIOGRAPHY: *T. Ruziev, 'A History of the Working Class in Pakistan', Moscow, 1980; 'Trade Unions of the World', (ed.) by F.J. Harper, Longman group, London, 1987.*

M.YU. MOROZOVA

Pakistan Workers' Federation (PWF)

Founded in 1966, it closely co-operates with the *United Workers Federation. The Federation comprised 106 trade unions of workers and employees of machine-building plants, textile factories, insurance companies, etc., and was active in Karachi, Hyderabad, Sukkur, Lahore, Gujranwala. For a long time the PWF was headed by Nabi Ahmad. The Federation is radical in orientation and it strives for the extending of trade union rights.

D.B. NOVOSELOV

Pakistan Writers' Guild

A professional organization of Pakistani writers founded in Karachi after Muhammad Ayub *Khan came to power. On 4 December 1958 a group of writers published an appeal to all authors to convene an All-Pakistan Writers' Organization. On 28-31 January 1959 the Conference adopted a manifesto and rules, and elected General Secretary Qudratullah Shahab, who held important posts in the Information Ministry and the President's Secretariat. President Ayub Khan made a speech at the opening session and donated Rupees 10,000. The leadership of the Pakistan Writers' Guild consisted of twenty-five authors, including Ghulam *Abbas, Qurratulain Hyder, Shaukat Siddiqi, Waqar Azim, Farigh Bukhari, Hajra *Masrur (*Urdu), Shaykh *Ayaz (*Sindhi); Ghulam Mustafa Tabassum (*Punjabi), Amir Hamza *Shinwari (*Pashto) and a group of Bengali writers. Regional executive committees were set up in Karachi, Lahore, Hyderabad, Peshawar, Multan, Rawalpindi and other cities. Many of them continued the work of the PPWA's local committees, banned in 1954. The conference appealed to the government to release all arrested writers, including the ex-members of PPWA. Including *Faiz Ahmad Faiz, Ahmad Nadim *Qasmi and others. The principles and aims of the Pakistan Writers' Guild, as formulated in the manifesto, determined its professional nature: to guarantee the freedom of speech and of the press, to protect the writers' rights and interests, to develop modern printing facilities, to organize co-operative publishing houses, protect copyright, and start a collective insurance system. The Pakistan Writers' Guild published the following literary journals: *Hamqalam* (Fellow-Writers), *Qalamkar* (Writer), both in Urdu, and *Literary Pakistan* in English (see English Literature). The Guild published works of Pakistani authors in English as well as overviews of the country's literary life. Copyright laws were worked out, and the decision was made to establish the *Pakistan Academy of Letters. In 1960 the annual Adamjee Prize was established. In 1962 annual prizes for literature in different Pakistani languages were established. The Writers' Guild was largely financed by the government and by private donations from industrialists and businessmen. Lack of political stability in the country, and the amorphous structure of the Writers' Guild gradually led to the dissolution of its various structures and eventually a complete shutdown.

N.V. GLEBOV

Palaeolithic

The early Stone Age or Palaeolithic period in Pakistan, which was influenced by the Palaeolithic peoples of central Asia and India. However, there is every reason to think that the Palaeolithic in Pakistan had specific features of its own. In 1983 members of the British Archaeological Mission discovered the site of Rawat, 12 km. to the southeast of Rawalpindi. The finds, associated with dense sandstone and cemented conglomerate, allowed R. Dennell to surmise that people first appeared in Pakistan some 2 million years ago. This speculation radically changes accepted ideas about the time people first came to Asia. A series of low hills were studied in the region of Pabbi Hills, to the south-west of *Jhelum. They are composed of alluvial deposits of the upper part Siwalik series. The age of these deposits was determined to be within the 2.0-1.2 million years range. A number of stone implements and production waste can be found on the deposits surface. Dennell believes that these are 1 million years old, or even older.

The finds belonging to the next age group came from the area of Din and Jalalpur. In both cases the artefacts, including three hand axes, were found in early conglomerates. Their age is determined as 500,000-400,000 years. These are the first Acheulian hand axes of Pakistan to be found in well-stratigraphed conditions. By analogy with neighbouring India, it is possible that the Acheulian culture survived in Pakistan up till the Upper Pleistocene (50,000 years). This explains why the age of hand axes found on the surface of river terraces and watersheds of the river *Soan on *Potwar Plateau can be different. Despite some serious doubts about the geological age of the finds from a boulder conglomerate from Potwar, one should mention large flakes of the so-called pre-Soan culture that are contemporary with the artefacts from Din and Jalalpur.

In the next period of the *Himalayan interglacial (400,000-300,000 years), there existed a pebble culture known as the ancient Soan culture, in parallel to the Acheulian culture.The Middle Palaeolithic, that corresponds to the Mousterian in Europe and Near East is represented by spectacular finds on the Potwar Plateau. There are reasons to believe that the Middle Palaeolithic of Pakistan coincided with the latter half of this period. The Middle Palaeolithic that is often called the Late Soan culture is mostly found on the Potwar Plateau on both sides of the Soan River from Rawat in the north to Kot Malarian in the south. Generally speaking, the Middle Palaeolithic i represented by an industry with implements on blade and flakes detached from pre-prepared cores. It is clo to the Mousterian culture but also includes develop pebble tools. Two lower levels of Sanghao near Mar also belong to the Middle Palaeolithic where diggi were undertaken by A.H. *Dani. The quartz implements from these levels partly resemble the Mousterian implements of the Near East and central Asia. At the same time they are similar to Newassa artefacts of India. The industry of the Late Soan and the lower levels of Sanghao belong to one and the same culture, that was a link between the central Asian seat of a Middle Palaeolithic culture and the Indian industries chronologically close to them.

So far, the Upper Palaeolithic has been inadequately studied. A site that yielded stone structures and a large amount of archaeological material belongs to its very beginning. It was found near Rawat and its age was determined as 45,000 years. It seems that the upper level in Sanghao belongs to a later period of the Upper Palaeolithic. The tools, while partly preserving old traditions, became noticeably smaller. New forms and microblades appeared which shows that the horizon existed for 20,000 years.

Periodization of the Stone Age in Pakistan shows that human traces can be found in all stages starting with a very early Lower Palaeolithic period and ending during the final stage of this period. However, the degree of our knowledge about the Palaeolithic in Pakistan and the geological substantiation of the site camps remain inadequate.

V.A. RANOV

Palejo, Rasul Bakhsh (1930–)

Political activist. A public and political figure of Pakistan and active participant in the *Sindhi movement, Palejo has been repeatedly arrested. In the 1980s Palejo was one of the organizers and leaders of Sindh Awami Tehrik (Sindhi Popular Movement). He served as General Secretary of the *Awami National Party.

YU.V. GANKOVSKY

[Pap]anek, Gustav F. (1929–)

[Econ]omist/Statesman. An economist, he was a research [associa]te in economics at Harvard University (USA), [adviser] to the Planning Commission, Pakistan (1954-58), [and serv]ed as a faculty member in the Department of [Economic]s at Boston University.

[illegible] *[Pak]istan's Development: Social Goals and Private [Incentives'], [C]ambridge, Mass, 1967; (ed.) 'Development [Policy: Theory] and Practice', Cambridge, Massachusetts,* [illegible]

YU.V. GANKOVSKY

Pargana

(Persian: region, district) The lowest administrative unit in the *Mughal empire, forming a division of the *sarkar* and consisting of individual villages (*mauza, mahal*). At the head of a *pargana* was a *Chaudhri* and a *Qanungo* (in North India), or a *Deshmuck* and a *Deshpande* (in Deccan), i.e., an administrative boss and his scribe, who were regarded as officials but in fact were the community elders.

L.B. ALAYEV

Parsi

The term Parsi refers to a member of the Zarathustrian faith, originally an inhabitant of Iran. The Zarathustrian religion has its origins in a time when the early *Aryans inhabited the northern Steppes of Central Asia. The prophet Zarathustra, or Zoroaster in Greek, preached his gospel at some time between 1700–1500 BC. Zarathustra preached two main concepts, that of Godhead, the All Wise Creator, *Ahura Mazda*, who governs the whole of creation by means of His wisdom and has six divine attributes. The second is that the doctrine of good and evil is purely ethical. It is for the individual to choose the good or evil in every situation in life. The wise choose good because of their innate rightmindedness. The unwise choose evil because of their deceptive mind. By this means the righteous ones achieve a state of higher consciousness through their correct choices. Zarathustra taught that people must choose for themselves, judge for themselves and decide for themselves whether to approve of the faith he taught. Freedom of choice is therefore at the basis of the faith. In the 7th century the region was conquered by the Arabs, following two decisive battles at Quadsia in 637 and Nehavand in 641. The Parsi communities moved out and traveled eastwards to make their home on the west coast of India.

M.R. KAZIMI

Pashto Academy

It was established in 1955 in Peshawar to promote studies of the language, literature, and history of the *Pashtuns, and to preserve publications, in *Pashto, of works of literature and scientce of other Pakistani peoples and nations of the world. There is a research centre for the study of the life, work, and literary heritage of Khushal Khan *Khattak at the Academy. The Academy maintains a specialized library and a publishing house that prints books in Pashto, *Khowar, Arabic, English, and *Urdu. It publishes a monthly literary magazine, *Pashtun,* and a quarterly, *Khushal Review.*

N.V. GLEBOV

Pashtun (also Pashtoon)

A people inhabiting Afghanistan (about 8 million) and Pakistan (about 13 million). Their religion is Islam and 98 per cent are *Sunnis, while the *Shia are only in Turi and Orakzai tribes in Pakistan. A considerable number of Pashtuns remain firmly devoted to their time-honoured common law (*Pashtunwali*), and traditional socio-economic relationships in their everyday life and culture. In the countryside, they still preserve some elements of the tribal system. The largest Pashtun tribes in Pakistan are the *Yusufzai, Tarklanri, *Wazir, *Afridi (Apridi), Orakzai, Khattak, Bangash, *Kakar, Turi, Momand (Mohmand), and Tarin.

BIBLIOGRAPHY: *Yuri Gankovsky, 'The People of Pakistan', Lahore, 1972, Muhammad Hayat Khan, 'Hayat-i Afghan', Lahore, 1964.*

YU.V. GANKOVSKY

Pashtunistan (Pakhtunistan) issue

See: Durand Line.

Pashtunwali

(Pakhtunwali, in Pashtu: Pashtun's code of honour) Common law, a collection of traditional moral norms determining the behaviour of the members of the *Pashtun community. Its basic principles are respect for elders (*myshr*), hospitality (*melmastiya*), blood feud, revenge (*badl* or *badal*), dignity, and pride (*ghyrat*).

BIBLIOGRAPHY: *K. Hadim, 'Pashtunwali', Kabul, 1332.*

YU.V. GANKOVSKY

Pashtu

Pashtu belongs to the south-eastern subgroup of the Eastern Iranian group of languages. Apart from Pashtu, this group includes Munjan and Pamir languages. Pashtu is the native tongue of the *Pashtuns. In Afghanistan, Pashtu has the status of a national language, along with Dari. It is spoken in the *North West Frontier Province, *Balochistan, the *Federally Administered Tribal Areas, *Punjab and *Sindh. In Afghanistan, Pashtu is mostly spoken in the south and south-west regions of the country. Pashtu is divided into more than fifty territorial and tribal dialects that have not, so far, been thoroughly studied. At present they are commonly united into two large groups; the western or Kandahar group and the eastern Peshawar, or Jalalabad-Peshawar group. Reliable facts concerning texts in Pashtu date from the fifteenth century. A continuous written tradition has existed since that time. The Pashtu script evolved on the basis of the Arabic-Persian alphabet, a number of signs being added to designate sounds peculiar to the language such as retroflex affricates, as well as some diphthongs. In all, the alphabet consists of forty-one letters.

At present, there are two variants of literary Pashtu. One variant evolved in Afghanistan, its centres being Kandahar, Jalalabad and Kabul, and the other variant in Pakistan centre on Peshawar. The two variants developed on different dialect bases. In Afghanistan, the basis is the Kandahar dialect; in Pakistan, it is the Peshawar-*Momand dialect. The conventions of literary Pashtu are at present at the evolutionary stage. There is a tendency towards closer unity of the two literary variants. Pashtu is the language of original literature. Of special interest is folklore, poetry, fairy tales, songs, legends, and proverbs.

BIBLIOGRAPHY: *YE.E. Bertels, 'The Structure of Pashtu', Leningrad, 1936 (in Russian); N.A. Dvoryankov, 'The Pashtu Language', Moscow, 1960 (in Russian); K.A. Lebedev, 'A Grammar of the Pashtu Language', Moscow, 1970 (in Russian); A.L. Gryunberg, 'An Outline of the Grammar of the Afghan Language' (Pashto), Leningrad, 1987 (in Russian); P.B. Zudin, 'Russian-Afghan Dictionary', Moscow, 1963; M.G. Aslanov, 'Afghan-Russian Dictionary', Moscow, 1966; K. QA. Lebedev, L.S. Yatsevich, Z.M. Kalinina, 'Russian-Pashtu Dictionary', Moscow, 1983.*

V.V. MOSHKALO

Pathan

1. Another name for *Pashtuns in Pakistan.

2. A corporate group of Muslims in Pakistan and South Asia. They are alleged to be descendants of Pashtuns (Afghani), who came to India with Muslim armies in ancient times and formed the upper gentry of the Muslim society in India. Later, they mixed with other Muslims, speaking different languages, but traditionally they are still called Pathans. Their names invariably contain the component *Khan.

BIBLIOGRAPHY: *'A Glossary of the Tribes and Castes of the Punjab and the North West Frontier Province', Lahore, 1978.*

S.F. LEVIN

Peasant Conference

(Urdu: *Kisan Jirga*) The Conference appeared in the *North West Frontier Province after the Second World War. In 1948-50 it led the peasants in their struggle to abolish landlordism and to cut the landlord's share of the yield. In 1956 and 1958 it headed peasant marches on Lahore. In 1962 when the ban on political parties and organizations was lifted, it resumed its activity and from 1969 to 1974 headed the tenants' struggle for property rights on the land they tilled. In a number of places it developed into armed seizure of land.

S.I. TANSYKBAEVA

Peasant Movement

It assumed massive scope in Pakistan in 1948-50. The main demand was for tenants' hereditary rights to cultivate land. The peasant struggle was best organized in Sindh, the Punjab and the NWFP. In the 1950s there were demands to stop the eviction of tenants and to distribute the newly irrigated state-owned land among landless peasants. In the 1960s two principal trends took shape in the peasant movement in Pakistan: the poor peasants fought to gain access to land, while the well-to-do peasants, whose position improved during the 1959 land reform, fought for a more favourable tax policy and purchase prices. The early 1970s were marked by mass actions of tenants in the NWFP. Their main demands were guarantees of their right to use land. In 1972, after Z.A. *Bhutto passed the law on land reform, only smallholders and tenants continued to take part in the peasant movement and struggles were entirely local. During the 1980s the main demand was for the banning of arbitrary evictions and rent increases. The situation was especially tense in the NWFP, where the difficulties were compounded by the arrival of three million Afghan refugees. In the 1980s the better off peasants took part in the struggle for democratization. They put forward general democratic slogans, including the lifting of martial law, the restoration of democracy, and general elections. The most vigorous actions against the government in 1983 and 1986 were in *Sindh. In recent years the focus of peasant discontent has shifted to the region of Okara in *Punjab, and particularly to the tenants on the large army-owned estates in that area. The leading peasant political organizations are the *Peasants and Workers Party (*Mazdur Kisan Party*) and the Sindh Metayers Committee (Sindh *Hari* Committee).

BIBLIOGRAPHY: *S.I. Tansykbaeva, 'The Peasants of Pakistan', Tashkent, 1969 (in Russian); V. I. Tyurin, 'Pakistan's Agrarian Problems', Saratov, 1968 (in Russian); M.Yu. Morozova, 'Modern Rural Pakistan', Moscow, 1986 (in Russian).*

M.YU. MOROZOVA

Peasant-and-Worker's Party

(*Krishak Sramik Party*) Founded in *East Pakistan in July 1953 by A.K. Fazlul *Haq, the Party headed the right wing of the Bengali national movement and advocated complete autonomy for East Pakistan and the recognition of Bengali as a national language. In January 1954 the Party headed the United Front of East Pakistan. In 1954-56 the Party's leaders led the provincial governments of East Pakistan. From 1958 to 1962 the Party was banned but, from 1962 to 1969, it was a member of the National Democratic Front and the *Muslim League government. It disappeared during the 1971 elections.

YU.V. GANKOVSKY

Peerbhoy, Adamjee, Sir (1845–1913)

A prominent industrialist and philanthropist, he founded the first tannery in western India. He presided over the first Annual Session of the *All-India Muslim League held at Karachi on 29 and 30 December 1907.

M.R. KAZIMI

People's Labour Bureau of Pakistan

(PLBP) Founded in the mid 1980s as a wing of the *Pakistan Peoples Party in the workers' movement. The Bureau's positions are strongest in *Sindh, where its provincial division, the People's Labour Bureau of *Sindh, had the support of more than 100 trade unions in 1986. The Bureau is influential in the workers' movement in Lahore, Rawalpindi, and other cities.

D.B. NOVOSELOV

People's Uprising in India

Known in English literature as the Sepoy Mutiny, this was a widespread uprising against British rule (see British India). Spreading over a considerable territory in northern India, it included Hindus and Muslims and all social strata of Indian society. The main reason for the uprising was increased exploitation by the British, conquest of princely territories and missionary activities to convert Hindus and Muslims to Christianity. By the mid-nineteenth century, the conquest and political subjugation of the Indian subcontinent had been concluded. All traditional economic ties and crafts were disrupted. The British agrarian policy undermined the village commune. Its upper class was deprived of the larger part of their land ownership. Many feudal lords were discontented with the annexation of several vassal principalities. The uprising began on 10 May 1857, with the mutiny of the soldiers ('sepoys') in the town of Meerut. Having defeated their British officers, the sepoys moved on to Delhi and seized it within a day. The insurgents proclaimed Bahadur Shah II, the last of the Mughal dynasty, King of India and appealed to all Indian peoples and chieftains to rise against the British. The insurgents set up a Council ('*Shura*') in Delhi, headed by Bakht Khan. However, the power of the Council extended only to the capital. During the uprising several large and small centres sprang up, but they lacked proper communication, a united command, and a concerted plan of action. The freedom fighters were committed to driving the British out of the country. To reinforce the royal armies located in India, additional forces from other colonies and even from England were brought in. The British army dealt several serious blows to the rebels, in the battles of Delhi, Kanpur, Jhansi, and Kalpi. By 1858 the organized uprising was suppressed but partisan fighting continued until 1859. The captured rebels were cruelly punished. The leaders of the uprising, such as Firuz Shah, Bahkt Khan, Nana Sahib, Lakshmi Baithe Rani of Jhansi, and Tantia Tope, were either killed in battle or executed after the suppression of the uprising. Hazrat Mahal, the wife of Wajid Ali Shah, after fighting the British, retreated to Nepal where she disappeared. On 1 November 1858 Queen Victoria issued a new policy withholding from the East-India Company the power over India and transferring it to the British crown, represented by the Viceroy and Governor-General of India.

On Pakistani territory, *Sindh was the main area involved in the uprising, primarily the districts of Karachi, Hyderabad, Shikarpur, and Jacobabad. The leaders of the uprising, Imam Bakhsh Khan and Alif Khan Tarin, were executed.

BIBLIOGRAPHY: *'People's Uprising in India. 1857–9', Moscow, 1957 (in Russian); Khudadad Khan, 'Lubb-i Tarikh-i Sindh', Karachi-Hyderabad, 1959; 'A History of the Freedom Movement', Vol. II, Karachi, 1960.*

P.M. SHASTITKO

Permanently Settled Lands in British India, The System of

A series of laws passed in 1859-1932, giving lease-holders permanent rights on land allotments, that were close to actual ownership. The land and tax laws, introduced by the British authorities at the turn of the nineteenth century, the permanent settlement system or *zamindari*, *mauzawar*, *ryotwari*, and were not satisfactory for the lease-holders. The British adopted the policy that those working on the land should own it because they determined the state of the agriculture. Some attempts were made to protect the lease-holders from extortion. In 1859 the Bengal Presidency issued the first law on land lease, which established the basis for future legislation. If a lease-holder had been paying a certain rent for twenty years he was entitled to go on paying the same rent, and the landlord could no longer raise it. If a lease-holder and his ancestors had been cultivating a certain plot of land for twelve years in a row, his family received the occupancy right. The rent could be raised only by a judgement of a court, and only in the case when the landowner could prove that he himself had to pay more in taxes. In 1868 the law was extended to Oudh. Similar laws, which gave wider rights to lease-holders, were passed in 1869 in the *Punjab, in 1873 and 1881 in the North-West Provinces. In the Central Provinces, lease-holders' rights were strengthened in 1863-70 while a land-tax system or malguzari, was introduced. These rights were codified by the laws of 1883 and 1898. Despite the imperfections of these laws, which left landowners with loopholes allowing them to continue exploitation, by the early 1880s lease-holders, who had the rights on the plot of land they cultivated, made up 40 per cent of all the lease-holders in the North-West Provinces (55 per cent of the leased land); in Oudh, they made up 75 per cent (80 per cent of the land); in the Punjab, 33 per cent (35 per cent of the land). In the Central Provinces, after the law was passed in 1898, only 13 per cent of the land remained in the hands of the peasants having no rights. The new Bengal law of 1885 clearly defined the rights of the landowners and the lease-holders. In particular, the occupancy right law was reformulated so that it was no longer possible to violate it by simply moving the lease-holder within one village. It was decreed that a census of all rights on the land should be conducted. Similar laws were also passed in 1886 in Oudh, in 1887 in the Punjab, in 1901 in the United Provinces. In 1845, it was amplified so that the census of land rights should be conducted regularly. In the twentieth century, laws on the lease of land were passed in those areas where peasant movements were active: in Oudh in 1921 (after the Eka uprising), in Bengal in 1928 and 1930, in the Malabar districts of Madras Presidency in 1930 (after the Mopla uprising), and in Assam in 1932. By 1947, the overwhelming majority of lease-holders were protected, but occupancy right became a commodity and often got into the hands of those not working the land.

L.B. ALAYEV

Persian Language and Literature of the Subcontinent

In the eleventh century, north-west India joined the *Ghaznavid Empire. Persian was adopted as the language of the royal court and for official correspondence. By the eleventh century the first local Persian-language poets, Abul Faraj Runi (d. 1091) and Masud Sad *Salman had already appeared in Lahore: Their work testifies to lively literary activities in Lahore. Their **qasidas* inspired numerous imitations, while the prison elegies of Masud started a new genre of *habsie,* prison lyrics. The formation of the *Delhi Sultanate in the twelfth century considerably extended the area of Persian-language literature involving non-Muslims, such as the Kayashta scribes. *Sufi fraternities played an important role in the spread of Persian-language literature by their use of **ghazals* and **rubai* in their ritual Sufi *samas* or recitals. The migration of poets from Iran and Central Asia to the courts of the Delhi Sultans and local rulers also promoted Persian language literature. During the thirteenth to fourteenth centuries, literary centres sprang up in Delhi, Multan, Peshawar, and Sialkot. Amir Khusrau *Dehlawi started the tradition of the poetic answers to Nizami's *Khamse,* and also enriched Persian language literature with a new genre of the chronicle-novel and the **masnawi*, devoted to various events of court life. The poetry of Amir Khusrau Dehlawi and Amir Hasan Sijzi (d. 1327) represent the flourishing of the *ghazal*. Amir Hasan is the author of the first Sufi allegory based on the subjects of love between a Muslim and a Hindu woman, and the burial ritual of burning in the positive Sufi context of the union of souls. Sufi lives and religious-philosophical treatises spawned new genres in Persian literature. Imitations of Firdousi's *Shah Nama* became increasingly more popular. The thirteenth century saw the flourishing of lexicography when the first Persian dictionaries appeared. *Tuti Nama* (The Book of the Parrot) is recreated in a prose version by Ziyauddin Nakhshabi (d. 1350). Non-Muslims also made important contributions to Persian literature. The poets Dinkar and Chandra Bhan Brahmin became well known. Regional literary schools appeared. The *Sindhi school, was represented by Jam Jun, Shaykh Hammad Jamali, whose work is tinged with Sufi motifs. The Deccan school, by Isami (b. 1311) whose early works—*Shah Nama-i-Hind* tells the story of the subjugation of the Deccan by the Delhi Sultanate. There was also a Lahore school. After the fall of the Delhi Sultanate Persian literature was centred in Malwa, Gujarat, Bengal, Golconda, Bijapur, Sindh, and the Punjab. In Kashmir, under Sultan Zayn-al-Abidin (1420-70), a translation school was set up, which produced excellent translations from Sanskrit into Persian and vice versa. For the first time *Mahabharata* and *Rajatarangini*, the history of the *Kashmiri rulers, were translated into Persian by Mullah Ahmad. In Gujarat, Persian literature was used by the ethnic Persian—*Zoroastrians. Bahman Keykobad ibn Hormozyar produced *Qissa-i-Sanjan* (The Story of Sanjan) about the migration of Zoroastrians into India.

Regional schools of Persian literature actively assimilated local legends and traditions as well as literary forms, and they promoted interpenetration of literatures. Some outstanding Sufis, such as Sayyid Gesudaraz (1318-1421), also participated in the literary process. Bilinguism and attention to local languages was characteristic of Sufi creativity that was primarily connected with their missionary work (see: 'Sufi Orders'). In the fifteenth century, famous poets included Jamali (d. 1535), Azari (d. 1461), Mullah Naziri Tusi (d. 1460), Isa Langotio (fifteenth century) and Jam Nindo (d. 1508). The sixteenth century marked a new stage in the development of Persian literature, connected with the formation of the *Mughal State. This falls into two periods: early Mughal (16th century to mid-18th century) and the decline of the *Mughal empire (mid-18th century to mid-19th century). The first period was a time of flourishing intellectual life, wide cultural exchanges, and establishment of libraries.

India became the leader in the Iranian-language development. Shaykh Faizi retells the love story of Nal and Damayanti in his narrative **Dastan*; Zuhuri (d. 1615) renders clear-cut genre features to his lyrical-confessional *Saqi Nama* (The Book of the Wine-Bearer). In the work of Sayyid Urfi, the *qasida* acquires a philosophical tenor. Other popular genres include history chronograms, riddles, and literary charades (Qasim Kahi, 1463-1580). In the work of these poets and also in the work of Anisi Shamlu (d. 1605), Naui

(d. 1610), Naziri Nishapuri and many others, the 'Indian style' became dominant, even affecting the prose (e.g. Zuhuri).

Translation flourished at the courts of Akbar and such patrons of the arts as Abdurrahim Khan-i-Khanan (1557-1628) and the Prince Dara Shikoh (1528-1615). Thanks to Faizi and Abd-al-Qadir Badauni (d. 1595), Persian literature preserved many literary and cultural monuments, from the *Upanishads* and *Mahabharata* to Tulsi Das's *Ramayana*. During the second late Mughal period lyrical and philosophical poetry came to the fore, but the lyrical characters are less elevated, with a stress on prosaic concerns such as 'bread and water'. Prominent in that period were Fani (d. 1670), Saib Tebrizi, Ghani Kashmiri (d. 1688), Shaukat Bukhari (d. 1695), Nasir Ali Sirhindi (d. 1697), and *Zebunissa (alias Makhfi) (d. 1702). The work of *Bedil concludes this period of the development of Persian literature.

Northern India produced fine examples of the narrative epic, based on subjects borrowed from local legends and traditions, such as tales about Hir and Ranjha, and Sassi and Punnu. While preserving the local colour, they were usually presented in a Sufi spirit. The highest literary achievements of the third period were made by Mirza *Ghalib whose Persian-language poetry reflects the influence of Bedil and Shaukat Bukhari. In the 1830s–40s Persian, as the language of clerical work, was replaced by Urdu and in the province of *Sindh by *Sindhi,. Nevertheless, the traditions of Persian literature did not become obsolete. They were enriched by the achievements of the new literature with its focus on the individual and society, social, political and patriotic themes, that previously had been alien to Persian literature. These new trends were visible in the works of various genres appearing in Sindh, *Kashmir, and the *Punjab and in the first half of the twentieth century. The period was brilliantly consummated in the poetry of Muhammad *Iqbal.

BIBLIOGRAPHY: *G. Aliev, 'Persian-Language Literature of India', Moscow, 1968 (in Russian); E. Bertels, 'History of Persian-Tajik Literature', Moscow, 1958 (in Russian); M.A. Ghani, 'History of Persian Language and Literature at the Moghal Court', Part 1-3, Allahabad, 1929-30; Hasan Hadi, 'Moghal Poetry', Madras, 1952; Hussain Iqbal, 'The Early Persian Poets of India', Patna, 1937; Kirmani Waris, 'Dreams Forgotten: An Anthology of Indo-Persian Poetry', Aligarh, 1984; S.B.F. Husaini, 'A Critical Study of Indo-Persian Literature during Sayyid and Lody Period', New Delhi, 1988; H.I. Sadarangani, 'Persian Poets of Sindh', Karachi, 1956; Tikku, 'Persian Poetry in Kashmir 1339-1846', Berkeley, 1971; J.S. Sital, 'Persian Language and Literature in the Punjab during the Sikh Period (1760-1849) and After', Lahore, 1944; S.A.H. Abidi, 'Hindustani Farsi Adab (Persian-Language Literature of India)', Delhi, 1984; Ahmad Idris, 'Sirhind Men Farsi Adab Persian-Language Literature of Sirhind', Delhi, 1988; Naimuddin, 'Hindustan Men Farsi Adab (Persian-Language Literature of India)', Delhi, 1985; Shibli Numani, 'Shir al-Ajam (Iranian Poetry)', Vols. 1-5, Tehran, 1937-60.*

N.I. PRIGARINA

Pervaz, Ahmed (1926–79)

Artist. One of the most prolific of the group of artists active from 1952 onwards achieved prominence at home and abroad, and was an inspirational figure. His visual dialogue via colour on a purely intuitive plane was a mind map of emotions. It was an inner compulsion that drove him to repeat a dynamic movement energized by exploding small abstract forms. A closer look shows that his forms were not identical nor static, but continuously evolving in the changing amorphous space, constantly challenging the eye to find a focus in the chaos. It is perhaps an affirmation of his tremendous talent that he could create endless variations to rescue his art from the commonplace. In 1978, a year before his death, he was awarded the Pride of Performance.

Peshawar Museum

It was founded in 1906. As a result of the excavations in *Gandhara, the museum has one of the finest collections of Gandhara sculpture together with the *Lahore Museum collection. The museum has in its collection the remains of Kanishka's coffin, one of the most valuable discoveries in the history of world art. The exhibition also includes a gallery of specimens of art of the peoples of north-west Pakistan and numismatic collections.

BIBLIOGRAPHY: *S.R. Dar, 'Museums in Pakistan', in Museology and Museum Problems in Pakistan, Lahore, 1981.*

N.K. KARPOVA

Peshawar Valley

A depression among the mountains in the central part of the *North West Frontier Province of Pakistan, in the valley of the *Kabul River. The territory is about 6,500 sq.km. extending 130 km. from west to east, and 80 km. from north to south. The rocky bottom of the valley is formed of Attock table slate covered by a thick layer of clayey alluvium. The north-eastern and south-western areas of the valley are criss-crossed by multitudinous gullies. The average annual precipitation is about 400 mm, with comparatively high winter temperatures. The climate is propitious for irrigation agriculture. About 70 per cent of the territory is ploughed up, mainly for wheat which occupies up to 40 per cent of the cultivated area, maize, sugar cane, and fodder crops. There are many orchards of pears, apples, peaches, grapes, apricots, figs, and dates. In the western part of the valley, on a tributary of the Kabul, stands the city of Peshawar, the capital of the North West Frontier Province. Connecting the Peshawar Valley with the *Kohat Plain, which lies to the south, is the *Kohat Pass. This scenic pass crosses the Kohat mountains, at a mean elevation of 1,000-1,500 meters.

M.YU. MOROZOVA

Phalura (also Phalura, Palola, Dangarik Dangarikwar)

Phalura belongs to the *Dardic group of the eastern subgroups of *Indo-Aryan languages. Its closest relationship is with *Shina. Phalura is spoken in several villages in the eastern side valleys of Chitral. There is a closely related dialect of Phalura called Sawi in Sau, East Afghanistan. The exact number of speakers is not known. Phalura has no written tradition. Traces of the influence of the pre-Indo-European substratum are observed, especially in phonology. There are loan words from Iranian languages.

BIBLIOGRAPHY: *D.I. Edelman, 'Dardic Languages', Moscow, 1965 (in Russian); G. Buddruss, 'Die Sprache von Sau in Ost Afghanistan (Beitrage zur Kenntnis des dardischen Phalura)', München, 1967; D.I. Edelman, 'The Dardic and Nuristani Languages', Moscow, 1983; G. Morgenstierne, 'Notes on Phalura, an Unknown Dardic Language of Chitral', Skrifter utgitt av det Norske Videnskaps Akademi i Oslo, II, Historisch-philosophische Klasse, 1940, No. 5, Oslo 1941.*

D.I. EDELMAN

Philology

The largest centres for the study of Pakistani languages are found in Pakistan: *Anjuman-i-Taraqqi-i-Urdu*, Karachi, was founded in 1903 by Abdul Haq. *Iqbal Academy (Lahore); *Bazm-i-Iqbal*, was founded in 1950 (see Iqbal Society). *Majlis-i-Taraqqi-i-Adab*, was established in 1950. The Pakistan Academy of Letters (Islamabad) has been active since 1976. The main regional centres of Pakistani philology are: *Sindhi Adabi* Board (Hyderabad, active since 1951); the Sindhi Academy (Jamshoro), the *Institute of Sindhology since 1964); the Punjabi Literary Academy (Lahore, set up in 1957); the *Pashto Academy (Peshawar, founded in 1955); the *Balochi Academy (Quetta, founded in 1966); the Brohi Academy (Quetta, established in 1966); and the Siraiki Academy (Multan and *Bahawalpur, established in 1961). The major academic centres of Pakistani philology are the Academies of Sciences of Uzbekistan and Tajikistan, the Institutes of Linguistics and Art Studies at the Russian Academy of Sciences, the School of Oriental and African Studies at London University (UK), Harvard (USA), and Charles University in Prague.

A.S. SUKHOCHEV

Pir

(Persian: an elderly, tutor) The head of a Muslim community or sect.

YU.V. GANKOVSKY

Pir Pagaro

(in Sindhi: turbaned pir) The title of the *pir* of the *Hurs. The title was introduced in *Sindh in the 1830s.

YU.V. GANKOVSKY

Pirak

This a settlement in *Balochistan in the valley of the river Kachhi, inhabited from the 18th to the 8th centuries BC. The French Archaeological Mission, headed by J.P. Jarriage, worked on the site from 1968 to 1974. It covers an area of 9 hectares, the layer excavated being 12 metres thick. There are fourteen construction horizons and three consecutive development stages. Phase I (15th-14th centuries BC) exhibits large pisé, or clang houses supplied with sewerage. 70 per cent of the pottery found can be described as coarse modelled ware, 20 per cent can be classified as painted pottery. There are numerous seals and clay figurines of 'horsemen' and horses. During Phase II (13th-12th centuries BC) the houses became smaller, and there were iron objects together with earlier ones made of bronze. No changes occurred in the pottery. Pisé houses with courtyards characterize Phase III (11th-8th centuries BC). Ninety per cent of the pottery was made according to the previous tradition but a group of grey-and-black wheeled pottery with grooved patterns appeared. There are arrows, axes and adzes among the iron objects, and also bronze seals with loops. There is great controversy over the origins of the culture.

BIBLIOGRAPHY: *J.P. Jarrige, M. Santoni, 'Fouilles de Pirak', Vols. I-II, Paris, 1979.*

N.M. VINOGRADOVA

Piran

(Persian: pirahan—dress, shirt) Part of the male and female *Kashmiri costume in India and Pakistan. It is usually made out of local wool and, sometimes, out of cotton or satin. A *piran* is a loose, wide shirt or a dress with long loose sleeves, an open neck with an opening that extends as far as the breast and slits on both sides. It has no fasteners. Men wear it belted. Often the neck, the front, the sleeves, and the hem are embroidered with chain-stitch, feather stitch, or satin-stitch. Embroidery motifs are typical Kashmiri variations of buta, a flowery design. *Pirans* are usually yellow, dark green, dark blue, azure, or red. The colour of the embroidery complements the fabric; for example pink embroidery on dark green fabric, bright yellow on azure, etc. Women wear *pirans* with *shalwars* made of the same fabric.

BIBLIOGRAPHY: *S.N. Dar, 'Costumes of India and Pakistan', Bombay, 1982.*

O.V. LYSTSOVA

Pirpur, Syed Muhammad Mehdi, Raja of (1896–1949)

Statesman. Syed Muhammad Mehdi was a leading Taluqdar of Oudh. He received his early education at the Colurin Taluqdar School, and graduated in 1920 from Canning College, Lucknow. He succeeded to the estate in February 1927. He was elected unopposed to the UP Legislative Council the same year. He became the Honorary Secretary of the British Indian Association of Oudh. He represented the Oudh Taluqdars in the *Round Table Conference. In 1932 he was made Raja on personal distinction. In 1936 he was awarded the Silver Jubilee Medal. The Raja of Pirpur's most notable contribution is what is popularly known as the Pirpur Report about the grievances of Muslims under the provincial rule of Congress.

M.R. KAZIMI

Pirzada, Abdul Hafeez (1935–)

Statesman. A Pakistani politician who is descended from a wealthy land-owning family, Pirzada graduated from in Karachi in 1954, continued his education in England, and became a lawyer by profession. From 1969 to 1970, he headed the Karachi branch of the *Pakistan Peoples Party and was elected Member of the Pakistan National Assembly in 1970 and 1977. As Law Minister, he was responsible for presenting the 1973 *Constitution. From December 1971 to June 1977 he was, in turn, Minister of Education, Minister of Information and Radio, and Minister for Inter-provincial Co-ordination. In 1985 he helped to organize the *Sindhi-*Balochi-*Pakhtun Front, which campaigned for transforming Pakistan into a confederation of four provinces.

YU.V. GANKOVSKY

Pirzada, Syed Sharifuddin (1923–)

Lawyer. Regarded as an outstanding legal brain, Pirzada graduated from Bombay University with a degree in Law and served as Attorney-General of Pakistan from 1964 to 1966 and again in 1978. He served as the Minister for Foreign Affairs from 1966 to 1968, Minister of Justice in 1983 and General Secretary of the Organization of Islamic Conference in the 1980s. From October 1999 he has been a member of Pakistan's National Security Council. He is currently Honorary Senior Adviser of Foreign Affair, Law, Justice and Human Rights.

WORKS: *' The Foundations of Pakistan', 2 Vols., Karachi, 1969, 1970.*

YU.V. GANKOVSKY

Pishkash (also Peshkash–gift)

In the *Delhi Sultanate, an annual tribute from vassal princes. In the *Mughal empire and *British India, Pishkash was a tax on **zamindars* of Bengal when their land-ownership had been settled.

K.A. ANTONOVA

Platts, J.T. (1830–1904)

Linguist. He was a British specialist in Persian, Urdu, and Hindi. Having graduated from Bedford U.K. College he served in India (1858-72) in the Benares College, the Sagar School, and the Central Provinces. He retired to the UK for health reasons, and began teaching the languages he had learned in India. In 1880 he was appointed a teacher of Persian at Oxford University. He was the author of a work on Urdu grammar, and his main work, *A Dictionary of Urdu, Classical Hindi and English,* embraced vast lexical material and gave a detailed description of all entries. Its words are cited in the Persian-Arabic script adopted for Urdu. Several editions were printed.

WORKS: *'A Grammar of the Hindustani or Urdu Language', London, 1874; 'A Dictionary of Urdu, Classical Hindi and English', London, 1884 (Reissued in two volumes, Moscow, 1959); 'A Grammar of the Persian Language', Oxford 1911 (with G.S.A. Ranking).*

V.P. LIPEROVSKY

PNCA (Pakistan National Council of the Arts)

The PNCA Performing Arts Group, once known as the PIA Arts Academy, was set up in the early seventies, during the Zulfiqar Ali *Bhutto years, and was meant to promote Pakistan's dance and music, both folk as well as classical, in other countries, and in particular those where the national airline flew. Renowned actor, Zia Mohyeddin, successfully led the Academy. But it was closed down, and during the Ziaul Haq regime, it was taken over by the Pakistan National Council of the Arts (PNCA), which is run by the Ministry of Culture. In 2001 the PNCA Performing Arts troupe was revived under Nighat Chaudhry, who was appointed the Director at PNCA, Karachi. By December 2001 Chaudhry had left, and Sheema Kermani trained a dance troupe of 10 female dancers, 10 male dancers, and 10 musicians, as the PNCA Artistic Director.

R. HUSAIN

Police in Pakistan

The police in each province are directly under the supervision of the Inspector General of Police who has deputies and assistants under him. The police force of a district is headed by a superintendent. In small towns and rural areas police precincts are headed by police inspectors and their deputies. Villages have police posts. Special police units fight interprovincial crime, such as smuggling. The country's police force is more than 100,000 in number, nearly half of which is located in the Punjab, with a considerable number concentrated in Islamabad. These units are under the Inspector-General of Police. The Federal Bureau of Investigations renders assistance to the police force, including technical assistance. A special research bureau has been set up to study the causes of crime; it has links with the country's universities and scientific centres. Police schools, colleges, and a Police Academy in Rawalpindi train policemen and provide refresher courses.

V. N. MOSKALENKO

Political Agency

These are special territorial-administrative regions with a form of government set up by the British in the north-west territory of *British India where the *Pashtun and *Balochi tribes live. The number and administrative boundaries of the political agencies have changed several times. In the early 1990s there were seven political agencies in Pakistan within the *Federally Administered Tribal Area (FATA); *Khyber, formed in 1878; *Kurram, formed in 1892; North *Waziristan, formed in 1895; South Waziristan, formed in 1895-96; Momand, formed in 1951; Orakzai, formed in 1973; Bajaur, formed in 1973. Their total area is 27,200 sq. km., with a population of 2.2 million (1981). Pakistan's criminal and civil law does not apply to the territory of the political agencies and taxes are not collected. The population of the political agencies settle their internal affairs on the basis of their common law or **Pashtunwali*. The federal authorities are represented in the FATA by the Governor of the NWFP. The administrative apparatus of each political agency is headed by the political agent; this apparatus consists of the agent's two assistants and several political *tahsildars* and *naib-tahsildars*, each of which controls situations in the territory of the settlement of a given tribe or clan. Two more political agencies–Dera Bugti and Kohlu–exist in the territory of the Sibi division in the province of *Balochistan.

YU.V. GANKOVSKY

Pop Music

A fast paced, modern genre of music that is considered typically western. Pakistani pop has transformed from the early days of Nazia/Zohaib Hassan, Alamgir and Muhammad Ali Shehki in the 1980's, to a full fledged

Pakistani Pop Music Band 'Strings'.

pop music industry in the post, 1990's era. Pakistani pop music has also made inroads into Indian cinema, with Pakistani pop and rock artists being hired to perform background soundtracks for Indian movies. Some landmarks of Pakistani pop and rock performers include *Junoon* who have the distinction of performing in the United Nations, the now disbanded *Awaz* who were the first sub-continental band to be aired on MTV, Strings (see image) who's songs have been included in the soundtrack of the Hollywood movie 'Spiderman 2', and Nusrat Fateh Ali Khan who fused sufi poetry with popular music to become another world-renowned exponent of Pakistani culture. Besides this, Pakistan's Adnan Sami Khan is the worlds' fastest keyboard player according to the Guinness Book of World Records. Although there is still a lot of confusion as to who started the pop music trend in Pakistan, however most fingers point towards Ahmad Rushdie with his **filmi* song titled '*coco-corina*'.

I. PIRACHA

Potohari

One of the northern mountain dialects belonging to *Lahnda, it serves as a basis for the formation of a language of the same name. Potohari is spoken in the northern part of the province of *Punjab, north of the *Salt Range as far as the river *Soan and further north to the area between the *Indus and the Soan. Rawalpindi and Islamabad come within the Potohari area. Phonologically, Potohari is close to *Punjabi. It has two tones and is without voiced aspirates.

BIBLIOGRAPHY: *G.A. Zograf, 'Languages of South Asia', Moscow, 1990 (in Russian); Yu.A. Smirnov, 'The Lendi Language', Moscow, 1970 (in Russian); G.A. Grierson, 'Linguistic Survey of India', Vol. 8, pt. 1, Calcutta, 1919; Yu.A. Smirnov, 'The Lahndi Language', Moscow, 1975.*

YU.V. ARESHKO
V.P. LIPEROVSKY

Potwar Plateau

This is a hilly plateau lying between the the *Indus Valley and the north of the *Salt Range. It lies between the rivers *Jhelum in the east and the *Indus in the west. The mean elevation above sea level is approximately 500-900 metres. Potwar is watered by the Rivers Haro and *Soan.

YU.V. GANKOVSKY

Presidency

An administrative-territorial unit in *British India. The name is derived from the title of the person who chaired the council of the main factory of the East-India Company. There were three presidencies: Fort William in Bengal embracing east, north and central India; Fort St. George in Madras which was responsible for matters in south and south-east India; and Bombay presidency in western India. At the head of each presidency was a governor, who possessed executive and at times legislative powers, and a council. Before 1833 presidencies were divided into districts, later into divisions consisting of several districts. Each presidency had its own legal and judicial system, and its own army. The governor of Bengal Presidency was simultaneously the governor-general of all of British India, and from 1858 also the viceroy for all the Indian vassal princes.

T.N. ZAGORODNIKOVA

Proto-Indian Writing

A system of writing developed by the *Harappan civilization about third millennium BC of the early second millennium BC. Samples of proto-Indian writing, such as inscribed seals, have been known to the since the 1850s. The main examples of inscriptive objects was found during the 1922-36 excavations of ancient cities of the *Indus Valley. At present, some 4,200 monuments of proto-Indian writing are known, including inscriptions on seals, on clay tablets, copper plates, stone slabs, ceramics, clay bracelets, bronze tools, and ivory rods. The monuments were discovered in the territory of Pakistan in sixty Harappan towns and settlements, as well as outside South Asia—in excavations of the ancient cultures of Mesopotamia (Ur, Lagash), Iran (Susa), Bahrein islands and Central Asia (Altyn-Tepe).

Proto-Indian writing comprises more than four hundred signs, of which some one hundred to one hundred and fifty are probably the work of scribes or allographs, of the geometrical and stylized drawing types. The drawing-like signs include pictures of objects, buildings, elements of the landscape, plants, animals, birds, insects, and human figures. The direction of writing is generally right to left though in some texts it is left to right, and sometimes running from left to right followed by a line runing from right to left or boustrophedon. Most inscriptions are three to five signs long, the longest being twenty-six signs long. Proto-Indian writing seems to be the result of a local pictographic tradition of ornamental elements and 'potters' signs' on ceramic objects from Rana-Ghundai, Kulli Mehragarh and other pre-Harappan cultures.

N.V. GUROV

Punjab

Punjab is a province in north-east Pakistan, lying chiefly in the lower valleys and alluvial covered northern flood plain of the Indus and its tributaries. It covers an area of 205,300 sq.km., 25.9 per cent of the total territory of Pakistan. The province consists of eight divisions: Lahore, Rawalpindi, Sargodha, Multan, *Bahawalpur, Dera Ghazi Khan, Faisalabad and Guranwala, and 34 districts. The provincial capital is Lahore. The population in 1998 was 72,585,430, representing 55.66 per cent of the population of Pakistan. The indigenous population is *Punjabi but in the south-west there is a considerable population of *Balochis, and *Pashtuns in the north west.

University of the Punjab in Lahore.

The new federal capital of Pakistan, Islamabad, although not regarded as a part of Punjab for administrative reasons, is located on the *Potwar Plateau in north-western Punjab. Economically Punjab is the most highly developed province of Pakistan. The economy is based chiefly upon diversified irrigated farming. Some six and a half million hectares of land are under cultivation, out of which 5 million hectares are irrigated. The main crops grown are wheat, covering about 40 per cent of the sown area in any year, gram, bajra, rice, jowar, corn, cotton and sugar cane. The province produces 77 per cent of the wheat crop, 43 per cent of the rice crop, 72 per cent of the cotton and sugar cane of Pakistan. Cattle, sheep and goat breeding, are practised in the northern and north western areas Mining in the area includes workings of coal, antimony, salt, limestone, gypsum and oil. Industry is also well developed with food and textile industries concentrated in Faisalabad and Multan. Light industry, mechanical engineering, metal working, the chemical industry and cement making are all represented. Cottage industries include metal working, carpet weaving and pottery making.

There is an ancient history of urban settlements in what is now Punjab. In the third to the second millennium BC the larger part of the area was inhabited by what is called the *Harappa civilization. At the turn of the first millennium bc it became, together with what is now called Afghanistan, the main area of settlement for the *Indo-Aryan tribes. At the end of the sixth century bc the western part of Punjab was acceded to the Persian empire and ruled by the *Achaemenids from 558 to 339 bc. In 327 bc the territory up to the *Beas river was conquered by Alexander of Macedonia. After his death in 323 bc, the area was seized by the *Mauryan empire, followed in turn by the Indo-Greek kingdom, the *Kushan state and the *Ephtalite state. When the latter fell in about ad 567 several small independent states sprang up in the territory of present Punjab.

In AD 764 Punjab was invaded by Arab conquerors. By the beginning of the eighth century they had taken Multan and in the twelfth century Punjab became a province in the empire of the *Ghaznavids, Their capital was moved to Lahore in 1161. Following the fall of the Ghaznavid empire, in 1206, Punjab was incorporated into the *Delhi sultanate until 1526. From 1526 to 1757 it was part of the *Mughal empire and it then fell to the *Durrani Empire until 1799. From 1799 to 1849 Punjab was a part of the *Sikh state founded by Maharajah Ranjit Singh (1799–1839). In 1849 the territory was conquered by Britain. On 14 August 1947 it was part of the united province of *West Pakistan. On 1 July 1970 it once again became Punjab province.

YU.V. GANKOVSKY

Punjab National Unionist Party

(PNUP) Founded in December 1923 in Lahore by a member of the *Muslim League, Mian Fazl-i-Husayn (1877-1936), a lawyer and a Member of the Punjab Legislative Assembly. The Party mostly represented the interests of predominantly Muslim *Punjabi landowners.

The Party was reorganized in 1935. Its leaders, Sikandar Hayat Khan, Malik Firoz Khan Noon, Khizar Hayat Khan Tiwana, Shah Nawaz Khan Mamdot, and Ahmad Yar Khan Daultana declared their intention to promote the development of the economy, education and culture of Punjab's agricultural regions; to reduce the electoral property qualifications; to increase the number of representatives of rural constituencies in Punjab's legislative organs; to bring down taxes and restrict usurer's interest rates. In 1937-42 the party's leader, Sikandar Hayat Khan, headed the provincial government of *Punjab. The Party ceased to exist in 1947.

YU.V. GANKOVSKY

Punjab Peasant Committee

(*Kisan Sabha*) Before it was banned in 1954, the *Communist Party of Pakistan controlled the Committee. It demanded abolition of landlordism and an end to lawlessness and massive eviction of peasants from the land, deeper agrarian reforms, abolition of land rent from the plots of less than five hectares, slashing down the water tax, and raising purchase prices. In June 1963 *Kisan Jirga*, Sindh *Hari* Committee and the peasant committees of the *Punjab, *Bahawalpur, and *Balochistan became branches of Pakistan's Peasant Committee. It was set up to fight landlordism, to discontinue evictions of lease-holders from the lands they tilled, to do away with the land tax on plots of up to five hectares, to lower the water tax, the taxes on diesel fuel, pesticides, etc.

YU.V. GANKOVSKY

Punjab Plain

The northern part of the Indo-Gangetic Plain in Pakistan and India, it ranges from the *Thal Desert in the west, to the Indus-Ganges watershed in the east. It is irrigated by a system of rivers that includes the *Jhelum, *Chenab, *Ravi, *Beas, and *Sutlej, which together form the Indus's biggest tributary, the Panjnad. The relief of the plain is generally flat with low hills. There is a thick network of gullies. The total slope of the surface is 1-2°. The absolute heights above sea level are within 150-350 metres. Deposits of river-alluvials predominate, though there are also deposits of coal, oil, salt, bauxites, graphite, etc. The climate is generally dry, but seasonally aaffected by monsoons. In May the mean temperature is 35°C; in January it is about 12-13°C, with occasional surface frosts. The annual precipitation varies from 150 mm in the west, to 700 mm in the east. More than 70 per cent of the precipitation falls during July and September. During floods the rivers often overflow extensively and change their course. The soils formed in modern and ancient alluvium are fertile if irrigated. The natural vegetation of the semi-desert type, consisting mainly of prickly shrubs, has been preserved mainly in the vicinity of watersheds. The greater part of the territory has been brought into agricultural production. Wheat and cotton are the main crops. The valley is one of the most ancient foci of civilization. It is densely populated. The major towns are Lahore, Multan, and Islamabad in Pakistan, and Amritsar and Chandigarh in India.

S.B. ROSTOTSKY

Punjab Public Library

It has been active since 1884 in Lahore. The collection includes 200,000 books, in *Urdu, Farsi, Arabic, *Punjabi, *Pashto, *Sindhi, and *Balochi and collections of Oriental manuscripts, rare Islamic books, and publications in Persian.

YU.V. GANKOVSKY

Punjabi Literary Academy

(Punjabi *Adabi* Academy) It was founded in 1957 in Lahore to promote and encourage the publishing of literary criticism, historical studies and other scholarship created in the *Punjab. The Academy publishes in *Punjabi, Persian, *Urdu, and English. Much attention is given to classical *Punjabi literature. A specialized library consists of 20,000 volumes.

N.V. GLEBOV

Punjabi Literature

This falls into two catagories:

1. The literature of the *Punjabi people written in Punjabi. A synthesis of various cultures determined the formation of the language and literature of the *Punjab, and its development. Its birth is connected with Multan. The first literary work dates back to the eighth century AD: *Sandeshrasak* (Poem-Epistle) by Addakman Multani. The hymns written in Old Punjabi date back to the tenth and eleventh centuries. Old Punjabi was taking shape in those days on the basis of *Apabhransha Shaureseni*, written by Siddhi, Nathi and Jogi preachers. The more famous among them were Gorakh Nath and Charpat Nath (890-990) who rejected pantheism and idol worship. They did not recognize the authority of the Vedas and Shastris, and condemned the decline of morals. Shaykh Farid Shakarganj made an important contribution to Punjabi literature with his work, based

on *Sufism and Bhakti, consisting of more than a hundred *saloks* (distyches) written in Multani, a dialect of Punjabi. The work of Shaykh Farid depicts a broad picture of the everyday life and mores of the village. With a clear connection with folklore, Shaykh Farid had many disciples and much of his writings have become popular sayings.

From the end of the fifteenth century, the development of literary genres in Punjabi literature were stimulated by Sikhism, which had been founded by Guru Nanak. Only a few of Guru Nanak's works hare come down to our day: *Japan ji* (Prayer), *Barah Manh* (Twelve Months), and *Asa di Var* (Hymn to Asa Melody). Guru Nanak wrote in colloquial Punjabi, thus extending the sphere of its usage. He made use of Indian and Persian metres, each with a melody of its own. Poems by Guru Nanak and other poet-preachers were collected in *Adigranath*—'The Book of Beginnings,' the sacred book of the Sikhs compiled in 1604 on the order of Arjun, the fifth guru of the Sikhs. The work of Shaykh Farid was also included. *Adigranth* was compiled and copied by the outstanding poet, Bhai Gurdas. It was written in the Gurmukhi alphabet, but other languages were also represented: *Lahnda, Pahari, Multani, Bengali, Marathi, Arabic, and Farsi. The works of Guru Gobind Singh (1666-1708), the last guru of the Sikhs, have been collected in *Dasam Granth*, 'The Book of the Tenth Guru', which also includes the autobiographical poem *Bacittar Natak* (Multicolored Drama), containing a historically accurate description of the period.

In the sixteenth century, a new genre appears in Punjabi literature: *Qissa-Kawi*, a romantic poem about love and immortal exploits in the name of love, usually ending in the death of the young lovers. This genre was strongly influenced by Persian and Arabic tradition such as Leila-Majnun and Yusuf-Zuleikha. The first writer in this genre in Punjabi literature was Damodar (1556-1605). He wrote the poem 'Hir-Ranjha', about the love of Hir, daughter of a rich tribal leader, for the shepherd Ranjha. Damodar sings of the power of love and defends noble human feelings. His heroine breaks the time honoured traditions of her ancestors and chooses a husband for herself. Damodar's poem contains a wealth of ethnographic information about medieval Punjab. This plot was later borrowed by other authors, and even in the twentieth century it continued to attract writers. Gurbakhsh Singh, a major Punjabi writer, wrote a prose rendering of the poem. The followers of *Qissa-Kawi* in Punjabi literature included Pilu ('Mirza-Sahiban') and Hafiz Barkhudar ('Yusuf-Zuleikha'). In the eighteenth century, Waris Shah wrote his famous poem 'Hir-Ranjha' based on the poem of the same name by Damodar it was noted for its figurative style, inventive metaphors and similes. In the sixteenth century, apart from *Qissa-Kawi*, late Sufi poetry also flourished. Its major representative, Shah Husain (1538-93), wrote poetry of a mystic nature. Another outstanding representative of the late Sufi poetry was Bulleh Shah, the follower of Shah Husain. His elegiac **qafi* were famous not only in India but also in Egypt and Iran.

In 1849 the Punjab was annexed by the British, giving a boost to patriotic and heroic poetry. Favoured genres were *var*—heroic tale, and *jang-nama*—war tale. Shah Muhammad (1782-1862) writes his *Jang-nama Singhan te Farangian da* (Tale of the Battle between the Sikhs and the English), devoted to the first Anglo-Sikh War (1845-6). He glorifies the courage of the Sikhs, their unity with Muslims and Hindus, and laments the fall of their state.

From the mid-nineteenth century missionary societies began book printing in the Punjab. They opened European style schools that taught subjects in *Urdu, neglecting the Punjabi language. In the latter quarter of the nineteenth century, a movement for the revival of literature in Punjabi arose among the Punjab's intelligentsia, who believed in the development of various literary genres reflecting the anti-colonial struggle in literature. The activities of societies like *Arya Samaj* and *Singh Sabha* played an important role in the movement. Bhai Wir Singh was one of the founders of contemporary Punjabi poetry (his collections include *Lahiran de har*—The Garlands of Waves, *Bijlian de har*—The Garlands of Lightning). He has several novels to his credit, the first prose works in contemporary Punjabi. The work of the poet Dhani Ram Chatric is an important contribution to the development of Punjabi poetry. In his writing about the hard lot of the farmer and about forced labour, he introduced a new hero into Punjabi literature—a simple toiler. Chatric published many collections of his poetry, including *Sandan vari* (Sandal Grove), *Kesar Kiari* (Saffron flower-bed), *Nawan Jahan* (New World).

The rise of the national liberation movement in the first decades of the twentieth century inspired great enthusiasm among Punjabi intellectuals. In 1926 progressive writers united into the *Punjabi Sabha* (Punjabi Literary Society). Chatric was its first president. The society aimed at promoting Punjabi language and literature among the Punjabi population regardless of their religious affiliations. The society was mainly engaged in educational work. The dramatist Ishwar Chander Nanda, the satirical writer Charan Singh Shahid, and the poet Puran Singh became prominent in Punjabi literature. When the All-India Progressive Writers' Association was established in 1936, young Punjabi writers such as Mulk Raj Anand, Kartar Singh Duggal, and Mohan Singh joined the organization.

2. The second category of the Punjab literature of Pakistan is the literature of the Pakistani Punjabis, written in the Punjabi language. It is genetically one with the Punjabi literature but there are essential distinctions. In the Middle Ages, in connection with the appearance of Sikhism, two trends in Punjabi literature revealed themselves. The Sikhism-oriented literature used Arabic and Persian script. In the Muslim branch, the influence of Persian poetry was apparent, while in the early twentieth century it was strongly influenced by major Urdu poets. It is precisely this branch that the Pakistani Punjabis consider their cultural heritage. As a result of a number of political and economic influences, Punjabi literature in the Arabic script remained less developed. Though most Punjabi poets were bilingual, they wrote primarily in Urdu. However, in 1926, the journal *Punjabi Darbar,* launched in Lyallpur, published ghazals and masnawi by Abdul Majid Salik, Hakim Nasir, Akhtar Lahori, Firozuddin Sharif, Dr Faqir and Joshhua Fazldin (the publisher). After the partition in 1947 a number of Urdu newspapers and magazines began carrying sections in Punjabi. In 1951 Faqir Muhammad Faqir launched the magazine *Punjabi* that mainly published traditional poetry written by the older generation. However, in those years, there were active attempts already amongst poets to bring literature closer to life, and to renovate its poetry. They included Chiragh Din Daman (Ustad Daman, d. 1984), Sufi Ghulam Mustafa Tabassum (1899-1978), and Abdul Majid Bhatti. Important contributions to the renovation of Punjabi poetry were made by Sharif Kunjahi, Ahmad Rahi (b. 1923), Baqi Siddiqi (1909-79), Arif Abdul Matin, Salim Kashar, and Salim-ar-Rahman Kiyani. Avant-garde experiments were attempted by Afzal Ahsan Randhawa, Sattar Sayyid, Ghulam Husain Sajid, and the founder of this trend—Najm Husain Sayyid (b. 1927). Munir Niazi (b. 1928) is another prominent Pakistani poet who published several books in Urdu and Punjabi, including a collection of his poetry, *Safar di Rat* (The Night of Travelling), 1960. Pakistani Punjabi literature was given a new opportunity for development by newly established journals, such as *Punjabi Adab* (Punjabi Literature), *Panj Darya* (Five Rivers), and *Punjabi Zaban* (Punjabi Language), the foundation of the Punjabi Adabi Academy (1957), Punjabi Literary Union (Punjabi Adabi Sangat), Pakistan Punjabi Adabi Board, and the Shah Husain Society (Majlis-i-Shah Husain).Two trends stand out in contemporary Punjabi poetry. The first is 'traditional' with *ghazal* remaining the main genre, without social themes. Noteworthy in this trend are Faqir Muhammad Faqir, Hakim Fazl, Pir Fazl Karim Gujarati, and Jawhar Jallandhari. The other trend strives to renovate poetry and bring it closer to the world aesthetic norm. Its proponents include Ahmad Rahi, Ahmad Salim (b. 1946) and Nadir Jajwi. The work of Laiq Babur (b. 1934), a graduate of Sorbonne University, organically combines traditional Sufi imagery and new European poetic techniques. Prominent in the poetry of the last decades are Mushtaq Sufi (b. 1949), Anis Nagi, Sultan Mahmud Ashufta, Safdar Mir, Rashid Anwar and Tanwir Bukhari. Artistic prose appeared much later. The first novel was written in the 1920s by Miranbakhsh Minhas. Joshua Fazldin published a novel and several short stories on rural themes. In 1947 Abdul Majid Bhatti published the novel *Theda* (A Kick). In the early 1960s A.A. Randhawa published his novel *Diwa te Darya* (The Candle and the River), and then a collection of short stories *Ran, Ghora, te Talwar* (Woman, Steed and Sword). The novel *Sanj* (Blood Ties) by Salim Khan Gimmi became a turning point in Punjabi literature. Other widely acclaimed writers include Ahmad Salim, Zafar Lashari, Hanif Choudhuri, Fakhr Zaman, Mustansir Tarrar and Ehsan Batalwi. Pakistan Punjabi literature also includes plays, intended for reading, and radio plays. Many dramatists regularly write for television. Well-known dramatists include Sajjad Haidar, Ashfaq Ahmad Khan, Munnu Bhai, Husain Sayid, Akram Butta, Agha Ashraf, Anwar Sajjad, and Salim Khan Gimmi.

Much work has been done to collect and publish the rich Punjabi folklore. Literary criticism appears in print, mainly studies on individual poets. The literary scholars of note include Mirza Maqbul Badahshani, Muhammad Kushta, Abdul Gafur Qureshi, Ainul Haq Faridkoti and Sarfraz Qazi. *Urdu literature continues to inspire Punjabi literature.

BIBLIOGRAPHY: *Mazhar Jameel, 'Guftugu' (Conversation), Karachi; A. Bausani, 'Storia delle letterature del Pakistan', Milano, 1958; I. Serebryakov, 'Punjabi Literature', Moscow, 1963 (in Russian); Lajwanti Rama Krishna, 'Punjabi Sufi Poets', London, 1938.*

A.S. SUKHOCHEV

Punjabi (Dress)

(also *shalwar-kameez*) A woman's two-part costume worn in Pakistan and India. It consists of a straight dress-shirt with long sleeves and slits on both sides (*kameez*) and loose pants (*shalwar*). Usually a Punjabi is worn with a **dupatta* (scarf) with the ends thrown from front to back. Traditionally worn by Muslim women, it was particularly widespread in the Punjab. Today, the Punjabi is highly popular among women of all social walks and confessions. The Punjabi can be made of varied materials, from simple cotton to silk or brocade, and may be decorated with embroidery and applique.

BIBLIOGRAPHY: *S.N. Dar, 'Costumes of India and Pakistan', Bombay, 1982.*

O.V. LYSTSOVA

Punjabi (Language)

It belongs to the *Indo-Aryan group of the Indo-European family of languages. Punjabi is spoken in the Pakistani province of Punjab and in a state of India of the same name where it is recognized as an official language. In the broader sense, according to the 1961 census the Punjabi language was in use, by about 60 per cent of the inhabitants of what was then *West Pakistan. At present, there is a clear distinction in everyday life between western Punjabi languages, of which the most prominent are *Seraiki, *Hindko and Potohari, and standard eastern Punjabi. Punjabi is based on the Majhi dialect found in the areas of Lahore and Amritsar. Apart from this, there exist about a dozen minor dialects.

The history of the Punjabi language begins in the twelfth or thirteenth centuries. Its standardization dates back to the sixteenth or seventeenth centuries, when it became the language of religious sermons in Sikh communities. In the nineteenth century, various modern genres of literature began to develop, but the difference between the Sikh Punjabi language in India and the Muslim Punjabi language in Pakistan had been retained.

BIBLIOGRAPHY: *Yu.A. Smirnov, 'A Grammar of the Punjabi Language', Moscow, 1976 (in Russian); N.I. Tolstaya, 'The Punjabi Language', Moscow, 1960 (in Russian); T.G. Bailey, 'A Punjabi Phonetic Reader', Lonon, 1914; T.F. Cummings, T.G. Bailey, 'Punjabi Manual and Grammar', Calcutta, 1925; H.S. Gill, H.A. Gleason, 'A Reference Grammar of Punjabi', Patiala, 1969; H.S. Gill, 'Linguistic Atlas of the Punjabi, Patiala', 1973.*

G.A. ZOGRAF

Punjabi (People)

A people in the north-western part of the South Asian subcontinent. The population is 100 million (estimated figure for 1990), out of which 70 million live in Pakistan, forming the bulk of the population in the Punjab province and the divisions of Hazara and Dera Ismail Khan (*North West Frontier Province). A considerable number of the Punjabi population resides in the northern region of the *Sindh Province and in the north-eastern region of *Balochistan Province. In India, Punjabis dominate the populations of the state of the Punjab and Haryana. Concentrations of Punjabis are found in the state of Jammu and *Kashmir and elsewhere in north-western India. Several tens of thousands of Punjabis live in Singapore, Sri Lanka, and Afghanistan. Some 75 per cent (estimation) of Punjabis are *Sunni Muslims (mostly in Pakistan); some are *Sikhs and Hindus (in India); 3 per cent of the Punjabis are *Christians, mainly linving in Sialkot District, Lahore division, and in India; about 1 per cent belong to the *Ahmadiya sect in Pakistan, India, and in Western Europe. Central and eastern Punjab are the main areas of Punjabis' ethnic consolidation, which began about 500AD. In its early stages, the process assimilated the local *Indo-Aryan population, the tribes of the Jats, *Gujars, and *Rajputs. In the early centuries of the second millennia AD they were joined by Turki, *Pashtun, Persian-Tajik, and *Balochi ethnic groups. The Sikh religion has played a dramatic role in Punjabi Sikhs' ethnic consolidation and in the formation of their culture and national psychology.

The Punjabi economy is based on ploughed farming (wheat, millet, corn, cotton, sugar cane), and cattle-breeding. Cottage industries are widespread, such as weaving, carpet and rug making, leather-working, metal-working, and wood and stone carving. Punjabis play an important role in the social and political life of Pakistan. 80 per cent of the armed forces and 70 per cent of the civil service bodies consist of Punjabis. The same is true concerning the national economy. The movement for establishing Khalistan, as a separate Independent state of the Sikhs is a serious force in India.

BIBLIOGRAPHY: *Yuri Gankovsky, 'The Peoples of Pakistan', Lahore 1972; D. Ibbetson, 'The Punjab Castes', Lahore, 1974; Z. Eglar, 'A Punjabi Village in Pakistan', N.Y., 1960; L.H. Griffin, 'Chiefs and Families of Note in Punjab', Vol. I-II, Lahore, 1909-10.*

YU.V. GANKOVSKY

Pushto Literature

This is the literature of the *Pashtuns in present-day Pakistan with traditions, folklore, both classics, and, similar to the Pashto literature of present-day Afghanistan. The most ancient and available written monument, *Da Shaykh Mali Daftar* (*Cadastre* Book of Shaykh Mali) dates back to the fifteenth century. Pashto literature has always been firmly rooted in folklore. Its distinctive feature is a close connection with public and political movements, both religious and liberation. In the sixteenth to seventeenth centuries, it was linked to the Roshanai movement and anti-Mughal movement. At this time, theological treatises written in rhymed prose appeared: *Khayr al-Bayan* (Annunciation) by Bayazid Ansari (1525-85), the founder of the Roshanai Sect, the quintessence of his pantheistic teaching, and *Makhzan al-Islam* (The Treasury of Islam) by Akhund Darweza (1533-1658), an answer to Bayazid Ansari from the standpoint of orthodox Islam. The same period produced a powerful stream of *Sufi and secular poetry that later made up the body of classical Pashto literature. The more outstanding classical authors include: Khushhal Khan *Khattak (1613-91), Abdurrahman (1632-1708), Abdulhamid (1660-1732), and Kazim Khan Shaida (1723-78). The turn of the century saw the move to new literature. It was then that writers turned to original plots. Mention should also be made of the innovative poetry of Fazl Mahmud Makhfi (1884-1947). In the 1920s and 30s, the national patriotic movement became more active. At this time, the progress of Pashto literature is directly connected with the struggle of the Pashtuns for independence. Some of the mid-century writers were among its leaders: Muhammad Khan Mir Hilali and Abdul Akbar. Munshi Ahmad Jan (1882-1951) and Sayid Rahat Zakheli (1886-1963) are regarded as the founders of contemporary Pashto literature. The latter headed a literary circle, '*Bazm-i-Adab*', established in Peshawar in 1937, and in his work strove to overcome ignorance and superstitions. From the end of the 1920s, writers combined enlightenment with national liberation and patriotic ideas. The enlightenment movement in literature was opposed by that based on orthodox Islam, led by Abdul Ali Kakar (1872-1945). Realistic and romantic trends began to take shape in literature, producing particularly successful results in prose.

Contemporary Pashto literature is noted for its brilliant shories story. Famous novelists include Master Abdul Karim (1908-61), Wali Muhammad Tufan and Qalandar Momund (b. 1930). The work of such writers as Mir Mahdi Shah Mahdi (b. 1926), Samandar Khan Samandar is romantic in spirit and addresses the more urgent topics of the day. Traditional poetry contains religious, mystic motifs, nature scenes, philosophical lyrics, and uses only classical genres, primarily *ghazals*. This trend is represented by Amir Hamza Shinwari, Samandar Khan Samandar who was awarded the title of '*Malik ash-Shuara*', Fazl Haq Shaida (1910-84), Rasul Rasa (b. 1910), Abdul Khaliq Khaliq (1895-1978). Realistic poetry is dominated by civic motifs such as the national liberation struggle, social justice, and humanitarian ideals. Prominent in this group are Ajmal Khattak, Muhammad Wali Tufan, Hashim Khalil and Sahibzada Muhammad Idris. Several poets combine traditional motifs and forms with Western poetry in their work: e.g., Abdul Ghani (b. 1916), the leader of the movement, and Muhammad Siddiq Shakir (b. 1948). Many authors write poetry, literary criticism, and plays as well as prose. Particularly famous are the plays by Sayyid Rahat Zakheli, Rashid Ali Dehqan, and Abdullah Jan Asr. Several literary journals are published in Pashto: *Pashto, Nangyalay* (Defender), *Rahbar* (Guide), *Al-Fallah* (Well-being), *Abasing* (The Indus).

BIBLIOGRAPHY: *G.F. Girs, 'Literature of the Undefeated People', Moscow, 1966 (in Russian); A. Bausani, 'Storia delle letterature del Pakistan', Milano, 1958; M.M. Kaleem, 'Pushto Literature. The Cultural Heritage of Pakistan', Karachi, 1955; Abdul Halim, 'Pashto Adab' (Pashto Literature), Peshawar (sa); A. Habibi, 'Da Pashto Adabiyato Tarikh' (History of Pashto Literature, Kabul, 1960.*

A.S. GERASIMOVA

***Chawkandi tombs** are located on the National Highway, about 8 kilometers from Malir City. They comprise of innumerable sand graves with unique carved motifs, dating from an early Muslim period in *Sindh.*

***Clifton Promenade** (1920) is a part of the Jehangir Kothari Parade. The kiosk at one end of the parade, with its elliptical roof structure, built in Jodhpur stone, has an octagonal seat in the centre and was used as a bandstand at the time. A temple of Shiva lies below the Parade, with rock gardens on both sides.*

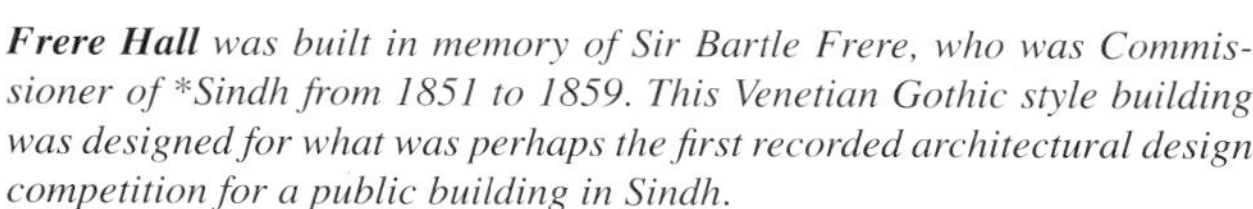

***Frere Hall** was built in memory of Sir Bartle Frere, who was Commissioner of *Sindh from 1851 to 1859. This Venetian Gothic style building was designed for what was perhaps the first recorded architectural design competition for a public building in Sindh.*

***Ziarat Residency** in *Balochistan, where *Quaid-i-Azam, Muhammad Ali *Jinnah spent the last days of his life.*

*The ***Northern Areas** of Pakistan are very beautiful and scenic places, like *Swat, Kalam, Naran, Bhurban, Murree and the set of Galiyats are very popular with local and foreign tourists.*

****Khyber Pass**, mountain pass in western Asia, the most important pass connecting Afghanistan and Pakistan, is controlled by Pakistan. The Khyber Pass winds northwest through Peshawar to Kabul.*

***Tarbela Dam**, the largest earth-filled dam in the world is 469 feet high and 2,264 feet thick at the base.*

***Lake Saiful Muluk** has a touch of the unreal about it, nestling 3,200 metres high. Legend has it that the Crown Prince of Persia, after whom the lake is named, hears about the beauty of the fairy Princess Badar Jamal—the daughter of King of Caucasus—and falls in love with her. This lake was their romantic rendezvous point.*

*The *__Lahore Fort__ was built by Akbar in 1560s. It is culmination of many buildings built over a period of time. The entrance to the fort is through the Alamgiri gate built in 1618 by Jahangir (see, Mughal Empire).*

The mausoleum of ****Rukn-i-Alam*** *is the glory of Multan. This dome is the Shrine of Sheikh Rukn-ud-Din Abul Fath commonly known by the title Rukn-i-Alam (pillar of the world).*

The ***Shah Faisal Mosque*** *in Islamabad is dedicated to the memory of the late King Faisal of Saudi Arabia. The mosque, at the time of creation, was considered to be the national mosque of the newly formed Islamic nation.*

Minar-e-Pakistan *marks the spot at which the *Muslim League on 23 March 1940 passed the resolution calling for the creation of the independent Muslim state of Pakistan (see, Lahore Resolution).*

Pakistan is one of the most prominent Textile producing countries in the world. Each area adds its own ethnic flavour to its garments, creating an interesting theme of colours and blends of design.

Please see the article on Textiles of Pakistan.

A unique style of jewellery adorns both men and women in Pakistan. For all levels of society jewellery often inherits regional styles and cultural motifs

Please see the article on Jewellery in Pakistan.

The evolution of Pakistani currency through the years. Initially, notes and coins carried inscriptions in Hindi, Urdu and English, however, subsequently Hindi was removed.

Please see the article on Pakistani Currency.

The evolution of Pakistani postal stamps through the years. Stamps show famous buildings, places, events, and people. Recent stamps also carry the government's web site address.

Please see the article on Pakistani Stamps.

Qadi

(Arabic, also *Qazi*) A judge in a Muslim community. The decisions passed by a *Qadi* must be based on the **Shariah,* Muslim religious law, rather than on common law, or the *adat* (custom).

YU.V. GANKOVSKY

Qadiani

See, Ahmadiya.

Qadiriya

A *Sufi order founded by Sheikh Abdul Qadir al-Gilani (b. 1077, Gilan, Iran–b. 1166, Baghdad), a *Sunni who followed Hanbali **madhab*. It is the oldest and most numerous Sufi order. The first Qadiriya community appeared in South Asia in the town of Uch-Sharif (district *Bahawalpur, *Punjab Province,). It was founded in 1482 by Sheikh Muhammad Ghaus (d. 1517). The followers of Qadiriya grew in number through the 16th to the 18th centuries. They are very tolerant towards other religions. Baghdad is a holy city as it is home to the main shrine of the Qadiriya founder. In modern times, Qadiriya have been taking an active part in the political life of the countries where Qadiriya communities exist chiefly in north and south Africa, and the Middle East.

YU.V. GANKOVSKY

Qadri, Syed Mohammad Afzal, Dr (1912–74)

Politician. Dr Qadri obtained a PhD in Zoology from Aligarh Muslim University, a further PhD from Cambridge and a DSc. He formulated a scheme for partition with Dr S. Zafrul *Hasan which he presented to the AIML leadership in 1939. Dr Qadri was a member of the *Islami Jama'at* cell formed by the Raja of *Mahmudabad within the *All-India Muslim League.

M.R. KAZIMI

Qaiyum, Abdul, Sahibzada Sir (1866–1937)

Statesman. Sir Abdul Qaiyum received both a traditional and school education. He entered military service in 1887 and was twice mentioned in despatches namely during the Khyber Black Mountain expedition (1888) and the Tirah expedition (1889). Subsequently, Abdul Qaiyum was inducted as political agent for *Chitral and *Khyber. He was an ardent advocate of progress, both educational and political, disclaiming the official notion that the NWFP was too backward for reform. In 1912 he became co-founder, with Sir George Roos-Keppel, of the Islamia College, Peshawar, which later became the University of Peshawar. In 1917 he was knighted. He was elected Member of the Legislative Council in 1923 and 1926. He became the first Minister for Education when the NWFP became a governor's province. He was awarded the *Kaiser-i-Hind* Gold Medal (1929). He was a delegate to the *Round Table Conference where he vigorously advocated reforms in his province. Abdul Qaiyum was sworn in as Chief Minister of the *North West Frontier Province on 22 April 1937 but on 3 September lost a vote of confidence. He died in December of the same year.

BIBLIOGRAPHY: *S. Ahmad, 'Sir Sahibzada Abdul Qayyum', Peshawar, 1989.*

YU.V. GANKOVSKY

Qasida

The *qasida*, as a poetic form, originated in pre-Islamic Arabia, of which the seven Suspended Odes were the most celebrated examples. It had four broad thematic categories and four parts. The themes were categorized as 1. *al-Madeeh*—praise 2. *al Wasf*—narrative especially relating to chivalry 3. *at-Hija*—satire—or lampoon and 4. *ar Ritha*—Elegy. The four parts were 1. *Tashbib*—or the opening. This portion deals with general, even different themes, to engage the attention of the audience 2. *Gurez*—digression. This was a device to connect the first portion to 3. which constituted the main body of the *qasida*, drawing its theme from any one of the four categories mentioned above. 4. lastly comes the entreaty and supplication addressed to the patron who has been praised, in expectation of receiving a reward.

The Arabic *qasida* retains a primitive vigour, both for the unaffected style, and because the subject of praise was rarely unworthy of it. In Persian, however, the subject was rarely worthy of the lavish praise. In Persian the diction was polished, the style ornate, elegant, but in the end somewhat hollow. The *Urdu *qasida* was modelled on the Persian, and the *al-Madeeh* category came to be identified with the *qasida* itself.

Qasidas started as a vehicle for professional poetry. They were composed in praise of kings, princes and other nobles. The parties tacitly understood the praises to be grossly exaggerated, but deserving of a handsome reward. *Qasidas* were also devotional in praise of the Holy Prophet (PBUH), the 12 *imams, caliphs and saints. Mirza Muhammad Rafi *Sauda (1706-81) is universally regarded as the pre-eminent poet of *qasida*, writing in praise of both spiritual and temporal overlords. In the following generation, his place was taken by Sheikh Muhammad Ibrahim *Zauq (1789-1884) the poet-laureate of the last Mughal, Bahadur Shah II. Another exponent of the style, Zafar, though religious by temperament, confined his *qasidas* to court personages. His contemporary Mirza Asadullah Khan *Ghalib (1797-1869) composed *qasidas* both in Persian and Urdu, both temporal and spiritual. His *magnum opus*, a *qasida* in praise of Imam Ali bin abi Talib (598-661), has become memorable as a sincere devotional poem by a sceptical poet. The court *qasida* died out as an art form with the demise of the old order, but the devotional *qasida* was carried forward, in the late 19th century by Mohsin Kakorvi (1826-1905) and Amir *Minai (1828-1900), in the early 20th century, by Safi Lucknowi (1863-1950), Qais Zangipuri (1895-1970), Jameel Mazhari (1904-80) and Muhammad Mustafa Jauhar (1895-1985) of whom only the last named migrated to Pakistan and gave the *qasida* an impetus in the new country.

Sauda wrote satires vividly depicting the instability and corruption of his age. Momin Khan Momin (1800-51) was the only renowned poet to approach the *al wasf* category in *qasida*. All the themes of the *qasida* are repeated in modern and contemporary poetry, but they are not considered *qasida* or **Haj* as they are not written in the classical form.

N.V. GLEBOV

Qasmi, Ahmad Nadeem (1916–)

Writer. Ahmad Shah (his real name) is a leading writer, essayist and public figure, who writes in *Urdu. He was educated in Cambellpur, Sheikhupura and *Bahawalpur. He first published his poetry in 1931 in the Lahore newspaper *Siyasat* ('Politics'). In 1935 he earned his BA degree from the University of the Punjab. For several years he was unemployed and made his living with occasional translations. In those years of semi-unemployment he met writers like Saadat Hasan *Manto, Krishan Chandar and Mumtaz *Husain, who introduced him into the literary life of the country. He took an active part in the work of the *Progressive Writers' Association. His work was published in magazines on a regular basis. From 1939, to 1942 his work as a tax inspector in Multan took him to various *Punjabi villages and gave him a chance to observe rural life. His impressions of those years laid the basis for many of his works in prose and poetry.

His poetry collection includes: *Dharkanen* ('Heartbeats') and *Rim Jhim* ('The Sound of Rain'), 1940-41; *Jalal-o-Jamal* ('Beauty and Glory'), 1947; *Shola-i-Gul* ('The Flame of Flowers'), 1953. His Collections of Short Stories are *Chopal* ('Village Assembly'), 1940; *Bagole* ('Whirlwinds'), 1941; *Tulu-o-Gharub* ('Sunrise and Sunset'); and *Abley* ('Curse'). 1946.

He edited the journals *Tahdhib-i-Niswan, Sawera* and *Adab-i-Latif,* and also worked at Peshawar Radio. Since 1948, Qasmi has been living in Lahore, heading the Progressive Writers' Association and publishing the official organ of the Association, the magazine *Nuqush*. He takes part in the work of various cultural and public organizations, appears in print with articles on politics and art, and publishes stories, poems, and pamphlets.

When Martial Law was imposed in October 1958, the magazine edited by Qasmi was closed down and he was arrested a number of times. Between the 1960s and 1980s, Qasmi published the following collections of stories: *Ghar se Ghar tak* ('From House to House', 1967) and *Kapas kay Phul* ('Cotton Flower,' 1947). He also published two collections of poetry, *Dasht-i-Wafa* ('The Desert of Faithfulness', 1963) and *Muhit* ('The Range of Life', 1975). He published the magazine *Fanun* ('Art') and has several articles on the history of literature to his credit, as well as a series of pen portraits. Qasmi is a winner of prestigious literary prizes of Pakistan. In 1963 he won the Adamjee Prize.

BIBLIOGRAPHY: *N. Glebov, A. Sukhochev, 'Urdu Literature', Moscow, 1967 (in Russian); R.A. Elizarova, A.S. Sukhochev, 'Progressive Writers of Pakistan', Tashkent, 1978 (in Russian).*

N.V. GLEBOV

Qaumi Mazdur Mahaz (QMM)

(National Workers Front) Founded in 1961, in the mid 1970s, this front united forty-one trade unions with 38,000 workers and employees of textile factories, auto repair shops, and air companies located in Karachi, Lahore, Rawalpindi, Multan, Faisalabad, and Quetta. The QMM was a member of the United Workers Federation. It stepped up its activities after the lifting of Martial Law in 1986. The QMM participated in the work of the action committee of *Sindh trade unions.

D. B. NOVOSYOLOV

Qawwali

This is a form of singing among darweshes or itinerant *Sufi musicians. *Qawwals* drove the participants in the rite into a state of religious ecstasy. It was in fact a special technique of singing **ghazals* based on a dispersal of segments of words through their prolonged intonational variation, usually *Urdu. The main form of the performance is juxtaposition of complex improvisations of one or two soloists with a characteristic refrain-like recurrence to the main musical idea performed by a group. The singing is accompanied by playing the **dhol*, the harmonica, the **tabla*, and by clapping. Performance of *qawwals* in traditional Muslim congregations requires close communication between musicians and audience. In the 20th century, *qawwalis* were performed in concerts and recorded. They were also introduced into films, sometimes in modernized form. The origin of *qawwali* is traditionally traced to Amir Khusro *Dehlawi. His works, both Persian and Bhasha, form the main part of the repertoire of most modern *qawwali*. In Pakistan, a new trend was set by late Ghulam Farid Sabri and his brother Maqbool Sabri (see image) and their group who make the art form more evocative than melodious. This trend was heightened by Nusrat Fateh Ali Khan who also introduced some western beats in his concerts.

Most popular exponents of Qawwali, the Sabri brothers.

M.I. KARATYGINA

Quaid-i-Azam

See, Jinnah, Muhammad Ali.

Quaid-i-Azam Academy

It was founded in 1976 in Karachi and was headed by Professor Sharif-ul-Mujahid. Scholars there study the life and activities of *Quaid-i-Azam* M.A. *Jinnah and the history of the Pakistan movement.

The Academy has a library with 12,000 volumes and an archive, and publishes the *Journal of Pakistan Studies* in English and *Urdu.

BIBLIOGRAPHY: *Muslim League Documents (the eighth volume appeared in 1990); Quaid-i-Azam: A Comprehensive Chronology. Vols. 1-4; Quaid-i-Azam's Speeches (1935-47; 1947-48).*

YU.V. GANKOVSKY

Quaid-i-Azam Library

Opened in Lahore in the late 1980s, it has the most modern library facilities for researchers and scholars. The *Quaid-i-Azam* is a reference library, arranges seminars, readings and recitals, symposia, and has a remarkably large collection of international journals, periodicals, films, and books, including rare selections. Membership is restricted to postgraduates and research scholars.

S.J. AHMAD

Quetta culture

This archaeological culture gets its name from the ware with distinctive ornaments found in the settlements in the Quetta valley in northern *Balochistan. There are about twenty excavated sites in all, including Kili-Ghul-Muhammad, Damb Saadat, Kechhi Beg and Karez. The largest of them is tell Damb Saadat (140 x 105 metres), the cultural layer of which is 14 metres thick. Three development Periods (I-III) can be identified. W.A. *Fairservis compares Period IV of Kili-Ghul-Muhammad, Kechhi Beg with Period I of Damb Saadat, and Karez with Period II of Damb Saadat. There are two radio-carbon dates for the earlier Period (Damb Saadat I)–3180 and 3150 BC; for the second Period (Damb Saadat II) there are three radio-carbon dates–3150, 2920 and 2630 BC. Archaeologists found brick walls of solid constructions in Damb Saadat (period III). The material remained the same throughout the three Periods. Clay anthropomorphic and zoomorphic figurines such as zebu, bone axes, copper objects (a dagger), stone implements, such as grain grinders, and sickles. The so-called Zhob figurines are found only in Period III. The Quetta ware is characterized by two colours, black on red, used for decoration in all the three Periods in Damb Saadat and polychrome decorations, the Kechhi Beg style, typical for Periods I-II of Damb Saadat. The Faiz Muhammad style was limited only by Period II of Damb Saadat. There are parallels between the pottery of Damb Saadat I-III and Mundigak (south Afghanistan) II-III.

BIBLIOGRAPHY: *Brigget and Raymond Allchin, 'The Rise of Civilization in India and Pakistan', Cambridge, 1982; W.A. Fairservis, 'The Roots of Ancient India', Chicago-London, 1975; 'Excavations in the Quetta Valley', New York, 1956.*

N.M. VINOGRADOVA

Quetta-Pishin Tableland

This area is situated in the north-eastern part of *Balochistan province between the ranges of Great *Brahui in the east and Sarlath in the west. It is the biggest oasis in Balochistan with a mean elevation of about 1,800 metres, and an area of 10,000 sq. km. It is a flat plain criss-crossed by numerous gullies, and has a precipitation of about 500 mm. a year. Coal deposits have been found here.

YU.V. GANKOVSKY

Qureshi, Ishtiaq Husain (1903–81)

Historian. A Pakistani historian of the Muslim community in South Asia, he served as a public and state figure. Ishtiaq Qureshi graduated from Delhi and Cambridge universities. He taught history in the universities of Delhi, Punjab (Lahore), and Columbia University (USA). He was Vice-Chancellor of the University of Karachi (1961-71), President of the Pakistan Historical Society (1967-70), and President of the Pakistan Political Science Association (1951-72). He took part in the Khilafat Movement and the Pakistan National Movement in Cambridge during the 1930s. He was a member of the Constituent Assembly of Pakistan and a member of the Pakistan Cabinet from 1949-54 serwing as Deputy Minister for Interior, Information and Broadcasting, and for Refugees and Rehabilitation, and also Minister of Education.

WORKS: *'The Pakistan Way of Life', Lahore, 1957; 'The Administration of the Sultanate of Delhi', Karachi, 1958; 'The Muslim Community of the Indo-Pakistan Subcontinent', The Hague, 1962; 'The Administration of the Mughal Empire', Karachi, 1966; 'Ulema in Politics', Karachi, 1972.*

YU.V. GANKOVSKY

Qureshi, Saleem M.M. (1931–)

Political Scientist. He is a political scientist and had been Professor of Political Science at the University of Alberta (Edmonton, Canada) since 1963. He graduated from Lucknow University in India in 1952 and continued his education at the University of Pennsylvania, USA, where he earned his doctorate in 1960. He taught political science in the humanities colleges and institutes in Karachi (1952-61) and then at McGill University, Montreal, Canada in 1961-62 and Saskatchewan University in 1962-63.

WORKS: *'Jinnah and the Making of the Nation', (s.l.) 1969.*

YU.V. GANKOVSKY

R

Radcliffe Award

Sir Cyril Radcliffe, the vice-chairman of the General Council of the English bar chaired the *Punjab and Bengal Boundary Commissions that were to demarcate the Indo-Pakistan boundaries following all the parties' acceptance of the principle of Partition. Radcliffe had been recommended for this appointment in part because he had no local knowledge of the territories that were to be divided. This was supposed to ensure his impartiality, but made a complex task more difficult, especially as Radcliffe only arrived in India on 8 July 1947 and power was to be transferred on 15 August. In the absence of agreement between the Congress and *Muslim League nominated members of the Commissions Radcliffe became the final arbiter. The boundary commissions were to take into consideration, 'other factors' as well as demography in making their award. This encouraged all the parties that made representations to the public sittings of the Commissions to push the boundary as far as possible in a direction that favoured their interests. Great controversy continues to surround the Boundary Award. It is claimed that the delay in its publication until three days after independence was a contributory factor in the Partition related violence. The award of the Muslim majority district of Gurdaspour to India which provided access to *Kashmir has been attributed to Mountbatten's influencing of the award. Moreover, it is also claimed based on circumstantial evidence that Mountbatten prevailed upon Radcliffe to award the Muslim majority tehsils of Zira and Ferozepore to India. It was the *Sikh community, however, that suffered the most from the partition. Radcliffe never returned to the subcontinent and burnt his papers relating to the boundary commission.

I. TALBOT

Radif

(Arabic: one sitting behind the horseman, co-traveller) A word or group of words in poetry that are reiterated unchanged after the rhyme, and are its compositional component. Sometimes *radif* can stand before the rhyme or even at the beginning of a poetic line. *Radif* is used in the poetry of the Middle East and South Asia.

N.V. GLEBOV

Radio in Pakistan

Radio Pakistan and the new State of Pakistan both came into being on the midnight of 14 August 1947. At that time, in the areas now constituting Pakistan, radio started with two small medium wave stations broadcasting for 18 hours a day with transmitting power of 15 kilowatts, covering 6 per cent of the area and 21 per cent of the population. There was no short wave transmitter and no radio station in the capital city. Towards the end of 2001, the 24 stations in the home service air about 375 hours of programmes in 21 languages, reaching 78 per cent of the area and 96 per cent of the country's population. Five stations have two channels and three also have FM service. The 10-hours world service is for overseas Pakistanis, while the 12 hours of external services are in 16 languages. There are 108 news bulletins, totalling 606 minutes. There are forty-six transmitters with radiating power of 3854 kilowatts. A five-hour Quranic channel and a seven-hour news and current affairs channel have been functioning since January 1998 and April 2001 respectively.

On 20 December 1972 Radio Pakistan was made a statutory organization, the 'Pakistan Broadcasting Corporation', to ensure effective operation and growth of broadcasting as a function-oriented public service.

After independence concerted steps were taken to make Radio Pakistan the 'voice of the nation'. A new set of programmes was conceived, new priorities and ratios fixed. The secular nature of the British empire period changed to more ethical and moral programmes in consonance with the aspirations of the new nation. To make up for the initial shortage of playwrights and good scripts, efforts were made to encourage playwrights for radio. Radio drama, besides providing healthy entertainment, was also used as a means to sensitize people about social and moral evils, and to propagate positive traditions and concepts. In music, Radio Pakistan alone patronized music and musicians, and kept alive the tradition of classical and folk music. A new form of **ghazal* singing was introduced, new orchestras created, new music talent found and polished, and a platform provided to potential singers. Through its farm broadcasts, radio provided expert advice and the latest farming information, leading to the adoption of better inputs and mechanical farming techniques, increase in per acre yield, and greater market access. This contribution to agriculture has been recognized internationally. Another achievement is the projection of regional cultures and their blending with the national ethos. Radio had played a very effective and important role in national affairs from the very beginning. Its role during emergencies was spontaneous and laudable. Under the broadcast strategy, introduced in January 1987, programmes were made more life related and result-oriented, with greater emphasis on current affairs and social service, and personalized one-to-one communication with the listener.

The near monopoly position of Radio Pakistan faced a severe challenge with the coming of television, which was initially manned by radio. After the initial setback and adjustment in its programmes, the challenge was met through efficient administration, better budgetary procedures, and by offering multilateral programmes, and above all stressing creativity and imagination for producing quality programmes. Despite the potential size of the audience being much larger than that of television, radio in Pakistan still remains a greatly under-utilized medium.

N. AHMAD

Raga

(Sanskrit: to colour) A multi-aspect concept used in the music of Pakistan and of all South Asia in several mutually complementary senses: 1. a sound equivalent of **ras*; an objective psycho-emotional state embodied in sound and synaptically associated with a definite deity, element of the universe, constellation or luminary, colour, natural sound, caste, as well as the time of day and season of the year; 2. a system of thinking based on the modal principle of development of musical material and linear mode of its unfolding and perception; 3. a sound series with an internally conditioned hierarchy of tones and rigid forms of their correlation; 4. a model or frame of a musical composition comprising a set of melodic cliches or tunes which embody, as a whole, a full code of grammatical and aesthetic norms of the given *raga*. 5. a musical composition based on a sequential mastering of *raga* as a sound sequence and optimal revelation of *raga* as a state.

As a musical term, *raga* was first introduced in the Brihaddeshi treatise in the 5th-9th centuries AD. Later it was developed by scholars. Musical thought, based on the *raga* principles (*ragdar*), went through a long process of development. In this process there were numerous points of contact between the evolution of the *raga* and the parallel *maqam* system that was widespread in Islamic countries. For centuries the search went on for the most convincing system of classification of *ragas*, their grouping in terms of psycho-emotional influence and acoustic laws. *Ragas* were subdivided into basic and derivative, male and female (*raga* and *ragini*), and so on. The most popular classifications are the mathematically demonstrated system of seventy-two sound series developed in the 17th century and the ten sound series classification evolved in the 20th century. The *raga* philosophy was reflected in medieval miniature painting.

I. PIRACHA

Rahimtoola, Habib Ibrahim (1912–91)

Statesman. Habib Rahimtoola was educated at St. Xaviers College and Government Law College in Bombay (now Mumbai). He was a member of the Government of India Food Delegation to the United Kingdom and the United States in 1946. He served as Pakistan's High Commissioner to the United Kingdom. He was the Governor of *Sindh from 1953 to 1955. In 1955 he was Governor of *Punjab.

YU.V. GANKOVSKY

Rahman, Shafiqur (1920–2000)

Writer. Author, physician, and soldier, Shafiqur Rahman was the *Urdu language humorist with the longest sustained popularity. Shafiqur Rahman wrote in an effortless style, commanding a wide range of idiomatic strains. He had a lyrical abandon to his prose. His humorous characters, outrageously drawn, were nevertheless appealing. Shafiqur Rahman was a humorist but not a satirist. This trait endeared him to millions, his books becoming a part of life for his readers.

Shafiqur Rahman's romantic or tragic stories were as well received as his humorous books. He imbued in them a pathos as tangible as that produced by war, hunger and disease. He retired as Surgeon–Rear Admiral in 1980 and in the same year he became founding Chairman of the *Pakistan Academy of Letters. He was awarded the *Hilal-i-Imtiaz* (Military).

BIBLIOGRAPHY: *S. Rashk (ed.) 'Urdu Punch Shafiqur Rahman Edition' (Rawalpindi, 1995); R. Pervin, 'Dr Shafiqur Rahman—Ek Muta'lia' (New Delhi, 1999).*

YU.V. GANKOVSKY

Rahman, Shaikh Mujibur (1920–75)

Political activist. A politician in Pakistan and the national founder figure of Bangladesh, Mujibur Rahman studied political science and law at Calcutta and Dhaka universities. One of the founders of the *Awami League in 1949, he served this Party in various capacities, including from 1949 to 1952 as Secretary, from 1952 to 1966 as General Secretary and from 1966 to 1974 as Chairman. In March-August 1975, Rahman became Chairman of the BAKSAL (*Bangladesh Krishak Shramik Awami* League). In 1945 Rahman was elected to the Bengal Legislative Assembly. He was a Member of the Pakistan *Constituent Assembly simultaneously with membership of the *East Pakistan Provincial Assembly following independence. In 1954 he was one of the prime leaders of the Jugto Front alliance that overwhelmed the *Pakistan Muslim League in elections to the East Pakistan Provincial assembly. In 1970 he was elected a Member of the National Assembly of Pakistan, leading his Awami League Party to a dramatic victory, a key event in the process that would lead to the break-up of Pakistan and the emergence of Bangladesh. Taken prisoner by the Pakistan Army in March 1971, he was released by Zulfiqar Ali *Bhutto in January 1972, to become the first Prime Minister of Bangladesh. From January to August of 1975 he served as President. In 1973 Rahman was awarded a 'Joliot-Curie' medal by the World Peace Council. He was assassinated in Dhaka, while still President, during a military *coup d'etat.*

BIBLIOGRAPHY: *L. Ziring, 'Bangladesh From Mujib to Ershad', Karachi, 1992.*

V.P. BAIDAKOV

Raja

(Sanskrit: king, ruler) Title of ruler of a principality in medieval India, Malaysia and on the island of Jawa (Indonesia). Other forms of this title are Rawal, Rao, Rai, Rana and Raya. The title of *raja* could also be assumed by major landowners who did not have sovereign rights. In antiquity, a tribal chief could also be called a *raja.*

T.N. ZAGORODNIKOVA

Rajasthani (Language)

Belonging to the *Indo-Aryan group of the Indo-European family of languages, Rajasthani does not have an official status. It is mainly spoken in the state of Rajasthan, India, and in the border areas of *Sindh, Pakistan. The language is represented by twenty dialects, usually grouped under several headings. The principal dialect of Rajasthani is Marwari. The literary language now develops on the basis of Marwari, which has a long literary tradition. The earliest monuments depicting Rajasthani literature date back to the 15th century.

BIBLIOGRAPHY: *P.A. Barannikov, 'Problems of Hindi as a National Language', Moscow, 1972 (in Russian); G.A. Zograf, 'The Languages of South Asia', Moscow, 1990 (in Russian); V.A. Chernyshev, 'The Dynamics of the Language Situation in North India', Moscow, 1978 (in Russian); Motilal Menariya, 'Rajasthani bhasha our sahitya', Prayag, 1951; G.A. Grierson, 'Linguistic Survey of India', Vol. 9, Indo-Aryan Family. Western Group, Pt. 2, Specimens of Rajasthani and Gujarati', Calcutta, 1904.*

V.A. CHERNYSHEV

Rajasthani (People)

A people speaking western dialects of the Rajasthani language, reminiscent of the *Sindhi language. They inhabit south-eastern areas of Pakistan, mainly the desert districts of Tharparkar, Nawabshah, and Hyderabad of the *Sindh Province. Their population was 153,000 in 1961—no later data is available. The main occupation is farming and the rearing of livestock. In cities, various crafts are practiced, such as weaving, stone carving, jewellery-making, enamelling, ceramic-making, etc.

YU.V. GANKOVSKY

Rajput

(rajput, Sanskrit: *rajaputra,* king's son, scion of a royal house) A common name for many warrior castes current in North India. They claim to have descended from the *Kshatriyas*, but most clans of Rajputs are descendants of the *Ephtalites and other tribes who came from the north-west and settled in the western part of India in the 5th and 6th centuries. In the 8th to 10th centuries the Rajput clans conquered almost all of north India, founding the states of Gurjara-Pratihara, Guhilot and others. Some ruling groups of the Munda, Gond and Bhil tribes in Central India have also been identified with the Rajputs. Some merchant castes, including the Khatri also call themselves Rajputs. In the time of the Muslim dynasties, the Rajputs formed the dominant caste of the rural population of north and central India, and a considerable proportion of **zamindars* in the *Mughal Empire and in the colonial period.

The Rajputs' principal occupations are agriculture and army service. Their way of life is highly regarded socially. They are allowed to eat meat and drink wine. The rules for giving girls away in marriage are very complicated, for they cannot be given away either to related clans or to lower ones. For this reason the custom of killing newborn girls was widespread until the middle of the 19th century but was later banned by the British.

L.B. ALAYEV

Ramazan

(also *Ramadhan*) *See*, *Sawm*.

Rana Ghundai

Near Loralai in Northern *Balochistan is an archaeological site of a multi-level settlement of resident land-tillers dating back to the 2nd millennium BC. In the 1940s and 50s, E.J. Ross and W.A. *Fairservis worked here. The lower levels of Rana Ghundai I yielded modelled pottery with traces of a basket, flint and bone implements and bones of domestic animals on it. This complex is also found in Kili-Ghul-Muhammad II. Wheeled pottery including vases on legs, the forms of which are close to the vessels of the Hissar culture, appeared in the Rana Ghundai II levels. As distinct from the Hissar pottery, they bear drawings of local animals, such as zebu and antelope. Rana Ghundai II, with its wheeled, painted pottery marks the heyday of the culture of land-tilling communities that were contemporaries of the *Harappan civilization. The periods Rana Ghundai IV and V saw a certain cultural decline. The pottery with basket imprints and the breeds of domestic cattle speak in favour of the local genesis of the land-tilling and cattle-breeding culture of the region. According to V. Gordon Childe, professional potters who resettled to Rana Ghundai from Western Asia brought wheeled painted pottery with them. D.H. Gordon and W.A. Fairservis believe that it was originated by infiltration of some of the western tribes into Balochistan.

BIBLIOGRAPHY: *E.J. Ross, 'A Chalcolithic Site in Northern Balochistan', Journal of Near Eastern Studies, 1946, Vol. 5, No. 4; W.A. Fairservis, 'Archaeological Surveys in the Zhob and Loralai Districts', West Pakistan, Anthropological Papers of the American Museum of Natural History, 1959, Vol. 47, Part 2, New York; D.H. Gordon, 'The Pre-Historic Background of Indian Culture', Bombay, 1958; V. Gordon Childe, 'New Light on the Most Ancient East', London, 1952.*

A.YA. SHCHETENKO

Rann of Kutch

The Rann of Kutch, consists of the Great Rann in the northern section, and Small Rann of the south-eastern part. They are marshy, salty lowlands up to 50 meters above sea level, located in western India, the state of Gujarat, and in Pakistan to the south-east of the Indus delta stretching into the *Arabian Sea. The lowlands spread 400 km., to the west of the Indus dud for 230 km., beyond the mouth of the Luni in the east. and for 230 km. The area extends from the *Thar Desert in the north to the Mandaw Plateau in the south. Formerly the Rann was a shallow sea bay, which rose as a result of tectonic processes. During the monsoon season, the Rann is flooded by the rivers and wind-driven sea water. During the dry season it is covered with bleached salt and black slime. The climate is tropical, dominated by the monsoons. The annual precipitation is within the range of 200-500 mm. In April and May dust storms occur there.

N.N. ALEXEEVA
S.B. ROSTOTSKY

Rashid, Abdur, Justice Mian Sir (1889–1981)

Statesman. Mian Abdur Rashid was educated at Forman Christian College, Lahore and Christ's College, Cambridge. He was called to the Bar from the Middle Temple in 1913. He served as Government Advocate Punjab from 1929 to 1930. He was elevated to the Lahore High Court in 1933 and served till 1946. He was Chief Justice of Lahore High Court (1946-48). He administered the oath of office to Quaid-i-Azam Mohammad Ali Jinnah, as the first Governor-General of Pakistan by virtue of being the senior most judge in Pakistan. From 1949 to 1954 Sir Abdur Rashid was the Chief Justice of Pakistan. During October to December 1953 Sir Abdur Rashid was acting Governor-General.

M.R. KAZIMI

Rashid, Noon Meem (1910–75)

Poet. Rashid was a poet writing in *Urdu. He received a traditional domestic education and in 1926-32 he studied at the Government Colleges in Lyallpur and Lahore. In his student days, he started reporting for the newspaper *Zamindar,* in which he published articles on Mirza *Ghalib, Muhammad *Iqbal and the plays of Imtiaz Ali *Taj. Considered among the pioneers of the Modernist movement in Urdu poetry, his first sonnets and *vers libre* appeared in Akhtar *Shirani's journal *Humayun*. In 1934 he became editor of a famous literary journal *Shahkar* ('Masterpiece'). In 1935 he joined the Indian Civil Service in Multan. He published several translations of Western and Russian authors. From the end of the 1930s he took part in the work of the Group of Art Lovers (*Halqa-i-Arbab-i-Zawq*). In 1939 he took a job with All-India Radio and, in 1943, he joined the army, serving in Iraq, Iran, Egypt and Sri Lanka. After 1947 he worked in *Radio Pakistan, heading its branches in Karachi, Lahore and Peshawar. From 1952 he occupied prominent positions in the UN, working in New York, London, Cairo, Jakarta and Karachi. He headed the Pakistan Information Centre in Tehran, where he appeared in the Iranian press. He joined a group of modernist poets and published a book of contemporary Persian poetry with Urdu translation. Rashid's work asserted the artist's independence from any ideology, emphasizing freedom of artistic choice and creative endeavours. He practised various traditional verse forms but preferred free verse. His thematic range was wide. He had three collections of poetry published: *Mawara* ('The Otherwordly', 1942), *Iran men Ajnabi* ('An Alien in Iran', 1955), and *La-Insan* ('The Antihuman', 1969). He was awarded several prestigious literary prizes. His book is entitled *La Masavi Insan*. Rashid's work has been compiled and published recently by Mavra Lahore under the title of *Kulliyat-i-Rashid* (1990). Rashid is also known for his fascination with existentialist philosophy and most of his poetry is philosophical in nature.

BIBLIOGRAPHY: *M. Hasan, 'Jadid Urdu Adab' (New Urdu Literature), Delhi, 1975; D.J. Matthews, C. Shackle, Shahrunuh Husain, 'Urdu Literature', London, 1985; A. Ahmad, N.M. Rashid, 'Shair aur Shakhs', Lahore, 1989, Karachi 2000; Jameel Jalibi (ed.) 'N.M. Rashid Ek Mutalia', Karachi, 1985.*

N.V. GLEBOV

Rashidi, Pir Hussamuddin (1911–82)

Historian. A Pakistani historian, philologist and public figure. Author of *History of Sindhi Literature* (Karachi, 1959), he also compiled an Anthology of Kashmiri Poetry in Persian in four volumes (Karachi, 1968-70). He was director of the Institute for the Study of Central and Western India (Karachi, 1973-82) and also served as President of the Society of Pakistan-Soviet Cultural Ties in the 1960s and 70s.

Noted author, Pir Hussamuddin Rashidi.

YU.V. GANKOVSKY

Ravi

The Ravi is the eastern tributary of the *Chenab in the basin of the River *Indus, and the middle of the five major rivers of *Punjab. It is 725 km. long and flows from north-east to south-west. Its source is on the south-eastern slope of the Pir-Panjal Range, at a height of some 4,000 metres. It cuts through the Dhaoladhari and Siwalik ranges and enters the Punjab Plain in the vicinity of the town of Pathankot (India). Approximately 100 km. of its course serves as the border between India and Pakistan. It is fed in the upper reaches mainly by glacial and sub-soil waters, and in the lower valley by rainfall. The regimen is determined by the monsoons. Floods occur in summer and are very high. The discharge is largely regulated by dams. The waters of the Ravi are extensively used for irrigation. The Upper *Bari Doab canal, with a hydro scheme at Madhopura, built in 1859, was the first big irrigation structure built in north-west India. According to the agreement between India and Pakistan signed in 1960, the use of water of the Ravi is controlled by India. The largest tributaries of the Ravi, the Degh to the west and the Sakki to the east, are connected to the River *Beas by a canal. The city of Lahore stands on the Ravi.

S.B. ROSTOTSKY

Rawalpindi Conspiracy

In February 1951, thirteen army officers and four civilians were arrested on conspiracy charges. The detainees included, among others, Chief of General Staff Major-General Akbar Khan, Begum Neseem Akbar Khan, Major M. Ishaq, Zafarullah Poshni, Air Commodore Mohammed Khan Janjua, major-General Nazir Ahmed, Brigadier Siddiq Khan, Brigadier Latif Khan, Sajjad Zaheer (Secretary, *Communist Party of Pakistan), and famous poet and then editor of the *Pakistan Times, Faiz Ahmed *Faiz. They were accused of conspiring with communists and revolutionary elements to bring about a military takeover against the government of Liaquat Ali *Khan. Husain Shaheed *Suhrawardy and other advocates defended them, the prosecution being led by A.K. Brohi before a tribunal headed by Justice Abdur Rahman from the Federal Court.

After few years of detention, all accused were set free. However, military personnel were expelled from service. The case is best known throughout Pakistan as the 'Rawalpindi conspiracy'.

BIBLIOGRAPHY: *Z. Hassan, 'The Times and Trial of the Pawalpindi Conspiracy, 1951 the First Coup Attempt in Pakistan, Karachi, OUP, 1999; DAWN Archives.*

M.R. KAZIMI

Rawshaniya

A Muslim sect founded by Bayazid Ansari (*c.* 1515–85), from Kaniguram in *Waziristan. He was given the name of *Pir Rawshan* (the father, or the teacher of light by his followers). Bayazid Ansari preached equality of all people before Allah. He opposed feudal lords and the **ulema* elite, and campaigned for the abolition of taxes and dues. Bayazid Ansari and his successors led the Rawshaniya movement, a popular *Pashtun movement (*c.* 1560–1638) against the local feudal lords and the Great Mughals. It played an important role in the ethnic consolidation of the Pashtuns, but it was suppressed in the years of Shah Jehan's rule (1627–58).

YU.V. GANKOVSKY

Rayat

(or *ryot*, Arabic: flock) A general term for tax-payers in Muslim countries. 1. In the tax instructions of the *Mughal Empire (India, 16th–18th centuries), the term was used to denote tax-payers, small and major landowners (**zamindar*, **maliks*, *arbabs*, **mirasdars*) who had extensive rights to land. 2. In the deeds and other documents of the same empire, *rayat* meant permanent or temporary tenants leasing land from *zamindars* and others. 3. During the British period *rayats* were persons who received land, at first on conditions of life-long tenancy, and later as their property, in the Madras and Bombay presidencies.

L.B. ALAYEV

Rechna Doab

From the initial letters of the river names, *Ravi and *Chenab, with the addition of *doab*, which means 'between rivers'. The territory between the Rivers Ravi and Chenab in *Punjab.

YU.V. GANKOVSKY

Red Shirts

(Persian: *surkhposh*; official name: *Khudai Khidmatgar*–the servants of God) Volunteer detachments of the *Pashtun national organization, the '*Pakhtun Jirga*'. It was established in 1929 in the *North-West Frontier Province. The Red Shirts took an oath to fight for the freedom of their land from British rule, to help the downtrodden, to resist their oppressors, and to obey their commanders unconditionally. The commander-in-chief (*Salar-i-azam*) of the Red Shirt Army was Khan Abdul Ghaffar *Khan, popularly known as '*Baacha* Khan'. In 1931 the size of the Red Shirt Army reached 200,000 men, predominantly peasants. They took an active part in the anti-British armed uprising of 1930–2, in the course of which 12,000 people were arrested and hundreds were shot.

BIBLIOGRAPHY: *Yuri Gankovsky, 'Nationalities Question and National Movements in Pakistan', Moscow, 1967 (in Russian); M. Yunus, 'Frontier Speaks', Bombay, 1947; Abdul Qaiyum, 'Gold and Guns on the Pathan Frontier', Bombay, 1945; W. Khan, 'Facts are Facts', New Delhi, 1987.*

YU.V. GANKOVSKY

Reisner, Igor Mikhailovich (1899—1958)

Historian. He was a historian of the East, and a professor who graduated from the Oriental Department of the Military Academy of the Red Army (1924). He worked at the People's Commissariat for Foreign Affairs in Afghanistan (1919-22), taught at the Moscow Institute of Oriental Studies, and headed the Sector of the East of the Historical Department of Moscow University (1934-58). He was sector head at the Institute of Oriental Studies of the USSR (1950-58). He was the author of books on the history of the Great Mughals, the *Durrani Empire, Afghanistan, and the Eastern *Pashtuns.

WORKS: *'Afghanistan', Moscow, 1929; 'Essays on the Class Struggle in India', Moscow, 1932; 'Feudal Development and State Formation among the Afghans', Moscow, 1954; 'Popular Movements in India in the 17th-18th Centuries', Moscow, 1961 (all in Russian).*

YU.V. GANKOVSKY

Rekhta

(mixed, scattered, Persian: *rikhtan*—to mix, to scatter) The name of a language and a literary form in *Urdu, popular in the 18th, early 19th century. *Rekhta* as a literary form was popular at the king's court in Delhi, and particularly in Lucknow with the poets of the Lucknow school.

BIBLIOGRAPHY: *H. Glebov, A. Sukhochev, 'Urdu Literature', Moscow, 1967 (in Russian).*

N.V. GLEBOV

Rekhti

A lyrical genre and poetic style practiced by poets in Delhi and Lucknow at the end of the eighteenth and in the early nineteenth century. Usually it was a **ghazal* in the name of a woman with words and idioms having a special meaning typical of the *Zanana* (female) language, the language of the ladies apartments. *Rekhti* is also known as 'flirting' poetry. Famous in this genre were: Insha Allah Khan *Insha (d. 1818), Saadat Yar Khan Rangin (d. 1834), and Mir Yar Ali Khan (Jan Sahab, d. 1897).

N.V. GLEBOV

Replaced wax (also known as Lost wax)

A technique of casting with a wax model, popular in Pakistan during antiquity and the Middle Ages. The earliest sculptures found using this technique are miniature sculptures of animals and human beings that came from centres of the *Harappa civilization. In the *Kushan empire (1st-3rd centuries AD), the development of the cult of worshipping divine characters of Buddhism, Jainism, and Hinduism gave an added impetus to casting sculpture. The classical monuments belong to the *Gupta epoch (4th-6th centuries), including the sculpture of four-faced Brahma from Mirpur Khas (5th century), now located in the *Lahore Museum use this technique. In the early Middle Ages the sculptures were mostly Buddhist, and close in style to those of *Kashmir. The spread of Islam nearly led to the extinction of the art of replaced wax in the territory that is now Pakistan.

The technique of casting was similar to the technique used in South Asia, as described in a number of canonic works, which used brass, or sometimes bronze. In the classical process, a sculpture was cast with all its details simultaneously. Apertures for pouring molten metal into the clay mould and for the discharge of air were made at the base of the sculpture.

E.V. GANEVSKAYA

Republican Party

Founded on 23 April 1956 in Lahore by a group of politicians of *West Pakistan who withdrew from the *Muslim League. The group included by such men as Dr Khan *Sahib, Malik Firoz Khan *Noon, M.G.A. Talpur, and S.M.K. *Leghari. The Party was mostly active in West Pakistan. The leaders of the Party declared that it did not have a religio-communal character, supported the idea of a single province of West Pakistan, and called for land reforms on condition that compensation for land was to be paid to the landowners. The Republican Party won over a majority of members of the West Pakistan's Legislative Assembly on 29 April 1956 and thus headed the provincial government. From September 1956 to October 1958 the Republican Party was a member of several coalitions that came to power in Pakistan.

BIBLIOGRAPHY: *Yuri Gankovsky, L.R. Gordon-Polonskaya, 'A History of Pakistan', Lahore, 1972.*

YU.V. GANKOVSKY

Resident

Until the 1770s, the head of a provincial office of the British East India Company or the head of district administration. Later, an official of the British administration in a vassal state or group of states, who controlled their home and foreign policy.

T.N. ZAGORODNIKOVA

Riaz, Fahmida (1946–)

Poet. Educated in Hyderabad and London, Fahmida Riaz is among the front rank of poets in *Urdu. From the outset, she refused to be stereotyped as a female poet and conform to what are generally regarded as the confines of 'proper' literary and creative traditions of poetry written by women. In her choice of themes, diction, allusion and similes, she broke from the inhibitions imposed on her gender. This was evident from the contents of her first collection of verse, *Paththar Ki Zaban* ('Tongue of Stone', 1967). With the publication of her second collection *Badan Dareeda* (*'The Torn Body'*), she emerged as a full-fledged iconoclast. The poem *Badan Dareeda,* which carried the same title as the collection, can be regarded as something of a landmark putting her in the same category as Ismat Chughtai when she wrote the short story *Lihaf.* If this, on the one hand, won her many admirers, especially among the modernists and the younger generation, she also became the target of criticism by traditionalists who believed she had transgressed into forbidden territory. However, Fahmida Riaz refused to be inhibited because she was a woman. Instead, she used her femininity as a weapon to expose the prudishness of the male-oriented traditions of Urdu poetry. She has since published four more collections of her verse–*Dhoop* ('Sun'*), Kya Tum Pura Chand Na Dekhogay ('Will you not look at the Full Moon'), Hamrakab ('Travelling Companion')* and *Aadmi Ki Zindigi (*'The Life of a Man'*).* Fahmida Riaz is also the author of several short stories and travelogues in Urdu,

Godavari about her wanderings in India and *Zinda Bahar Lane* about Bangladesh.

Fahmida Riaz is also an unrelenting social critic and has been active in several human rights movements. She was among the writers who campaigned against General Ziaul *Haq's military rule and the execution of Z.A. *Bhutto, and had to suffer the wrath of the authorities and a period of self-exile. She has travelled widely and lectured at universities and cultural forums in England and the US. Fahmida Riaz was given the Himmett-Hellman Award by Human Rights Watch, New York, in 1997.

M.H. ASKARI

Round Table Conferences 1930–32

Three Round Table conferences were hosted at St, James' Palace, in London, by Prime minister Ramsay Macdonald. These followed the setting up of the Statutory Commission under Sir John Simon in 1927. The *Simon Commission had been boycotted and then overtaken by the *Nehru Report and *Fourteen Points. The atmosphere had become that of protest and dissent, with Pandit Motilal Nehru insisting on full independence. In an attempt to break the political deadlock the Viceroy invited 58 delegates, all leaders of public opinion in India, to a Round Table Conference with the aim of formulating the future constitution of India.

First Round Table Conference, 21 November 1930–19 January 1931: This was inaugurated by King George V. The delegates agreed to the replacement of diarchy, where the two powers ruled jointly, by representative provincial government, and to the predomination of the Indian power at the centre. Essentially a federation was proposed and the rulers of the various princely states expressed their willingness to join at that stage. However the issues of communal representation could not be resolved, with major differences over the number and proportion of representatives a religion based community could send to the legislature. The separation of *Sindh from Bombay was also hotly debated. The first RTC therefore failed to produce a positive outcome. Meanwhile in India the well-known poet and activist, Sir Allama Mohammad *Iqbal, whilst presiding over the annual December session of the AIML at Allahabad, called for the creation of a Muslim State in the north west region of India. Earlier that year, on 5 April, Mahatma Mohandas Karamchand Gandhi symbolically broke the Salt laws by marching to Dandi beach, causing Congress agitation to build to a climax. The Civil Disobedience Movement continued to agitate until March 1931, when Viceroy Lord Irwin and Gandhi signed a pact, calling for the release of the non-violent category of political prisoners. This pact paved the way for Gandhi to attend the second RTC.

Second Round Table Conference, 7 September–1 December 1931: This session was attended by a number of new delegates including Sir Mohammed *Iqbal, Pandit Madan Mohan Malaviya and Gandhi as the sole representative of Congress. Despite the early conciliatory gestures of Gandhi and the earnest efforts of Sir Mohammed *Shafi and M.A. *Jinnah, communal differences could not be reconciled. Liberals including Sir Chimanlal Setalvad, Srinava Shastri and Sir Tej Bahadur Sapru were in favour of a settlement, but other delegates including Malaviya opposed them. On 8 October Gandhi announced that his efforts at mediation had failed. He asked the Muslim delegates to oppose the granting of separate electorates to the depressed classes of Hindu. The Muslim delegates undertook to abide by any agreement Gandhi could arrive at with Dr B.R. Ambedkar, leader of the depressed classes, but could not reasonably oppose the extension to others of the same rights they had claimed for themselves. The Second Session decided to separate Sindh from Bombay and to make NWFP a governor's province. At this session the princes withdrew their willingness to join any proposed Indian Federation. The *Communal Award announced on the 16 April 1932 retained separate electorates for Muslim and extended this right to the depressed Hindu classes, but the weightage system reduced the Muslim majorities in Punjab and Bengal. In protest Gandhi started a fast on 20 September which ceased on 26.

Third Round Table Conference, 17 November–24 December 1932: This session was almost inconsequential, as it was not attended by Gandhi, and Jinnah was not invited to take part. He later maintained that this was because of his insistence on the Fourteen Points. He had displeased the Hindus for criticizing what he saw as their underhand activities, he had displeased the princes and he infuriated the British parliament by terming the RTC a fraud. On 27 November he had charged the chairman of the Federal Structure sub-committee with being pro-Hindu. Nevertheless, even without the two major players, the delegates drew up a plan for constitutional reforms, published in the white paper dated 17 March 1933. Many of the proposals were later embodied in the Government of India Act, 1935.

The Round Table Conferences did not achieve any meaningful advance, but they did serve to mirror more sharply the differences between Indian factions and interests. Delegates from the Muslim majority provinces, such as Sir Fazle *Hussain and Sir Mohammad Shafi, were in favour of greater provincial autonomy with no weightage for minorities. The weightage principle was seen by them as reducing the statutory Muslim majorities in Punjab and Bengal, without substantially altering the position of Muslims in minority provinces such as Uttar Pradesh and Bihar. The Conferences also threw into stark relief the differences of views, regarding the constitutional demands of Muslims, between liberal Hindu leaders such as Setalvad and communal Hindu leaders such as Malaviya. These differences seriously limited the efforts of the British prime minister to resolve the problem of Indian independence.

BIBLIOGRAPHY: *Parliamentary Papers and HMSO. Publication: Cmd. 3738 (1931), Proceedings of the Indian Round Table Conference: First Session Cmd. 3997 (1932), Proceedings of the Indian Round Table Conference. Second Session. Cmd. 4238 (1933), Report and Proceedings of the Indian Round Table Conference Third Session. (b) K.H. Khurshid, Memories of Jinnah (Karachi, 1990); David Page, Prelude to Partition (Karachi, 1987), Chimanlal H. Setalvad, Recollections and Reflections (Bombay, 1946.); Jahan Ara Shahnawaz, Father and Daughter (Lahore, 1971).*

M.R. KAZIMI

Rubai

The *rubai* consists of four lines, generally having a rhyme scheme of a a b a, but in rare cases aaaa in which case it is called *musarrah*. All quatrains or poems of four lines are not considered *rubai* but only those conforming to set prosodic conventions. These are twenty-four variations of the *Hazaj Akhram* and *Hazaj Akhrab*. The *rubai* had its origin in Saffavid Iran during the reign of Yaqub bin Lais (d. 878). The first preserved Persian rubai was composed by Shaikh Abul Hasan Khirqani (d. 1034). Other important poets were Baba Tahir Uryan Hamdani and Saheb Sultan. Abu Said Abul Khair, who was born towards the end of the 10th century introduced the theme of *Sufism in *rubai*. It was the 19th Century free translation into English by Edward Fitzgerald of the poet Omar Khayyam (d.1123), little known in his own country, that was responsible for introducing *rubai* worldwide.

In Urdu, the earliest *rubai* is traced to Mir Abdul Qadir Hyderabadi (Deccan) who lived before 1700. From the 18th century onwards almost every **Dewan* or **Kulliyat* contained some *Rubiyat*, but never received more than passing attention from the masters. In the 19th century the *rubai* became a form subservient to the marsiya popularised by *Anis, *Dabir and other contemporaries to depict the tragedy of Karbala and related moral and didactic subjects. Piarey Saheb Rashid (1846-1917) made the ravages of old age his constant theme. The Urdu *rubai* blossomed only in the 20th century. Shad Azimabadi (1846-1927), Yas Yagana Changezi (1884-1956), Jagat Mohan Lal Rawan (1889-1934), Firaq Gorakhpuri (1896-1982), Amjad Hyderabadi (1908-19), and Ijtiba Rizvi (1908-88) are the main exponents. In Pakistan, four names stand out: Josh *Malihabadi, Abu Jafar Kashfi, Sadequain Ahmad Naqvi, and Syed Maqsud Zahidi. The *rubai* was especially attuned to the poetic genius of Josh whose output rivals Omar Khayyam in the universality of appeal and outstrips him the range of themes. Loud and raucous in political satires, Josh achieves a soft and delicate diction in *rubai*, their aspect ethereal and style translucent. Abu Jafar Kashfi reverted to the traditional and didactic manner. The *rubaiyat* of *Sadequain are about seemingly commonplace themes, descending even to gauche familiarity, but are nevertheless evocative and engrossing.

BIBLIOGRAPHY: *F. Fatehpuri, 'Urdu Rubai ka Irtiqa' (The Evolution of Urdu Rubai) Karachi, 1962.*

M.R. KAZIMI

Rukn

(Arabic: pillar, support; plural: *arkan*) The basic religious rules and main religious duties obligatory for any Muslim. Otherwise known as the five pillars of Islam, the rules and duties are the confession of faith (*shahada*), prayer (**salat*), fasting (**sawm*), alms (**zakat*), and pilgrimage (**haj*).

YU.V. GANKOVSKY

Rukn-i-Alam

A monument of Pakistan's medieval culture this mausoleum in Multan was built of fired brick in 1320-24. It has features characteristic of the architecture of the *Delhi Sultanate. The two-tiered, domed octagonal tomb has massive walls inclined inward, with buttress

A Dehli Sultanate monument, the *Rukn-i-Alam.*

towers that remind us that the edifice also served as a fortress. The mausoleum's compact building is crowned with a spherical dome with a height of 34.5 metres and the thickness of the walls in the first tier is 4 metres. The second tier is embellished with arched window openings in ornamental frames and with a crenulated parapet.

A.B. RALLEV

Russia-Pakistan Relations

Relations between Pakistan and Russia date from the Cold War era when Russia was the main component of the Union of Soviet Socialist Republics. Thus not only strategic configurations but also ideological concerns became a factor during the formative phase of these relations. An *All-India Muslim League leader, Yousuf Haroon, contacted the Soviet Foreign Minister, W.M. Molotov, to secure help for Pakistan, but the Pakistani leadership discarded his attempt, perhaps under pressure from the British. Three days after independence Prime Minister Liaquat Ali *Khan stated clearly that Pakistan would follow a policy of non-alignment. On 7 September 1947 the founder and first Governor-General of Pakistan, M.A. *Jinnah stated in cabinet that 'Pakistan was a democracy and communism does not flourish in the soil of Islam', meaning manifestly that Pakistan was favourably inclined to the West. He added the proviso that this should be done 'without however going out of our way to annoy Russia'. In the subsequent meeting on 11 September Jinnah's stand was strengthened when he noted that among all countries, only Russia had not sent a congratulatory message on the creation of Pakistan. Moscow was informed that the British Embassy would represent Pakistan's interests in the Soviet Union. Meanwhile a delegation had gone to Washington seeking monetary help, in return for which Pakistan would block the progress of Communism in Asia. However, formal relations were established with, on 1 May 1948.

Well within a year, Liaquat grew disenchanted with the West because of lukewarm support over the *Kashmir dispute. When the Indian Prime Minister was invited to the US, the Soviet Union looked for an opening in South Asia. On 2 June 1949 Liaquat Ali Khan was invited to visit the Soviet Union. On 7 June he announced his acceptance and proposed 20 August 1949 as the date of the visit. It was against this backdrop that Liaquat stated on 10 June that 'Pakistan cannot afford to wait. She must take her friends where she finds them.'. But from then on the Soviet Union back-pedalled. On 19 July Liaquat was informed that the date of his visit had been advanced and he must arrive on 15 August. Since this would have meant his absence from Pakistan during its first Independence Day after the death of its founder, Liaquat proposed 18 August but from that time on the Soviet Union never set the dates again till Liaquat's assassination (16 October 1951).

On 31 December 1949 the Pakistan Ambassador to the USSR assumed his post, but it was only in March of the following year that the Soviet Ambassador arrived in Pakistan. In a development following Liaquat's assassination, the famous historian Arnold Joseph Toynbee expressed the view that the USSR would bear down on Pakistan, seeking the warm water port of Karachi. This created greater suspicion of Russia but also alerted the US to the need of pre-empting such a move. In 1954 Pakistan signed its first military pact with the US in Manila, on the 8 September. This was followed by the Baghdad Pact on 24 February 1955 and a bilateral agreement on 5 March 1959. The USSR, which until then had been distant but neutral, turned hostile. N. Bulganin and N. Khrushchev, Prime Minister and First Secretary of the Communist Party respectively, visited India and Afghanistan, supporting the host countries on the Kashmir and **Pakhtunistan* disputes. From then on the USSR vetoed every UN resolution on Kashmir. During this phase, on 7 May 1960, a U2 American spy plane, having taken off from near Peshawar, was shot down over Soviet territory. Nikita Khrushchev directly threatened Pakistan with reprisals.

One year later, on 4 March 1961, the Fuel and Power Minister of Pakistan, Z.A. *Bhutto, negotiated an oil and gas exploration agreement with the Soviet Union. At the time of the Sino-Indian war in April 1965 President Ayub *Khan made a state visit to the USSR. After the outbreak of the 1965 war the Soviet Union inched closer to Pakistan, Alexei Kosygin acknowledging that there was a dispute over Kashmir. After the ceasefire, the USSR hosted the *Tashkent Conference. President Ayub again went to Moscow in September 1967. In April 1968 and in May 1969 Kosygin visited Pakistan and made a token arms deal.

The Tashkent Declaration was unpopular in Pakistan, but the people had hopes with Soviet neutrality. These hopes, however, were shattered upon the outbreak of the political crisis in the eastern wing of Pakistan, when Pakistan brought the feuding USA and the People's Republic of China together on 15 July 1971. President

Nicolai Podgorny threatened President Yahya *Khan over the military action, which began on 25 March 1971. President Yahya Khan in his reply referred to the Soviet role in Hungary and Poland. A meeting between the two presidents in Tehran was not cordial. An Indo-Soviet Treaty of Co-operation was signed, under which the Russians warned Pakistan that any action against *Awami League terrorists would be treated as an act of war. During the December 1971 debate in the UNSC, the Soviet Union vetoed every proposal for ceasefire, making Pakistani withdrawal from its own territory a condition for peace.

President Z.A. Bhutto made an official visit to the USSR on 16-18 March 1972, but was told plainly by his hosts that the Soviet Union would act in the same manner in a similar situation. This was interpreted as a Soviet invitation to secession of the NWFP and *Balochistan provinces. Z.A. Bhutto's second visit from 24-26 October 1974 was far more cordial. Nevertheless, the Brezhnev plan to include the 'States of Hindustan' in a security arrangement showed that Indian hegemony over South Asia was the linchpin of Soviet policy.

Relations with the Soviet Union deteriorated when the Soviet army invaded Afghanistan in 1979, practically threatening the borders of Pakistan. In this situation the US again extended help to Pakistan against the Soviet threat. General Ziaul *Haq tried to maintain relations regardless, but his visits to Moscow during state funerals proved futile. The Soviet withdrawal from Afghanistan was covered by the 14 April 1988 *Geneva Agreement. The Soviet troops left on 15 February 1989.

The Soviet withdrawal and the subsequent break-up of the USSR raised hopes about a new era of relations with Russia. Pakistan had withdrawn from US-sponsored military pacts and had joined the Non-Aligned Movement, and Russia had shed its Communist ideology. Optimism marked the discourse of A.U. Alexeyev, the Russian Ambassador, before a Karachi audience on 24 December 1995. He said state and national interests, not ideology would guide the foreign policy of Russia. Strategic and ideological imperatives had the same effect, however, mainly because of two irritants. These were Pakistan's support to the Taliban regime in Afghanistan, and Russia's conviction that the Taliban were behind fomenting resistance in Chechnya. There was renewed hope when Presidents Vladimir Putin and Pervez *Musharraf met in September 2000 on the sidelines of the UN Millennium Summit. These were followed through the same month by the visit of special envoy Sergey Yasterzhembsky, who proposed treaties relating to extradition, drug trafficking, smuggling, and terrorism, but no concrete progress was made, despite Pakistan's stated position that it considers Chechnya a part of Russia.

In October 2000 President V. Putin visited India, made the suggestion that Russia would mediate on Kashmir if both India and Pakistan wished it, and reaffirmed outright support to the Indian position on Kashmir. During this visit Putin signed a new Defence Pact which Indian sources described as being more comprehensive than its 1971 predecessor. With Pakistan having to withdraw support from the Taliban in the aftermath of the 11 September 2001 terrorists attacks on the US, a major source of contention had gone. Russia recently helped Pakistan launch a satellite.

BIBLIOGRAPHY: *M.A. Popatia, 'Pakistan's Relations with the Soviet Union 1947-1979', Karachi, 1988; H. Malik, 'Soviet-Pakistan Relations and Post-Soviet Dynamics', London, 1994.*

M.R. KAZIMI

Ruswa, Mirza Muhammad Hadi (1857–1931)

Writer. Ruswa was one of the pioneers of the *Urdu novel. He came from an impoverished aristocratic family and had a technical education. His first poetic attempts were a failure. Ruswa wrote one of the first literary plays in *Urdu, intended for reading rather than enacting, *Drama of Leila and Majnun,* written in 1898. Ruswa's main contributions to Urdu literature were his novels, carrying the idea of Muslim enlightenment in India: *Umrao Jan Ada* (1899), *Ifsha-i-Raz* ('Secrets Disclosed', 1896), *Zat-i-Sharif* ('The Noble Self'), *Sharif-Zada* ('The Young Nobleman', 1900), and *Akhtari Begum. Umrao Jan Ada* is about a Lucknow courtesan and is regarded as a classic Urdu novel.

WORKS: *'Umrao Jan Ada', Delhi, 1982; 'Zat-i-Sharif', Delhi, 1983; 'Sharif-Zada', Delhi, 1984; 'Muraqqa-i-Leila-o-Majnun', Allahabad, 1928; 'Akhtari-Begum', Karachi (undated).*

BIBLIOGRAPHY: *A.S. Sukhochev, 'From the Dastan to the Novel', Moscow, 1971 (in Russian); A.A. Suvorova, 'The Sources of New Indian Drama', Moscow, 1985 (in Russian); M.B.A. Marharwi, 'Mirza Muhammad Hadi Ruswa: Sawaneh-i-Hayat aur Adabi Karnama', Lahore, 1963.*

A.A. SUVOROVA

S

SAARC (South Asian Association for Regional Cooperation)

The Association was founded in December 1985, at the first meeting between the heads of state and governments of South Asian countries in Dhaka, the capital of Bangladesh. In accordance with SAARC'S Declaration and Charter, Pakistan, India, Bhutan, Bangladesh, Nepal, Sri Lanka, and the Maldives, with a total population of more than a billion, became members of this transnational organisation on terms of sovereign equality. SAARC's declared objectives are to ensure peace, stability and accord in the region; to work for the freedom, social justice, and economic prosperity of all the partners linked by affinity of culture and history; to move towards mutual understanding, good-neighbourly relations and meaningful cooperation; also to foster collective defence of coordinated positions on the restructuring of the world system of trade and economy. One of the tasks of the association is to establish purely economic relations in the so-called non-conflict areas, which so far do not include production, trade, and finance. Questions of bilateral relations and links with the outside world, as well as all acute international problems of regional and global levels, do not come within the purview of the association.

The practical work of the organisation began at an extremely low intra-regional level. The volume of trade between the member countries amounts to only two to three per cent of the total volume. Member countries' links are oriented towards extra-regional relations. Reserve stocks of food (200,000 tons) have been accumulated, Rs 400,000,000 from a voluntary fund have been expended, agreements have been concluded on scientific and meteorological issues, as well as on health services, agriculture, television, anti-terrorist activity, etc. However, SAARC's potential is limited by the difficult situation on the subcontinent and because of the existence of numerous areas of conflict, confrontation, and tension. The future of the Association depends on the positive development of relations among South Asian states and their neighbours. The eleventh SAARC summit took place in Kathmandu, Nepal, on 6 January 2002. There was modest progress in the form of the proposal to create a South Asian Economic Union. Although SAARC does not allow discussion of bilateral issues, the Indo-Pakistan tension took its toll even there. President Pervez *Musharraf crossed the floor to shake hands with the Indian Prime Minister Atal Bihari Vajpayee, however no immediate political results emerged.

On 7 March 2002, SAARC Information Ministers assembled at Islamabad and one month later, at the same venue, SAARC Finance Ministers met and drew up a plan of action for poverty reduction. On 9 December 2002, the Government of Pakistan announced the postponement of the Twelfth summit scheduled to be held in Islamabad in January 2003.

This Twelfth Summit was finally held on 4 to 6 January 2004. During the summit Indo-Pakistan leaders agreed to a composite dialogue on issues including *Kashmir. An additional protocol against terrorism was signed and the security of small states, constituting the majority, was addressed by affirming the UN Charter. One major development was the reaffirmation and signing of the framework agreement on South Asian Free Trade Area (SAFTA). The Thirteenth Summit is to be held at Dhaka, Bangladesh in January 2005.

G.P. KOLYKHALOVA

Sabk-i-Hindi

(Indian Style, otherwise known as New Manner—*Tarz-i-Nou*, *Sabk-i-Safawi*, Indian School—*Maktab-i-Hindi*) This is one of the three main trends in *Persian literature, the other two being Khorasan and Iraqi styles. The beginning of *Sabk-i-Hindi* dates back to the 14th to 16th century. The term was already used by Amir Khusrau *Dehlawi however the sources of *Sabk-i-Hindi* can be traced back to the Herat School of poetry and Baba Fighani (d. 1516). The development of the style coincided with the migration of some poets from Safawid Iran to the court of the Mughals (16th to 17th century). Many representatives of this style were Iranians by birth including Urfi Shirazi, Naziri Nishapuri, Saib Tebrizi, Zuhuri Turshizi, Kalim Kashani, and Ghazali Mashhadi. They arrived in India and remained there for most of their lives.

Other practitioners of this style were the natives of South Asia such as Faizi, Nami, Dara Shikoh, Ghani Kashmiri, Muhsin Fani, Nasir Ali Sirhindi, and Mirza Abdul Qadir *Bedil. *Sabk-i-Hindi* was popular in the literatures of Afghanistan and Central Asia, and had a great influence on *Urdu literature. *Sabk-i-Hindi* originated within the Iraqi style as a result of its stylistic and genre development.

Two periods can be singled out in its history (early 16th century to the beginning of the 17th century) and late (17th to 18th century), and it existed until the 20th century. During the first period, literature tended to be pithy and aphoristic in style, with meaningful poetic imagery. In the second period the same processes led to the excessive sophistication of poetic expression, which is particularly true of Bedil. *Sabk-i-Hindi* resorts to the more complex poetic devices and an extensive layer of colloquial vocabulary is introduced to enhance the expressiveness of the verse. The genre range is extended to include **ghazals*, **qasidas*, **masnawi*, **qita*. The philosophical **qasida* and *saqi nama*—confessional lyrical poem, became well established. Chronogram (**tarikh*) became popular as well as all sorts of literary games—riddles, coded texts, anagrams, etc.

BIBLIOGRAPHY: *E. Bertels, 'On the Indian Style in Persian Poetry', in: Charisteria Orientalia praecipue ad Parsian pertineuta, Prague, 1956; Z.G. Riziev, 'Indian Style in Farsi Poetry of the Late 16th to 17th Centuries, Tashkent, 1971 (in Russian); Bausani A., Contributio a una definizioni dello 'stilo indiano' 'dello poesia persiana', Annali Instituto Universario Orientale di Napoli, V. VII, Napoli, 1957; Hadi Hasan, 'Moghal Poetry', Madras, 1952; Heinz W., 'Der Indische Stil in der Pesischen Literatur', Wiesbaden, 1973.*

N.I. PRIGARINA

Sadequain (1930–87)

Artist. A rare visionary, Sadequain was able to bridge the gulf between disparate groups in society. At the age of 31 his work won recognition at the 1961 Paris Biennale. Sadequain had a prolific career and much of his work is displayed in public places. Like Diego Rivera, he celebrated the role of the proletariat. His early mural, based on the dignity of labour is housed in the Mangla Dam, near Islamabad. His painted ceilings in the *Lahore Museum and Frere Hall in Karachi present an epic view of man's destiny as envisaged in the poetry of *Iqbal. His canvas was encyclopedic and he looked at universal themes from classical literature to social activism. His most critically acclaimed works are from 'The Cactus Series', in which he immortalized the humble wild cactus of coastal *Sindh. During his life Sadequain became a cult figure with a large following from all walks of life. In the 1970's he acquired nation-wide fame for his rendering of Quranic verses on canvas. Sadequain's influential position in Pakistan's art history cannot be challenged.

One of Pakistan's foremost artists, Sadequain.

Frere Hall, where Sadequain painted the ceiling.

N. FARRUKH

Safi, Ibn-i- (1928–80)

Writer. Born Asrar Ahmad, Ibn-i-Safi (his pen name) was a popular author, whose thrillers and detective novels became best-sellers throughout the *Urdu-speaking world. He wrote two series of novels, beginning in the 1950s with *Jasoosi Dunya* ('World of Espionage') and the *Imran Series* (Imran being the name of the lead character). His characters, such as Imran, Colonel Ahmad Kamal Faridi and Captain Hamid, captured the imagination of the people. His novels were set in an imaginary country called 'Pak Asia' whose antagonist was the futuristic 'Zero Land'. Ibn-i-Safi had a very readable style, wrote poetry occasionally and, in the prefaces to his detective stories, made moral, religious and political comments, mostly of a conservative nature.

M.R. KAZIMI

Said, Hakim Muhammad (1921–98)

Public figure/Stateman. Hakim Said was a public figure in Pakistan and a specialist in Eastern medicine. In

Philanthropist, Hakim Said.

1940 he graduated from the Ayurvedic and Unani College in Delhi. He was President of the *Hamdard Foundation in Pakistan and was founder and President of the teaching and research complex *Madinat al-Hikmat* (City of Learning) near Karachi. He was advisor to the President of Pakistan on *Tibb* (medicine and public health) with the rank of Federal Minister (1979-82). He was also a member of the National Geographic Society of Pakistan and served as Board Member of many international medical organisations, including the Royal Society of Health, London, and the International Union of Health Education, Paris. Also a member of the British Society of the History of Science, Hakim Said was an essayist, an author of academic publications and an organiser and leader of many international forums, such as the Millenary of Al-Beruni, in Pakistan, 1973. He was the winner of many international awards, including the Islamic Medicine Prize (Kuwait). the Avicenna Prize (USSR, 1989) and the Pakistani order *Sitara-i-Imtiaz* (The Star of Distinction), 1966. He was sadly assassinated in 1998.

L.A. VASILYEVA

Saifi, Zafar Saeed (1943–)

Scientist. Zafar Saeed Saifi graduated from DJ Science College in 1961, took his MSc at the University of Karachi in 1963, which he later joined and rose to become Vice-Chancellor in 2001. He received his PhD in Pharmaceutical Chemistry from the University of London. Z.S. Saifi organised the first International Pharmaceutical Conference in Pakistan in 1992. His area of research and specialisation is isotopes in medicines, standardisation of homeopathic medicines and their potency, and the effects of ecology on the poisonous ingredients of drugs.

M.R. KAZIMI

Salat

(Arabic: prayer; Persian—*namaz*) The ritual canonical prayer performed five times a day. One of the five 'pillars of faith' (**rukn*) in Islam. Each Friday at noon, Friday congregational prayers (*salat al-juma*) are offered, in the mosque (*masjid-i Juma*, or *masjid-i Jami*).

YU.V. GANKOVSKY

Salok

(from the Sanskirt, *shloka*) A poetic form used in the medieval literatures of Western India, in the languages of Apabhramsha, Rajasthani, *Gujarati, *Punjabi, and Braj. Not to be confused with Sanskirt *shloka*. Gujarat and Rajasthan have a marriage folk tradition: the newlyweds exchange *distiches—shloka* (in the local pronunciation—*salok*) in the form of questions and answers borrowed from collections of classical wisdom. This poetic genre became widespread. *Adi Granth,* the *Sikh scripture, the most important literary monument in *Punjabi literature, is written in the form of *salok*. Salok metres are varied: **doha* predominates, but metres can include *soratha, shyam ullas, haripad, sar, gita. Adi Granth* includes distiches by Kabir, also called *salok*. *Salok* has many genre versions. It can be composed independently (*muktak*) or can be incorporated into a larger work.

YU.V. TSVETKOV

Salt Range

East to west mountain range in Pakistan, of which the average height is 671 metres. The highest peak is Sakesar, at 1,525 metres. The spurs of the Salt Range begin in the *Jhelum district. Here, the Yogitilla and Barkala revers have their sources. The range traverses the *Indus near Kalabagh and stretches south into the *Bannu and Dera Ismail Khan districts. Economically viable deposits of salt, coal, and oil are prospected in Balkassar, Dhulain, and elsewhere.

YU.V. GANKOVSKY

Sami (1743–1850)

Poet. This *Sindhi language poet's real name was Chanrai Bachumal Dattaramani; he is, however, commonly known as *Sami*, which is a distortion from Sanskrit *Swami*. The son of a textile merchant, Sami travelled extensively in West India and Central Asia. In his poems, written in the style of **salok*, he promoted the philosophy of the *Vedanta*. Sami's heritage comprises paraphrases of a number of Bhakti and *Sufi poets. His works were collected, systematised and published in three volumes by Kaudomal Ch. Khilnani (1890, 1898, 1914). Sami's work is an example of the synthesis of Hindu-Muslim philosophies in Sindhi poetry.

BIBLIOGRAPHY: *Lakhraj Aziz, 'Sami', Delhi, 1965 (in Sindhi); L.H. Ajwani, 'History of Sindhi Literature', New Delhi, 1977; Gurdial Mallik, 'Divine Dwellers in the Desert', Karachi, 1949.*

A.S. SUKHOCHEV

Sammi

A special dance without any songs or music. Women of the *Punjab traditionally dance *Sammi*. The dancers dress in bright coloured *kurtas* and full flowing skirts called *lehngas*. A particular silver hair ornament is associated with this dance. It is in reality a dance-drama, portraying a story of love and longing.

R. HUSAIN

Sanghao

Near Mardan in northern Pakistan, Sanghao is an archaeological site 27 metres deep and 12 metres wide, formed in Pleistocene conglomerates. A.H. *Dani launched excavations in 1962 that were carried on by M. Salim. The cultural layer yielded thousands of tools made of quartz, which is very unusual for the Stone Age, that makes their identification very difficult. Those who studied this collection offered varied opinions. There is no doubt, however, that some experts identify it with the Middle and Upper *Palaeolithic and probably Mesolithic. In this way, the time of settlement can be estimated as five to ten thousand years. The industry of the lower levels can be compared with the industry of the late *Soan culture. Both exhibit influence of a western Mousterian culture of which they probably were the easternmost out-post. The upper levels are Kushanic and post-Kushanic.

BIBLIOGRAPHY: *A.H. Dani, 'Sanghao Cave Excavations, the First Season, 1963,' Ancient Pakistan, I, 1964; M. Salim, 'Handaxe Collections of Northern Pakistan,' Journal of Central Asia, 4/1, 1981.*

V.A. RANOV

Sangi (1851–1924)

Poet. Mir Abdul Husain (his real name) was a *Sindhi language poet who also wrote in *Urdu and Persian. He belonged to the *Talpur family, whose ancestors had ruled in *Sindh until the middle of the nineteenth century. His two-volume **diwan* in Sindhi (1904) includes 450 **ghazals* and 230 **kafi*. While faithfully following the canons of Persian poetry, Sangi made wide use of folk imagery and local scenes. His lyric verse sang of love and feminine beauty and is marked with optimism. It did much to establish the *ghazal* in Sindhi poetry and to enrich it with folk imagery.

BIBLIOGRAPHY: *Pir Husamuddin Rashdi, 'Sindhi Adab' (Sindhi Literature), Karachi (undated); L.H. Ajwani, 'History of Sindhi Literature', New Delhi, 1977.*

A.S. SUKHOCHEV

Sangit

The term used in the art of Pakistan and India to denote a synthesis of the arts of music (both vocal and instrumental), dance and drama. In this kind of syncretic whole the leading aesthetic positions belong to music, in view of which the term sangit is sometimes interpreted simply as 'music', especially in the musical culture of antiquity and the Middle Ages.

E.M. GOROKHOVIK

Santur

A string instrument similar to a dulcimer, widely used in Pakistan, India, and, the Middle East. It consists of a wooden sounding board with numerous strings. Every four strings are tuned to a definite pitch. In recent times a shell resonator was added to the instrument. The *santur* accompanies *Sufi songs and is also used as a solo instrument in *Hindustani.

E.M. GOROKHOVIK

Sarangi

A string bow instrument of widespread use in Pakistan, India, and other countries of South Asia and Middle East. It has many local varieties with at least three principal types that vary in size. The *sarangi* consists of a hollow wooden body with a parchment covered sounding board and a neck to which three or four primary strings and some thirty resonant strings are fixed. The bow is arc-shaped, with horsehair stretched between the two ends. The *sarangi* is played in such a way that the strings are not fully pressed against the neck. It is used to accompany singing and dancing and as a solo instrument. Bundu Khan of Pakistan is one of the best known *sarangi* players.

E.M. GOROKHOVIK

Sardar

(from Persian *sar* meaning head: warlord, chieftain) The head, usually hereditary, of a tribe or clan of *Pashtuns, *Balochis, or *Brahuis. In *Balochistan the *Sardar* continues to wield traditional power, known as the '*sardari* system' (*sardari nizam*). Repeated attempts by the federal government of Pakistan to abolish this system in the 1960s and 1970s were of no avail.

YU.V. GANKOVSKY

Sari

An unsewn female garment worn in India, Pakistan and Bangladesh. It is a length of cloth, 100-120 cm. wide and 5 to 9 metres long dyed and ornamented. The design is either made in the process of weaving, or is printed or embroidered. The design can be evenly distributed over the entire length of the fabric or concentrated along the hem, about. 5-7 metre of one end (*pallu*), more heavily decorated than the other. Various weaving techniques are used. In recent decades *saris* are sometimes made out of synthetic fabrics.

Women doing menial tasks wear simple short saries with no other clothes underneath. Normally women wear long *saris* with a petticoat and a small tight blouse called a *choli*, leaving the midriff bare. According to tradition, the colour of the *sari* should match the season or correspond to a festive occasion or family holiday.

N.R. GUSEVA

Sarinda

A string plucked and bowed instrument similar in shape to a violin used when playing classical music. Three primary strings, one of gut and two of metal, are fixed on the wooden frame. The *sarinda* accompanies singing or is played in combination with the flute.

I. PIRACHA

Sarkar

(in Farsi, head, chief, overseer) 1. administrative and fiscal districts under the Mughals (*See*, *Suba*)

2. in *British India, the Indian name for the East India Company.

K.A. ANTONOVA

Sarmast, Sachal (1739–1829)

Poet. The real name of this very well known *Sufi poet was Abdul Wahhab. His pseudonym means 'Intoxicated with the Truth'. He is known as *Shair-i-Haft Zaban*, or 'Poet of Seven Languages', since he wrote poetry in Arabic, Persian, *Sindhi, *Seraiki, Hindi, *Urdu and *Punjabi. He was born in *Sindh into the family of the **darwesh*-poet Salahuddin Moragi. In his verse he was a follower of Shah Abdul Latif *Bhitai, while in *Sufism he considered Attar (1136-1229) his teacher. Sachal Sarmast's poetry is characterised by a blend of lyricism and protest against religious orthodoxy. His favourite forms were **kafi* and **doha*. In addition to singing praises to his heavenly beloved, the universal spirit, he also rejoiced in earthly pleasures. Sachal Sarmast's poetry was collected, commented on and published by literary scholars M.K. Beg (1902), Aga Sufi (1933), Jethmal Parsram, Kaliyan Adwani and others.

BIBLIOGRAPHY: *Pir Husamuddin Rashdi, 'Sindhi Adab', Karachi, (s.a.); L.H. Ajwani, 'History of Sindhi Literature', New Delhi, 1977.*

A.S. SUKHOCHEV

Sarod

(From Farsi, *surud* meaning tune, melody) A stringed instrument of the lute type, played in South Asia and countries in the Middle East. It has a deep wooden frame with figured hollows on the sides. The lower part is covered with parchment. The polished-steel upper part has nine primary and fifteen resonant strings, played with a plectrum of wood or ivory. The *sarod* is distinguishable by its light, noble sound, which is capable of conveying the finest emotional nuances. A prototype of this instrument is presumed to be the *rabab* of Iran and Afghanistan, which has survived various changes to its construction. The *rabab* was introduced to the genre of *Hindustani music by Muhammad Hashim Khan Bangash, the founder of a musical dynasty represented by the well-known *sarod* players of the twentieth century, Hafiz Ali Khan and his son, Amjad Ali Khan.

I. PIRACHA

Sarshar, Rattanath (1846–1903)

Novelist. Rattanath Dar (his real name) was an *Urdu-language novelist, born into the family of a Brahmin. He graduated from a Muslim **madrasah* and went on to Canning College in Lucknow. Sarshar spoke Persian, Arabic, and English. He began his literary career as a journalist and editor of the newspaper *Awadh Akhbar,* in which he serialised his best known novel *Fasana-i-Azad* ('The Story of Azad'). One can trace the influence of the prose Urdu **dastans* in his work as well as the ideas of the Muslim enlightenment (Aligarh Movement) and the influence of European realist literature (Dickens, Thackeray and particularly Cervantes). All his novels depict the life of the Muslim community in Lucknow and include *Jam-i-Sarshar* ('Sarshar's Goblet', 1887), and *Sair-i-Kohsar* ('Mountain Journey', 1890). Together with Nazir Ahmad and Abdul Halim Sharar, Sarshar had a significant influence on the establishment of the novel in *Urdu literature.

BIBLIOGRAPHY: *A.S. Sukhochev, 'From the Dastan to the Novel', Moscow, 1971; Latif Husain Adid, 'Sarshar ki Nawalingari' (Sarshar's Novels), Karachi, 1961.*

A.S. SUKHOCHEV

Sauda, Mirza Muhammad Rafi (1714–81)

Poet. An *Urdu language poet, Rafi Sauda was one of the 'four pillars' of Urdu poetry. He came from a family of rich Afghan merchants. He called himself a disciple of the poet Hatim and belonged to the circle of the poet Arzu (1689-1756). In 1757 he left Delhi and settled in Farrukhabad at the court of the Chief Minister of the *Mughal Empire, Imad al-Mulk. In 1770 he was appointed poet laureate of Oudh. Sauda's pamphlets satirised his rivals, religious figures, military commanders, ignorant physicians and pedantic scholars. Sauda founded the genre of Satire in *Urdu literature and his **qasidas* were written in the style of *Shahr-i-Ashob,* describing the decline of Delhi in the middle of the 18th century after the invasions of Nadir Shah, the Afghans, *Jats and others. Sauda's poems, like the work of his contemporary *Mir Taqi Mir, reflected the socio-political crisis of the late Mughal Empire. They created a new critical and tragic attitude of poetry towards reality.

WORKS: *'Kulliyat', Delhi, 1966; 'Kalam-i-Sauda', Aligarh, 1965.*

BIBLIOGRAPHY: *Shaykh Chand, 'Sauda', Aurangabad, 1936; Khaliq Anjum, 'Mirza Rafi Sauda', Aligarh, 1966; R. Russel, Khurshid ul-Islam, 'Three Moghal Poets', Cambridge, 1968; M.A.R. Barker, Shah Abdul Salam, 'Classical Urdu Poetry', Vol. II, Ithaca, 1977.*

A.S. SUKHOCHEV

Saudi-Pakistan relations

Saudi Arabia has had very warm relations with Pakistan from the very beginning of Pakistans inception. These diplomatic ties began to develop intensely in the mid 1970s, under the Z.A. *Bhutto leadership. In 1974 Faisal and Bhutto co-hosted the second Islamic Summit in Lahore. The policy of expanding political, economic, and other links was continued under the Ziaul *Haq regime. Ever since Riaz-al-Khatib, the Saudi Ambassador, had attempted to mediate between the PPP and PNA in 1977, Ziaul Haq maintained contacts with Saudi leaders and co-ordinated his tactics on a number of important international issues, including the problem of the Middle East. In the 1980s an important factor in the consolidation of Saudi-Pakistan relations was co-ordination of their policies on Afghanistan. Starting in the early 1980s several agreements on defence co-operation were signed, to replace the 1976 agreement. As a result, military-political links intensified. Pakistan helped Saudi Arabia in the training of military personnel. In the 1980s, Pakistani military contingents were regularly contracted out to Saudi Arabia.

The second *Pakistan Peoples Party government, which came to power in 1988, attached great significance to the development of Saudi-Pakistan relations. Prime Minister Benazir *Bhutto visited Saudi Arabia in 1989 and 1990. In August 1990 the government of Ghulam Mustafa *Jatoi declared that it was sending a contingent of Pakistani troops to Saudi Arabia in view of the occupation of Kuwait by the Iraqi army. In October 1991 President Ghulam Ishaq *Khan visited Saudi Arabia. Since then almost every Pakistani leader has visited Saudi Arabia. With the Saudi economy coming under pressure following the Kuwait-Iraq War, financial help was less forthcoming, but the two countries' recognition of the Taliban in Afghanistan formed a bond, apart from religious ties.

R.M. MUKIMJANOVA

Sawm

(Arabic: fast) Fasting in the ninth month (Arabic: *Ramadan*, Persian: *Ramazan*) of the Muslim lunar year. One of the five 'pillars of faith' in Islam (**rukn*). During the thirty days of *Ramadan* an adult Muslim is required to abstain from food, drink, and sex between sunrise and sunset. Exceptions are made for those who are old, sick, pregnant, or travelling. *Ramadan* concludes with the festival of *Id ul-Fitr*.

YU.V. GANKOVSKY

Sayyid (also Syed)

1. Descendants of the Prophet Muhammad, his cousin and son-in-law, Ali, and his daughter Fatima. A hereditary Muslim title.

2. An elite corporate group of Muslims in south Asia. In Pakistan, certain Muslim circles claim the title of Sayyid without being direct descendants of the Prophet and his family. A case in point are the Abbasids, the

descendants of Abbas, Ali's uncle. Sayyids belong to different social groups, but mainly to the ruling classes and to *ulema* elite in particular.

S.F. LEVIN

Sayyid, Mumtaz Husain (1919–92)

Literary Critic. He was a Pakistani critic and literary historian writing in *Urdu. He was educated in the universities of Allahabad, Aligarh and Agra and took part in the activities of the *Pakistan Progressive Writers' Association. As a critic, he focused his attention on the question of the social determination of literature. His books include: *Naqd-i-Hayat* ('Criticism of Life', 1950), *Adabi Masail* ('Literary Problems', 1954), *Nayi Qadren* ('New Values', 1955), *Adab aur Shaoor* ('Literature and Consciousness', 1959), and *Naqd-i-Harf* ('Criticism of the Letter', 1985). His monographs *Ghalib* (1969) and *Amir Khusrau Dehlawi, Life and Poetry* (1976) have been awarded the Daud Prize. Mumtaz Husain is widely regarded as having the best critical faculty among his contemporaries.

BIBLIOGRAPHY: *A.S. Jafri, 'Taraqqipasand', Aligarh, 1951; 'Tulu-i-Afkar', (ed.) Husain Anjum, Karachi, August 1992; Muhammad Reza Kazimi, 'Tab-i-Sukhan', Karachi. 1994.*

A.S. SUKHOCHEV

Schimmel, Annemarie (1922–2003)

Islamic Researcher. Annemarie Schimmel was a world renowned scholar of Islam, who devoted her life to fostering a better understanding of Islam and the Muslim world in the West. An author of nearly 100 books and monographs, she was a distinguished expert on Islam in South Asia and a leading scholar of Islamic literature, mysticism and culture. Prof. Schimmel also translated Persian, *Urdu, Arabic, *Sindhi and Turkish poetry and literature into English and German. She first visited Pakistan in 1958 and continued to make many visits after that. She translated Allama Muhammad *Iqbal's *Javidnama* into German verse. Pakistan honoured her with the *Hilal-e-Imtiaz*, its highest civil award, and a fine tree-lined avenue in Lahore is named after her.

Renowned scholar, Annemarie Schimmel.

Annemarie Schimmel was born and educated in Germany. She was awarded a doctorate in Islamic languages and civilizations by the University of Berlin at the age of 19, and a second doctorate in history of religions by the University of Marburg. She was Professor Emerita of Indo-Muslim Culture in the Department of Near Eastern Languages and Civilizations at Harvard University from 1967 until her retirement in 1992.

The impact of her work has been felt all over the Muslim world, especially in South Asia, Turkey, and the Arab world. In recognition of her extraordinary scholarship, she received many honorary doctorates and prestigious awards from governments and institutions worldwide.

Her numerous publications include *Gabriel's Wing: A Study into the Religious Ideas of Sir Muhammad Iqbal* (Leiden, 1963); *Islamic Literatures of India* (Weisbaden, 1973); Sindhi Literature (Weisbaden, 1974); *Classical Urdu Literature* (Weisbaden, 1975); *Mystical Dimensions of Islam* (University of North Carolina Press, 1975); *The Triumphal Sun: A Study of the Works of Jalaloddin Rumi* (London, 1975); *Islam in the Indian Subcontinent* (Leiden, 1980); *As Through a Veil: Mystical Poetry in Islam* (New York, 1982); *Das Mysterium der Zahl* (Cologne, 1984); *And Muhammad is His Messenger* (Chapel Hill, 1985); *A Two-Coloured Brocade: The Imagery of Persian Poetry* (New York, 1992); Make a Shield from Wisdom (London, 1993); and *Deciphering the Signs of God: A Phenomenological Approach to Islam* (Edinburgh, 1994).

S.D. SEREBRYANI

Scientific Society of Pakistan

The Scientific Society of Pakistan (SSP) was founded in 1955 by three scientists who had their early education at Aligarh University. The main objective of the SSP is the promotion of science and technology in the *Urdu language. The society publishes Urdu journals such as *Jadid Society* (Modern Society) and *Science Bachoon kay Liye* (Science for Children), and organizes annual science conferences where research papers and the entire proceedings are in Urdu. The SSP has so far organized over twenty conferences in major cities of Pakistan (Karachi, Lahore, Faisalabad, Quetta, Islamabad) at which environmental scientists and engineers participated.

T. NAIM

Seep

A quarterly publication from Karachi founded in April 1963. Edited by Naseem Durrani, this journal was published with the aim of promoting the works of new and budding writers, allowing them to rub shoulders with established masters. A whole generation of writers has grown up with *Seep* and has flourished.

M.R. KAZIMI

Seraiki (also Multani)

Belonging to the *Indo-Aryan group of the Indo-European family, Seraiki is spoken mainly in the southern part of the *Punjab Province. Until recently, Seraiki was treated as a West Punjabi (*Lahnda, Lendi) dialect. Only in the last two or three decades has a cultural movement pushed for its recognition as a local language and for the development of *Seraiki literature. Some samples of writing in Seraiki since the 18th century have survived. Seraiki uses the Arabic script with a number of added signs. Structurally, Seraiki is distinctly different from *Punjabi.

BIBLIOGRAPHY: *Yu.A. Smirnov, 'The Lendi Language', Moscow, 1970 (in Russian); C. Shackle, 'The Seraiki Language of Central Pakistan: A Reference Grammar', London, 1976.*

G.A. ZOGRAF

Seraiki Literature

This has a long history dating to the Sultanate period, (12th Century). Until the middle of the 20th century it was either orally transmitted or remained confined to manuscripts. It was only with the launching of the journal *Akhtar* from Multan in 1964 that *Seraiki acquired modern means of circulation. The legendary Seraiki poets of the classical age drew their imagery from every day rustic scenes even in mystic themes. This aspect of Seraiki literature is striking and persists even now in all traditional forms of poetry, even in **Marsia* (elegies on the more recent tragedy of Karbala). *Sachal Sarmast (d. 1780) is a legendary Seraiki poet. Khwaja Farid (1855-1901) of Mithan Kot, who died early in the 20th century, brought forward the *Sufi and classic tradition.

Seraiki is a language that has its origins in the contiguous districts of *Sindh and the *Punjab, excluding the central districts of these provinces where *Sindhi and *Punjabi literatures flourish. The bulk of Seraiki literature relates to the first half of the 20th century and most of it is politically inclined. Seraiki writers and poets were in the vanguard of the Pakistan Movement and, after independence, they were concerned with regional and social issues. The lead was taken by the renowned poet Ghulam Rasul Dadda, who personally participated in the national movement and composed patriotic songs and anthems. His 'Salutation to the Pakistan Flag' was sung throughout the Seraiki region. Immediately after independence in 1947 the poems of Faiz Mohammad Dilchasp reflect the fervour of the people and the optimism which pervaded that generation. This patriotic fervour was heightened during the 1965 War. Apart from Dilchasp a large array of poets including Suroor Karbalai, Iqbal Sokri, Janbaz Jatoi and Bahar Multani composed war poems of considerable literary merit expressing the fervour of the common man.

Seraiki fiction remains very strong in social depiction, for example all the characters found in Munir Ahmad Alavi's novel *Apni Rat Jo Pani Thi'i* and Zafar Lashari's novel *Pahaj.* A notable example is Mohammad Ismail Ahmadani's novel *Cholian*, in which the crisis before and after the creation of a new state is vividly depicted. The reformist zeal has fired writers like Nazir Leghari, Batul Rahmani, Sabiha Qureshi and Munir Malik among others. Social reform is represented also in humour and satire. Faruq Atash and Aslam Qureshi are the most prominent writers of this genre. One of the main social issues dealt with, by Seraiki writers is education. Because of feudal resistance to the opening of schools in their locality or villages people have been forced to send their wards to towns and cities. Munir Alavi's novel recounts the experience of such a family that has sent a younger brother to break the bonds of illiteracy constricting them. Female education faces resistance from many sides, and Musarrat Kalanchvi devotes a play, *Gahnan,* to this theme. It ends on an optimistic note however, the older generation finally relenting and allowing girls access to education. Seraiki literature also promotes Seraiki cultural identity, surrounded as it is by Sindhis and Punjabis, and weighed under *Urdu and English. Mohammad Ismail Ahmadani's *Peet de Pindh* represents this aspiration.

BIBLIOGRAPHY: *Mohammad Aslam Rasulpuri, 'Pakistani Muashara our Seraiki Adab', in: S.H.M. Jafri and Ahmad Salim (eds.).*

G.A. ZOGRAF

Shafi, Mohammad, Mian Sir (1869–1932)

Political activist. Mian Mohammad Shafi belonged to the Baghbanpura locality of Lahore. He was the first Secretary of the Punjab *Muslim League. Mian Mohammad Shafi was nominated to the Punjab Legislative Council in 1909. He presided over the All-India Urdu Conference at Poona (now Pune). Mian Mohammad Shafi attended the Delhi Durbar in 1911. In 1912 he became Member of the Imperial Legislative Council. He presided over the 1913 Lucknow session. He was an ardent advocate of separate electorates but was against the provision of positive rote discrimination to minorities that acted to reduce the Muslim majority in the *Punjab and Bengal. It was for this reason that he opposed the *Lucknow Pact. M.A. *Jinnah charge-sheeted him for this opposition and the *Punjab body of the Muslim League was disaffiliated in favour of the faction, which was then led by Sir Fazli *Husain. Sir Mohammad Shafi gave evidence against British officers before the Hunter Committee. He served as Education Member, Viceroy's Executive Council (1919–24). He was President of the AIML in 1927, when he favoured co-operation with the *Simon Commission. This led to a split in the AIML. Shafi remained the President of the main body, while first Sir Mohammad Yaqub and then M.A. Jinnah became President of the non-cooperative faction. Dr Saifuddin *Kitchlew, the original Honorary Secretary, went over to Jinnah, while Sir Mohammad *Iqbal joined Shafi as Honorary Secretary. The stand of Sir Mohammad Shafi was vindicated when the *Delhi Muslim Proposals were cast out of the *Nehru Report. He co-operated with Jinnah in the issuance of the *Fourteen Points. He served briefly as President of the AIML in 1928, when both factions merged.

WORKS: *'Some Important Indian Problems', Lahore, 1930.*

BIBLIOGRAPHY: *Jahan Ara Shahnawaz, 'Father and Daughter', Lahore, 1971.*

M.R. KAZIMI

Shafii

Followers of the Shafii *madhab* philosophy. Its founder and eponym was Muhammad ibn-Idris al-Shafii (d. 820). Another famous Shafii theologian was Abu Hamid Muhammad al-Ghazali (1058–1111). In the Middle Ages, Shafii *madhab* was widespread in the Arab world and Iran. Today it is dominant in Egypt, east Africa, and Indonesia. Prominent Shafiis included *Ghaznavid sultans and *Ghurid sultans.

YU.V. GANKOVSKY

Shahada

(in Arabic: Evidence) From the Arabic verb *Shahida*—to witness. A confession of faith and one of the five pillars of Islam (**rukn*). The *shahada* contains two main Islamic articles of faith: monotheism—*tauhid*, and the recognition of Muhammad (PBUH) as Allah's last Prophet, which is expressed in the statement 'There is no God except Allah, and Muhammad is his Prophet'.

YU.V. GANKOVSKY

Shahi (also Shahiya)

A ruling dynasty of a state existing in the 7th-11th centuries on the territory of modern north-west Pakistan and south-east Afghanistan, occupying the valley of the *Kabul River, *Peshawar plain, and the lands between the *Indus and the *Chenab. The *Shahi* capital was Udabhandpura, also known in Muslim sources as *Vaihand* or *Vaihind*, located near the town of Attock in the *North-west Frontier Province. In 982–1022 the *Shahi* state was conquered by the *Ghaznavids.

YU.V. GANKOVSKY

Shahnai

A wooden wind instrument that is found in South Asia. It is made of ebony and has a double reed made of palm-leaf which is inserted in the aperture with a thin copper or silver plate. Three to nine holes are drilled in the body of the *shahnai* and the bell of the pipe is flared and made of metal. The length varies from 20 to 10 cm. depending on the variety of the *shahnai*. *Shahnai* belongs to the family of musical instruments whose sound is regarded as 'favourable'. The sound is strident, strong, and piercing. The instrument is used in traditional, ritual, and cultic performances that form the basis of *naubat* ensembles, with other types of the *shahnai* and percussion instruments such as the **dhol*, a double ended drum. The instrument is assumed to have originated in central Asia, The earliest mention of it is in 5th to 9th century sources. The first pictures of the modern *shahnai* are on 16th century miniatures. In the 1940s, as a result of the improvements in the technique of playing the shahnai by the musician Ustad Bismillah Khan, this instrument was introduced into the sphere of classical music. During the second half of the 20th century the shahnai also came into use in popular music.

I. PIRACHA

Shaikh

1. The leader of a Muslim religious community, the spiritual advisor.

2. A corporate group of Muslims in South Asia, mostly based in the *Punjab in Pakistan. They claim Arab descent. The most popular Shaikh names are: Qureshi, Ansari, Siddiqi, Faruqi, and Usmani. Each name indicates the origin of its owner. Quraysh represents the Arab clan which gave birth to the prophet Muhammad (PBUH). Ansar represents a helper and the first followers of the prophet in Medina. Siddiqi derives its name from the first caliph, Abu Bakr al-Siddiq. Faruq is from one of the names of the second caliph, Umar. Usmani is the name derived from the third caliph, Usman, etc.

BIBLIOGRAPHY: *'A Glossary of the Tribes and Castes of the Punjab and North West Frontier Province', Lahore, 1978.*

S.F. LEVIN

Shaka (also Sakas)

Iranian tribes of the northeastern group. At the end of the 1st millennium BC, they settled in Bactria, Arachosia, and north-west India. The Shakas were subordinate to the Graeco-Bactrians and Indo-Greek rulers. In the 1st millennium BC they founded their own Indo-Shaka (Indo-Scythian) kingdoms. The ruler of *Taxila, Maues (Moga), seized lands as far as central India and assumed the title King of Kings. His successor Az I also called himself the King of Kings. Numismatic material reveals Hellenic influence and Shaka cultural assimilation with the Indians. Towards the end of the 1st century AD the power of the Shaka kings in India weakened, giving way to the Indo-Parthians and then to the Kushan Empire. Until the end of the 5th century Shaka dynasties, such as western Kshatraps, Kshahahratas and Kardamakas, competed for power with the Satawahanas in the areas near Maharashtra, southern Gujarat and Kathiawar.

BIBLIOGRAPHY: *J.T. van Lohuizen de Leeuw, 'The Scythian Period', Leiden, 1949.*

A.A. VIGASIN

Shakir, Pervin (1953–94)

Poet. Pervin Shakir was a poet who took the *Urdu literary world by storm in the 1970s. Her debut was a significant event as Urdu poetry, otherwise dominated by male emotional attitudes, was confronted by a fresh, uninhibited poetic expression of female love. Inevitably naive at the beginning, Pervin Shakir's poetry matured in theme and expression but, throughout her literary career, her poems remained essentially feminine, although never feminist. In time she moved matters of political concern. Pervin Shakir infused much needed glamour into the literary scene after the despondency following the 1971 military defeat. Her style was strikingly individual and her lyricism was sustained through her four volumes of poetry from *Khushboo* ('Sweet Scent') to *Inkar* ('Refusal'). In her **ghazals* her couplets were thematically connected, a departure from the norm, and her free verse was very compact in construction. Her complete works were published as *Mah-i-Tamam* in the year of her death. Pervin Shakir was awarded the President's Pride of Performance medal. She was engaged in literary research in the United States and research on the causes of the separation of *East Pakistan, when she was killed in a car crash.

F. MUSHTAQ

Shalimar

1. Famous gardens in Pakistan 8 km. east of Lahore. The gardens were laid out in 1637 by Ali Mardan Khan on the orders of Shah Jahan, a Mughal ruler. The gardens follow a formal plan with terraces, water reservoirs, fountains, and pavilions. The gardens cover some 80 acres.

2. A cultural centre in Pakistan that includes radio, TV, a national film corporation, and a gramophone records firm. The centre plays an important role in the popularization of national art.

A.S. ALPATOVA

Sharar, Abdul Halim (1860–1926)

Writer. Abdul Halim (his real name) was a novelist and dramatist who wrote in *Urdu. He was born in the family of a *hakim* (physician) and given a traditional Muslim education. Sharar is the pioneer of the historical novel in Urdu. He followed the principles of 'enlightening realism'. His novels idealise the Muslim past, juxtaposing Muslim with European invaders and proposing complete faith in the enlightened ruler and his wisdom. He has some thirty novels to his credit: *Malik al-Aziz wa Warjana* (1888), *Hasan wa Anjelina* (1889), *Mansur wa Mohana* (1890), *Firdaws-i-Barin* ('Paradise', 1899), *Zawal-i-Baghdad* ('The Fall of Baghdad', 1912). Sharar also published essays, plays, and poetry. He edited the journals *Mahshar* ('Doomsday', 1881) and *Dilgudaz* ('Caressing the Heart', 1887). Sharar's work is a cross between Urdu prose **dastans* and Western historical novels, such as those of Sir Walter Scott.

BIBLIOGRAPHY: *A.S. Sukhochev, 'From the Dastan to the Novel', Moscow, 1971 (in Russian); Faiz Ahmad Faiz, 'Mizan' (Scales), Lahore, 1962; Jafar Reza, 'Abdul Halim Sharar', Delhi, 1988.*

A.S. SUKHOCHEV

Shariat

(Arabic for the right way, law) Muslim law regulating religious, civil, family, criminal relations, and norms of everyday life of the followers of Islam.

YU.V. GANKOVSKY

Sharif al-Mujahid (1926–)

Historian. He is a Pakistani historian and sociologist, and professor at the University of Karachi. He graduated from the University of Madras, and continued his education at the universities of McGill (Montreal, Canada) and Syracuse (USA). Sharif al-Mujahid headed the chair of journalism of the University of Karachi (1955-72). He helped publish the Journal of the Pakistan Historical Society (1965-67), and was one of the authors of the multivolume *History of the Freedom Movement* (Karachi, 1957-70), as well as founding Director of the Quaid-i-Azam Academy in Karachi.

WORKS: *'Quaid-i-Azam Jinnah: Studies in Interpretation', Karachi, 1981.*

YU.V. GANKOVSKY

Sharif, Mohammad Nawaz, Mian (1950–)

Twice Prime Minister of Pakistan. A Pakistani politician with ancestral roots in *Kashmir. Prior to 1947 Sharif's family resided in East *Punjab. He has been a highly successful businessman owning a steel plant, a sugar mill and several textile factories. In the early 1980s he was Minister of Finance in the Punjab provincial government and in 1985 was elected as a Member of the National Assembly of Pakistan and to the Provincial Assembly of Punjab. He served as Chief Minister of Punjab province from 1985 to 1988. He later became the leader of the *Pakistan Muslim League in the 1988 elections. This way his party secured majority of seats in the Punjab province allowing him a further term as Chief Minister, while the *Pakistan People's Party formed the Federal government. In 1990, he spearheaded the formation of the *Islami Jamhuri Ittehad* electoral alliance that won the elections of that year, defeating the Pakistan People's Party. He assumed the office of Prime Minister.

Former Prime Minister of Pakistan and Industrialist, Nawaz Sharif.

Sharif's first government was noteworthy for the acceleration of the processes of liberalization of foreign exchange, encouragement of the private sector and the general opening-up of the economy that had commenced earlier. Privatization of the State-owned sector of the economy also commenced. However, in the province of *Sindh a virtual reign of terror was unleashed on supporters of the opposition by the MQM-dominated provincial government of Jam Sadiq Ali. The subsequent Army action against some members of the MQM led to disaffection. There were also serious allegations of high-handedness, cronyism and outright corruption against the government.

Sharif's government was dismissed by President G.I. *Khan on 18 April 1993, but was restored by the Supreme Court on 26 May. Sharif is the only Prime Minister, so far, to have been restored by judicial process. The stalemate continued and both President G.I. Khan and Nawaz Sharif resigned on 18 May 1993. After a brief interregnum, under the caretaker government of Muin Qureshi, new elections brought in a PPP government for a second term under Benazir *Bhutto. This was in turn dismissed in 1996. In the elections held in that year the hitherto split mandates that had been manifested in the last three election results, were altered, and the Pakistan Muslim League was elected with massive majorities, bringing Sharif to power once again. During his second term Pakistan went openly nuclear in response to India's nuclear tests. The economic sanctions that followed, proved calamitous for Pakistan's already weakening economy. Meanwhile relations with India dramatically improved with the visit of that country's Prime Minister to Pakistan. This improvement proved to be short-lived with the breaking out of the internationally unpopular Kargil crisis. There were numerous allegations of corruption and, when called upon by the Supreme Court to answer some of these, Sharif ran foul of the judiciary and the infamous incident of the storming of the Supreme Court by members of his Party occurred. Sharif sought to consolidate his hold on office in 1997 by bringing in a President (Rafiq *Tarrar) believed to be more pliable to his wishes, and then by seeking the passage of constitutional amendments that would greatly enhance his powers as Prime Minister. He was removed in a military *coup* in October 1999 by General Parvez *Musharraf. After being tried and found guilty of aircraft hijacking he was pardoned and exiled to Saudi Arabia on 10 December 2000.

YU.V. GANKOVSKY

Sharif, S.M. (1880–1972)

Politician. Syed Mohammad Sharif received his MA from Patna College and Barrister-at-Law from Cambridge. He was the Secretary of the Reception Committee to the 1938 AIML Annual Session at Patna. He became a member of the AIML Working Committee in 1940. He was the author of the *Sharif Report*—an investigative report on the plight of Muslims in Bihar during the Congress Ministry of 1937–39.

M.R. KAZIMI

Sheikh

See, Shaikh.

Sherwani, Latif Ahmad (1917–99)

Scholar. (Pseudonym Shamloo Latif Ahmad Sherwani was Deputy Secretary of the Indian Institute of International Affairs in 1945. He served the Pakistan Institute of International Affairs from 1947 and was on the board of editors of its journal *Pakistan Horizon*. As a Nuffield scholar (1954-55) he was associated with Henry Kissinger, Philip Talbot, and Ralph Braibanti among others. He participated in the Harvard University International Summer Seminar. On his return Latif Ahmad Sherwani taught at the Pakistan Study Centre, Department of International Relations and Department of History, University of Karachi.

WORKS: *'India, China and Pakistan', Karachi, 1967; 'The Founder of Pakistan', Karachi 1976; 'Pakistan, China and America', Karachi, 1980; 'The Partition of India and Mountbatten', Karachi, 1986; (ed.) (as Shamloo) 'The Speeches and Statements of Iqbal', Lahore, 1944; 'Pakistan Resolution to Pakistan', Karachi, 1969; 'Pakistan in the Making', Karachi, 1987.*

SHARIFUL MUJAHID

Sherwani (also Achkan)

A male garment worn in Pakistan and India. It is a knee-length jacket with long narrow sleeves, buttoned from the collar to the waist. The collar is upright and tight around the neck. Open slits on both sides extend from the waist to the knee. The lower part is loose, with characteristic pleats resembling an English frock-coat. The present-day design of sherwanis took shape during the turn of the century as a combination of Indian and European clothing styles. A *sherwani* was originally worn by wealthy city-dwellers, the aristocracy, and higher military ranks. After 1947, the *sherwani* came to be used as formal dress. Traditionally, a *sherwani* is worn with **paijama* or *churidar paijama* and a cap. In Pakistan it is worn with a *shalwar*.

O.V. LYSTSOVA

Shia

(In Arabic: Partisan) The Quran (XXXVII: 83) refers to Abraham as the Shia of Noah. In the first Civil War, the terms *'Shia of Usman'* and *'Shia of Ali'* gained recognition. Ultimately the *'Shia of Ali'* came to be known simply as Shia. Shias recognize only Ali and his progeny through Fatima, the Prophet's (PBUH) daughter, to be the rightful *Imams or caliphs. Their largest denomination is *Ithna-Ashari* or 'twelvers', believing in twelve Imams from *Ali bin abi Talib* to **Mahdi* the son of Hasan al Askari, believed by the Shias to be alive and in occultation. Among their particular tenets is a belief in 'justice' as an attribute of God and the infallibility of all prophets and imams as well as Fatima, the Prophet's daughter. The Shias believe in *muta* or temporary marriage. For its origin see Quran (IV: 24), and *Taqqaya,* or dissimulation of faith, if life is endangered, see Quran (XVI: 106) again for polemics. The Shias, like *Sunnis, believe in *Hadith, but they also include the sayings of the twelve Imams in this corpus. The main Shia books of Hadith are: Muhammad bin Yaqub al Kulaini (d. 940) ed., *al Kafi*; Sheikh Saduq bin Babuyah (d. 991) ed., *Man La Yadhurul Faqih;* Sheikh at Taifa Muhammad al Tusi (d. 1068) *Tahzib-al-Ahkam* and *al-Istibsar*. The other sacred texts are the sermons, epistles and maxims of Ali, edited by Sharif Razi (d. 1014) under the title *Nahjul Balagha*, and the prayers of the fourth Imam Ali Zain-ul-Abidin (d. 712) *Sahifat-al-Sajjadia*, entitled. The jurisprudence of the Shiites was codified by the sixth Imam, Jafar, as Sadiq (d. 765), and hence is known as *Fiqh-i-Jafaria*. After the occultation of the twelfth Imam (872) the Shias were led by four *nawabs, or deputies, and thereafter the leadership of the Shiites went to the Marja, a Grand Ayatullah. The two seats of learning that produced **ulema* and **Mujtahids* are Najaf in Iraq and Qum in Iran.

Shiism came to South Asia, first in the Deccan, where the kings were Shia, and thereafter in Oudh, where the first public Friday prayers of the Shia took place. During the freedom movement the Shias formed a party, the *All-India Shia Conference led by Maharajkumar Amir Hyder of Mahmudabad. However, most of them joined the *All-India Muslim League, in which they were well represented. In the early years of Pakistan the Shias were considered a generally progressive community, producing writers, poets, lawyers, and student activists, as well as politicians. The informal but acknowledged leaders of the Shia community were *Zakirs,* scholars who recounted the tragedy of Kerbala (680), in which the third Imam Husain bin Ali, a grandson of the Prophet (PBUH), was martyred. The two leading *Zakirs* have been Allama Rashid Turabi (1908–1973) and Allama Talib Jauhari (b. 1940).

The Iranian Revolution of 1979 had a spill-over in Pakistan, when the clergy, leaders of prayers and custodians of the mosques revitalised the religious party *Tehrik-i-Nifaz-i-Fiqh-i-Jafaria.* Now known simply as *Tehrik-i-Jafaria,* it was led by Mufti Jafar Husain, Allama Ariful Husaini (d. 1988) and Allama Sajid Naqvi. Another faction, led by Allama Hamid Musawi, is regarded as moderate, leaning less on Iranian clerics.

M.R. KAZIMI

Shina (also Sina)

Shina belongs to the *Dardic group of the eastern subgroup of the *Indo-Aryan languages. Shina is spoken in the northern *Kashmir valley, mainly in *Gilgit, Tangir, *Chilas, Astor, *Kohistan, the valleys of the Gurez and Tilel, as well as in the valley of the Dras. Shina speakers live there along with *Kashmiri speakers and speakers of the Purik Tibetan dialect. The Dahhaun dialect, isolated from the others, is spoken east of the principal area, and is surrounded by Tibetan dialects, in particular Balti. The principal dialects of Shina are Gilgiti and Astori. Similar to the Astori are Gurezi, Drasi, Kohistani, Chilasi, and others. At present, a writing system has been developed on the basis of an *Urdu modification of the Arabic script.

BIBLIOGRAPHY: *D.I. Edelman, 'Dardic Languages', Moscow, 1965 (in Russian); T.G. Bailey, 'Grammar of the Shina (Sina) Language', London, 1924; id., 'Studies in North Indian Languages', London, 1938; D.I. Edelman, 'The Dardic and Nuristani Languages', Moscow, 1983; G.A. Grierson, 'Linguistic Survey of India', Vol. VIII, pt. II, Calcutta, 1919; Vol. I, pt. I, Calcutta, 1927.*

D.I. EDELMAN

Shinwari, Amir Hamza (1907–94)

Poet/Writer. Abu al-Murad Hamza Shinwari (his real name) was a poet and writer who wrote in *Pashto and in *Urdu. A graduate of the Islamia College in Peshawar, Shinwari wrote poetry in which religious-mystical motifs predominated. These were combined with humanitarian and patriotic themes. His favourite form is the traditional **ghazal* enriched with modern imagery. His prose is of a publicist nature for example travel notes about his trip to Kabul, such as *Nawai Pashtun*—'The new Pashtun' and meditations on *Sufi themes. His works, including *Jwandun* ('Life') and *Tajalliyat* ('Radiance') are a glorification of the heroic struggle of the *Pashtuns against foreign invaders. In 1950 he led a literary group called *Bazm-i-Adabi* (Literary Circle), intended for a narrow circle of lovers of elitist literature. Shinwari's works are widely known among the Pashtuns of Pakistan and Afghanistan and have been translated into Urdu and Russian.

WORKS: *Collections of poetry: 'Da Zra Awar' (The Voice of the Heart), 1948; Ghazawani (Noble Impulses), 1956, Peshawar; 'Da Khaibar Wajmi' (The Breath of Khaiber), Kabul, 1968; prose: Nawi Chapi (New Waves), Peshawar, 1957.*

BIBLIOGRAPHY: *G.F. Girs, 'Literature of the Undefeated People', Moscow, 1966 (in Russian); Abdurrauf Benawa, 'Osani Likwal', Vol. 1, Kabul, 1961.*

A.S. GERASIMOVA

Shirani, Akhtar (1905–48)

Poet. Muhammad Daud Khan (his real name) was an *Urdu language poet. He received a traditional Muslim education and studied Persian and Arabic literature and language under the tutorship of his father, Hafiz Mahmud Shirani, who taught at the Oriental College in Lahore. While studying at the Oriental College, Akhtar started writing poetry and regularly published his poems, essays, and feature stories in local newspapers and magazines. Akhtar Shirani published his own literary journal *Khayalistan* ('Land of Thought') and also edited well-known publications such as *Humayun* (late 1930s) and *Shahrah* ('The Highway',1941). Shirani's romantic lyrics are full of vitality and emotional tension. His poetry enjoyed great popularity among the youth. His **ghazals*, **nazm* and songs made up eight collections of verse published in the 1930s and 1940s: *Phulon ke Git* ('Songs of the Flowers'), *Lala-i-Tur* ('Tulips of Sinai'), *Naghma-i-Haram*, and *Tayur-i-Awara* ('Vagabond Birds'). His collected works have been edited by M. Yunus Hasni, Lahore 1993.

BIBLIOGRAPHY: *'Nairang-i-Khiyal' (ed.) Yusuf Hasan Khan, Lahore, 1948; M. Yunus Hasani, 'Jadid Urdu Shairi aur Akhtar Shirani', Karachi, 1976.*

N.V. GLEBOV

Shloka

See, *Salok*.

Shruti

(From Sanskrit: 'that which is heard') A system of organization of sound space in Indian classical music and at the same time a minimal microtone magnitude. In terms of theory the musical tradition in Pakistan and India subdivides the octave into twenty-two unequal *shruti*. Just like all the other components of musical texture, *shruti* is the carrier of the psycho-emotional code, or *ras*. In the practice of classical music, both northern or *Hindustani and southern or Karnataka, *shrutis* are not independent tones. Instead they are correlated with seven *swara* tones and play a part in the musical development mostly as various microinterval ornaments. The *shruti* system is a distinctive feature of the high tradition of musical culture, a symbol of its development and refinement. It is practically absent in the regional genres and forms.

I. PIRACHA

Siddiqui, M. Raziuddin (1905–98)

Scientist. M. Raziuddin Siddiqui was educated at the Osmania University, then at the universities of Cambridge and Leipzig. He served as Vice-Chancellor of the universities of Peshawar (1953–58) and Sindh (1960–64) and as the first Vice-Chancellor of Islamabad University (1964–72). He was regarded as an authority in the field of non-linear partial differential equations, as well as in the areas of quantum mechanics and the theory of relativity. He was awarded the *Hilal-i-Imtiaz* by the President of Pakistan.

M.R. KAZIMI

Siddiqui, Salimuzzaman (1897–1994)

Scientist. Salimuzzaman Siddiqui obtained his MSc from Aligarh Muslim Univerity (AMU) in 1919, after which he proceeded to University College, London, and the University of Frankfurt returning in 1927. For almost ten years he remained associated with Hakim Ajmal Khaṇ in the *Tibbiya* College and patented Ajmalin. In 1940 he was appointed Director, Indian Council for Scientific and Industrial Research. He established the Pakistan Council of Scientific and Industrial Research in 1951 and remained its Chairman till 1966. He founded the Husain Ebrahim Jamal Institute of Chemistry in the University of Karachi. His area of specialization was alkaloids, triterpenoids flavonids, the correlation of Chemical Structure and Physiological Activity. Salimuzzaman Siddiqui secured over fifty patents. He was awarded a MBE (Member of the British Empire) in 1944.

M.R. KAZIMI

Sikander, Shahzia (1969–)

Artist. Born in Lahore she received her art training there, at the National College of Arts. She took her Master in Fine Arts degree in 1995 at the Rhode Island School of Design, specializing in miniature painting. She found wide acclaim as she expanded the constraints of this form of painting, with its formal and highly stylized conceptual boundaries. By bringing her personal experiences into this often impersonal art form she has blended eastern focus with western creativity and thereby moved miniature painting into the sphere of contemporary art.

She is interested in exploring both sides of the Muslim and Hindu traditions, often combining imagery from both in one painting. Sikander also creates murals and, in what she has labeled 'performances', has experimented with wearing the veil in public-something she never did in Pakistan. She seeks to subvert stereotypes and in particular that of the Pakistani woman.

Shahzia Sikander has received a number of awards including the Honorary Artist award from the Pakistan Ministry of Culture and *National Council of the Arts. She lives and works in New York and Texas.

N. FARRUKH

Sikh

(in Punjabi 'pupil') The followers of Sikhism. They total approximately 20 million (1991 estimate) in number. The majority of Sikhs live in India in the state of *Punjab, constituting over 60 per cent of its population. There are numerous Sikh communities in the United States, Canada, and England. According to the 1981 census there were approximately 2600 Sikhs in Pakistan (0.003 per cent of the population), mainly living in the Punjab.

Sikhism is a monotheistic religion that appeared in the Punjab at the turn of the 16th century. Sikh dogmas were largely influenced by Bhakti movement and *Sufism. Sikhism was founded by the *Guru* Nanak (1469–1539). He preached monotheism and the equality of all Sikhs before God. He rejected idol-worship and castes, and called upon his followers to take an active part in the affairs of the world. The *Guru* Anger (1539–52), one of the nine *gurus* who followed Guru Nanak, introduced the Gurmukhi script as special Sikh writing. The script was devised on the basis of several north Indian scripts. The holy book of the Sikhs, *Adi Granth* (the Book of Beginning), began to be compiled in 1604 under the order of the Guru Arjun (1581–1606). Apart from pronouncements by the Guru Nanak, it also included poetry by the great Bhakti poet, Kabir (*c.* 1380–1418), and by some *Sufi preachers. The holy temple of the Sikhs, the Golden Temple, is located in the city of Amritsar in East Punjab, India. (*See* also Khalsa, Sikh State).

E.YU. VANINA

'Silk Letters' Conspiracy

An episode in the Indian national-liberation struggle, so named because members of the radical organization of Indian Muslims wrote their secret plans on lengths of silk that felt into the hands of the British authorities. The leaders of the organization, Maulana Mahmud al-Hasan and Ubaydullah Sindhi, were connected with an Indian 'provisional government' in Kabul (Afghanistan). The organization planned an armed uprising of Indian Muslims with the support of Afghan armies, and possibly the armies of other Muslim states, to overthrow British rule and proclaim a republic. The leaders of the conspiracy tried to establish contacts with the underground Hindu organizations in India. The participants of the conspiracy were arrested. Mahmud Hasan was exiled to Malta.

BIBLIOGRAPHY: *'Sedition Committee Report of 1918', London, 1919.*

A.V. RAIKOV

Sikh State

This sprang up in India as a result of the national movement of *Punjabi peasants, tradesmen, and artisans against the *Mughal and the *Durrani Empires. Proclaimed in 1763 in Amritsar by the Sikh *Khalsa, Sikhism became the ideology of the rebels. From 1748 the military operations were commanded by **Sardars* at the head of *Jathas*, or armed detachments, of *Sikhs. In the early 1760s, the conquered regions of the *Punjab were divided into twelve small *Misals*, or principalities. Between 1799 and 1811, they united under the power of Ranjit Singh, who founded a united Sikh State to the west of the *Sutlej River. It existed until 1849.

BIBLIOGRAPHY: *N.I. Semyonova, 'The Sikh State', Moscow, 1958 (in Russian); I.M. Reisner, 'Popular Movements in India in the 17th-18th Centuries', Moscow, 1961 (in Russian); H.R. Gupta, 'A History of the Sikhs: 1739-99', Simla, 1952; J.D. Cunningham, 'History of the Sikhs', Calcutta, 1949.*

YU.V. GANKOVSKY

Sikh Uprisings

Lasting from the 1620s to the mid-18th century, the Uprisings were preceded by a long history of the formation of Sikhism as a peaceful religion (**Khalsa*), professing one of the Bhakti teachings. In the 1620s, the Sikh armed uprising was triggered by the execution of Guru Arjun (1582–1607) on the Great Mughal Jahangir's orders. The *Sikh movement quickly developed into an anti-Mughal war waged by peasants, craftsmen and tradesmen. The uprising flared up in the *Punjab and then spread into the neighbouring regions of north and northwest India. The rebel strongholds were the Sikh religious centre of Amritsar and the fortresses of Anandpur, Paonta and Gurdaspur.

The movement gained momentum dramatically under the tenth *guru*, Govind Singh (1660–1708), who introduced a number of important reforms in the Sikh community. He abolished the position of hereditary *guru,* and the hereditary agents (*'Masands')* who collected taxes for the *guru*'s upkeep. He gave the power to the Sikh community itself, which led to considerable democratisation of the movement, contrary to the wishes of its moderate wing. *Guru* Govind Singh armed to separate the Sikhs from other religious communities and simultaneously do away with caste inequality. He therefore introduced a special hairstyle and style of clothing for the Sikhs, as well as an initiation ceremony and the title of Singh ('Lion') to be added to the name of each Sikh. The Sikhs succeeded in scoring a number of victories over the Mughal army but in 1705, with the help of the local *Rajas, the Mughals seized Anandpur. In 1708 *Guru* Govind Singh was killed, but the uprising continued under the leadership of Banda Bahadur. He won back from the Mughals the fortresses of Sirhind and Saharanpur. Despite repeated defeats sustained by his army, Banda Bahadur assembled new forces again and again. The movement gradually assumed the character of a peasant war. This is why the local landlords and merchants, who initially supported the anti-Mughal struggle, started backing away from it. In 1715, after a nine-month siege, Gurdaspur fell. Banda Bahadur and other rebel leaders were executed. However, the Sikhs continued their warfare and, after the downfall of the

*Mughal empire, they restored their strength. They played an important role in the struggle against the *Durrani *padishahs* in the second half of the 18th century. (See: also Sikh State.)

BIBLIOGRAPHY: *I.M. Reisner, 'People's Movements in India in 17th-18th Centuries', Moscow, 1961 (in Russian); K.Z. Ashrafyan, 'Sikhism in India's Socio-Political Life (16th century-early 1980s)', in: Religions of the World History and Modern Day, Moscow, 1987 (in Russian).*

E.YU. VANINA

Simla Agreement

This agreement was signed by President Zulfikar Ali *Bhutto of Pakistan and Prime Minister Indira Gandhi of India at Simla on 2 July 1972. It followed the 1971 Indo-Pakistan War during which India had intervened in an internal constitutional crisis in Pakistan and militarily severed its eastern province. The Simla Agreement ignored the UNSC Resolution 307 of 21 December 1971, which had called for withdrawal of troops to respective territories 'which fully respect the ceasefire line' (of 1949). However, the principles and the purposes of the United Nations Charter were invoked in order to govern the relations between the two countries, and that, in accordance with the UN Charter, the two countries would refrain from the threat or the use of force against the territorial integrity or political independence of each other.

On *Kashmir it was decided that the Line of Control, resulting from the 17 December 1971 ceasefire, 'shall be respected by both sides without prejudice to the recognized position of either side. Neither side shall seek to alter it unilaterally, irrespective of mutual differences and legal interpretations. Both sides further undertake to refrain from the threat or the use of force in resolutions of this line.' In the concluding paragraph it was stated that the modalities had to be set for a final settlement of Jammu and Kashmir.

The issues besides Kashmir, which remained unsettled, were the repatriation of prisoners of war and civil internees, and the resumption of diplomatic relations. The issues which were settled were the re-establishment of postal and telegraph links, maritime communications, scientific and cultural co-operation, and the cessation of hostile propaganda.

The Simla Agreement faced criticism in both countries. Mahmud Azam Faruqi of **Jamaat-i-Islami* of Pakistan supported an Indian interpretation that the Agreement precluded reference to the UN, while Atal Bihari Vajpayee of the Jan Sangh of India, contended that President Bhutto had succeeded in reopening the *Kashmir issue. Despite bitterness and violations, the Simla Agreement stands.

BIBLIOGRAPHY: *'White Paper on Jammu and Kashmir Dispute', Ministry of Foreign Affairs, Pakistan; G.S. Bhargava, 'Success or Surrender? The Simla Summit', New Delhi, 1972-73; Rafi Raza, 'Zulfikar Ali Bhutto and Pakistan 1967-77', Karachi, 1997.*

M.R. KAZIMI

Simla Conference, 1945

The Simla Conference of 1945 resulted from an attempt by the wartime Viceroy, Lord Wavell, to break the political deadlock and install an Interim Government, representative of Indian parties. The Viceroy and the Commander-in-Chief would continue to be British, in accordance with the *Cripps Mission, as long as the war with Japan lasted. The Interim Government would continue working under the government of India Act, 1935.

The Viceroy broadcast his proposals on 14 June and announced the release of the Congress Working Committee members, detained since the 1942 Quit India Movement. The Conference opened on 25 June and the Viceroy announced its failure on 14 July, attributing the blame to himself. The Conference actually failed because Quaid-i-Azam Mohammad Ali *Jinnah, President of the *All-India Muslim League, insisted that, since his party was the sole spokesman for the Indian Muslims, no other political party had the right to nominate a Muslim to the Viceroy's Executive Council. This contention was unacceptable to the Congress and the Viceroy, and thus the Conference failed. Objectively, the stand of the AIML could not be upheld in the light of its dismal showing in the last 1937 elections. Before the AIML delegation left Simla it called for fresh elections.

As an aside to the Conference, the leader of the AIML in the Indian Council of State held out the hope to V.P. *Menon, the Reforms Commissioner, that, if the Honorary Secretary of the AIML, Liaquat Ali *Khan, were approached, a way could be found out of the impasse. The subsequent discussion between Liaquat Ali Khan and V.P. Menon was not productive. Despite this, Viceroy Lord Wavell made an attempt to see Liaquat Ali Khan over the head of M.A. Jinnah but Liaquat, in deference to Jinnah's wishes, did not accept the Viceroy's invitation.

BIBLIOGRAPHY: *N. Mansergh and E.W.R. Lumby (eds.), 'The Transfer of Power' London, 1974; V.P. Menon, 'The Transfer of Power in India', Princeton, 1957; Pender ell Moon (ed.), 'Wavell: The Viceroy's Journal' Karachi, 1974; Khalid B. Sayeed, 'Pakistan: The Formative Phase' Karachi, 1969.*

M.R. KAZIMI

Simla Deputation, 1906

The Simla Deputation was a gathering of thirty-five Muslim notables of India led by Sir Sultan Mohammad Shah *Aga Khan III to present demands before Viceroy Lord Minto on 1 October 1906 at Simla. Mohsinul *Mulk was Secretary of the Delegation. The main demand was separate electorates and weightage for minorities in the legislatures. Under this system the Muslim voters, of whom separate registers would be maintained, would vote for Muslim candidates representing a variety of parties or interests. The members of the Deputation had argued that, although Muslims constituted fourteen per cent of the population of the United Provinces, under joint electorates they had not been able to secure a single seat. The delegates also pressed for Aligarh College to be raised to the status of a University as well as for a greater share for Muslims in government services.

However, The Deputation members, refused to accommodate the demand of Bengali delegates that the partition of Bengal be maintained, although Hindu/Congress opposition to the partition of *Bengal the previous year had been the main cause of Muslim awakening.

Muslim political consciousness had been awakening since the dawn of the 20th century and Sir Syed Ahmad *Khan's policy of loyalty to the British and the eschewing of political activity was now being thought inadequate. Muslims organized an *Urdu Defence Council against the anti-Urdu, pro-Hindi bill of Sir Anthony McDonnell, Deputy-Governor of UP, in 1900. The same year Muslim delegates from all over India had assembled at the Lucknow residence of Hamid Ali Khan, Barrister-at-Law, and had mooted forming a political party called the *Muslim League of India. This proposal was not immediately followed up. It was to take Hindu communal opposition to the partition of Bengal in 1905 to galvanize Muslims into action.

Mohammad Ali's statement during the *Khilafat Movement, that the Simla Deputation had been a 'command performance', has been used by Dr Rajendra Prasad and others to create doubts about the bona fides of the Deputation. The allegation that Viceroy Lord Minto had connived behind the scenes to receive a delegation of Muslims is not borne out by his correspondence, or by the non-committal nature of his reply to the Muslim delegation, nor by his resistance to the proposal of granting separate electorates.

In a letter of 8 August 1906 to the Secretary of State, the Viceroy wrote that he have not have the time to think over the advisability of receiving a Muslim delegation, but was inclined to do so. On 2 May 1909 Lord Minto telegraphed the Secretary of State that separate electorates for Muslims were manifestly impractical and that he had made no such suggestion.

Thus, contrary to a popular notion, the main demand of the Muslim delegates–separate electorates–had not been immediately or unreservedly accepted by Lord Minto. Replying to the Deputation, he had merely said that the demand was worthy of sympathetic consideration.

Sir Adamjee Peerbhoy, presiding over the first session of the *All-India Muslim League at Karachi in 1907, had admitted that the Viceroy had neither committed himself nor the government to separate electorates.

Separate electorates were included in the Government of India Act, 1909 (Morely-Minto Reforms) by the efforts of the Honorary Secretary of the AIML, Syed Hasan Bilgrami, when he was living in London. Bilgrami's main argument had been that in some constituencies registers for Muslim voters were maintained separately, and the practice only needed to be made universal and given statutory protection.

On the Muslim side, the timing of the Deputation had not been planned in advance. *Aga Khan III was on his way to China and had to break his journey at Sri Lanka in order to lead the delegation. The Simla Deputation preceded, but did not encourage, the foundation of the All-India Muslim League.

BIBLIOGRAPHY: *Mohammad Salim Ahmad, 'The All India Muslim League', Bahawalpur, 1988, [contains the names of the delegates]; John Buchan, 'Lord Minto-A Memoir', London, 1924'; Ram Gopal, 'Indian Muslims' London, 1959, [Contains the text of the Deputations Memorial and the Viceroy's reply]; John Morley, 'Recollections', 2 vols. London, 1917; Rajendra Prasad, 'India Divided', Bombay, 1947; Francis Robinson, 'Separatism among Indian Muslims', Cambridge, 1974; Matiur Rahman, From Consultation to Confrontation, London, 1970; Syed Razi Wasti, 'Lord Minto and the Indian Nationalist Movement', Oxford, 1964.*

M.R. KAZIMI

Simon Commission, 1927

This was a Statutory Commission, named after its president Sir John Simon, set up to draw up the new Constitution of India to succeed the Montagu-Chelmsford Reforms, i.e. *The Government of India Act, 1919*. The timing of the appointment of this Commission was disruptive, since this was the one time when the British quite openly played the divide and rule game. The Congress and the *Muslim League had arrived at a new constitutional settlement in succession to the *Lucknow Pact of 1916, based on joint electorates. The *Delhi Muslim Proposals of 20 March 1927 had been accepted by the Indian National Congress in its May session at Bombay. On the grounds that the Simon Commission had no Indian member, the Congress and a sizeable bloc of the *All-India Muslim League decided to boycott the Commission.

The President of the All-India Muslim League at that time was Sir Mohammad *Shafi and the Honorary Secretary was Dr Saifuddin *Kitchlew. The president was in favour of co-operation with the Simon Commission while Kitchlew was against co-operation. This led to a split in the All-India Muslim League. M.A. *Jinnah, who had resigned from Congress in the 1920 Nagpur session during which he was insulted, preferred a split in the ranks of the Muslim League, rather than leaving the Congress isolated at this juncture. The AIML led by Sir M. Shafi held the 19th session in Lahore, while the dissenting group held its session at Calcutta on 30 December 1927, with Sir Mohammad Yaqub presiding. Ultimately, M.A. Jinnah assumed the presidency of the pro-boycott faction and joined the Congress party in setting up an All Parties committee, under Pandit Motilal Nehru, to draft a Constitution for India, as the native substitute for the Simon Commission.

The Simon Commission paid two visits to India, the first from February to March 1928 and the second from October 1928 to April 1929. The Commission published its Report, which recommended the granting of provincial autonomy and responsible government at the Centre. The Simon Commission also suggested that a council for Greater India be formed, which would include both *British India and the Princely states. The report of the Simon Commission was never placed before the British Parliament but was consulted during the *Round Table Conferences.

The Simon Commission had no other effect than to split the AIML temporarily and abort the *Delhi Muslim Proposals, agreed upon between the Muslim League and Congress. The *Nehru Report (q.v.) and the *Fourteen Points followed.

BIBLIOGRAPHY: *C.F. Andrews, 'India and the Simon Report' London, 1930; Khalid B. Sayeed, 'Pakistan. The Formative Phase', Karachi, 1978; S.M. Burke and S.A.D. Qureshi, 'The British Raj in India', Karachi, 1995.*

M.R. KAZIMI

Sindh (also Sind)

Sindh is a historical and geographical division and a province in south-eastern Pakistan, in the basin of the lower *Indus. Its area is 140,900 sq.km. Its population 29,991,000 (1998). The indigenous population is *Sindhi. In Karachi, Hyderabad and in other major cities, **Muhajirs* or incomers predominate. Sindh consists of four divisions: Sukkur, Hyderabad, Karachi, and Larkana, and twenty-one districts. The capital is Karachi, a major economic centre and a sea port, accounting for almost half of the industrial production of the country. Other industrial centres are Hyderabad and Sukkur. The more developed industries include textile, food, chemicals, ferrous metallurgy, mechanical engineering, and metal working. In the *Indus Valley they practice diversified, irrigated, commodity farming 50 per cent of which is rice, 15 per cent wheat and sugar cane and 30 per cent cotton. Cattle breeding and fishing are also practised. In the third and the first half of the second millennia BC, one of the main centres of the *Harappan Civilization—*Mohenjo-Daro—was on Sindh territory. At the end of the sixth century BC, Sindh was included in the ancient Persian empire of the *Achaemenids. In 327-25 BC, it was conquered by Alexander of Macedonia. Subsequently it was probably part of the *Maurya Empire. During the fifth and sixth centuries it fell under the *White Huns or *Ephtalite rule. In 711 it was conquered by the Arabs and accompanied by the spread of Islam. In the first half of the eleventh century it was under vassalage of the *Ghaznavids and in 1591 Sindh was conquered by Akbar. It became independent at the beginning of the eighteenth century under the local dynasties of the Kalhoro and the *Talpur, but in the second half of the century became a vassal state of the Afghan kings of the *Durrani dynasty. In 1843 Sindh was annexed by Britain and remained a part of the Bombay Presidency until 1936. From 1936 to 1947 it was a province of *British India. In August 1947 it joined the newly created Pakistan. From 1955 to 1970 it was part of the united province of *West Pakistan. On 1 July 1970 it was resurrected as Sindh province.

YU.V. GANKOVSKY

Sindh Hari Committee

Set up in 1937, the Committee was an influential peasant association. It advocated abolition of landlordism without compensation to the landlords, and distribution of their lands among landless peasants or peasants with little land. It wanted to stop the practice of driving the *haris* from the land they tilled, to cut down taxes, and revise the water and land taxes. In the 1980s the agrarian conflicts in the *Sindh countryside became politicized as a result of the Committee's activities. It organized protest meetings, demanded the restoration of democracy, the general elections, and the holding of release of all political prisoners. Peasants were involved in anti-government disturbances in 1983 and 1986.

S.I. TANSYKBAEVA

Sindh Lowlands

An area of flood plain Located to the south of the confluence of the *Indus and the rivers of the *Punjab.

The Sindh Lowlands slope less than 15 cm. every kilometer, contributing to the slowing of the river flow. This leads to the rivers deporting over 90,000,000 cu. meters of soiled matter in the form of alluvial sedimentation every year.

M. STONEY

Sindh Women's Movement, (also SWM, Sindhiani Tehrik)

The SWM was organized in 1982 to defend the rights of women, fight discriminatory laws, and work for democracy and peace. It has branches in all cities of the *Sindh province.

N.A. ZAMARAEVA

Sindhi, Abdul Majid (1889–1978)

Political activist. Sheikh Abdul Majid Sindhi was born to a Hindu family of Thatta and was originally named Jethanand. He converted to Islam in 1908. He was educated at Sindh Madrasah, Karachi. He was editor of the journal *Al-Amin*. He was jailed for participating in the *Reshmi Roomal* Movement (*Silk Letters Movement) (1916–18). He was appointed Convenor of the Sindh Khilafat Committee and was jailed again. Abdul Majid Sindhi edited *Al-Wahid* and in 1938 he founded the Sindh Azad Party. When the 1937 elections were approaching he joined the Sindh Muslim League Parliamentary Board, but the Sindh Azad Party was still retained as an independent entity. Adbul Majid Sindhi defeated Sir Shahnawaz *Bhutto in the 1937 Provincial Assembly elections standing in the Larkana Constituency. In the Assembly he joined Sir Ghulam Husain *Hidayatullah's Sindh Muslim Party. He was a member of the AIML Council from 1937 to 1938. In 1938 he became President of the Sindh Muslim League. His organizational abilities proved invaluable and ML offices were established in almost all Sindh districts. He was defeated by Sir Abdullah *Haroon for the post of President of the Sindh Muslim League. Between 1941–42 he was Finance Minister in the Sindh cabinet under Mir Bandeh Ali. In 1944 he was briefly allied with the *Azad* group of Maula Bakhsh. He was appointed Chairman of the Committee of Action of the SML by G.M. *Syed. After the creation of Pakistan Shaikh Abdul Majid became less politically active.

BIBLIOGRAPHY: *'Khan Mohammad Panwhar' (ed.), Abdul Majid Sindhi, Hyderabad.*

M.R. KAZIMI

Sindhi (Language)

As part of the north-western *Indo-Aryan group of languages, *Sindhi is mainly spoken in the Pakistani province of Sindh and in the Indian states of Maharashtra, Gujarat and Rajasthan. In both countries, the language is used in education, culture and literature.

The dialects of Sindhi are: Vicholi, occupying a central position and forming the basis of the literary language; *Seraiki, the northern dialect; Lasi, spoken in coda round Lasbela; Lari, along the lower reaches of the river *Indus; Thareli, an intermediate stage between Sindhi and Rajasthani; and Kachhi, an intermediate stage between Sindhi and Gujarati.

BIBLIOGRAPHY: *R.P. Yegoroga, 'The Sindhi Language', Moscow, 1966, in Russian; E. Trumpp, 'Grammar of the Sindhi Language', London, 1872.*

G.A. ZOGRAF

Sindhi Literature Board

(Sindhi *Adabi* Board): It was founded in 1951 in Hyderabad (*Sindh), to promote *Sindhi language and literature. The Board is headed by nine people, including the Vice-Chancellor of the Sindh University in Hyderabad. The Board publishes collections of Sindhi folklore, poetry, studies of the history of Sindh and ancient manuscripts in Arabic and Farsi. The publications are in Sindhi, Persian, Arabic, *Urdu and English. They are also responsible for translations into Sindhi of world classics such as works by Dostoyevski and Tolstoy. Since 1955 they have been publishing a quarterly journal *Mehran*.

BIBLIOGRAPHY: *'Sindhi Adabi Board. A Brief Introduction', Hyderabad (s.a.).*

M.K. SAFOLOV

Sindhi Literature

Sindhi literature has a long and rich folklore tradition. Many epics of historic-heroic, romantic and fairytale nature have been passed down via this literature. These include: *Rai Diach, Laila and Chanesar, Umar and Marvi, Sassi and Punhun, Momal and Rano, Nuri and Tamachi, Sukhni and Mehar.* In numerous versions, these legends and *dastans* provide plots and images to poets and novelists of *Sindh and the neighbouring regions.

The first written pieces date back to the end of the reign of the Sumra dynasty (1051-1351). The chronicles of the Samma dynasty (1351-1520) mention the name of Shaikh Hamad ibn Rashiduddin Jamali (d. 1362) and contain an excerpt from a poem by Shaikh Ishaq Ahangar (d. 1497). But it was only with the work of Qazi Kazan (d. 1551), author of religious mystical verse in the genre of *shloka, that Sindhi literature was first properly recorded. From the 16th century, at the court of Sindhi rulers, the influence of the Persian language grew. Poetry written in the Sindhi language was mainly popular in *Sufi and religious circles and developed in the direction of folklore. The more noted poets of the period include: Shah Abdul Karim Bulari (1536-1620), Shah Inayat, Makhdum Nuh Halakhundi (c. 1505-1950) and Abu-al-Hasan (b. 1661).

The local *Kalhora dynasty patronized Sindhi-language poets in the time of such classical poets as Shah Abdul Latif *Bhitai, Sachal *Sarmast, and Sami, who derived their inspiration in folk poetry. Other prominent poets of those times are Makhdum Ziyauddin Thattawi (d. 1759), Makhdum Abdul Khaliq Thattawi, Sahibdino Faqir (1687-1785), Pir Muhammad Baka, and Makhdum Abdur Rahim (b. 1739).

From the middle of the 18th century such genres as **kafi*, **wai*, and **doha*, began to be overshadowed by Persian genres. The major poets of this period were Rohal Faqir (d. 1782), Dalpat (d. 1841), Bedil *Rohri Sabit Ali Shah (1740-1810), who wrote Persian-style **qasidas* and **marsias*, and Khalifa Gul Muhammad (1808-11 to 1855-6), the author of the first **diwan* in Sindhi. Alongside poetry in the style of *aruz*, poetry in the traditional Sindhi prosody was also written.

At the end of the 19th century an enlightenment movement was born in Sindh, led by Mirza Qalich *Beg, K.C. Khilnani (1844-1916), Dayaram *Gidumal and others. Translations were made from Farsi, Urdu, Bengali and English. Among these poets were Mir Abdul Husain Khan Sangi, Haji Ghulam Shah Gada (1826-1916), and Bhojraj Motwani (1867-1920). Modern prose genres also originated at that time. The first prose works in Sindhi literature were the short stories of Ghulam *Husain (1853), the translation of the 'Gospel According to St John' (1853), and a prose version of Saadi's *Gulistan*. Most of the prose works of the second half of the 19th century are free translations. Mirza Qalich Beg is the author of the first novel in Sindhi, entitled *Zinat*. Pritamdas Hukumatrai wrote his novel *Ajabbhet* (Strange Comparisons) in 1892. The novelists were the first to depict the real life of the *Sindhi people.

Drama appeared in Sindhi literature only at the end of the 19th century. The Sindhi College in Karachi became a theatre centre where the Amateur Dramatic Society was founded in 1894. They staged and published fifteen plays, mostly dramatizations of various episodes from *Mahabharata* and *Ramayana*, translations and renderings of Kalidasa, Shakespeare, Gogol's *Inspector-General*, Ibsen's *Pillars of Society*, and, only occasionally, original works. The absence of professional theatre prevented the dramatic arts from developing. The major prose writers were, as a rule, also dramatists. Prominent among them was K.C. Khilnani, Mirza Qalich Beg, Dayaram Gidumal and Parmanand Mevaram (b. 1866).

In the 1930s a progressive, largely realistic, trend became predominant, with a strong influence of the All-India Progressive Writers' Association. Sindhi writers established their own organizations, such as *Jamaat-ush-Shuara-i-Sindh* (Society of Sindhi Poets), *Sindhi Adabi Sangat* (Sindh Literary Union, 1947), with branches in various cities of Pakistan. Characters drawn from life appeared in Sindhi literature—farmers, craftsmen, petty clerks, and intellectuals. The leading theme of that period was the national liberation struggle and restructuring of society. Literary studies and criticism originated at about that time too.

After independence in 1947, Hindu Sindhis moved to India. Sindhi literature was written in two different states, which affected its nature. In Pakistan, Sindhi writers were affiliated with *Mehran* magazine, the

Sindhi *Adabi* Board (1951), and the Sindhi Academy. In India the journals *Hindvasi, Nayi Dunya Kahani,* came out haphazardly.

The Pakistan-based Sindhi poets include Shaikh *Ayaz, Muhammad Bakhsh Wasif, Hari Dilgir, and Abdur Razzaq Raz. Among the prose writers, mention must be made of Jamaluddin *Abro, Tanwir *Abbasi, Shamsher Haydari, Ayaz Qadri, Rashid Bhatti, and Rasul Bakhsh Palejo. In poetry one can observe the departure from *aruz* norms as poets turned to free verse and purely Sindhi genres. Realistic trends predominated *avant-garde* style was hardly ever practised.

In the 20th century, studies into classical and contemporary Sindhi literature were made on a wider scale. The more noted literary scholars and critics are Muhammad Siddiq Memon (1890-1958), Pir Husamuddin Rashdi (1911-82), Nabi Bakhsh Baloch, Lal Singh Ajwani (1899-1976), Agha Sufi Ghulam Nabi, Asadullah Behud Husaini (b. 1931), and G.M. Shahwani.

BIBLIOGRAPHY: *I.D. Serebryakov, 'Literatures of the Indian Peoples', Moscow, 1985 (in Russian); Pir Husamuddin Rashdi, 'Sindhi Adab', Karachi (s.a.); Mazhar Jamil, 'Guftugu' (Conversation), Karachi, 1986; L.H. Ajwani, 'History of Sindhi Literature', Delhi, 1977; Gurdayal Mullik, 'Divine Dwellers in the Desert', Karachi, 1949; Annemarie Schimmel 'Sindhi Literature', Wiesbaden, 1974; H.T. Sorley, 'Shah Abdul Latif of Bhit', Karachi, 1989.*

A.S. SUKHOCHEV

Sindhi (People)

A people in Pakistan inhabiting the *Sindh Province, and also the Lasbela, Kalat districts in the *Balochistan Province and the Rahimyar Khan district in the *Punjab Province. The total Sindh population in Pakistan is 30.4 million. Ninety-eight per cent are Muslims, mostly *Sunnis. About 2.5 million Sindhis live in north-western India. They are largely Hindu refugees from Sindh who moved to India after 1947, and their descendants. Sindhi ethnogenesis can be traced to *Indo-Aryan people and tribal unions that formed in the first millennia BC in the lower reaches of the Indus (Patalae, Massanoi, Musikanos, and others).

Taking part in the Sindhi ethnogenesis were the early indigenous populations (prior to the Indo-European period); the *Shaka and *Ephtalite tribes in the 2nd through fifth century BC; some *Balochi and *Brahui tribes in the 15th-16th centuries. They penetrated Sindh from the west and north-west and were eventually assimilated Jat clans also migrated here from South Punjab.

Traditional occupations include farming on the fertile alluvial soils of the *Indus Valley (grain, pulses, oilseeds, vegetable, fruit), cattle-breeding, handicrafts in urban areas, and sea trade and fishing.

Sindhi culture is rooted in ancient times (*see* Mohenjo-Daro). It has absorbed many different elements, but, by the turn of the second millennium, it was already perceived as a distinctive single entity. A number of medieval works and cultural figures are well known. The 17th-18th centuries saw the creation of several classical Sindhi works (Sayyid Abdul Karim, Makhdum Abdullah Nariyawaro, Shah Abdul Latif *Bhitai).

BIBLIOGRAPHY: *M.K. Kudryavtsev, 'The Sindhi', South Asian Nations, Moscow, 1963 (in Russian); Yuri Gankovsky, 'The Peoples of Pakistan', Lahore, 1972.*

YU.V. GANKOVSKY

Sindhi, Ubaydullah (1872–1944)

Theologian. A Muslim theologian and public figure in *British India, Sindhi was born into a Sikh family, later converting to Islam and attending the Muslim school in *Deoband from 1888 to 1890. He taught at religious schools in Deoband, Delhi and elsewhere, and took an active part in the national liberation movement. Sindhi lived in Afghanistan from August 1915 to November 1922. He was a member of the Indian provisional government, which was established in Kabul by Raja Mahendra Pratap and Maulana Barakatullah, and headed the Kabul branch of the Indian National Congress. In 1922 he visited Moscow. From 1922 to 1926 he lived in Turkey and, from 1926–39 in Hijaz. In March 1939 he returned to British India where he founded and led the party '*Jamna-Narbada-Sindh-Sagar*' which aimed at reorganizing the administrative-territorial system of British India on linguo-cultural principles.

WORKS: *'Kabul mein sat sal', Lahore, 1955 (in Urdu); 'Shah Waliy Allah aur unki Siyasi Tahrik', Lahore, 1970 (in Urdu).*

BIBLIOGRAPHY: *Muhammad Sarwar, 'Talimat Maulana Ubaydullah Sindhi', Lahore, 1955 (in Urdu); H. Malik, 'Muslim Nationalism in India and Pakistan', Washington, 1963; G. Allana, 'Our Freedom Fighters', Karachi, 1969.*

YU.V. GANKOVSKY

Sindhi-Balochi-Pakhtun Front

(SBPF) Founded in 1985 in London by a group of political emigrants from Pakistan including Mumtaz Bhutto, Z.A. *Bhutto's cousin, A.H. *Pirzada, former minister in the government of the *Pakistan Peoples Party in 1972-77, and Ataullah Khan Mengal. The objective of the Front was to transform Pakistan into a confederation of the four provinces (*Punjab, *Sindh, *North West Frontier and *Balochistan) in which the central government would only control foreign policy, defence and currency.

O.V. PLESHOV

Singh, Bhai Vir (1872–1957)

Poet. A poet and writer in *Punjabi, Bhai Vir Singh grew up in a literary family. He was a brilliant scholar and was conversant in ancient Indian and *Persian literature as well as *English literature. Bhai Vir Singh took part in the *Sikh movement at the end of the 19th century. He published a newspaper *Khalsa Samachar* (Khalsa News). His work is strongly influenced by Sikhism and *Sufism and is noted for its vivid descriptions of nature, exalted emotions and lofty humanism.

WORKS: *'Sundari', Amritsar, 1897; 'Bijai Singh', Amritsar, 1899; 'Satwant Kaur', Amritsar, 1900; 'Baba Naudh Singh, Amritsar, 1921'. 'Lahiran de har', Amritsar, 1921; 'Matak hulare', Amritsar, 1922; 'Bijlian de har, Amritsar', 1927; 'Mere saia jio', Amritsar, 1955.*

BIBLIOGRAPHY: *Madan Mohan Singh, 'Bhai Vir dia racnava', Amritsar (undated); Sarmukh Singh Amol, 'Bhai Vir Singh', Amritsar, 1949; Narula, Narindar Singh, 'Bhai Vir Singh', Ludhiana, 1951; Harbans Singh, 'Bhai Vir Singh te unha di racna', Ludhiana, 1951.*

N.I. TOLSTAYA

Sinjrani

This area of about 15,000 sq. km in the district of *Chagai, *Balochistan province, is situated between the east-west lying Chagai Hills in the north and Ras Koh Range in the south. It consists of a flat plain covered with sandhills and it abounds in salt lakes (*hamun*) that become dry in summer.

M.U. MOROZOVA

Sino-Pakistan agreements

A number of treaties and agreements between Pakistan and China were signed in the 1960s and 1980s.

The agreement on the demarcation of the border between the Chinese People's Republic and the Pakistan-controlled areas of Jammu and *Kashmir was signed on 2 March 1963 in Beijing. The text includes a clause stating the border's temporary character. When the question of Kashmir's fate is finally settled, the Chinese government will enter into negotiations with whichever state is established as having jurisdiction over Jammu and Kashmir. The agreement on the establishment of a direct air link was concluded in August 1963.

The development of trade between the two countries began with the signing of a trade agreement on 5 January 1963. This agreement granted the two parties most favoured nation status. Specific trade conditions, including trade in the border areas, were defined in agreements and protocols signed in 1964. Economic co-operation was based on agreements that included a Chinese loan to Pakistan of $60 million, in order to construct a heavy machine-building complex in *Taxila (1965); a $40 million loan (1968), and $200 million for the completion of the Fourth Five-Year Plan of Pakistan's development (1970). These loans were interest-free and for long terms stretching to twenty years and more. A number of agreements and protocols were signed in the 1980s. (See also Sino-Pakistan Relations).

BIBLIOGRAPHY: *V.N. Moskalenko, 'Pakistan's Foreign Policy', Moscow, 1984 (in Russian); R.M. Mukimjanova, 'Pakistan, South Asia and US Policy', Moscow, 1974.*

R.M. MIKIMJANOVA

Sino-Pakistan relations

Pakistan was one of the first countries to recognize the People's Republic of China in 1949. By 1951 fully-fledged diplomatic relations were established. The Pakistani Prime Minister Mohammad Ali *Bogra struck a rapport with his Chinese counterpart Zhou EnLai during the *Bandung Conference of 1955, which Pakistan had co-sponsored. Prime Minister Huseyn Shahid *Suhrawardy visited China in October 1956 and Zhou EnLai paid a return visit in March 1957.

At the outbreak of the Sino-Indian conflict of 1959 President Ayub *Khan of Pakistan offered India joint defence against China, which Indian Premier Jawaharlal Nehru inexplicably refused. At this stage successive Pakistan Foreign Ministers M.A. *Bogra and Zulfikar Ali *Bhutto were able to cement ties with China.

In March 1963 a Sino-Pakistan agreement was signed demarcating the border between China (Sinkiang-

Uighur Autonomous Region) and the Pakistan-controlled territory of *Kashmir. Agreements were also signed on trade and the establishment of direct air communication between Pakistan and China (*see* Sino-Pakistan agreements).

In 1970 President Yahya *Khan helped the US establish links with China. After a clandestine visit to China from Pakistan by US Secretary of State Dr Henry Kissinger, it was announced on 15 July 1970 that US President Richard Nixon would visit China. This led indirectly to the signing of the Indo-Soviet Treaty of Friendship in August 1971, which neutralized Chinese help to Pakistan during the 1971 War.

During the 1960s Pakistan actively supported China's bid to restore its seat in the United Nations and opposed the US 'two Chinas' formula. Pakistan supported the General Assembly resolution which led to the restoration of China's seat in the United Nations and simultaneous expulsion of Taiwan on 25 October 1971.

China supported Pakistan in the development of industry, energy and other spheres. In particular, China helped Pakistan to develop a machine-building complex at Taxila. In 1971 the first section of the *Karakoram Highway between *Gilgit and the Chinese border was completed, while the highway construction was completed in the late 1970s.

Z.A. *Bhutto's government regarded Sino-Pakistan relations as an important factor in consolidating Pakistan's position in Asia. Bhutto visited China in January and February 1972, in May 1974 and in May 1976. US arms deliveries during this period were limited. China became one of the main sources of arms for Pakistan, and China also helped Pakistan develop its munitions factories.

In the late 1970s and 1980s, politicians of both countries maintained close contact concerning the Soviet intervention in Afghanistan and other international issues. Pakistan supported China's position on Cambodia. Co-operation between the two nations in military areas continued. Economic and trade links developed.

Benazir *Bhutto's government announced its policy to further improve relations with China and in February 1989 she visited China.

During the 1980s-90s, relations between China and Pakistan remained stable and friendly. They covered a variety of areas including politics, economics and military. In November 1989 Li Peng, head of the Chinese government, visited Pakistan. In November 1989 China agreed to help Pakistan in the development of nuclear energy and to deliver equipment for a nuclear power plant. In the summer of 1990 Pakistan launched a satellite from Chinese territory. The satellite was thrust into orbit by a Chinese rocket carrier. In February 1991 Pakistan's Premier, Nawaz *Sharif, paid a visit to China.

A change of leadership in China and Pakistan had not significantly altered bilateral relations nor, initially, had the end of the Cold War. With the emergence in the 1990s of USA as the sole super power, Sino-American relations had receded as a factor. Sino-Indian relations improved. By 16 December 1994 the first proposal were made for joint military exercises with. This co-operation grew against the backdrop of Pakistani support for the Taliban regime in Afghanistan. The year 2003 marked a number of developments which showed that friendship with Pakistan remained a basic anchor, while changes on all fronts took place. On 19 June 2003 when India had blocked Pakistan's membership of the *Association of South East Asian Nations (ASEAN) China publicly and vociferously supported admitting Pakistan. This forum was widely perceived as an alliance forming a block of China, Russia, South Asia and South East Asia against the growing influence of the United States.

On 4 November 2003 President Pervez *Musharraf visited China and, consequence of talks with Prime Minister Hu Jintao, both countries undertook to enhance defence co-operation. However Pakistan's pro-Taliban policy cast its shadow aver the proposals. The neutralization of North Korea made adjustments necessary on a global scale, and the incursion of Islamic militants into the Xinjiang province with an Uighur Muslim presence raised concerns, causing China to balance its relations with India and Pakistan. On 2 October Chinese troops killed a influential Muslim, presumably from Pakistan. On 22 October 2003 China and Pakistan conducted joint Naval exercises, the first such exercise China had conducted with any country. During the following month China conducted similar naval exercises with India. Somewhat more seriously China expelled seven hundred Pakistani traders from Xinjiang, albeit under a 1985 agreement. This action carried political overtones as China had already flooded the consumer goods market of Pakistan. However this as yet represented a modification and not deviation from policy. Normalization of Sino-Indian relations could improve prospects of making South Asia a nuclear free zone. Both China and Pakistan have protested against US sanctions for alleged transfer of Nuclear technology.

The following Pakistani projects have been undertaken with Chinese aid: The Karakorum Highway, the heavy mechanical complex of *Taxila, the heavy electrical complex at Kot Najibullah, The machine tool factory at Karachi, Guddu Thermal Power Station, SPARK, an agricultural co-operation programme and the Saindak Metalurgy Project. Strategically the most important on-going project is the development of the Gwadar Sea Port. In sphere of defence, it is the jointly developed fighter aircraft JF-17 Thunder.

BIBLIOGRAPHY: *Sultan M. Khan, 'Memories and Reflections' London, 1997; Anwar Husain Syed, 'China and Pakistan: Diplomacy of an Entente Cordiale', Amherst, 1973.*

V.F. URLYAPOV

Sitar

A plucked string instrument, it is one of the most widely used musical instruments in South Asia. The neck is made of wood, with a wooden or pumpkin-shell resonator, sometimes inlaid with ivory or mother-of-pearl. There are six or seven primary strings and, under these, from seven to eleven resonant ones fixed on a neck that has from sixteen to twenty-two moveable brass or silver frets. The *sitar* is played with a wire plectrum worn on the index finger of the right hand. Playing the *sitar* demands a complex and highly developed technique. There are two main schools of sitar playing, of which the major Pakistani representatives are Imdad Hussain, Raees Khan, and Sharif Khan Poonchwala.

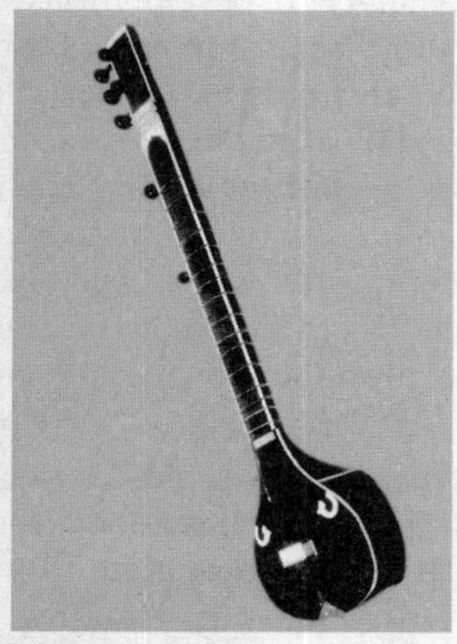

Sitar, a traditional musical instrument.

I. PIRACHA

Soan Culture

The Soan culture is a *Paleolithic culture of India and Pakistan, which was identified in the late 1930s as a result of the studies conducted by the Cambridge-Yale expedition to the *Potwar Plateau in Northern Pakistan. Tools made from chopping pebbles and flaked tools (racloirs and points) are characteristic of the culture. The Soan culture became synonymous with a 'pebble culture' despite a Western technical tradition (the Levallois technique) evident at the later stage. According to the findings by H. Terra and T.T. Paterson, it was divided into four stages that can be compared with the *Himalayas' four interglacial periods. Later, the Soan culture was identified in India as well. Here it was first found in the north, in eastern *Punjab, in the valleys of the *Beas, Sirsa and other rivers.

Later, this culture was also discovered further to the south, in Durkadi on the river Narbada (Maharashtra). H.L. Movius, an American archaeologist, published several works in 1944 that presented the Soan culture as one of the major elements of the Asian Palaeolithic. The pebble tools were made by striking on one side with the result that the working edge cuts on one or both sides. The pebble crust is also preserved on the tools. The tradition of pebble tools and the specific pebble technique makes the Asian Palaeolithic different from the Afro-European Palaeolithic. Neither in India nor in Pakistan does the Soan culture have a definite chronological framework. A tentative assessment suggests a wide temporal range, from 500,000 to 40,000 years. Currently there are doubts about the culture's earliest stages, the pre-Soan and ancient Soan, while the best represented later Soan (100–40 thousand years) is believed to be a result of a Mousterian culture. The periodisation of Soan, based on the Himalayan interglacial sequence, is equally tentative.

BIBLIOGRAPHY: *H. De Terra and T.T. Paterson, 'Studies in Ice Age of India and Associated Human Culture', Washington, 1939; H.L. Movius, 'Early Man in Pleistocene Stratigraphy in Southern and Eastern Asia', Papers of the Peabody Museum of Anthropology and Ethnology, XIX/3, 1944; D. Stiles, 'Palaeolithic Artifacts in Siwalik and Post, Siwalik Deposits of Northern Pakistan', Kroeber Anthropological Society Papers, Nos. 53/54, 1978.*

V.A. RANOV

Socialist Party of Pakistan

(SPP) Founded in March 1971 by a group of members of the *Communist Party of Pakistan. SPP leaders declared their resolution to unite all Marxists who are free from dogmatic attitudes. In February 1975 the second conference adopted SPP's programme, which proclaimed the party's ultimate goal of creating a socialist society free from oppression and exploitation. After April 1978 the SPP repeatedly spoke out in favour of normalization of *Afghanistan-Pakistan relations. During the 1988 general elections the SPP formed a Democratic Front together with five other left-wing parties.

O.V. PLESHOV

Society of Ismaili Reforms

(*Barbhai*) Appearing in India in 1840, the Society did not recognize the holiness and absolute power of *Aga Khan I, the spiritual leader of the *Khoja sect. Ten years later, Aga Khan, whose position of higher authority was confirmed by the special resolution of the Supreme Court of Bombay (1866), excommunicated the Society from the Khoja sect. However, the Society still retains its influence in India and Pakistan. The reformist movement also gained momentum among another South Asian community, Bohra. The reformers of *Bohra teaching refuse to recognize the current leader as the living, yet secret, imam endowed with the grace which is transferred from one **imam* to the next, emanating from Ali and Fatima. They also refuse to pay a special tax into the sect's fund.

A. NIYAZI

South-East Asia Treaty Organization (also SEATO)

A military-political regional organization founded on 8 September 1955 in Manila, and based on the 19 February 1955 treaty on collective defence in South-East Asia (Manila Pact). The Organization included Australia, Great Britain, New Zealand, Pakistan, the United States, Thailand, the Philippines and France. SEATO's military and economic measures were extended, apart from the full members in the region, to include Cambodia, Laos, South Vietnam, and later, Malaysia. The headquarters were located in Bangkok, Thailand. The highest ranking body was the SEATO Council, consisting of Ministers for Foreign Affairs of the member countries. The council had two agencies under it: one for civilian affairs, the general secretariat; another for military affairs, the military planning department. The treaty on collective defence obliged the member countries to react to armed aggression against a member state or territory in accordance with constitutional procedures. Mechanisms for mutual consultations were designed. SEATO had no separate armed forces of its own. In September 1975 the decision was taken, in view of the events in Indo-China, to dissolve the organization. Pakistan had already left in 1972. In June 1977 SEATO ceased to exist.

BIBLIOGRAPHY: *'SEATO, 1954-60', Bangkok, 1960.*

V.F. URLYAPOV

Space research

Despite the considerable squeeze on resources, Pakistan decided to embark on a limited programme of space research. A report of the National Science Commission headed by Professor Abdus *Salam in 1959 proposed the formation of a Space and Upper Atmospheric Research Commission (SUPARCO) reporting directly to the President of Pakistan. SUPARCO has concentrated on three broad areas: building rockets to carry out scientific experiments, developing geo-stationary satellites, and remote sensing data. SUPARCO has developed and constructed 'sounding' rockets, which can lift a scientific payload of between 66-110 1bs to heights varying from 124-310 miles. In 1990 SUPARCO designed and launched its first satellite, BADR-B, into a low circular orbit. The satellite was launched on board a Chinese vehicle in 'piggyback' mode. BADR-B, a 154 lb satellite, is shortly to be placed into a sun-synchronous circular orbit at about 620 miles altitude. SUPARCO also provides facilities to download remote sensing data from the US Landsat satellite, as well as the French Spot satellite.

T. NAIM

Spain, James W. (1926–)

Political Scientist. A sociologist, diplomat, and political scientist he graduated from Columbia University (New York, USA) and received his doctorate there in 1959. Since 1951 he has worked at the State Department (USA) and was Vice-Consul in Karachi (1951-53); a member of the Council of Political Planning; Director, Bureau of Research and Analysis—Near East and South Asia, Director of Pakistan and Afghanistan Affairs (1963-68); chargé d'affaires in Islamabad (Pakistan, 1969); Consul General in Istanbul (Turkey, 1970), and other posts. Spain conducted field research in the *North West Frontier Province on a grant from the Ford Foundation in the 1950s. He has also lectured at the University of Florida.

WORKS: *'The Way of the Pathans', London, 1962 (2nd ed. Karachi, 1972); 'The Pathan Borderland', The Hague, 1963.*

YU.V. GANKOVSKY

State Structure of Pakistan

Pakistan is a federal parliamentary republic. Its official name is the Islamic Republic of Pakistan. The head of state is the President, elected for five years by members of both houses of parliament and of provincial assemblies. The President must be guided in his work by recommendations of the cabinet of ministers and its head, the Chief Minister. Pakistan's highest legislative organ is parliament. It consists of two chambers, the lower house, the National Assembly, and the upper house, the Senate. The National Assembly consists of 237 deputies. It is elected for five years by general direct secret ballot. The elections are conducted by two electorates, the Muslim and the non-Muslim; the latter includes all of Pakistan's religious minorities. The Senate consists of 87 members. The bulk of the deputies, 56 members, are elected by the deputies of provincial legislative assemblies; the rest are elected by members of the National Assembly. The leader of the party which has a majority in the National Assembly is appointed Prime Minister by the President. On the Prime Minister's recommendation, the President appoints members of the government. The government is collectively responsible to the National Assembly and resigns if the chamber expresses lack of confidence in the government.

The highest official in a province is the Governor, who is appointed by the President. The province's legislative organ, the provincial assembly, is elected by the province's population for a term of five years. The leader of a party group which has the majority in the house is appointed Chief Minister by the Governor. The Governor then appoints members of the government on the Chief Minister's recommendation. Each province has its own police force. The most important issues of state defence, foreign relations, currency matters, etc., are entrusted to the federal authorities.

There are four provinces plus the Federal Capital Territory and the *Federally Administered Territorial Area (FATA). The Federal Capital Territory of Islamabad and the FATA are run by the federal authorities. Pakistan also has a complex system of local government institutions.

Pakistan's judicial system is headed by the Supreme Court, appointed by the President, who also appoints the Chief Justice of Pakistan and the members and Chief Justices of the High Courts in the provinces. All members of the administrative apparatus belong to the Civil Service of Pakistan. They are divided into 22 ranks, the first being the lowest.

V.N. MOSKALENKO

Stein, Marc Aurel (1862–1943)

Archeologist. Stein was an Indologist who became a British subject in 1904. He was educated in Budapest, Dresden, Vienna University (1879-80), Leipzig University (1880), Tubingen University (1881-84), Cambridge and Oxford (1884-85), and the Ludwig Military Academy in Vienna (1885). Late in 1887 he came to India where he became Director of the Oriental College, Lahore. In 1888 he was keeper of archives at the University of Punjab and in 1899 he headed the Calcutta Madrasah. In 1891 he worked on *Rajatarangini*, or a Chronicle of the Kings of *Kashmir. He published its Sanskrit text in 1892 and in 1900 its translation with a commentary. In 1903 he was inspector of the Archaeological Survey of India in the *North West Frontier Province and *Balochistan, and became Inspector General and Chief of the Archaeological Inspection in the frontier regions in 1911. He organized and headed several large-scale expeditions into Central Asia, including the Pamirs. He discovered and described hundreds of archaeological sites in Sinkiang and western China, gathering a huge collection of cultural and historical evidence that embraced the period from the Neolithic to the developed Middle Ages. These monuments, especially the Buddhist monuments, yielded a vast amount of material on the ties between India, Central Asia, and China. He conducted important research in Kashmir, the NWFP and the neighbouring Iranian regions, where he discovered and partially excavated Eneolithic (Copper age) sites. His scientific interests stretched as far as western Iran and Mesopotamia. His vast scientific legacy is kept in Indian museums and the British Museum. A doctor of sciences and bearer of the Order of the Indian Empire (1910), he was a member of many geographic societies, of the British Academy and others.

WORKS: *'Zoroastrian Deities on Indo-Scythian Coins', London, 1887 (Reprinted from the Oriental and Babylonian Record, 1887); 'Kalhana's Rajatarangini, a Chronicle of the Kings of Kashmir'. (Translation With an Introduction, Commentary and Appendices by M.A. Stein), Vols. 1-2, Westminster, 1900; 'Serindia, Detailed Report of Explorations in central Asia and Western-most China', Vols. 1-5, Oxford 1921; 'Archaeological Reconnaissance in North-Western India and South-Western Iran', London, 1937.*

BIBLIOGRAPHY: *F.H. Andrews, 'Sir Aurel Stein: The Man—Indian Art and Letters', New Series, Vol. XVIII, No. 2, Second Issue for 1944; L. Rasonyi, 'Stein Aurel es hagyateks', Budapest, 1960; J. Mirsky, 'Sir Aurel Stein, Archaeological Explorer', Chicago and London, 1977.*

N.P. KOCHERGINA

Suba (also Subah)

(Arabic for side) A province in the Great *Mughal empire. There were twelve of them in the late 16th century, and twenty by the beginning of the 18th. Administratively, each *suba* was divided into several **sarkars*. The latter consisted of districts known as mahal or *parganah*. The ruler of a *suba* was called *faujdar or subadar* and the head of a *mahal* or *parganah, amil.*

BIBLIOGRAPHY: *I.H. Qureshi, 'The Administration of the Mughal Empire', Karachi, 1966.*

YU.V. GANKOVSKY

Subadar

(From Arabic and Farsi) 1. In the *Mughal Empire, vicegerent, ruler of a suba or province.

2. In *British India, a senior officer's rank which was given to Indians serving in the colonial army equal to Captain in the British units.

YU.V. GANKOVSKY

Sufi Literature

A collection of literature in different languages conveying *Sufi ideas that gave birth to a multitude of literary works—religious, philosophical and artistic—in many Asian countries. Of particular artistic merit is Sufi poetry. Sophisticated metaphors, symbolism and motifs of great poetic power in the works of the more outstanding Sufi poets created a special psychological depth, and humanistic idealization of man's potential. This influenced the ideological and artistic significance of the best samples of Sufi literature that developed its own system of symbolism in poetry. Real-life objects were interpreted as abstract symbols representing Sufi notions, which in turn could be perceived by the reader as lofty poetic expressions of ideal love, friendship and free human spirit. *Sufism found its most consummate expression in the tenth to 15th centuries in the Farsi poetry of Iran, South Asia and other Muslim countries in the Farsi poetry of Iran, South Asia and other Muslim countries.

In the early period of Sufi literature, the work of Abdallah Ansari (d. 1089) was outstanding. He enriched his verse with rhymed prose and is credited with the first Sufi **ghazals*. Ibn al-Arabi (1165-1240) was another noted Sufi author, writing in Arabic. His work had considerable influence on Sufi literatures in all Muslim countries. Classical poetry of epic and didactic nature *(*masnawi)* and lyrical verse (*ghazals*) make up the creative heritage of the great Sufi poets of the twelfth to 13th centuries: Abul Maj Sanai (died c. 1141)—*Hadiqat al-Haqaiq* (The Garden of the Truth), Fariduddin Attar (died c. 1225)—*Mantiq at Tayr* (The Conversation of Birds); Jalaluddin Rumi (1207-73)—*Masnawi-i-Maanawi* (Spiritual *Masnawi*). These works expressed protest against social injustice in the light of heavenly justice, they condemned cruel rulers, falsehood, and fanaticism. The poetic forms they used tend towards folk song, parable, and fairytale. Such great masters as Nizami (c. 1141-1209), Saadi (c. 1210-92), Hafiz (1325-90) and Jami (1414-92) produced masterpieces of humanistic poetry by their original use of various motifs from Sufi mysticism.

In the Turkic languages Sufi literature first appeared in Central Asia and then in Azerbaijan and Turkey. Many Turkic poets also wrote poetry in Farsi and Arabic: Ahmad Yasavi (d. 1166), Sultan Veled (1226-1312), Imamuddin Nasimi (1369-1417), Qasim al-Anwar (dc 1433), Lutfi (c. 1367-1463), Yunus Emre (died 1320), Mir Ali Sher Nawai (1441-1501) who rose to great heights of active humanism, and Makhdum Kuli (1733-82). In South Asia, the most eminent Sufi authors are Hasan Dehlawi (1257-1336), Amir Khusrow *Dehlawi, Mir Taqi *Mir, Mir *Dard, Shah Abdul Latif *Bhitai, Madho Lal Husain (1539-99), Sachal *Sarmast, Mirza Abdul Qadir *Bedil, Bulleh Shah (d. c. 1758), Waris *Shah, Fazl Shah (d. 1890), and Ghulam Farid (d. 1901).

Sufi literature in *Pashto is represented by the leaders of the Rahshanai movement: Bayazid Ansari, Mira Khan Ansari, and Abdurrahman Mohmand (late 17th and early 18th century).

BIBLIOGRAPHY: *E. Bertels, 'Sufism and Sufi Literature', Moscow, 1965 (in Russian); G.Yu. Aliev, 'Persian-language Literature of India', Moscow, 1968 (in Russian); A. Schimmel, 'Mystical Dimensions of Islam', Chapel Hill, 1975.*

I.S. BRAGINSKY

Sufi Orders

(*Silsila* or *Tariqat*—literally: 'a mystic way', from the Arabic *taraqa*—to embark on a journey, to go) *Sufi orders appeared in the 11th-14th centuries by the merging of existing individual *Sunni and *Shia communities and Sufi groups. In the 15th-19th centuries, new Sufi orders branched off from the original orders, called *usuls*. Each Sufi order is named after its founder and is ruled by his successors. There is an hierarchy of ranks. Each order has its own philosophic and theological doctrine and its own mystic rituals designed to lead one towards spiritual perfection. The number of steps on the way to spiritual perfection varies from four to nine. The ties connecting a rank-and-file Sufi (*murid) to his spiritual adviser (*Sheikh, *pir, *murshid) remain unbreakable for life. A Sufi order is headed by a **wali* (also: *qutb*—the pole of the world). In the local branches he is represented by a *naqib* (in Arabic—a representative, head) or **khalif*. Rank-and-file members, called *faqir* or **derwish*, can be hermits and wandering mendicants (*qalandar*), or they can live at home with their families. Some of the latter belong to the aristocracy.

The first Sufi orders—*Chishtiya, *Suhrawardiya, *Naqshbandiya, Qadiriya and Kubrawiya—appeared in the territory of Pakistan and other South Asian countries, as far back as the 13th-14th centuries (*see* also Sufism.

BIBLIOGRAPHY: *I.P. Petrushevsky, 'Islam in Iran', Leningrad, 1966 (in Russian); J.S. Trimingham, 'The Sufi Orders in Islam', Oxford, 1971; Aziz Ahmad, 'Islam in India', Edinburgh, 1969.*

YU.V. GANKOVSKY

Sufi

(derives from the Arabic word 'Sufi' meaning dressed in a hair shirt, plural: *sifiya*—ascetic, mystic, *fakir*, adherent of the mystic or ascetic trend in Islam (*see* Sufism) A member of a *Sufi order or fraternity. A Sufi who had attained the highest degree of spiritual perfection was called a '*fani*', meaning 'one who had merged with the heavenly being', from the Arabic word *fania*—to disappear. (*See also Sufism.*)

YU.V. GANKOVSKY

Sufism

(also: *Tasawwuf*, from the Arabic '*Suf*'—coarse woollen cloth, hair shirt; hence—*sufi*) A mystic and ascetic trend in Islam aiming at closer union with God, knowing God, and merging with Him. It appeared in the 8th century. In the 9th century, Sufism split into a moderate and an extremist trend. The former believed in strict observance of the *Sharia, the latter was shaped under the impact of pantheistic philosophy. In Pakistani territory, Sufism appeared in the 8th century. In the 11th-12th centuries the first *Sufi orders emerged. Since the 13th century in Pakistan and in other areas of South Asia, the *Chishtiya, *Suhrawardiya, and *Naqshbandiya orders were particularly active. Since the 14th century, Qadiriya and Kubrawiya orders have been active. Missionary work and the idea of social equality were conducive to the spread of Islam. In the late Middle Ages, as well as in modern times, Sufism, taking the form of popular Islam with its faith in miracles and the cults of the saints—*awliya*, became widespread among peasantry, urban traders and craftsmen in South Asia. Sufism had a significant influence on the formation of such movements as Bhakti, Sikhism and Rawshaniya. Sufi influence can also be traced through literature to Pakistani languages, such as *Punjabi, *Sindhi, *Pashtu, *Balochi, *Urdu, *Kashmiri, and to other South Asian literatures. Famous Sufi poets include Sultan Bahu, Bulhe Shah, Waris Shah, Ghulam Farid and Shah Abdul Latif *Bhitai.

YU.V. GANKOVSKY

Suhrawardiya

A *Sufi order, founded by and named after the *Sunni *Sheikh, Shihabuddin Abu Hafs Umar Suhrawardi (*c.* 1145–1235), a resident of Baghdad. The poet and philosopher Saadi (*c.* 1203–92) was one of his disciples. In South Asia, this order has been active since the early 13th century. Of particular importance for its spread in *Sindh and the *Punjab were the activities of Sheikh Bahauddin Zakariya of Khurasan (1182–1268), the founder of the Suhrawardiya community in Multan. Suhrawardi Sheikhs enjoyed great influence at the court of the *Delhi Sultanate. They carried on active missionary work. Suhrawardi influence is evidenced by the fact that in 1443, Sheikh Yusuf, the head of the Multan community of Suhrawardis, was elected the governor of south-west Punjab and north Sindh. Suhrawardis follow Hanafi **Madhab*.

YU.V. GANKOVSKY

Suhrawardy, Huseyn Shaheed (1893–1963)

Prime Minister of Pakistan (1956–57).

Prime Minister of Pakistan from 1956 to 1957. H.S. Suhrawardy received his degree from Oxford and became a lawyer by profession. From 1921 to 1947 he was a member of the Bengal Legislative Council. From 1937 to 1947 he remained one of the front-rank leaders of the *Muslim League in Bengal. From 1937 to 1945 he served variously as

Minister for Labour, Finance, and Health H.S. Suhrawardy was the first leader to reject the *Nehru Report. From 1946 until August 1947 he served as the Bengal Chief Minister and Minister for the Interior. In April 1946, at the Muslim League Legislators' Convention in Delhi, he proposed the resolution on the formation of the united independent Muslim state of Pakistan. The *Lahore Resolution of 1940 had proposed the establishment of two independent states in the subcontinent. In 1946, during the Calcutta and Noakhali riots, he travelled with and worked alongside Mahatma Gandhi to help restore communal peace. After partition, Suhrawardy gave asylum to Bihari refugees. In 1950, he insisted on Pakistan's secession from the British Commonwealth and, in 1951, he called for the establishment of a non-aligned union of Muslim states. He headed the right wing of the *Awami League and played a major role in the massive electoral triumph of the Jugto Front alliance in the 1954 East Bengal elections. From December 1954 to August 1955 he was Minister for Justice of Pakistan. From September 1956 to October 1957 Suhrawardy served as the Prime Minister of Pakistan. After Ayub *Khan's seizure of power in October 1958 he was disqualified from holding any office under the Elective Bodies Disqualification Order (EBDO) and was the only political personality to challenge the EBDO Tribunal in the superior Courts, but without success.

WORKS: *H.R. Talukdar (ed.), 'Memoirs of Huseyn Shaheed Suhrawardy', Dhaka, 1987.*

BIBLIOGRAPHY: *Shaista Ikramullah, 'Husain Shaheed Suhrawardy', Karachi, 1991; Raghib Ahsan, H.S. Suhrawardy and the Inner History of the United Bengal Scheme, Karachi, 1951.*

YU.V. GANKOVSKY

Sui

The biggest deposit of natural gas in Pakistan. It is situated in the border area between the *Punjab Plain and the southern spurs of the *Sulaiman Range in the eastern part of *Balochistan Province. The gas deposits are assessed at 200,000 million cu. metres. The gas, which is under high pressure, contains about 90 per cent methane, with a calorific value of about 8,000 kcal/cu metres. The deposit was discovered in 1952, and its exploitation began in 1955, with the completion of the first section of the Sui-Karachi pipeline. Later the gas was supplied to Larkana, Dadu, Lahore and Peshawar. In the mid-1960s, the overall production of gas constituted 1,500 million cu metres, by 1980 it reached 7,500 million cu metres and by the late 1980s it exceeded 12,000 million cu metres a year. In 1989-90 Sui accounted for almost 60 per cent of the entire gas production in the country. A system of pipelines brings a large part of it to the Karachi industrial district.

M.YU. MOROZOVA

Sulaiman Mountains

This range stretches from the River Gomal in the north to the Bugti and Marri Mountains in the south. The highest peak is *Takht-i-Sulaiman* (Solomon's Throne), 3,385 metres. The Sulaiman Range runs for approximately 777 km, along the eastern fringe of the Iranian Plateau. It consists of two parallel ranges, which slope steeply in towards the valley of the *Indus. The rock structure consists mainly of limestone and sandstone. On the western slopes lie dry steppes and deserts. On the eastern slopes there are patches of sparse woods and leaf-bearing forests and savannahs. On the edge of the southern spur of the Sulaiman Range, where it borders the *Punjab Plain, lies the biggest deposit of natural gas in Pakistan, the *Sui Gas Field.

YU.V. GANKOVSKY

Sunnah

(in Arabic: a road to follow; a tradition, a legend) Deeds, pronouncements, and resolutions of the Prophet Muhammad (PBUH) concerning various aspects of Islam and the life of a Muslim community (*umma*). They are recorded in *ahadith* (*Sunni) and in *khabars* (*Shia) and accepted by Muslims as guidance in their religious, public, political and personal lives. The Sunnah is the second most important source, after the Quran, of Muslim law.

YU.V. GANKOVSKY

Sunni

(Arabic: '*ahl al-Sunna*'—the people of Sunnah: The adherents of the Sunnah). *See*, Sunnism.

YU.V. GANKOVSKY

Sunnism

This is the major sect of Islam, constituting an overwhelming majority, including the Muslims of Pakistan. Sunnism means literally following the Sunnah, precepts of the Holy Prophet Muhammad (PBUH), *Sunnis follow the early republican Caliphs, the Rightly Guided Caliphs (*Khulafa-i-Rashidin*): Abu

Bakr (r 632–4) Umar (r 634–44) Usman (r 644-56) and Ali (r 656-61). Belief in the dynastic and monarchical caliphs of the Ummayad, Abbasid, and Ottoman dynasties is optional in practice. The Sunnis recognize Abdullah bin Zubayr as Caliph as against Marwan I (r. 684) and Abdul Malik (r. 685–705). The Sunni theory of the Caliphate holds that the office should be filled by the process of *Shura* (consultation) or election, nomination or by acclamation. *Imarat-al-Istila*, emirate by seizure, is also recognized as a valid source of authority, when it is in the interest of public order, otherwise the preferable nominee had been one who did not put forward his own candidature. The Caliph had to be a Muslim adult, sound of mind and body and initially he had to belong to the tribe of the Qureish. This condition was dropped when Sultan Salim I, the Ottoman, siezed the Caliphate. During the conflicts between the Murjites, who believed in suspending judgement on a Muslim till the Day of Judgement, and the Kharijites, who declared sinners to be infidels, the Sunnis tended to favour the Murjites.

In the conflict between the Asharites and the Mutazilites, the Sunnis support the Asharites. The main bone of contention is the status of the Quran. The Mutazilites—the Rationalists, influenced by Greek philosophy—believe in a created Quran, with the implication that its injunctions could be understood by reason and theoretically could be modified by the decision of a 'divinely inspired person' to suit the circumstance. The Asharites believe in an uncreated Quran which is eternal and immutable. The Mutazilites assert the free will of man, and the Asharites, predestination. Here again, Sunnis incline to the Asharite view. The appellation *Sunnah wal Jamaa* was adopted in the reign of Harun Rashid (r. 786–809). Some scholars consider Murjites and Asharites identical with the Sunnis, but there is no formal decision that excommunicates Kharijites and Mutazilites from the fold of the Sunnis. The Sunnis are followers of the four schools of jurisprudence (see *Madhab*).

In Pakistan, Sunnis identified as Barelwis are the followers of Ahmad Reza Khan, with emphasis on love and reverence for the Holy Prophet as the central article of faith. They are open to Sufi influence, revere saints such as Abdul Qadir Jilani of Baghdad, Moinuddin Chishti of Ajmer, Nizamuddin Aulia of Delhi and visit their shrines.

Sunnis of the Barelwi sect are organised politically under the party **Jamiat-ul-Ulema-i-Pakistan* founded in 1970 and headed by Shah Ahmad *Noorani. Sunni Tehrik led by M. Ilyas Qadri has lately become popular.

YU.V. GANKOVSKY

Sutlej

(Setlej, Satlaj; in ancient Greek—Zarados; in the Vadas—Sutudir; in Chinese—Lanchuhe) Below the confluence with the *Beas the river is sometimes called Ghara and below the mouth of the *Chenab it is called Panjnad or Five Rivers, from the number of major rivers flowing together. These are the Sutlej, Beas, Chanab, *Ravi and *Jhelum. The Sutlej rises between the sources of the *Indus and the Brahmaputra. From its source on the southern slope of the Kailas Range, at a height of nearly 6,000 metres above seal level, the river flows through China, India, and Pakistan. It is the southernmost river in *Punjab and the biggest tributary of the Indus from its eastern side. The Sutlej is about 1,500 km. long and its basin is 395,000 sq. km in area. In its upper reaches the river flows from east south east to north west and pursues its course along the broad valley that divides the *Himalayas from Tibet. The river then turns in the general direction of flow from north-east to south-west. In the upper reaches the *Sutlej passes through Mansarowar and Langak lakes. After forcing its way across Himalayan ridges and foothills in a narrow valley with innumerable rapids, the river emerges into the Punjab Plain near the town of Rupar.

Approximately 120 km. of its course serve as the border between India and Pakistan. In Pakistan the river is fed in its upper reaches mainly from the glaciers. Through the mountains it is fed by meltwater and by subsoil waters, and chiefly by rainfall in the plain. There is a strong variation of discharge over the seasons. During the floods in July and August the discharge at Rupar reaches 20,000 cu. meters per sec., while at its slowest it is barely 100 cu. metres per sec. The average figure is 500 cu. metres per sec. The discharge is largely regulated by several dams.

The water of the Sutlej is extensively used for irrigation. There was a dispute between Pakistan and India, lasting from 1947 to 1960, concerning the distribution of the waters. The dispute ended in the signing of the Indus Water Treaty agreement in 1960. During the high-water season, the Sutlej is navigable on separate sectors of its course. The major tributaries are the Chenab and Beas from the west. The biggest cities on the river are Nangal in India and *Bahawalpur in Pakistan.

S.B. ROSTOTSKY

Suvorova, Anna Aronovna (1949–)

Linguist. An expert on *Urdu *belles-lettres*, translator, and art critic. A DSc in Philology, she graduated from the Institute of Oriental Languages at Moscow University (1971). She is a research member at the Institute of Oriental Studies. Her main spheres of interest are classical literature in Urdu, graphic arts and theatre of Pakistan and India, medieval Muslim culture, and Sufism. She translated **Dastans* of Nihal Chand Lahori (1974), Khalil Ali Khan Ashq (1981), and others into Russian.

WORKS: *'Indian Love Poems'; 'Mathnawi', Moscow 1992; 'Poetics of the Urdu Dastans', Moscow, 1979; 'At the Source of the New Indian Drama', Moscow, 1985;]In Search of a Theatre. Drama Works of India and Pakistan of the Twentieth Century', Moscow, 1988 (all in Russian).*

A.S. SUKHOCHEV

Suyurghal

(From Mongolian; the other name for it was *madad-i-maash*, Persian for livelihood) A category of feudal land ownership in India during the 15th to the 18th centuries. Also lands granted by the state to Muslim religious establishments (mosques, *mazars*, etc.), *sheikhs or **pirs* of Islamic religious orders. *Suyurghal* owners often had tax and administrative immunity and could pass on the grants of land to their heirs. The suyurghal was not linked with public service. (See also *Waqf*.)

BIBLIOGRAPHY: *K.Z. Ashrafyan, The Agrarian System in North India (13th–mid 18th centuries)', Moscow, 1965 (in, Russian); I.H. Qureshi, Administration of the Mughal Empire, Karachi, 1966.*

YU.V. GANKOVSKY

Swat

A historical and geographical area in the *North West Frontier Province, consisting of 16,000 sq.km. It is populated by *Pashtun, *Yusufzai and *Kohistani tribes. The area includes *Kohistan, a mountainous region in the north covered by deodar and cypress forests, and the Swat Valley which is not more than 20 km. wide. This is an area of intensive farming and gardening. On the fertile lands along the Swat river there are many famous historic and cultural settlements. The Swat Valley is rich with beautiful landscapes, highland resorts, and famous historic monuments that attract tourists and sightseers. Swat's capital is Saidu Sharif. In the middle of the 19th century Swat appeared as a Princely State.

Akhund Abdul Ghafur (c. 1794-1877) was the first ruler, or *Wali*. On 3 May 1926 his grandson, Mian Gul Abdul Wadud, signed an 'Agreement of Mutual Friendship' with the British authorities. On 11 November 1947 the Swat state acceded to Pakistan and was abolished in 1955.

BIBLIOGRAPHY: *V.A. Romodin, 'Dir and Swat', in: Countries and People of the East, issue one (In Russian), Moscow, 1959; W.A. Wilcox, 'Pakistan', New York, 1963.*

M.YU. MOROZOVA

Swat Culture

The Gandhara Burial Culture is an ancient culture in the territory of the *Swat district in northern Pakistan. To date, some thirty-five burials and six settlements have been studied by the joint efforts of Pakistani and Italian archaeologists. The most prominent of the sites are at Timargarh, Loebanr I, Katelai I, Butkara II, Zarif Karun and numerous settlements of Ghaligai, Aligram and Birkot Ghundai. The stratigraphy of multi-level settlements allows archaeologists to determine the culture's chronological limits to its origins. It also allows the recreation of the general picture of settlement of the Swat and the neighbouring valley from the 3rd millennium BC to the mid-1st millennium BC. The earliest evidence of a pre-Swat culture came from Ghaligai I (radio-carbon dates 2230-70; 2295-55 BC). The next stages–Ghaligai II and III continued to flourish uninterrupted until the mid-2nd millennium BC (1505-1400 BC). The Swat culture took shape in the Ghaligai IV period on the basis of the local Neolithic sites and the culture of late *Harappa. A new ethnic group, that brought cremation with it, penetrated the Swat valley at the end of Ghaligai IV. The Swat culture burials, with the exception of the necropolis of Kherai Ghaligai IV, are connected with the Ghaligai V-VII periods. The stratigraphy of the Balambat settlement determines the finishing pointor, terminus *ante quem,* for the Swat cultures. There the burials and refuse heaps of the Swat culture's latest stage are directly covered with Achaemenid constructions. The Swat culture fits into the period between the 15th and 6th centuries BC.

The Swat population tilled land and bred cattle. All the sites were close to rivers, on top of or on slopes of hills or in valleys. First, people lived in dug-outs (Birkot Ghundai, Loebanr III), later in rectangular dwellings of a unified layout. Several chronological periods and phases that are organically connected can be identified in the necropolises. In some cases (Timargarh) the burials were marked with stone rings. In the majority of cases the grave was a pit with side chambers, the lower pit being walled up and closed with stone slabs. There were two types of burials: complete or partial burial in the ground (inhumation) and cremation in urns or on the grave bottom. The bodies were placed in contracted positions, women on their left and men on their right sides. There was no definite orientation but the head was normally placed in the direction of the nearest mountain. Burial goods consisted of vessels, metal and bone objects and figurines resembling animals and people. Several anthropological types could be identified among the Swat population: Mediterranean, proto-Europoid, Vedoid, or proto-Australoid, and Mongoloid.

Throughout its history, the Swat culture maintained contacts with its neighbours–with *Kashmir and indirectly with China at an early stage, with the southern cultures of the Indus Valley and Balochistan of the late Harappan time and with northeastern Iran (Hissar II B-III B). To a certain extent the land tilling sites in northern Afghanistan and southern Central Asia of the 2nd millennium BC can be compared with the Swat culture, there being typological similarities in pottery and metal objects. It is still unclear whether Swat was in the zone of direct contacts with the south of central Asia. Neither chronology nor the cultural context supports the idea that the Swat necropoli appeared under the influence of the steppe Bronze cultures (Beshkent and Wakhsh sites).

BIBLIOGRAPHY: *H. Müller-Karpe, 'Jungbronzezeitlich-früheisenzeitliche Graberfelder der Swat-Kultur in Nord Pakistan'. Münich, 1983; C. Silvi Antonini, G. Stacul, 'The Protohistoric Graveyards of Swat (Pakistan)', Rome, 1972; 'Timargarh and Gandhara Grave Culture', AP. 3, 1967.*

N.M. VINOGRADOVA

Syed, Anwar Husain (1926–)

Scholar. He entered the Government College in Lahore, from where he received his bachelor's degree in economics and philosophy in 1946. As a supporter of the *Muslim League party that demanded the creation of Pakistan, he joined a number of other young people from his college to campaign for this party's nominees in the critical elections held in 1945 and 1946. A few days after the emergence of Pakistan on 14 August 1947 the Syeds moved from India to Pakistan. While in Lahore, Anwar Syed worked for Dayal Singh Trust and, at the same time, studied economics at the University of the *Punjab. He received a master's degree in 1951, became a lecturer in economics at the Government College (Lahore), won a Fulbright scholarship to study in the United States and entered the University of Chicago in the autumn of 1952. He wrote a doctoral dissertation on Walter Lippmann's Philosophy of International Politics, and was awarded a PhD at the end of 1956. He was editor of *Polity*, the journal of the North-Eastern Political Science Association, for five years (1980-86), and has served on various committees and councils of the university of Massa Chuselts, including the Faculty Senate of which he was chairman for some time. In addition to numerous articles in professional journals, he is the author of several books.

WORKS: *'Walter Lippmann's Philosophy of International Politics', Philadelphia: University of Pennsylvania Press, 1963; 'The Political Theory of American Local Government' New York: Random House, 1966; 'China and Pakistan: Diplomacy of an Entente Cordiale', Amherst: University of Massachusetts Press, 1973; Pakistan: Islam, Politics, and National Solidarity, New York: Praeger, 1982; 'The Discourse and Politics of Zulfikar Ali Bhutto', New York: St Martin's Press, 1992.*

YU.V. GANKOVSKY

Syed, Ghulam Murtaza (1904–95)

Politician. Syed was a participant in the *Khilafat Movement of 1920 and in the movement for the separation of *Sindh from the Bombay Presidency in the 1930s. After the formation of Pakistan in 1947 he became a noted leader of the *Sindhi movement and, in 1948, helped organize and lead the Sindh *Awami Mahaz*. In 1955 he began to voice his opposition to the unification of *West Pakistan into a single unit. He became a leader of the National Awami Party in 1957 and in 1988 became the President of the Sindh *National Alliance.

WORKS: *'Struggle for New Sindh', Karachi, 1949; 'Muslim League-ki-Mukhalifat Kiyon', Shikarpur (in Urdu).*

BIBLIOGRAPHY: *V.F. Ageev, 'Modern History of Sindh', Moscow, 1986; M.S. Korejo, 'G.M. Syed, An Analysis of his Political Perspectives', Karachi, 1999.*

YU.V. GANKOVSKY

Symonds, Richard (1918–)

Scholar. He took his MA in Modern History at the University of Oxford. Richard Symonds was Deputy

Director of Relief and Rehabilitation in Bengal during the Great Famine and served till 1945. He thereafter joined the United Nations. He was senior Research Officer at the University Institute of Commonwealth Studies at Oxford (1962-65). In 1965 he was Visiting Professor at the University of Sussex and has been Senior Research Associate with Queen Elizabeth House, Oxford. Richard Symond's relief work brought him in close association with Mahatma Gandhi. He was personally acquainted with all the stalwarts of independence and partition, including M. A. *Jinnah, Liaquat Ali *Khan and Jawaharlal Nehru. Richard Symonds wrote the first book on Pakistan and has recently published his personal memoirs of the independence era.

WORKS: *The Making of Pakistan, London, 1950; In the Margins of Independence, Karachi, 2001.*

M.R. KAZIMI

T

Tabla

A *Tabla* is a set of two small drums found in Pakistani musical culture. A *Tabla* consists of a small wooden drum called *sidda* (*tabla, dayan, or dahina*) and a larger metal one called *dagga* (*banya*). The *sidda* is played with the fingers and palm of the right hand, while the *dagga* is played with fingers, palm and wrist of the left hand. The pair of *tabla* is positioned on two ring shaped bundles called *chutta*, consisting of plant fiber wrapped in cloth.

I. PIRACHA

Taj, Imtiaz Ali (1900–70)

Writer. Syed Imtiaz Ali (his real name) was an *Urdu-language dramatist, prose writer, and filmmaker. His father was a teacher and his mother was an author of children's literature. He graduated from Government College, Lahore. He work is chiefly categorised as romantic

His main work, the historical drama *Anarkali* (written in 1922, published in 1931), was a classic of *Urdu literature. *Anarkali* contains the main motifs of romantic tragedy: great passions, doomed love and the tragedy of life, conveyed through the characters of Emperor Akbar, Prince Salim and the dancer Anarkali. The play is considered a model literary play for reading and has been filmed a number of times.

In the 1930s Taj worked in the amateur theatre and cinema, directed the Lahore theatre company 'Al-Hamra', and wrote one-act plays. He produced a number of popular films, for which he had also written screenplays: *Shahr se Dur* ('Far from the City'), *Dhamki* ('Threat'), and *Gulnar*. In 1958 he was elected President of the Society for the Promotion of Urdu Literature (*Anjuman Taraqqi-i-Urdu*). After 1968 he published the series *Classical Urdu Drama*.

WORKS: *'Anarkali'; 'Kahaniyan' (Stories), Lahore.*

BIBLIOGRAPHY: *A.A. Suvorova, 'The Sources of New Indian Drama', Moscow, 1985 (in Russian); A.A. Suvorova, 'In Search of the Theatre: Twentieth-Century Drama of India and Pakistan', Moscow, 1988 (in Russian); A.L. Siddiqi, 'Imtiaz Ali Taj', Karachi (undated).*

A.S. GEVASIMOVA

Takhallus

(Arabic: to be safe, sheltered) A pen name or pseudonym chosen by the author or given by a mentor. The poet's *takhallus* is usually included in the *maqta*, the concluding verse (**bait*) of a **ghazal*, and is one of its formal characteristics. The term is used in the literatures of the Middle East and South Asia.

N.V. GLEBOV

Tal

This is the fundamental principle of the temporal structuring of the sound flow in the music of South Asia. As a system of structuring musical time, *tal* relies on a complex code of grammatical forms. It has a self-sufficing artistic and informative content - a semantic counterpart of the **raga* principle.

The teaching of the art of *tal* is based on memorising syllabic meanings correlated with types of percussion and rhythmical configurations. These are also used for written notation of the rhythmical series. The play of the musician's imagination is manifested, among other things, in the intentional shifts of the rhythmical pattern in relation to the normative *tal* pattern. In the *Hindustani tradition, the accentuation of, or play on, strong intervals, *sams* (beginning and end of a cycle) and **khalis* (the middle of the cycle are of great significance. The greatest possibilities for the expression of artistic individuality and of the principles of a given **gharana* are offered by the art of *kaida*-original presentation of rhythmical themes for improvisation based on lending a semantic and accentual form, specific for the given *gharana*, to typical rhythmical models.

The *tal* principle had been known and used from the earliest times. The term is also used with particular meanings: 1. clapping of hands in marking the rhythm during dancing or singing; 2. bronze cymbals used for the same purpose.

I. PIRACHA

Taliban

See, Afghanistan-Pakistan Relations.

Talpurs

1. A *Balochi tribe, until the 17th century, a branch of Leghari tribe. Most of the Talpurs settled in *Sindh but individual Talpur settlements also developed in the south-west *Punjab;

2. A dynasty of Sindh rulers of Baloch extraction, who ruled from 1784–1843. They were defeated at the Battle of Miani by Sir Charles Napier, after which Sindh was annexed by the British. In the princely state of Khairpur a Talpur continued to rule until 1955;

3. An agricultural clan in Sindh, genetically connected with the aristocracy of the Balochi tribe of Talpurs.

BIBLIOGRAPHY: *V.F. Ageev, 'British Conquest of Sindh', Moscow, 1979 (in Russian); V.F. Ageev, 'Modern History of Sindh', Moscow, 1986 (in Russian); Khudadad Khan, 'Lubb-i Tarikh-i Sindh', Karachi-Hyderabad, 1959; M.K.B. Marry Baloch, 'Search-light on Balochs and Balochistan', Karachi, 1974.*

YU.V. GANKOVSKY

Talukdar

(from Arabic and Urdu *taluqa*) Hereditary major landowner in North India in the 17th–19th centuries; a military vassal of the *Mughal Empire. In the course of the colonial wars, they lost many of their possessions and partly merged with **zamindars*.

YU.V. GANKOVSKY

Taluqa

(Arabic: connection, dependence; Urdu: possession, estate, power) Territorial unit in India. In the *Mughal Empire and the states which became its heirs, *taluqa* was an inherited but alienable private land property owned on condition of payment of a fixed tax and granted by the treasury or any private individual (**zamindar*, mostly in Bengal). *Taluqas* were abolished during the British conquest and the land and fiscal reforms changed to a permanent settlement system and *mahalwari*. In South India *taluqa* designated an administrative unit, a part of a district (the same as *tehsil* in north India).

L.B. ALAYEV

Tappa

Tappa is the most traditional, age old and anonymous form of *Pushto poetry. It is a popular form of folk poetry that is meant to be sung. The first line is shorter than the second line, with nine syllables where as the second line has thirteen syllables. The themes of *tappa* are wide ranging, from the romantic to reflective and war. It is generally addressed to the beloved. The modern poets who have contributed to the popularity and the scholarship of *tappa* are Amir Hamza *Shinwari, Syed Rasul Rasa, Abdul Ghani Khan, and most notably Partan Puhilla.

BIBLIOGRAPHY: *Partau Rohilla (ed.) 'Tappay', Islamabad, 1979.*

N.V. GLEBOV

Tarana

Originally meant the ecstatic singing of *Sufis based on chanting mystical combinations of separate syllables or sacred expressions e.g. *tu dani*, 'You know', *Ya* Ali, 'O Ali' in Farsi. These are often included in **khiyal* compositions either as a slow introductory part instead of the *alap* or in the climax zone resulting from a previous whipping up of an ecstatic state. Since *khiyals* themselves are sung in Braj, while *taranas* use segments of Persian words, the modern listener perceives them merely as fast virtuoso sections in which the singer uses meaningless syllables to demonstrate his varied vocal techniques, in nasal notes.

I. PIRACHA

Tarikh

(Arabic: date, chronology, history) A poetic figure, a chronogram of some event that is written in code in a work of literature using a system of digital representation of the Arabic letters, **abjad* or *jumal*. *Abjad* is the first word out of eight meaningless words using letters that correspond to numbers, from one to one thousand. These words are only used to make up chronograms. Chronograms code dates of, birth and death of poets, generals, rulers, construction of famous buildings, completion of literary works, etc. An example is the famous Persian classic *Qissa-i-Chahar Darwesh* ('A Story of Four Deweshes'), that was translated into *Urdu by the poet Mir Aman who called it *Bagh-o-Bahar* ('The Garden and Spring'). The sum of the digital representations of this chronogram reveals the date when the work was completed—1217, the year of *hijra*. Chronograms not exceeding two or three words, and indicating not just the year, but also the month and day, are considered particularly successful. The *Abjad* system is also employed in everyday life. For example documents and letters in Urdu often begin with the number 786 which corresponds to the Muslim sacred formula, recited before starting important business:

Bismi'llah ar-rahman ar'rahim! (In the name of Allah, gracious and merciful!). Tarikh was widely used in the literatures of the Middle East and South Asia.

BIBLIOGRAPHY: *R. Musulmankulov, 'Persian-Tajik Classical Poetics', Moscow, 1989 (in Russian); Q.D. Pybus, 'Urdu Prosody and Rhetoric', Lahore, 1924.*

N.V. GLEBOV

Tariqa-i Muhammadiya

(Muhammad's (PBUH) way) An organisation of Muslim fundamentalists established in the 1820s in northern India by Sayyid Ahmad *Barelwi, who in his teaching combined the traditions of the Sufi orders of *Chishtiya, Qadiriya and *Naqshbandiya. He preached the egalitarian ideas of early Islam and called upon believers to follow the precepts contained in the Quran and the *Sunnah. Members of the organisation were supposed to strictly observe the Shariah. In 1826 Sayyid Ahmad Barelwi announced **jihad* against the Sikhs. *Tariqa-i Muhammadiya* had much in common with the fundamentalist teaching of the Arabian *Wahhabi. This is why, in scholarly literature, members of the movement (*mujahiddeen*) are often called Indian Wahhabis. However, unlike the Arabian Wahhabi who belonged to Hanbali **madhab*, *Tariqa-i Muhammadiya* did not recognise any of the four *Sunni *madhabs*. After Barelwi's death in 1831, the *mujahiddeen* continued an armed struggle against the *Sikhs, and later, against the British.

A. NIYAZI

Tariqat

(a mystic way, from the Arabic *taraqa*—embark on a journey, to go) A fraternity, order. (see 'Sufi Orders') as opposed to Shariat. In Sufi parlance *Tariqat* means that path to God, where the seeker in an ecstatic state ignores ritual and legal obligations.

A. NIYAZI

Tarjiband

See, Tarkibband.

Tarkibband

(Persian: organised strophe) A strophic form of verse with mixed rhyme, that is widespread in the poetry of the Middle East and South Asia. The strophe consists of a certain number of verses (**baits*), specific for a given poem, with the same rhyme (monorhyme). The strophe is concluded with a double-rhymed *bait*. In the subsequent strophes the monorhyme and the double rhyme of the concluding bait change.

The most frequently occurring *tarkibband* is *tarjiband* (in Persian, retrieved, repeated) when the double rhyme of the concluding *bait* remain unchanged.

The concluding *bait* can be repeated in each strophe without any variations, as a refrain. Such *bait* is called *bait-i-wasila* (connecting *bait*), and it is supposed to be connected thematically with each strophe. Both *tarkibband* and *tarjiband* have been employed in Persian poetry since the tenth century. In the 19th to 20th centuries they became the favoured form of civic-minded lyrical verse. In *Urdu literature these strophic forms are used in the innovative poetry of Mir Taqi *Mir, Nazir *Akbarabadi, Altaf Husain *Hali, Muhammad *Iqbal, and Josh *Malihabadi.

BIBLIOGRAPHY: *In. Glebov, A. Sukhachev, 'Urdu Literature', Moscow, 1967 (in Russian); Abdul Wahid, 'Anthology of Contemporary Urdu Poetry', Lahore-Karachi (undated, in Urdu).*

N.V. GLEBOV

Tarrar, Mohammad Rafique, Justice (1929–)

President of Pakistan from 1997 to 2001. Rafique Tarrar obtained his LLB from Punjab University Law College and began practice in Gujranwala. He was appointed Additional Sessions Judge in October 1966 and District and Sessions Judge in 1967. He was elevated to the bench of the Lahore High Court in 1974 and became its Chief Justice on 13 December 1989. He was elevated to the Supreme Court bench in 1991 and retired in 1994.

During his career as a Judge, Justice Tarrar was a member of the Election Commission. He was on the Supreme Court bench that restored the government of Nawaz *Sharif in 1993 and was a member of the inquiry committee set up to probe the death of General Asif Nawaz.

Justice Tarrar was elected Senator on the Pakistan *Muslim League ticket in March 1997. He became President of Pakistan on 31 December 1997. He remained President after General Parvez *Musharraf overthrew the government of Nawaz Sharif and assumed the office of 'Chief Executive'. He was obliged to resign as a result of a new Provisional Constitution Order on 20 June 2001.

M.R. KAZIMI

Tasawwuf

See, Sufism.

Tashkent Declaration

The Tashkent Summit was an attempt to restore the order disrupted by the September 1965 Indo-Pakistan War over *Kashmir. The US and the USSR had the common objective of isolating and discrediting China and bolstering India, therefore they preferred terms less than the settlement of the *Kashmir dispute. The *USSR had originally issued the invitation in the initial stages of the war when Pakistan had the upper hand. Pakistan's Foreign Minister stated in Moscow in November 1965 that his country had accepted the offer of talks unconditionally.

The Indian objective was to secure a No-War Pact from Pakistan so as to permanently freeze the Kashmir dispute. Pakistan wanted a self-executing mechanism for the proposed UN held plebiscite in Kashmir. The Indian delegation was led by Prime Minister Lal Bahadur Shastri, the Pakistani delegation by President M. Ayub *Khan, the host delegation by Chairman, Council of Ministers, Alexei N. Kosygin. Tashkent, the capital of Uzbekistan, was then in the USSR. The talks lasted from 4 to 10 January 1966. India had opposed the drawing up of an agenda. The Tashkent Declaration signed on 10 January 1966, secured the reaffirmation by both India and Pakistan of their obligation 'under the United Nations Charter', not to resort to force and instead to adopt peaceful means. The only mention of the cause of the conflict was as follows: 'It was against this background that Jammu and Kashmir was discussed, and each of the sides set forth its respective positions'. Armed forces were to be withdrawn to the positions as they were before 5 August 1965, prisoners of war would be repatriated, and diplomatic relations restored. There was also provision for non-interference in the internal matters of each country, hostile propaganda would be discouraged, and both sides would create conditions to prevent the exodus of people.

However, after the signing ceremony, Kosygin asked Shastri to solve the Kashmir problem. Shastri offered minor adjustments along the ceasefire line which Pakistan rejected. The Indian reaction to the Declaration was naturally favourable; the death of Shastri in Tashkent (10 January 1966) sanctified the Declaration for Indians.

BIBLIOGRAPHY: *Iqbal Akhund, 'Memoirs of a Bystander', Karachi, 1s997; Altaf Gauhar, 'Ayub Khan: Pakistan's First Military Ruler', Lahore, 1993; Roedad Khan (ed.), 'The American Papers', Karachi, 1999; Kuldip Nayar, 'India: the Critical Years', New Delhi, 1971; Mahboob A. Popatia, 'Pakistan's Relations with the Soviet Union 1947-1979', Karachi, 1988; Hafeez Malik, 'Soviet-Pakistan Relations', London. 1994.*

YU.V. GANKOVSKY

Taqlid

(Arabic: connection, following, from *qalada*—to tie up) The duty of any Muslim, including theologians, is to follow the **madhab* and to obey decisions concerning Muslim law (*see Fatwa.*) Every Muslim (called *Muqallid*—follower, disciple), including rank-and-file theologians, is duty-bound to recognize the authority of the **Mujtahid*, follow his instructions and accompany him if necessary.

YU.V. GANKOVSKY

Taqqaya

(Arabic: support, refuge, mainly dissimulation) A rule by which Muslims are supposed to conceal their faith in cases of danger. It is followed by *Shia sects (except Zaidi Shias) (see also Shias and Shiaism).

YU.V. GANKOVSKY

Taxila

(Sansk. *Taksasila*) Taxila is an ancient city 35 km. to the north-west of contemporary Rawalpindi, at the crossroads of the major routes leading from the valleys of the Ganges and *Indus to western Asia through Iran, and to the inner Asian regions and China through central Asia or *Kashmir. From the 6th-5th centuries BC to the 5th century AD Taxila was one of the major political and cultural centres of *Gandhara. One comes across references to it in many historical sources including works by Panini, Graeco-Roman authors and stories of Chinese pilgrims, in the *Mahabharata*, the *Puranas* and *Jatakas*. Its geographical location was determined back in the 19th century. Systematic studies started in 1913 by J. *Marshall*, head of the Archaeological Service of India, and continued until 1924. In 1944-5 A. Ghosh, an Indian archaeologist, made new diggings smaller in scale, and he verified some of Marshall's points. In recent years a Pakistani expedition headed by A.H. *Dani has worked in Taxila.

Several fortified settlements of Taxila have survived. The oldest of them is found on Bhir Mound covering an area over 1000 x 600 metres. It was surrounded with an adobe wall and was dated to the 4th-2nd centuries BC. A large monumental building with numerous rooms and a rectangular hall was found. The Sirkap fortified settlement lies to the north-east of it. This was a well-planned city (1300-1400 x 800 metres) with straight streets that crossed at right angles and a stone defence wall. It existed from the late 3rd, early 2nd century BC to the early 2nd century AD. Archaeologists uncovered well-planned living quarters, a large building thought to be the royal palace, a temple and several stupas. The third fortified settlement Sirsukh was larger than the two others. It covered an area of 1.3x1.0 km. and is believed to date from the 1st century AD. It was destroyed by the *Ephtalites (*White Huns) in about 460. The Jandial temple with traces of Hellenistic traditions, Buddhist monasteries of the 2nd-5th centuries with stupas and sculptures (Dharmarajika, Mohra-Moradu, Jaulian and others) have been excavated and studied in the Taxila environs by a number of archaeologists including Sir Moretimer Wheeler. Taxila has been a UNESCO world Heritage Site since 1980.

BIBLIOGRAPHY: *G.F. Ilyin, 'Ancient Indian City of Taxila', Moscow, 1958 (in Russian); J. Marshall, 'Taxila', Vols. I-III, Cambridge, 1951; J. Marshall, 'A Guide to Taxila', Cambridge, 1960; A. Dani, 'The Historic City of Taxila', Tokyo, 1986.*

B.YA. STAVISKY

Tazkira

A poetic anthology of the literature of the Middle East and South Asia, compiled in the Middle Ages. *Tazkira* includes information about poets and their selected works, with short explanatory notes and critical remarks. *Tazkira* is characterised by dynastic-chronological and geographic principles in arranging the material. Although many *tazkira* are influenced by the notions of their times, their appraisals are subjective and the information is often incorrect. Yet some of them are unique sources of early classical poetry. Examples include: *Lubab al-Albab* ('The Heart of the Essence') by Muhammad *Aufi, one of the first anthologies of Persian poetry, compiled in India in c. 1220, and *Niqat al-Shuara* ('Notes about Poets'), the first anthology of Urdu poetry, compiled by Mir Taqi *Mir (c. 1752).

N.V. GLEBOV

Tazmin

Tazmin is a form of *Urdu poetry in which extra lines are added to the **ghazal* or *sher* (distich) of other renowned poets. Ghalib's *tazmin* of Bahadur Shah Zafar's *ghazal* consists of suffixing a third line rhyming with the second. The usual form is to then add three lines rhyming with the first line—making five lines in all. Nakhshab's *Tazmin* of Nizam Shah Rampuri's *ghazal* is one of the most prominent examples of *Tazmin*. Josh *Malihabadi wrote a *tazmin* of his own poem 'Baghi Insan' (Rebellious Man). Iqbal's mode was to compose complete poems and prefix them to a couplet of a classical Persian poet.

N.V. GLEBOV

Tebhaga

A movement of peasant sharecroppers in Bengal in 1946–7 demanding two-thirds of the harvest for themselves instead of the customary half. The *Tebhaga* movement spread almost all over Bengal but was particularly active in eleven districts. The movement involved approximately five million sharecropper families.

In Bengal the sharecropper's harvest had to be delivered to the threshing floor of the lands owner (*jotedar*), who shared out the crop as he saw fit. Sharecroppers began to share out their crops themselves on peasants' threshing floors according to their own demands. The authorities and *jotedars* suppressed the movement with force but it continued to spread. The *Tebhaga* movement ceased to exist only after the Partition of Bengal between India and Pakistan. The governments of independent India and Pakistan passed laws on lease-holding that were supposed to satisfy the demands of the sharecroppers. But to translate these laws into practice required more struggle.

BIBLIOGRAPHY: *S. Sen, 'Agrarian Struggle in Bengal. 1946-7', New Delhi, 1972; M.A. Rasul, 'Tebhaga Struggle of Bengal', New Delhi, 1986.*

A.M. MELNIKOV

Television

Television broadcasts are the most popular and the most convenient source of entertainment and information in Pakistan. For a long time Pakistan Television (PTV) had a monopoly, but unlike the film industry (see Cinema in Pakistan) it sought to raise the artistic quality of drama and related programmes. Religious programmes had a considerable impact.

The first two television stations were set up on an experimental basis, in Lahore on 26 November 1964 and Dhaka on 25 December 1964. After three months Pakistan Television was established in the public sector. The following stations have since been established: Rawalpindi on March 1967, Karachi on 2 November 1967, Quetta on 26 November 1974, and Peshawar on 5 December 1974. The Islamabad station came up in 1987 with which the Rawalpindi station was merged.

Television began with very meagre resources, only two cameras operated by two cameramen. The processing started in a shed on the premises of the Lahore Radio station. However, the talent pool was enormous. Lahore was home to Pakistan's film industry, but it drew the majority of its artists from radio and theatre. Radio artists had a different voice modulation to that required in television but they adapted to the new medium effortlessly. For religious, literary, and sports broadcasts, the talent pool of the radio was trawled.

In the field of drama, Pakistan Television was an instant hit because its output had far greater literary and artistic merit than the slapstick, loud, bombastic films that were being churned out to a captive cinema audience. Black and white TV was treated as a medium rather than a constraint, establishing an artistic link with the New Theatre Films of Calcutta, which produced classics of a non-glamorous genre.

Literary classics were successfully produced. The first serial was based on Shaukat Siddiqui's *Khuda ki Basti* in which the underworld of Karachi was potrayed with stark realism. The cast of this serial included veterans like Mohammad Yusuf, Mahmud Ali, and Zafar Siddiqui. The second serial was Khalid Saeed Butt's *Raat ki Ankhen* about the world of smuggling. Shabbir Shah's *Jhok Syyal* remained obscure in print but fired the imagination of viewers once it was depicted on the mini-screen.

Adaptations have also made a distinct contribution: *Crime and Punishment* in which Talat Husain shone as Raskolnikov; Turgenev's *Father and Sons* which brought Rahat Kazimi into the limelight. Stars of the small screen include Kamal Ahmad Rizvi, Mahboob Alam, Usman Pirzada, Uzma Gilani, Roohi Bano the late Ghazala Rafique, Tahira Naqvi, and Khalida Riasat.

Noteworthy among dramatists are Ashfaque Ahmad and Amjad Islam Amjad, who wrote *Qurrat ul Ain* and *Waris* respectively. From among the classics the works of Saadat Hasan *Manto have been made into a serial, the play *Badshahat ka Khatima* carrying truly memorable performances by Kamal Ahmad Rizvi and Ghazala Rafique. Kamal Ahmad Rizvi's fame rests mainly on the serial *Alif Noon* with Rafi Khawar playing Hardy to Rizvi's Laurel. This was comedy albeit with a strong social content. At first only minor misdemeanours were satirised but Rizvi progressively enlarged his net to catch the big fish. The *Alif Noon* serial is the subject of a long literary analysis by Alain Desoulieres. Other popular humorous series include *Intizar Farmaiya* and *Hullo, Hullo* written by Athar Shah Khan who also played the lead role.

Adding romance to humour was the formula adopted by Hasina Moin, who has written hits such as *Shehzori, Ankahi,* and *Tanhaiyian*. She leans somewhat on P.G. Wodehouse but completely localises her settings and characters with a finesse that is incomparable. Humour is also featured in stage programmes, for example Shoaib Hashmi's *Tal Matol*. *Studio 2* by Anwar Maqsud and Moin Akhtar, and the combination of stage and skits in Shoaib Mansur's *Fifty-Fifty* have been effective means of reform.

Quiz programmes like *Kasauti, Sheeshay ka Ghar,* and *Neelam Ghar* were also popular.

Religious scholars lectured on exegesis, traditions, and morality and some speakers established a countrywide reputation through these programmes.

Literary programmes were rarely given prime time coverage except for drama and fiction, and poetry recitals, book reviews, literary discourse and interviews with famous literary personalities wereinfrequently featured.

Music programmes suffered somewhat for being monaural but the most original popular music came from television, notably Nayyara Noor singing the lyrics of Faiz Ahmad *Faiz. Pop music dominates these days but classical music is still not forgotten and is featured on late night programmes.

Sport events like live telecasts of cricket and hockey are one of the prominent mainstays of television. When these are relayed almost all other programmes except news broadcasts are put into abeyance.

News broadcasts are edited by state officials who are often criticised for giving exclusive coverage to political leaders. The news is widely viewed. Pakistan, surrounded as it is by satellite channels, is poised to enter the digital age.

A. MIR

Tehrik-i-Istiqlal

(TI, or Independent Movement) A political party founded in February 1970 by retired Air Marshal M. Asghar *Khan. The TI called for a revision of foreign policy, a rejection of orientation towards the United States, improvement of relations with China and the setting up of a confederation with Afghanistan. After 1971 the TI opposed the recognition of Bangladesh. It also demanded the resignation of the PPP government headed by Z.A. *Bhutto and called for an early general election. In 1979 the party opposed military regime and TI's leaders were subjected to reprisals. In 1981 TI joined the *Movement for Restoration of Democracy but left it in 1986 declaring that it was 'infected with Bhuttoism'. In the 1988 elections TI formed the *Pakistan Awami Ittehad* jointly with the **Jamiat-ul-Ulema-i-Pakistan* group, led by Shah Ahmad *Noorani, and a group from the Muslim League, led by M. Khan *Junejo. In its 1988 election manifesto TI proposed serious populist measures, calling for encouragement of private enterprise, but failed to win a single seat in the National Assembly and the provincial legislative government.

O.V. PLESHOV

Thal

This is a sand desert between the rivers *Indus and *Jhelum. The central part consists of uninterrupted sands and dunes. In the north, there are clayey deposits, hence agriculture is possible with the use of tubewells.

YU.V. GANKOVSKY

Thar

(from t'hul—the local name for sandhills) Between the *Indus and the *Sutlej in the north-east and the Arawalli Range in the south-east lies a region of deserts and semi-deserts covering an area of about 300,000 sq.km. On the borderlands of Pakistan and India, in the south-west, the Thar merges with the *Punjab Plain. The western part is in the zone of a bazim filled with alluvial deposits of the Indus, the eastern part lies on the Indian Platform. The relief is flat with an elevation of between 350 and 450 metres above sea level at the foot of the Arawalli Range, and below 100 metres in the west and as low as 20 metres in the south-west. About 90 per cent of the surface is covered with wind blown, or aeolian, sands. In the northern and western parts, 58 per cent of the territory is made up of dunes that range in height from 10 to 80 metres.

The climate is subtropical continental, with an annual precipitation varying from 120 mm. in the west to 500 mm. in the east. The major part of the rainfall occurs between July and September. In the dry regions there may be no rainfall at all for more than two years. The mean maximum temperature in summer is 40°C and in winter, 22-28°C. The mean minimum temperature is 22°C and 4°C respectively. Evaporation is up to 3,000 mm. a year. In May and June dust storms are frequent. Surface water is practically absent and underground water usually lies at considerable depth and is very salty.

Vegetation includes solitary trees, up to 4 metres high, and drought resistant shrubs such as caligonum, saksaul, ephedra, tamarisk and acacia. Grasses sprout following the autumn rains. The population consists mainly of semi-nomadic cattle-breeders. In the oases and along river valleys there is some irrigated agriculture. Deposits of coal have been found. These are mainly lignite with a potential economic significance. Oil had been found in the Indian sector of the Thar and it is possible that the strata extend into the Pakistan sector. Other minerals include gas, phosphorites, apatite and copper ores.

S.B. ROSTOTSKY

Thari, Dances of the

Danced in the Tharparkar desert (*see*, image) in Sindh. These include Rasooro, Dandan Rand, Mitco and Chakar Rand. The Thari women wear brilliant traditional *ghagras, cholis and *dupattas*, but the most

Women carrying water in the Tharparkar.

striking features of their appearance are the white bangles worn by them, stretching from the wrist to the shoulder. The Rasooro is a stick dance performed by women. A woman plays the **dhol* and some women sing songs to the accompaniment of its beat.

Eight to ten men perform the Dandan Rand holding a stick in one hand and a silk handkerchief in the other. The *dhol* player accompanying the dancers also sings the songs. A male performs *Mitco* solo, but sometimes it is also danced by women, for instance on the occasion of their son's wedding. The *Chakar Rand* is traditionally performed by Thari Muslims. A male dancer performs it with a sword in his hand.

R. HUSAIN

Third June 1947 Plan

This Plan was the basis for the transfer of power by the British to the two dominions of India and Pakistan on 14/15 August 1947. It is also known as the Mountbatten Plan, after the last British Viceroy, under whose authority it was devised. The Plan was announced simultaneously in the House of Lords, the House of Commons and Viceregal House in New Delhi. This was the second such plan despatched by the Viceroy. The earlier plan sought to transfer power to provinces or confederations of provinces. It was rejected by Jawaharlal Nehru, Vice-Chairman of the Viceroy's Executive Council, who wanted unity with provision of non-accession to be made the basis of the plan, rather than the reverse i.e. for provinces to be vested with power with a provision for unification. Nehru's objections were upheld. The Provinces were stripped of the option to become independent of both India and Pakistan, most notably Bengal, where such a move had the blessings of the *All-India Muslim League leadership. V.P. Menon was asked to draft the new Plan.

Under the 3 June 1947 Plan the British would transfer power to two successor authorities, Congress and the *Muslim League, meaning in territorial terms the dominions of India and Pakistan, which would remain within the British Commonwealth. As for the princely states such as *Kashmir or Hyderabad, the paramountcy of the British Crown was not to be transferred to the successor dominions. Consequently, it would stand terminated and constitutionally a third option of remaining independent, and not joining either Dominion, was kept open for the States, while being denied to the Provinces.

The Indian Independence Act 1947 was enacted to give effect to the 3 June 1947 Plan. This Act, which received Royal assent on 18 June, expressly provided for the partition of the *Punjab and Bengal, which would cease to exist as they then stood. The Indian Independence Act provided for the continuation of the Government of India Act 1935 until the Dominions drew up their own respective Constitutions. Each Governor-General could adapt the 1935 Act to suit the particular requirement of his Dominion. The office of the Secretary of State for India would be abolished.

Congress was the first party to accept the basis of the 3 June 1947 Plan by calling for the partition of the Punjab and Bengal, thus signifying their assent to the Partition of India. It was, conversely, the partition of these two Provinces that prevented the AIML from according enthusiastic and immediate acceptance to the Plan. The Quaid-i-Azam, Muhammad Ali *Jinnah, could concede only a personal and provisional nod of acceptance. Lord Mountbatten had threatened him with the permanent loss of Pakistan if he did not give an immediate and firm acceptance, but this threat left M.A. Jinnah unperturbed. Lord Mountbatten then took upon himself to speak for the AIML Council and expressed willingness to accept the blame if the AIML Council refused to ratify the Plan.

The partition of two Provinces caused the 3 June 1947 Plan a rough passage in the AIML Council's meeting of 9 June in New Delhi. Prominent members favoured rejection because the territorial limits of the proposed Pakistan merely corresponded to those already contained in C. Rajgopalacharia's offer of 1944. Maulana Hasrat Mohani's was the most vociferous voice of dissent, taking severe exception to the acceptance of a truncated Pakistan. M.A. Jinnah replied that he had not accepted the Plan and it was for the AIML Council to accept or reject it. He had no wish to prejudge the Council. However, there could be no modification in the Plan, which had to be accepted or rejected as a whole. Prof. Abdur Rahim (Bengal) preferred rejection and to fight for the original Pakistan demand. Abul Hashim, General Secretary of the Bengal Muslim League criticized the 3 June 1947 Plan for not giving his Province the freedom to choose its own independent status. However, Abdul Hamid (Assam) expressed the prevailing sentiment when he said that, as a Muslim who would have to stay in India, 'If according to this Plan the majority of the Muslims become free, I prefer to remain as a slave.' The most memorable words were spoken by Sir Ghulam Husayn *Hidayatullah, Chief Minister of Sindh, 'We will rapidly industrialise our country and provide a haven of refuge to Muslim traders and craftsmen who would choose to migrate to *Sindh from the Muslim minority provinces. We have removed the consideration of *Sindhi or non-Sindhi from our province and we will see that Sindh will soon progress far.'

The AIML Council accepted the Plan under protest, authorising its President, M.A. Jinnah to take any further necessary action.

This was unacceptable to the Congress leaders, Jawaharlal Nehru and Sardar Vallabhai Patel, who wanted a clear-cut acceptance from M.A. Jinnah before Congress ratified the Plan. Liaquat Ali *Khan countered Sardar Patel by reminding him that, after the AIML had accepted the *Cabinet Mission Plan, Congress had defeated them by putting so many reservations that the AIML had to pull out. Lord Mountbatten cut the knot by offering to accept undertakings for both parties simultaneously. The AIML in turn undertook to term their acceptance 'a compromise settlement.' With this exercise, the stage was set for the creation of Pakistan.

BIBLIOGRAPHY: *N. Mansergh and E.W.R. Lumby, (eds.), 'Constitutional Relations Between Britain and India: The Transfer of Power', Vol. xi., (London, 1982); Z.H. Zaidi et al. (eds.), 'Jinnah Papers, First Series, Vol. II', Islamabad; Larry Collins and Dominique Lapierre, 'Mountbatten and the Partition of India', Colombo, 1982; L.A. Sherwani, 'The Partition of India and Mountbatten', Karachi, 1986.*

S.B. ROSTOTSKY

Thumri

A vocal tradition in South Asia that emerged through a synthesis of aesthetic and musical-theoretical principles of classical music and elements of the traditional musical culture of Oudh, now Uttar Perdesh In India. *Thumri* began to evolve in the 16th-17th centuries, reaching its peak by the second half of the 19th century, especially in Lucknow at the court of the Nawab Wajid Ali Shah (1847-56). At first *thumri* was closely linked with the art of dancing, but later it became an independent musical genre. *Thumri* is marked by lightness of expression and lyrical-romantic character, relying mostly on texts dealing with the subject of love and developing such types of *ragas as sadness and eroticism. The most important schools of *thumri* at present are those of the *Punjab, Lucknow, and Varanasi. The most outstanding performers in the *thumri* genre are (*Bare*) Ghulam Ali Khan, Fayyaz Khan, Begum Akhtar and Barkat Ali Khan. In Pakistan the most famous exponents are Roshan Ara Begum, Iqbal Bano (see image) and Tahira Syed.

Legendary singer, Iqbal Bano.

I. PIRACHA

Tonga

(Urdu: *tanga*) A light, two-wheel horse-drawn coach for two or four passengers. Despite the development of motor transport, the *tonga* is still used in the cities of India and Pakistan.

M.YU. MOROZOVA

Toreutics

Metalwork familiar to Pakistan territory since the Chalcolithic Age. The *Harappa civilization left behind miniature figurines of human beings and animals cast in metal, the most famous of these being the female dancer from *Mohenjo-Daro, as well as small items made of gold, silver, electron, copper and gilded bronze. The art of toreutics is discussed in the Vedas, the Ramayana, and the Mahabharata.

Various types of tooling and metal ornamenting were known in the ancient and medieval tradition. Excellent specimens of coins (numismatics) and decorative chasing have survived from the Kushan period (cf. the reliquary with a Kanishka dating found near Peshawar), as have cast sculptures from the *Gupta period (see Replaced wax). The spread of Islamic culture made popular the technique of incrustation (damascene work) used in ornamenting weapons. Particularly valued were steel or iron inlaid with gold in a process that lends the background a bluish shade. In the late Middle Ages and in modern times inlays were also made on decorative objects of everyday use.

Metal utensils, like jugs of the *aftaba* and *surahi* type, *samovars*, basins for ablutions, trays, **huqqas*, sets for preparing betel, etc., were widely used in everyday life. The favourite type of decor was engraving, of which two techniques were in use. Engraving was combined with chasing and notching. Ornaments were mostly fine floral and geometrical designs, solidly covering large surfaces. Inscriptions in Arabic characters were often woven into the ornament. Muslims preferred copper plates and dishes; Hindus preferred brass ones made of 'bell metal' constituted of four parts of copper and one part of tin.

The principal centres of production were Lahore, Multan, Peshawar and Karachi. The traditions of metalwork and ornamenting metal objects have survived in Pakistan to the present day.

E.V. GANEVSKAYA

Tripartite Declaration of India, Pakistan, and Bangladesh

The Declaration was signed in Delhi on 9 April 1974 by representatives of the three states. Relations had normalised, following an acute political crisis and war in 1971. The *Simla Agreement of 2 July 1972 and the Delhi Agreement between India and Pakistan, concluded on 28 August 1973, on the mutual repatriation of military personnel and civilians, and the recognition of the Republic of Bangladesh by Pakistan on 22 February 1974. This enabled the three parties to negotiate face to face. In the Delhi Agreement the three parties declared themselves to be vitally interested in peace and progress, in the normalisation of relations and in the establishment of lasting peace in the subcontinent. The declaration helped to conclude the repatriation of 400,000 citizens of Pakistan and Bangladesh in accord with the United Nations High Commissioner's statement on 1 July 1974.

YU.V GANKOVSKY

Tufan, Wali Muhammad (1919–83)

Poet. Wali Muhammad (his real name) was a poet, writer and public figure, who wrote in *Urdu and *Pashto. He took part in the national liberation movement of the Pashtuns and his work is permeated with patriotic ideas. Particularly successful were his *nazm*, but he also wrote **ghazals* and **rubai*, all of which are romantically coloured.

WORKS: *Manjara ('Bud'), collection of rubai; Ghorzang ('Thrust'), 1973, collection of verse; Dewa ('Lamp'), collection of stories.*

BIBLIOGRAPHY: *H. Khail, 'Pashtany Likwal' (Pashto Writers), Vol. 1., Peshawar; A. Benawa, 'Osani Likwal' (Contemporary Writers), Vol. II, Kabul, 1962.*

A.S. GERASIMOVA

Turkey-Pakistan relations

These relations have developed in political and military areas. The two countries support each other on the *Kashmir and Cyprus problems (*see*, Kashmir Dispute). From 1965 to 1975, when the United States ceased to supply arms to Pakistan, the latter received spare parts for its military equipment from Turkey. In the 1980s and early 1990s the two countries co-operated in the production of weapons and regularly exchanged visits by military officials. The top leaders of Pakistan and Turkey have maintained contact on vital issues of international politics (cf. the visits to Ankara of M. Ziaul *Haq in 1987 and of Benazir *Bhutto in May 1989; the visit of President Kenan Evren to Islamabad in February 1989, etc.).

(See also Central Treaty Organization; Economic Cooperation Organization.)

R.M. MUKIMJANOVA

U

Udergam

(Also Udegram, Udigram) Called Ora by classical authors, this was an ancient city in the *Swat district, to the northeast of Barikot (*North-West Frontier Province). The archaeological excavations suggest that it consisted of two parts: the lower part, tentatively called 'The *Bazaar*', and the elevated one, tentatively called 'The Castle'. The diggings were conducted in 1956-7 by an Italian expedition headed by Prof G. Gullini.

The *Bazaar* was probably the city proper. Diggings reveal seven levels, the lower ones dating back to the 4th century BC while the upper ones date to the 4th century AD. The houses were built in blocks on both sides of the streets. In the second level (Graeco-Bactrian and Indo-Parthian time), the streets look like stretches of well-trodden earth with slate fragments. Each block is divided into two parts–the living part and the shop. Rectangular shops have small rooms at the back and the living rooms being grouped around a central courtyard. In some houses there was a pool in the courtyard, made of perfectly fitted slate plates. The houses were also made of slate plates kept together by clay mortar. In some cases the wooden ceilings were supported with wooden columns. There were fireplaces in every house.

The Castle stood on a high rock surrounded by walls with tower-like counterforces. Probably this was the ruler's residence. One could get to the castle by an imposing stairway. The complex consists of numerous rooms divided with corridors. This part yielded twelve periods, starting with the 2nd century AD. The importance of the Castle appears to have further increased when people left the *Bazaar* in the 5th century AD. The coins and archaeological evidence show that the Castle preserved its significance in the *Ghaznavid period. As recently as the 13th and 14th centuries AD, a Buddhist community stayed there for some time. There is a fragmented representation of Buddha dated to this time.

BIBLIOGRAPHY: *G. Gullini, 'Udergam', IsMEO, Reports and Memoirs, Vol. 1, Rome, 1962; D. Faccena, 'A Guide to the Excavations in Swat (Pakistan)', 1956-62, Rome, 1964.*

B.A. LITVINSKY

Ulema

(plural of *Alim*, 'learned men') There is no priesthood in Islam, but a class of *Ulema* gradually emerged, especially when rulers became dependant on scholars for knowledge of the Law (*Sharia*). *Ulema* progressively acquired influence over the common Muslims. *Ulema*, as a class, have the following verse of the Holy Quran (IX: 122) as a basis:

'Why should there not turn up from every division (of Muslims), a group in order that they might understand the Faith deeper, and when they return to their people, they might admonish them so that their brethren can also improve their conduct by resisting (from possible mistakes).'

YU.V. GANKOVSKY

Umayyads

A dynasty of **khalifas* ruling in AD 661–750, founded by Muawiyah I (661–80), a descendant of the Meccan clan of Umayya of the Arab tribe of Quraysh. Their capital was Damascus. Under the Umayyads the conquest of North Africa was completed. They also seized the Pyrenees, central Asia, *Sindh and southwest *Punjab. The Umayyads were overthrown in 750, as a result of an uprising led by Abu Muslim in eastern Iran, and power was taken over by the Abbasid dynasty (750–1258, capital: Baghdad). A branch of the Umayyad dynasty continued to rule in Spain (756-1031).

YU.V. GANKOVSKY

Umma

(from the Arabic: people, plural: *umam*) A muslim community, Muslims collectively.

YU.V. GANKOVSKY

Unionist Party

See, Punjab National Unionist Party.

United Democratic Front

Founded in 1973 by political parties in Pakistan, opposed to the *Pakistan Peoples Party government headed by Z.A. *Bhutto. The Front united the Pakistan *Muslim League, the *National Awami Party, **Jamaat-*

i-Islami, **Jamiat-ul-Ulema-i-Islam*, **Jamiat-ul-Ulema-i-Pakistan*, the Pakistan Democratic Party, and **Khaksar Tehrik*. The United Democratic Front was headed by the leader of the Pakistan Muslim League, Shah Mardan Shah Pir Pagaro.

YU.V. GANKOVSKY

United Workers' Federation

(UWF) Founded in 1977. It works for the unity of trade union actions in defence of workers' interests.

BIBLIOGRAPHY: *T. Ruziev, 'A History of the Working Class of Pakistan', Moscow, 1980, (in Russian).*

M.YU. MOROZOVA

Urdu

Urdu is a modern literary language belonging to the *Indo-Aryan group of the Indo-European family of languages. It is the national language of Pakistan and one of the fifteen languages recognized by the Constitution of India. It has the status of an official language in *Kashmir, Uttar Pradesh together with Hindi, and in some districts of the states of Bihar and Andhra Pradesh together with Hindi and Telugu respectively.

In Pakistan, Urdu is an important element of bilingualism or multilingualism. The Urdu-speaking population is unevenly distributed, gravitating towards the major cities of Karachi, Islamabad, Rawalpindi, Lahore, Multan, Hyderabad and their respective districts. Under Pakistani conditions, the leading role in the standardization of Urdu belongs to Lahore and Karachi. In India, Urdu speakers are mostly Muslims. They mainly reside in Delhi, Lucknow, Mumbai, and Hyderabad (Deccan).

Urdu dates back to *Khari-boli* or'stable speech', a supra-dialectal type of everyday speech that developed in the eleventh-thirteenth centuries in the Delhi/Meerut/Agra region, which originally included Lahore. This was a zone of intense contact between Muslim newcomers speaking Turkic and Iranian languages and the local population. This form of speech later functioned as an inter-regional language called in Persian *Hindavi or *Hindi 'the Indian language', or Dehlawi 'the Delhi language'. It was brought to the Deccan, South India, by the Delhi sultans' warriors, *Sufi missionaries and migrants from the north. This form of speech, in its southern variety of *Dakhini or Dakhni, acquired the status of a court and literary language in the Muslim state of Bahmani and later, in the principalities of Bijapur and Golconda. The literary tradition of Dakhini (of the fourteenth-seventeenth centuries) became the connecting link between the birth of literary creativity in *Khari-boli* which covers the period from the twelfth to early fourteenth centuries and the development in north India of a stable literary tradition in two languages, Urdu and Hindi. In the first quarter of the eighteenth century the poetic successor of Dakhini in north India, which came to be called *Rekhta* ('mixed', 'scattered'), marked the beginning, of Urdu as a language different from Hindi. The name 'Urdu' itself appeared at the end of the eighteenth century. It replaced Persian in the poetry of north India, and in the early nineteenth century, also became firmly established in prose. Being linked with the Muslim cultural tradition, Urdu emerges as the Persianized literary language, succeeding the *Khari-boli* dialect, or *Hindustani.

The structural affinity of Urdu and modern literary Hindi is explained by their genetic identity. They differ in the writing systems; Hindi uses the Devanagari script, and vocabulary, which is distinctly different from the primordial stock and is also represented by old 'loan' words. Urdu is based on words of Persian, Turkic and Arabic origin, of which the functional parallels in Hindi are Sanskritisms.

Following the formation of Pakistan in 1947, Urdu has functioned under different conditions in India and Pakistan. This has led to a growing divergence in Pakistani and Indian Urdu, both in vocabulary and phonetics. In Pakistan, the functions of Urdu have been considerably extended, and it is treated as an instrument of integration of the country and of the expression of the Muslim community. Hence, there is a tendency towards further Persianization and Arabization of Urdu. This is manifested in such processes as the development of scientific-technical and socio-political terminology, and the standardization of pronunciation and spelling.

BIBLIOGRAPHY: *Z.M. Dymshits, 'The Urdu Language', Moscow, 1962 (in Russian); G.A. Zograf, 'Hindustani at the End of the 18th and in the Beginning of the 19th Century', Moscow, 1961 (in Russian); T. Khalmurzayev, 'The Status of Urdu in Modern India and the Tendencies of Its Development', Tashkent, 1979 (in Russian); A.N. Shamatov, 'Classical Dakhini (17th Century South Hindustani)', Moscow, 1974 (in Russian); 'A. Rai, A House Divided. The Origin and Development of Hindi/Hindavi', New Delhi, 1984.*

V.P. LIPEROVSKY

Urdu Academy

It was set up in 1957 in Lahore to promote the *Urdu language and literature, and to print scientific and technical books in Urdu and English, dealing with education, industry, agriculture, business, and administration. The Academy has published collections of articles on nuclear power engineering, cosmic technology, chemistry, electricity, and magnetism.

N.V. GLEBOV

Urdu Literature

The literature of the peoples of South Asia written in the *Urdu language. In its early period, the Urdu language was called *Hindawi, *Dakhini, and *Rekhta. The term Urdu was first used at the end of the eighteenth century. From its start, Urdu literature was under the strong influence of religious philosophy of Islam, particularly *Sufism, and related with * Persian literature and Persian literature of India. Most of the genre forms came from Persian classical literature. Indian folklore was another source. These two influences distinguished Urdu Literature, as a cultural synthesis, from other literatures of the subcontinent.

Individual poems in Hindawi appeared as early as the end of the thirteenth century and early fourteenth century (Amir Khusraw *Dehlawi). Hindawi was also used in their sermons by the Sumnani *Sufis in the twelfth century, (Hamiduddin Nagori, d. 1274) and others. Historically the uninterrupted tradition of Urdu literature, evolved in the Muslim principalities of Deccan and Gujarat, beginning in the fourteenth century, when the Hindawi language and Persian literature were brought to South India.

Urdu literature in the south (Dakhini) was made up of Instructions by such Sufis as Gesudaraz (d. 1421), Miranji (d. 1499), Fakhruddin Nizami (1397–1422) in the Bahmanid state and by Shah Ahmad (d. 1446), Muhammad Jiw Jan (d. 1515), and Shaikh Muhammad Huba (1539–1614) in Gujarat who turned to local plots, folklore and local poetic forms in their work.

The 16th–17th centuries saw the heyday of south Urdu literature in the Deccan principalities of Bijapur and Golconda. The Bijapur school was characterized by an Indian influence, drawing on local subjects and poetic forms. Examples include *Kulliyat* by Abdullah Adil Shah (1638–73), **masnawi Chandabadan was Mahiyar* by Muqimi, and *Gulshan-i-Ishq* (The Flower Bed of Love) by Nusrati. The Golconda school is characterized by strict adherence to the rules of the Persian-language poetry: *Kulliyat* by Quli Qutb Shah, *masnawi Tuti Nama* (The Book of the Parrot) and *Sayf al-Mulk wa Badi al-Jamal* by Ghawwasi, and *masnawi Qutb Mushtari* by Mullah Wajhi. The latter, a Sufi allegory, *Sab Ras* (All the Races, 1634) is a classic of Urdu prose in the Deccan.

The conquest of Deccan in the seventeenth century by the Great Mughals (see, Mughal Empire) marked the beginning of the decline of southern Urdu literature. Its centre moved to the north. At the court of the Delhi Shahs and at other cultural centres of the north, Rekhta poetry was cultivated, which had inherited the experience of the Deccan School through Muhammad Wali's **Diwan* and the works. In the work of Abru (d. 1750), Arzu (1689–1756), Hatim (1699–1791), Urdu literature evolved into its literary norm.

The downfall of the *Mughal Empire in the second half of the eighteenth century caused a crisis in public life which in turn gave birth to feelings of doom that we find in Urdu literature of that period. At the same time, the second half of the eighteenth century is considered to be the 'Golden Age' of Urdu literature when Delhi boasted such celebrities as the Sufi poet Mir Dard, Muhammad Rafi *Sauda, famous for his satirical **qasidas*, and Mir Taqi *Mir, the trend-setter in the genre of the philosophical and love *ghazal*, and the author of the classical *masnawi* Mir Hasan. The humanistic traditions of Urdu literature were in much evidence in the poetry of Nazir Akbarabadi, who never followed the canons of the court poetry.

After the decline of the Delhi school, the centre of Urdu literature moved to the princely state of Oudh, Rampur, Hyderabad and elsewhere. In the capital of Oudh, the Lucknow School flourished. Its characteristic features include complex sophisticated forms and content: the poetry of Imam Bakhsh Nasikh, Haydar Ali Aatish, the erotic Rekhti poetry of Rangin (1755–1834), Jan Sahib (1818–97), masnawi *Gulzar-i-Nasim* (Nasim's Flower Bed, 1833) by Daya Shankar Nasim, *Zehr-i-Ishq* (The Poison of Love, 1860) by Mirza Shawq. Also well-developed are the Shia elegy—**marsia* (Mir *Anis, Mirza Dabir), and artistic prose (Inshallah Khan Insha, Rajab Ali Surur). Some poets followed the Delhi tradition (Mir Soz, Mushafi).

The first half of the nineteenth century marked the end of the classical Urdu literature. Its main proponents were Ibrahim Zawq (1789–1854), Momin (1800–51) and particularly Mirza *Ghalib whose lyrical *Diwan-i-Urdu* still serves as a criterion of poetic perfection. The Farsi poetry and prose of Ghalib had a great influence on the subsequent development of Urdu literature. Its classical period was concluded by the work of Amir Minai (1828–1900) and Nawab Mirza Khan Dagh Dehlawi (1831–1905).

By the end of the eighteenth century, an uninterrupted tradition of prose-writing established itself. Popular **dastans* with fairytale and fantastic plots appeared, mainly in adaptations of Sanskrit and Persian plots. With the founding of Fort William College in Calcutta in 1800 and Delhi College in 1827, a steady stream of translation of works from Eastern and Western languages began preparing the way for original works of Urdu literature. The 1840s was the time of educational and didactic literature, e.g., Ram Chandar and his journals *Muhib-i-Hind* (India's Friend) and *Fawaid un-Niazirin* (Readers' Benefit) which began coming out in 1837.

The later nineteenth century was the stage of enlightenment in Urdu literature. The ideological leader of this trend was Sir Sayyid Ahmad *Khan. Its centres were the Aligarh College (1878), the 'Scientific Society' headed by Sayyid Ahmad Khan (1866), and the weekly *Tahzib-al-Akhlaq* (Moral Education, 1870). Numerous translations from the English and other European languages, including the spread of Rolusseau's ideas of natural education and the role of reason in the cognitive processes, encroached all genres of Urdu literature in the late nineteenth century.

There was intensive development of the novel-adventure (Rattanath Sarshar), historical (Abdul Halim Sharar), and social (Muhammad Hadi Ruswa). Particularly noteworthy are theatrical novels of Sajjad Husain (1856–1915) and the short stories and poems in the Lucknow-based satirical magazine *Awadh Punch* (1877–1912).

Enlightenment determined the direction of the new trends in poetry, represented by Altaf Husain *Hali and Muhammad Husain *Azad. The poetic reform affected by these two poets in 1874 in Lahore gave birth to the so-called 'natural poetry.' Which assimilated some of the features of English romanticism. With their theoretical essays and their poetry, Hali, Azad and Shibli Numani laid the way for Muhammad *Iqbal.

In the verse of Hasrat Mohani (1875–1951) and other poets of his circle, one can find first occurrances socialist ideas. Evolution of the short story started with Prem Chand and Sajjad Hyder Yaldram. Prem Chand proved to be a source of inspiration for the realist school of fiction which merged with the Progressive Writers Movement (1936), while Yaldram inspired the *belle-letters* school, and early humorists like Farhatullah Beg.

In the 1930s, the role of Urdu literature in the public life grew. Literary organizations sprang up; the largest was the All-India Progressive Writers' Association, which was established in 1936 by young writers, including Sajjad *Zaheer, Mulk Raj Anand, Muhammad Din Tasir and others. The Association was supported by such eminent figures as Rabindranath Tagore, Prem Chand, Abdul Haq and other luminaries. During the 1930–50s, the Association redirected the development of Urdu literature. The poets Josh, Jamil Mazhari, Faiz Ahmad *Faiz, Ali Sardar Jafri, Kayfi Azmi, Makhdum Mohiuddin, Ahmad Nadim *Qasmi, the prose writers Saadat Hasan *Manto, Krishan Chandar, Khwaja Ahmad Abbas, Raziya, the critics and essayists Sajjad Zaheer, Ehtisham Husain and other took part in the process. Anti-feudal and anti-colonial trends in the work of the members of the Association in the pre-independence period established its reputation among the public. Simultaneously, other literary organizations were active. In 1939, *Halqa-i-Arbab-i-Zawq* (Circle of Art Lovers) was founded in Lahore. Its members adhered to formal-aesthetic criteria in art. After independence and the partition of India into two sovereign states, Urdu literature acquired new features.

The *Pakistan Progressive Writers' Association became the successor of the All-India Progressive Writers' Association. However, in 1954, it was banned. The *Pakistan Writers' Guild, in 1959, was actually a trade union for the writing profession. The unstable economic position of most writers, and that of journals and publishing houses hampered the publication of serious literature. Book publishing concentrated on catering to the less demanding readers.

A.A. SUVOROVA
A.S. SUKHOCHEV

Eventually, the Progressive Writers Association became a victim of state suppression. Extreme ideological exclusiveness and factional strife had already weakened the movement. Writers of the right wing also felt the pressure of religious groups. As a result, Qurratulain *Hyder (1926–), resentful of the tirade against her masterpiece *Aag Ka Darya* ('River of Fire', 1959), re-migrated to India.

The Urdu novel achieved its apogee with *Aag Ka darya*, and during the same era, Shaukat Siddiqui (1923–) published *Khuda Ki Basti* '(God's Dwelling') that became an overnight success because of its strong social realism. Novels had generally trailed behind short stories, but at intervals, powerful novels have surfaced, written by authors who originally made their reputation as short story writers. *Angan*, by Khadija *Mastur, was another classic Urdu novel.

By 1960, the experimental short story became the dominant trend in Pakistan. The experimental technique (symbolism in Urdu) was led by Intizar Husain (1925–) and Enwer Sajjad (1934–) followed closely by Masud Ashar and Arsh Siddiqui (1927–97). Intizar Husain invoked Islamic traditions, and Indian mythology for his symbolism and adopted the style of chronicles (*Dastan*). The symbols of Enwer Sajjad came from social and medical terms, Masud Ashar employed symbolism for producing protest literature against despotism in Pakistan—he wrote mainly against the Ziaul *Haq regime (1977–88). Arsh Siddiqui concentrated on spiritual themes. Khalida Husain (1938–) received recognition rather late, but her mysterious and inscrutable style and themes have already left a lasting impression on Urdu fiction. Other lady fiction writers who have lately dominated the scene are Zahida Hina (1946–) and Firdous Haider.

Belonging more to Khalida Husain's generation but representing the second phase of experimental fiction in Pakistan are Rasheed Amjad (1940–) and Muhammad Mansha Yâd (1937–), Rasheed Amjad has sought to break both the linguistic and story structure while M. Mansha Yâd has drawn his symbols from the rural milieu and folk tales.

The fiction scenes today have representatives from all forms and generations. The neo-classical strand is best depicted by Ghulam-us-Saqlain Naqvi (1923–2003). Among the modernists, the figure of Mazhar-ul-Islam (1949–) looms large; he blends imagination and abstraction to present haunting comments on daylight reality. Hasan Manzar uses introspection to condemn bigotry and hypocrisy.

In the realm of poetry, the most celebrated names were Hafeez Jallandhari, N.M. *Rashid, and Faiz Ahmad *Faiz until the migration of Josh *Malihabadi to Pakistan in 1956.

Hafiz Jallandhari had already made his major contributions before partition, but he composed memorable verses here including the national anthem of Pakistan. Josh made his more meritorious contribution to devotional poetry, wrote some of his most touching love poetry amidst some protest poems reflecting self-pity. As a skeptic and a poet with deep metaphysical insight, Nazar Muhammad Rashid (1910–75) turned his blank verse into abstract illuminations and formations. He projected the enigmatic, bizarre and weird aspects of life, thereby extending the boundaries of poetry, absorbing themes hitherto the preserve of prose. His contemporary, Miraji (1909–49) became a cult figure, and was far more influential than Rashid, but was nevertheless, an inferior poet. Faiz Ahmad Faiz (1911–84) was an exponent of Marxist ideology; intellectually, his poems are less satisfying than Rashid's, but he was a consummate artist with words. His neo-classical control over light and shade combined with his rich lyricism have brought him critical approval and popular acclaim. Another contemporary, Aziz Hamid Madani (1922–91), displayed subtle abstractions, subdued tones, and therefore, could faithfully portray the more elusive strands of urban consciousness during the early years of Pakistan. Majid Amjad (1914–74) and Wazir Agha (1922–) were more at home in a rural setting and were successful in giving an epic dimension to pastoral themes.

Modern poets with a classical background were Ahsan *Danish and Ahmad Nadeem *Qasmi (1916–). Also active on the literary front were Zahir Kashmiri (1919–95), Saba Akbarabad (d. 1991), Saifuddin Saif (1921–93).

Side by side, with a generation of neo-classical poets, a generation of post modern poets started to attract attention. They were, Iftikhar Jalib (1936–), Mubarak Ahmad (d. 2001), and Qamar Jamil (d. 2000). They even penetrated the fortress of the hidebound *ghazal* and transformed it into an *avante guarde* art form. These writers also included Javed Shahin, Iqbal Sajid, Zafar Iqbal and Anwar Shaur (1943–) and but before they could displace the earlier generations, the 1965 war broke out. The demands of national solidarity dissolved the difference between generations. Himayat Ali Shair (1932–) composed a poem 'Blood' that conveyed the sentiment of the nation. Jamiluddin *Aali (1926–), Rais Amrohvi (d. 1988) and Safdar Mir (d. 1998), all rose to the occasion, and equalled in literary merit, the revolutionary works of 1919–47.

The Tashkent Declaration (1966) was popularly viewed in *West Pakistan as a betrayal, and resentment over it gave rise to protest poetry on an unprecedented scale. Habib Jalib (1929–93) became the voice of the people and raised national feeling to a pitch that prepared the ground for the ultimate election victory in 1970 of the leftist *Pakistan Peoples' Party in *Sindh and *Punjab. Habib Jalib was echoed by Yunus Sharar (1946–) and a number of young poets who had not come to the fore during the 1965 war itself.

The 1971 war and the secession of Bangladesh resulted in the largest migration of Urdu writers. The migration from Delhi to Lucknow in the nineteenth century and the cross-migration in 1947, dislocated far fewer writers. Before these writers joined the mainstream, they produced another crop of riot literature, but literature on this riot remained one sided and had a smaller span then the partition literature. Ahmad Nadeem Qasmi wrote poems like *Twenty-Five Words* and Faiz Ahmad Faiz contributed a poem lamenting the separation of the two wings of Pakistan. The writers from *East Pakistan formed a distinct entity.

Among the poets who became instantly popular after the separation, were Iqbal Azim (1913–2000) and Suroor Barabankvi (1927–80). Other poets who made their reputation more steadily are Jamil Azimabadi (1924–), Akhtar Payami (1930–), Salahuddin Muhammad, Saif Hasanpuri, Afsar Mahpuri (d. 1996), Adeeb Suhail (1927–), Akhtar Lucknowi (1935–95), Pasha Rahman, Zaki Azar (1940–90), Saba Ikram (1945–), Yawar Aman (1942–), Iftikhar Ajmal (1942–) and Javed Rasul Jauhar (1968–).

The fiction writers are Shahzad Manzar (1933–97), Ali Haider Mallik (1944–), Umm-i-Ammara, Shahnaz Pervin (1947–), Ahmad Zainudin (1939–) and Nurul Huda Syed (1942–). To this circle gathered Qamar Abbas Nadim (1946–81) and A. Khayyam (1943–). Among leading critics were Nazir Siddiqui (1930–2001), Mahmud Wajid (1933–) and Hanif Fauq (1926–).

After these writers had settled down, the 1980s saw Peshawar become the capital of Urdu poetry with such luminaries as Farigh Bukhari (1917–97), Raza Hamdani (1916–94), Qatil Shifai (1919–2001), Ahmad Faraz (1930–), Mohsin Ahsan (1932–), and Akhtar Peshawari. Almost all of these poets participated in political struggles, giving both revolution and lyricism a new impetus.

The same decade saw the domination of feminist love poetry. Female poets were rare, but not unknown, and early in the twentieth century, Zahida Khatun Sherwani and Ummat-ur-Rauf Nasrin were perceived to have broken the male monopoly over poetry. Later on, Ada Jafri (1924–), Pervin Fana Syed and Zahra Nigah gained respect and recognition for their literary merit. This poetry turned feminist with the advent of Kishwar Naheed (1940–) and Fahmida *Riaz (1924–). Feminist issues and grievances were broadcast, to be amplified later by Sara Shagufta and Azra Abbas (1950–). The ingredient of glamour remained elusive until the advent of Pervin Shakir (1952–94). A poet of exceptional sensibility and erudition, she was able to add real literary lustre to her reputation before her untimely death. Since then the inhibitions felt by women diminished over time, and without being avowedly feminist, a number of them have held the field by enlarging their canvas. They are Shahida Hasan (1953–), Tanvir Anjum (1956–), Mansura Ahmad, Shabnam Shakil, Fatima Hasan (1953–) and Fouqia Mushtaq (1968–).

The 1970s and 1980s also witnessed emigration of Urdu writers to the West and the Middle East. In these countries, expertise received encouragement to continue their cultural activities and even set up Urdu press facilities.

Mention should also be made of religious scholars who composed poetry. They formed an island in the history of Urdu literature because of their excessive veneration of classical forms. It is incidental that their poetry, even avowedly devotional, had metaphysical overtones. They are Abul Ala Maudoodi (1903–79), Rasheed Turabi (1908–73), Kausar Niazi (1934–93) and Talib Jauhari (1940–); only the last named has made concessions to modern forms and themes. As prose writers, Abul Ala Maudoodi and Rashid Turabi have been hailed as great stylists and rhetoricians.

In sharp contrast to the **ulema*, are prose poems in Urdu. Contemporary writing is characterised by prose poems in poetry, experimental stories in fiction, structuralism in its latest manifestation, stylistic in literary criticism. But so far, only experimental stories have met with acceptance; prose poets and structuralists are still trying to find converts by theoretical arguments rather than by the intrinsic value of their output. The more successful practitioners of this have been Afzal Ahmad Syed (1946–), Mubarak Ahmad (d. 2001), Qamar Jameel (d. 2000), Sara Shagufta and Ahmad Hamesh. Kishwar Naheed also excels in this genre.

The Japanese *haiku* has found much greater acceptance, not only at the popular but also at the critical level. The leading exponents are Mohsin Bhopali (1938–), Muhammad Rais Alvi (1946–), Qamar Sahiri (1943–2001), Farasat Rizvi (1954–), Ada Jafri (1924–) and Tajdar Adil (1947–).

The writers who introduced to Urdu readers the literature of the regional languages of Pakistan by translating, interpreting and even writing critical histories are Kamilul Qadri, Afaz Siddiqui (1928–) and Wafa Rashidi (1926–). Shaikh Mubarak *Ayaz (1923–97), the greatest modern *Sindhi poet, also wrote directly in Urdu.

Drama in Urdu has never been able to compete with other forms of Urdu literature. Aga Hashr Kashmiri (d. 1934) and Ahsan Lucknowi (1859–1930) were considered better poets and critics than dramatists but with the advent of television in Pakistan (1964), the trend was reversed. Teleplays became a major art form and gave dramatists a reputation which overshadowed their considerable merit in other fields. Ashfaq Ahmad (1923–) acquired great eminence as a short story writer before writing teleplays. His wife Bano Qudsia (1928–) had established hereself as a novelist and Amjad Islam Amjad (1944–) as a poet. Even Kamal Ahmad Rizvi (1930–), prolific as he is on the mini screen, has more publications than plays to his credit. Only Khwaja Moinuddin (1924–71) and Anwar Maqsood (1941–) seem to have confined their literary talent to teleplays.

The **ghazal* has proved to be the most resilient form of Urdu poetry and at present three different strands of *ghazal*: neo-classical, modern and post-modern *ghazals* simultaneously claim the attention of readers. Tabish Dehlavi (1911–), Nusrat Zaidi and Saqi Amrohvi and John Elia (1936–) are some of its most famous exponents.

Ghazal writers are led by Ahmad Faraz, whose lilting lyricism and political protest continue to captivate. On the other side of the spectrum is Zafar Iqbal who made a deliberate dictional and thematic reformation of the *ghazal*, but still, the traditional strains of his *ghazal* continue to haunt. Javed Shaheen (1942–) and Anwar Sha'ur (1943–) have seen to it that the post modern diction strtikes its roots.

The pre-eminent *ghazal* poets are Iftikhar Arif (1944–) and Sahar Ansari (1941–) who have kept the flame of skeptic and speculative philosophy alive. Hasan Akbar Kamal (1946–), whose lyricism is laced with erudition, and Nasir Turabi (1945–) whose classical hinterland sets his modern idiom most effectively; Tajdar Adil (1954–) has also a distinct voice. The most dominant figure however, remains Munir Niazi (1928–).

The **nazm* broke its early modernistic mould with Akhtar Husan Jafri (1932–92), and now he has been succeeded by a later generation including Zeeshan Sahil (1961–), Saiduddin (1953–).

The *Pakistan Progressive Writers Association has been revived effectively by Hasan Abidi (1929–) Muslim Shamim (1939–) and Rahat Saeed (1939–).

As Urdu literature enters the new millennium, fiction is dominated by symbolism, poetry by abstraction and criticism by structuralism. Still a survey written even a decade later might need to alter the perspective as now seen.

A.H. MALLIK

Urs

(Arabic: wedding) A celebratory ritual widespread among Islamic peoples of South Asia. The ritual has two meanings. The first is the festivities on the occasion of a marriage, a wedding feast. The second is the feast on the occasion of a death anniversary of a revered sufi or other religious authority (**wali*).

In the first instance, *urs* implies escorting the bride into the bridegroom's house followed by the signing of the marriage contract and a wedding feast. In different ages and areas inhabited by Muslims, wedding ceremonies have varied, sometimes lasting for weeks.

In the second instance *urs* interprets a *sufi's death as a marriage of the lover, the mystic, to his beloved the Creator. During *urs* festivities thousands of pilgrims visit sufi monasteries to pay homage to the saint. They perform funeral rites and distribute amulets and free food. *Pirs* read the Quran. Sometimes *urs* includes music and drama performances.

A. NIYAZI

Usmani, Ishrat Husain (1917–92)

Scientist. I.H. Usmani's formal schooling started late, when he was admitted directly into the seventh class. He earned his MSc and PhD from Imperial College, London in 1950. On his return to Pakistan he entered the Central Superior Services and rose to be Chief Controller of Imports and Exports. He came to the notice of President Ayub *Khan who inducted him as Chairman of the *Pakistan Atomic Energy Commission. He redesigned and expanded the Nillour Research Reactor and established the PINSTECH. It was primarily due to his efforts that Pakistan's first atomic energy plant at Kanupp near Karachi could be inaugurated in 1972.

T. NAIM

US–Pakistan relations

Diplomatic relations between Pakistan and the United States of America began at the height of the Cold War. Each had a different set of reasons for seeking an alliance. Pakistan needed assistance against India which had withheld Pakistan's military assets while war had broken out in *Kashmir. The US identified a strategic need to encircle the communist states, the USSR and the People's Republic of China. The lead in establishing relations was taken by Pakistan when, in October 1947, a Pakistani delegation led by Mir Laiq Ali offered the country's services to counter any Soviet influence in the region in return for the sum of $ 2 billion.

The US viewed Pakistan sympathetically and supported its position on Kashmir in the United Nations. Liaquat Ali *Khan, the first Prime Minister of Pakistan, visited the United States in 1950. The visit was successful however Liaquat held back from sending Pakistan troops to Korea and from a formal military alliance. Subsequently under the Governor-Generalship of Ghulam *Mohammad, military pacts including those of CENTO originally Baghdad Pact, and SEATO were signed in 1954 and a Mutual Assistance Agreement in 1959. These pacts enabled Pakistan to gather a large arsenal, specially in the Air Force. Pakistan was called the most 'allied ally' of the US during the 1950s.

Taking this as an excuse, the Prime Minister of India, Jawaharlal Nehru, resiled from his promise of holding a plebiscite in Kashmir. The Soviet Union thereafter recognized Kashmir as a part of India and began to veto every resolution which called for a plebiscite.

President D.D. Eisenhower visited Pakistan and President M. Ayub *Khan made a visit to the United States, where he told Congress, on 12 July 1960, that the US could land its troops in Pakistan whenever it wished. These pacts benefited Pakistan militarily but diplomatically affected its non-aligned status.

During the 1962 Sino-Indian War, it was revealed that the US had an agreement with India as well. During the 1971 war US officials referred to supplementary commitments to Pakistan which encompassed the threat from India as well. The truth behind such transcripts still awaits confirmation. Meanwhile Pakistan continued to honour its side of the bargain. In 1960 an American U2 spy plane which had taken off from Pakistan was shot down over Soviet territory.

Pakistan's growing relations with China, and America's action of arming India, became sources of contention. Relations with the US remained cold when the 1965 Indo-Pakistan War broke out. The US imposed an arms and aid embargo on both India and Pakistan, but this harmed only Pakistan as India had an alternative source of supply from the USSR.

Relations remained sour until 1970 when the US revised its policy towards China and sought Pakistan's help in establishing contact.

The United States' so-called 'tilt' towards Pakistan lasted till the end of the Gerald Ford era when Pakistan, in response to the 1974 Indian nuclear test, started its own nuclear programme. Pakistan's pursuit of a defensive nuclear armoury seemed unreasonable to the Jimmy Carter Democratic Administration. This phase continued till 1979 when the USSR directly invaded Afghanistan.

Pakistan became a frontline country and under both Jimmy Carter and Ronald Reagan received massive military and financial aid. The Pakistan military government under Ziaul *Haq took advantage of the lifting of American pressure and went ahead with the nuclearization programme. One other consequence of the Afghan War to both the US and Pakistan was the induction and arming of Islamic military groups from Afghanistan itself and the Middle East, against the Soviet Union. After the Soviet withdrawal from Afghanistan, in 1989, this policy was to have catastrophic consequences for both countries.

In the short term, Pakistan faced a diminished status after the Soviet withdrawal from Afghanistan. Within two years the Soviet Union was fragmented. With the end of the Cold War, the United States felt safe in resuming its nuclear non-proliferation programme, again making Pakistan and not India, which had already gone nuclear in 1974, their target. For this purpose, a spate of legislation proceeded from the US.

Apart from mutual agreements, there have been, several pieces of US legislation concerning Pakistan. The first was the Symington Amendment of 1976, aimed at stopping air and arms sale, as well as military training. This was followed by the Glenn Amendment of 1977, which stopped aid to non-weapon countries importing uranium enrichment technology, and barred assistance to countries importing reprocessing technology. This was exactly what Pakistan wished to import from France. This amendment was first invoked by President Jimmy Carter on 6 April 1979, two days after Zulfiqar Ali *Bhutto, the Pakistani Prime Minister who was to sign the deal with France, was executed.

The Pressler Amendment of 1985 was Pakistan specific, because it was initially designed to enable Pakistan to receive US aid during the Soviet-Afghan war, by suspending the Symington Amendment if the US President certified that Pakistan was not pursuing a nuclear weapon programme.

During this time, the United States reaffirmed the 1959 bilateral areement with Pakistan relating to aggression from a communist or a communist dominated state.

In 1989 US President George Bush refused to certify that Pakistan did not possess a nuclear weapon and aid was halted.

Senator Hank Brown moved an amendment in 1995, which was endorsed by President Bill Clinton in 1996. The Brown Amendment did not seek to repeal or modify the Pressler Amendment. It only allowed economic and limited military aid. On 17 July 1999 Senator Tom Harkin and John Warner had the Symington Amendment effectively altered to suit Pakistan. The subsequent missile and democracy sanctions have been short lived.

The restoration of democracy in Pakistan brought about a thaw in mutual relations. President Bill Clinton said on the occasion of Benazir *Bhutto's visit that it was wrong on the part of the US to retain both the F16 planes and the money. In November 1995 Senator Hank Brown moved his own amendment which restored Pakistan-US co-operation in economic and non-military matters. The Brown Amendment did not moderate or repeal the Pressler Amendment but improved bilateral relations immensely.

A lobby which sought to isolate Pakistan was still powerful in the United States when, in May 1998, Pakistan responded to the Indian nuclear tests conducted earlier. USA-Pakistan relations took another plunge. The rationale of Pakistan's decision was not called into question at this time, but unhappiness nevertheless prevailed that Pakistan had not bowed to US pressure and had taken defensive measures. US officials had been unperturbed when India seized Kargil from Pakistan in 1965, which partly contributed to the outbreak of war that year, and also when Indian violated the line of control by taking Siachen. However the nuclear portents of the crisis had an alarming effect when Pakistan irregulars occupied Kargil in 1999. Pakistan was forced to withdraw under international military pressure, led by the US, which was quite indifferent to the merits of Pakistan's cause.

This distrust was heightened in October 1999, when Pakistan once again came under military rule. President Bill Clinton showed his displeasure by making a stop of only a few hours in Pakistan on 26 March 2000, during which he delivered a televised homily. By contrast his visits to India and Bangladesh had been extended and cordial. On Kashmir, the US's historical position was that a UN-sponsored plebiscite was still binding, but it had refused to intervene in the dispute unless India also joined Pakistan in seeking the US as an intermediary.

The new George W. Bush administration indicated that it would objectively review bilateral relations, when the 11 September 2001 terrorist attacks took place in Washington and New York. The first statement to issue forth regarding bilateral relations was that the rules had changed. The prime suspect was located in Afghanistan and, in an ironic twist, Pakistan again became a frontline state, this time being held responsible for the deeds of the puritanical rulers of Afghanistan, the Taliban.

The Taliban were the residue of the Islamic militant groups jointly fostered by the US and Pakistan to combat Soviet occupation. After the Soviet withdrawal the Taliban turned against the US and put pressure on Pakistan to the point of effecting an aberration in Pakistan's foreign policy. To date, Pakistan has shown willingness to co-operate with the US, resulting in some domestic unrest, but the long-term effects of this confrontation on US-Pakistan relations still remain to be seen. After the 11 September 2001 terrorist attacks on the US, Pakistan joined the US coalition. This has improved relations. President Pervez *Musharraf was received warmly in the US during a visit from 12 to 15 February 2002.

During the whole of 2003, and until the time of writing this entry, US Pakistan relations remained chequered. On 15 March 2003 US waived democracy-related sanctions against Pakistan. On 24 March US imposed sanctions against the Khan Research Laboratories (KRL) nuclear facility. On 3 April US waived $1 billion in debt payable by Pakistan. On 8 April, during a seminar at Johns Hopkins University, the majority view was that Pakistan posed a greater threat than Iraq. On 10 April, the US Secretary of State, Colin Powell, rebutted the assertion of the Indian Foreign Minister, Yashwant Sinha, that there was a stronger case for military action against Pakistan than Iraq. He also stressed that the situation across the Line of Control in Kashmir was 'difficult'. Pakistan, for its part joined the US coalition against Afghanistan, but refused to endorse the action against Iraq.

On 22 June 2003 US and Pakistani troops conducted a joint patrol on the eastern borders of Afghanistan. Three days later during talks with President Pervez Musharraf, President George W. Bush announced a $3 billion, five year assistance programme for Pakistan. This decision was not popular with the American academia. On 31 October 2003 the assistant secretary of state defended US aid to Pakistan by citing its excellent support for the US war on terrorism and the aid given by Pakistan's agencies to apprehend 500 Al-Qaeda suspects. The same day a strong statement was made in Congress calling for an impartial plebiscite in Kashmir.

On 10 January 2004, Deputy Secretary of State Richard Armitage said he did not ascribe all violence across the LoC in Kashmir to the Government of Pakistan.

Following investigations top nuclear scientists, including Dr A.Q. Khan, were interrogated and as a result, A.Q. *Khan admitted that he had been involved in nuclear proliferation. He submitted a mercy petition and was pardoned. The US State Department has appreciated such steps although it has been deemed the opportunity to interview Dr Khan. Thus, present day relations though warm, are equivocal and ambivalent. On 19 October 2004 Secretary of State Colin Powell announced in Islamabad the designation of Pakistan as a Major Non-NATO ally.

In the latest developments, nuclear proliferation issues are alternating with the US efforts to end a military standoff between India and Pakistan, which began on 13 December 2001.

BIBLIOGRAPHY: *F.N. Bajwa, 'Pakistan and the West', Karachi, 1996; M.R. Beschloss, 'Mayday: Eisenhower, Khrushchev and the U2 Affair', New York, 1986; D. Kux, 'The United States and Pakistan, Disenchanted Allies', Karachi, 2001; Leo Rose (ed.), 'United States–Pakistan Relation', Berkeley, 1987; S.R.T. Kheli, 'The United States and Pakistan', New York, 1982.*

M.R. KAZIMI

V

Vanaspati

(Sanskrit: *vanas-pati*—lord of the forest) A general term for hydrogenated vegetable oils, such as coconut, nut, etc., which solidify at room temperature, resembling margarine. They are used in cooking instead of expensive *ghee* (clarified butter).

O.N. BOBYLEVA

Viqarul Mulk, Nawab (1841–1917)

Politician. Nawab Mushtaq Husain, Viqarul Mulk, was orphaned at an early age and struggled to complete his education. After qualifying, he first became a schoolteacher, then joined the British Service in 1859, rising to *serishtidar*. He thereafter served in the domain of the Nizam of Hyderabad but left after a factional strife. Viqarul Mulk was the principal leader to favour the foundation of a Muslim political party. He first made an attempt in 1901 in Lucknow. When the idea of forming the *All-India Muslim League was floated, Viqarul Mulk supported it, while Nawab *Mohsinul Mulk was initially averse to it. When the AIML was nevertheless founded, Viqarul Mulk and Mohsinul Mulk were made joint Honorary Secretaries. In 1907, when Mohsinul Mulk died, Viqarul Mulk became secretary of both the AIML as well as the Aligarh College. Ultimately, he decided to retain the Secretaryship of the College, agreeing to become a Vice-President of the AIML. Viqarul Mulk braved out a crisis at Aligarh College when the entire British faculty had threatened to resign as a result of the imposition of the supremacy of the Board of Trustees. Nawab Viqarul Mulk used his influence to prevent the AIML's deflection of the demand of separate electorates as well as preventing its London branch from becoming independent.

BIBLIOGRAPHY: *M.I. Nadvi, 'Viqar-ul-Hayat', 2nd ed., Karachi, 1984; M.A. Zuberi, 'Tazkira-i-Viqar', Aligarh, 1938.*

M.R. KAZIMI

Waheed, Saida (1917–)

Political activist. Begum Saida Waheed is a pioneer social worker who participated actively in the Pakistan Liberation Movement as a member of the *All-India Muslim League. In 1940 she participated in the conference where the Pakistan Resolution calling for the establishment of Pakistan was adopted. She responded to the call of M.A. *Jinnah by organizing the Punjab *Muslim League women's wing as its joint secretary.

In the early 1940s she was elected an officer of the Lahore Hospital Welfare Society, Punjab Children's Aid Society and the *Anjuman-e-Himayat-e-Islam* Orphanage and Women's Education Committees. After 1947 she helped to reorganize these institutions and also served as the first Honorary Secretary of the Women's Relief Committee. As a founder member of the *All Pakistan Women's Association and Honorary General Secretary of APWA *Punjab, She helped to establish eight primary schools for girls, and a cottage industries workshop. She also re-organized the *Dar ul-Niswan* Industrial Home. She helped in achieving international recognition for APWA.

In 1952 she founded the Family Planning Association of Pakistan, which was recognized by the Pakistan Government. It was affiliated with the International Planned Parenthood Federation (IPPF) through her efforts. She served as a Board Member and Vice-President (IPPF) for a period of ten years. In recognition of her outstanding voluntary work for social services she was awarded *Tamgha-e-Quaid-i-Azam* in 1959.

Since 1971 she has devoted all her creative energies, physical and material resources towards the planning, creation, and development of the 410-bed Fatima Memorial Hospital. In 1999 she was awarded a Gold Medal by the Pakistan Movements Workers Trust in recognition of her role and contribution in the freedom movement. On World Population Day (July 11, 2002) Saida Waheed was awarded Lifetime Achievement Award by the President of Pakistan in recognition of her efforts for the welfare of the community and for her lifetime contribution in founding and developing the Family Planning Movement in Pakistan.

H. MALIK

Wahhabi

1. Sunni Muslims, followers of the religion-political movement that appeared in Arabia in the 18th century. The founder, Muhammad ibn-Abd al-Wahhab (1703-87), called for *jihad* in the name of creating a state on the principles of early Islam. He also believed in cleansing Islam from innovations and cults of the saints. He denounced social inequality, luxury and greed.

2. In South Asia, the name Wahhabi is often applied to the followers of Sayyid Ahmad Barelwi (1786–1831). The term was first introduced in the 1860-70s by W.W. Hunter, an English administrator scholar, who noted great similarity between the teachings of both Barelwi and Wahhab. However, many scholars in India and Pakistan believe that this similarity is superficial and only applies to common principles. In fact, Sayyid Ahmad Barelwi and his successor Shah Ismail were the followers of Shah Waliullah in Pakistani and Indian historical writing.

L.R. GORDON

Wai

A genre form of a small lyrical poem, in medieval *Sindhi poetry. It mainly occurs in the works of Shah Inayat (1625-1713) and Shah Abdul Latif *Bhitai's *Shah Jo Risalo* (Epistle), in which each chapter (**sur*) is concluded with a *wai*. The *wai* usually speaks of unfortunate lovers suffering in separation. Their pain is interpreted in the mystic *Sufi sense. After the development of the genre by Shah Abdul Latif the *wai* has been classified as a variety of **kafi*.

BIBLIOGRAPHY: *L.H. Ajwani, 'History of Sindhi Literature', New Delhi, 1970; H.J. Sorley, 'Shah Abdul Latif of Bhit', Karachi, 1989.*

A.S. SUKHOCHEV

Wali

(plural: *awliya*, from Arabic verb *walia*—to be close; to rule, to manage) A ruler, protector, or master. It is also used for a devotee, someone close to God. *Waliullah* is an epithet applied to Ali, the fourth righteous **khalif*, son-in-law and cousin of the Prophet Muhammad (PBUH).

YU.V. GANKOVSKY

Waliullah (1922–71)

Writer. Sayyid Waliullah was a Bengali-language Pakistani writer, dramatist, and journalist. In 1943 he graduated from a college in East Bengal with a Bachelor's degree in economics. He went on to Calcutta University and contributed to the *Statesman* newspaper. After 1947 he worked in *Radio Pakistan in Dhaka and Karachi. From 1951 he was in the diplomatic service of Pakistan and served in India, Australia, Indonesia, the United Kingdom, West Germany and France, and also in the Ministry of Information and Broadcasting. From 1967 to 1970 he worked for UNESCO. He published three collections of stories, three plays and three novels: *Lal Shalu* ('The Red Tree of Shalu', 1949), *Chander Omabosha* ('New Moon', 1964), *Kando, Nodi, Kando!* ('Cry, River, Cry', 1968). His first novel *Lal Shalu* brought him international acclaim and was translated into French (1963), English (1967), and Czech (1974). The novel depicts the life of an East Bengali Muslim village. In 1960 Sayyid Waliullah received the Pen Club Award, in 1961 the Prize of the Bangla Academy and in 1965 the Adamjee Prize, the most prestigious in Pakistan.

WORKS: *'Tree Without Roots', London, 1967; 'L'arbre sans racines', Paris, 1963. A.J. Shamsuddin, 'Kando, Nodi, Kando by Sayyid Waliullah, in: Bengali Academy Journal, Dhaka, Vol. 1, No. 1, April 1970.*

S.D. SEREBRYANY

Waqf

(Arabic: plural of *auqaf* from the Arabic verb *waqafa*—to devote, to bequeath, to intend for a trust) Personal property and real estate exempted from taxes, the income from which goes for the maintenance of religious and charity organizations or corporations such as **mazars*, **madrasas*, **masjids*, hospitals, etc. *Waqf* is instituted by a *waqif*, who may appoint a manager (*mutawalli*) of the property donated. Terms of donation are defined in a special document called *waqf-nama* and are ratified and stamped by a **qadi* (*qazi*). *Waqf* is inalienable, cannot be transferred or removed, and can be of two types. The first is basic, when the *waqif* loses all rights to the property donated; the second is the common, when the *waqif* and his successors keep the right to a part of the income from the property donated.

According to Pakistan's *Constitution (1973), the management of *waqfs* is exercised by the Federal Ministry of Religious Affairs and Minorities Affairs through special departments established in all the provinces.

YU.V. GANKOVSKY

Waris Shah (1735–98)

Poet. Waris Shah was a *Punjabi-language poet who made an important contribution to the genre of the romantic poem, *qissa-kavi*, that came to *Punjabi literature from Persian classical poetry. His best known work is *Heer and Ranjha* (1775), a long epic poem about the tragic love of a rich peasant girl for a shepherd flute-player. The poem contains vivid scenes of peasant life.

N.I. TOLSTAYA

Wasti, Syed Razi (1929–1999)

Scholar. Syed Razi Wasti earned his MA from Punjab University he did his BA (Hons) in History from the University of London in 1959, and also obtained his PhD from the University of London. He served as professor and head of the Department of History, Government College, Lahore. He was Director of the Historical Research Institute (1965–69). Syed Razi Wasti was awarded the *Quaid-i-Azam centenary Gold Medal in 1976 and the Allama *Iqbal centenary Gold Medal in 1977.

WORKS: *'Lord Minto and the Indian Nationalist Movement. 1905–1910', Oxford, 1964; 'The Political Triangle in India', Lahore, 1976; (ed.) 'Memoirs and other Writings of Syed Amir Ali', Lahore, 1968.*

H. MALIK

Wazir

A *Pashtun tribe, from the Kerlarni group of tribes. Wazirs have two branches: Darwesh *Khel (or Musa Darwesh Khel), and Masud (or Mahsud Wazir). They inhabit the political agencies of North *Waziristan and South Waziristan. Wazir settlements also occur in the districts of *Bannu and Dera Ismail Khan in the *North West Frontier Province. The population is estimated to be more than 600,000.

BIBLIOGRAPHY: *L. Temirkhanov, 'Eastern Pashtuns: Main Issues of Modern History', Moscow, 1987 (in Russian); A.S. Ahmed, 'Tribes and States in Central and South Asia', in: Asian Affairs, Vol. XI, Part II, London, 1980.*

YU.V. GANKOVSKY

Waziristan

A historical-geographical region in the north-west of Pakistan, between the rivers *Kurram and Gomal. Its area is about 30,000 sq.km. Administratively, it forms part of the *Federally Administered Tribal Areas (FATA) and is subdivided into two political agencies—Northern Waziristan and Southern Waziristan. The northern part is a heavily mountainous area, interspersed with fertile valleys in the lower reaches of the rivers Kurram, Kaitu and Tochi. The population was 357,867 in 1998, the capital is the town of Miramshah. The southern part is an arid barren area with a population 423,592 (1998). The capital is Wana. The most numerous tribe in Waziristan is the *Pashtun tribe of *Wazirs who are mainly engaged in cattle-breeding. They are also known to be excellent craftsmen. Other tribes include Dawar (Daur), *Bhitasni, to name just two. Waziristan preserved its independence until the second half of the nineteenth century. In 1893, it was annexed to British India. Since August 1947, it has been part of Pakistan.

M.YU. MOROZOVA

Wazir Khan Mosque

The Wazir Khan Mosque lies within the walls of the Old City of Lahore. It was built in 1634 and is one of the treasures of architecture in Lahore. The Mosque follows the rectangular floor pattern with octagonal minarets at each corner. The minarets are 10 metres in diameter and are crowned with domed kiosks. The high portal entry is decorated with fine floral and geometrical parti-coloured ornaments of glazed tiles. The red brick inner walls of the courtyard are decorated with panels of glazed mosaics and inscriptions.

A.B. RALLEV

Wesh

(in *Pashtu: division, sharing, a share in inheritance) A tradition of regular re-allotment of land among Pakistan *Pashtuns.

YU.V. GANKOVSKY

West Pakistan

According to the 1956 and 1962 Constitutions, one of the two provinces of the Federal Islamic Republic of Pakistan, covering an area of some 807,000 sq.km. It was divided into twelve divisions plus the *Federally Administered Tribal Areas consisting of six agencies. The administrative centre was Lahore. The heads of the executive authority, or Governors, were appointed by the President. The Governors in their turn appointed members of the provincial government. Legislative power was in the hands of the Provincial Legislative Assembly, elected for five years. The province of West Pakistan was abolished by a decree of President A.M. Yahya *Khan of 30 March 1970. In its place, four autonomous provinces, *Punjab, *Sindh, *Balochistan, and the NWFP, were re-established, as well as the federally administered Islamabad Capital Territory.

BIBLIOGRAPHY: *Yuri Gankovsky, V.N. Moskalenko, 'The Three Constitutions of Pakistan', Lahore, 1978.*

YU.V. GANKOVSKY

Wheeler, Sir Robert Eric Mortimer (1890–1976)

Archaeologist. He was a British archaeologist and one of the founders of the Indian and Pakistan archaeological school. From 1913, and after an interval for the First World War, he studied Roman Britain and the Roman provinces in general. He later studied Oriental archaeology and in 1944 he headed the Indian Archaeological Survey. In 1947 he became an archaeological consultant for the Pakistan government. His diggings in the Indus valley, books on the ancient history of the East and cultural ties between Rome and India and other countries and regions of the ancient world, won him worldwide recognition.

WORKS: *'Early India and Pakistan to Asoka', London, 1959; 'Charsada, a Metropolis of the North-West Frontier', Oxford, 1962; 'The Indus Civilization', Cambridge, 1960; 'Five Thousand Years of Pakistan', London, 1950.*

B.YA. STAVISKY

White Huns

See, Ephtalites.

Wichitra Wina

A variety of the **wina*, it has six primary and numerous auxiliary strings. While performing, the *wina* player holds a wire plectrum in his right hand and a small glass disc for dampening sound in his left. It is commonly used in the classical music of Pakistan and north India, and also in certain forms of popular music.

I. PIRACHA

Wicker work

This has been practised in Pakistan since antiquity. Wicker items can often be seen in rural homes, but they are used in cities too. Wicker items are made of grass, twigs, bamboo, reeds, palm leaves, and wheat straw.

Wicker baskets of various sizes and forms are used for storing and carrying foodstuffs, mostly grain, but also vegetables, fruit, and sweets. A famous product of the *Punjab is a spiral pattern basket woven out of wild grass. Parts of these baskets are fastened together by palm leaves. Their decorative ornament is reminiscent of *phulkari* embroideries. In the *Punjab, *Sindh, and *Balochistan baskets are often embellished with shells, beads, and feathers, which makes them especially striking. *Dabbi* baskets, used for storing bread are distinguished by fine craftsmanship and expressive austerity of form. These are woven out of wheat straw. Baskets in Sindh are characterized by lattice-like patterns. Baskets used by snake charmers are remarkable for their detailed craftsmanship. Traditionally, only men take part in their manufacture. Sandals and bags from Balochistan woven out of palmetto leaves are extremely elegant. Mats are woven out of grass and leaves of various kinds. They are used to cover floors and are also used temporary shelters.

O.V. LYSTSOVA

Wilcox, Wayne Ayres (1932–74)

Scholar. He was an American Orientalist, political scholar, and historian. He was Professor of Political Science at Columbia University, New York. He studied at Pardue University from 1950-54 and Columbia from 1955-58. In 1960 he received a doctorate from Columbia. He was Research Fellow of the Institute of War and Peace Studies of Columbia University (1961-66); Senior Research Fellow of the RAND Corporation (1967-71); Consultant, Department of State on the problems of the Middle East and Southern Asia; and cultural attaché at the US Embassy in Britain (1971-74). Wilcox organized the Pakistan Council of the US Asian Society, was its first president, and headed the Pakistan Centre at Columbia University. He died in an air crash.

WORKS: *'Pakistan. Consolidation of a Nation', New York, 1968; 'India, Pakistan and the Rise of China', New York, 1964; 'Asia and United States Policy', Englewood Cliffs, New Jersey, 1967; 'The Emergence of Bangladesh', Washington, 1973.*

YU.V. GANKOVSKY

Wina

(also *Bina*, Veena) One of the most ancient Indian plucked string instruments of the lute type. Sometimes the word *wina* is used when referring to musical instruments in general. In its many varieties, the *wina* was the most prominent instrument in musical culture throughout South Asia. Two varieties of the *wina* survived the *rudra* and the *saraswati*, which became the prototype of the modern *wina*. It is a lute with a long curving neck, twenty-four frets and two resonators. The main resonator is in the form of a wooden cup, or a pumpkin shell, and another at the other end of the neck that also serves as support. It has four main strings and three resonant ones.

I. PIRACHA

Wolpert, Stanley (1937–)

Scholar. Distinguished Professor of South Asian History, Stanley Wolpert visited India for the first time as a Marine Engineer in 1948, and has since that time remained a student of Indo-Pakistani History, which he has taught at UCLA since 1958. Professor Wolpert is the author of eighteen books on South Asian History.

WORKS: *'New History of India', sixth edition New Delhi 2001, 1977; 'Nine Hours To Rama', New York, 1962; 'Tilak and Gokhale', California, 1962; 'Morley and India', Berkeley, 1967; 'Roots of Confrontation in South Asia', 1982; 'Jinnah of Pakistan', New York, 1984; 'Zulfi Bhutto of Pakistan', New York, 1993; 'Nehru: A Tryst With Destiny', New York, 1996; 'Gandhi's Passion: The Life and Legacy of Mahatma Gandhi', New York, 2001.*

YU.V. GANKOVSKY

Women's Action Forum

(WAF) This organisation was set up in September 1981 in Karachi. It united the liberal and progressive women's organizations of the country, including the Democratic Women's Association of Pakistan, the All-Pakistan Women's Association, the Lahore Club of Working Women and others.

The *Shariat Court's decision to flog a 15-year-old girl caused a general outburst of indignation among women and motivated them to join together to protect their rights. The WAF is not an organization in the strict sense of the word: it is a group that influences public opinion and looks into women's problems. It has neither president nor any other administrators. The programme of action is determined by the Working Committee, convened once a month. WAF is in fact a constantly growing network of women's organizations brought together by shared aims: to upgrade the status of Pakistani women; protect their legal, social and economic rights; contribute to women's higher level of political awareness and education, realization of international charters and conventions on the rights of women.

The WAF examines national legislation and attracts the attention of the government, public opinion, and the press to the legal acts that infringe upon women's rights.

The Forum gives free legal assistance, conducts seminars and symposiums on the problems concerning women from all walks of life, organizes mass demonstrations and campaigns in defence of women's rights. Every year it marks International Women's Day (8 March).

WAF assumed considerable prominence during the military rule of General Ziaul *Haq, when it was able to mount visible campaigns to arouse public opinion against the bigoted excesses of that regime. It has remained an active and energetic entity and had led to the formation of different organisation such as JAC (Joint Action Committee) and War Against Rape (WAR) with special emphases. WAF is still an umbrella organisation and has branches is all large cities of the country.

F.A. ABDRAKHMANOVA

Wriggins, W. Howard (1918–)

Political Scientist. He is a political scientist and diplomat; professor of political science, director of the Southern Asia Institute; and head of the Pakistan Centre of Columbia University, New York. After graduating from the University of Chicago, he received his doctorate from Yale (USA) in 1952 and then taught at Yale and Johns Hopkins (USA). From 1958-60 Wriggins headed the Department of Foreign Policy of the Library of Congress of the US. in 1961-67 he worked at the US State Department and in 1973-74 he taught at Oxford University. He has studied and organized a great number of research projects on the political problems of Pakistan and Southern Asia.

WORKS: *(ed.) 'Pakistan in Transition', Islamabad, 1975.*

YU.V. GANKOVSKY

Y

Yaktara

This is a very simple variety of a long lute used in Pakistan. It has one or more open strings and a round pumpkin-shell resonator. The hole is sometimes covered with stretched leather. It is used to accompany singing in the itinerant musicians' tradition.

I. PIRACHA

Yaqub, Mohammad, Maulvi Sir (1879–1942)

Statesman. A graduate of Aligarh University, Maulvi Mohammad Yaqub was elected to the Indian Legislative Assembly in 1923. He served as it's Deputy-President between 1927 and 1930. In 1930 he became it's President. Sir Mohammad Yaqub joined the *All-India Muslim League in 1907. In 1908 he became an office bearer of the London branch. Sir Mohammad Yaqub had opposed the non-cooperation policies of the Ali Brothers, but was bitterly critical of Britain's Turkish policy while presiding over the AIML Calcutta session. This represented the faction having broken away from Sir Mohammad *Shafi because it did not wish to co-operate with the *Simon Commission.

Sir Mohammad Yaqub became Honorary Secretary of the All-India Muslim League in February 1928 but, by 17 August, he faced a no-confidence motion, which he survived as a result of *Jinnah's support. He resisted behind-the-scenes efforts by Sir Fazli *Husain to wind up the AIML by merging it with the All-India Muslim Conference. When Sir Zafrullah *Khan resigned as President of the AIML to join the Viceroy's Executive Council, the Acting President Mian Abdul Aziz arbitrarily declared the post of Honorary Secretary vacant. On 28 May 1933 Mian Abdul Aziz was himself removed from office. Sir Mohammad Yaqub was brought back as Secretary when Hafiz Hidayat Husain resigned. In 1936 Sir Mohammad Yaqub retired, offering his support to the new incumbent Liaquat Ali *Khan. In 1937 Sir Mohammad Yaqub veered away from the AIML and inclined to the British sponsored National Agriculturist Party. In 1938 Sir Mohammad Yaqub joined the Viceroy's Executive Council as an acting member, representing the Council of State, and remained a member until his death.

YU.V. GANKOVSKY

Yueh-Chih (Yeh-Chi)

See, Ephtalites.

Yusufi, Mushtaque Ahmad (1925–)

Writer. A banker by profession, Mushtaque Ahmad Yusufi, was the first post-partition humorist to achieve popularity and critical acclaim. His satire is sharper than that of his contemporaries and he debunks nostalgia, social oddities and eccentricities based on complacency and ignorance. He shuns romance and sentiment, expressing his sparkling wit and perception in a style that is epigrammatic and alliterative. His autobiography *Zar Guzasht*, has a warmth his earlier essays and his latest book not evident in *Ab-i-Gum,* transcends the limits of mirth to give a sense of pathos to the fringes of his humour. He was awarded the *Hilal-i-Imtiaz* in 2001.

WORKS: *'Chiragh Taley', Lahore, 1961; 'Khakam Badahan', 1969; 'Zar Guzasht', 1976; 'Ab-i-Gum', Karachi, 1989.*

BIBLIOGRAPHY: *N. Durrani (ed.) Seep Special Number, Karachi, 1968.*

A.S. SUKHOCHEV

Yusufzai

A *Pashtun tribe, belonging to the Sarbani group of tribes. They fall into two branches: the highlanders and the lowlanders. The highland Yusufzais live in the *Dir and *Swat districts of the *North West Frontier Province. Their main clans are the Maliza, or Mallezai, Akozai, Isazai, and the Iliaszai. The lowland Yusufzais inhabit the northern areas of the *Peshawar Valley. Their clans are the Utmanzai, and Usmanzai, of the Razar. All the lowland Yusufzais are also known by a common name: Mandan or Mandanr. The total population is 1.5 million (estimation).

BIBLIOGRAPHY: *L. Temirkhanov, 'Eastern Pashtuns: Main Issues of Modern History', Moscow, 1987 (in Russian); H.W. Bellew, 'A General Report on the Yusufzais', Lahore, 1977.*

YU.V. GANKOVSKY

Z

Zafrul Hasan, Dr Syed (1879–1949)

Scholar. Dr Syed Zafrul Hasan was born in Ambala, East Punjab and was educated at the Aligarh Muslim University (AMU). He continued his education in Germany where he obtained his PhD. He joined the AMU Department of Philosophy as lecturer and retired as professor. He was the co-author, with Dr S. Afzal *Qadri of *The Problem of Indian Muslims and its Solution* (Aligarh, 1939). He died in Rawalpindi two years after partition.

YU.V. GANKOVSKY

Zaidi

A moderate *Shia sect founded by Zaid ibn-Ali (d. 6 January 740). Zaidi religious dogmas are similar to Sunni ones. They reject the holy nature of *imamat* and the 'hidden imam', and they do not practice **taqayyia*. They had a state in Yemen and followers in Oman till the mid 20th century.

M.R. KAZIMI

Zaidi, Zafar Hasnain (1939–2001)

Scientist. Zafar H. Zaidi studied for his MSc in Chemistry at the University of *Sindh in 1963, and for his PhD at Leeds University in 1968. He was associated with the Pakistan Council of Scientific and Industrial Research (1968–78). He joined the University of Karachi as Associate Professor in the Husain Ebrahim Jamal Institute of Chemistry in 1978 and was appointed Vice-Chancellor of the University of Karachi in 1997. He died in office. Z.H. Zaidi founded the teaching of, and research in, protein chemistry in Pakistan.

M.R. KAZIMI

Zakat

(Arabic: purification, purity) A Muslim tax in favour of the poor. One of the five **rukns*, 'pillars of faith', of Islam. The general rate is 2.5 per cent of unused monetary worth of an individual.

YU.V. GANKOVSKY

Zaman, Fakhar (1940–)

Writer/Poet. Fakhar Zaman is a *Punjabi language writer and poet. He has to his credit several collections of verse and the novel *Sentenced to Death*. Zaman was also a noted public figure, who was persecuted under the Ziaul *Haq regime for his links with the opposition of the time. His novel, a synthesis of the best achievements of critical realism and modernism, has been translated into Urdu, Hindi, English and Ukrainian.

WORKS: *'Bandivan', Amritsar, 1981.*

I.D. SEREBRYAKOV

Zaman, Mukhtar (1924–2003)

Writer/Journalist. Mukhtar Zaman was a student activist before independence. He served as Secretary-General of the All India Muslim Students Federation in 1946-47. He started his career as a journalist on the *Morning News* of Calcutta. He was assigned to report on the birth of Pakistan from Dhaka. He subsequently joined the *Morning News* there. Among his professional assignments was working for BBC Urdu Service in London and serving as Director-General of the Associated Press of Pakistan. During the years preceding independence, he came into close contact with the founders of Pakistan. During the Organization of the Islamic Summit Conference in Lahore in 1947, he was able to interview most of the leaders. In the *Urdu language he was regarded as a humorist for the essays titled *Baton Ke Kharboozay* ('The Melons of Conversation'). He was on the editorial board of *Ghalib,* the Urdu quarterly founded by Faiz Ahmed *Faiz.

WORKS: *'Students Role in the Pakistan Movement', Karachi, 1978.*

YU.V. GANKOVSKY

Zamindar

(Persian: *zamin*, land, plus the suffix *dar* denoting an owner) Owner of a plot of land or another source of income in India in the sixteenth to twentieth centuries. In the *Mughal empire the term *zamindar* was used with three different meanings:

1. Tax-payer possessing hereditary alienable rights on his land, and constituting the upper crust of the village community. This stratum was well represented in the Gangetic Valley and in Rajasthan. In Bengal, part of Bihar, Orissa, northern Andhra and Gujarat, *zamindar* tax-payers were mostly large-scale landowners subletting land to smaller holders.

2. A middleman in the collection of taxes, head of a larger community, a *Chaudhri (see,* Chaudhury) in north India, or *Deshmukh* and *Deshpande* in Maharashtra. It was stipulated that the middlemen could retain up to 10 per cent of the tax money for themselves. In fact, they usually appropriated more than 10 per cent.

3. Vassal princes who were duty-bound to the Mughals to serve them or pay tribute–*pishkash*. These three strata had one thing in common–they had hereditary rights as distinct from the **jagirdars* and government officials. In the colonial period a landowner in north India either payed a fixed tax (see: Permanently Settled Lands, the system of) or a tax which changed every thirty years (*mahalwari*). *Zamindar* land-ownership was abolished in the 1950s by redemption in East Bengal and India.

BIBLIOGRAPHY: *L.B. Alayev, 'Village Community in North India', Moscow, 1981 (in Russian); S.N. Hasan, 'Zamindars under the Mughals–Land Control and Social Struggle in Indian History, Madison, 1969.*

L.B. ALAYEV

Zaheer, Sajjad (1905–73)

Writer. Sajjad Zaheer was a writer and public figure who wrote in *Urdu. Coming from an aristocratic family, he graduated from Lucknow University and later from Oxford. He became a member of the Communist Party of India in 1930 and served as General Secretary of the All-India Progressive Writers Association. He edited a number of newspapers, published by the Communist Party of India, while pursuing his own writing career as a novelist. His collection of five stories *Angare* ('Sparks', 1932) was banned. His famous writings Bimar ('Invalid'), a play; *London-ki ek Raat* ('A Night in London', 1937), a short novel; *Roushnai* ('Light', 1956), reminiscences about the setting up of the All-India Association of Progressive Writers; *Pighla Nilam* ('Melted Sapphire', 1964), a collection of poems; *Zikr-i-Hafiz* ('A Memoir about Hafiz'), a literary study; *Sajjad Zaheer ke Mazamin* ('Articles'), published posthumously in 1979. He translated many works from English and French. Sajjad took part in the Solidarity Movement of Afro-Asian Writers.

BIBLIOGRAPHY: *A.Q. Abdali, 'Banne-Bhai', Asansol, 1986; A. Ahmad, 'Sajjad Zaheer', Karachi 1992; A. Ahmad (ed.), 'Banne-Bhai', Karachi, 1991.*

A.S. SUKHOCHEV

Zarubin, Ivan Ivanovich (1887–1964)

Scholar. He was a specialist in Eastern studies, linguist and ethnographer, and the founder of the *Balochi studies in Russia. After graduating from St. Petersburg University (1912) and the Department of Law at Kharkov University he became a professor, working mainly in two institutions: the Museum of Anthropology and Ethnography where he headed the department of the Muslim peoples of Central Asia, and the Institute of Language and Thinking. Zarubin lectured at the Leningrad Institute of Living Oriental Languages, at Leningrad University, and courses for national minorities at the Herzen Teacher Training Institute in Leningrad. He organized expeditions to study the languages and cultures of the peoples of the East in the Pamirs (1914-15), in Central Asia (1918), Tajikistan (1926-27), and Turkmenistan (1928-29).

WORKS: *'On the Studies of the Balochi Language and Folklore,' in: Notes of the Collegium of Oriental Scholars, Vol. 5, 1930 (in Russian); 'Balochi Fairytales', Part I, Leningrad, 1932, Part 3, Moscow-Leningrad, 1949.*

V.V. MOSHKALO

Zebunnisa (1639–1702)

Princess/Poetess. A Mughal royal princess, Zebunnisa was a Persian-language poetess who wrote under the pseudonym '*Makhfi*'. The elder daughter of Emperor Aurangzeb, her poetic talent and erudition won her public admiration in her time. After the failed *coup* of Prince Muhammad Akbar against Aurangzeb in 1681, Zebunnisa, as a party to the conspiracy, was punished by her father with life imprisonment in the Salimgarh Fortress.

Zebunnisa left nearly 4,000 verses and Persian **ghazals,* enriching them with the Indian style. Her meditative lyrical verse is imbued with her personal tragedy and her unfulfilled wishes. She compiled a commentary of the Quran, *Zeb-i-Tafasir* ('The Beauty of Interpretation'). *(See also: Sabk-i-Hindi).*

BIBLIOGRAPHY: *G.Yu. Aliev, 'Persian-language Literature of India', Moscow, 1968 (in Russian).*

M.M. OSINOVA

Zhob

1. A river in the north-east of *Balochistan province in Pakistan, approximately 320 km. long. It is the southern tributary of the Gomal and flows from the south-west towards the north-east through a wide valley covered with sandhills. The river dries up in summer, but the underground waters are very near to the surface. More than 400 water springs scatter the slopes.

2. A district in the Quetta region, Balochistan province. Its area covers 27,129 sq.km. with a population of 362,000 (1981). The administrative centre is the town of Zhob, (*see*, Zhob Plateau) with a population of 38,380 people in 1998.

YU.V. GANKOVSKY

Zhob Culture

This Neolithic culture has sites in the Zhob valley in northern *Balochistan. A. Stein in 1927 and W.A. *Fairservis in 1950 studied the Periano Ghundai and Mughal Ghundai settlements. The upper level in Periano Ghundai was disturbed by secondary burials with cremations made in urns, and was identified by Fairservis of a phase of Zhob culture; S. Piggott was the first to identify Zhob culture, guiding himself by the typical patterns of oxen on vessels. Brick houses on stone foundations were discovered in Periano Ghundai. Finds of clay female figurines of the Mother-goddess (*see,* Quetta Culture), figurines of humped oxen (zebu), stone leaf-shaped arrows and copper, alabaster and bone implements were made. The wares have black patterns against a red background. The patterns are zoomorphic and geometric and include goats and oxen. There are analogies with the pre-*Harappan sites in Balochistan, the culture of Quetta and the neighbouring settlements of Loralai–Rana Ghundai and Dabar Kot.

BIBLIOGRAPHY: *A. Stein, 'An Archaeological Tour in Waziristan and Northern Balochistan. Memoirs of the Archaeological Survey of India', No. 37, 1929; W.A. Fairservis, 'The Roots of Ancient India', Chicago and London, 1957.*

N.M. VINOGRADOVA

Zhob Plateau

This mountainous region in the north of Balochistan borders on the Sulaiman Mountains to the east. It forms part of the Iranian Plateau and consists of several ranges and highlands of up to 3,500 metres and higher upto 3,578 metres. The climate is sharply continental and arid. The vegetation is predominantly of desert and dry steppe variety. The mountain slopes are overgrown with mountain and savannah flora, subtropical forests, and spare growths of trees. Saksaul thickets, tamarisk, juniper, and milk vetch are widespread. There are small irrigated areas where wheat, barley, peas, melons, gourds, and fodder grasses are grown. The mountain slopes are used for grazing. In the valleys there are orchards of apricot trees, almond, peaches, pears, apple trees, and fig palms. Chromite mining is of economic importance to this region.

M.YU. MOROZOVA

Zoroastrians

See, Parsi.

Zikri

(Arabic: *Zakara*—to mention, *zikr*—mention, rememberance of Allah's name) A *Sufi sect founded by Sayid Muhammad Jaunpuri (1443–1504). In 1459 he performed Haj in Mecca. In 1499 he announced himself a Mahdi. Later he was forced to emigrate to *Sindh. His followers practice **taqayyia*. Currently, a community of Zikris lives in *Balochistan.

YU.V. GANKOVSKY

Ziring, Lawrence (1928–)

Scholar. Professor of Political Science and Director, Development Administration Programmes at Western Michigan University. Dr Ziring began his tenure at WMU in 1967, having taught earlier at Columbia University, 1960-61, Lafayette College, 1961-64, and Syracuse University 1964-67. His major fields of are international relations, law and organization, and interest comparative government. Dr Ziring has also served as a Syracuse/Ford Foundation Advisor, Pakistan Administrative Staff College, 1964-66, and Visiting Professor, Dhaka University, Bangladesh, 1959-60 (then *East Pakistan), and again in 1986 under contract with the Asia Foundation.

Dr Ziring was educated at Columbia University where he received his BS degree in 1955, a Masters in International Affairs in 1957, and PhD in 1962. He also holds a certificate in Persian Studies from Princeton University, 1961. He was the first American in the Pakistan Studies Programme at Columbia University, studying with Dr Ishtiaq Hussain Qureshi from 1955 to 1960. Columbia University Fellowships enabled him to study in Pakistan in 1957 and 1959-60. It was during his last Columbia sponsored programme that he was recruited to teach political science in the Department of Political Science, Dhaka University. During this period

Dr Ziring also held a National Defence Education Fellowship.

Dr Ziring's doctoral dissertation is titled 'The Failure of Democracy in Pakistan: East Pakistan and the Central Government, 1947-58.'

WORKS: *The Ayub Khan Era: Politics in Pakistan, 1958-69 (Syracuse, 1971); Pakistan: The Long View, Duke, 1977; Pakistan: The Enigma of Political Development (Dawson, Kent, 1980); The Subcontinent in World Politics, Praeger, 1982; Pakistan's Foreign Policy with S.M. Burke, second edition, 1990; Bangladesh from Mujib to Ershad, Oxford, 1992.*

YU.V. GANKOVSKY

Zograf, Georgy Alexandrovich (1928–)

Scholar. A philologist, specializing in Oriental studies, he graduated from the Oriental department of Leningrad University (1951) and studied the grammatical structure of Urdu and other new Indo-European languages. He translated works by Mir Amman, Mirza Ruswa, Kh. A. Abbas, Krishan Chandar, Yashpal, and others into Russian. A DSc (Philology), Zograf was also a research member of the Leningrad Branch of the Institute of Oriental Studies of RAS from 1954.

WORKS: *'Description of the Manuscripts in Hindi and Punjabi at the Institute of Oriental Studies', Moscow, 1960; 'Languages of India, Pakistan, Ceylon and Nepal', Moscow, 1960; 'Hindustani at the Turn of the Twentieth Century', Moscow, 1961; 'The Languages of Southern Asia', Moscow, 1990 (all in Russian).*

A.S. SUKHOCHEV

HISTORICAL PREVIEW PRE-1947

Ian Talbot

The genesis of Pakistan can be traced to the emergence of Muslim separatism in the closing decades of the nineteenth century. Separatist sentiment was institutionalised with the formation in December 1906 of the *All-India Muslim League. Its creation was precipitated by anxieties arising from the prospect of further constitutional reform and the Hindu revivalism surrounding the *swadeshi* movement in Bengal. The attempt to give territorial expression to Muslim separatist sentiment dates to Mohammad *Iqbal's 1930 *Muslim League Presidential address. He called for a Muslim State in North West India encompassing the *North West Frontier Province, *Punjab, *Sindh and *Balochistan. Three years later Chaudhuri Rahmat Ali, in a pamphlet entitled *Now or Never* coined the term 'Pakistan.'

The schemes for Pakistan drawn up in the early 1930s, however, only entered the realm of practical politics after the experience of Congress rule in India from 1937-39. The Congress, despite winning popular Muslim support only in the Frontier, formed governments in 7 out of 11 of India's provinces. The Muslim League had itself done poorly in the elections, especially in the Muslim majority provinces, with the exception of Bengal. In what was to become the pivotal province of the freedom struggle, the Punjab, it had been eclipsed by the cross-community Unionist Party. The period of Congress government brought home for the first time to many Muslims that they would be ruled by a Hindu dominated Congress once the British had left. This experience helped to create common interests which had been lacking earlier between politicians in the Muslim minority and majority provinces. Celebrations were held throughout India on 22 December 1939 when the Congress ministries resigned in the wake of the Viceroy declaring war on India's behalf. The Muslim League took advantage during the war years of the conflict between the Congress and the colonial state. It exploited the vacuum created by the imprisonment of many Congress leaders following the British repression of the 1942 'Quit India' movement.

Simultaneously the Pakistan demand provided a popular rallying cry for the Muslim community. Pakistan was not mentioned by name, although the 1940 *Lahore Resolution was subsequently dubbed the Pakistan Resolution. Its third paragraph called for the grouping of contiguous Muslim majority areas in north-west and north-east India into 'Independent States in which the constituent units would be autonomous and sovereign.' The Pakistan demand's status was raised by the *Cripps Mission which arrived in India in 1942. Although the Mission failed, it conceded in theory the future partition of India. Further crucial events in the increasing support for the Muslim League struggle were *Jinnah's political success at the expense of Gandhi in September 1944 and the Viceroy Lord Wavell in July 1945; he manoeuvred Gandhi during their negotiations in Bombay into accepting the Partition of India in theory; at the Simla Conference he successfully demanded that all Muslim members of the Indian Executive Council should belong to the Muslim League. This outcome was a bitter blow for the Unionists who had sought a seat. The Muslim League thus approached the crucial 1946 elections in the Punjab in a greatly strengthened position.

The Muslim League breakthrough in the Punjab paved the way for Pakistan. It was only, however, with the failure of the 1946 *Cabinet Mission that the partition of India became virtually inevitable. Agreement was not finally reached until the 3 June Plan 1947 (see, Third June Plan). The Pakistan which emerged was a 'moth eaten' state shorn of the East Punjab and West Bengal. Its birth was accompanied by horrific massacres which sparked off unforeseen mass migrations of around 12 million people each way across the Indo-Pakistan border.

THE PARTITION OF BENGAL

The partition of Bengal took effect on 16 October 1905. The action was based on sound administrative grounds given that the province at the time contained about a quarter of the total population of *British India. The decision was unpopular because of the lack of consultation. It also coincided with economic distress among the educated classes because of the impact of inflation on their fixed incomes following four successive poor rice harvests. Many upper class Hindus saw the resulting creation of an eastern Muslim province as imperial divide and rule strategy. Muslims had not at first urged partition, but rallied to its maintenance in the face of an increasingly virulent campaign.

The *swadeshi* campaign against the partition involved the boycott of British goods. The movement spread from Calcutta to the rural hinterland. The campaign was popularised by students and local newspapers attached to the so-called extremist wing of the Congress. In a foretaste of later Gandhian campaigns, foreign cloth was burned and National Schools and colleges established. The patriotic song *Bande Mataram* ('Hail Mother') became a rallying cry for the movement. Its aggressive Hindu imagery alienated Muslims and provided a catalyst for the formation of a separate Muslim political party.

CABINET MISSION PLAN

The decision in January 1946 to send a three member Cabinet Mission comprising of Pethick-Lawrence, Stafford Cripps and A.V. Alexander to India fulfilled the British promise of discussions on the form of a constitution making body following the holding of elections. The issue had not become whether power would be transferred but the form of the post-imperial order. The Mission's preferred option was for a united India on strategic grounds. By mid-June it appeared that a plan had been agreed for the grouping of provinces into three sections and with a central government confined to control of defence, foreign affairs and communications. The Muslim League had accepted the scheme because of the autonomy it gave to the six Muslim provinces, although this fell short of a sovereign Pakistan. The Congress wanted a much stronger centre and Nehru's hedging around the future working of the grouping element led the League to withdraw its acceptance on 29 July 1946. The British then went ahead with the establishment of a Congress only 14 member Interim Government. This forced the League into adopting direct action. This course of action following from the failure of the Federal scheme of the Cabinet Mission meant that the Partition of the subcontinent became virtually inevitable.

CRIPPS MISSION

Sir Stafford Cripps, the Leader of the Commons was sent by Churchill to India in March 1942. The background to his mission was the growing Japanese threat following the fall of Singapore and the need to demonstrate good faith to the Americans who were now war-time allies, but had traditionally voiced anti-Imperialist sentiment. Cripps promised India dominion status at the end of the war. In the short term all that was on offer, however, was an expansion of the Viceroy's Executive Council. Crucially there was to be no Indian control over defence. The Cripps Offer held out for the Muslim League support in theory for the Pakistan demand in that it included a proviso that no part of India could be forced to join the post-war arrangements. The Mission failed to the relief of Churchill because of Gandhi's opposition within the Congress. Its rejection led to the British repression of the ensuing Quit India movement. Many of the Congress leaders spent the final three years of the war in jail. Jinnah was able to take advantage of this in consolidating the Muslim League's position.

DELIVERANCE DAY

On 22 December 1939, the *All-India Muslim League celebrated a day of deliverance throughout India following the resignation of the provincial Congress ministries. They had relinquished power on the order of the Congress high command. The action was designed in protest at the Viceroy Lord Linlithgow's declaration without consultation that India was at war. The Pirpur Report of November 1938 had highlighted Muslim grievances in Congress run provinces. The Shareef Report which dealt especially with Bihar followed a year later. Jinnah dubbed the resignations a deliverance from the 'tyranny, oppression and injustice' of the Congress Governments. Deliverance Day meetings were held in mosques and public places after the *Jumma* (Friday) prayers. They marked an important step in forging Muslim unity in advance of the raising of the Pakistan demand. Ceremonial activity included the hoisting of the Muslim League flag and the presence of detachments of the Muslim National Guards.

KHILAFAT MOVEMENT

From the first decade of the twentieth century onwards a section of North Indian Muslims led by the brothers Muhammad and Shaukat *Ali became concerned about western encroachment on the power of the Turkish Sultan who held responsibility for safeguarding the Islamic holy sites of Mecca and Medina and was accorded the status of *Khalifah* or spiritual head of the worldwide Muslim community. This pan-Islamic sentiment intensified with Turkey's defeat in the First World War which further undermined the *Khalifah*'s status. The Khilafat campaign brought together younger politicians, a section of the **ulema* and was used by Gandhi to bring Muslim support into his wider nationalist campaigns. The Khilafat struggle was the largest Muslim mass mobilisation before the Pakistan movement. It marked a high point of Hindu-Muslim co-operation in the agitation against the colonial state. Nevertheless such leaders as Muhammad Ali even at this time only accepted Gandhi's attachment to non-violence as a political expediency. The Moplah rebellion within India (August-December 1921) revived Hindu-Muslim tensions. The decisive blow to the Khilafat movement, however, was dealt by events in Turkey. The rise in secular nationalism was marked by the abolition of the office of *Khalifah* in March 1924.

KHUDAI KHIDMATGAR (ALSO RED SHIRTS)

The *Khudai Khidmatgars* (Servants of God) were powerful exponents of *Pushtun nationalism and of resistance to colonial rule. The *Khudai Khidmatgars* were established in November 1929 by Abdul Ghaffar *Khan on quasi-military lines. Abdul Ghaffar Khan's message was one of social and religious reform through education. He also articulated grievances against the large pro-British landowning *Khans. The *Khudai Khidmatgars* were popularly known as the Red Shirts because their uniforms were dyed with red brick dust. They received support from the Congress especially from the time of the 1930 Civil Disobedience campaign onwards in which a number of Red Shirts were killed. They represented important allies for the Congress as the Pakistan Movement intensified. Abdul Ghaffar Khan because of his simple lifestyle, deeply religious, but non-communal outlook and commitment to the cause of Indian independence by means of non-violent struggle, became dubbed as the 'Frontier Gandhi.' It was only after the 1946 elections which installed another *Khudai Khidmatgar* government that the Muslim League began to achieve a breakthrough in the Frontier region. The *Khudai Khidmatgars* peacefully boycotted the July 1947 referendum which recorded support for accession to Pakistan. The *Khudai Khidmatgar*/Congress ministry remained in office at the time of Pakistan's creation.

KRISHAK PRAJA PARTY

Fazlul *Haq, the leading Bengali politician founded the Krishak Praja Party in April 1936. It appealed to *Bengali speaking professionals and to the tenant class. It fared especially well in the East Bengal constituencies in the 1937 provincial elections and formed a coalition government with the Muslim League until December 1941. After Haq's split with the Muslim League, it formed a component of the Progressive Coalition Assembly Party which survived in office until March 1943. By the time of the crucial 1946 provincial elections it had lost many supporters to the Muslim League. It had developed a broad base of support under the dynamic leadership of its General secretary Abul Hashim from November 1943 onwards. The Bengal League boasted the largest grassroots support of any provincial branch of the All-India Muslim League with a membership of over a million. After independence the Krishak Praja Party supporters formed the nucleus of a new party led by Fazlul Haq called the Krishak Sramik Party. This triumphed in the Spring 1954 *East Pakistan provincial elections.

LAHORE RESOLUTION

Historical resolution of the Muslim League demanding an independent state. The period of provincial Congress rule from 1937-9 questioned whether separate electorates would adequately safeguard Muslim interests when power was fully devolved into Indian hands. The ground was laid for the Muslim League's adoption of a scheme for a Muslim homeland following the deliberations of the October 1938 Sindh Provincial Muslim League Conference. The following March, Jinnah chaired a Muslim League Subcommittee which considered schemes for India's political future. This formed the background to the historic 1940 Lahore Muslim League Session. The Lahore Resolution did not mention Pakistan by name, although it became subsequently called the Pakistan Resolution. Its third paragraph called for the grouping of contiguous Muslim majority areas in north-west and north-east India into 'Independent States in which the constituent units would be autonomous and sovereign.' In 1946 the plural 'States' was removed from the wording to end any ambiguity that a confederal arrangement was anticipated in the Pakistan scheme. The Lahore Resolution provided a demand around which previously regionally divided Indian Muslim politicians could rally.

LUCKNOW PACT

Agreement between the Muslim League and Congress in 1916. The Lucknow Pact (1916) was the only occasion in modern Indian history in which the Muslim League and the Congress came to a voluntary agreement about the political future of India. The Pact provided Congress acquiescence to many of the safeguards that the Muslim League had been demanding since its formation, such as separate electorates and weightage in the Legislative Councils of those provinces in which they formed a minority of the population. In return Congress secured support for its home rule demands. Jinnah's role in bringing the Congress and the Muslim League together earned him the title, 'ambassador of Hindu-Muslim unity.' The new political environment at the end of the First World War dealt a blow to hopes that the Pact would have a lasting effect on Indian politics. The Lucknow Pact in any case was not an agreement between the whole of the Muslim and Hindu communities, but reflected the views of sections of their tiny political elites. The Muslim League had only around 800 members at the time of the Pact.

PROVINCIAL ELECTIONS–1937

The 1935 Government of India Act introduced the new constitutional development of provincial autonomy, thereby devolving more power than ever before into Indian hands. Property and educational qualifications meant that only between 1 in 7 and 1 in 10 of the population was enfranchised. Nevertheless, the elections were an important test of political opinion. The polls revealed that the Congress outside of the Frontier where it was allied with the *Khudai Khidmatgars* could not command widespread Muslim support. It had fought only 58 out of 482 Muslim seats in the provincial elections, winning just 26 of these contests. The Muslim League revealed its historic weakness in the Muslim majority provinces. It failed to capture a single seat in Sindh and the Frontier and won just one seat in the Punjab. Its best performance in the future Pakistan areas was in Bengal where it won 39 seats, three more than the Krishak Praja Party, although it polled less votes. The League's best performance was in its United Provinces heartland where it won 29 out of 64 Muslim seats. The Congress's success in the Hindu constituencies ensured that it won 716 out of 1585 seats in the provincial legislative assemblies. It was thus able to form governments in 7 of India's 11 provinces.

PROVINCIAL ELECTIONS–1946

If the Pakistan demand was to have any credibility, it was vital for the Muslim League to reverse its poor showing in the 1937 polls in the Muslim majority provinces. Its greatest breakthrough was in the Punjab which Jinnah had dubbed the 'cornerstone of Pakistan.' It recorded victories in 75 out of 86 Muslim seats in the former Unionist heartland. This opened the way for Pakistan, although the remaining Unionists soldiered on in a coalition with the Congress and the Panthic Sikhs in the 175 member Assembly. In Bengal the League also turned the tables on its Krishak Praja Party opponents and captured 115 out of 123 Muslim constituencies. In Sindh the situation was finally balanced between the League and its opponents, until a second election in December returned a clear Muslim League majority. The *Khudai Khidmatgars* still held sway in the Frontier, but a year later the Referendum campaign on Pakistan was won by the League. The earlier provincial election successes in Bengal and the Punjab had made the Pakistan demand a reality because they registered in terms the colonial state regarded as legitimate, Muslim support for a separate homeland.

RADCLIFFE AWARD

The award of land division between India and Pakistan in 1947. Sir Cyril Radcliffe, the vice-chairman of the General Council of the English Bar chaired the Punjab and Bengal Boundary Commissions that were to demarcate the Indo-Pakistan boundaries following all the parties' acceptance of the principle of Partition. Radcliffe had been recommended for this appointment in part because he had no local knowledge of the territories that were to be divided. This was supposed to ensure his impartiality, but made a complex task more difficult, especially as Radcliffe only arrived in India on 8 July 1947 and power was to be transferred on 15 August. In the absence of agreement between the Congress and Muslim League nominated members of the Commissions, Radcliffe became the final arbiter. The boundary commissions were to take into consideration, 'other factors' as well as demography in making their award. This encouraged all the parties that made representations to the public sittings of the Commissions to push the boundary as far as possible in a direction that favoured their interests. Great controversy continues to surround the Boundary Award. It is claimed that the delay in its publication until three days after independence was a contributory factor in the Partition related violence. The award of the Muslim majority district of Gurdaspur to India which provided access to *Kashmir has been attributed to Mountbatten's influencing of the award. Moreover, it is also claimed based on circumstantial evidence that Mountbatten prevailed upon Radcliffe to award the Muslim majority tehsils of Zira and Ferozepur to India. It was the Sikh community, however, that suffered the most from the Partition. Radcliffe never returned to the subcontinent and burnt his papers relating to the boundary commission.

SIMLA CONFERENCE

A conference convened at Simla by Lord Wavell in June 1945 to form a more representative Indian Executive Council. This was expected to pave the way for a new constitution making body. The conference foundered on the issue of Muslim representation. Jinnah made the demand that all Muslim members should be drawn from the Muslim League. He also put forward the demand that any measure to which Muslims objected could only be carried by a two thirds majority. The Unionist Party sought one representative on the Council. Wavell took personal responsibility for the conference's failure. A less determined negotiator than Jinnah might have bowed to the Viceroy's pressure regarding Unionist representation. In the event, both Jinnah's and the Muslim League's status was raised by deadlocking the conference. The Unionist Party suffered a major setback. The conference thus marks an important landmark in the progress towards the achievement of Pakistan.

SIMLA DEPUTATION

A body of 35 Muslims who met Viceroy Lord Minto at Simla on 1 October 1906. In their address, they claimed for a 'fair share' in any expansion of Indian representation. This was to be made with reference to the Indian Muslim community's political importance and contribution to the defence of the empire as well as its numerical strength. The deputation raised the issue of separate electorates with the viceroy. The background to the deputation was the experience especially in the United Provinces of Muslim under-representation in elected local bodies and the use by Hindu leaders of such bodies to restrict cow slaughter and to alter procession routes at festival times. While some Indian nationalist writers have maintained that the deputation was encouraged by the British as a 'command performance', there is little evidence for this. The initiative for the deputation came from Mohsinul *Mulk the secretary of the Aligarh College. The British nevertheless welcomed the fact that there was a body of Indian opinion that stood outside the Congress. They also accorded the deputation with a greater representative character than it really possessed. There was, for example, just one Bengal representative, while there were 11 from the United Provinces. Muslims from the latter region were to have a similarly dominant role in the All-India Muslim League whose creation followed on from the Simla deputation.

SIMON COMMISSION

A Commission formed to work out a constitution for pre-partition India. The Simon Commission was appointed in 1927 to review the working of the 1919 constitutional reforms. The all-British composition of the commission aroused considerable Indian opposition. Lord Birkenhead, the Secretary of State for India justified this on the grounds that Indians could not agree on a constitution themselves. The Congress boycotted the Commission's proceedings. The All-India Muslim League was divided on the matter. One section under the leadership of the *Punjabi politician Sir Muhammad *Shafi presented its case to the Commission. The Jinnah faction of the League joined the Congress boycott. In a riposte to the Commission, the Congress called an All-Parties Conference to produce a draft constitution. Its deliberations produced the *Nehru Report. This recommended joint mixed electorates, and reservation of seats for Muslims in the minority provinces alone. When Jinnah's call for a reservation of seats on population basis in Punjab and Bengal was rejected along with a call for a one third Muslim representation in the Central Legislature, he withdrew from the All-Parties Convention. In March 1929 he formulated his famous 'Fourteen Points' which demanded among other safeguards the maintenance of separate electorates. Some historians have seen the failure to achieve an agreement in the wake of the Simon Commission as a significant event on the way to the creation of Pakistan.

THIRD JUNE PLAN 1947

The plan on the basis of which Pakistan and India were divided. On 3 June 1947 Mountbatten announced that India would be partitioned. The British would transfer power to the separate states of India and Pakistan on the basis of Dominion Status. Jinnah had very reluctantly acquiesced to the Plan as it involved the partition of Punjab and Bengal and therefore the creation of a truncated and 'moth-eaten' Pakistan. The Congress was willing to accept a partition involving a truncated Pakistan in return for immediate independence and the possibility of constructing a strong government at the centre. Jinnah was sidelined during the final negotiations which resulted in the Plan's announcement. The acceptance of the Plan was followed by the establishment of a Partition Committee comprising of Vallabhbhai Patel, Rajendra Prasad, Liaquat Ali *Khan and Abdur Rab Nishtar to decide on the division of assets and the establishment of a boundary commission to demarcate the new boundaries of Punjab and Bengal.

PHYSICAL GEOGRAPHY

Milly Stoney

Location

The Islamic Republic of Pakistan lies in the north-west of the South Asian subcontinent. It covers an area of 796,096 sq.km. and has a population of almost 150 million.

The state flag is a green cloth with a white vertical band running along the flagstaff, and a white crescent and star centred against the green background. The coat of arms consists of a crescent and star over a shield surrounded by a wreath. On the shield are depicted a cotton flower, a tea-bush, jute, and wheat. Underneath the wreath there is a ribbon with the *Urdu inscription, '*Faith, Unity, Discipline*'.

In addition to the Georgian calendar, the Muslim lunar calendar is also used (see, Addendum 5). Muslim holidays are celebrated according to this calendar.

Pakistan is a Federal Republic and is headed by a president. It is a member of the British Commonwealth.

Administratively, Pakistan is divided into four provinces, the Federal Capital Area, the *Federally Administered Tribal Areas (FATA), and Federally Administered Northern Areas (FANA).

Province/Area	Area in thousand sq. km.	Population in millions (1998 census)
Balochistan	347,190	6,511
Punjab	205,344	72,585
NWFP	4,521	17,555
Sindh	140,814	29,991
FATA	27,220	3,138
FANA	7,805	—
Islamabad	906	805
Total area	796,095	130,579

The national anthem of Pakistan (lyrics by poet Hafeez *Jalandhari) begins with the words: 'May it prosper, the sacred land!'

PHYSICAL GEOGRAPHY

Pakistan lies between 23°35' and 37°05' northern latitudes and 60°50' and 75°30' longitutdes it is bordered by Afghanistan to the west and north-west, China to the north-east, and India to the east. To the south, it meets the *Arabian Sea.

The north east to south-west extent of the country is about 1700 km., and its east-west width is approximately 1000 km. In the north and wast, nearly 60% of the land area is mountanous terrain and incised tableland topography. The remaining area consists of alluvial plains of the *Indus River system and the Thar and Cholistan Deserts. The offshore Exclusive Economic Zone covers over 231,674 sq.km. in the Arabian Sea.

A great diversity of landforms characterize the physiography of Pakistan: ranging from high mountain belts, including K-2, the second highest mountain in the world, the glaciers of the *Himalayas, the *Karakoram, *Hindu Kush, and *Pamirs, the fertile plains of the Indus River and it's tributaries, the sandy deserts of Thar and Cholistan to the coastal beaches of the Arabian Sea. The bent mountain belts of the western part of Pakistan are significant physiographic features.

GEOLOGY

The physical geography of Pakistan, ranging from the high mountain belts of the Himalayas, Karakoram, Hindu Kush and Pamirs to the low alluvial plains of the *Indus Valley can best be understood by first examining the underlying geological structure of the area.

Pakistan is truly the geologist's 'wonderland'. Field exposures of complex features are excellent. Add to this the setting of Pakistan in the framework of the modern concept of plate tectonics and the area can be seen as unique. Within an area of approximately 800,000 sq.km. there are clear features relating to important tectonic junctions of difference interacting plates and microplates. No other region in the world has mountain belts that bend so often and so severely. The structures include such geological features as arcs, arches, festoons, garlands, harpin bends, inflections, loves, nodes, oroclines, re-entrants, sailents, sweeps, syntaxes and knots. Here geologists can find a living textbook of features to be explored.

About 600 million years ago the Precambrian metamorphic rocks were laid down as a part of the hot molten magma welling up from the earths lower crust and cooling, known as igneous rock, into an area called the Indian Shield. Over the next 450 million years, during the geological eras known as Palaeozoic and Mesozoic, the region experienced considerable rises and falls or oscillations, particularly along its western edge, sometimes receiving marine deposits or sediments, and at ther times none. For instance during the Palaeozoic, the region was divided into large marine and terrestrial basins separated by intervening swells of rock that received little or no accumulation of sediments. The source of shale, mud and clay rocks (pelites) and rocks compressed from fragments, conglomerates and breccias (clastics) was chiefly from the Indian Shield to the east. The rise and fall of the landmass is marked by regional unconformities during a lengthy period from the late Proterozoic to the Permian period. Sediments from the later part of this period are gound throughout the Himalayas.

During the Mesozoic era the pattern of deposits became even more complex largely due to the structural twisting and streching and general deformation of the landmass. It was at this time that the supercontinent of the Gondwana landmass began to split into a number of continents riding on tectonic plates. In the southern hemisphere this included Africa, Australia, South America, Antarctica, India and a number of micro-continents. As evidence of this rock structure shows a major unconformity at the base of the Jurassic period. A number of developing rift structures and fault systems associated with the rifts, both traverse as well as parallel to the rift direction have been identified. Geological studies have shown that at this period the Indo-Pakistan plate was travelling at some 0.7 centimeters per year towards the north. Basaltic rocks, volvanic ingneous in origin, welled up. These are known as the Deccan Trap in the south east Pakistan and the Punjal Trap in the north.

During the Early Jurassic to Eocene period the Neo-Tehys Ocean formed between the Indo-Pakistan plate and the Eurasian plate. This sea laid down deposits of marine rock sequences while volcanic rocks continues to accumulate at the margins and on the Indo-Pakistan plate. In the Late Cretaceous period, with the northward drift accelerating to an amazing speed of 16 centimeters per year, the two plates collided and began to link up, or suture. The earlier rock sequences deposited on the western edge of the Indian Sheild were extrememly deformed during this northward migration of the Indo-Pakistan plate and now lie as a north-south Fold-Thrust Belt in Pakistan along with fragments of what were oceanic island arcs, snake-like ridges called ophiolites with mixtures of rocks and a variety of structures called melanges in geological descriptions.

Following the collision with the Eurasian plate, the northward drift slowed to the 2 to 5 cm. per year of the present day. The movement besides drigting to the north also has an anti-clockwise rotation. This causes stresses and therefore has tectonic implications on the western margin. The compressional stresses have re-activated the east-west faults lying deep under the Indus, Thar and Kutch basins resulting in significantly frequent seismic activity in the region.

Currently Pakistan lies on the western rift margin of the Indo-Pakistan subcontinental plate. The territory is on the junction of three plates – the north western corner of the Indian plate; the southern part of the Afghan shield, composed of a crystalline base of Precambrian rocks surrounded by a platform of flat sedimentary rocks (a craton) which has not undergone much plate tectonic activity; and the northern part of the Arabian Oceanic plate which is sliding, or subducting, benearth the adjoining plate.

The fact that the major part of Pakistan is an active zone of frequent siesmic activity along it's north-western margin as well as the Indus Basin has serious implications for engineering structures and potential loss of life.

Mineral Deposits

The main mineral deposits are based on sediment complexes of the edge of the platform and the folded area. According to 1990 estimates, the known deposits of mineral resources are as follows, oil: 6.6 million tons in the *Potwar Plateau—Dhuliyan, Joyamair, Balkassar; natural gas: 600 billion cubic metres at *Sui, and also Marri, Uch, Larkana; coal: 600 million tons in the *Salt Range, trans-Indus *Punjab, Quetta with recent deposits yet to be exploited in the Thar desert area; iron ore: 600 million tons at Kalabagh; rock salt: 40 million tons at Khewra, in the vicinity of the Salt Range, trans-Indus Punjab, and the *Kohat district. There are also deposits of chromites at Hindubagh, manganese at *Lasbela, *Kalat and *Zhob; copper and lead in *Chitral, *Kalat, and Lasbela; arsenic in Chitral. Deposits of zinc, bauxites, antimony, brimstone, gypsum, magnesite, limestone, and clay are also to be found.

Hydrography

The larger part of Pakistan falls within the basin of the Indus Valley. The western regions have an outflow into the Arabian Sea or, in parts of Balochistan, have an internal flow. The overall annual flow in the Indus Valley is 220 billion cubic metres, of which the upper Indus itself accounts for 53 per cent, the *Jhelum 13 per cent, the *Chenab 14 per cent, the *Ravi 6 per cent, and the *Sutlej 16 per cent. According to the type of water supply, the rivers can be divided into predominantly glacier-fed (the Indus and the *Mastuj), mixed supply (the Sutlej and the Chenab), snow and rain-fed (the Jhelum and the Ravi), and only rain-fed (mainly small rivers such as the *Hub, Poraly and Hingol). The river flow in summer is 10-15 times more than in winter. Some rivers dry up completely during winter and spring.

As a protection against floods, the banks of some rivers are lined with earth embankments. A considerable portion of the flow is used for irrigation. In the Indus Valley, more than 50 per cent, 120 billion cu.metres, is used. Pakistan's irrigation system includes 43 main canals with a total length of 62,820 km. The area under irrigation is 16 million hectares or 77 per cent of the cultivated land. Prior to the partition of the subcontinent into India and Pakistan in 1947, over 13 million hectares of the Indus plains were irrigated by a network of over 50, 000 kms of canals. With the division of the Punjab, a lengthy dispute began over the control and use of the canal waters. This was principally because the actual headwaters over the major rivers vital to Pakistan began their course in Indian territory. The rivers Jhelum, Chenab, Ravi and Sutlej were all at risk and the threat to Pakistan's agriculture was great. India threatened to disrupt the flow and at one time actually did cut off water to the Pakistan Punjab. The World Bank assisted in negotiating a treaty in 1960 (see, Indus Basin, Agreement on the) whereby Pakistan could feel less threatened, however the agreement is somewhat delicate and frequently causes problems. In an attempt to develop the countries own water resources, Pakistan built a series of diversionary canals which fed water from the Jhelum to the Chenab and from the Ravi to the Sutlej. The Mangla and Tarbela dams were built. Barrages, designed to create headwaters from which the irrigation systems would be developed were constructed at Kalabagha, Chashma, Taunsa, Guddu and Hyderababd on the Indus, at Sidhnai on the Ravi, and at Mallsi on the Sutlej. The present system of canals is one of the most extensive in the world. The earliest canals were unlined and this has led to a tragic amount of water logging and salinity, a problem which is yet to be solved. The Indus River Supply Agreement continues to present political and economic difficulties.

Climate

Pakistan has a predominantly dry, tropical climate, with some subtropical areas. In the northern mountains there is altitudinal zonation with frequent frosts as low as –20ºC in winter in the higher lands. In the western mountains and higlands July temperatures can rise to 20-25ºC. In January, the temperature in the Indus Valley fluctuates between 10ºC and 18ºC and rises to an average of 35ºC and occasionally as high as 50ºC in July. The average temperature in July in the southern and south-eastern deserts is up to 35ºC, with Sibi in the Kacchi Desert of Balochistan known as the hottest place on earth. On the coast July temperatures, about 29ºC, drop to a modest 20ºC in the winter.

In the Indus Valley and in the northern mountains, most of the precipitation occurs during the period of south-westerly monsoons (July-September). In the territory of the Iranian Plateau, the maximum precipitation occurs in winter and spring. On the coast, the annual precipitation is 150–200 mm.; in Sindh 100-200 mm. (in the Thar Desert—up to 50mm. in some places); in parts of the valleys and plateaus of the north-west of the country, 1,000–1,500 mm. a year.

Evaporation exceeds the annual average several times over e.g. in Lahore, more than three times, in Jacobabad, 25 times. Therefore, agriculture is only possible with irrigation. The uneven distribution of precipitation during the year determines the rhythm of farming in Pakistan. Two main seasons can be singled out: Kharif, immidetly before the monsoon season, when moisture loving crops are planted, such as rice, sugar cane, cotton, and corn; and Rabi, when wheat, barley, pulses and millet are planted.

Soils

Pakistan's land amounts to 57.8 million hectares, including 5.4 per cent forests, 4.5 per cent soils unsuitable for cultivation, 18 per cent suitable for cultivation but lying unused, 9.1 per cent lying fallow, the cultivated area proper occupies 26.9 per cent of the territory. The overall cultivated area, including areas sown more than once a year, amounts to 19.8 million hectares (1990).

Pakistani soils are divided into four categories in terms of potential fertility. Highly fertile soils cover 26 per cent of the land surface. Soils that are potentially fertile, but in need of recultivation comprise 14 per cent. Soils with low fertility potential requiring costly amelioration measures cover 34 per cent of the area and those unsuitable for farming, 26 per cent. The recent rapid development of irrigation in the plains has shaply intensified the processes of salinity and waterlogging. It is estimated that currently over 50,000 hectares of land are spoiled annually made unusable for agriculture. The cutting of forests, faulty cultivation of the hillsides, and intensive cattle grazing have caused rapid wind and gully erosion are adding to the depredation of the land.

The soils in the mountain areas in the north and north-east vary with altitude. The low dry hills and the valleys are covered with a variety of mountain-grey earth. Higher up, one finds mountain-forest brown soils with groves of holm oak. Still higher up the soil turns into a bleached sandy clay poor in humus or podzol which supports coniferous forests. The highlands are covered with sub-alpine and alpine meadow-steppe and mountain-desert soils.

The Indus Valley territory can be divided into two main soil types. In the humid regions south of the foothills the soils are principally brown and grey-brown. In Central Punjab, where the main centers of irrigation farming lie, there are grey earth tracts. During conditions of sufficient humidity, meadow-grey earth, meadow-grey brown, and other types of soils also develop.

In the Thar desert, located in the south-east, the soils are sandy. In the west in Balochistan, there is a variety of soils characteristic of arid conditions such as mountain-grey earth, grey-brown desert soil, saline soils, fine grained crused soils or *takyrs*, mountain-brown soils, which are covered by drought resistant or xerophytic forests.

Relief

The northern and north-western regions of the country are mainly occupied by mountains and highlands. The eastern and south-eastern regions consist of that valley of the Indus which forms the western part of the Indus-Ganges Plain.

The Highland Rim

Some of the highest mountain ranges in the world are situated in the far north. These form the Himalayas, the Karakoram and the Hindu Kush. Included as part of the Himalayas is the notable outliner, the monadnock *Nanga Parbat*, rising to 8,125 meters. The highest peak in the Hindu Kush Range is Mount Trichmir, 7,690 metres above sea level. In the Karakorams, the second highest mountain in the world, K-2, rises to 8,616 meters. This northern territory is criss-crossed by deep gorges and river valleys, and the peaks are snow-capped and covered with some of the longest glaciers in the world, outside the polar regions. The high mountain area also includes the *Hinduraj Range, south of the River *Mastuj, or Chitral valley. Towards the valley of the Indus, the mountain ranges become progressively lower, making way for large basins, such as Kohat, *Bannu and the *Peshawar Valley.

Coastline

The entire coastline of Pakistan is 850 km. long, and runs from west to east. It is divided into two sections. The western coast of the *Makran, 560 km long, is low, slightly indented, with occasional active mud volcanoes. The eastern section, the Indus delta proper, stretches across 290 km., and consists of frequently flooded lowlands with numerous streams, often changing their course, and forming bights and lagoons. The solid flow of the Indus is 435 million tons per annum. Along the coast are sand banks and several islands. The Arabian Sea offshore shelf is up to 120 km. wide, narrowing to 35 km. at the western Makran coast end. The shelf finishes at a depth of 90 meters and is indented with underwater canyons reaching to a depth of 2,500 meters.

There are two tides per day, with a tidal range of over 5 meters in spring. Minimal surface temperatures in January and February range from 24°C to a maximum of 28°C in June.

The salt content varies from 35 per cent to 36 per cent.

Recent studies have shown that from July to December, during the south west monsoons, a low level atmospheric wind called the Findlater Jet drives a north eastward drift along the coast. This turns southwards along the coast of India. During this period there is high productivity of fish. From February to June the weaker North Easterly monsoon blows and lesser south flowing currents result in much lower productivity.

The Arabian Sea is one of the most productive fishing grounds in the world, although it is currently at risk due to over-fishing by factory ships and their fleets. Tuna, Sardinella, Flying fish, Sea-Cods, Southern

Herring, reef fish, shrimp and prawn are abundant. The industry is mainly concentrated in the shelf regions.

Bibliography: Statistical Yearbook of Pakistan, 2004; Pakistan 2004 – Statistical Pocketbook; Insight Guide – Pakistan; Pakistan Handbook – Isobel Shaw; Footprint Pakistan Handbook – David Winter & Ivan Mannhem; Pakistan Travellers Handbook – M Hanif Raza.

DEMOGRAPHY

Milly Stoney

Pakistan is one of the most densely populated countries in the world. A large percentage of the population is rural and a significant proportion semi-nomadic, tending herds and moving when drought affects the land. There have also been a number of political changes to the boundaries of the area over the past century. Statistical criteria and headings under which figures were collected have also varied over time making population estimates subject to caveats as below.

CENSUS RECORDS

Under British rule (see, British India), the country's population was covered by censuses from 1872. In all, there have been thirteen censuses, five of them in the years since independence. The most recent was in taken in 1998. The census of 9 February–1 March 1951 was the first to take into account the conditions of land leasing, the position of agricultural labourers and landowners, and housing conditions. Many women were not included in the records. This has been a characteristic feature of all Pakistani censuses. The distribution of the population by age is largely inaccurate as birth records are uncommon especially in rural areas. More or less accurate data for the standard five-yearly intervals for all the age groups have been obtained only for Karachi.

The 12 January–1 February 1961 census recorded the birth rate, educational level, and occupational breakdown of the population for the first time. Compared with the previous census, the age limit for obtaining data on the workforce was lowered. The results of the census were published in ten volumes. There were also several volumes published on separate districts.

The 16–30 September 1972 is a selective study of 300,000 individual holdings. Compared to the 1961 census, the number of headings in collected data was reduced and some of the headings became criteria for sampling. Preliminary results were published in 1973, and final ones, in 1976-8. Only two volumes on the selective study have so far been published.

The 1 March 1981 census was preceded by collecting data on housing. For the first time, the census was conducted in tribal areas. Afghan refugees, however, were not covered by the census. Detailed data on geography, history, and economy were included. Final results have been appearing since 1983 in six bulletins, five volumes of records on dwellings, and sixty-nine volumes on individual districts. Another census was held in 1998. A number of bulletins and some district records have been published. Figures for the period since the census have been largely projections and extrapolations based on the 1998 statistics.

These limitations must be borne in mind when using the statistics and information below.

POPULATION

The population has risen from 65.31 millions in 1972 to 130.6 millions in 1998, the most recently conducted official census. The current estimated total is 148.72 millions (Federal Bureau of Statistics, Pakistan Statistical Year Book 2004). Pakistan's population density was 106 persons per sq.km. in 1981 and rose to 142 persons per sq.km. in 1991 and in 1998 was estimated to be 164 persons per sq.km. This is higher than the world's average, currently 34 people per sq.km, and that of developing countries, currently 43 persons per sq.km. However there is considerable variation in the provinces where the population density is unevenly distributed, depending upon the terrain. The average ranges from 19 per sq.km in *Balochistan to 359 persons per sq.km in the *Punjab. (1998).

REGIONAL POPULATION STATISTICS 1981, 1998 CENSUS RETURNS

Region/Province	Population (1981 census) 000s	Population (1998 census) 000s	Area (sq.km.)	Density 1981 (Person per sq.km.)	Density 1998 (Person per sq.km.)
Islamabad	340	805	906	376	889
Punjab	47,292	73,621	205,344	230	359
Sindh	19,028	30,440	140,914	135	216
N.W.F.P.	11,061	17,744	74,521	148	238
Balochistan	4,332	6,566	347,190	12	19
FATA	2,198,	3,176	27,220	81	117
FANA	No records				

The annual population growth from 1960 through the 1980s was 3.1 per cent. Growth rates during the 1990s slowed to 2.94% per annum and further to 2.06% in 2001 with a recent United Nations Population Fund report (2004) estimating that the growth rate has fallen to 1.9% between 1998 and 2004.

In 1950 for each 1,000 women the figures showed a population of 1,164 men. In 1998, for each 1,000 women there were 1,080 men. The ratio would appear to have leveled out, but the male ratio seems to be appreciably larger than could be expected. Experts would point out, however, that there is a considerable under-reporting of women in the census in many areas. The average life expectancy for men has risen from 34 in 1950 to 59.3 years in 1998, and for women the rise has been from 34 to 66.7 years in the same period. There continues to be a high infant mortality rate of 77 per 1,000 live births. Statistics show that the average marriage age is 24.3 years for men and 18.9 years for women although there is a bias toward younger women marrying in rural areas as shown in the 1998 census returns. The figures show that in the cohort 15 – 19 years of age there was a total of 3,570,574 of whom 2,395,230 (67%) were classified as rural and 1,175,344 (33%) as urban. In that age group 1,040,450 (43%) rural women were already married in contrast to 300,706 (25%) for urban women.

MIGRATION

Migration is a common phenomenon in Pakistan.

Inter-regional migration involves the flow of population from Punjab to the west and south-west towards Sindh. There is also an influx of migrants into the southern regions, from the *North West Frontier Province to Balochistan and Sindh. The influence of migration flows becomes more and more important and influential in many regions; it was most strikingly felt, in recent years, in Karachi, Peshawar and in northern Balochistan, partly due to the sharply increased flow of refugees from Afghanistan.

Historically the majority of the population has gravitated towards areas of irrigated agriculture. In the most populated province, Punjab, the greatest concentration of the population was, for a long time, in the eastern districts of Lahore, Sialkot, Gujranwala and Sheikhupura with the development of the irrigated 'doab' farmlands. In the late 1970s and early 1980s, the greatest population movement was to the west and south-west of these districts. Lahore remains one of the most populous and fastest growing districts in Punjab. In 1951, there were only eight districts with a population of more than one million in Punjab. In 1981 the number rose to eleven, the districts with the administrative centres in Faisalabad (4.7 million), Multan (4.1 million), Sahiwal (3.6 million), and Lahore (3.5 million) comprising more than 35 per cent of the entire population of the province.

The chief causes of migration have been the poor conditions of subsistence farming, the persisting drought and waterlogged conditions in many formerly productive areas, and the generally higher wages and opportunities reputedly available in the larger urban areas. Many of the migrant workers have been the male members of the family, leaving the women to tend the often increasingly marginal farm land and flocks.

During the latest census period alone, about six million people, i.e. between 8 and 10 per cent of the entire population, changed location. 43 per cent moved from one village to another, 44 per cent moved from the countryside to towns, and 12 per cent from one town to another. About 30 per cent of the migrants moved to another province, half of them to Sindh, and mainly to Karachi.

IMMIGRATION, EMIGRATION AND RETURNEES

Internal and external migration peaked as a direct result of politics in several periods: 1. after the division of *British India in 1947-50; 2. during the formation of the Republic of Bangladesh in place of former *East Pakistan in 1971; 3. in the 1980s, as a result of the aggravation of the internal political situation and the Soviet war in Afghanistan.

REFUGEES

Refugees have been coming to Pakistan from India since 1947. By 1951, Muslim refugees numbered nearly 6.5 million. During the same period 5.5 million Hindus and *Sikhs moved from Pakistan to India. Refugee settlement was largely determined by ethnic origin. *Punjabi Muslims preferred to settle in the Pakistan Punjab, among people linguistically and culturally similar. Eighty per cent of the refugees from India settled in the Punjab, where they constituted 26 per cent of the population.

There has also been a considerable influx of refugees into the Karachi District of southern Sindh throughout the period since partition. Refugees constituted 45.4 per cent of the District population according to the 1951 data. This was mainly due to job availability and better business opportunities for refugees from India, with skills and business experience. The availability of housing and land were other important factors. Since 1971, when East Pakistan became the Republic of Bangladesh, tens of thousands of Urdu-speaking refugees have moved to Karachi.

During the 1980s a new wave of refugees was caused by the Soviet war in Afghanistan, prompting approximately three million people to migrate to Pakistan. A further influx came into Pakistan in 2001 during the American action in Afghanistan. These families settled mainly in the North West Frontier Province, but colonies of Afghan people are to be found in all the major cities.

Refugees still remain a major determining factor in the socio-economic situation in the areas of their settlement. Inter-ethnic conflicts in Karachi and other *Sindhi cities, clashes among the local population and the refugees from Afghanistan in the North West Frontier Province and northern Balochistan have often compelled the government to bring in troops and to impose curfews, as well as resort to other extreme and extraordinary measures in order to maintain law and order.

The end of the 1970s saw the peak of the Pakistani labour force migration to the countries of the Persian Gulf in search of jobs and opportunities. Since then the Pakistani population abroad has been growing more steadily. Despite continuing emigration, Pakistan's population is annually replenished by more than 15,000 returnees i.e. people who had previously left the country in search of employment. These are mostly unqualified workers and labourers.

Currently some two million Pakistanis live abroad, about 75 per cent of these in the Persian Gulf countries, the remaining 25 per cent in Western Europe and the United States.

POPULATION GROWTH TRENDS

The degree of urbanization in Pakistan is lower than in most developing countries. Though the rate of urban growth has been slowing, it still remains high. Between the 1951 and 1961 censuses it was 4.9 %; this reduced to 4.7% over the next ten years. From 1972 to 1981 it was 4.3 % and slowed still further to 3.5%

between 1981 and 1998. At this rate, the urban population will double in 20 years. The urban growth rate is almost 1.5 times more than the rural growth rate and 1.3 times more than the overall rate for the country.

COMPARATIVE URBAN/RURAL POPULATION GROWTH 1981, 1998. (IN THOUSANDS)

Region/ Province	Population 1981	Population 1998	Population 1981	Population 1998	Growth rate of Region/Province
Islamabad	204	529	136	276	5.19
Punjab	13,051	23,019	34,241	50,602	2.64
Sindh	8,243	14,839	10,766	15,600	2.80
N.W.F.P.	1,665	2,994	9,396	14,749	2.82
Balochistan	677	1,568	3,655	4,997	2.47
FATA	na	85	2,199	3091	2.19

URBAN AREAS

More than 35% of the population is currently concentrated in urban areas with 6% in the largest 8 cities. In 1981, among the 400 urban settlements, there were three cities with a population of over a million: Karachi, Lahore and Faisalabad. By 1998 Rawalpindi, Multan, Hyderabad and Gujranwala had reached over a million inhabitants, increasing the number to seven cities, with further population centers ready to break the million mark.

In Sindh, the most polarized urban/rural province, the urban population constitutes over 48.9 per cent of the entire population of the province. The largest city, Karachi, was home to some 9.26 million people in the 1998 census and in 2004 is estimated to house more than 11 million people, making it one of the most populous cities on earth.

By 2010, the overall national population is expected to be 195 million people, and by 2035, 280 million people. Half of the population is expected to be urban.

Sindh is the most urbanized province. This is due to its rapid industrial development, linked to its favourable geographical position. Internal migration is also a major factor. People from other provinces mainly migrate to Sindh province. There is in addition considerable migration from the rural areas of the province to the main city, Karachi. The urban population in this province is 48.9 per cent and keeps growing with rates twice as high as those of the rural population. Karachi is Pakistan's 'sea gate'. Karachi is also the heart of the country's transport communications. Its population is estimated to be 11 million, almost 22 per cent of the country's entire urban population.

More than 53 per cent of Pakistani urban dwellers are concentrated in the Punjab.The province boasts five cities with populations exceeding half a million. Three quarters of all Pakistan's towns with a population greater than 100,000 are situated in the Punjab, and the province takes the leading place in having the greatest number of urban settlements of all types, in population density, and in size.

The North West Frontier Province is a largely rural province. Peshawar, the capital, has a population of just over 1 million, Mardan, the next town of any size just over a quarter of a million and Mingora has a population of just over 100,000. Only 48 settlements number over 5,000 urban residents.

The population distribution in Balochistan is very unusual. Quetta accounts for more than 36 per cent of the urban population with just over half a million people. Urbanization is low with 77 per cent of the province categorized as rural dwellers. There are several administrative districts in NWFP and Balochistan that have no urban population.

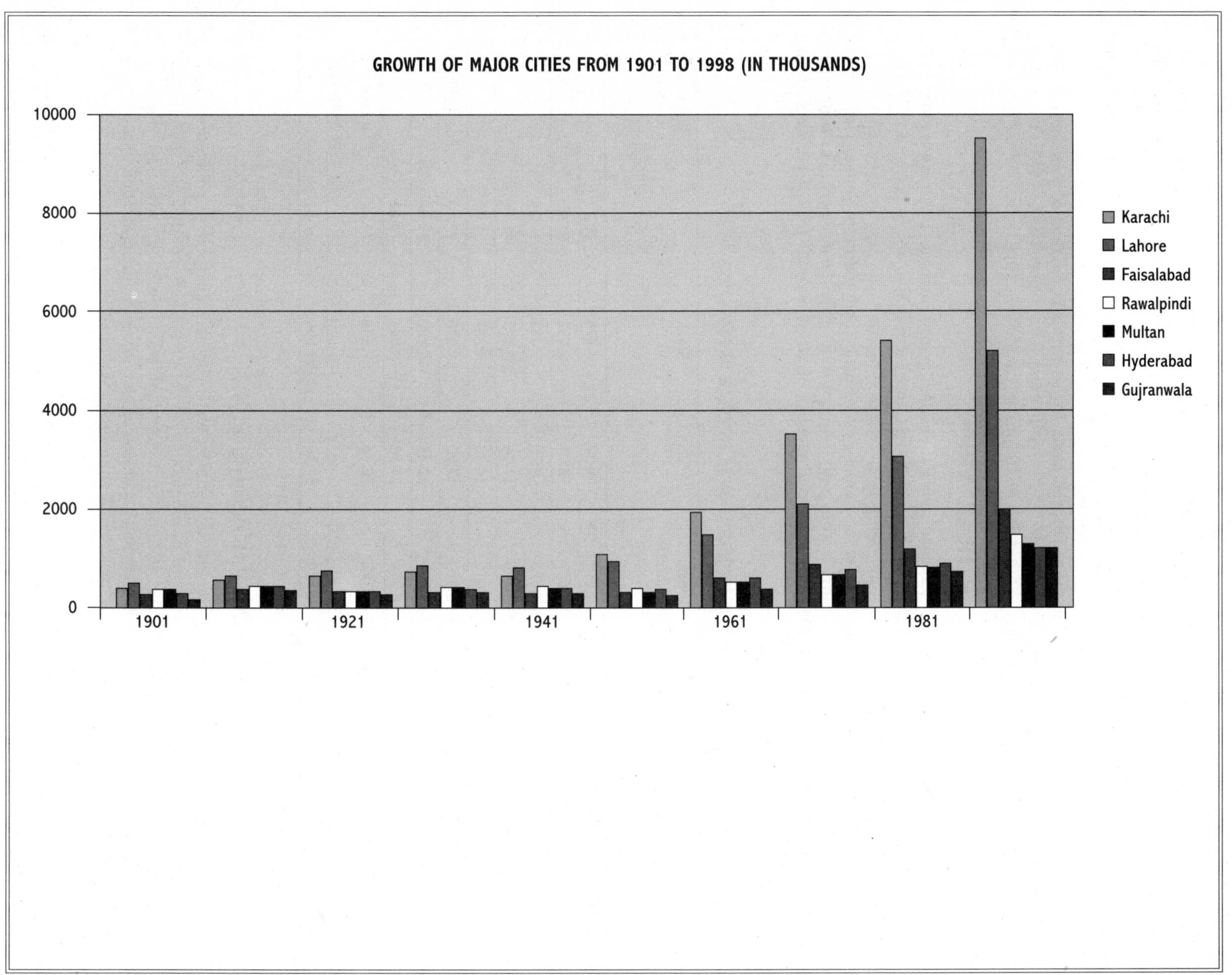
GROWTH OF MAJOR CITIES FROM 1901 TO 1998 (IN THOUSANDS)
10000
8000
6000
4000
2000
0
1901
1921
1941
1961
1981
Karachi
Lahore
Faisalabad
Rawalpindi
Multan
Hyderabad
Gujranwala

The majority of the urban population is concentrated in the larger cities. By 1961, cities with a population over 500,000 incorporated more than one-third of urban dwellers, in 1972 almost half of urban dwellers, and at the most recent census in 1998, 53.5 per cent.

In 1961, about 25% of all urban residents lived in large towns with the population from 100,000 to 500,000. By 1981, only 12.1% lived in such towns and in 1998, 17% per cent.

There has also been a dramatic fall in the number of small towns with a population of less than 10,000. Their share of the urban population was 10.2 per cent in 1961, and only 3 per cent in 1981. The actual number of such towns diminished from 185 in 1961 to 105 in 1981 and 62 in 1998.

RURAL AREAS

In 1998 an estimated 67.5% of the total Pakistani population was classed as rural. There were more than 45,000 settlements classed as villages in 1998 of which 57 per cent were in Punjab, 16 per cent in NWFP, 14 per cent in Balochistan and 13 per cent in Sindh.

Extensive farm holdings are characteristic of Punjab, Balochistan and northern Sindh. Throughout Pakistan 24 per cent of the total farmland is held by only two per cent of the landowners. The proportion is greatest in Balochistan where 10 per cent of the total number of farms account for 5.3 per cent of the provincial farm area.

URBAN AND RURAL POPULATION IN PAKISTAN IN 1901-1998

Year	Total Population in Millions Census data	Total Population Corrected	Urban Population	%	Rural Population	%	Historical Context
1901	16.756		1.619	9.77	14.975	90.23	Pre-partition
1911	19.382		1.689	8.71	17.693	91.29	
1921	21.109		2.058	9.75	19.051	90.25	
1931	23.542		2.769	11.76	20.773	88.24	
1941	28.282		4.015	14.20	24.267	85.80	
1951	33.740	38.940	6.970	17.90	31.970	82.10	Post-partition
1961	42.880	50.067	11.204	22.38	38.862	77.62	
1972	64.892	66.6129	16.774	25.18	49.844	74.82	
1981	84.253	88.119	25.272	28.68	62.846	71.32	Post secession of Bangladesh
1998	131.500		32.500	32.50	99.000	67.50	

DEMOGRAPHIC POLICY

Policy is determined by government institutions and aims at restricting the rapid rate of population growth which resulted in the almost fourfold increase of the population between 1947 and 1992. Despite the high growth rate of the Gross Domestic Product (GDP), demographic overloading, along with other factors, is seen as an obstacle to the growth of investment and expansion of technological modernization of production. The government of Pakistan has allocated considerable funds to programmes that restrict population growth and promote family planning.

A family planning policy was initiated in the 1950s, and was implemented through women's voluntary societies. A number of consulting centres were set up. In 1963, the Family Planning Council was organized; and in 1965, the national programmes for demographic policy and family planning were formulated. In 1976, an inquiry into the state of affairs showed the programme to be ineffective. The new 1980 programme for family planning set more limited goals. These goals sought to cover 14 per cent of the population by 1995 and 21 per cent by 2000. The sixth plan for development envisaged the setting up of 900 family planning centres that would serve 30,000 people each.

At the beginning of the 1990s, the programme covered approximately 40 per cent of the female population in their fertile ages. This is far below the target figure of 4.6 million. An estimated 0.62 millions of births, or 31.3 per cent of the target number, have been avoided. On the whole, the realisation of the programme lags behind the target figures of 49.8 %. The attainment of the goal—involvement of 11 million women in the programme and prevention of two million births by 1993 did not materialize. A more realistic and promising approach, which takes into account the influence of such socio-economic determinants of population growth as family welfare, has since been adopted.

RATES OF POPULATION INCREASE

Census years	Rate of increase between Census	Levelled out increase rates	Rates of Natural Increase
1901-11	1.58	1.58	0.16
1911-21	0.86	0.86	0.54
1921-31	1.10	1.10	0.04
1931-41	1.85	1.85	0.97
1941-51	1.78	1.78	1.38
1951-61	2.43	3.17	2.80
1961-71	3.67	3.08	2.70
1971-81	3.06	3.06	3.20
1981-98	2.6	2.6	2.3

CURRENT DEMOGRAPHIC STATUS

The demographic situation in the country is presently a cause for concern. Although the annual population growth rates dropped to 2.6% in 1998, given this population growth rate, the country's population doubles approximately every 27 years.

At the beginning of the century the 1901 census indicated that the overall birth rate level was about 48 per cent, the mortality rate was 42.6 per cent. Average life expectancy was exceedingly low by present day standards, at 24 years. The main causes for the high ratio of early deaths were infectious diseases and parasites such as malaria, tuberculosis, stomach infections and intestinal worms. However, despite widespread disease and high mortality rates, the high marriage and birth rates ensured slow but constant rates of population growth.

Starting in the 1970s, a decrease in child mortality, and the overall decrease of mortality, improved the demographic indices.

The levelling out of mortality rates in different age groups indicates a decrease in a number of factors including life threatening diseases. Men's average life expectancy from 1980 to 1985 was 53 years; women's was 52. This index varies considerably, however, from area to area, reflecting a greater territorial mobility of younger men migrating to the cities in search of work. On the whole however, the population reproduction model must be regarded as high in terms of the types worked out by the Population Department of the United Nations.

The age structure is marked by the preponderance of the younger age groups, which is projected to continue. In both urban and rural areas the under-30s constitute almost 50% of the population. The average family size is five persons. The average age of marriage is 18 for men and 16 for women, but there is a much lower average age of marriage for women in rural areas.

THE WORKING POPULATION

In the early 1950s, the economically active population stood at about 9.6 million people. In 1991, they numbered 32.8 million. In the 1998 census, despite the increase in population, this had decreased to 21.85 millions. Of these 7.95 millions were in the urban areas and 13.9 millions in the rural areas. The annual growth rate of the employed population was 2.6 per cent in the 1980s, below the general population growth rate of 3.1% during that period. In 1991, the number of the unemployed reached 10 per cent of the population. In the 1998 census over 3.7 million people reported that they were looking for work or had been laid off.

The prospective Twenty-Year Plan for 1965-1985 set the task of reducing unemployment from 20 per cent of the economically active population to 4 per cent. This target figure was not achieved. Three to four times as many able-bodied people are for all practical purposes unemployed as are working. Unemployment and under employment remains one of the most serious economic, as well as political, problems. This is made worse since unemployment includes a considerable portion of young people who are nominally literate and 'educated'.

Literacy is hard to define because of the difference in the methods of book-keeping and questionnaires. According to the 1951 census, any person who could read, even without understanding the meaning of the text, was registered as literate. In 1961, understanding of the text was required. In 1972, a literate person was required to be able to read and write, while fully understanding the meaning of the text. A definition of literacy is still being discussed.

Literacy in Pakistan is generally very low—43.9 per cent in 1998, and growth from 1947 to 1998 has been very slow. Literacy is considerably higher among males (54.81 per cent) than among females (32.02 per cent), and much higher in cities (63.08 per cent) than in the countryside (33.64 per cent). Despite the growing involvement of a wider strata of the population in primary education, the number of illiterate persons keeps increasing, by approximately one million a year.

The development of the economically active population is closely linked with changes in social attitudes and opportunities. It took Pakistan forty years to bring the share of those employed in agriculture down to below 50 per cent, given the relatively high rural population growth rates.

The sex and age structure of the economically active population and efforts to change the dynamics of this structure are a severe problem

In the second half of the 1980s, the share of the population classed as persons of employable ages was 53 per cent. This proportion is the highest in South Asia because Pakistani statistics include all persons over 10. A considerable gap exists between the potential labour resources and the real resources, i.e. the same population minus those not employed in social production who are mostly women, caste beggars and the landless very poor.

The highest levels of economic activity are achieved in the age brackets between 30 and 35. The period of economic activity ends very early, generally at the age of 45 to 50. The apparent productive economic activity of women is twelve to fifteen times lower than that of men. The share of the population involved in unskilled labour is still very high.

A characteristic of Pakistan's economy is its division into two labour markets—the modern and the traditional. In the traditional sector of the economy, labour resources are used under conditions of extreme poverty and an inadequately developed social infrastructure. This results in poor health, low labour activity, low standards of education and vocational training.

MAJOR URBAN AREAS OF PAKISTAN

Islamabad

This is the capital of Pakistan. In 1959, the decision was taken to transfer the capital from Karachi to Islamabad. In the early 1960s, the construction of the new capital began. The city was designed by the Greek architect Doxidiadis. Islamabad has developed as an administrative centre, a seat of various state and government bodies, such as the parliament, presidential palace, cabinet secretariat, and diplomatic missions. A major centre of education and science, it is the location of the Quaid-i-Azam University, named after the founding father of Pakistan, Muhammad Ali *Jinnah. It is also the home of the Pakistan Institute of Nuclear Science and Technology (see image), the Pakistan Institute of Development Economics, and the Institute of Strategic Studies. Individual industrial enterprises forming part of the Rawalpindi industrial zone are also found in the capital. Islamabad is famous for its parks, the largest of which is the Fatima Jinnah Park. The main sightseeing attraction is Faisal mosque (see center-piece for image), which is built in a modernistic style.

The Pakistan Institute of Nuclear Science and Technology at night time.

AREA, POPULATION AND DENSITY BY PROVINCE AND DISTRICT

Islamabad

Area (sq km)	Population of the Administrative area	Population of the city	Density per sq km	Urban %
906	805,235	524,500	889	65.7

Punjab Province

Province/District	Area (sq.km.)	Population of Administrative District (1998)	Population of city/town (1998)	Density per sq.km.	Urban %
Punjab Province	205,345	73,621,290		359	31.3
Attock	6,857	1,274,935	1,265	186	21.3
Bahawalpur	24,830	2,433,091	352,744	98	27.3
Dera Ghazi Khan	11,922	1,643,118	188,149	138	13.9
Daud Khel		22,387			
Faisalabad	5,856	5,429,547	1,997,427	927	42.7
Gujranwala	3,622	3,400,940	1,124,729	939	50.5
Gujrat	3,192	2,048,008	250,121	642	27.7
Jhang	8,809	2,834,545	292,214	322	23.4
Jhelum	3,587	936,957	127,940	261	27.7
Kasur	3,995	2,375,875	241,649	595	22.8
Lahore	1,772	6,318,745	5,063,499	3,566	82.4
Multan	3,720	3,116,851	1,182,441	838	42.2
Murree		21,413			
Okara	4,377	2,232,992	200,901	510	23.0
Rawalpindi	5,286	3,363,911	1,406,214	636	53.2
Sahiwal	3,201	1,843,194	207,388	576	16.4
Sargodha	5,854	2,665,979	455,360	455	28.1
Sheikhupura	5,960	3,321,029	271,875	557	26.2
Sialkot	3,016	2,723,481	417,597	903	26.2
Taxila		48,115			
Wah		198,431			
Wazirabad		89,652			

PUNJABI CITIES OF THE SHAHI ROAD AND GRAND TRUNK ROAD

Lahore

Lahore is situated close to the River *Ravi where the original *Shahi* Road, or Imperial Road, built in the 1540s by emperor Sher Shah Suri, passed through from Delhi to Kabul. Under British rule the road was later extended as far as Calcutta and re-named Grand Trunk Road. The city is currently the administrative centre of *Punjab Province. The city rose to fame at the end of the tenth century under the *Ghaznavid dynasty, but its importance fell in the Great Mughal era of the 15th Century. At the turn of the seventeenth century it became the capital of the *Mughal Empire. During the eighteenth and early nineteenth centuries it fell into decline once more only to come to life again as the capital of the *Sikh state from 1799-1839 initially under Ranjit Singh. In the first half of the twentieth century Lahore developed as a major cultural, educational and scientific center under British rule. The campus of Punjab University, the oldest in the country, is located here. It is also home to the University of Engineering and Technology (UET) and many prestigious colleges and well known medical establishments including the Mayo Hospital.

Lahore is a major economic centre with a stock exchange and branches of commercial banks and insurance companies, only second in importance to Karachi nationally. Lahore is also the headquarters of the Water and Power Development Authority, the Railway Administration and the Central Railway Depot, with a railcar repair shop in nearby Mughalpura.

The city is famous for its textile industry, machine-building plants, tractor, bicycle and motorcycle manufacturing, the production of industrial and household electric devices, a match factory, furniture making factories, tanneries, various small-scale industries, arts and handicrafts.

As a major cultural center it is the headquarters of the Arts Council of Pakistan and it is the site of the internationally famous *Lahore Fort and *Lahore Museum. Lahore is a major religious centre attracting numerous pilgrims to the tombs of Data Ganj Bakhsh, and Mian Mir; and the *Badshahi Mosque, with the resting place of the poet and philosopher Allama Muhammad *Iqbal at its entrance. Tourism is of importance and among further attractions are the picturesque Sikh *gurudwara*, the palace of Ranjit Singh, the tomb of the Mughal Emperor Jahangir on the opposite river bank to the fort, and, last but not least, the world-famous *Shalimar Gardens.

Gujranwala

Gujranwala lies on the reclaimed land, or *doab*, between the *Chenab and the *Ravi rivers. Once situated on the Grand Trunk Road, the town is now by-passed. It is a major trade centre situated in the area growing high-quality rice, sugarcane and wheat. It has a main bazaar covering an area of over one kilometer square. It also has a large-scale textile industry, sugar factories, and well developed weaving and cottage industries. Steel making and various forms of metal-working have led to the production of manufactured goods such as household electric appliances including fans, air-conditioners and refrigerators. Rubber, soap, plastics and bathroom suites are also manufactured. There are many *mosques* and *madrasahs*. The town is the birthplace of the Maharaja Ranjit Singh, a nineteenth century Sikh ruler of the Punjab, and consequently there are still many fine Sikh buildings.

Wazirabad

Sited close to the Chenab river, it is an important railway junction. The Alexandra railway bridge, named after the Princess Alexandra of Wales, was built across the Chenab in 1876. It is 3 km. long, which at the time of building was the longest in South Asia.

Known for its cottage industries and handicrafts, Wazirabad's traditional crafts include hardware, simple lathes, instruments and tools, knife-making and metal-working for everyday needs

Gujrat

The town is located close to the Chenab west bank, and was originally close to the route of the old Grand Trunk Road, but is now by-passed. The site probably dates back to the time of the Emperor Akbar, although there are claims that it can be traced back to the 5th Century BC ruler Bachan Pal of the *Rajput dynasty. There may also be some truth in the legend that Alexander the Great defeated King Puru (Poros) in the vicinity in the 4th Century BC. British troops scored a decisive victory here over the Sikhs in 1849. Gujrat is famous for its pottery, furniture-making, metalwork, crockery, and china. Between here and Lahore are some of the best *Basmati rice paddies and prime vegetable growing areas in Pakistan.

Jhelum

It was named after the *Jhelum River on whose northwest bank the city lies, at the point where the Potwar Plateau ends and the very flat Punjab Plain stretches away to the south into India. Jhelum is a relatively modern town, although an ancient mound on the opposite bank of the river has yielded archaeological items dating back to the Greek and Hindu periods. It is also mentioned in the Mahabharata. The Rohtas Fort constructed by Sher Shah Suri is nearby. Modern Jhelum is known as a timber-trading centre with several sawmills and warehouses. Other industrial enterprises include salt production. There is also a cantonment.

Rawalpindi

The city dates back to pre-Mughul times although little remains as evidence. It was of importance during the 16th century when it was a settlement on the Imperial road, later known as the Grand Trunk Road from Delhi to Kabul. It was later captured by a Sikh sardar in 1765. The city was taken by Ranjit Singh in the early 19th century. The British government developed it as a garrison town following its capture in 1849. It became a centre of trade with *Kashmir. The city served as Pakistan's interim capital in the 1960s and is now regarded as a twin city with the capital, Islamabad.

Rawalpindi is a major trade, industrial, political, and cultural centre. Textile, glass-making and food industries, scrap metal plants and a small oil refinery are located in the city. Many national newspapers and other periodicals are published here and there are several printing presses. Rawalpindi boasts many colleges, the most famous being Gordon College. The General Headquarters (GHQ) of the Pakistan army is also situated in Rawalpindi.

Wah

Wah lies some 16 Kms. from the Margalla Pass off the Peshawar section of the road. Originally a place where the Mughal emperor Akbar laid out gardens in the late 16th century it is now known for its defence industries such as plants for repairing and assembling tanks, fire-arms, aeroplanes, military uniform making factories and cement factories.

Attock

Attock is a district in the Rawalpindi division and the city is located on a historical crossing point of the Indus. The Shahi road and later the Grand Trunk Road used this crossing. There is also a rail bridge here used by the Islamabad-Peshawar track. The main sightseeing attraction is the fort built by Mughal Emperor Akbar, an imposing monument of Mughal architecture. (The population statistics for the city include those for the cantonment.)

TRADING CENTRES OF THE DOABS

The *Indus Valley is believed to have been one of the major centres of an agriculturally based civilization for over two millennia. During the 19th century methods of irrigation were developed and these enabled large tracts of land between the Indus and its tributaries to be used to a much greater extent than had previously been possible. The land that had at one time been unproductive desert was now provided with a water supply that made it possible to grow cash crops such as cotton, *basmati* rice, and many other varieties of warm - temperate and sub-tropical grains and vegetables, as well as the rearing of beef and dairy cattle.

The flat irrigated lands between the rivers are called *Doabs*: between the Beas and Ravi lies the earliest land to have been irrigated in the 1860s, the **Bari Doab*; between the Chenab and Ravi is the **Rechna Doab*; between Jhelum and Chenab is the **Jhech Doab* developed between 1905 and 1917. Between the Indus and the Jhelum lies the most recently developed area forming part of what was the *Thal Desert and known as the Sagar Doab.

A number of major towns and cities have developed as a result of the farming activities in the surrounding land. Some were settled only after the doab irrigation scheme was started.

Kasur

Sited between the Ravi and Sutlej close to the Indian border south of Lahore, this is a major grain and cattle-trading centre and consequently tanneries and the leather industry have developed. There is a shrine to Bulleh Shah, a *sufi mystic, to which pilgrims flock at the celebration of the **urs*, or death commemoration, of the saint.

Faisalabad

Faisalabad was founded in 1890 as a centre of the 'settlers' colony' on the Lower Chenab Canal, when the area was first irrigated and agriculture made possible. Between 1890 and 1976 the city was called Lyallpur after J.B. Lyall, the English governor of the Punjab. It was then named Faisalabad in honour of King Faisal of Saudi Arabia. Until the 1980s, it was one of the fastest growing cities in the country. A major textile centre, it is home to the largest textile factories in the country as well as small-scale weaving shops. There are more than 50,000 looms in the city. The wholesale grain trade and agricultural sciences and technical centres are located here. The campus of the Agricultural University, the Agricultural Scientific-Research Institute and a number of seed selection stations are also sited in the area.

Jhang

Jhang was formed by the linking of two towns adjacent to the Chenab River, Jhang, known since the fifteenth century, and Maghiana, known since the eighteenth century. It lies in the heart of the Punjab cotton belt. The town of Jhang is known for its weaving industry. Factories here produce army uniforms and regulation wool blankets, carpets, flat cotton rugs *(daris or dhurries*), and cotton bedspreads *(khes)*.

Okara

Okara is sited south of Lahore on the main route to Multan. It lies to the north east of the ancient site of *Harappa. The town developed in the early twentieth century, in a period when newly-reclaimed lands began to open up as a result of the construction of a complex of irrigation canals. The local economy specializes in the grain trade, food industries and textiles.

Sahiwal

Sahiwal was founded in 1865. It is sited between Lahore and Multan and 20km to the east of the ancient site of Harappa. Until the 1970s, it was called Montgomery in honour of the Lieutenant-Governor of the Punjab, Sir Robert Montgomery (1859-65). It grew up as a canal colony when scrub land was irrigated. It is now at the heart of the cotton growing area. Sahiwal is a trade centre, with large-scale food and textile industries. It is well known for its dairy and beef industries and biscuit factories

Bahawalpur

Founded in 1748 by Nawab Bahawal Khan, after whom it was named, it was the capital of *Bahawalpur princely state until 1955 when the state was abolished. Today it is the administrative centre of the division of the same name and the main town serving the *Cholistan Desert. The city is a major trade centre, dealing mainly in the food industry and large-scale light manufacturing industry. It is also home to a university and several colleges. Bahawalpur is known as a centre for Islamic study and is the location of a theological college, *Jamia Abbasia*.

Sargodha

Sargodha was founded in 1903 in connection with the opening up of newly-reclaimed land, as a town in the area of 'colonies on canals'. It is sited on the flat plain with rich soils. It is famous for its agriculture, the organization of which is based on a feudalistic style of society. It has several textile mills and food industries associated with its agricultural hinterland. It is also home to a major airforce base, an aerodrome and Air Force College.

Multan

Multan is one of the oldest cities in South Asia. It lies at the heart of a vast region embracing the south and south-west of the Punjab, northern *Sindh, part of *Balochistan and *North West Frontier Province. Situated at the junction of a number of important ancient trade routes and what was once the confluence of the Chenab and Ravi rivers, archaeological and written evidence suggests that it has been a well defended, wealthy city for more than 2,000 years. In 712 AD, it was conquered by the Arabian general Muhammad bin Qasim. Later, in 1005, it was included in the Kingdom of the Ghaznavids and the Ghaurids. Tamurlane *(Tamburlane)* took the town in 1398. At one time it was the capital of a semi-independent state, then a provincial centre of the Great Mughal Empire, and capital of the Afghan Empire under the Durranis (see, Durrani Empire). In 1818, it was taken over by Ranjit Singh. From 1849 to 1947, it was the capital of the Punjab in British India.

Modern Multan has oil-refineries, chemical plants, textile factories, and food factories. It is famous for its cotton trade of which it is the centre for a large hinterland, leading to a spinning and weaving industry producing carpets and rugs. Because of the agricultural region surrounding the city it has also become well known as a centre for the hide and skin trade over the past 200 years. Handicrafts, including laquered wood, inlaid work and jewellery, traditional shoes called *khussa*, camel skin work, silk textiles, embroidered costumes, and plaid-making are also major industries. Traditional painted and glazed ceramics are still made here and there is an Institute of Blue Pottery Development dedicated to ensuring that the skills and techniques of manufacture are retained. Multan is also a centre of the grain and fruit trade, chiefly wheat, cotton, mango and palm dates.

Pilgrims visit the tombs of Bahauddin Zakariya Multani, known for his missionary work, and Shah **Rukn-i-Alam* among others. The ancient fort citadel and part of the fortification wall still exist. There is a university and a cantonment.

Daud Khel

Lying south of the old town of Kalabagh and close to the Jinnah Barrage, the town has chemical, pharmaceutical, and cement industries. In the 1970s it was called Iskandarabad, in honour of President *Iskandar Mirza.

Dera Ghazi Khan

The town is the administrative centre of the division of the same name. It was founded in the fifteenth century by Mir Ghazi Khan, the **Sardar* of the *Balochi* tribe of *Rind*. It was originally in Balochistan but boundary changes made by the British, for administrative and strategic reasons, transferred it into the Punjab. Following the flood of 1910-11, when the banks of the Indus were breached, with disastrous results, the present-day town was rebuilt 9 kms further upstream, on more organized lines.

The town is a trading and industrial centre. It is also known for handicrafts of lacquer, wood and leather work. It also produces date palm baskets, rope-weaving and textiles. The town is a well-known Muslim religious centre.

Sheikhupura

Sheikhupura was founded during the Great Mughal period, when it was named after the Sheikh of Emperor Jehangir. The town saw its heyday during Jahangir's reign. A beautiful palace was built and *Hiran Minar* gardens were laid out in the environs of the town during this period in 1616. It is now a trade and industrial centre, specializing in textile manufacture.

Sialkot

Situated in the *Himalayan foothills 70 km. from the river Chenab and close to the Indian border, Sialkot is known to have existed since the 2nd century B.C. It is identified with Sakala, the capital of the Greek-Indian Kingdom, and later of the *Ephtalites' state. From the eighth century it was part of Kashmir. In the eleventh century it joined the Ghaznavid Empire and the *Delhi Sultanate. Sialkot has always been a major manufacturing centre, the craftsmen of the Mughal period being famous for fine swords and daggers.

It is now a major industrial and trade centre, specializing in the production of high-quality sports goods, surgical instruments (see image), saddles, musical instruments, bench tools and small lathes. The development of surgical instrument production resulted from a need to repair and replace equipment for the American Mission Hospitals in 1905. It is frequently quoted that more bagpipes are made in Sialkot than in Scotland.

There are altogether some 500 factories in Sialkot employing about 100,000 people.

Sialkot was the birth place of the poet philosopher Allama Muhammad *Iqbal. His house is a centre of pilgrimage and there is a public library named after him. There are several educational and theologian centres, and a number of famous mosques.

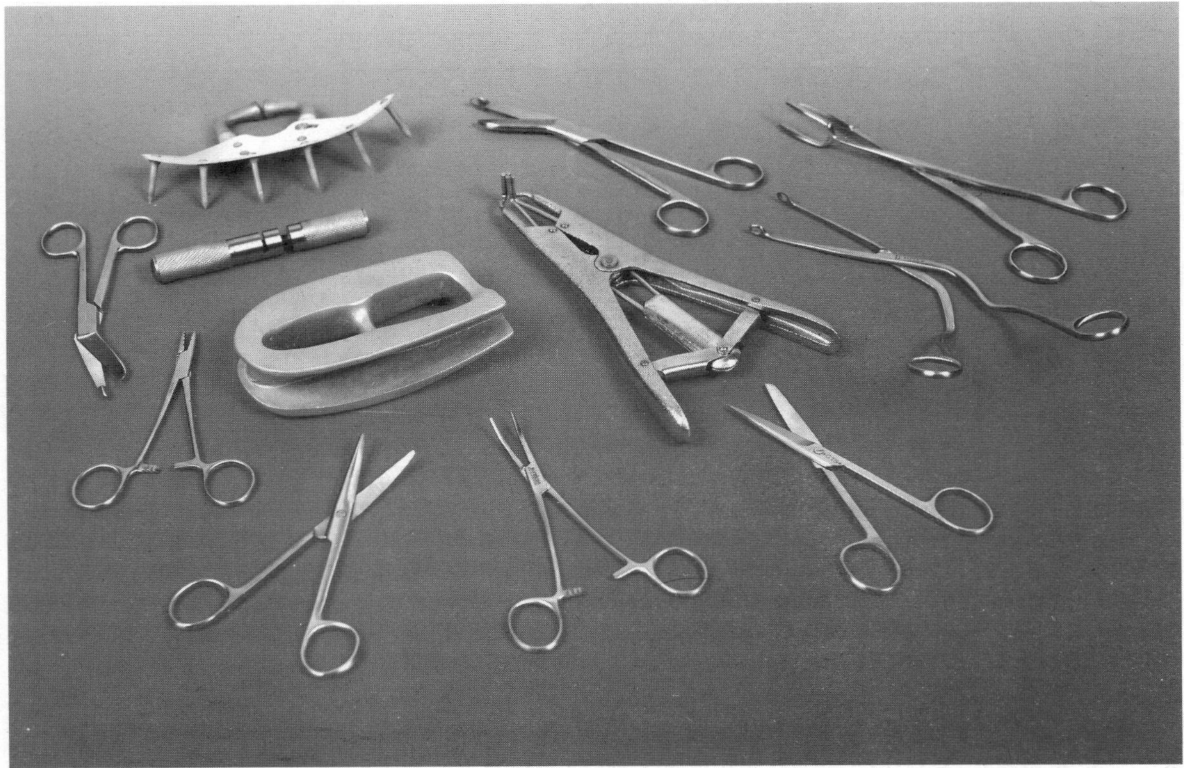

A selection of surgical instruments from Sialkot.

Taxila

(Sanskrit: Taksasila): Situated in the foothills of the Himalayas, 30 km. from Islamabad. Taxila is the site of an archaeological complex which has considerable historical and cultural importance. According to Aramaic inscriptions on archaeological finds, Taxila used to be part of *Achaemenid empire. After the campaigns of Alexander the Great it was included in the *Mauryan Empire. Under King Asoka, Taxila became a Buddhist centre. In about 1000 AD the city was seized by the Saka and then by the *Kushans. Later, it was razed by the Ephtalites.

At the end of the 1960s, several heavy engineering plants and casting and forging plants were built in the area with help from China.

SINDH PROVINCE

Karachi

Karachi, with its recently established industrial outport of Port Quasim, is the largest city in Pakistan. Situated on the shore of the Arabian Sea it is the administrative centre of Sindh Province. Karachi has existed as a sea port on the Arabian Sea coast since the end of the eighteenth century. Under the Sindh rulers of the Talpur dynasty, Karachi was the main port city of Sindh. During British rule, the city expanded quickly. From 1843 to 1947 Karachi was the capital of Sindh Province, it later became the capital city of the province within the Bombay Presidency. From 1947 to 1959 Karachi was the capital of Pakistan.

Province/District	Area (sq km)	Population of Administrative District (1998)	Population of city/town (1998)	Density per sq.km.	Urban%
Sindh	140,914	30,439,893		216	48.8
Hyderabad	5,519	2,891,488	1,151,274	524	50.8
Jacobabad	**5,278**	**1,425,572**	137,733	**270**	**24.4**
Karachi	**1,259**	**8,874,906**	9,269, 265	**7,049**	
[Karachi East]	139	2,746,014		19,756	100
[Karachi West]	929	2,105,923		2,267	90.7
[Karachi South]	122	1,745,038		14,304	100
[Karachi Central]	69	2,277,931		33,014	100
[Malir]	2,268	981,412		433	67.3
Port Qasim					
Sukkur	5,165	908,373	329,176	176	50.9
Thatta	17,355	1,113,194	36,915	64	11.2

Karachi is the country's largest manufacturing and scientific center. It has the campus of the country's main university, several prestigious colleges, and scientific research institutions such as the Aga Khan University of Medical Sciences and the centre of Eastern Medicine of the Hamdard foundation. The city boasts museums, libraries and exhibition halls. The city is the main trading centre for Pakistan with banks, branches of foreign banks, head offices of insurance companies, a stock exchange and cotton exchange. The Karachi international airport caters to a majority of the worlds' airlines. There is also a naval base of considerable importance.

There are a great many of modern multi-storey buildings, luxury hotels and trade centres. Architecturally the most interesting streets are in the central area. The buildings are of local pink limestone and sandstone built between the two world wars. The most picturesque road is the Clifton promenade built in the British period. Quaid-i-Azam M. A. Jinnah's Tomb is one of the main sightseeing attractions.

Port Qasim

One of the two main ports in Pakistan, it was named after Muhammad bin Qasim, high commander in the service of the Omeyad Khalif Walid (705-15), who conquered Sindh in 711-13. The construction of the port in the coastal area of Sindh Province began in 1977. The first stage was completed by 30th June 1989. Construction costs amounted to 6.6 billion rupees. In 1986-8, the turnover of goods exceeded 6.5 million tons.

The port has a hinterland where various heavy industries are being developed.

Hyderabad

Hyderabad was founded in 1768 by Mian Ghulam Shah (1758-71), the ruler of Sindh and founder of the *Kalhora dynasty, who made it his capital. The Kalhora's were followed by the Talpurs under whom it remained the main city of Sindh. The walls of the fortress still exist, and the rulers' palace has been turned into a museum.

Second, after Karachi, in importance as a political and economic centre of Sindh, Hyderabad is an area of large-scale industries, and houses a branch of the Sindh Industrial Trading Estates, with its headquarters in Karachi. There are large-scale cement, chemical, textile and food factories. It is an educational center having the Sindh University campus at Jamshoro in the suburbs of the city.

Jacobabad

The administrative centre of the Jacobabad district, Jacobabad is situated in the north-west of Sindh in the Indus Valley. It is connected with Sukkur and Quetta by a railway line and a highway. Jacobabad has the reputation of being the hottest area in Pakistan with high temperatures of 50°C. in summer and an intensely arid climate.

Sukkur

Located in the northern Sindh Plain on the Indus River, it has been known since the eighth century AD, and was the capital of Upper Sindh for over 2,000 years. Pilgrims are attracted to its tombs and mosques. The main sightseeing attractions are the inclined **minar* of Mir Muhammad Masum and the medieval fortress Bakkhar. The Sukkur Barrage is not far from the town and is probably its main claim to fame. Below the barrage the river is only 200 metres wide, but above it the Indus River can be up to 20km wide. Seven major canals lead off the barrage to form a massive network of canals feeding the farmlands of Sindh and enabling almost 3 million hectares of desert to be brought into productive use. The main canals are the Nara to the east, the Khairpur and the Rohri Canal running closest to the east bank of the Indus. The early smaller canals leading off the main feeders were often badly sited cutting across natural drainage, sometimes not lined, and have been badly maintained. This has led to a severe problem of waterlogging and salinisation. Seepage can absorb up to one third of the useful water with a further third lost due to evaporation. Water percolating down has led to a rise in the water table leaving standing water on fields subject to evaporation. The combination leaves a layer of salts and minerals making the land unusable.

Thatta

The town is of considerable cultural and historical interest, known since ancient times under different names. In the Middle Ages, Thatta was an important political centre. Sited on a hill above the town is a series of tombs and graves of famous rulers. The 'City of the Dead' on Makli Hill is a monument dating back to the

13th to 16th centuries. In the town itself the Jamia Masjid, built under Shah Jehan, is the main sightseeing attraction.

North West Frontier Province

Province/District/Town	Area (sq km)	Population of Administrative District (1998)	Population of city/town (1998)	Density per sq.km.	Urban %
NWFP	74,521	17,743,645		238	16.9
Bannu	1,227	675,667		551	7.1
Kohat	2,545	562,644	94,647	221	27.0
Mardan	1,632	1,460,100	244,511	895	20.2
Nathiagali					
Peshawar	1,257	2,026,851	988,005	1,612	48.5

Bannu

The town of *Bannu is situated in an almost circular basin on the *Kurram River where it leaves the *Kohat and *Wazir hills and was originally a trading route between the Indus Valley and Kabul. It is referred to as 'Pona' in 404 AD by a Chinese pilgrim Fa-Hien. At that time there was a Buddhist monastery housing 3,000 monks. During the period when the town was held by Ranjit Singh it was named Dulipshehr and was re-named Edwardesbad under British rule. In 1903 it became Bannu. The town, surrounded by palm trees and mango orchards, now has a spacious cantonment and a crowded market centre and is in an area of richly irrigated, densely populated and wooded farmland.

Kohat

The present-day city was founded in the middle of the 18th century, although there have been settlements close to the north-south Kohat Pass through the Safed Koh Range from Peshawar to the Kohat Plains and the Indus Valley for many centuries. It was known for its salt trade and as a stronghold of the British regime in *Pushtun lands. Now a trade centre, Kohat has many small-scale industries. It is chiefly a garrison town.

Mardan

Mardan lies on the east bank of the *Swat River between Peshawar and the Swat Valley and controlling entry to the Malakand Pass from the south. Mardan is now a trade centre, mainly dealing in the sugar and tobacco industries. It is also a cantonment. Mardan was built in the mid-nineteenth century as a stronghold of the British authorities although evidence of earlier *Gandhara period Buddhist settlements dating back as 40 AD has been excavated in the area most notably at *Takht-e-Bahi*.

Peshawar

(ancient name: Purushapura) It is the capital of the North West Frontier Province. Peshawar is one of the oldest cities in Asia, once the capital of the Kushan Empire. From 1849 to independence in 1947, it was under British rule. It is a major trade centre on the way to Afghanistan and a major terminal on the motorway and railway line, which connects Karachi and the southern regions of the country with the north. Peshawar is home to a large-scale food industry. It is a major educational centre, having the campus of the Peshawar University and the Institute of Radiotherapy and Nuclear Medicine located here. It is also a religious centre of importance and there are many mosques and *mazars*. There is a cantonment. The main architectural attraction is the Bala Hisar fortress and its defence walls.

Balochistan

Province/District/Town	Area (sq km)	Population of Administrative District	Population of city/town	Density per sq.km.	Urban %
Balochistan	347,190	6,565,885		19	23.9
Kalat	6,622	237,834	22,559	36	14.2
Quetta	2,653	759,941	560,307	286	74.4

Kalat

(Persian: Fortress) In the Middle Ages the town was called Kalat-i Sehwa, or Kalat-i Balochi. In the seventeenth and eighteenth centuries it was the capital of the Kalat princely state, in vassalage to the Great Mughals and the Shahs of Iran and Afghanistan. From the second half of the nineteenth century until 1947, Kalat was the capital of a Balochi princely state, a vassal to British India. From 31 March 1948 to 1955 it was the centre of a princely state in West Pakistan. From 1955 to 1970 it was the centre of the Balochistan division of West Pakistan. Now a major local trade centre, Kalat is also known for its magnificent orchards.

Quetta

Known in the Middle Ages as Rasulabad, then Shol or Shalkot, it is now the administrative centre of Balochistan province. A major trade and transport centre close to the Iranian and Afghan borders, Quetta has many textile factories and food factories. A cantonment, comprising one-fifth of the city's population, has been here since the colonial days. It is home to an Army College, military schools, the University, the Geological Survey of Pakistan, the Geodetic Institute, the latter chiefly because Quetta is located in an active seismic zone. The city was almost completely destroyed during the 1935 earthquake in which 20,000 people were killed.

Note: Statistical data has been taken from the Statistical Division, Government of Pakistan.

ECONOMIC POLICY, GROWTH AND POVERTY IN HISTORICAL PERSPECTIVE

Akmal Hussain

The study of history, since it reconstructs the past, is essentially conducted from the vantage point of present concerns. Pakistan's present policy challenge is to achieve a level and structure of economic growth that can rapidly reduce poverty. In an attempt to trace the genesis of the problem, this article provides a historical analysis of the emergence of an economic structure that: 1. constrained the capacity of GDP growth to reduce poverty, 2. constrained the potential to achieve a high GDP growth on a sustainable basis.

The policies of various political regimes have not only been distinct but have had a profound impact on institutions and the structure and growth of the economy. Therefore in examining Pakistan's economic history it is useful to periodize it in terms of political regimes rather than simply in terms of five-year plans.

The emerging architecture of Pakistan's economy is founded in its institutional structure and the nature of governance. Therefore, in tracing Pakistan's economic history we have indicated, albeit briefly, the relationship between the practice of power by governments, the process of institutional decay and the nature of Pakistan's economic growth process[1].

I. THE AYUB REGIME (1958-69): GROWTH, INEQUALITY AND LOAN DEPENDENCE

The military *coup d'etat*, which brought General Ayub *Khan into power, established the dominance of military and bureaucracy in Pakistan's power structure. The associated political system while it weakened the nascent democratic institutions of the legislature, press and the judiciary, constituted authoritarian power behind a civilian facade called 'basic democracy'. The economic strategy of the government, while it induced rapid GDP growth, sharply accentuated inter-personal and inter-regional inequalities, which generated explosive political tensions. These tensions erupted in a mass movement against President Ayub Khan in *West Pakistan and a national independence movement in *East Pakistan that culminated in the emergence of the new state of Bangladesh.

I.1 Industrial Growth, Inequality and Loan Dependence

The decade of the 1960s is seen by many as the 'golden age' in terms of the high growth rates achieved through the provision of subsidies and tariff protection to industry and an elite farmer strategy in agriculture. It was also a period when the mould was set for the emergence of an economic structure that was to lock Pakistan's economy into increasing income inequality, a narrow and inefficient industrial base, and increasing loan dependence, for the next four decades.

Following the Korean boom in 1953, the government had introduced a policy framework for inducing the large profits of traders in jute and raw cotton to flow into the manufacturing sector. This was attempted through a policy of encouraging the domestic production of consumer goods through a variety of protection measures during the 1950s[2].

During the 1960s import substitution industrial growth in the consumer goods sector, was more systematically encouraged by the government. This was done by means of a wide range of protection measures for domestic manufacturers. These included high import tariffs on imported consumer goods, cheap credit, and in some cases direct import controls on competing imports. At the same time, there was removal of import controls (established earlier in the 1955) on industrial raw materials and machinery. In addition to various forms of protection, new incentives were offered for exports. These included the Bonus Voucher Scheme[3], tax rebates, tax exemptions and accelerated depreciation allowances to increase post tax profits.

The magnitude of protection provided by the government to private sector industry was such that it enabled domestic manufacturers to earn large rupee profits on the production of goods that were not internationally competitive. It has been estimated[4] that during the 1960s, Pakistan's main industries (when input costs and output values are both measured in dollar terms) were producing negative value added. Indirect subsidies such as the Bonus Voucher Scheme combined with the overvalued exchange rate, enabled domestic manufacturers to earn large rupee profits on exports that brought no gain to the economy in terms of foreign exchange.

It has been argued that the phenomenon of negative value added in industry was an important reason why during the 1960s, inspite of import substitution and large export volumes, foreign exchange shortages persisted[5]. This set the 'mould' for Pakistan's narrow export base (concentration on the low value added end of textiles) and the associated debt problem, which persisted for the next three decades. For example (see chart 1), the share of the traditional textile industry in total exports far from falling, in fact increased from 30% in the decade of the 1960s to 50 per cent in the decade of the 1990s.

CHART 1
PERIOD AVERAGES OF EXPORTS OF VARIOUS COMMODITY GROUPS AS A % OF TOTAL EXPORTS OF PAKISTAN

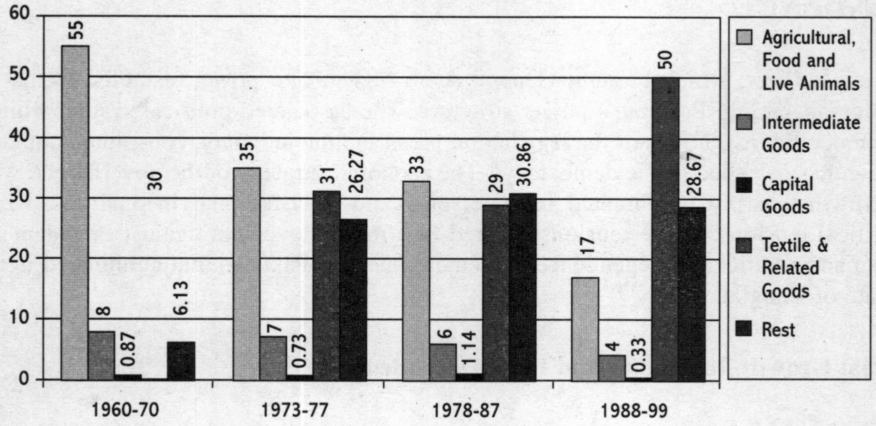

The government during the 1960s adopted a deliberate policy of concentrating national income in the hands of the upper income groups.[6] The economic basis of this policy was the assumption that the rich save a larger proportion of their income and hence a higher national savings rate could be achieved with an unequal distribution of income (the target savings rate being 25 per cent of GDP). In practice while the policy of distributing incomes in favour of the economic elite succeeded, the assumption that it would raise domestic savings over time failed to materialize. It has been estimated that 15 per cent of the resources annually generated in the rural sector were transferred to the urban industrialists and 63 to 85 per cent of these transferred resources went into increased urban consumption.[7] Far from raising the domestic savings rate to 25%, the actual savings rate never rose above 12 per cent.[8]

The failure of the economic elite to save out of their increased income during the 1960s, resulted in a sharp increase in the requirement of foreign aid. According to official figures, gross foreign aid inflows increased from US $ 373 million in 1950-55 to US $ 2,701 million in 1965-70. The rapid increase in foreign aid was accompanied by a change in its composition from grants to higher interest loans[9]. Consequently the debt-servicing burden rose dramatically. Debt servicing as a percentage of foreign exchange earnings which was 4.2 per cent in 1960-61, increased to 34.5 per cent by 1971-72. The magnitude of this figure did not fall for the next three decades and by the year 2000 it was even higher at 40 per cent.

Given the policy of re-distributing incomes in favour of the rich, it is not surprising that by the end of the 1960s a small group of families with inter-locking directorates dominated industry, banking and insurance in Pakistan.[10] In terms of value added 46 per cent of the value added in the large scale manufacturing sector originated in firms controlled by only 43 families.

In banking, the degree of concentration was even greater than industry. For example, seven family banks constituted 91.6 per cent of private domestic deposits and 84.4 per cent of earning assets. Furthermore, State Bank compilation of balance sheets of listed companies indicates that the family banks tended to provide loans to industrial companies controlled by the same families.[11] The insurance industry, although smaller in size than banking, also had a high degree of concentration of ownership. Forty-three industrial families controlling 75.6 per cent of the assets of Pakistani insurance companies tended to favour industrial companies owned by the same group.[12]

Not only were the 43 families dominating industry, insurance and banking, but also had considerable power over government agencies sanctioning industrial projects. PICIC (Pakistan Industrial Credit and Investment Corporation) was the agency responsible for sanctioning large-scale industrial projects. Out of the 21 directors of PICIC, seven were from the 43 leading industrial families and were actively involved in the public sector financial institutions that directly affected their private economic interests.

During the process of rapid economic growth of the 1960s, while an exclusive and highly monopolistic class was amassing wealth, the majority of Pakistan's population was suffering an absolute decline in its living standards. For example, the per capita consumption of foodgrain of the poorest 60 per cent of Pakistan's urban population declined from an index of 100 in 1963-64 to 96.1 in 1969-70. The decline was even greater over the same period in the case of the poorest 60 per cent of rural population. In their case, per capita consumption of foodgrain declined from an index of 100 in 1963-64 to only 91 in 1969-70.[13] There was an even larger decline in the real wages in the industry: In the decade and a half ending in 1967, real wages in the industry declined by 25 per cent.[14] According to one estimate, in 1971-72, poverty in the rural sector was so acute that 82 per cent of rural households could not afford to provide even 2,100 calories per day per family member.[15]

In an economy where there were significant differences in the infrastructure facilities available in the different provinces, there was a tendency for investment based on private profitability to be concentrated in the relatively developed regions. Consequently regional disparities would tend to widen over time. This is in fact what happened in the case of Pakistan. The *Punjab and the *Sindh provinces, which had relatively more developed infrastructure, attracted a larger proportion of industrial investment than the other provinces. In Sindh, however, the growth in income was mainly in Karachi and Hyderabad. Thus, economic disparities widened not only between East and West Pakistan, but also between the provinces within West Pakistan.

During the 1960s, the factor which accelerated the growth of regional income disparities within what is Pakistan today was the differential impact of agricultural growth associated with the so-called 'Green Revolution'. Since the yield increase associated with the adoption of high yield varieties of food grain required irrigation, and since the Punjab and Sindh had a relatively larger proportion of their area under irrigation, they experienced much faster growth in their incomes, compared to *Balochistan and the *North West Frontier Province.[16]

I.2 Agriculture Growth and the Structure of Poverty

The failure to conduct an effective land reform in Pakistan had resulted in a continued concentration of landownership in the hands of a few big landlords. Thus, in 1972, 30 per cent of total farm area was owned by large landowners (owning 150 acres and above). The overall picture of Pakistan's agrarian structure has been that these large landowners have rented out most of their land to small and medium-sized tenants (i.e., tenants operating below 25 acres).

In a doctoral thesis[17] it has been shown that given this agrarian structure, when the 'Green Revolution' technology became available in the late 1960s the larger landowners found it profitable to resume some of their rented out land for self-cultivation on large farms using hired labour and capital investment. Consequently there was a growing economic polarization of rural society. While the landlords' incomes increased, those of the poor peasantry declined relatively, as they faced a reduction in their operated farm area and in many cases growing landlessness.[18] For example in the case of farms in the size class 150 acres and above, the increase in the farm area during the period 1960 to 1978, constituted half their total farm area in 1978. In terms of the source of increase, 65 per cent of the increase in area of large farms came through resumption of formerly rented out land. That this resumption was accompanied by growing landlessness of the poor peasantry is indicated by the fact that in the period 1960 to 1973 about 0.8 million tenants became landless wage labourers. Of the total rural wage labourers in Pakistan in 1973, as many as 43% had entered this category as the result of proletarianization of the poor peasantry[19].

The polarization of rural society and increased landlessness of the poor peasantry was associated with increased peasant dependence in the face of rural markets for agricultural inputs and outputs that were mediated by large landlords. In the pre 'Green Revolution' period, the poor tenant relied on the landlord simply for the *use* of the land but used the government's canal water, his own seeds and animal manure. In the post 'Green Revolution' period however, since the political and social power of the landlord remained intact, the peasant began to rely on the landlord for the *purchase of inputs*. (e.g. HYV seeds, chemical fertilizers, pesticides, the landlord's tube-well water, for a seasonally flexible supply of irrigation, and credit). Thus, in many (though not all) cases, the dependence of the poor peasant intensified with the commercialization of agriculture in the sense that now his very re-constitution of the production cycle annually depended on the intercession of the landlord. At the same time due to the reduction in his operated area following land resumption, the tenant was obliged to complement his income by working as a wage labourer part of the time at a wage rate below the market rate in deference to the landlord's power. (Conversely, the landlord's management of the owner cultivated section of his land was facilitated through this tied source of labour supply). This phenomenon persists till today[20].

Thus, the 'commercialization of agriculture' in a situation where landlords and the local power structure controlled markets for inputs and outputs, brought new mechanisms for the reproduction of rural poverty, even though overall agricultural growth accelerated. The high rate of agricultural growth during the Ayub regime could not be sustained in subsequent years. Yet the mechanisms of reproducing rural poverty that had emerged in this period, persisted over the next four decades.

II. THE BHUTTO REGIME (1973-77): GROWTH, NATIONALIZATION AND THE FISCAL CRISIS

The Ayub regime had instituted policies, which resulted in a concentration of incomes in the hands of a nascent industrial elite while real wages declined and poverty increased. In the resultant social tensions, Z.A. *Bhutto emerged as a champion of the poor to lead a mass movement for overthrowing the Ayub government. Support for the newly formed *Pakistan People's Party (PPP) led by Bhutto came not only from workers and peasants but also from elements of the urban middle classes seeking reform. Conservative landlords also gravitated to the PPP, because of their antagonism to an industrial elite that was appropriating a growing share of economic resources.

Soon after 1973 there was a purge of radical middle class element from the PPP, and the achievement of a dominant position within the party by the landed elite. Consequently there was an institutional rupture between the PPP and the mass base amongst the workers and peasants. This set the stage for economic measures that were socialist in form, while actually serving to strengthen the landed elite and widening the economic base for state patronage.

One of the most important initiatives of the PPP government was the nationalization in 1972 of 43 large industrial units in the capital and intermediate goods sectors such as cement, fertilizers, oil refining, engineering and chemicals. Just three years later the government nationalized the cooking oil industry and then flour milling, cotton ginning and rice husking mills.

While the first set of nationalizations impacted the 'monopoly capitalists', the second set of nationalizations in 1976 by contrast hit the medium and small sized entrepreneurs. Therefore nationalization in this regime cannot be seen in terms of state intervention for greater equity. Rather the rapid increase in the size of the public sector served to widen the resource base of the regime for the practice of the traditional form of power through state patronage. This involved the state intervening to redistribute resources arbitrarily to those who had access to its patronage.[21]

II.1 Nationalization, Investment and Growth

Let us now briefly indicate the implications of the economic measures in this period on investment, growth and the budget deficit. Private investment as a percentage of GDP in the Bhutto period (1973/74 to 1977/78) declined sharply to 4.8 per cent compared to 8.2 per cent in the preceding period 1960/61 to 1972/73 (See table 1). The nationalization of heavy industries shook the confidence of the private sector and was a factor in the declining investment[22].

It may be pertinent to point out, that the decline in private sector manufacturing as a percentage of the GDP, had already begun eight years before the Bhutto period, after the 1965 war.[23] So while the nationalization and subsequent economic measures cannot be said to have *caused* the decline in private investment, they certainly intensified it.

The decline in private sector investment in the post 1965 period as a whole, (as opposed to its sharp deceleration during the nationalization phase), can be attributed[24] to three underlying factors: 1. foreign capital inflows fell sharply after the 1965 war, 2. the manufacturing sector in a situation of declining domestic demand was unable to meet the challenge of exports due to high production costs in traditional industries, and 3. entrepreneurs did not diversify into non traditional industries where there was considerable growth potential.

TABLE 1
PERIOD AVERAGES OF GROSS INVESTMENT* AS A % OF GDP

Average During	GFCF (Total) as % of GDP (Current Prices)	GFCF (Private) as % of GDP (Current Prices)	GFCF (Public) as % of GDP (Current Prices)
1960-1973	15.28	8.21	7.26
1973-1978	15.50	4.79	10.71
1978-1988	16.77	7.10	9.66
1988-1993	17.95	9.22	8.73
1993-1998	16.31	9.32	7.36
1998-2000	13.26	8.10	5.31

SOURCE: Economic Survey, Government of Pakistan (G.O.P.), Economic Advisor's Wing, Finance Division, Various Issues.

Note: *GFCF is Gross Fixed Capital Formation

We find that unlike manufacturing investment, the decline in the total private sector investment as a percentage of the GDP was more than compensated by an increase in the total public sector investment. Thus, the overall investment/GDP ratio during the Bhutto period reached 15.5%, which was slightly higher than in the preceding period (see Table 1). Yet inspite of an increase in the total investment/GDP ratio, the growth rate of GDP declined compared to the preceding period (as table 2 shows, GDP growth during the Bhutto period was about 5% compared to 6.3% in the earlier 1960-73 period). This is indicative of a decline in the productivity of investment (i.e. an increase in the incremental capital output ratio).

The question is, what caused the decline in the capacity of investment to generate growth? The answer lies in the fact that not only was most of the investment in the period emanating from the public sector, but that a large proportion of this investment was going into unproductive spheres: Defence and public administration were the fastest growing sectors of the economy (11.4%) while the commodity producing sector was growing at only 2.21% during the period. Even in the productive sector, the lion's share of the public investment went into the Steel Mill (see, Pakistan Steel Mill) project beginning in 1973. The project using an obsolete Soviet design, involved a technology that was both capital intensive and inefficient. Consequently, the tendency of declining productivity of investment was exacerbated.

Even in the existing manufacturing industries in the public sector while some industries showed good profits to start with, there was a sharp decline in the rates of return on investment, due to a combination of poor management of existing units and improper location of new units on political grounds[25]. Thus, the lowering of GDP growth inspite of an increase in investment in the Bhutto period occurred because of two sets of factors: (a) concentration of public sector investment in the unproductive sectors of defence and administration, and (b) economically inefficient investment decisions in the public sector industries based on political considerations, with respect to technology choice, geographic location, and production management.

II.2 Governance and the Emerging Fiscal Crisis

Let us now briefly discuss the implications of the political and economic measures of the government during this period for the budget.

The problem of the government's dependence on financial borrowing as we have indicated, started in the Ayub period, when the obligation of maintaining a large military and bureaucratic apparatus combined with the imperatives of providing huge subsidies to both agriculture and industry: For agriculture in the form of subsidized inputs (water, fertilizer, pesticides) as part of the elite farmer strategy; for industry in terms of explicit and implicit subsidies such as an over-valued exchange rate, subsidized credit and tax incentives to an industrial sector that was inefficient and lacked export competitiveness.

In the Z.A. Bhutto period, budget deficits widened further as expenditures on defence and administration increased sharply. Higher defence expenditures were part of the policy of refurbishing the defence establishment. Large expenditures on government administration arose mainly out of the decision to build new para-military institutions such as the Federal Security Force. The bureaucracy was also enlarged and re-structured through the policy of 'lateral entry' which enabled loyalists outside the civil services cadre to be appointed at the upper and middle echelons[26].

Apart from the increased expenditures on defence and administration, the budget was additionally burdened by the losses of the public sector industries. The deficits in these industries were generated by their poor performance on the one hand and the pricing policy on the other. Nationalized units under official pressure to suppress price increases inspite of rising costs, were recovering not much more than their operating costs. Consequently, internally generated funds could finance only 7%[27] of the investment undertaken, thereby necessitating heavy borrowing from the government.

As government expenditures increased, the ability to finance them from tax revenue was constrained by two factors: (a) The slow down in GDP growth, and (b) the government's inability to improve the coverage of direct taxation. As a consequence, the deficit increased rapidly. The government attempted to control the rising budget deficit by reducing subsidies on consumption goods and increasing indirect taxation. However even these measures failed to reduce the budget deficit in the face of rising current expenditures. Therefore monetary expansion was resorted to, resulting in accelerated inflation.

The financial constraint following the large non-development expenditures, severely restricted the funds available for development, and hence enfeebled the two initiatives that were designed to benefit the poor: the National Development Volunteer Programme (NDVP) and the Peoples Work Programme. The former aimed at providing employment to the educated unemployed and the latter to generate employment for the rural poor through labour intensive projects. Both programmes were marginalized due to budgetary constraints.[28]

The social consequences of these financial measures were to have a profound impact on the political strength of the Bhutto regime. Withdrawal of subsidies on consumption goods together with higher inflation rates squeezed the real income of the middle and lower middle classes. This served to accentuate the resentment amongst middle class commercial elements that had followed the nationalization of the small and medium sized food processing units in 1976. These urban *petit bourgeois* elements had in 1968-69 fuelled the anti-Ayub agitation that had catapulted Bhutto into power. They now joined the street demonstrations in 1977 that led to his downfall.

III. THE ZIA REGIME (1977-89): ECONOMIC GROWTH, RELIGIOUS EXTREMISM AND THE PRELUDE TO RECESSION

The various political regimes that came into power were characterized not only by their distinct economic policies, but also by the specific ideologies through which they legitimized themselves for the practice of political power. The Ayub regime propounded modernization and economic development. The Z.A. Bhutto regime donned the mantle of redeeming the poor through socialism. The Ziaul *Haq regime sought to institutionalize military rule through the garb of a coercive and obscurantist version of 'Islamic' ideology. Indeed the design and implementation of economic policy in various periods was conditioned by the politics of each regime.

III.1 Religious Extremism and Fiscal Space

In the pursuit of this power objective, the democratic *constitution of 1973 was set aside and draconian measures of military courts, arbitrary arrests, amputation of hands and public lashing were introduced. Pakistan's society, by and large, was historically characterized by cultural diversity, democratic aspirations and a religious perspective rooted in tolerance and humanism. This was one of the reasons why the founding father, *Quaid-e-Azam Muhammad Ali *Jinnah conceived of Pakistan's polity as democratic and pluralistic with religious belief to be a matter concerning the individual rather than the state.[29]

In attempting to restructure such a state and society into a theocracy, the government undertook two kinds of initiatives: First, measures designed to subordinate to executive authority, institutions of state and civil society such as the judiciary and the press, which if allowed to function independently could check governmental power[30].

The second set of measures towards a theocratic state sought to inculcate obscurantist views and induced a narrowing of the human mind. It involved a suspension of the sensibility of love and reason underlying the religious tradition signified in Pakistan's folk culture[31].

Advocacy for a theocratic social order was conducted through the state controlled television and press[32] and governmental financing of new mosque schools (*madrassas*)[33] in small towns and rural areas many of which were linked with militant religious organizations involved in the Afghan war.

Political and economic support was sought from the U.S. by offering to play the role of a front line state in the Afghan guerilla war against the occupying Soviet army. (see, US-Pakistan Relations) Accordingly, Pakistan obtained a package of U.S. $ 3.2 billion in financial loans and relatively sophisticated military hardware. Moreover, with the support from the U.S., Pakistan was able to get additional fiscal space by getting its foreign debt rescheduled, and increased private foreign capital inflows. These official and private capital inflows played an important role in stimulating macro economic growth in this period. They also helped establish a small though powerful political constituency within state and society, for a theocratic form of military dictatorship.

III.2 Economic Growth and the Prelude to Recession

The rapidly growing debt servicing burden together with a slow down of GDP growth and government revenues that had occurred at the end of the Bhutto period would have placed crippling fiscal and political pressures on the Zia regime but for two factors: (a) the generous financial support received from the West, and (b) the acceleration in the inflow of remittances from the Middle East which increased from US $ 0.5 billion in 1978 to US $ 3.2 billion in 1984. These remittances not only eased balance of payments pressures, but also potential political pressures, directly benefiting about 10 million people, predominantly in the lower middle class and working class strata.[34]

TABLE 2
PERIOD AVERAGES OF THE PERCENTAGE SHARE OF SELECTED MACRO-ECONOMIC INDICATORS IN THE GDP OF PAKISTAN.

Average During	Real GDP Growth % (Market Prices)	Domestic Savings as % of GDP	Average Export Growth %	Exports as % of GDP	Trade Balance as % of GDP	Workers Remittances as % of GDP	Debt Servicing as % of GDP
1960-1973	6.26	12.99	16.19	4.57	-5.11		1.28
1973-1978	4.99	7.29	10.31	8.79	-7.27		2.04
1978-1988	6.6	8.15	14.33	9.59	-8.66	7.71	2.44
1988-1993	4.92	12.99	9.19	13.01	-5.00	4.54	3.02
1993-1998	3.14	14.98	5.15	13.50	-3.99	2.55	3.48
1998-2000	4.17		0.16	13.69	-2.33	1.71	2.55

SOURCE: Economic Survey, Government of Pakistan (G.O.P.), Economic Advisor's Wing, Finance Division, Various Issues.

As it was, the easing of budgetary pressures together with good harvests and the construction and consumption booms associated with Middle East remittances, helped stimulate economic growth. As table 2 shows, GDP growth increased from about 5% during the Z.A. Bhutto period i.e. (1973-77) to 6.6% during the Zia period (1978-88). The data show that this acceleration in the GDP growth was induced to some extent by increased investment: The gross fixed capital formation as a percentage of the GDP increased from 15.5% in the Bhutto period to 16.8% in the Zia period. (Table 1).

There was a strategic shift from the 'socialist' policies of nationalization, and the large public sector in the Bhutto period, to denationalization and a greater role assigned to the private sector in the growth process. In this context the Zia regime offered a number of incentives to the private sector such as low interest credit, duty free imports of selected capital goods, tax holidays and accelerated depreciation allowances. These inducements combined with high aggregate demand associated with consumption expenditures from Middle East remittances, and increased investment in housing, created a favourable climate for new investment. Private sector gross fixed investment increased from 4.79% of the GDP in the Bhutto period to 7.10% in the Zia regime (See Table 1). The public sector gross fixed capital formation as a percentage of the GDP however declined slightly from 10.7% in the preceding period to 9.7 % in the Zia period. The data on the manufacturing sector is also consistent with these findings and show a substantial acceleration in the growth of overall manufacturing from 5.5% in the 1970s to 8.21 % in the 1980s. In terms of the composition of investment in the large scale manufacturing sector as table 3 shows, there appears to be a significant acceleration in the investment in the intermediate and capital growth sectors, whose percentage share in the total manufacturing increased from about 43% at the end of the Bhutto period to about 50% in the mid 1980s. (The share fell again in the late 1980s and 1990s). This is consistent with the boom in the construction sector and the secondary multiplier effects in the intermediate and capital goods sectors.

TABLE 3

TOTAL INVESTMENTS IN VARIOUS INDUSTRIES AS A % OF TOTAL INVESTMENT IN ALL INDUSTRIES IN THE LARGE SCALE MANUFACTURING SECTOR OF PAKISTAN.*

Years	Investment in All Consumer Goods	Investment in Intermediate & Capital Goods	Investment in Textile & Related Goods	Investment in all other Industries
1964-65	22.7	25.2	41.1	11.1
1966-67	28.7	30.8	37.3	3.1
1970-71	31.8	27.3	38.0	2.9
1976-77	31.2	22.1	17.9	28.8
1977-78	23.6	43.2	23.7	9.6
1982-83	18.0	49.7	21.5	10.7
1983-84	24.5	57.2	17.9	0.3
1987-88	29.4	21.8	37.4	11.4
1990-91	28.7	24.6	44.4	2.2

SOURCE: Census of Manufacturing Industries, FBS, Statistics Division, Govt. of Pakistan. Various Issues.

Notes:

1. The CMI data represents only the large scale manufacturing sector in the economy.
2. The compilation of CMI data is conducted through mail enquiry supplemented by field visits. The questionnaires are issued to the factories as per list of manufacturing establishments maintained on the basis of monthly statements of registrations and cancellations received from the provincial Chief inspectors of Factories, Directorates of Labour Welfare of the Provinces.
3. Large scale manufacturing industries are those which employ 20 workers or more on any one given day of the year for manufacturing activity.
4. Manufacturing activity is defined as the mechanical or chemical transformation of inorganic or organic substances into new products whether the work is performed by power driven machines or by hand or whether it is done in a factory or in the worker's house. The assembly of component parts of manufactured products was also considered as manufacturing.
5. Investments here refer to all fixed assets consisting of land and building, plant and machinery and other fixed assets which are expected to have a productive life of more than one year and are in use by the establishment for the manufacturing activity.
6. Investments for a year include additions made during the year minus any sales of fixed assets during that year. These consist of, both Pakistan made and imports, and assets made for own use.

* Data refers to the figures obtained from the industries/establishments included in the census and does not represent the figures as a whole for the economy of Pakistan.

Although the GDP growth rate during the Zia period did increase, yet this higher growth rate could not be expected to be maintained because of continued poor performance of three strategic factors that sustain growth over time: a. The domestic savings rate continued to remain below 10% compared to a required rate of over 20%. b. Exports as a percentage of GDP continued to remain below 10% and did not register any substantial increase (see table 2). c. Inadequate investment in social and economic infrastructure. As defence and debt servicing expenditure increased, the Annual Development Programme (ADP) through which much of the infrastructure projects were funded, began to get constricted. As table 4 shows, ADP expenditure as a percentage of GDP fell from an average of 7.4% in the Z.A. Bhutto period, to 6.2% in the Zia period.

TABLE 4
ADP AS A PERCENTAGE OF GDP PERIOD AVERAGES

Average During	ADP as a% of GDP
1972/73 to 1976/77	7.4
1977/78 to 1986/87	6.24
1987/88 to 1996/97	4.26
1997/98 to 1999/2000	3.5

SOURCE: Economic Survey, GOP, Economic Advisor's Wing, Finance Division, Various Issues.

It is not surprising that when the cushion of foreign loans and debt relief was withdrawn at the end of the Afghan War, the underlying structural constraints to GDP growth began to manifest themselves: Debt servicing pressures resulting from the low savings rates, high borrowings and balance of payments deficits related with low export growth and poor infrastructure, combined to pull down the GDP growth into a protracted economic recession in the 1990s. Average annual GDP growth rate declined from 6.3% in the decade of the 1980s to 4.2% in the decade of the 1990s (See Table 5). The sharp decline in GDP growth was accompanied by a dramatic increase in poverty: The percentage of population below the poverty line was 17% in 1987 and rose to 34% in the 1999-2000. At the same time, the seeds of social conflict sown with the breeding of religious militant groups, began to erupt and feed off the growing poverty and unemployment. These armed extremist groups in time began to erode the writ of the State: In the post Zia period this became an important factor in constraining private sector investment and GDP growth, a constraint that continues to remain to this day.

IV. THE DEMOCRATIC INTERLUDE (1989-99): THE DEEPENING CRISIS OF ECONOMY AND STATE

The decade of the 1990s was marked by democratically elected regimes attempting to practice authoritarian forms of power within an ostensibly democratic order. This was combined with the use of public office for private wealth[35]. These features of governance during the 1990s, intensified to a critical level by the late 1990s, the three key elements of the crisis that threatened the State: a. A collapsing economy. b. The threat to the life and property of citizens resulting from rampant crime, and the emergence of armed militant groups of religious extremists. c. The erosion of many of the institutions of democratic and effective governance. Establishing competent and honest democratic governments to address these elements of the national crisis were necessary for winning greater political space for civilian rule in the undoubtedly constrained democratic structure. As it was the failure to deepen democracy, undermined even its existing fragile form.

IV.1 Economic Growth, Employment and Poverty in the 1990s

During the decade of the 1990s, political instability, historically unprecedented corruption in governance, and the worsening law and order situation perhaps had a significant adverse effect on private investment and GDP growth.

An important factor in the sharp slow down in GDP growth and increase in poverty was the particular way in which the government addressed the fiscal crisis, which reached a critical level during this period. The government having adopted a Structural Adjustment Programme (SAP) under the auspices of the IMF, undertook the necessary reduction in public expenditure through a sharp reduction in development expenditure rather than in unproductive expenditure. (Development expenditure as a percentage of GDP fell from 7.4% in the 1970s to 3.5% in the 1990s. By contrast the government's unproductive expenditure remained at the same high level (See Chart 3). This severely restricted urgently needed public investment in infrastructure and poverty reduction projects thereby simultaneously slowing down GDP growth and accentuating poverty.

Similarly the necessary increase in tax revenues was attempted not through an increase in direct taxation, but rather through indirect taxation. Since indirect taxation has a regressive effect on income distribution the increase in indirect taxation worsened poverty. For example evidence on the incidence of the tax burden by income group in Pakistan following the adoption of SAP, shows that the tax burden as a percentage of income was highest at 6.8%, for the lowest income group and lowest at –4.3%, for the highest income group[36]. Thus the tax burden on the poor increased and on the rich declined.

The particular choice of policy instruments used to pursue the reduction in the budget deficit stipulated in the SAP, thus contributed to slowing down growth and increasing poverty. Apart from this, the sequencing of the measures adopted further exacerbated the adverse effect on GDP growth and poverty. For example the increase in interest rates required by the Structural Adjustment Programme was initiated before rather than after the reduction in the budget deficit. Consequently, as interest rates rose sharply, so did the government's debt servicing burden and thereby an even more drastic reduction in development expenditure[37].

Yet these factors merely accentuated the tendency for declining growth that was rooted in structural factors, which were manifest even in the 1980s[38]. The failure of successive governments to address the deteriorating infrastructure and the emerging financial crisis further exacerbated the unfavorable environment for investment. As table 1 shows, total investment (as a percentage of GDP) declined from 17.9% in the period 1988-93 to 16.3% in the period 1993-1998. The decline in the overall investment was due to the fact that while the private sector investment did not increase (it remained around 9%), the public sector investment declined sharply from 8.7% at the end of the 1980s to 5.3% at the end of the 1990s.

While GDP growth declined during the 1990s (from 6.3% in the 1980s to 4.2% in the 1990s), employment growth continued to remain at a low level of 2.4% since the 1980s. This indicates that the employment problem persisted during the 1990s. At the same time the growth of labour productivity declined (see Table 5), which served to push real wages downwards[39].

TABLE 5

GROWTH OF GDP, EMPLOYMENT AND PRODUCTIVITY IN TWO DECADES

Per cent

GROWTH	1980s	1990s
1. GDP GROWTH	6.3	4.2
2. EMPLOYMENT GROWTH (TOTAL)	2.4	2.4
(i) Agriculture	1.9	1.6
(ii) Manufacturing	1.4	-0.4
3. PRODUCTIVITY GROWTH (TOTAL)	3.9	1.8
(i) Agriculture	2	1.7
(ii) Manufacturing	7	4.6

SOURCE: NOMAAN MAJID, PAKISTAN: AN EMPLOYMENT STRATEGY, ILO/SAAT, DECEMBER 1997 (Mimeo), TABLE A5, PAGE 58.

Evidence on sectoral employment elasticities shows that employment elasticities in both agriculture and industry declined during the 1990s. Thus the adverse effect on poverty of slower GDP growth rates in the 1990s was accentuated by this structural constraint to employment generation in agriculture and industry. Another structural dimension of the process of poverty creation in this period was located in the increased fluctuations in agricultural output which was pointed out in a recent study.[40] It indicates that under conditions of declining input productivity, when higher input/acre is required to maintain yields, the subsistence farmers with fewer resources are likely to suffer a greater than average decline in yields compared to large farmers. At the same time, due to lack of savings to fall back on, they are relatively more vulnerable to bad harvests under conditions of unstable growth.[41] Consequently, slower and more unstable growth during the 1990s could be expected to be accompanied by growing poverty and inequality. The evidence shows that this is precisely what happened during the 1990s: The Gini coefficient, which is a measure of the degree of inequality, increased from 26.85 in 1992-93 to 30.19 in 1998-99. Similarly the percentage of the population below the poverty line (calorific intake basis) was 26.6% in 1992-93, and increased to 32% in 1998-99[42].

V. POSTSCRIPT: THE MUSHARRAF REGIME AND THE ECHOES OF HISTORY

The multifaceted crisis of economy, society and state had reached a critical point by the end of the 1990s. This set the stage for the collapse of the formal democratic structure within which the contention for power between the military and elected political leadership had been conducted during the 1990s. President *Musharraf's government formulated a comprehensive set of reforms aimed at reviving the economy, and establishing the institutional basis for improved governance. At the same time through a number of constitutional amendments the political system was restructured. The powers of the President were enhanced even as he retained the post of Chief of Army Staff (COAS), and the National Security Council was created to ensure 'political stability' and 'continuity' of economic reforms. Thus the new political dispensation signifies the institutionalization of military power within a political structure in which an elected government also has a role to play.

During the regime of President Musharraf, economic policies combined with the changed international environment following 9/11, have enabled a substantial improvement in macro economic indicators: The GDP growth rate has accelerated to over 6 per cent in the last two years, the debt servicing burden has become tolerable, the budget deficit has been brought down substantially and State Bank reserves have

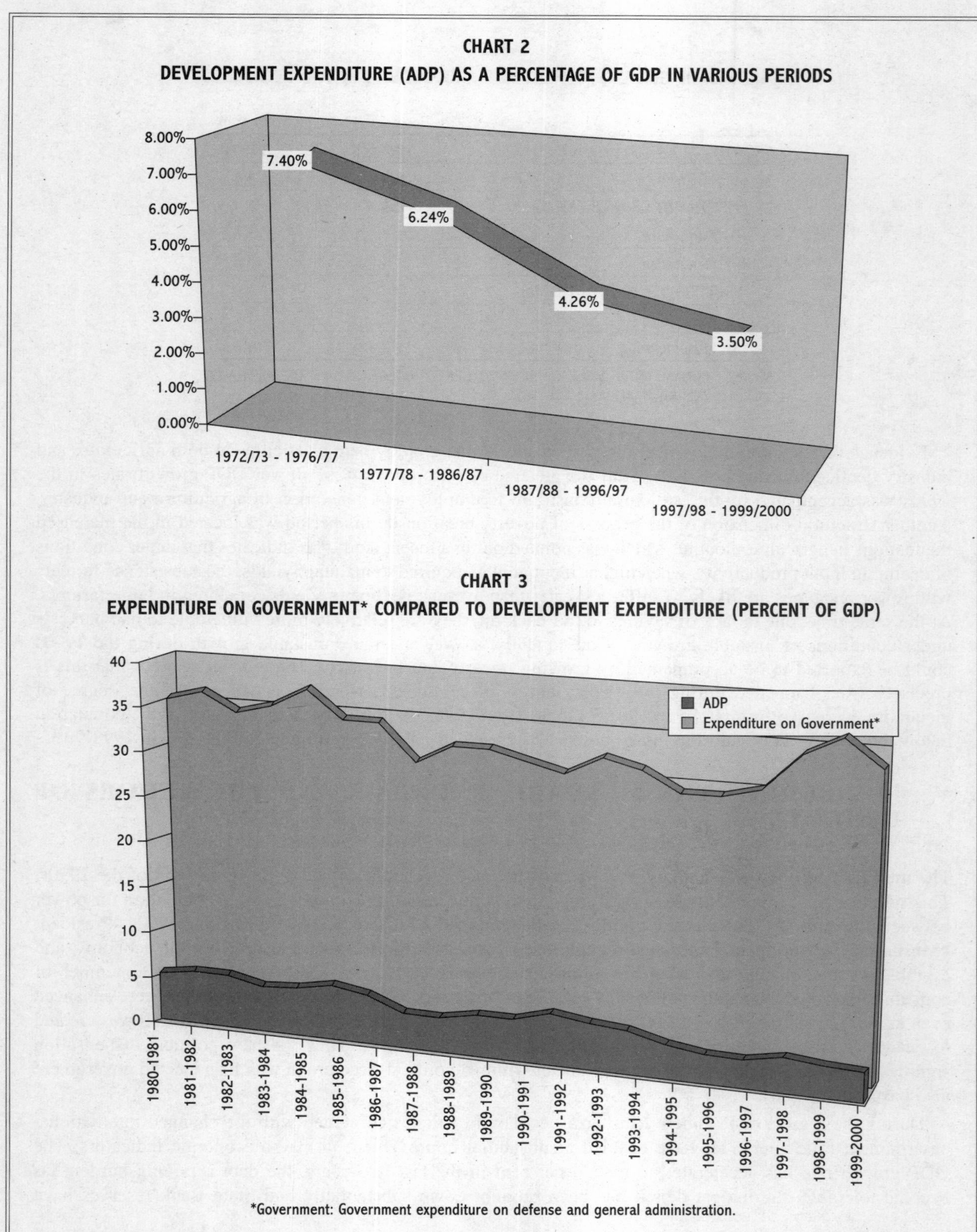
CHART 2
DEVELOPMENT EXPENDITURE (ADP) AS A PERCENTAGE OF GDP IN VARIOUS PERIODS
8.00%
7.00%
6.00%
5.00%
4.00%
3.00%
2.00%
1.00%
0.00%
7.40%
6.24%
4.26%
3.50%
1972/73 - 1976/77
1977/78 - 1986/87
1987/88 - 1996/97
1997/98 - 1999/2000
CHART 3
EXPENDITURE ON GOVERNMENT* COMPARED TO DEVELOPMENT EXPENDITURE (PERCENT OF GDP)
40
35
30
25
20
15
10
5
0
ADP
Expenditure on Government*
1980-1981
1981-1982
1982-1983
1983-1984
1984-1985
1985-1986
1986-1987
1987-1988
1988-1989
1989-1990
1990-1991
1991-1992
1992-1993
1993-1994
1994-1995
1995-1996
1996-1997
1997-1998
1998-1999
1999-2000
*Government: Government expenditure on defense and general administration.

reached record levels. However, inspite of the recent sharp acceleration in GDP growth there has been no significant reduction in poverty. At the same time the question remains of whether this high GDP growth can be sustained. This is because recent high GDP growth has been predicated essentially on the large scale-manufacturing sector, and within this sector it is relatively narrowly based in the growth of just three industries: (a) Consumer durables (particularly automobiles), (b) Construction, (c) Textiles.

Three economic challenges confront the country: a. To restructure the economic growth process so as to enhance its capacity for poverty reduction, b. To broaden the basis of GDP growth and make it sustainable, c. To establish the writ of the State, a viable democratic structure and a culture of tolerance. These are necessary conditions for achieving a substantial and sustained increase in private sector investment, both domestic and foreign. They are equally necessary for building a future for the people of Pakistan that is better than the past.

List of References

1. Amjad, Rashid, 1982. 'Private Industrial Investment in Pakistan, 1960-1970', Cambridge University Press, London.
2. Amjad, Rashid, Solving Pakistan's Poverty Puzzle: Who Should We Believe? What Should We Do?, PIDE 19th Annual General Meeting and Conference, 13th–15th January, 2004, Islamabad.
3. Burki, Shahid Javed, 2004. 'Pakistan, Fifty Years of Nationhood', Vanguard, Lahore.
4. Government of Pakistan, Planning Commission, The Third Five Year Plan, 1965-70, Karachi.
5. Government of Pakistan, Federal Bureau of Statistics, Islamabad, April 2001, (Mimeo).
6. Government of Pakistan, Finance Division. Economic Survey, 1974, Islamabad
7. Griffin, K. and Khan, A. R. 'Growth and Inequality in Pakistan'. Macmillan, London.
8. Hamid, N. 'The Burden of Capitalist Growth, A Study of Real Wages in Pakistan'. Pakistan Economic and Social Review, Spring 1974.
9. Hamid, N. and Hussain, Akmal: 'Regional Inequalities and Capitalist Development', Pakistan Economic and Social Review, Autumn 1974.
10. Hussain, Akmal, 2004. 'Institutions, Economic Structure and Poverty in Pakistan', South Asia Economic Journal, Volume 5, Number 1, January-June 2004, SAGE Publications, London and Delhi.
11. Hussain, Akmal, 1980. 'Impact of Agricultural Growth on Changes in the Agrarian Structure of Pakistan with Special Reference to the Punjab Province'. D. Phil Thesis, University of Sussex.
12. Hussain, Akmal, et.al, 2003. 'Pakistan National Human Development Report, 2003', UNDP, Oxford University Press, Karachi.
13. Hussain, Akmal, 1988. 'Strategic Issues in Pakistan's Economic Policy'. Progressive Publishers.
14. Hussain, Akmal, 1999. 'Employment Generation, Poverty Alleviation and Growth in Pakistan's Rural Sector: Policies for Institutional Change'. Report prepared for the International Labour Organization, Country Employment Policy Review, Pakistan, ILO/CEPR.
15. Jillani et. al. 'Labour Migration'. PIDE Research Report No. 126.

16. Kemal, A. R., 1999. 'Patterns and Growth of Pakistan's Industrial Sector', in Khan, Shahrukh Rafi (ed.), 'Fifty Years of Pakistan's Economy'. Oxford University Press, Karachi.
17. Khan, Zia ul Hasan, 1995. 'Rise of Sectarianism in Pakistan: Causes and Implications'. Research Paper (Mimeo), Pakistan Administrative Staff College, Lahore.
18. Majid, Nomaan. 'Pakistan: An Employment Strategy'. ILO/SAAT, December 1997.
19. Munir, Muhammad, 1979. 'From Jinnah to Zia', Vanguard Books, Lahore.
20. Naseem, S. M., 1977. 'Rural Poverty and Landlessness in Asia'. ILO Report, Geneva.
21. Noman, Omar, 1988. 'The Political Economy of Pakistan, 1947-85'. Routledge, Kegan and Paul, London.
22. Pasha, Hafiz, 1999. 'Fifty Years of Finance in Pakistan: A Trend Analysis' in Khan, Shahrukh Rafi (ed.) Fifty Years of Pakistan's Economy, OUP, Karachi.
23. Rahim, Sikander, 'Myths of Economic Development'. Lahore School of Economics, Occasional Paper No. 10, February 2001.
24. Report of the Task Force on Poverty Eradication: Overcoming Poverty, May 1997.
25. Soligo and Stern, J. J., 1965. 'Tariff Protection, Imports Substitution and Investment Efficiency, The Pakistan Development'.
26. Syed, Najam Hussain, 1986. 'Recurrent Patterns in Punjabi Poetry' Second Edition. Punjab Adbi Markaz, Lahore.
27. The Daily Dawn, 12th July 1977, Karachi.
28. White, L. J. 'Industrial Concentration and Economic Power in Pakistan'. Princeton University Press.

NOTES

1. For a more detailed analysis of the relationship between the practice of political power, the process of institutional decay, and the economic structure, See: Akmal Hussain, Institutions, Economic Structure and Poverty in Pakistan, South Asia Economic Journal, Volume 5, Number 1, January-June 2004, SAGE Publications, London and Delhi, 2004.
2. Consequently the growth in manufacturing industry during the decade of the 1950s was impressive at 8.1 per cent, although overall growth in GNP remained at a relatively low level at 3.4 per cent. This was primarily because of slow growth in the agriculture sector (2.3 per cent), which was the predominant sector in the economy. See: Shahid Javed Burki: Pakistan, Fifty Years of Nationhood, Vanguard, Lahore, 2004, Table 3.3, Page 100.
3. The Bonus Voucher Scheme enabled exports of certain manufactured goods to receive in addition to the rupee revenue of their exports, bonus vouchers equivalent to a specified percentage of the foreign exchange earned. The vouchers could be sold in the market (to potential importers) for a price usually 150 to 180 per cent above the face value. Thus the exporter not only earned the rupee revenues from exports but also an additional premium through sale of the bonus vouchers.
4. Soligo, and J.J. Stern, Tariff Protection, imports substitution and investment efficiency, The Pakistan Development, 1965, Pages 249-70.
5. Sikander Rahim: Myths of Economic Development, Lahore School of Economics, Occasional Paper No.10, February 2001.
6. 'It is clear that the distribution of national production should be such as to favour the savings sectors', Government of Pakistan, Planning Commission, The Third Five Year Plan, 1965-70, Karachi, Page 33.
7. K. Griffin: Financing Development Plans in Pakistan, in K. Griffin and A.R. Khan, Growth and Inequality in Pakistan, Macmillan, London Page 41-42.
8. Ibid. Page 133.
9. For example, during 1950-55 grant and grant type assistance constituted 73% of total foreign aid. By 1965-70 this type of assistance had declined to only 9% of total foreign aid. See: Economic Survey, Government of Pakistan, Finance Division, Islamabad, 1974, Page 133.
10. For a detailed analysis of this phenomenon, see: Rashid Amjad: Private Industrial Investment in Pakistan, 1960-1970, London, Cambridge University Press, 1982.
11. L.J. White: Industrial Concentration and Economic Power in Pakistan, Princeton University Press, Page 63.

12. The major industrial families and entrepreneurs were a fairly closely-knit group. Not only did many of them have caste and kinship relations, but members of the families tended to sit on each other's boards of directors. For example about one-third of the seats on the boards of directors of companies controlled by the forty-three families were occupied by members of other families within the forty-three. See: L.J. White, op.cit., Pages 74-75.
13. N. Hamid, The Burden of Capitalist Growth, A study of Real Wages in Pakistan, Pakistan Economic and Social Review, Spring 1974.
14. K. Griffin and A.R. Khan, op.cit. Pages 204-205.
15. S.M. Naseem: Rural Poverty and Landlessness in Asia, ILO Report, Geneva, 1977.
16. Naved Hamid and Akmal Hussain: 'Regional Inequalities and Capitalist Development', Pakistan Economic and Social Review, Autumn 1974.
17. Akmal Hussain: Impact of Agricultural Growth on Changes in the Agrarian Structure of Pakistan, with Special Reference to the Punjab Province, D.Phil. Thesis, University of Sussex 1980. Also see: Akmal Hussain: Strategic Issues in Pakistan's Economic Policy: Technical Change and Social Polarization in Rural Punjab, Chapter 4, Progressive Publishers, June 1988.
18. See: Akmal Hussain, D. Phil Thesis, op.cit.
19. See: Akmal Hussain, Strategic Issues in Pakistan's Economic Policy, op.cit. Page 187
20. This phenomenon was first analyzed in a Doctoral Thesis: Akmal Hussain, D. Phil Thesis, op.cit.

    For the latest survey evidence, See: Akmal Hussain et.al, Pakistan National Human Development Report, 2003, Chapter 3, Section IV, UNDP, Oxford University Press, Karachi, 2003.
21. Omar Noman, The Political Economy of Pakistan, 1947-85, Routledge Kegan and Paul, London 1988, Page 79.
22. The trend may have been reinforced by a second set of measures during this period. These included a devaluation of the exchange rate, which placed large and small-scale industry at par with respect to the rupee cost of imported inputs (i.e. the indirect subsidy provided to large scale manufacturing industry through an overvalued exchange rate, was withdrawn). At the same time, direct subsidies to manufacturing were significantly cut down, import duties on finished goods were reduced and anti-monopoly measures along with price controls were instituted. It is not surprising that domestic manufacturers who had been bred on government support, responded by further reducing investment.
23. See A.R. Kemal: Patterns of Growth in Pakistan's Industrial Sector, in Shahrukh Rafi Khan (ed.). Fifty Years of Pakistan's Economy, O.U.P, Karachi 1999, Page 158.
24. Ibid, Page 158.
25. Omar Noman: The Political Economy of Pakistan, op.cit. Page 80.
26. Defence expenditure as a percentage of GDP increased from 2.7% in 1965 to 6.7% in 1974-75. Similarly general administration as a percentage of GDP increased from 1.1% in 1964-65 to as much as 1.8% in 1974-75, see: Hafiz Pasha: 'Fifty Years of Finance in Pakistan: A Trend Analysis', in Shahrukh Rafi Khan (ed.), Fifty Years of Pakistan's Economy, OUP, Karachi, 1999. Pages 209, Table-3.
27. Omar Noman, op. cit. Page 82.
28. Omar Noman, op.cit. Page 122.
29. 'You may belong to any religion or caste or creed ___ that has nothing to do with the business of the state...We are starting with this fundamental principle that we are all citizens and equal citizens of one state.... Now, I think we should keep that in front of us as our ideal and you will find that in the course of time Hindus would cease to be Hindus and Muslims would cease to be Muslims, not in the religious sense, because that is the personal faith of each individual but in the political sense as citizens of the state.'

    Speech of Mohammad Ali Jinnah as President of the Constituent Assembly, August 11, 1947, cited in Muhammad Munir, from Jinnah to Zia, Vanguard Books, Lahore 1979, Page 29-30.
30. In the case of the judiciary its essential powers to scrutinize the legality of martial law or the orders of military courts were abolished. The judicial protection against arbitrary detention of a citizen embodied in the right to Habeas Corpus was eliminated for the first time in Pakistan.

    In the case of the press, an attempt was made to subordinate it to State authority. President Zia ul Haq declared: 'Democracy means freedom of the Press, Martial Law its very negation'. The Daily Dawn, 12th July 1977. In the pursuit of this policy, press control measures were introduced. The government constituted committees at the district level to ensure that articles repugnant to the ideology of Pakistan were not published. Those members of the press who had refused to acquiesce faced state repression. A number of newspapers were banned and journalists were arrested and given flogging sentences by military courts.
31. The hero Ranjha is celebrated as the synthesis of love and reason, See: Najam Hosain Syed, Recurrent Patterns in Punjabi Poetry, Punjab Adbi Markaz, Lahore, Second edition, 1986.
32. Omar Noman, The Political Economy of Pakistan, op.cit., Page 124.

33. According to an official report of the police department, a number of madrassas were only providing religious education. Yet as many as 42 per cent of them in the Punjab alone, were actively promoting sectarian violence through a well conceived indoctrination process. As this new kind of madrassas emerged and grew during the Zia regime, so did sectarian violence. For example, the number of sectarian killings increased from 22 during the period 1987-89, to 166 during the period 1993-95 in the Punjab. See, Zia ul Hassan Khan: Rise of Sectarianism in Pakistan: Causes and Implications, Research Paper (Mimeo), Pakistan Administrative Staff College, Lahore, 1995.
34. As many as 78.9% of emigrants to the Middle East were production workers See: Jillani et.al. Labour Migration PIDE, Research Report No. 126.
35. For a detailed analysis and estimates of corruption during this period, see: Shahid Javed Burki: Pakistan, Fifty Years of Nationhood, op.cit., chapter 5.
36. Overcoming Poverty, The Report of the Task Force on Poverty Eradication, May 1997, Page 6.
37. This was pointed out by Rashid Amjad, in his paper titled: Solving Pakistan's Poverty Puzzle: Who Should We Believe? What Should We Do? Paper presented at the PIDE 19th Annual General Meeting and Conference, 13th–15th January, 2004, Islamabad.
38. A 1987 study by Akmal Hussain had argued that the high growth experience of the preceding three decades may not be sustainable in the next decade due to structural constraints rooted in deteriorating infrastructure, low savings rates and slow export growth: '...if present trends continue, we may be faced with the stark possibility that high GDP growth may not be sustainable over the next *five years*...' (Emphasis added). See: Akmal Hussain: Strategic Issues in Pakistan's Economic Policy, op.cit., Page xviii.
39. An ILO study suggests that real wages of casual hired labour (which is the predominant form of hired labour in Pakistan) declined in both agriculture and industry, during the 1990s. See: Noman Majid: Pakistan: An Employment Strategy, ILO/SAAT, December 1997, Pages 34 and 35.
40. Akmal Hussain: Employment Generation, Poverty Alleviation and Growth in Pakistan's Rural Sector: Policies for Institutional Change, ILO/CEPR, Mimeo, 1999. This study analyses the structural factors that slowed down agricultural growth and increased its variability from year to year.
41. Ibid. Page 4.
42. Federal Bureau of Statistics, Government of Pakistan, April 2001, (Mimeo).

358

TOURISM

Milly Stoney

Pakistan has been called 'Tourist Asia's best kept secret'. With its huge range of physical features and landscapes, ancient archaeological sites and historical legacy dating back to the dawn of civilization plus a reputation for hospitality among its people, this should be a country with a thriving tourist industry.

The figures show a different picture, however. The number of tourists visiting Pakistan in the year 2000 was just over half a million, providing Rs. 84.4 million in foreign exchange receipts, and this has remained approximately the same over the following three years. The majority of such tourists came from Europe (257,000) and South Asia (109,000). It could be conjectured that the South Asian cohort were making visits to family members, 28% coming from Afghanistan and 66% from India, bringing the actual tourist figures down still further.

The combination of a lack of an indigenous tourist industry of any size to support investment in the infra-structure needed for development to take place, and the general world security concerns in recent years, tourism on any significant scale has been held back.

As a result of these factors Pakistan is currently a possible destination of special interest tourism only. Such responsible tourists, who are interested in seeing places in terms of geography, history, culture, wildlife, sports, adventure and environment are, as yet, small in number. This is, however, now recognized as an expanding segment world wide.

Outdoor tourism involving such pursuits as back-packing, walking, mountaineering and fishing could be well catered for in the northern areas, with the attractions of the fantastic scenery of the *Hindu Kush, *Karakorams and *Himalayas.

PRE-HISTORY AND THE INDUS VALLEY CIVILISATION

The landscape of Pakistan offers a huge range of locations to visit in terms of the sites and remains of civilizations and empires. The pre-historic sites, dating back to 6,000 BC, so far identified and excavated have been chiefly in the *Punjab, in *Balochistan and the *North West Frontier Province. In Balochistan a comparatively recent archaeological find of several ancient villages pre-dates the *Indus Valley Civilization and provides indications of a flourishing trade route through this region, in those very distant times.

However it is for the world famous sites of *Moenjodaro in *Sindh and *Harappa in Punjab that Pakistan is renowned. The Moenjodaro remains are the site of one of the world's most spectacular, earliest known and most developed civilizations referred to by archaeologists as the Indus Valley Civilization. The area is known to have flourished from the 3rd to the 2nd millennium BC.

Harappa in Punjab is about the same size and is contemporaneous with Moenjodaro. It flourished in the 3rd millennium BC. There are remains of a citadel, granaries, brick kilns, and a drainage system and fortification—the signs of the well-developed urban township associated only with the Indus Valley Civilization. Archaeologists have found here what are reputed to be the earliest written words ever discovered. Moenjodaro itself has been designated a World Heritage Site by UNESCO.

It is believed that these Indus Valley sites, of which there are in fact over 400, mark some of the world's earliest settled farming communities. They developed at about the same time as the Mesopotamian and Egyptian empires. The serious paucity of visitors is illustrated by the figures of those spending time at the Moenjodaro. In the year 2000 there were 560 foreign and 40,632 local visitors. In 2002 the number of foreign visitors had dropped to 200, but local visitors had remained almost the same, at 49,688 (Dept. of Archaeological Museum, Govt. of Pakistan).

At *Amri, in Sindh, pottery shards dating back to 3000 BC and bricks similar to those used in Moenjodaro are found scattered over a large area. The people of Amri may have pre-dated those of the Indus Valley Civilization but disappeared around 2500 BC. Chak Purbane Sival in the Punjab, 13 miles south of Harappa, is a big mound where pottery and other artifacts have been discovered, calling archaeologists to uncover yet another township of the Indus Valley.

GANDHARA AND THE BUDDHIST LEGACY

Buddhism came from north-east India, to be practised in what is now Pakistan, 230 years after the Buddha's death. It was here that the religion of peace flourished and spread north eastward into the Far East. Lord Buddha's cremation ashes were housed in Stupas, several of which are still found in Sindh and Punjab, but mostly in NWFP, particularly *Swat.

In Sindh the most famous Stupa is on the mound behind the remains of Moenjodaro. In the sixth century BC the evolving priesthood and practice of Buddhism was brought to the developing Persian Province of *Gandhara, now in northern Pakistan, under Darius the Great. From the fourth century BC one of the most important universities of the ancient world was located in Gandhara at *Taxila, now in NWFP and close to modern Islamabad. Originally named Taksashila its history can be traced back to the 5th century BC. The Sanskrit language was formalized here and Emperor Asok *Maurya made it a great seat of Buddhism. It was in this area that, uniquely, Greek art and Buddhism merged.

The Taxila site houses several Stupas still venerated by visiting Buddhists. These include the Kunal Stupa, Jaulian Stupa, Mohra Moradu Stupa, Pippala Stupa and the shrine of the Double-Headed Eagle. The exceptionally fine small museum at the heart of Taxila, with its examples of graeco-buddhist statuary and the extensive Buddhist remains, attracts visitors in reasonable numbers. This is possibly helped by its proximity to the national capital. In 2002, however, the museum recorded only 6,423 foreign and 67,465 local visitors, compared with 20,636 and 80,937 in 2001. Taxila has been designated as a World Heritage Site by UNESCO

Other Buddhist sites are to be found in the Swat Valley, from where the Nyingma order of Buddhist priests travelled and took the faith into Tibet and yet further afield to Mongolia, China, Korea and Japan. In 2002 the museum here recorded 91 foreign and 12,590 local visitors, less than half the number visiting in 2000.

At Charsadda in NWFP there are impressive remains of a 1st century AD well constructed and compact Buddhist monastery and nearby prayer halls, built 500 meters up the hill. The NWFP has in its territory several Stupas and accompanying monasteries such as the Mekha-Sanda Stupa, Chanak-Dheri Stupa, Sahri Stupa, Gumbat Stupa, Shingerdaar Stupa and Butkara Stupa. At Jahanabad in Swat there is a four meter high rock carving of Lord Buddha, shown sitting cross legged in meditation

Gandhara came under the heel of Alexander the Great between 327 and 325 BC. His reputed route was Taxila, the *Salt Range, and along the *Beas River to its confluence with the *Indus. At Sehwan Sharif, in Sindh, said to be the oldest living town he built a fort, the ruins of which still remain. From here he is believed to have sailed to the *Arabian Sea then headed westwards along the Makran Desert in Balochistan. As a conqueror he has left few memorials other than images of his head on coins minted in Gandhara and, it is said, many blue eyed, blonde haired children!

THE MAURYAN EMPIRE

From the third century BC to the sixth century AD the area that is now Pakistan lay at the western edge of the *Mauryan Empire, the capital of which lay at Patna on the Ganges far to the east. The greatest of the Mauryan rulers was Asoka who reigned in the middle of the third century BC. The region became a buffer zone between Indian and Persian influence and a route by which invaders entered from the north and west to sweep across the Punjab. These included the Bactrian Greeks, who developed the second city of Taxila at Sirkap; the Scythians whose path through the mountains is marked by rock carving at *Chilas on the Karakoram Highway; the Parthians; the *Kushans and the *White Huns.

Dipalpur in the Punjab some 17 miles from Okara, is an ancient township reputedly as old as Harappa. It is studded with ancient buildings and Scythian coins and other artifacts have been found here. All of the invaders seem to have left their mark on the remarkable buildings at Taxila. In a strategic location on one branch of the Silk Route, plus the site's religious importance as a place of Buddhist pilgrimage, the settlement was able to thrive until the middle of the 5th century, after which the invading forces destroyed many of the buildings and the seat of learning was no longer inhabited.

The Sassanians and Turks, and finally in 870 AD the Hindu Shahis succeeded in taking the territory around the Indus valley. Hindu shrines and places of pilgrimage are situated mainly on the borderlands of India and Pakistan and in the desert areas of Sindh and Balochistan. Populations of semi-nomadic herdsmen travel the waste lands, largely ignoring the national borders, and continue their ancient traditions. Small villages, such as Islamkot with its five Hindu temples, lie scattered throughout the desert areas with inhabitants who still adhere to the Hindu faith. Among the best known shrines are the *Nag Devta*, (snake), temple at Mithi, the Bodhisar and Gori Jain Temples and Anchlasar Baoli, near Nagar Parkar in the *Thar desert, where Hindu women bathe in the sacred waters as a cure for infertility; Babu Lal Jasraaj at Dipalpur near Okara where there is a Hindu temple still in use; the cave of the Kalka Shrine at Bhatti near Sukkur, dedicated to *Kali Devi*; the ancient complexes of Kallar Kahar and Ketas in the Salt Range, dedicated to Lord Shiva and the 8th century Malot Temple in the same area.

There is a site dedicated to Durga, in a huge cave near Hinglaj, on the banks of the Hingol river near Lasbela, in Balochistan. The Hindu shrine dates back to the 6th century, and is said to be second in importance only to the Jagannath Temple in India. Here there is also the Muslim shrine of Bib Nani. It is said, however, that the cave has a sacred history dating much further back into the Indus Valley civilisation when the goddess Nania was worshipped her some 5,000 years ago

THE COMING OF ISLAM

In 711 AD an Arab commander, Muhammad bin Qasim, arrived with cavalry forces at the southern reaches of the Indus, with the determined intention of suppressing the piracy that had been troubling the Arab coastal shipping trade. He had been preceded by Mohammad Bin Harun whose tomb, a domed square building of brick and mud mortar, is located at Bela. Bin Harun had conquered Makran but had not been able to proceed further. Bin Qasim, however, established a fortress at Daibul, now known as Bhambhore, in Sindh, and converted the local population to Islam.

Bhambore was already a well-planned city port with a flourishing trade 14 centuries ago. The archaeological remains of the settlement include the earliest-known mosque in Pakistan.

Bin Qasim continued his advance northwards taking Niran, near Hyderabad, where his forces crossed the Indus by the now famous bridge of boats, and scattered the forces of the Brahmin ruler, King Dahir. Capturing Brahminabad the Arab forces built their own city of Mansura and continued their advance as far as Multan. This city had a renowned ancient golden temple dedicated to the sun god, Aditya, and the conquerors felt that with so much gold in their possession they need go no further. For three centuries this was the northernmost city of the Sindh province of the Ommayid Empire, based in Damascus. The Ommayids were succeeded by the Abbasid caliphs in Baghdad.

Meanwhile Islam was also entering the area from the North Western regions. Evidence of this can be found in the Museum at Peshawar, where a stone tablet is inscribed in both Sanskrit and Arabic. This establishes the presence of Islam in the Tochi valley of *Waziristan as early as 857. By the 11th century the Turkish rulers of Afghanistan under Mahmud Ghazni led a series of raids against Hindu temples and Lahore was developed as an Islamic centre in the Punjab.

Mass conversions to Islam took place at this time in the Punjab. The offer of conversion to Islam was taken up by many of the lower caste Hindus of Sindh, as an opportunity to free themselves from the shackles of the caste system and its virtual slavery. Hinduism and Buddhism were allowed to flourish, however, and those who did not choose to convert were permitted to continue in their faiths. Scholars from the Indus Valley were welcomed at the caliphate court in Baghdad and their works on medicine, mathematics, philosophy and astronomy were translated into Arabic.

The Tomb of Sultan Kutbuddin Aibek, in Lahore, neglected for some time has been rebuilt and is a major attraction. So also is the Tomb of Shah *Rukn-i-Alam at Multan *circa* 1324. This two-storey, inward inclining, brick structure, with a simple dome topped with a high finial, is decorated in traditional blue and turquoise tiles.

Uchchh Sharif, an ancient town dating back to a time before Alexander the Great, sited near the confluence of the *Chenab and *Sutlej was taken by bin Qasim in 711 AD after a siege of 11 days. It is traditionally held that in the 8th century the Brahmin ruler of the area, Chach, invented and gave his name to the game of chess. The town became the capital of a wealthy kingdom in the 13th and 14th centuries. It was a centre of culture and learning at that time and the remains of a number of beautifully decorated tombs still stand as a reminder of the brief flowering of Uchchh.

Rhotas Fort on the Kahan river, close to the city of *Jhelum south of Islamabad is a spectacular example of Muslim military architecture. Built by Sher Shah Suri in 1543 it took a decade to complete. It is designated as a World Heritage Site by UNESCO.

THE SUFI TRADITIONS

From the 11th century onwards the conversion of the vast territories of northern India to Islam went hand in hand with the conquest of the land by the forces of the Sultans. It was the influence of the great **sheikhs*, or **pirs*, of the *Sufi orders who attracted local converts through their remarkable reputation as wonder-workers. Their deep spiritual message, ideas of tolerance, and special teaching and techniques of reaching spiritual enlightenment made for the most successful missionary movement in the subcontinent. There are many shrines to the *Sufi saints, some in remote places. These often have special days of celebration, or **Urs*, when crowds flock to the shrine and remain through the early hours in contemplation and taking part in Qawwali, as the singing of mystical songs to the accompaniment of drums and stringed instruments are known.

Abdullah Shah Ghazi in Karachi is the resting place of the 9th century saint or *pir*. He is venerated as the patron-saint of the city and several miracles are attributed to him. Crowds gather here on a Thursday evening to take part in the music. At Bhitshah in Sindh there is the shrine of Shah Abdul Latif Bhitai, one of the most revered Sufi saints [1689–1752]. A philosopher, poet, author and musician, Sufi mysticism is the soul of his writings most of which are in his book, *Shah jo Risaalo*, which has been translated into several world languages. The pir's urs, or festival of commemoration, in the Islamic month of Safar, is celebrated with a huge fair and classical and folk music concerts throughout three days and nights. The Bhit Shah Cultural Committee makes annual Latif Awards to the best singers. At Nurpur, near Islamabad a shrine is similarly dedicated to Syed Abdul Latif Shah, the venerated 17th century Sufi saint whose many miracles are remembered every year at the annual *urs* celebrated with music and a fair.

In Lahore there is the shrine of the venerated Data Ganj Bakhsh, associated with scholarship and the basic texts of Sufism. Other major shrines are located at Golra Sharif in Islamabad and Pakpattan in Punjab. The sufi saints' '*urs*' are without doubt the most musical occasions with some of the most interesting cultural and folkloric activities in Pakistan.

THE MUGHAL TREASURES OF PAKISTAN

In 1526, at the Battle of Panipat, near Delhi, raiders from Afghanistan under the leadership of Babur of Farghana a descendent of Tamurlane and Genghis Khan, defeated Sultan Ibrahim Lodi ending the *Delhi Sultanate. Thus the Mongul, or as it is better known–Mughal (see, Mughal Empire)–dynasty began its long and glittering rule until 1793, with one short break between 1539-1545, when Sher Shah Suri took over the empire. The territory over which the Mughals ruled extended from the Oxus river in the west to the Ganges and west Bengal in the east. The southern reaches of the empire were the wastelands of the Rajasthan Desert. The Mughals supported the cultural and intellectual development of an empire of some 150 million people over a period of 267 years, producing a legacy of many exquisite and majestic world famous relics.

Of all the cities in Pakistan, Lahore contains perhaps the greatest collection of both buildings, and works of art in the form of miniature paintings of the Mughal period. Two UNESCO World Heritage sites, the Fort (see, Lahore Fort) and the *Shalimar Gardens are located within the city. The walls of the old city date back to this period, although much has fallen into decay or been replaced.

*Lahore Fort is the archetype of mughal architecture and remains one of the city's most impressive structures. The Emperor Akbar the Great (1556-1605 - grandson of the first Mughul Emperor Babur), lived and administered his empire from here, from 1585, as did his successors. The Fort houses the marvellous *Sheesh Mahal* or Hall of Mirrors; the *Naulakkha*, an exquisite small pavilion once decorated in pietra dura, a delicate inlay of precious and semi-precious stones; the *Moti Masjid*; the Hall of Public Audiences and the Chamber of Private Audience. Subsequent additions include the personal residences of emperors Jahangir and Shah Jahan. Part of the fort is being restored under the auspices of various international organisations.

The **Badshahi* Mosque *(*masjid)* was built in 1674 by Aurangzeb, the last of the great emperors. Locates facing the fort, is one of the world's largest mosques. It houses some of the holiest relics for Muslims. It has four octagonal towers as well as four smaller minarets. The smaller Wazir Khan Mosque, built in 1634 is located deep in the heart of the old walled city. Flamboyantly decorated in painted tiles the interior is a striking example of Mughal delight in the use of colour and complex design.

Among the many other treasures of the period in and around Lahore are the world famous Shalimar Gardens, a superbly constructed white marble pleasure garden of water and quiet greenery, established by Shah Jahan (1627-58). The *Hiran Minar*, built by the Emperor Jehangir (1605-27) and set in charming environs is also a visual treasure, demonstrating Mughal architectural genius. It was built on water as a monument dedicated to Jehangir's pet antelope.

Mughal craftsmansip and decorative arts are visible in the structure of Jahangir's Tomb, built on the orders of Shahjahan but overseen by the Empress Noorjahan (also known as Nur Jahan) for her husband and in Noorjehan's Tomb and Anarkali's Tomb. Anarkali is said to have been buried alive by the Emperor Akbar in 1599 and the story of immortal love of a prince for a slave girl has entered into legend. The mausoleum is currently the store and offices of the Punjab Archives and access to the tomb is severely restricted.

Although the Shalimar Gardens are world renowned, foreign visitors numbers were 8,558 in 2000 but only 319 in 2002. Similarly the Lahore Fort went from 7,706 to 2,906 foreign visitors in the same period. Local visitors to the Fort remained relatively constant at around one and a quarter millions and the Shalimar Gardens visitors were 318,111 in 2000 and 395,547 in 2002.

The lengthy period of Mughal rule has, not surprisingly, left evidence of its architectural flowering in many other locations in Pakistan, despite the depradations of later rulers and including the present day neglect. These include the Bala Hissar fort in Peshawar, originally built by Babur the founder of the dynasty, and currently a subject of controversy as a result of unauthorized construction work likely to alter the ancient façade; the Shahjahani Mosque in Thatta with its internal arches decorated in *Sindhi turquoise, blue and white tiles and some of the tombs in the necropolis above the town. The Thatta complex has been designated a World Heritage site by UNESCO.

Umarkot Fort, also in Sindh was built in 1746 and is reputedly the birthplace of Emperor Akbar the Great. The town is home to unique embroideries, handicraft and snake charmers. It also houses a museum with Emperor-related exhibits.

One of the first gardens in the Mughal style was laid out by Babur, in 1519, at Kallar Kahar in the Salt Range. At Wah, in the Punjab close to the Margalla Pass, on the Peshawar road Akbar laid out a further pleasure resort in the late 16th century in the same style as Lahore's Shalimar Garden. Although much is overgrown and decayed, traces of the garden design can still be identified.

On a simpler scale than grand architecture and extensive pleasure gardens, but culturally of significance, the Mughal legacy includes the love of intricate design in ornate jewellery and inlaid work seen throughout Pakistan, and many of the motifs used in carpet making.

Probably the most important practical legacy of the Mughal dynasty was to continue the construction of the *Shahi*, or Imperial, road from Delhi to Kabul, commenced by Sher Shah Suri during his short reign in the 16th century. This highway enabled the speedy transmission of information throughout the empire. It was later enlarged and extended by the British to form the Grand Trunk Road from Calcutta to Kabul to facilitate troop movements. Much of the GT road route is still in use today. Many towns sprang up and villages developed into large towns along the edge of the road and at important river crossings, passes, crossroads and junctions, including Rawalpindi. A short section of the original cobbled 16th century road lies to the left of the new road leading up to the Margalla Pass.

THE SIKH KINGDOM

In 1764, following a period of gradual decline in Mughal power, the *Sikhs defeated Ahmad Shah Durani and by 1799 the Afghans had conceded Lahore to the Sikh warrior ruler, Ranjit Singh. Although historically a singularly unimposing man himself, he was able to make good use of his political and military abilities to make himself master of Hazara, Peshawar and *Kashmir for over 40 years. His political intrigues included siding with the British during the First Afghan War. He died in 1839.

The founder of Sikhism, Guru Nanak was born near Lahore in 1469 and although the political capital of the Sikh territory was Lahore, the spiritual capital was Amritsar.

During Sikh rule, although some remarkable buildings were constructed, many of the Mughal treasures were ransacked or destroyed. This was particularly the case in Lahore where many of the beautiful *pietra dura* inlays were deprived of their precious stones, and quantities of gold and large slabs of marble were removed to embellish to Golden Temple in Amritsar.

The chief Sikh buildings of note in Lahore are the *Gurdwara*, or shrine, of Arjan Singh, and the Ranjit Singh *Samadhi* (memorial), which houses the Maharajah's cremated remains and was built in 1848 in a combination of Hindu and Mughal styles

The birthplace of Ranjit Singh was in Gujranwala and the town still has some fine Sikh buildings, notably the Maharajah's Hunting Lodge.

At Narowal, near the *Ravi river, is the *Gurdwara* Kartarpur *Sahib*, built in 1911 to mark the place where Guru Nanak settled and spent his final days.

Close to Wah and Taxila, at Hasan Abdal, the Sikh Temple of the Guru's Palm, or *Panja Sahib* is a centre of pilgrimage associated with Guru Nanak, the founder of the Sikh faith. The complex of buildings and a large tank commemorate the miracle of fresh water springing forth from a rock.

THE REMAINS OF THE RAJ–FEATS OF ENGINEERING

In the middle of the 19th century the British East India Company changed from being a trading concern to annexing territory on behalf of the British Government. In Sindh following a geographical survey, the impetus was both to use the *Indus River as a trading route and to use the area as a frontier to counter Russian expansion toward the Indian Ocean. Similarly Balochistan and the North West Frontier Province were regarded as strategically important. It is for this reason that the chief remnants of the British period are primarily linked to the rapid movement of troops, for example the Grand Trunk Road and the railway system, and secondarily to the development of agriculture in the form of irrigation, dams and barrages.

The canal system in the Punjab was begun in 1886, in an area close to Multan using the Sutlej River. In 1892 the Lower Chenab Canal was opened and proved such a success that a very ambitious project was undertaken to irrigate the area to the south of Lahore using the *Jhelum, *Chenab and *Ravi. All three rivers were linked by a criss-cross pattern of channels and enabled the area to be settled by canal colonies based on irrigated agriculture.

Some architecture of note remains from this period, namely large public buildings in Lahore such as the Museum (see, Lahore Museum) and the Punjab High Court in a style known as Mughal-Gothic. A few similar buildings exist in Karachi, but are falling into decay and disuse, gradually being replaced by concrete high rise offices.

Most typical of the Raj period is Murree, a mountain resort in the Rawalpindi district of the Punjab. It is situated at an altitude of 2,287 metres above sea level, 64 km. from Rawalpindi. This town developed as a result of the British rule, when the administration migrated into the Margalla hills to escape the summer heat of Rawalpindi. It is still a popular holiday resort and a number of schools and military establishments are based here. Murree has led to further hill resorts being developed in the areas known as the *Gallis*, most notably Nathia Galli.

WILDLIFE SITES AND NATURAL PHENOMENA

Although not regarded as spectacularly rich in wildlife Pakistan does possess a number of reserves offering the keen ornithologist opportunities to observe rare species of birds as well as large numbers of migratory flocks, chiefly as a result of location on the Indus Flyway from central Asia, north of the *Himalayas, to the warmer climes of south Asia and east Africa.

There are 11 national parks; Kirthar in Sindh; Darun Hingol and Hazerganj Chiltan in Balochistan; Margalla, Chinji and Lal Suhandra in Punjab; Chitral Gol and Ayubia in the North West Frontier Province; Khunjerab and Deosai in *Northern Areas and Matcharia in Azad Jammu and *Kashmir (see, Azad Kashmir). In addition to these there are over 100 wildlife sanctuaries, game reserves and wilderness parks. In some cases permits are given for hunting and shooting of rare species with the intention that the money so raised is dedicated to the preservation of the habitat and protection of the small populations of that animal or bird.

Among the many physical features of interest to specialist visitors the mountain regions must count as among the most spectacular in the world. Significant glaciers such as Siachen, Biafo, Boltoro and Batura, all over 50 km long lie in the area. Many of the most challenging peaks in the world are located here such as K-2, Nanga Parbat and the four peaks of Gasherbrum. Pakistan can boast of no less than 36 peaks within the top 100 highest peaks of the world. Many of the facilities in such northerly locations as Karimabad have geared themselves up to equip expeditions and a significant part of the population have relied, in the past, upon such expeditions for employment as porters and guides, only to find that of recent years visitor numbers have dwindled. The hotel, restaurant and souvenir trades have been similarly affected by the drop in numbers of foreign guests and a general lack of local visitors from Pakistan itself.

For the less agile there is an opportunity to visit Khewra, the site of a salt mine in the Salt Range. This ancient mine, which has produced rock salt since the time of Alexander the Great according to local legend, is a working mine. Facilities have, however, been developed and improved to make this into a worthwhile location for visiting tourists.

LIVING HISTORY AND CULTURE

Colourful crafts and traditional products are to be found in every region of Pakistan. The desert areas of Cholistan and Thar are especially rich in the production of handicrafts, chiefly made by women in the semi-nomadic family groups. Pottery in mainly blues and white and *susi*, a woven cloth in vegetable died colours from the area of Hala, north of Hyderabad, can be found in local markets.

Culturally diverse and unique communities continue to live largely traditional lives in some of the more remote valleys of the north of Pakistan. Most notably these include the Hunza valley centred around *Gilgit and Karimabad; *Chitral beyond the Shandur Pass under the massive *Hindu Kush range where the culture of the 3,000 *Kalash people is struggling to remain unchanged by outside influences; and Skardu, in the far north eastern tip of Pakistan, with its hinterland of the Deosai plateau. The plateau lies below the *Karakoram range with Nanga Parbat in the background. It is well known for its wildlife and especially the flora abundant on the 3,000 sq. km of rolling grassland at an average height of 4,000 metres.

Festivals are chiefly linked to the *Urs* of the *Sufi* saints (see above). Two notable exceptions are the traditional Horse and Cattle Show held in Lahore and Sibi each February or March, and the *Basant* or Spring festival in Lahore. This urban celebration of the advent of spring has grown into a truly cosmopolitan festival celebrating the season and is marked by kite flying, music, dance and food events. It has grown into a very colourful festival attracting tourists from all over the country and from abroad.

Even politics, in this remarkable country, can make for a sight worth seeing as those who have visited the Waga border crossing, near Lahore, for the evening flag lowering ceremony can confirm. Here a virtual ballet takes place with rivalry for smartness of manoeuvre being the ‘battle ground’ in no-mans land between the Pakistani and Indian borders. With enthusiastic and good humoured cheering and singing to encourage the tallest of soldiers to compete for mock aggressive behaviour the tourist will find a unique photographic opportunity.

SPORT

The north of Pakistan claims to be the original home of Polo, and some communities there, notably Gilgit and Chitral, continue to play the game in a more regulated form than the Buzkashi version played in Peshawar. However the true love of the Pakistani male is cricket. Street cricket is played wherever a few people can gather to relax and a ball can be found. Serious matches are played between neighbourhoods on the local roads, especially on a Sunday, making walking and driving hazardous. The international circuit of matches are watched keenly and the home team is a constant source of discussion.

Pakistan has the potential to be able to offer a number of attractions for the Special Interest tourist, including unique examples of geology, archaeology, history, architecture, culture, engineering or sports. Adventure holidays such as mountaineering, trekking, hiking, desert safaris, birdwatching, horse riding, camel or yak riding could be planned. Add to these the thrill of driving the spectacular Karakoram Highway on the highest metalled road in the world, riding the steam railway up the *Khyber Pass or sailing, deep-sea fishing and scuba diving in the *Arabian Sea, plus the generous hospitality of the population at large - Pakistan has the unrealized possibility of benefiting from an expanding tourist industry.

FAUNA OF PAKISTAN

T.J. Roberts

Pakistan as a whole experiences an arid sub-tropical climate with very high summer temperatures and average annual rainfall of less than 250mm. This climate allows only a semi-desert vegetation over both the Indus plains and the dry mountainous plateau of the western and north-western regions. A cooler, more moist climate can only be found in limited areas such as the Himalayan and foothill belt running east-west across the northern part of the country. Despite the limitations of climate, Pakistan has a surprising variety of reptiles. There are two species of crocodiles, eight freshwater and two salt water turtles, two land tortoises, 88 lizards, and 72 species of snakes, including fourteen which live in the sea, and which have been recorded in her coastal waters.

This variety is largely explained by the adaptations evolved by reptiles of many thousands of years. For example reptiles throughout the planet are abundant because they have developed a very efficient reproductive system and are less dependent upon water of moisture than their more primitive vertebrate ancestors, fish and amphibians. They have also adapted a hard skin that is resistant to desiccation and loss of precious body moisture, often protected by horny scales. Reptiles have also inherited, from more primitive moisture-dependent amphibia, a comparatively low rate of metabolism and an ability to maintain body temperature apart from external heat sources such as sunlight or warm substrates. This has enabled them to colonize both hot arid regions and cold alpine regions. The low metabolic rate also means that they are able to survive for long periods without food, having very low energy requirements compared to warm blooded animals. Fertilized eggs are protected with a tough parchment-like shell and some species even carry the fertilized gee internally until live young are born. Reptiles may protect their developing embryos by burying their eggs in a hole excavated in the ground.

Reptiles are surprisingly in external appearance and anatomy. Turtles and tortoises have a rigid trunk and body encased in a bony shell. Most reptiles however, have a lizard-like shape, including the large crocodilians. Snakes and some lizards have long cylindrical bodies, the former without limbs. Snakes have forked tongues which are mainly sensory organs of taste, picking up molecules from the atmosphere. The flicking tongue give messages to a special gland called Jacobson's Organ located inside the palate of the mouth. They have no eyelids, and cannot close their eyes, nor external ears, but can detect vibrations through sensitized areas under the throat. Lizards do have transparent eyelids, and external ear flaps, some with tongues like ours, others like the Monitor Lizards with forked snake-like tongues.

THE CROCODILE FAMILY

Until the 1950s, the Mugger of March Crocodile (*Crododiles palustris*) was widespread throughout the province of *Sindh. Exploitation of its skin to make decorative shoes, handbags and luggage led to its virtual disappearance by the 1980s. Only a small remnant population survived in the seeping lakes of Snaghar District. Fortunately, the Sindh Wildlife Management Board designated part of this area as a sanctuary for the Mugger and there is now a healthy population surviving within the sanctuary area. There is also a thriving colony of captive snub-nosed crocodiles attached to the tomb of a local Sufi saint at Mangho Pir, near Karachi, reputed to have special healing powers for skin problems.

The fish eating Ghavial Crocodile (*Gavialis gangeticus*), however, has become virtually extinct in Pakistan. It was always confined to the main river system and the construction of irrigation barrages, as well as persecution by fishing tribes resident on the Indus had reduced its numbers severely. A captive breeding programme has led to a partial recovery currently exists in Pakistan.

THE TORTOISE AND TURTLE FAMILIES

The Starred Tortoise (*Geochelone elegans*), only found in extreme southern Sindh coastal areas, was historically collected for its attractively patterned shell. It has become virtually extinct within Pakistan, though a few survive in the border areas of *Tharparkar. In *Balochistan and the *North West Frontier Province the Afghan Four Toed Tortoise (*Testudo horesrield*) still survives in good number.

THE MARINE TURTLE

Pakistan has internationally important breeding beaches for the green turtle (*Chelonia mydas*), a herbivorous species living on seaweed, and the smaller Olive Ridley (*Lepidochelyhs olivacea*). The larger, green turtle is threatened with extinction throughout the world. Predators such as feral dogs and Monitor Lizards account for the destruction of clutches of eggs in unprotected nests and many hatchlings are eaten by Ghost Crabs (*Ocypoda rotundata*), before they can reach the sea. Both turtle eggs and parts of its meat are highly prized for human consumption in many far-eastern countries where breeding beaches are heavily exploited. The beaches of Pakistan are therefore of international importance in the conservation of this endangered species Here, World Wildlife Fund Pakistan and the Sindh Wildlife Management Board have successfully operated a conservation scheme, with turtle eggs being recovered from natural nests and allowed to hatch in protected enclosures. Public awareness of the scheme and the significance of the turtle beach is being encouraged through schools and tourist visits.

THE LIZARD FAMILIES

Among the lizards there are few truly Oriental Families of Indo-Chinese faunal origin, but many of African origin or with affinities to the great Iranian Basin. Among the important families represented in Pakistan are the Geckonids. Despite their soft warty skin and delicate bodies they are surprisingly widespread in all habitats, including pure desert. No less than 36 species have been recorded in Pakistan. Many of them, such as the Leopard or Fat-Tailed Gecko (*Eublepharis macularius*) and the Blotched Gecko (*Hemidactylus triedrus*), are brightly coloured and of great herpetological interest. The genus *Hemidactylus* is of interest because it includes the familiar House or Wall Geckos, which occupy inhabited rooms and are actually beneficial in preying upon mosquitos and other insects. The Yellow Bellied House Gecko (*H. flaviventris*) is common throughout the Plains, while in Balochistan the Persian Gecko (*H. persicus*) is more typical.

Another large family comprises the Agamidae Lizards with many species adapted to the drier rocky places. The are widespread in the mountains including the far north. The males are territorial, often with brightly coloured throats or head appendages, which they use in display to drive off rival males and attract females. In Sindh *Kohistan, the large Yellow-Headed Rock Agama (*Agama nupta fusca*), with a black body and sulphur yellow spiny outgrowth around its neck, is one such example. The greatest concentration of endemic lizards, including many small Toad Agama such as the Black-Tailed Toad Agama (*Pheynocephalus maculatus*) are found in the *Chagai desert.

The family Scincidae are characterized by rather smooth shiny bodies which are usually long slim and snake-like, often with limbs which are reduced in size. Some have colonized the highest alpine meadows in the far north, such as the Glacier Skink (*Scinella ladacense*), and they can appear plentiful even in suburban gardens during and after the monsoon season.

The largest lizards in Pakistan are the Monitor Lizards (*Varanus*). There is one common species, the Desert Monitor (*V. griseus*), and the more widespread less common Indian Monitor (*V. bengalensis*), while in south-western Balochistan the more colourfully patterned Transcaspian Desert Monitor (*V. caspius*) can be found. A big specimen of the Indian Monitor can measure as long as 1.75m. These powerful daytime hunting lizards can easily climb trees and will hunt and eat small birds, Northern Palm Squirrels and small reptiles.

Two other frequently found lizards with differing appearances are the common garden lizard and the spiny tailed lizard. The garden lizard (*Calotes versicolor*) with its whip tail, has crest of lance shaped scales along its back. It hides among trees or bush foliage and along desert tracks waiting for unsuspecting insects. The spiny tailed lizard (*Uromastix hardwidckei*), with wrinkled olive yellow skin and a thick corrugated spiny tail, scuttles along the ground with surprising speed at the approach of a vehicle, diving suddenly into one of its vertical tunnels.

SNAKES

Snakes have always given rise to fear because of some of the species being venomous. Out of the 72 species recorded in Pakistan, only about seven are in fact dangerously poisonous to man. In the croplands snakes are actually valuable and important controllers of rodent pests, particularly Bandicoot rice-feeding rats, as well as Roof Rats in urban area.

The so-called Elapid, or Rear-Fanged poisonous snakes, have small mouths and cannot inject venom into their prey without chewing, so that there have rarely been any recorded cases of fatal bites. The long hollow-fanged Viper family is, however, much more dangerous, since their fangs are hinged and open downwards when the snake pens its mouth wide to strike. All the Sea Snakes are highly venomous but in temperament extremely shy and inoffensive. Fishermen pick them out of their nets with bare hands and casually toss them back into the sea without harm.

Among the more noteworthy families are the Boidae, which kill their prey not by biting, but by suffocation, wrapping their coils tightly around their victims. The huge Rock Python (*Python molurus*) had become very rare due to collecting by professional snake charmers. Three much smaller members are the common Earth Boa or Two Headed Snake (*Eryx johni*), the more beautifully patterned Sand Boa (*E. conicus*), and the rare Taretary Sand Boa (*E. tataricus*) found in Balochistan.

A large family known as Colubrid Snakes includes many rather thin whip-like snakes that can travel swiftly over even the roughest rocky surfaces. These include the Cliff Racer (*Coluber rhodorachis*), Glossy Bellied Racer (*C. ventromaculatus*) and the rather aggressive large orange-pink and black blotched Royal Snake or Diadem Rat Snake (*Sphalerosophis atriceps*). This common and handsome snake is a favourite with snake charmers. Though non-venomous, it will bite readily if handled.

Of particular interest to those studying reptiles, or Herpetologists, are the desert-adapted snakes belonging to the genus *Lytorhynchus* or Awl Headed Snakes, which specialize in living in drifting sand dunes. They are adept at burrowing under the sand in one smooth flowing movement and disappearing from sight, often lying hidden in ambush for unwary prey. There are three such species in Pakistan, including the pale yellow and black banded Maynard's Awl Headed Snake (*L. maynardi*) a native of the Chagai desert and feeds on small gecko and Lacertid lizards.

Perhaps one of the most frequently encountered and second largest snake in Pakistan is the *Dhaman* or Rat Snake (*Ptyas mucosas*), which can grow to a length of 3.5 metres (over 11 feet). Usually adults are black in colour but young specimens can be olive yellow, each scale beautifully outlined in black. They are harmless but will rear up when cornered and are often wantonly killed despite their value to farmers in disposing of vermin.

VENOMOUS VARIETIES

Of the dangerous venomous snakes the diminutive Saw Scaled Viper (*Echis carinatus*), which rarely grows more than 45 cm in length, is the cause of most fatal snake bites. It is aggressive in temperament, fond of climbing into bushes and trees to ambush its prey and prefers dry rocky areas. It gets its name from the curiously keeled scales along its flanks which make a hissing sound when rubbed together. The threat or warning gesture of this snake before attack is to coil in an 'S' shape and rub these scales together producing a rustling sound.

The Indian Cobra (*Naja naja*) is equally widespread in Pakistan and will normally slip away in the grass if it detects the approach of heavy footfalls. This snake is mainly a nocturnal hunter and seeks all sorts of warm-blooded prey, as well as lizards and amphibians. When threatened, it will typically raise the forepart of its body off the ground, dilating the hood in the well-known heart shaped outline.

The viper family is quite distinct, with a relatively thick short body, a narrow tail at the caudal end, and a rather broad diamond shaped head with a restricted neck behind. Most are rought scaled with zig-zag darker patterns along the back and flanks. The largest of these is Russell's Viper (*Vvipera russelli*), which prefers moist grassy laces and is found in all four provinces. It is most handsomely marked with lozenge shaped areas outlined in black and white. In the dry mountainous country of Balochistan two venomous vipers are found. The Persian Horned Viper (*Pseudocerastes persicus*) and the Levantine Viper (*Macrovipera lebetina*). In the sand dune areas of the Chagai Desert, the specialist leaf Nosed Viper (*Eristicophis macmahonii*) can be quite plentiful. This is one of the pit vipers, with heat sensor pits in the front of the nose, capable of detecting minute variations in surface temperature. The viper can thus detect the proximity of warm-blooded desert rodents–their main prey. Another is the Himalayan Pit viper (*Gloydius himalayanus*) which may live at altitudes of up to 2700 metres (9,000 ft), and must hibernate for nearly eight months of the year while snow carpets the ground.

MAN VERSUS REPTILES

Turning to the relationship of reptiles with human beings, a professional tribe of snake catchers called *jhogis*, live in Pakistan and earn a living either clearing farmsteads of snakes at the request of the owners or exhibiting so-called performing snakes. They also skin snakes for the fancy leather trade and provide a supply of live venomous specimens to the National Health Laboratories in Islamabad for the preparation of anti-venom serum. The actions of the *jhogis* limit the population of snakes and have caused all the larger more spectacular species to become rare.

The manufacture of small leather goods from reptile skins had also greatly increased in recent decades and the skin of Cobra hoods, the chequered Keelback Water Snake (*Xenochrophis piscatory*), as well as Monitor lizards, are all much in demand for making watch straps, belts, ladies handbags and shoes. There is little regulation of the trade in such skins, both for export and domestic consumption. Because of their economic value in controlling rodent pests, especially in the rice growing tracts, experts suggest that the reptile skin trade should be monitored and regulated to prevent the current trend of over-exploitation. Sadly the snake and lizard population is diminishing. People in many rural areas still believe that harmless geckos are deadly poisonous, particularly the Turkestan Plate Tailed Gecko (*Teratoscincus scincus*) in the Chagai Desert and that the *Dhaman* Snake steals milk form cows at night There is also a belief that the Krait (*Bungrarus caruleus*), which feeds exclusively on other snakes and normally flees from man, kills sleeping humans merely by rising up and breathing upon their faces. The introduction into school curricula of more balanced information about the value of reptiles and the harmlessness of most snakes would certainly help to dispel many superstitions still widely held.

T.J. ROBERTS

BIRDS OF PAKISTAN

New techniques of comparing minute strips of DNA molecules through an electron microscope, taken from an animal or bird's tissues, have now enabled biologists to compare closely related species and even to differentiate between relatives from a population of the same spieces. This has opened up new avenues in the classification of birds, so that the number of bird species now identified worldwide is increasing. Between 9941 and 9881 species of birds exist worldwide. Pakistan has 668 of this world total of identified species of birds. Pakistan is quite rich in species diversity despite the arid climate and terrain including large areas of sand dune deserts and barren rocky mountains. This is partly explained by Pakistan's strategic location at the junction of three major zoo-geographic regions. To the east is the Oriental Faunal zone, to the south-west the Ethiopian Faunal zone, and to the north-west and north, the great Palearctic Faunal zone.

Birds are much more mobile than mammals and can travel long distances each year in order to take advantage of favourable climate and obtain food. Pakistan provides wintering ground for a large number of migrant birds that are barred from central Asia and further north by cold winters. Despite the formidable barrier of the *Himalayas, the great *Indus River had created a route through the mountain chains, used by birds of many species over centuries. The importance of this route for birds entering the whole subcontinent, including India and Sri Lanka, was first recognised at an internationally sponsored conference in Ankara, Turkey, in 1967. Subsequently, its importance was further emphasized in 1971 at the Ramsar Conference in Iran, when the *Indus Valley was designated as the fourth most important 'Flyway' for migrant birds in the world.

MIGRATORY BIRDS

The Himalayan and *Karakoram Mountain chains also provide a suitable environment for many summer breeding birds that migrate only short distances down to the foothills or adjacent plains during winter where warmer weather provides a continuous supply of food for insect eating birds. Winter where warmer weather provides a continuous supply of food for insect eating birds. Examples of such local migrants are the chats and thrushes, and many tiny warblers such as the Lesser Whitethroat (*Sylvia curruca*), as well as the Great Tit (*Parus major*), and Himalayan Tree Creeper (*Certhia himalayana*).

Along the western borders spring and autumn migrant birds cross the *Arabian Sea from the Somalia region of the horn of Africa including the Eurasian Bee-Eater (*Merops apiastur*), Eurasian Roller (*Coppracisu garrlus*), a part of the Eurasion population of the common Cuckoo (*Cuculsu canorus*), and Hoopoe (*Upupa epops*). Some of this migrant population remains in Pakistan while the remainder travel further north to breed in the Central Asian republics of Tajikistan and Kazakhstan. The migrant movement of birds is complicated since some species, confined to India during the winter months, migrate northwards into Pakistan after the onset of the monsoon to breed. At this time, desert areas spring to life with temporary annual grasses and an abundance of insect life. The Yellow Wattled Plover (*Hoplopterus malabaricus*), Savannah Nightjar (*Caprimulgus affinis*), and Red Turtle Dove (*Streptopelil tranquebarica*) are examples of this movement in a north-westerly direction into Pakistan for summer breeding.

PAKISTAN'S UNIQUE SONGSTERS

Pakistan is important to a few species of birds that are unique to the area and largely confined within the borders of the country. The riverine thickets and forests along the banks of the Indus and its tributaries support four such examples: The White Tailed Stonechat (*Saxicola leucura*), the Long Tailed Grass Warbler (*Prini burnesii* burnesii), Jordan's babbler (*Chrysomma altirostris*), and the Yellow Bellied Wren Warbler (*Prinia flaviventris*). All these species have in north east India, but on both sides of the subcontinent their populations are very small and vulnerable to extinction, except for the Yellow Bellied Wren Warbler. In Pakistan, this bird has adapted to canal irrigation and spread into seepage swamps along many of the major canals.

MAN'S FLYING NEIGHBOURS

A few species of birds have adapted to living near human beings and hence they have become widespread and common with the growth of human settlement. They are known as commensal species. Examples include the House Crow (Corvus splendens), the Common Myna (Acridotheres tristis), and the House Sparrow (Passer domestics). In some areas of the Punjab, migrant sparrows have become serious pests to wheat crops, clinging to ripening ears and pecking out grains. The great increase in citrus orchards has led to a corresponding increase in the Rose Ringed Parakeet (*Psittacula krameri*) population as their beaks are sharp enough to pierce the tough rind of ripening oranges.

With increased interest and skills in observing birds, birdwatchers continue to identify new species that have not previously been recorded in Pakistan. Examples include the Dotterel (Charadrisu morinellus) and Woodchat Shrike (*Lanius senator*). In both cases, recordings have been substantiated by photographs.

Among the most beautiful birds in Pakistan is the Paradise Flycatcher (*Terpsiphone paradisi*), with its long white tail streamers and the Western Tragopan Pheasant (*Tragopan melanocephalus*), with gorgeous patterns in its plumage. The delicate violet tones of the little White Browed Tit Warbler (*Leptopoecile sohiae*) make it especially attractive. The Niltava (*Niltava sundara*) with its feather of black and iridescent blue contrasting with bright orange makes a thrilling sight as it flits through the dappled sunlight of a forest glade.

HALEJI LAKE WILDLIFE SANCTUARY

Haleji Lake, a wildlife sanctuary near Karachi, shelters thousands of water birds, including as many as 14 different species of duck especially in the winter. Migratory birds such as the Garganey (*Anas querquedula*), the Widgeon (*A. penelope*) and Brahminy duck (*Tadorna ferruginea*) can be found. Throughout the year there are resident species include Spot Billed Ducks (*Anas peocilorhyncha*), Cotton Teal (*Nettapus coromandelianus*), and Lesser Whistling Teal (*Dendrocygna javanicca*). Among the diving ducks are members of the Pochard family (*Aythya spp*).

SOARING HUNTERS

Many of the larger Raptors are to be seen in the highlands, soaring in the updrafts. Smaller varieties are to be spotted gliding over the desert areas in search of prey. One may find Steppe Eagles (*Aquila nepalensi*), Imperial Eagles (*A. heliaca*), the Brahminy Kite (*Haliastur Indus*) and the Booted Eagle (*Hieraaetus pennatus*). Among the scavengers are the vulture family the Griffon (*Gyps fulvus*), the White Backed (*G. bengalensis*), the Cinerous (*Aegypius mondachus*), and Egyptian Vultures (*Neophron percnopterus*).

SUMMER MUSICIANS

During summers in Kalam in *Swat, *Kohistan, the territorial songs of seven kinds of thrushes can be heard, all within the same small area. These include Tickell's Thrush (*Turdus unicolor*) and the Mistle Thrush (*T. viscivorous*). At higher altitudes the Chestnut Bellied Bock Thrush (*Monticola rufivventris*) can be found.

The look-alike Leaf Warblers present a challenge even to the experienced orinithologist, especially as they flit so rapidly and constantly amongst the foliage, never offering a clear view However, their songs, once learned, are all distinctive. The Naltar Valley in *Gilgit shelters Hume's Yellow Browed Leaf Warbler (*Phylloscopus proregulus*), Tickell's Leaf Warbler (*P. affinis*) and the Western Crowned Leaf Warbler (*P. occipitalis*), all breeding in close proximity.

EXPLOITATION BY MAN

Some of the larger and more spectacular birds have almost disappeared from Pakistan as a result of ruthless exploitation. Since the late 1960s, the hunting of falcons by visiting Arab dignitaries has led to a huge demand for certain larger wild falcon species that are trapped for sale each year often when they enter Pakistan's winter migrants. Enormous sums of money are paid for good female specimens. These tend to be larger and heavier than the males. As a direct result of this demand certain birds such as the Asker Falcon (*Falco charge*), the Peregrine (*Falco peregrines*) and even the resident Lager (*Falco juggler*) are becoming rare in Pakistan. Black Francolins, Cheer Pheasants, Monal Pheasants, and Houbara Bustards, as well as several Falcon species, are all disappearing from loss of habitat and excessive hunting. People capture birds for trade as well as falconry. Hundreds of black and grey francolins (*Francolinus francolinus* and *F. pondicerianus*) are trapped annually and kept as fighting and call birds while flocks of small grass finches or munias such as the Red Avadavit (*Amandava amandava*) are captured every year for the aviary trade. Eggs and chicks from the breeding colonies of Pinted Stork and White Ibis are robbed for export to private zoos. Fortunately, people are becoming aware of the loss, and the World Wide Fund for Nature, a non-government organization based in Lahore, now has an active conservation programme with regional offices in every province. Awareness and a sense of responsibility for the Pakistan wildlife heritage is steadily being nourished in order to ensure that the pleasure that this diversity of birds gives today is passed on to future generations.

MAMMALS OF PAKISTAN

On planet earth the Kingdom of mammals is represented by some 4,630 species by latest count. Despite its unfavourable climate for many animals, Pakistan has 167 mammal species. The extremes of temperatures, from 47°C (120°F) throughout the *Indus Plains and in many parts of the Frontier and Balochistan, to very low winter temperatures, down to -27°C (-12°F) in the plateau region of Balochistan, limit all but the sparsest and hardiest of plant growth, which forms the basis of the food chain upon which all mammals depend. Nevertheless, 43 species of rodents and 44 species of bats have been recorded within Pakistan. The country compares favourably in the rich variety of its mammalian fauna with much larger countries and regions. This diversity is partly explained by the strategic location of the country, lying at the intersection of three major Zoogeographic regions 1. To the east the Oriental Faunal zone, 2. to the south-west the Ethiopian Faunal zone, and 3. to the north-west and north, the great Palearctic Faunal zone.

However these Zoogeographic boundaries are not fixed. Unlike isolated large islands such as Madagascar or island continents such as North America, which often develop distinct indigenous plants and animals that are not found elsewhere, Pakistan, as part of a subcontinent, must share its fauna with adjoining countries both to the east and west. Animals that are believed to have originated in any of the three zoogeographic regions mentioned above, and that are characteristic of these funal zones, are able to spread across into other adjacent major zoogeographical zones wherever they find suitable living conditions.

ENDEMIC SPECIES

However, there are a few species that survive largely within Pakistan's boundaries and are known as endemic to the area. These are rare or absent elsewhere. They include the Woolly Flying Squirrel (*Eupetaurus cinereous*) and the Markhor (*Capra falconeri*) in the dry mountains of the far north. In Balochistan, Hotson's Jerboa (*Allactaga hotsoni*), the Balochistan Pigmy Jerboa (*salpingotus Michaelis*), and the Mouse-like Hamster (*Callomyscus bailwardi*) can be found. Because of their unique distribution and specialized ecology, they are all of great scientific interest and Pakistan has a special responsibility to ensure their preservation.

Since 1947, when Pakistan became an independent state, there has been a huge increase in the human population, from about 35 million to over 147 million as currently estimated (2003 Federal Bureau of Statistics). With this rapid increase there have also been dramatic changes to the countryside in order to develop the necessary resources to support this burgeoning population. The result has been a drastic shrinking of the surviving numbers of all the larger and more spectacular animals, most of which are intolerant of human disturbances, as well as being dependant upon large areas of suitable habitat. Such areas have largely been replaced by cultivated crops, or depleted by excessive competition for fodder from domestic grazing livestock, or by deforestation and jungle clearance. This latter has been both for agricultural development and the demand for timber for fuel or building material. Irrigation schemes have caused the uncultivated tracts of riverine forest or cane grass (*Saccharum spp.*) to dry out or be replaced by cultivation. Industrial development has aggravated the pollution of rivers and wetland areas, the home of many specialized mammals.

With 60% of the area mountainous and most of it arid and precipitous, Pakistan provides a unique refuge for some of the world's most spectacular mammals adapted to living in such conditions. This includes the Wild Goat or Persian Pasang, the Markhor or screw horned goat, and the Himalayan Ibex. Also adapted to gentler mountain slopes and ravines are the Urial or Asiatic Red Sheep, and the magnificent Marco Polo Sheep. The mature rams can grow huge spiralling horns measuring up to 144 cms from tip to tip. Predators surviving in these mountainous areas include Tibetan Wolf, the Himalayan Lynx, and the rare and elusive Sonw Leopard. In the sub-alpine regions the Grey Goral, a small horned goat-antelope still survives. Higher up in the alpine zone the diminutive Musk Deer, much persecuted for its valuable musk pod, is now very rare.

Amongst the host of tiny mammals are a number of specially adapted rodents living in the sand dune deserts of Balochistan, sharing ancestry with central Asian species. These include the Balochistan Pigmy Jerboa, two species of Five Toed Small Jerboas, Hjiary Footed Gerbils, and Mouse-like Hamsters. Specialist mountain desert rodents, such as the Aftghan Mole Vole (*Ellobius fuscocapillus*), have been replaced by the Short Tailed Mole Vvole (*Nesokia indica*). The Balochistan Gerbil (*Gerbnillus nanus*) had been driven out by the larger and more aggressive Antelope Rat (*Tatera indica*).

Pakistan also has a wealth of small carnivores or predatory mammals. These include four species of fox, including the King Fox (*Vulpes cana*), which as a very restricted world distribution and about whose life habits little is known. There are two species of otters, three species of civet cats, and four species of martens and weasels. There are six species of small wild cats, including the beautiful Leopard Cat (*Felsi bengalensis*) and the very rare Sand Cat (*F. margarita*), now confined to the Chagai Desert in south-western Balochistan. There have been changes in the mammal population during the past century, with many desert-adapted species becoming rare as they are replaced by more aggressive and adaptable species, able to take advantage of the increase in irrigation schemes, tree plantations and a more mesic or moist climate.

Only a few mammals are adapted to exploit man's activity and proximity. This includes some that have become agricultural pests, such as the Wild Boar, the Crested Porcupine, and the Short Tailed Mole Rat. Sadly, animals such as thee Indian Wild Ass or Onager, the Nilgai, Blackbuck, Chinkara Gazelles, Hog Deer, and Urial Wild Sheep are all thereatened with extinction with the area. These animals, like the Urial and Wild goat, now confined to one or two small populations in special sanctuaries. These diminishing populations are vulnerable to fatal transmissible diseases from domestic animals.

T.J. ROBERTS

Historic accounts reveal that in the mid-sixteenth century the Mughal Emperor Babur hunted the Great One-Horned Indian Rhimo in what is now a part of Swat and Attock District while former rulers of Bahawalpur State hunted the tiger in the riverine thickets of the Indus River as late as 1910. The Swamp Deer or Barasingha (*Cervus duvauceli*) still survived in the riverine forest of Sindh until the end of the nineteenth century.

In 1992, many of the nations of the world gathered for an international conference in Brazil to consider the damaging effects of over-exploitation of natural resources to our planet. Among the issues discussed were ways of preserving the natural wealth of the earth: rich food sources harvested from the oceans; valuable medicines and timber from forests and sources of precious fresh water upon which depend river environments and wetlands. This conference resulted in a 'Bio-Diversity Action Plan' to which over a hundred nations, including Pakistan, have signed up. We are committed to preserving our vanishing wildlife, both large and small. In this way we will maintain the health of our planet and the environment human beings need in order to maintain the quality of life and for our own health ad ultimate survival. Protecting the Flora and Fauna is an essential part of this imperative.

MILLY STONEY

EDUCATION IN PAKISTAN

Tariq Rahman

Pakistan inherited an unjust and class-oriented educational system from *British India which remains essentially unchanged to this day. The government schools, teaching through the medium of the vernacular languages (*Urdu and *Sindhi) are either free or very inexpensive because of which they cater to the lower-middle and working classes. Private schools, teaching through the medium of English, are for the middle and upper classes. Out of these schools those that run on the lines of elitist English Public Schools are mostly influenced, or controlled in some degree (generally through boards of governors), by the military and subsidized by the state in various ways. Children from poor, rural or religious families often study in Islamic seminaries (*madrassas*) where education, boarding, lodging and books are mostly free.

Higher and professional education is conducted in colleges, professional institutions and universities. Colleges are affiliated with universities so that the bachelors', and even the masters', degrees they give are conferred by the universities after a centralized examination. Some universities, however, do not affiliate and follow the American semester system with considerable autonomy in teaching and evaluation.

The trend since 1947 has been a tremendous increase in the number of all institutions which still lags behind the number of potential students because of the population growth. To give advantage to people from less developed areas in admissions and employment, the government created a 'quota' for them according to which every demographic group would be guaranteed a number of seats. This, however, created much resentment among the educated urban youth, who belonged to communicate with reduced quota, and were therefore losing jobs to less educated, but demographically dominant residents of a region.

The major change witnessed in the era of market economy and globalization is that privatization of education is increasing at all levels. As a result, quality education is fast becoming a very expensive commodity which is out of the reach of all except the elite of the country. Thus, while the products of expensive English-medium schools met those of the vernacular schools in colleges and universities in college, they remain separated from them even at that level since they can afford expensive private institutions of higher education. This further implies that state institutions at all levels are being ghettoized and are perceived as being stagnant and sub-standard. They are also losing those few above average faculty members who joined them despite the general trend of opting for lucrative, financially rewarding and powerful jobs.

The academic work ethic encourages goal-oriented study (even it be memorization) because of which even the products of vernacular medium schools, despite their handicap in English, do well as professionals in the international corporate sector. As their textbooks are in English they can compete with other students in foreign universities. Academia, however, does not attract the best students, therefore Pakistan lags behind other countries in teaching and research.

Ultimately, however, the system has considerable room for improvement. There is a dire need to create scientists, social scientists and artists of world class, though the existing system does produce professionals of a high caliber.

BIBLIOGRAPHY: *K.K. Aziz, The Murder of History in Pakistan (Lahore, 1993); Hayes, Louis.B., The Crisis of Education in Pakistan (Lahore, 1987); P. Hoodbhoy, (ed), Education and the State: Fifty Years of Pakistan (Karachi, 1998); International Advisory Group, Pakistan: Madrassas, Extremism and the Military (Islambad, 2002); Khalid, S.M., Deeni Madaris Mein Taleem (Islamabad, 2002); Nayyar, A.H. and Salim, Ahmed.(eds), The Subtle Subversion: The State of Curricula and Textbooks in Pakistan (Islamabad, 2003); Rahman, Tariq., Language, Ideology and Power: Language Learning Among the Muslims of Pakistan and North India (Karachi, 2002) and Denizens of Alien Worlds: A Study of Education, Inequality and Polarization in Pakistan (Karachi, 2004); Saigol, Rubina., Knowledge and Identity: Articulation of Gender in Educational Discourse in Pakistan (Lahore, 1995) and Symbolic Violence: Curriculum, Pedagogy and Society (Lahore, 2000).*

PUPPETRY IN PAKISTAN

(Lahore Museum of Puppetry)

The Rafi Peer Theatre Workshop

Rafi Peer Theatre Workshop is the oldest private performance arts company in Pakistan. It was founded by Rafi Peerzada in 1947 as the *Pakistan Drama Markaz* for the progress and development of performing arts. In 1974, it was renamed Rafi Peer Theatre Workshop (RPTW). For the past 26 years the RPTW has produced considerable amount of serious pioneering work for the progress of dramatic arts.

New programs and workshops produced at regular intervals. The productions are backed either by private sponsors or depend entirely on ticket sales. Since 1974, the Theatre Workshop has acquired some assets of its own e.g. scores of puppets, sets, props, theatre lighting equipment and sound equipment. The rentals from the latter help support the activities of the workshop.

At the time of its establishment in 1974, the aims and objectives of the Rafi Peer Theatre Workshop were developed after careful consideration. It was clearly established that the theatre workshop would serve the community and society through the promotion of performing arts. By providing meaningful entertainment, it aimed to educate, entertain, and bring about awareness of issues that concern Pakistan's people and society. The idea was to use the potential of performing arts to its fullest and work towards the fulfilment of its declared objectives through direct mass communication.

Rafi Peer Theatre Workshop has come a long way since 1974. It is a pioneer organization of its kind which has produced innumerable programs reaching out to audiences all over urban and rural Pakistan. It is the first group that has done extensive work for the development of theatre with its focus on youth and children.

The RPTW has now set up a Museum of Puppetry in Lahore alongwith a training institute and a theatre. It is a unique museum, where the masterpieces of international puppeteers from different cultures and backgrounds are exhibited for students, connoisseurs and followers of this art form. The Museum of Puppetry promotes human values such as peace and mutual understanding between peoples irrespective of who they are.

OBJECTIVES OF THE MUSEUM OF PUPPETRY

1. Educational and recreational programs designed to meet the needs of children in Pakistan. Included in this are the intellectually gifted as well as the mentally retarded, and especially the culturally and economically disadvantaged children, who have been born into an environment lacking books, playing space and a creative environment.
2. Develop special programs and educational packages for schools. Develop educational work with children and hold workshops for school teachers and in order to teach them simple puppetry.
3. Preservation of folk puppets and folk theatre forms by creating opportunities for innovative work available to folk artists.
4. Continue to develop and implement professional training programs for puppeteers all over Pakistan.
5. Produce documentary films on puppets and the art of puppetry in Pakistan. Films will be launched soon which are dedicated to the puppet festivals of 1992 and 1994, titled 'World of Puppetry'.
6. Creating opportunities for research work on puppetry and teaching for students.
7. Develop opportunities for foreign groups to visit Pakistan regarding development work on puppetry in Pakistan, i.e. research, publication and teaching.

8. Producing a regular newsletter of UNIMA Pakistan. Facilitate in the development of literature on various aspects of puppetry in Pakistan.
9. To organize National Puppet Festivals regularly and more frequently.
10. Promote the art of puppetry through the organisation of conferences, seminars, lectures, workshops and meetings at the Museum with local, national and international puppeteers.

The RPTW has collected a large number of puppets, posters, paintings, photographs, slides, documented material, video films, props and other material over the years. Most of these exhibits have been developed by the RPTW during the course of this various activities and some of the exhibits have been presented by foreign delegates as their contribution towards the Museum of Puppetry.

EXHIBITS

1. 2,160 Puppets from Rafi Peer Theatre Workshop.
2. 1,110 International puppets from Pakistan, Uzbekistan, Indonesia, China, Japan, Iran, Greece, Sweden, England, USA, Slovenia, Russia, Poland, New Zealand, Sri Lanka, Malaysia, Thailand, Combodia, Equador & India.
3. 350 Masks.
4. 175 Props.
5. 250 Glove Puppets.
6. 175 Scenography and props.
7. 650 collection posters from various puppet companies.
8. 24 French poster collection on puppets from all ages.
9. 2,000 Photographs of puppet players and their work.
10. 1,500 Slides of various puppet groups.
11. 240 Books on puppet theatre.
12. 2,100 Biographical references on various puppet players of more than 70 countries.
13. 1,690 Video tapes, depicting works of puppet players of more than 30 countries.
14. 16,000 minutes of reference material on International Puppet Festival, Pakistan, 1992, 1994, 1996 & 1998. Includes interviews of performers and lectures.

VIDEO REFERENCE LIBRARY

- 180 paintings on puppets.
- 132 cartoons depicting puppets with political satire.
- 6,500 letters of various puppet players.

These exhibits are Rafi Peer Theatre Workshop's contribution towards the Museum of Puppetry.

STATUS OF CURRENT MUSEUM ACTIVITIES:

At this stage the Museum is working on a film, based on folk puppeteers. This film is called 'The Dying Art' which will be completed soon. The Museum is planning to acquire more puppets of historical significance. The Museum will also acquire books, videos and other related literature for its library and training programme.

The folk arts and puppet preservation program will set up a Museum, which will house permanent exhibitions on various folk arts, showing their origins and traditions. It will send out its own exhibitions and invite exhibitions from all over the world.

RECURRENT ACTIVITIES:

1. Organize Exhibits.
2. Organize Seminars/Workshop/Lectures/Meetings on Puppetry and Related Art Forms.
3. Organize Video Material. Arrange Video Shows.
4. Publications and Video Films on Puppetry.
5. Identify and Support Folk Puppet Theatre and Puppeteers.
6. Support Puppet Theatre Activities.
7. Organize Puppet Plays/Festival on Local, National, Regional and International Scales.

The Museum will support itself through membership, sponsorship of activities and Museum entrance ticket sales.

DANCE IN PAKISTAN

Rumana Husain

Pakistan's human history dates back to the stone age, but one of the earliest examples of organised urban settlement in the heart of this land is the spectacular site of *Moenjodaro and *Harappa, dating 2,500 BC to 1,700 BC. These two cities belong to the *Indus Valley Civilisation. The famous bronze figurine of a dancing girl (of *Dravidian stock) found from the ruins of this ancient civilisation, bears testimony to the fact that dance is an age-old practice of this region.

There are two main traditions of dance and music in most countries of the world: Folk and Classical, and Pakistan is no exception.

FOLK DANCES

The folk dances of Pakistan are generally associated with the celebration of festive occasions such as the birth of a child, a marriage, religious devotion, etc. They are also celebrations for seasons of harvesting and the advent of spring. Folk dance, like everywhere else in the world, is truly the common person's spontaneous celebration, in which he or she is joined by a group of other revellers.

There are only a few mixed dances in Pakistan. There are some that are danced only by men, and some that are danced only by women. Folk dances from the four provinces of Pakistan have their own distinct flavour. Adding to their individuality are the different costumes and musical instruments accompanying the dances.

BAMQA

A dance from *Balochistan. It is a mixed dance of men and women danced to the beat of the drum and the sonorous sound of the **shehnai* (a type of flute music).

LEVA

Supposed to be of African origin. In Karachi's Lyari area, one can see *Leva* performed by the people living there. These are the people whose forefathers migrated from African countries. They introduced *Leva* to the *Baloch community, who have been settled in Karachi for a long time. *Leva* is danced with a wild swagger and fast movements of the dancers, to the rhythmic beat of the drums, and is quite unique in its style. While *Leva* is given the status of an 'outsiders dance' by the Baloch, *Latti* and *Hambo* are dances of the ancient indigenous people of Balochistan.

JHOOMAR (ALSO GHOOMAR)

(literally meaning spinning or going around) is the name given to two different kinds of dances. One is a dance from Balochistan whereas the other is from the *Punjab. This dance is very much part of Punjab's folk heritage. It is a graceful dance based on a *Jhoomar* rhythm. Dancers circle around the drummer and sing graceful lyrics as they dance. In Multan, Muzaffargarh and *Bahawalpur, women perform the *Jhoomar*. It is a romantic dance, beginning with a circle, but breaking and forming patterns as it progresses–much like the patterns in a kaleidoscope. In *Jhelum, men perform it, but it is quite different from the women's dance.

LUDDI

A dance for both men and women, but they don't dance together. It is a victory dance where people do special movements of their heads. It is usually danced when the fields have been prepared for sowing. The costume worn by the dancers is a simple loose shirt with a *lacha* or sarong. The dancers put one hand on their backs and the other hand in front of their faces. The body movement is sinuous, snake-like. There is also a drummer in the centre of the dance. *Luddi* may or may not be accompanied by songs.

SAMMI

A special dance without any songs or music. Women of the Punjab traditionally dance *Sammi*. The dancers dress in bright coloured *kurtas* (loose traditional shirts) and full flowing skirts called *lehngas*. A particular silver hair ornament is associated with this dance. It is in reality a dance-drama, portraying a story of love and longing.

KIKLI

A dance of young girls performed in pairs. The dancers face each other, cross their arms, and hold each other's hands, whirling around and singing folk songs. The girls stretch themselves backwards and forwards and whirl in a circle. Sometimes four girls join hands to perform this dance. Often the songs are devoted to the themes of relationship with the in-laws.

BHANGRA

Originally performed by the men of *Gujrat, Jhelum and Wazirabad districts to celebrate the success of a harvest or at the onset of spring. Now people in all urban areas of the country perform *Bhangra* at wedding parties and other happy occasions with great abandon. *Bhangra* is performed in villages as well as the cities, with large drums, called **dhols*, and the dancers encircle, leap and laugh. It is a most invigorating dance. It has now become so popular that it has gained international recognition, especially in the UK.

GIDDA

Punjab's most famous folk dance for women. It can be danced by as few as two dancers. Women enact verses called *bolis* and folk poetry. The subject matter of these *bolis* include a wide range: arguments with the father-in-law to political affairs. The dance rhythm is set by the *dhols* and the distinctive hand claps of the dancers.

DHAMMAAL (ALSO JULLI, ATHAN)

Dances associated with mysticism. Pakistan is a land of mystics and shrines. People flock to these shrines in large numbers. The *Sufi saints and poets who lie in their graves in these shrines are revered throughout Pakistan, and devotees come bare feet, dancing and twirling, singing spiritual songs. In particular, the death anniversaries or **urs* of these men are celebrated with fervour each year. Drums are beaten, soul-inspiring music is played, and onlookers dance in ecstasy. The *Dhammaal* is similar to the *Bhangra*.

Holy men or **pirs* who generally dance in their hermitages or *khangahs* performs *Julli*. They perform the dance while sitting. Sometimes they dance around a saint's grave. Normally the dancer wears black.

ATHAN

A dance of religious students, who sing praises of Allah and the Prophet (PBUH) as they dance. It is possible that this dance may be an influence of the 'whirling dervishes' of Konya, Turkey, who are associated with the Sufi teachings of Maulana Jalaluddin Rumi.

KHATTAK

The most popular of the dances from the North West Frontier Province. The Pathan men, known for their warrior-like nature, perform this dance by holding either big handkerchiefs or swords. There are many variations of the dance, as each tribe has its own style. In Hazara, the *Khattak* is performed to the accompaniment of wooden clappers, much like the Spanish castanets. Wearing embroidered waistcoats with the traditional *shalwar kameez* costume, the dancers normally dance in a circle, which becomes bigger when more men join in when the tempo of the drum increases.

LAKHTAI

A dance from the frontier province, but unlike the *Khattak*, *Lakhtai* can sometimes be performed solo.

DANCES OF THE KAFIRS

Danced by the *Kalash Valleys of Rumbur, Bunboret and Birir that lie within Chitral in the North-West Frontier Province. These are quite distinct. These valleys are the home of a primitive pagan tribe–the Kafirs. They wear black robes and elaborate headdresses as well as colourful bead and silver jewellery. The Kafirs have a religion and culture of their own. There is much dancing in the celebration of all their festivals and special occasions, whereby the elders chant legends with drum accompaniment and the women dance arm-in-arm in a circle.

DANCES OF THE THARI

Danced in the Tharparkar desert in Sindh, this includes *Rasooro*, *Dandan rand*, *Mitco* and *Chakar rand*. The Thari women are clad in brilliant traditional *ghagras, cholis and dopattas*, but the most striking feature of their appearance are the white bangles worn by them from the wrist to the shoulder. The *Rasooro* is a stick dance performed by women. A woman plays the *dhol* and some women sing songs to the accompaniment of its beat.

Eight to ten men perform the *Dandan* rand holding a stick in one hand and a silk handkerchief in the other one. The *dhol* player accompanying the dancers also sings the songs. A male performs *Mitco* solo, but sometimes it is also danced by women on the occasion of their son's wedding. The *Chakar Rand* is traditionally performed by Thari Muslims. A male dancer performs it with a sword in his hand.

DANDIA

Dandia has gained popularity as a special dance in celebration of a wedding particularly in Karachi. It originates from the Gujrati speaking Hindu and Muslim communities of India from where dances such as *Raas*, *Garba*, etc. have also originated. The *dandiyaas* or two short sticks are held in each hand of all the dancers. Ideally, two circles formed by men and women move in clockwise and anti-clockwise directions. Romantic songs are sung on the occasion. *Raas* is a very energetic, colourful and playful, providing opportunity for acting and exchanging messages through eye contact. Many romances therefore bloom during these performances and the dances are particularly popular among the younger generation.

CLASSICAL DANCES

Unlike folk dances, the genre of classical dance is highly specialised and individualistic. Its training is arduous and requires devotion as well as a keen understanding of classical music.

Unfortunately, dance has been the least encouraged and supported art form in Pakistan. Classical dance in particular, is rejected by orthodox religious leaders. A vast populace does not have either an education or the exposure to realise that it has been part of our cultural heritage, which flourished for millennia in the lands of South Asia. In the absence of any state support to this art form, vulgar dances in commercial films or at the infamous *kothas* or houses of ill repute are what the masses have been exposed to.

In this harsh landscape, only a few exponents of classical dance have managed to survive. *Bharata Natyam* and *Kathak* are two distinct classical dances performed and taught in Pakistan, while those who perform the *Bharata Natyam*, are also well-versed with other styles, like *Odissi* and *Manipuri*. The classical dancer's costume, jewellery and make-up are quite elaborate and colourful.

BHARATA NATYAM

Evolved in southern India. The long history of this stylised dance has been well recorded both in visual and textual documents. These dance traditions were the heritage of performers who were part of the courts of kings or performers who were part of religious traditions. In Pakistan, the statuette of the dancing girl of Moenjodaro, with her limbs and hip frozen in a particular pose, evokes those traditions.

It was in the nineteen thirties that pioneers like Rukmini Devi and Krishna Iyer revived dancing traditions and set the tone for the *Bharata Natyam* dance of today. It is one of the most evolved art form, that relates to all the aspects of human existence: body, psyche and the soul.

A peculiar style or stance of *Bharata Natyam* is *arai mandi* or half bent knees position. The dancer combines body movements, eyes, head and neck movements, facial expressions and hand gestures in a repertoire that normally begins by salutations to the gods, the *guru* and the audience. A*bhinaya* or *nritya* is the expressional aspect of dance, which is performed after the first two dance items called *Allarippu* and *Jatiswaram*, which are purely abstract. *Tillana* is the final item in the *Bharata Natyam* repertoire, and is another excellent example of pure and abstract dance. It is entirely governed by the scintillating musical score and incorporates intricate foot-work and sculpturesque poses.

GHANSHYAMS

In the early years of Pakistan's existence, the Ghanshyams were instrumental in inculcating a love for dance in many of their students. A dedicated couple, they ran a school of dancing, in Karachi, called the Rhythmic Arts Academy. Daughter Tara later joined them in teaching various dances. Every few months the three staged a public performance. Besides their repertoire of *Bharata Natyam* and other styles, Mr Ghanshyam's Peacock Dance was also well-received by audiences. The Ghanshyams had to leave the country in 1983 under pressure of the Ziaul *Haq martial law regime, leaving a big vacuum.

SHEEMA KERMANI

As a teenager, she had started learning dance with the Ghanshyams. She then earned a degree at the Croydon College of Arts in London and gained prominence and popularity in the *Bharata Natyam* and *Odissi* styles of dance. Later, she pursued dance in India with Leela Samson, Mayadhar Raut, and Aloka Pannikar. She has been holding dance classes and performing ever since 1984. Kermani has extended the classical dance genre into theatre productions under the banner of *Tehrik-e-Niswan* (Women's Movement), which was established in 1980. Amjad Ansari, Sadia Khan and Mani Chau are some of Kermani's outstanding students, who perform, choreograph and teach on their own.

INDU MITHA

In Islamabad, Indu Mitha has been performing and teaching *Bharata Natyam*. She learned in the *Kalakshetra* mode from Lalita Shastri and trained in the *Uday Shankar* style of modern dance at the Zoresh Institute, Lahore, before partition. Tehreema Mitha is her daughter, who studied Fine Arts from the National College of Arts in Lahore and later established her own dance production house under Tehreema Aabvaan Dance Productions. She now lives in the USA.

ODISSI

A style of dance that came into existence in the state of Orissa in India, and the style emerged from a confluence of scholars, teachers of traditional dance, and musicians.

MANIPURI

A style that comes from the state of Manipur in the northeast region of India. Its lyrical movements boast of a tradition beginning as early as 154 AD.

Pakistani dancers who perform *Bharata Natyam*, also perform the *Odissi* and *Manipuri*, but it is rare that other styles, e.g. the *Kuchipudi*, *Mohini Attam* or the highly theatrical dance from the southern state of Kerala in India, called *Kathakali*, are ever learnt or performed here.

KATHAK

A dance that traces its origins to the nomadic bards of ancient northern India, known as *Kathaks*, or storytellers. These bards, performing in village squares and temple courtyards, mostly specialised in recounting mythological and moral tales. Their recitals were embellished with hand gestures and facial expressions. With the advent of the Mughul rule (see, Mughal Empire) in India (11th-18th centuries), *Kathak* was transformed. It got out from the temple and became a court dance performed for entertainment. The *Mughul emperors patronised it and refined its different aspects. It is known for its sparkling footwork, swift whirling movements and understated *abhinaya* or mime. After the power of the Moghal Empire declined, *Kathak* was patronised by minor princely states. Wajid Ali Shah, the Nawab of Oudh, founded the famed *Lucknow *Gharana* or Lucknow School. Lucknow, Banaras and Jaipur are recognised as the three schools where this art was nurtured and refined.

The *Kathak* footwork is matched by the accompanying percussion instruments such as **tabla* and *pakhawaj*, and *jugalbandi* or a friendly competition, a sort of rhythmic wizardry, between the dancer and percussionists. It is often a source of delightful entertainment. The dance movements include numerous pirouettes executed at lightning speed and ending in statuesque poses.

Kathak can be danced with a wide variety of music, such as classical songs, e.g. **Thumri, Dadra, Kajri, Hori* and *Darbari* and **Ghazals* or *Urdu love poetry that includes themes of admiration, infatuation, and separation. Dance dramas based on Hindu mythological epics or any musical composition or film song based on **raga* can blend with a Kathak performance.

It is believed that *Kathak* and Flamenco (a Spanish dance) traditions have common roots. Gypsies from India carried the tradition to the Middle East and Europe. In the Andalusia region of Southern Spain, it blended with other cultural influences, evolving into the emotional and highly dramatic dance known today as Flamenco.

In Pakistan, Maharaj Ghulam Husain Kathak–the grand old man of *Kathak*, who danced in the Lucknow *Gharana* style and dedicated his life to this art form, taught until his death in Lahore a few years ago.

Madam Azurie (Owned a dance school in Karachi. She arrived from Bombay where she had worked in the movies), Rafi Anwar (Got his training in India. After migrating to Pakistan, the *Kathak* dancer became a popular 'peacock dance' performer, but he also taught *Kathak* for several years until he passed away), Zareen Suleman (Popularly known as '*Panna*'), and Amy Minwala, are other dancers who popularised *Kathak* on stage and in films.

PNCA

The PNCA Performing Arts Group, once known as the PIA Arts Academy, was set up in the early seventies. It was set up during the Zulfiqar Ali *Bhutto years, and was meant to promote Pakistan's dance and music (both folk as well as classical) in other countries, in particular those where the national airline flew.

Renowned actor, Zia Mohyeddin, successfully led the academy. But it was closed down, and then during the Ziaul Haq regime, it was taken over by the Pakistan National Council of the Arts (PNCA), which is run by the Ministry of Culture.

In 2001, the PNCA Performing Arts troupe was revived under Nighat Chaudhry, who was appointed the Director at PNCA, Karachi. By December 2001, Chaudhry had left, and presently Sheema Kermani trains the troupe: 10 female dancers, 10 male dancers, and 10 musicians, as the PNCA Artistic Director.

NAHID SIDDIQUI

Gained international acclaim for *Kathak*. She was associated with the PNCA as its star performer. She began training in the seventies, tutored by Maharaj Ghulam Hussain Kathak. Siddiqui left Pakistan in 1979 after her *Kathak* programme on the state-owned television channel was banned. She lives in Birmingham. From Great Britian she has travelled, researched about classical dances and enlarged her repertoire, working with the great Indian *Kathak* artist, teacher and choreographer, Birju Maharaj.

Siddiqui has recieved several awards, including The International Dance Award, presented in 1991; Time-Out Award at the National Theatre in London; Faiz Ahmed *Faiz Foundation Award in Lahore; British Cultural Award in 1992; the Digital Award in 1993; and the Pride of Performance by the Pakistan Government in 1994. Siddiqui has performed, taught, and achieved international fame during her stay in her adopted home. Nahid Siddiqui & Co has been working from England since 1991. The Arts Council of Great Britian has funded the company. She now commutes between the UK and Pakistan, and continues to perform as well as teach in both countries.

NIGHAT CHAUDHRY

Born in Pakistan but grew up in Britain, where she studied ballet and contemporary dance, and trained in *Kathak* with Nahid Siddiqui. Subsequently, she won a scholarship for a three-year course at Kathak Kendra in Delhi, where she studied under late Pandit Durga Lal and his disciple Uma Dogra in Bombay. Chaudhry also divides her time between two countries–Pakistan and the USA.

FASIH-UR-RAHMAN

Continues the legacy of Maharaj Ghulam Husain Kathak. He is the only male *Kathak* dancer in the country to have attained great prominence in the field. He performs internationally, and has had shows in the United States, United Kingdom and Japan. He lives in Lahore, where he performs and teaches, but from time to time he holds *Kathak* workshops in Karachi as well. He began learning the art when he was ten years old, under the tutelage of the legendary *Kathak guru Maharaj*, and is dancing since 1977. Rahman has attended training workshops with the famous dancer Kumidini Lakhia in London, UK, and in her hometown, Ahmedabad, India. He has also trained with Birju Maharaj.

SHAYMA SAIYID

Studied Kathak from Maharaj Ghulam Husain in Lahore, also from Nighat Chaudhry, and a year of *Odissi* with Sheema Kermani in Karachi. She has held several performances in both cities. She joined the Grinnell College Dance Troupe in the United States, where she went for her studies in 1989. In New York City she joined the Barnard College Dance Department at Columbia University, also attending the NY Summer Dance Intensive, culminating in a public performance. In Washington DC, she joined the Joy of Motion Dance Center and Dance Place. She taught and performed *Kathak* at these places. Saiyid lives in Toronto, Canada, where she teaches and performs.

JAHANARA AKHLAQ

She was only 24 when she, and her father–a renowned artist–Professor Zahoor-ul-Akhlaq, were brutally murdered in Lahore in 1999. Akhlaq had devoted 19 years to learn *Kathak*, initially with Nahid Siddiqui and later with the Chandralekha Dance Company in Chennai, India. Akhlaq had her first solo performance in 1993.

Sources: Folk Heritage of Pakistan 1977, published by the Institute of Folk Heritage, Islamabad; Pakistan-Tradition and Change by Khawar Mumtaz and Yameema Mitha, published by Oxford University Press; Zia Mohyeddin column: The Peacock Dance; Beena Sarwar article: PNCA-A Classical Revival?; Alexandra Ramanova article: Indian Classical Dance-A Universal Art; Kathryn Hansen article: Classical Dance Re-emerges in Pakistan, Samar 8-1997; Leela Samson article: Kathak-Indian Classical Dance; Online source: http://www.fortunecity.com/victorian/parkwood/388/Bharatha-Natyam.

VISUAL ARTS OF PAKISTAN

Niilofur Farrukh

GENESIS

The ancient settlements of Mehrgarh, *Moenjodaro and *Harrapa are linked to each other by a strong and diverse craft tradition that can be seen as the genesis of creative expression in the areas included in Pakistan. It is widely believed that two religious images were conceived and crafted here, one of *Shiva*, the reigning deities of the Hindu pantheon and centuries later of Lord Buddha, the founder of Buddhism.

Excavations reveal that the creative mind was inspired by religion, function and entertainment. In the ancient settlements located in the Southern part of the country, like Mehrgarh, *Kot Diji, Moenjodaro and Harrapa, a pottery tradition flourished which has left behind very interesting vessels. Potters achieved such high standards that the vessels successfully concealed all signs of the techniques used in its creation. High temperature stoneware fired through a complex system was invented for wide bangles, the use of which was exclusive to figures of authority.

The potter not only created outstanding pottery but evolved a symbolic pattern dedicated to each tribe. This embellished earthenware, with stylized animals, fish, birds, *pipal* leaf and geometric patterns in polychrome clay slips. The human form used in an inventive way created icons of religious and social significance. The Mother Goddess in terracotta, the Dancing Girl, cast from the lost wax technique in bronze and the High Priest successfully creates a visual impact. The varied linear iconography that support the script on the Indus seals (see, Indus Valley Civilisation) tell us of the ability of the artist to work with a wide range of mediums, including terracotta, steatite and marble.

In crafts, similar skills were adapted to bead making in widespread factories in Harrapa, which suggests the export of jewelry made from carnelian, agate, gold and faience beads. Evidence has led archeologists to conclude that the organized production of craft was the engine of the economy of this trading community. The discovery of *Indus Valley seals in far-off locations reinforces the fact that these superior and innovative crafts were in demand and held in high esteem.

The *Gandhara Art, dedicated to the veneration of Lord Buddha, emerged from the foothills of the *Himalayas in the *North Western Frontier Province in the first century AD. It combined the skills of the local stone carvers with Greek Hellenistic imagery as interpreted by the Buddhist descendants of Alexander's legions, who settled in this area.

The most significant contribution of this art is the introduction of the image of Buddha, which gradually replaced the symbols of the lotus and footprints, conventional depiction of him in the earlier religious imagery. Once Buddhism became the first religion to commit its scriptures to writing, it was followed by the development of 'the art of the book' in South Asia. The canonical texts were informed by the linear style of the frescos of *Ajanta* and *Ellora*. The horizontal format was dictated by the palm-leaf substrate. Written with the pressing action of a metal stylus, with ink and pigment brushed over it, the narrative illustrations were dominated by red, blue, orange, gold and black. This art progressed under the patronage of the Pala rulers of Bengal from the 7th to the 12th century. Gradually these manuscripts included Jain and Hindu scriptures and went into greater production all over India.

The famed Mughal *Miniature was a continuum of the visual arts tradition as it synthesized the indigenous with the Persian miniature style introduced by Emperor Humayum who commissioned two Persian painters to set up the regal studios.

During Emperor Akbar reign, Mughal Miniature moved away from the traditional Persian epics both in style and subject. He commissioned illustrated books on Christianity, Hinduism and Zoroastrianism and an elaborate history of Islam to commemorate the first millenium since the *Hijra*, was also completed in his studios.

Encouragement to innovators during this period led to an artistic investigation of the European Renaissance prints and tapestries that had been brought to him as gifts. An awareness of new perspective techniques used in Renaissance Europe followed and gradually began to influence spatial depth in the works.

Jehangir used miniature painting extensively as a tool for documentation. In portraits, authenticity was sought and an artist was even sent to the Persian court to get the likeness of the ruler for the court paintings. Court personages were religiously portrayed with resemblance instead of labelled stock figures.

Flora and fauna was a popular genre, compiled in *Muraqas* or personal albums these individual paintings are framed with elaborate borders bearing traditional arabesque motifs sometimes even landscapes and scenes of daily life.

The manuscript of *Padshahnamah* epitomizes Shah Jehan's taste for opulence. A great builder, he favored the depiction of the court in full splendor.

During the reign of Aurangzeb, an orthodox Muslim, the artisans suffered from neglect. Most paintings show him in his old age and are based on record conquests, court ceremonies. The emperor is frequently shown in meetings with holy men or performing his prayers. As the *Mughal Empire disintegrated into smaller kingdoms, its artists found new patrons in the smaller courts.

In the *Punjab, a Sikh School of Painting under the patronage of Maharaja Ranjit Singh took root. This served to glorify the religious and political leadership of the *Sikhs. Bright clear colours favoured by the community influenced the palette of the paintings and it was characterised by their physical features and costumes. In the later period, European realism crept into paintings as European portraitists were increasingly commissioned at the court. The artistic preferences of the ruler frequently led to changes that sometimes gave birth to a distinctive style. This resulted in various provincial schools of miniature painting that reflect the synthesis of the traditional genre with local cultural and religious influences.

With the advent of colonial rule, art practice underwent a major change. The transition from court to personal patronage put great financial strain on the artist and for survival he had to sell art in the bazaars. During these years there was an influx of British officials and their families who were keen to collect pictures of exotic India and its people and artists obliged them and a new niche for drawings and naturalistic aquarelles was created. The hybrid style that developed came to be known as the Company School of Painting.

This was a time of great social and cultural up-heavel. As the colonial race consolidated its power, it's strategy included culture invention. In 1853, Trevelyan said 'The only means at our disposal of preventing revolution is to set the natives on a process of European improvement.' Their aim was to train a group of individuals who would be, according to another Englishman, Macaulay, 'Indian in blood and colour but British in taste, in opinions, in morals and intellect.' To execute this a network of Victorian style craft schools and art academies were set up in the major cities of India under the British, from 1850 onwards. In Lahore, the Mayo School of Art was founded in 1875.

On the agenda was also a systematic disruption of the strong craft base of India to allow the import of industrial products of Great Britain. Once the sons of artists and artisans began to leave their ancestral practice, craft went into decline and this was evident only 28 years after the first school was established, when India was invited to participate in the 1878 Paris craft show.

The delinking of the craftsman from his community and source of raw material was a critical interference in the cultural pattern of India and resulted in a break from the traditional practice of the guild system patterned on the *ustad-shagird* (student-teacher) relationship. The academy and apprentice were philosophically polarized, one emphasized a link with the community needs and a shared creative ethos while the other was Eurocentric and hegemonic, with stress on design for mass production.

The art school produced a new breed of artists, who in art historian W.G. Archer's words, '**... remained,** in practice a pathetic outsider.'

From Calcutta, where the first art academy was set up, emerged the nationalist movement of The New Bengal School in the late 19th century, which focused on the integration of indigenous art and themes. Based on the ideals of the *Swadeshi* Movement spearheaded by Rabindranath Tagore, the artists of The New Bengal School revived cultural and religious themes along with traditional art practices. The graduates from these art academies formed two separate trajectories in painting that informed the Pakistani Art Movement.

EXPERIMENTS WITHIN THE TRADITIONAL GENRES

Abdur Rehman Chughtai, (1894–1975) a celebrated exponent of The New Bengal School, was among the leading painters of Lahore at the time of the Partition in 1947. Chughtai began his painting career in 1916 and got early recognition in various parts of India.

In keeping with the revivalist spirit of The New Bengal School, he sought inspiration from the Mughal Miniature and the '*Naqsh*' or patterns of the Islamic decorative arts. His themes borrowed from popular folklore, Hindu Mythology and Islamic epics.

Chughtai had a distinctive style of painting. The elongated elegant human figure is always central to his work, which he portrayed in a linear iconography with a soft wash, resulting in ethereal ambience. In soft, clear tones emerged exquisite details of costume, jewellery, architecture, landscape, flora and fauna.

Chughtai's work echoed the creative sensibilities of his people. In *Muraq-i-Chughtai* and *Amal-i-Chughtai,* his famous illustrations of the verses of *Ghalib and *Iqbal, he gave a contemporary interpretation to the classical tradition of Persian painting.

The self-taught **Ustad Allah Baksh** (1895–1978) had a natural talent for landscape painting. His early apprenticeship with a backdrop painter initiated him into this genre. During his association with the Court of Patiala, the *Ustad* (teacher) had the opportunity to closely study the Raja's European Collection and this was perhaps what influenced him to adopt this popular style of naturalism. Landscape, folk stories and Hindu mythology gave him considerable fame as a painter of Krishna themes in Lahore.

Talism-i-hoshruba, one of Ustad Allah Baksh's most memorable works assimilates high drama with the narrative, a quality informed by his long career in the world of theatre.

A stylization crept into his landscape and he used imaginative shapes in bold colours to depict anthropomorphic and formations in the later years. The School of Landscape Painting that has emerged from Lahore can be traced to his long distinguished career.

Two well-known portraitists in India relocated themselves in Karachi. Fayzee Rahamin and S.H. Askari where exponents of the European style, which had taken root in the post-Mughal courts and was now popular among the new social elite of the region.

Fayzee Rahamin (1880–1964), a student of John Singer Sargent had won recognition for his murals on the inner dome at the New Delhi Secretariat, painted around 1926. His work combines western portrait painting techniques with traditional Indian art. His Portrait of the Begum of Janjira is redolent of the Mughal court portraits.

In his portraits the features of his subjects are treated with an ethereal translucent quality that became the hallmark of his work. In 1952 he gifted his art collection to the city of Karachi.

Syed Hasan Askari (1907–1969) was an exponent of Academic Realism pioneered by Raja Ravi Varma in the 19th century. He can be called a modern day equivalent of the court portraitist as his oeuvre (works) mainly consisted of commissioned works for the social and political elite of the country. His portraits have a ceremonial formality. Askari presented an idealized image often enhanced by opulent formal attire.

Miniature painting had been largely eclipsed by western genres but several dedicated painters like Haji Mohmmed Sharif and Ustad Shujaullah kept it alive.

Haji Mohammed Sharif (1889–1978) belonged to a long line of miniaturists who had been in the employ of the Maharaja of Patiala. Following his exhibition in London in 1942, his talent was widely recognized and he was made the Member of the British Empire.

In 1945 he joined the Mayo School of Art where he taught for nearly two decades. In the true tradition of this pursuit of art he reproduced many works of the equestrian portraits, which he made of various Mughal emperors and their consorts.

Ustad Shujaullah (1912–1980) as a young man had received training in Kangra, Rajput, Deccani and Mughal schools of miniature painting. A preference for the Mughal style is seen in his strong skills of *'Naqqashi'*or design making. Elaborately designed borders characterize his miniature paintings.

The Modernist Expression

Fully aware of their place in history, the manifesto of the artists of nascent Pakistan could not escape the spirit of the time. The political and social leadership inspired by poet Iqbal's message of '*khudi*', the awakening of individualism and self-ambition, began to focus on a robust intellectual, economic and social participation in the modern age.

These views found resonance among the aspiring modernists of Pakistan and they looked at the new aesthetics of modern art as a manifestation of a technological and industrial progress leading to economic freedom, as it had done in the West. Modern art also seemed to be the chosen visual language that was compatible with the national poet philosophy of *'khudi'* or ego as a dynamo that propels man towards personal success. In this milieu, traditionalism in art seemed inadequate to articulate the dreams and fears of a generation poised to enter a new era of freedom.

Ahmed Pervaz, Sheikh Safdar, Shemza, Moyene Najmi and Ali Imam founded the Lahore Art Circle in the early 1950's. This paradigm shift manifested itself in art and experiments with the modern idiom provided a framework to re-examine a familiar cultural terrain. This early exploration of the new idiom was a purely visual response to what the pioneers had been exposed to through colour plates and black and white printed reproductions in magazines and art books. None of them were fully cognizant with the philosophies that energized the Schools of Paris; by default their lack of formal education led to an eclecticism that opened a new space for inventive work.

For each of these artists, modernism did not mean a denial of their legacy, experiences and affinities, but an engagemen. A similar movement led by Zainul Abedin was initiated in the Eastern wing of Pakistan.

Zubeida Agha (1922–1997), had the honor to be the first modernist to hold a solo show as early as 1949 in Karachi. She received formal art education in artist Sanyal's studio and later by Mario Perlingieri, a prisoner of war who has received some training from Picasso. Later at St Martins School of Art and Ecole de Beaux in Paris she had exposure to some of best modernists of the time. She was an influential figure on the art scene for half a century, both as a strong advocate of Modern Art as the director of The Contemporary Art Gallery in Rawalpindi, which she founded and ran and an activist in the campaign for the National Gallery.

Her personal style of painting alluded to child-like simplicity of form and a preference for pure bright hues in the 1950's. Gradually her imagery became non-figurative with colours and forms evocative of emotions and moods.

Anna Molka Ahmed (1917–1994), was instrumental in establishing formal art education for women in the country when she founded the Fine Arts Department of the Punjab University. She had a great fascination for the landscape of *Punjab and was often seen painting on location accompanied her students in villages and venues in the city sites to capture the immediacy of the environment with quick impasto strokes in vibrant hues.

Besides landscapes and portraits, Anna-Molka painted memorial scenes of the 1965 war. Philosophical themes like death, *'kismet'*and hell. She painted large murals with great passionate energy; she is the only Pakistani woman painter to attempt murals on this scale.

Pragmatic Anna Molka emphasized teaching as a way to sustain art practice. With her students in institutions all over Pakistan, modernism was able to make inroads in smaller towns

Ahmed Pervaz (1926–1979), the most prolific of the group achieved prominence at home and abroad, and was an inspirational figure. His visual dialogue via colour at a purely intuitive plane was a mind map of emotions. It was an inner compulsion that drove him to repeat a dynamic movement energized by exploding small abstract forms. A closer look shows that his forms were not identical, nor static but continuously evolving in the changing amorphous space, constantly challenging the eye to find a focus in chaos. Maybe it is an affirmation of his tremendous talent that he could create endless variations to rescue his art from the commonplace. In 1978, a year before his death, he was awarded the Pride of Performance.

Shakir Ali (1916–1975), with his extensive exposure to modernism first at Slade School of Art in the UK and later at School of Industrial Design in Prague provided him with aesthetic strategies to frame his personal experiences and traditional references into a contemporary philosophy. The artist's work can be distinctly divided into two groups, one of formalistic innovation with a preoccupation with 'the significant form' and an emotive body of work that interprets the vibrant *Rajput miniature in a modernist's tribute.

He headed the National College of Art, the country's largest art school, where he encouraged students to discover new ways of seeing through the prism of a modern thinker. The cultural interface found in his work is also visible in his house-turned museum in Lahore, where the minimalist interior showcases a collection of vibrant crafts, meticulously collected for their enduring aesthetic appeal.

Ali Imam (1924–2002?), Settled in Karachi where, as the head, he introduced a modern curriculum at The Central Institute of Arts and Crafts. When he left it in 1970 to establish the Indus Gallery, the longest running commercial gallery of the country and a cultural institution in its own right, he successfully cultivated a group of discerning art buyers in the country's financial center.

With all these preoccupations, Ali Imam's painting career took a back seat. Although he was never a prolific painter his work was always in demand. In his art he referenced the figurative tradition in painting and used textural techniques to create visually enigmatic effects under a veil of white to create a signature canvas.

Laila Shahzada (1928–94), in the 1960s series won recognition when her Driftmood were exhibited in Karachi. In a highly intuitively response she transformed driftwood found on the beaches of Karachi to flame like images. Work followed her inner vision as she looked to various themes and genres, which included images from the Indus Valley Civilization and Taxila. Before her death in 1986 she was working on mountain landscapes with an underlying surrealist quality.

Sadequain (1930–1987), A rare visionary, *Sadequain was able to bridge the gulf between the disparate groups in society. At the age of 31 his work won recognition at the 1961 Paris Biennale. Sadequain had a prolific career and much of his work is displayed in public places. Like Diego Rivera, he celebrated the role of the proletariat. His early mural, based on the dignity of labour is housed in the Mangla Dam, near Islamabad. His painted ceiling in the *Lahore Museum and Frere Hall in Karachi present an epic view of man's destiny as envisaged in the poetry of poet Iqbal.

His canvas was encyclopedic and he looked at universal themes from classical literature to social activism. His most critically acclaimed works are from 'The Cactus Series' in which he immortalized the humble wild cactus of coastal *Sindh. During his life, Sadequain became a cult figure with a large following from all walks of life. In the 70's he got nationwide fame for his rendering of Quranic verses. Sadequain's influential position in Pakistan's art history cannot be denied.

The Changing Syntax of Calligraphy

Calligraphy was appropriated both as a cultural and religious icon and innovations point to two distinct streams of thought, artists like Hanif Ramay, Gulgee and Sadequain preferred to retain the integrity of the word.

For **Hanif Ramay** (1931–), one of the first modern artists to discover possibilities within calligraphy explored the curvilinear script in his art to organize space with stylized words. His asymmetrical compositions have a strong graphic quality.

Gulgee's (1926–) who began his career as a portraitist in the expressionist mode, he discovered action painting in a collaborative experiment with a visiting American artist. For the monumental calligraphic painting that followed he made gesture painting his point of departure. A deeper exploration of this new genre reconnects him to the grand calligraphers of the Islamic tradition. He has prolifically experimented with calligraphy and succeeded in stretching its creative limits.

It was **Sadequain's** calligraphic works that broke class barriers as people thronged the gallery. As an heir to the strong calligraphic tradition of Amroha, Sadequain's calligraphic paintings looked to the meaning of the text and created calligrams informed by a constructivist vocabulary.

Shemza (1928–1985) looked beyond the meaning and transform texts into spatial and rhythmic patterns well beyond their function of communication. Modernists like Rashid Arshad, Zahoorul Akhlaq and Jamil Naqsh have exploited the design potential of the calligraphic script.

Artists from both wings of the country were instrumental in shaping the art movement of Pakistan. From *East Pakistan (present day Bangladesh) Zainul Abedin, Mubinal Azim, S.M. Sultan, Aminul Islam, Kibria, Murtaza Basir among others were influential both as artists and teachers.

A CONFIDENT VISUAL DIALOGUE

1970s

Held in Karachi in 1973, National Show saw the emergence of new trajectories in Pakistani art. The generation that came of age was the one that had attended Pakistan's art academies and had begun to shape a distinct national art movement.

Bashir Mirza (1941–?), remembered crossing over from Amritsar on his father's shoulders. The images of violence that haunted his childhood often found their way in his angst filled drawings. The 'Lonely Girl' series that caused a stir on the art scene announced the modern woman of Pakistan with the hope to banish forever the timid damsels from the canvas. At different periods of his career his style has varied. In the 'Lonely Girl', the gentle strokes blend primary colours into a smooth surfaces, while in his later Acrylic Series of the 90's an almost textural violence clash to craft images. He continued to dominate the scene with his brash innovations.

Zahoorul Akhlaq (1941–1999), returned from the UK to interface with the world as a global citizen. His oeuvre did not appropriate but question as he expressed a preference for the conceptual. The nuclear mushroom within the format of the '*farman*' or the royal decree suggests a subtext beyond the cross pollination of visual symbols.

In his extensive travels round the world and teaching sabbaticals, Zahoor continued to intellectually process different aesthetics through his artistic skills as a painter, printmaker and sculptor.

Jamil Naqsh's (1938–), visual thesis of 'Woman and Pigeon', which propelled him to the forefront of art history started in the 1970s. This consummate draughtsman may have limited his theme but he expanded its formalist investigation through different techniques, like pointillism that later gave way to skillful washes as he worked to master the forms in countless variations. When he embraced calligraphy it was with the meticulous attention of a miniaturist.

Op-Art served as a visual device in **Colin David's** (1957–), paintings. The black and white background design with its linear optical illusion forms an ever-changing relationship with the form, which was either a nude or figure. It is always the dynamic 'patterned' space rather than the form that holds the interest of the viewer. The nude became the painter's forte and in later series it was set against verdant landscapes.

Lubna Latif Agha (1945–), a graduate of the Karachi School of Art was recognized as an outstanding talent and honored with a solo show at Indus Gallery. Behind the veil of glacial white, molten crimson waited to flow from the fissures, Lubna's intensely emotive works were read as the statements of 'a body denied' or 'a wounded spirit' and broke the silence of the disenfranchised. After several successful shows she left for the USA where she settled with her family. In the 90's Lubna returned sporadically with canvases informed by the alienation and social concerns.

The **Zuberi** sisters have played a significant role both as co-founders of Karachi's very first 'Karachi School of Art'. Rabia is a well-known sculptor and Hajra who shifted to Islamabad has made a place for herself as a watercolorist from the school of Oriental Wash Painting.

The Landscape Painting of Punjab began to make its presence felt in the late 60s and early 70s. It can be read as a vital link with the rural sensibility of a people with a strong land culture. Sometimes landscape painting shows a resilience that transcends mere genre into the realm of the personal. Among its distinguished exponents are Khalid Iqbal, Saeed Akthar, Ghulam Rasul, Zulqarnain Haider, Ijazul Hassan, Shahid Jalal, Ajaz Anwar, Ghulam Mustafa, Zubeida Javed, Shahid Jalal, Nazir Ahmed and Pirzada Najm-ul-Hasan. A large number of them are graduates from the Fine Arts Department of the Punjab University, who had been inspired by their mentor Anna Molka Ahmed.

Khalid Iqbal paints the villages and fields of Punjab with a reverence bordering on the spiritual. On the restful montage of verdant nature, Ijazul Hassan mounted violent images of war and social conflict to depict a world of inequality and violence.

Mussarat Mirza's art is born out of her empathy for hometown Sukkur, the timeless life on the *Indus River that flows by it and its arid environs.

Through the 90's to the new century **Kaleem Khan** and his students in Quetta various artists like **Imtiaz Hussain** in Peshawar continue to be inspired by the expanse of the rugged terrain.

Raja Changez Sultan's portrayal of the mountain is sensuous, the layers of colour washes soften the stone mammoth into an enigmatic creature clothed with sheathes of light and mist.

The formalistic values of portrait paintings never gained their pre-independence significance. The few painters who contributed to it are Nagi, and later Saeed Akthar, Guljee, Eqbal Mehdi and Athar Jamal.

JEWELLERY OF PAKISTAN

Mahrukh Yousaf

Jewellery is the pride and passion of women in all cultures. It has an artistic and cultural significance as much for historians, archaeologists, and anthropologists, as for everyone else. It keeps our traditions alive handed down through the ages, and provides an ideological entity to our people.

Jewellery, like everything else, has followed an evolutionary path from prehistoric times to the present age, and yet had retained its basic purpose of adornment for the human body. For rural folk it is not just a piece of adornment for a special occasion but a complete ensemble. They carry jewellery as part of themselves without a hint of ostentation. For the urban woman it is an accessory to her dress and a complement to good grooming. Yet for some jewellery has amuletic properties.

Universally, jewellery is considered a safe investment. Precious metals such as gold, pladium and silver were an ideal form of savings which were not affected by migration or change of currencies. They were easily portable, exchangeable, concealable and useable at all times. For the common people, who had little opportunity of productive investment of savings or diversion from the endless drudgery of life, acquisition of jewellery became a yard stick of success and it's giving away the highest token of affection. This trend, coupled with the patronage of Mughal rulers (see, Mughal Empire), gave rise to communities of highly skilled craftsmen (*sunnars*) in every town and special bazaars known as '*Sarafa bazaar*' catering to the requirements of its populace.

In the rural societies of Pakistan the amounted quality of jewellery used marks the prestige and social status of that person. The higher the status the more artistic and elaborate the jewellery. In urban societies jewellery is regarded as a status symbol of wealth and a means of displaying power.

The jewellery trend in Pakistan has been greatly influenced by its history and multidimensional heritage. The *Indus Valley gave the world three most ancient civilizations namely *Gandhara, *Moenjadaro and *Harappa and to Pakistan 5,000 years of rich history and culture. These cultures were very sophisticated in all walks of life including crafts. The archaeological finds of these civilizations all suggest that the use of jewellery was widespread and its craftsmanship was artistic and sophisticated. The skilfully rendered terracotta figurines, the seals, statues and beads all give ample evidence of it. The famous bronze dancing girl had her arms encircled with bangles and a necklace adorned her neck. The statues of other priestly figures and noblemen show all the various articles of jewellery, from armlets to girdles and head ornaments to necklaces. This formed the basis of our traditional and contemporary jewellery. In its onward journey the designs of jewellery were influenced by hellinistic trends followed by the strong Mughal era styles and inventions.

Fine arts and jewellery has had a profound influence of the Mughul period in the subcontinent. Mughals were connoisseurs of arts and crafts. First Emperor Akbar and then Empress Noorjehan patronized jewellers and a number of new jewelled ornaments were designed for nobility. Noorjehan is credited with having made several outstanding inventions, such as the '*Guluband*', '*Karan Phool*', '*Jhoomer*', etc.

One aspect of Pakistani culture which increased the popularity of the use of jewellery is making a conscious effort toward bedecking our brides. Every part of a woman's body has a lavish piece of appropriate jewellery to decorate it. Accompanied with an elaborate ensemble, *hennaed* hands and fresh flowers in her hair she appears beautiful to the delight of one and all. Another important aspect of popular fashion is the requirement of jewellery to enhance the ensemble, matching pieces with colour co-ordination for ears, neck, hands and feet.

MATERIALS USED IN JEWELLERY MAKING

In prehistoric times, the basic and easily available materials for the making of jewellery were bones, shells, stones, seeds and feathers. The discovery of metals later on added a whole new dimension to this craft. Copper, bronze, silver and then gold were used along with, firstly the crude stones, pieces of glass and beads. The commonest of all materials were beads of a variety of shapes, sizes and colour. Later semi-precious stones such as agate, jadeite, carnelian, amethyst, jasper, rock crystal, garnet and lapis lazuli were used to add colour. The introduction of precious stones such as rubies, emeralds, sapphires and diamonds, both cut and uncut, added shine and lustre to the ornaments. Gold and silver being the most malleable and ductile materials respectively lent themselves to this craft very well. An interesting point to note is that the cords used in jewellery are also very important. Beautifully twisted gold, silver or coloured threads, tied with tassels, beads and pom poms form an integral part of it.

Pakistan is rich in ancient mineral deposits which have crystallised into precious stones such as rubies and emeralds, as well as semi precious ones such as tourmaline, jade, topaz, kunzite, garnet, aquamarine, fluorite and lapis lazuli. The *Northern Areas, *Kalat, *Swat, *Chitral, Hunza, *Dir, *Gilgit, parts of Balochistan and NWFP are rich in these minerals. To qualify as gemstone, a mineral must possess durability, ability to withstand abrasion, scratches, corrosion, chemical effects and the bleaching effect of light,

With the development of machines, the manufacture and widespread use of modern materials such as plastic, imitation pearls, stones and the acceptance of alloys, a large variety of jewellery is available to all levels of society.

TOOLS UTILIZED

Crucible tongs, mallet, chasing tools, saw frames, shears, anvils, doming punches, ring sticks, pliers, draw plate, doming blocks, scribes and crucibles.

DESIGNS

Earlier motifs were reproductions of the shapes of flora and fauna, the sun, moon and stars, the restless waves on the sea shore, the silhouette of the majestic mountains, the variety of living beings such as fish, peacock, serpent and the butterfly. The Mughal influence on design brought geometry based on the symmetry found in nature and a lot of stylization of motifs. As Islam forbids the reproduction of the human form, Muslims turned towards calligraphy and arabesque. Present day design is a confluence of the indigenous, the oriental and western influences on this art form.

TECHNIQUES OF CRAFTING JEWELLERY

'*Awkaz*' or Repousse: In this method the design is punched in relief on the metal sheet followed by chasing and engraving. The metal is worked on a bed of warm pitch with the help of a chisel and hammer. The designs are mostly memorized by the artisan. The front side is then given a finish.

'*Chitai*' or Chasing and Engraving: In chasing, the tool makes an indentation in the metal by pressure. But the displaced metal still forms part of the pattern. In engraving, the tool actually gouges out a portion of the metal leaving a clear thin line.

'*Sadakari*': It is the open work technique where the designs are first drawn on paper which is glued on the metal. The surface is worked entirely by hand with the help of a saw, forming delicate cutwork patterns.

***'Cuttuck'* or Filigree**: It is perhaps the earliest form of ornamentation of jewellery; the surface is adorned by fine wire which is twisted, plaited, spiralled and curled. The wire is then cut into the delicate tracery of design.

***'Minakari'* or Enamelling**: The method of coating paint on metals with mineral oxides, in a manner that the colour adheres to the surface is called *minakari* or enamelling.

'Kundan': It is the earliest form of encrustation or inlay in which thin metal strips are bent round to form a cell, then soldered to the ornaments surface and filled with enamel paste which is made to adhere by fire. This method helps to increase the light and shade through the transparent colours.

Most of the surfaces of jewellery items are a combination of two or three techniques. But the first stage in production is the drawing of the ornaments' sketch by the designer. The design is then etched on a tin plate which serves as a cut out.

Sunars or goldsmiths are highly skilled and respected most from among the community of artisans. Every technique has a master craftsman and one piece of jewellery might travel through four or five *sunars* for a particular embellishment before its completion.

While jewellery fashions are changing, the tools and techniques used have changed little over the years. They remain age old and workmanship is carried out entirely by hand.

SPECIAL CHARACTERISTICS OF FOLK, TRADITIONAL AND CONTEMPORARY JEWELLERY

Folk Jewellery is predominantly fashioned out of gild, mixed metal and silver. Besides being relatively inexpensive it is steeped in popular belief that it has properties of protection against the evil eye. Colour is added to the ornament with the use of beads, glass, mirrors, jingles along with cords and tassels. Each individual piece of ornament is crafted lovingly and is a marvel of manual skill. The motifs reflect appreciation of nature and include flowers, leaves, animal shapes, crescent, stars and the tree of life. Jewellery worn by the rural woman is usually large and sturdy, suiting the lifestyle of the people of the soil.

Traditional Jewellery reflects the influences brought to this part of the world especially during the Muslim rule from Mesopotamia (modern day Iraq), Afghanistan, Turkey, Iran and Central Asia. Islam provided new inspiration, injecting freshness and vitality to the designs and providing a cultural bridge between the existing trends and new ideas from outside. Traditional jewellery especially from urban centres of excellence was basically made of gold with incorporation of translucent precious or semi-precious stones along with pearls. The designs were motifs of rosettes and leaf scrolls in a multitude of variations and permutations to give an impression of flowing patterns of arabesque. The wearing of nine coloured stones—*Nauratan* was traditional and considered a protection from evil influences.

The contemporary trend Is centred round bold conception and simplicity in design. It is a moving away from the highly stylised and intricate designs of traditional jewellery. The emphasis now is on the purity of line, form, shape and colour. The use of single, large sized precious or semi precious stones is also in vogue. Traditional colour schemes have given place to a non-traditional and modern colour palette. Shapes have been simplified to basic squares, rounds and rectangles. Harder metals such as pladium, white gold and platinum have become the desired materials for the new ornaments. Gold chains supporting pendants and *taweez* have an alternate in strings of cut or uncut beads of precious and semi precious stones. Dull polishes and matt effects are in demand. The idea is to create a uniquely different effect often in abstraction.

Imitation Jewellery Is cheaper using copper, brass, bone, glass stones and beads. It has proved to be of great value for the majority who cannot afford to acquire real gold and gems jewellery.

DESCRIPTIONS OF THE POPULAR ITEMS OF TRADITIONAL JEWELLERY

Angothi

Finger rings of countless designs are called *angothis.*

Bali

These are small round metallic earrings. The tradition is to have baby girls' ears pierced around the age of 3-6 months using *balis* of pure gold.

Baley

These are large round metallic rings often with some beads or pearls in the rings or as a jingling fringe at the lower edge.

Bazuband

It is a jewelled band tied above the elbow. Sometimes these are in the form of amulet cases in varying shapes of square, round, rectangle or circular discs hooked one after another in rows and tied round the arm with cord.

Bindiya

Is a forehead ornament made of a small pendant fixed to a *dori* (chain) to fix on the hair.

Bundey

A wide term used for a huge variety of studs for the ears.

Challa

These are broad strip toe rings for the feet. The metallic band may be plain or have a motif on the top.

Champakali

It is a necklace and is so called because the fringe is made up of a row of *champa* (Indian magnolia) buds. These buds may be small or big, jewelled or plain.

Chandbali

Moon shaped earrings embellished with stones and fringed with pearls on petals or miniature *peepal* (a type of tree common to India and Pakistan) leaves.

Chandanhaar

It is made up of long strings–two, three, or five of cut floral motifs linked together to form a chain. The chains are fixed to triangle ornaments to fall on either side of the neck.

Chorian

These are bangles of a multitude of designs and variations. These are usually made of rings of solid bars in the form of thin strips with ends soldered to form a circle. The designs are chased on the surface.

Qumerband or Qumerpatti

It is a girdle round the waist, and was once commonly used specially by the nobility (both men and women) on state functions. The gold or silver bands were bejewelled and adorned with trinkets. This item never became popular with Muslim women.

Dastband

A flexible bracelet made of jewelled discs fixed on strands of pearls.

Dastphool

It is meant for the back of the hand. A flower shaped ornament is linked with chains to the bangle on the wrist on one side and with five rings for the fingers on the other side.

Guluband

An elaborate bejewelled necklace whose ornaments are linked with strands of pearls.

Gulshan Patti

A lighter and modern version of *pazeb*. These are both anklets.

Haar

Haars are made of chains mostly hanging lower down on the breast and maybe made of metallic chains, pearls, beads and precious stones.

Hansli

A collar type necklace graduating from a thick centre to tapered ends. Sometimes it is of hollow metal and often filled with lac.

Janshan

Grows out of an amulet to be tied round the upper arm.

Jhanjhan

It is made of a hollow tube with pebbles inside. When worn on the ankles they make a sweet jingling sound while walking.

Jhoomer

Designed by Empress Noorjehan it is a head ornament worn slightly to the left of the head. The shape is pyramidal, studded with stones or glass pieces and a fringe of beads or pearls at the base. It is supported by a chain or string which is hooked to the hair at the back.

Jhularian
Are earrings of multitiered strands hanging from tops.

Jhumkey
These earrings comprise of a flower from which hangs a dome shaped pendulum fringed with bells, beads or pearls.

Kangan
Stylised bangles. When thin metallic strips with deep grooves cut into the outer edge so as to form pointed needles are placed between the side *chooris* the piece becomes a *kangan.*

Kara
A bangle. It may be a ring of solid bar, a hollow tube around a core of lac or a stiff bangle with open ends shaped like heads of birds, animals or flowers.

Karan Phool
A large floral disc with bell shaped pendulum fringed with either pearls or stone drops. The whole ornament is bejewelled.

Lacchey
Are anklets made of thin coiled rings forming a band to go round the ankle.

Lowng
Are nose pins made of very tiny studs usually round or flower shaped often with a gem or diamond in its centre.

Lachcha
A jewelled choker about 1 ½ inch broad with a fringe of pearls and stone drops.

Machli
A jewelled semi circle with a fish shaped pendant suspended from its outer edge.

Magar
These are chandelier like elaborate long earrings having three or more ornaments linked together.

Nuth
A nose ornament worn at the weddings by brides. It is a thin, large gold loop having a central pearl with a ruby bead on either side. The loop is hooked to the ear by a chain. A tiny simple gold ring worn on one of the nostrils is a nose *bali.*

Paunchi
A very highly rated bracelet. It comprises of three rows of small drops with hooks strung on cords.

Pazeb
An anklet comprising a strap overlaid with creepers or a floral pattern in the open fringe of drops on leaves with or without jingles.

Sarpech
Aigrette or turban ornament, popular with monarchs of the Mughal era.

Satlara
A long necklace with seven identical strands of pearls, hanging one a little lower than the other, with individual pendants.

Tauq-
A looser variety of *hansli*.

Teeka
A head ornament usually worn by brides. A pendant is held in the middle of the forehead and kept in place by a chain hooked in the hair. The pendant is generally circular, crescent shaped disc set with stones and intricately filigreed and fringed.

Thoday
Stiff anklets made of jewelled metallic round band with open stylized ends.

Zanjeer
Two or three waist length chains for the neck of interlinked filigreed floral discs.

DESCRIPTIONS OF POPULAR ITEMS OF FOLK JEWELLERY

Aarsi
A large mirror studded round ring used at weddings. In traditional marriages, the bride and groom see each other in the mirror for the first time after the wedding.

Agothiun
A flat silver toe ring with a bunch of silver bells or a motif on top.

Angushtri
A four, five or more petalled flower-shaped finger ring.

Bahien
Stiff, carved bangles trimmed with bells.

Bahugan/Bahuto
About four inch broad, stiff bangles narrow at the wrist and broad at the upper end. They are usually carved and engraved in a trellis design.

Bakkal
Stone studded, embossed hair clips, trimmed with small trinkets.

Bali
Small earrings.

Bangray
Stiff bangles with filigree work and embossed stone studded knobs at the mouth.

Batwa
An embossed, purse like, hollow pendant, trimmed with bells on long chains.

Beenti
Finger rings in various shapes.

Bolo
A dome shaped finger ring of silver and coloured beads.

Buttonay
A long chain of alternate embossed pieces and silver hooks linked together to form a panel, with buttons attached to the back.

Chiskoor
A cap ornament of conical, silver pieces with filigree work, trimmed with bells on chains, strung in a row.

Cholay
A carved, stone studded pendant on two or more chains, held together with brackets at either end.

Choora
A spiral, spring like bangle made in a replica of a coiled snake.

Choori
Bangles or bracelets in a variety of designs.

Chooro
A stiff bangle with engraved, geometric patterns and a screw at the mouth.

Choti Phool
A hair ornament of embossed, silver pieces trimmed with bells or sequins on chains.

Chowkli
A necklace of broad, loose stone and glass studded pieces attached together and trimmed with heavy chains and bells.

Dabbi
A small box with a lid, in a variety of shapes, used to keep either snuff or perfume.

Dawni
A forehead ornament, similar to *singaar patti*.

Dhoree
A heavy pendant hanging on heavy silver chains held together with brackets and trimmed with coins or coin shaped trinkets.

Didey
Stiff, long, engraved earrings with betel leaf shaped ornaments.

Dolan
A necklace of oblong, hollow, barrel shaped amulets strung on a cord.

Gani
(Animal jewellery) Individual ornaments of mixed metals, sewn on a leather band or cord, trimmed with jingles, used to adorn the neck of a bull.

Ghabriyun
Loose, flexible anklets.

Ghamo Hameel
Long, narrow, carved pieces, linked together to form a broad necklace with *kundan* motifs attached on it and trimmed with bells on chains.

Goag
Two embossed silver balls attached with a hook in the centre, strung on a cotton cord along with beads and pom poms.

Gog
A cap of mirror work, with a dome shaped, silver embossed ornament in the centre of the top, with a pom pom attached to it.

Gokhroo
A bracelet of two or three strands of diamond-cut silver beads, strung on a cord.

Goshwaray
Elongated, dome shaped earrings with trimmings of bells on chains or beads.

Guluband
Heavy, engraved silver or *kundan* pieces held together to form a choker. It is trimmed with bells, coins or sequins.

Gumzi
Finger ring of floral motifs with a raised bead-like centre.

Gutta
Finger rings of various shapes and designs.

Haar
A common name for necklaces.

Hameel
Heavy floral chains with motifs of fish attached to the chain and trimmed with trinkets.

Happo Karay
Flat, stiff anklets adorned with bells and going round the ankle in a shoe like curve.

Huss
A stiff, tapering neck band with trimmings.

Istank
A flat, inch-wide, tapering, engraved, brass bangle with an open mouth.

Jappay
It is also called '*Nara-pani*'. A round, tapering stick, with a loop or hole at the broad end, used for inserting string in pyjama belts.

Jeegband
A costume ornament of stone-studded, floral shaped buttons on chains.

Jhumkay
Carved, embossed, dome shaped earrings, hanging from a ring or a floral disc. (*Jhumkay* for horses are big with pom poms attached to them and hang from a cotton cord).

Jijra
Costume ornament of hollow, embossed amulets, trimmed with bells hanging from long chains.

Jubbay
Dome-shaped buttons for the costume.

Kachkol
A boat-shaped, cup-like pendant hanging from one or more chains.

Kali
Engraved, *kundan* amulet, trimmed with bells and interlinked with silver hooks.

Kameez Gutty
A costume ornament consisting of five strands of silver bells of varying lengths.

Kamsai
Hair ornament made of three long, hollow, cylindrical pieces trimmed with bells and attached to a ring.

Kandur
Earrings with a round disc on the *bali* and a lower round motif trimmed with bells.

Kangan
Rounded, silver bangles, engraved or stone studded and closed with screws.

Kanta
Stiff, long earrings with some motif at the lower end.

Kara
Stiff, broad, lacy, trellis design bangles with trimmings. The mouth is open with motif of an animal at the ends.

Kari
A three inch broad, stiff, hollow, rounded on the outside bangle, engraved in a honey-comb design.

Kariyo
Stiff, rounded, silver anklets with open, flattened edges.

Kau
Stiff, flat, embossed bangles.

Khoppo Karay
Flat, silver anklets adorned with a raised motif in front and going round the ankle in a shoe like curve.

Koka
Nose pin, usually in a small floral shape.

Kubbay
A costume ornament of dome-shaped buttons used by the bride.

Lachchey:
Anklets for children consisting of rows of chains joined at intervals with embossed silver pieces.

Lakhtai
Costume ornament of *kundan* pieces trimmed with bells and linked together with chains.

Lakat
Pendant in assorted shapes.

Lanegan
Hollow, stone-studded amulets, trimmed with bells and strung on strands of chains.

Las Gutty
Costume ornament of rows of silver beads attached on to a cotton band.

Lawangeen
A long chain made of two strings of cardamoms with *alaichi* intermittent silver amulets and coral beads. There is usually a pendant in the centre. It is used as perfume by the wearer.

Makkay Karay
Round, hollow bangles with open mouths.

Malangi Mankay
String of multi coloured, glass beads.

Mardani Mankay
String of stone beads, collected from archaeological sites and worn by mystics.

Mathe Ji Patti
Forehead ornament of silver pieces, trimmed with trinkets.

Motti
Beads of any kind and pearls.

Mundri
Finger rings, usually of floral design, in *kundan*, *meenakari* work or stone studded.

Mushti

Dhol (cylinder) shaped and round, carved silver beads, strung on wire along with silver pieces. Sometimes it has a large, round, scalloped edged pendant.

Nama

A square, flat, embossed pendant, trimmed with bells or diamond shaped trinkets.

Nasbi/Nasbiun:

Nose pin of a small round floral disc on a thin silver ring.

Ogai

A round, tapering, stiff neckband with an open mouth at the back. The two ends of the mouth are engraved or embossed.

Pachay Panhar

Silver brackets and hooks are interlinked to form a broad necklace, trimmed with *betel leaf shaped trinkets.

Pachwaiz

A big, carved, triangular piece with filigree work and trimmed at the lower edge with trinkets.

Panja

A bangle with five finger rings attached to it with chains.

Panjangla

Four or five almond shaped, finger rings, joined together with chains.

Paranda

Embossed, dome shaped ornaments, trimmed with bells and attached to black cotton cords, used as hair extensions, plaited with the hair.

Pathlo

A large betel leaf shaped pendant, trimmed with trinkets and hanging on a chain.

Pathrigari Zanzeeri

A costume ornament of chains with trimmings of flat silver trinkets.

Pazeb/Paayel

Anklets of narrow, carved, individual pieces, linked together to form a flexible chain.

Phlaskor

A costume ornament of five, big, ceramic stones with pure silver mountings and stitched on to a cotton band.

Phumman
A pair of coloured fluffs with silver, dome shaped toppings.

Pontay
Animal jewellery consisting of seven round, big, hollow balls, trimmed with bells and strung on cord to tie around a horse's ankles.

96. Ranjo Haar: An embossed, hollow, purse shaped pendant trimmed with jingles on chains. It is used for keeping charcoal powder, serving as eye-liner for women.

Saggi/Spagiun
Same as *Paranda*.

Sapbaeen
Plain, flat, spiral, silver bangle like a coiled snake.

Sargul
A jewellery of a round or square or dome shaped ornament, trimmed with bells and attached to a chain with a hook at the other end.

Sarpatti
One ornament hangs on the forehead linked to a diamond shaped piece with a hook. On either side are two chains with bells which are fastened behind the ears.

Seenaband
A costume ornament of long, metallic chains stitched on to a cotton band.

Seena Moti
A costume ornament of metallic buttons on long chains trimmed with bells and jingles.

Shaglay
Anklets for children made of figure eight silver hooks, linked together and trimmed with bells.

Shankosi
Blue, porcelain buttons, embedded in metal frames and trimmed with bells on chains.

Silsila
Cap ornament of silver motifs, stone or bead studded, with filigree work and trimmed with bells, strung in a row.

Singaar Patti
A crescent shaped centre piece linked to a chain with a hook hangs on the forehead. On either side are two broad chains trimmed with bells which go at the back of the ears.

Surmadani
A container for *kohl* which comes in a variety of shapes. It is about three inches high with a hollow middle portion to keep the *kohl.* The ornamental cap has an applicator attached to it.

Tali Patar
A heart shaped pendant trimmed with small hollow, leaf shaped trinkets.

Taveej/Tavees/Taveezona
A square, embossed, *kundan*, stone studded or *meenakari* pendant, trimmed with bells and hung on a chain or cord.

Tayat
A hollow amulet, strung on a cord for holding tavees (religious inscriptions).

Teek/Tika
A forehead jewellery of a round or drop shaped, embossed or *kundan* piece, trimmed with beads or pearls, attached to a string with a hook.

Totay
A costume ornament of a somewhat triangular shaped piece bearing a replica of two parrots with their backs to each other. It is ornamented with twist silver wire work and trimmed with bells on chains.

Trora
Figure of eight silver rings, interlinked to resemble a basket weave and forming a broad, flexible anklet.

Varlo
A neckband of a curved silver rod, with two cone shaped, wire wrapped ends which lock into a floral motif in front of the neck.

Verka
Stiff, thin anklets for children, trimmed with bells at intervals.

Walay
Earrings with floral motifs and trimmings of bunches of bells.

Walwin
Earrings made of several twist wire, silver rings of various sizes, with a small plain disc or hollow ball at the mouth.

Zabadan
A small, hollow, ball like pendant used for keeping perfume.

All through the relatively short history of Pakistan, jewellery has been in constant demand of its women, hence the rise of very highly skilled gold and silver smiths and the evolution in design and technique. Pakistan is engaged in exporting its mineral wealth in the form of precious and semi- precious stones. Pakistani jewellery is also sold by private enterprise internationally.

The immense range and impeccable quality of Pakistani jewellery is acknowledged in international markets amongst the most discerning connoisseurs. Each ornament is a mute token to the centuries of tradition, technique, imagination and creativity to satisfy man's search for beauty.

TEXTILES OF PAKISTAN

Mahrukh Yousaf

Exquisite textiles emerge from the simple poetry of hands, weaving warp and weft, and shuttling the bobbin in and out of the yarn which is fixed on the loom. It is a labour of love for the weaver who may weave a whole story into the fabric, or fantasize his dreams into the design, giving it the colour of his desires and wishes.

INTRODUCTION AND HISTORICAL PERSPECTIVE

Pakistan has the distinction of being accepted as the first home of cotton, where the earliest piece of woven cloth was found amidst the ruins of its ancient riverine civilization. The craft of weaving cloth and embellishing it with dyeing, printing, and embroidery is the long standing heritage of this country. However, the fragile and perishable nature of fabrics has prevented one from effectively tracing the origins of ancient designs and development of embroideries on textiles. In spite of the test of time, this art has been perpetuated in all parts of Pakistan and continues to gain widespread patronage from the rural population. In fact the rural woman has been the principal figure in keeping this tradition alive and deserves sole credit for preserving the custom of enhancing the beauty of textiles with colours, prints, weaves and embroideries.

The history of evolution of the textile industry is steeped in antiquity. The indigenous product reflected the evidence of cotton cultivation and sheep farming in the area now comprising Pakistan. Both cotton cloth and woollen fabrics were produced. The art of dyeing the fibres with natural, vegetable dyes was also prevalent as was indicated by unearthing of a well equipped dyer's workshop at *Moenjodaro (seat of one of the ancient riverine civilizations). Other excavations of that period revealed various spindle whorls, bobbins and figurines which were draped with long shawls, girdles and turban-like headgear. The first colour on fabrics was red—considered a life depicting colour and the motifs on it were in black. The earliest motifs were symbolic such as the *Swastika* symbolising the movement of the four seasons, and the *Trefoil* representing the human form and symbolic of the power of the sun, water, and earth. *Trefoil* is revealed on the tunic of the King Priest, unearthed in *Taxila. The other motifs included re-productions in simple miniature forms of plant and animal life. Then there were diamonds and triangles and squares surrounded by multilinear lines often found to this day in the traditional '*Rilli*' (patchwork) *of Sindh.

Further evolution in textiles was brought by the *Aryans from Central Asia, who introduced more elaborate and complex looms for weaving cotton, wool and silk cloth. It is also assumed in general that the Central Asian invaders introduced stitched clothing to replace draping of cloth around the human body. '*Namda*' (rug as well as a saddle), a felted woollen mat was in great demand during that period and surprisingly has survived to this day in various styles and forms.

The *Gandhara period's lasting influence on the cotton cloth is its fine quality which endeared it far and wide. It had 60 ends and 20 picks per inch and was made of 34 count threads. This same cotton muslin was used to wrap mummies in Egypt. During this time the use of strong symbolic motifs such as the 'Lotus' depicting the heart of the universe and immortality, the '*Peepal*' leaf of the banyan tree under which Buddha meditated and the 'Rosette' was common. The 'Paisley', locally known as the '*Kairi*' became an all time favourite motif. It was usually further enhanced by floral tracery both within and the outer edges of the focal shape. It is extremely popular in *Kashmir and dominates various patterns used for embellishing shawls and household linens. Other decorative elements of this period include the peacock and its feathers commonly known as '*Mayur*' and '*Mayur pankh*'. It is believed to be endowed with protective powers as the peacock enjoys the superior status of a sun-bird. All sun symbols used in designs on textiles denoted protection from evil sources of energy.

About this time cotton and woollen cloth, woven in the areas now comprising Pakistan, was shipped to Syria, Egypt and other Mediterranean countries and traded in exchange of other commodities. These fabrics were noted for their fine quality reflecting the cultural and artistic evolution reached in textiles. More and more variations of natural dyes were being used made from the indigenous indigo, lac, saffron and madder. A noted Arab traveller, Suleman Tajir, observed that the cotton fabric known as '*mulmul*'or muslin was so fine that it could easily pass through a finger ring.

During this period some Chinese decorative styles travelled to this area via the Silk route in the mountain ranges of the North. This is evident from the use of cloud bands, cliff tops, dragons, birds and floral motifs on the embroideries, especially those of Kashmir. For Chinese styles of embroidery, silk cloth was the choice of material.

The art of 'Calligraphy'(beautiful stylised handwriting, done with a special pen or brush) as a decorative element was Arab influence introduced via the visiting missionaries and traders and firmly established as a unique art form inspiring textile design. The Islamic colours of indigo, blue and turquoise representing the night skies and the day sky became a very popular colour combination and were extensively used in tiles for architectural purposes.

The textile tradition continued and flourished, receiving a tremendous boost under the Moghuls (see, Mughal Empire) who were connoisseurs of art and beauty. The state patronage encouraged the already skilled weavers to excel. Interesting silk, satin, velvet and *banarsi* (silk interwoven with gold and silver threads) fabrics were manufactured introducing jacquard weaves. Cultural centres of textile design and manufacture were established at Hala, Nasarpur, Gumbat, Thatta, Rohri and Sehwan. The Islamic influence had replaced the figurative motifs with arabesque and infinite variations of repetitive geometric patterns that gave a mosaic like effect. With the use of gold and silver thread fabrics became rich and glamorous such as brocades and tissues (*tulle*) to cater to the adornment of the ruling elite of the kingdom. Delhi, Agra and Lahore became the capital cities of production of these lavish fabrics. Subsequently the textile industry reached its zenith and became a highly industrialized empire. The variety of cloth made was not only enough for the huge domestic consumption but there was surplus, enough for trade and export. Spinning wheels and looms were found in most homes. Conservative estimate records that fifty types of cotton, woollen and silk fabrics existed and it was noted by a Portuguese officer, Antonio Boccaro, that in the 16th century there were 30,000 looms in Thatta alone. Textile weaving as a craft and the weavers were held in high esteem.

Ready availability of raw material, the nature of the landscape, the climate, the natural vocation of the people, and the demand of the finished product all contributed in making this industry successful as well as sophisticated. The imagination of the people gave very artistic names to some of the most popular fabrics such as '*Aab-e-rawan*' (running water), '*Shabnam*' (evening dew) and '*Baft hawa*' (woven air).

This period of zenith of the textile industry was followed by four centuries of foreign invasion and rule over the sub-continent. The British era proved unduly harsh to the textile industry. Absence of patronage, coupled with the beginnings of industrialization, almost saw the end of the highly valued handloom production of cloth and near demise of skilled weavers and artisans. The western invaders were looking for a big market for their own products and their economic strategy was to replace the handloom with power looms which would quadruple the production of textiles to meet the world requirement at very competitive prices. The entire stocks of raw cotton from *Punjab and *Sindh were shipped to Great Britain for the utilisation at the textile mills of Lancashire. This spelled ruin for the home textile industry which suffered a great set back.

The process of revival of small and cottage textile industry began with the creation of Pakistan. Being the fifth largest producer of cotton the economy was dependant on it as a cash crop for export purposes. The Korean War provided a boom to the economy, and Pakistan for the first time launched a massive drive to set up a textile industry. It developed a large enough power-loom industry to meet the domestic requirement as well as produce a substantial surplus for export. Within a short span of time it was exporting yarn and coarse cloth instead of just raw cotton. With the passage of time the structure of export gradually underwent a change and Pakistan started exporting fine cloth and cotton made ups like clothing, sheeting, towels etc. Share of cotton and cotton exports in the GDP of Pakistan also increased considerably.

SPINNING AND WEAVING

Ancient and traditional methods of spinning and weaving persist with little change. Eight to ten people get together in workshops to weave cloth on either 'pit looms' (looms are partly inside huge pits dug in the ground with treadles suspended on string lams) or 'floor looms' fitted on frames on the floor. The weavers use the hand propelled shuttle as the maximum width of cloth is 36 inches. The complete yardage is rolled on a front beam.

The warp is prepared in the age old manner where stakes are driven into the ground in a row and the artisans, carrying a trellis filled with cones of warp threads walk back and forth to measure out their warp. Usually done in the open, fields and backyards are their workshops. Dressing the looms is also a simple technique. Original warp threads are tied to the ends of the new ones and pulled through the heddles and the reed. When a new pattern is required, the reeds and harnesses are tied together and threaded in one stroke over a few days.

The same steps are adapted to different types of looms. For cloth of bigger width, hand shuttles are replaced by semi-automatic fly shuttles and when producing cloth for commercial purposes semi-automatic and automatic machines are used for warping and dressing. The basic old systems are juxtaposed with most modern equipment to achieve a variety of complex results.

Spinning was always done on a floor spinning wheel called '*Charkha*'. The *charkha* is made of a wooden drum wheel that has two discs separated by a cylinder and held together by lacing cords. The spinner squatting on the floor turns the wheel to revolve the spindle, and the other hand feeds the fibre to be spun. Spinning of yarn was and is a daily activity of most homes especially in rural areas of Sindh and Punjab. The process of spinning has undergone a big change and home spun yarn used for centuries has been replaced since the last 25 to 30 years with mill spun cotton, silk and woollen fibres which find their way into the hands of the most remotely located weavers.

THE MEN BEHIND THE LOOMS—THE WEAVERS

The highly valued and respected community of weavers were sadly dispersed from their close knit units due to political upheaval in the sub-continent at the time of partition. A large influx of refugee craftspeople from India found their way to Pakistan bringing with them a rich harvest of highly skilled hands. The life style of the weavers remains almost unchanged. They work on commission and according to specifications given by the buyer. A middle man finances them to carry out the orders.

The weavers, commonly known as '*Jolahas*' numbered approximately 300,000 country wide in 1970. The textile arts, their glory and international acclaim is entirely due to these industrious workers.

KHADDAR (COARSE COTTON)

A type of cloth. It is the earliest and simplest form of cotton weave and the most comfortable for human apparel. A breathing fabric, it remains cool in summer and warm in winter and is the most popular for the national dress of Pakistan—*shalwar*/**kurta* (baggy pants and loose shirt). *Khaddar* lends itself beautifully for all types of intricate embroideries both traditional and contemporary. It is made in a wide range of thickness, texture and design and is available in different colours.

KHES

A cotton textile sheet/blanket which has a patterned and bound double weave fabric. *Khes* is extensively used all over Pakistan and has been put to multifarious needs especially of household linens. The important centres of *khes* production are Gumbat, Multan, Nasarpur and Sargodha. All the variety of designs in *khes* weaving is based on a geometric grid. They are traditionally woven in pairs and stitched together to create a 3 yard length. Each centre has adopted a distinct tradition of its own in colour and design and is identified by it.

LUNGI

Lower part of traditional dress. It is a sarong like wrap and is used by both men, who call it the '*Tehmad*' and by women who call it the '*Lacha*', in Sindh it is called '*Sash*'. The *lungi* is widely used in rural areas of both Punjab and Sindh as it is found very comfortable because of the weather, as well as the rural occupation. The traditional pattern of the *lungi* is of small squares, stripes or boxes with bold borders all around in vivid contrasting colours. It is about 3 yards in length and 27 inches in width. Noted centres of *lungi* productions are Pakpattan, Multan, Jhang, Hyderabad and Karachi. However Multani *lungis* are considered more attractive and glamorous due to the intricacy of design in border stripes along with a solid colour.

In the present age, the urbanites are using *lungis* for shirts, skirts as well as curtains and cushion covers.

SUSSI

A fabric of the pre-Christian era, *sussi* is finely woven thin striped cotton made in both monochromatic colour schemes or in multi colours. *Sindhi women traditionally use *sussi* to tailor their *shalwars*. The modern woman has found many non-traditional uses for it. It was and is exported to the West especially England. Multan, Tando Mohammed Khan and Gumbat are noted areas for production of *sussi*. This material is no longer confined to cotton fibre but is manufactured also in silk and silk blends. It comes in widths of 19 inches; 24 inches and 18 yards of it can be daily woven per loom. '*Garbi*' and '*Molhra*' are varieties of *sussi* with subtle variation in stripe design.

PATTI

A thick solid-colour woollen cloth extensively used in the remote and cold mountainous region of Chitral and *Gilgit. Both men and women are involved in its production as women spin the yarn and men weave the cloth on very simple spinning wheels and triangle floor looms. The width of *patti* is a mere 14 inches, 20 inches and the colours are a natural white or shades of tan and grey. The *patti* is used to make the traditional '*Chogas*' (cloak), winter jackets, coats, waist coat and caps with rolled brims.

SHAWLS OF PAKISTAN

Locally known as '*Chaddar*' these are used all over the country both by men and women. The size, thickness, the colour and embellishment styles differ from region to region based on climatic conditions.

The Sindhi version known as '*Khatha*'are light-weight made of cotton or woollen blend in shades of white with borders in a variety of colours. The *chaddars* used in North West Frontier Province and the *Northern Areas are larger in size, heavier in weight and are in tones and shades of grey, brown and khaki with tapestry like borders to them. The Swati style shawls are finished with multicolour borders and fringes. *Balochistan specializes in camel hair shawls which are a favourite of tourists in Pakistan. However, the most beautiful and intricately woven, as well as embroidered is made in *Kashmir (see, Kashmiri Shawls). The variety ranges from the traditional patterned woven *Pashmina* to the embroidered ones with patterns of dainty foliated motifs, *chenar* leaf and almond shaped designs and the all time favourite paisleys. There is a huge market for these shawls both locally and internationally.

SILK

An expensive and high quality silk. This is associated with a higher social status or is used on festive occasions such as marriage celebrations or religious holidays such as '*Eid*'.

Pakistan may rightly boast for producing excellent silk and its variations in the form of satins, brocades and *banarsi* silk.

Being soft to touch and lustrous to the eyes, it is liked by one and all. Silk was produced in the sub-continent since the first millennium BC and was sent west to Europe, where it became very popular. During the Mughal era seri-culture and silk weaving was especially encouraged. It not only catered to the requirements of the royalty and the vastly increased local demand, but also to the ready market of the Middle East and the West. Initially, silk yarn was imported from China and later on from Iran and Central Asia. The position is still the same. Multan, Lahore and Karachi are the major silk producing cities.

BANARSI SILK

Silk encrusted with gold and silver yarn. It is considered precious. It is woven in plain and jacquard weaves. Special mention must be made of '*Saris*' (a traditional female dress of the sub-continent) worn by women with intricate, graceful, elegant borders and *pallu* (one end of the six yard fabric used for the *sari*) of *banarsi* work. The patterns are '*Butidar*' (small motifs at regular intervals) and '*Beldar*' (scroll and creepers). *Banarsi* silk weaving is done on cottage industry basis and often under contract to big orders by retailers. In Pakistan, Khairpur, Lahore and Karachi are the big centres of production of these rich *banarsi* silks and brocades.

EMBELLISHMENT OF TEXTILES

Dyeing and Printing

Dyeing of fabrics is a thriving business all over Pakistan and it is done both at home as well as at commercial locations. There are about five different ways of dyeing fabrics to further enhance their appearance.

- **Simple dyeing**: The cloth is dipped into the dye prepared in boiling water to which dye and a little salt is added. After the fabric thoroughly soaks the dye, it is then dipped into a tub of cold water for the superfluous dye to bleed before drying it. The dyers are all highly skilled and experienced in making the required tones and shades of any colour hue.

- **Resist dyeing**: It is known as '*Bandhini*' or the 'Tie and Dye', method of dyeing, which is symbolic of youth and romance. Wax coated yarn is used to tie small knots around the area of cloth which is not to be dyed. After the entire pattern is tied, usually on a geometric grid, the fabric is dipped in the prepared dye. Once the fabric dries the knots are removed and the cloth ironed, revealing very interesting designs.

- **Batik**: It is another method of resist dyeing where the design or the areas not to be dyed are covered with molten wax. When the fabric is dipped in the dye solution, the area not covered with wax is dyed and the wax covered areas absorb the colour in a network of cracks, which form in the wax when the cloth is wrung to rid it of the excess of dye solution. This gives the finished fabric a very eye catching appearance.

- **Block Printing**: This type of printing requires wooden blocks which are made of *shisham* (rosewood) wood on which intricate designs are traced. Using only a chisel and a hammer, the design motifs are chiselled out to a depth of ¼ inch leaving the remaining area standing in relief. When a motif is composed of more than one colour, then an equal number of blocks of the same motif are needed for printing. In such a case, each block has a specific area of design engraved on it to cater to the need for a different colour for that part of the motif. A single motif may need anything from 2 to 12 blocks to complete the details. The art of block printing is spread all over the country and each region caters to the regional taste in colour and design. An impressive international export in hand block printed fabrics was established by the sub-continent long before the creation of Pakistan. This young country has been able to maintain the tradition with a lot of initiative and creativity to cater to modern day demand. The '*Calicos*' and '*Chintz*' are very popular in the West for their upholstery, curtain material, bedspreads and quilts. For cotton floor rugs, block designs depict animals, birds and the tree of life. The tools used and the craftsmanship is age old. The simple workshops hold padded tables, a huge number of blocks stored on shelves and in baskets along with vats of dyes. Dyes are mostly vegetable dyes such as indigo, madder, turmeric, & pomegranate rind along with the recent addition of some synthetic dyes to suit the present day choice of colours.

- **Ajrak**: It is the most ancient art of block printing, typical of the Sindhi tradition. *Ajrak* has always remained in fashion and is in great demand both for personal apparel as well as household linen. *Ajrak* printing differs from regular block printing in its technique. The fabric is first washed and softened with oils, soap & soda ash. A mordant iron sulphates resist, and then a solution of chalk & gum is stamped on the cloth. It is then dipped into a series of dye baths. The whole thing is covered with either powdered cow dung or rice bran to fix the three mixtures. The pattern printed with resist remains white and where mordant is used the dye only adheres to the print. Customarily, colours used are red, blue, black and white. The designs are mostly stylised geometrical configurations typical of the Sindhi style. A traditional *Ajrak* has a composition of vertical and horizontal borders with properly patterned corner motifs surrounding a central area of overall patterns. The value of *Ajrak* is determined by the quality of cloth, dyes & craftsmanship and the number & intricacy of the borders.

- **Wax printing and painting**: The tribal belt of the NWFP area of Pakistan uses this traditional technique of printing with wax. The *Afridi tribe is well known for this craft which is practiced in Peshawar and Quetta and has also spread to Lahore and Karachi. The artisans rely on family formulae of making dough like wax paste made with lime and safflower oil. The maker puts a small portion of the paste on his hand and pulls out fine filaments of the material with a stylus, attaching it to one point on the cloth. Then he stretches it to sketch the straight lines and curves that make up the whole picture. The design is dusted over with multicoloured, gold or silver powdered pigments. Popular items of production are scarves, stoles, table cloths and cushion covers.

EMBROIDERIES

The ingenuity of women's nimble hands in embroidery was, and is a perennial source of joy. They display all their passion for colour in embroideries by an instinctive, rhythmic repetition, producing fabrics of breathtaking beauty. The task encompasses a series of sub-activities such as preparing the design outline, stretching the fabric on a frame, considering colour options, choosing the stitches and selection of the design theme. Only in Kashmir do the men folk share this labour of love with the women. The range of this traditional craft of embellishing fabrics, dating back to the riverine civilization, is vast only if one realises that every piece of cloth or garment may be ornamented with embroideries. The zenith of this craft was reached during the Mughal period as the nobility not only patronised the craft but added further innovations to it.

SOME REGIONAL STYLES OF EMBROIDERIES

Balochistan: *Balochi embroideries are characterised by their bold designs and vivid colour combinations. The background chosen is usually red, home-spun cotton material or the natural beige colour of the fibre. Balochi embroidery is considered the finest in the country and acclaimed all over the world. Using a variety of very fine stitches such as the '*hurmutch*' (a grid of cross stitches further interlaced with thread) chain stitches and the buttonhole stitch. The latter is used to fix small, round pieces of mirrors within the pattern reflecting pin-points of light, creating a shimmering effect and highlighting the design. '*Pushk*' (a loose shirt) is a unique item used both in Balochistan and Sindh. It has an embroidered front with matching cuffs and a long pouch in the middle of the lower half of its front.

Northern Areas & NWFP: Bold geometric motifs in the basic primary colours dominate the embroideries of these cold climate areas. The designs, especially of *Swat embroidery bear traces of Greek influence. The embroidery is done on shirts, shawls, belts caps and '*choghas*' (loose cloaks) which are all made of the locally woven '*patti*' cloth.

Kashmir: The *Kashmiri embroideries are renowned for their sophistication of colour scheme and design. Drawing inspiration from the natural beauty of their surroundings, they typically design the *Chenar* leaf, paisley, creepers, lotus, fruits, birds & cypress cones in myriad variations. The most subtle aspect of the Kashmiri embroidery known as '*Kashida-kari*' is their '*Do-Rukha*' meaning two sided style in which there is no right or wrong side which gives it an excellent finish.

'*Gabbas*' are another embroidered item which is typically Kashmiri. These are mats fully covered with chain stitch embroidery depicting scenes of hunting, war, weddings, farm & rural activities. This ancient craft of the *Gandhara period is being acknowledged for its sophisticated composition and artistic craftsmanship, increasing the demand in the international market as wall hangings.

Punjab: '*Phulkari*' meaning flower craft is the style of embroidery peculiar to the Punjab and the Hazara district. Using simple darn stitch the embroidery is worked on soft, home-spun *khaddar* cloth creating labyrinths of geometrical patterns that give a mosaic like effect. The quality of workmanship is judged by the smoothness at the back that can come only from the evenness of the stitches. Originally this work was done with silk yarn but now both cotton as well as synthetic yarns is being used.

Traditionally *Phulkaris* were worn by brides and bride-grooms. The modern day use of it is as a very formal shawl or wall hanging. The dominant colours are bright and dark such as crimson, shocking pink, green, orange, purple, mustard and white.

Sindh: The most elaborately done piece of embroidery is on '*Guj*' the bride's wedding shirt. As soon as a girl is born in the family, the mother would put the first stitches on cloth to be made into a *guj* for the girl's marriage. It is a labour of love for the family who make sure that it is ready in good time for the event. The entire shirt is fully covered with intricate embroidery and mirror work and is a piece of art. The shawls with embroidery all over are known as '*Abochnais*' for females and '*Malirs*' for males. The '*Bochani*' is a scarf for the bridegroom.

Sindh also excels in the special craft of making '*Rilli*' which is a multi purpose sheet serving as a bedspread, a blanket, a saddle or a shawl. The patchwork is associated with the *Sufis who stitched together old scraps of cloths to make jackets, *chaddars* and caps as a mark of humility. Fine strips or squares of cloth are folded and cut out to compose geometric motifs which are painstakingly sewn onto a plain soft cotton sheet. Usually *rillis* are multicoloured and sometimes black & white. *Rillis* are also made in parts of Balochistan and *Cholistan besides Sindh.

CONCLUSION

Pakistan, inheriting an ancient historical background, stands high with a long record of technical and aesthetic achievements in the field of cotton cultivation, cotton manufactures and decorative cotton/silk textiles.

The weavers and craft men were guided in their search for excellence by an insatiable urge for beauty through the artistic interpretation of nature, symbolism of certain motifs as protection from evil. The traditional and intellectual leaning of Islamic art towards the abstract, leant enormous scope to patterns which were ideally suited to textile weaves and designs. Inspiration was also drawn from the Mughul architecture, miniature paintings and elaborate carpet weaving. All contributed towards the superb ornamentation of textiles in Pakistan.

Today Pakistan is the fourth largest producer of cotton, the third largest exporter of raw cotton and a leading exporter of yarn in the world. Its textile manufacture is not only prospering, but its export earns valuable foreign exchange for the country.

Textile Industry's contribution to the GDP is 11% and it employs 40% of the total workforce in the country. The industry consumes all the cotton produced in the country and imports large quantities to satisfy its growing demand.

- Number of textile mills is 453 of which 54 are integrated units and 399 are spinning units.
- Number of spindles is 7.6 million of which 83% are effectively utilised.
- Number of rotors is 70,000 and their capacity utilisation is 47%.
- Total production of cotton yarn in 2003 was 1,818.3 thousand tones.
- Installed capacity of looms in integrated units is 10,299 of which 4,947 are being effectively utilised.
- Independent weaving units have 23,622 looms installed in them of which 27,000 are effectively utilised.
- Power looms installed capacity is 225,358 of which 190,000 are working.

The export of textiles, cotton made-ups and cotton amounts to a little over 12 billion dollars. The main importers of these products are the developed countries of the West where a textile quota regime is in operation under the GATT (General Agreement on Tarrifs and Trade, a WTO standard). Textile and clothing export will cease to be governed by quotas placed by major importers on 31 December 2004 as the agreement among nations governing international trade in textile and clothing will lapse. There is now a consensus among most analysts that Pakistan will be one of the main beneficiaries of the end of quotas. It is likely to double its share in the international textile market that is currently estimated at 360 billion dollars. At present, Pakistan's share is slightly more than 2% of the world trade in textile and clothing. It could rise to 5% over the next five year, amounting to 25 billion dollars.

CLAY CRAFTS OF PAKISTAN

Nilofur Farrukh

Clay crafts of Pakistan include the vast repertoire of the *kumbhar* (potter) and *kashigar* (glazed design maker) of the country. Complex and rich in its diversity, Pakistan's traditional pottery has been impacted by three cultural dialogues that have left tangible evidence in techniques of production. This influence comes from Iran in the West and India in the East and during the last decade, industrialization has led to the use of electric potter wheels and gas firing.

Trade caravans and invaders that traversed mountains, deserts and river plains of this region brought with them fresh ideas and techniques that were absorbed into our ancient indigenous conventions. This constant interface with new cultures has left an imprint on the people, its customs and craft practices, particularly ceramics.

Pakistani ceramic tradition survives unchanged in the rural sanctuaries of crafts. Major onslaughts like the colonial strategies aimed at creating South Asia into a market for British manufactured goods, included tax on Indian craft imports, and an attempt to delink the craftsmen from their environment by sending their sons to art academies, were all attempts to systematically undermined their production. The Mayo School of Art, Lahore, where the student body constituted mainly of the sons of artisans till 1959, had a curriculum that not only detached the artisans from the ethos of their ancestral professions, but also robbed them of the pride they took in their skills.

Unlike this superimposed system, the second assault to this tradition has come from the change in consumer habits spawned by aggressive industrialization in the last five decades.

Ironically, poverty has saved and preserved the craft tradition, since people simply do not have the buying power to purchase other products.

The other smaller groups of patrons come from among the well-to-do urban dwellers. Motivated by a combination of disenchantment with mass produced wares and a need for cultural identity have also come to the rescue of the marginalized artisans.

The potter or *kumbhar*, as he is locally known in the south, and *kulal* in the North has always been prolific and skillful. His extended family, through a collaborative practice, functioned like a factory, producing all the functional ware to satisfy the needs of a given settlement. In a practical sense the *kumbhar* was equivalent to a product designer as he was required to make choices regarding the structure and appearance of the object as well as the strategy for making it. It's true that his priority was not to put a stamp of originality but often to reproduce the existing design with excellence.

The *kumbhar* works with the most rudimentary of tools and basic equipment combined a deep understanding of his medium, he not only builds and fires with consummate skill but makes intelligent design interventions to improve the product.

Two distinct kinds of clay crafts exist in Pakistan, the unglazed earthenware, which is largely utilitarian, and glazed ware which varies from architectural ornaments to functional vessels.

Unglazed containers for consumption, cleansing and cooking constituted the largest part of the production. The vocabulary of forms evolved around climatic needs and cultural influences. The water container is central to pottery production and has somehow managed to retain its popularity. It varies from large storage vessels that act like immobile reservoirs to smaller vessels that are used to deliver water to them. Each region has its own distinct style of containers dictated by culture, living and dietary habits and climate. Besides the *matka*, the most commonly known water pitcher, many variations can be found in different regions.

Combining early Indo- Greek influence with later Middle Eastern links, the pottery of Balochistan is dictated by the nomadic life of its dwellers and extreme seasonal temperatures. The strong limestone content in the clay serves as effective insulation.

In the North West Frontier Province, the *Patakai* is used mainly to carry water on camel caravan journeys. It resembles the pilgrim's flask and its origin can be traced back to the Indo-Greek influence. A similar shaped bottle is used by local mountain trekkers in the Valley of *Swat. The water container reserved for personal use is widely known as the *kuza*.

This small vessel with a spout is practical for '*vazu*' or the ritual washing of face, hand and feet before prayer by Muslims. It is also used to carry out the last rites of a person. In some areas the *kuza* for men and women can be identified by their size and surface pattern.

'*Roti*' which means bread is synonymous with food in many regional dialects. Wheat and other cereals are consumed in the form of thin, flat bread cooked on a griddle or in a sunken clay oven called *tandoor*. This is such an integral part of the domestic kitchen that special vessels are made for kneading the dough, resting it and finally cooking it.

To light up the village lanes and homes with simple *dia* (oil lamps) and more elaborate stands continue to complete with kerocene, lanterns in unelectrified villages.

These meticulously crafted lamp stands from Swat were used to burn resinous wood. No longer in demand, this elaborate tradition can find no willing apprentices. And today, only one eighty-year-old woman is left with the expertise to make these stands.

The only unglazed non-utilitarian pottery in Pakistan is the Paperware of Ahmedpur East. This fragile pottery is defined by a perforated arabesque design that echoes the forms and ornamentations of Islamic pierced metal-ware.

Press molded and dressed with clay with heavy mica content its exuberant designs epitomize the spirit of the decorative arts. In an attempt to keep up with the times and cater to the urban market ashtrays, lamp bases and platters have been added to more traditional forms.

Compared to earthenware production, which is widespread, Pakistan has only a handful of centers of glazed pottery. Its five main centers are located in Hala, Nusserpur, Quetta, Multan and Peshawar.

The master '*kashigars*' of Nusserpur traces their origin to Iran and Afghanistan. Their ancestors where brought to *Sindh by Mughal Emperor Shahjehan (see, Mughal Empire) to undertake the tilework of the mosque he built in Thatta.

Many generations later, they continues to embellish monuments with his glazed tiles and architectural ornaments.

A similar settlement in Hala, not very far from Nusserpur has expanded into glazed functional ware production mostly for the tourist and the urban market. Floral and geometric patterns are adapted for flowerpots, platters, vases and tabletops.

The tiles are used extensively for *mazars*, mosques and *havelis* for wall decorations. An urban market has also developed but, since the demand is mainly for floor tiles, the traditional craftsman with his limited resources is finding it difficult to compete with the durability and variety of industrially produced tiles.

The glazing techniques are very basic, and fired between 950–1,050°C.

The leatherware is covered with an '*astar*' or engobe. Clayslip with lead glazes mostly used for hollow ware and siliceous slip with alkaline glaze that is used for flatware like tiles and plates. Three pigments are commonly used cobalt oxide to give blue, copper oxide to give turquoise and copper oxide mixed with lead and chromium oxide to give green. In Hala, the glazed ware is less rigid in design and combines a wider palette and combination of motifs.

In Multani pottery, a siliceous slip forms the engobe, which after drying is decorated with patterns primarily in the limited palette of cobalt blue from cobalt oxide, turquoise black copper oxide and white. A few new colors like green, brown and yellow are being added.

In Multan the intervention of the Small Potteries has helped to provide jobs to potters but neglected the tradition. The rather bland slip-cast pottery produced in the small potteries have adopted Chinese motifs which have a global flavor and are far removed from the traditions of the place.

Among the domestic glazed ware bowls, urns and deep platters from the area around Peshawar and Pabbi have a distinct iconographic affinity to wares from pottery centers in neighboring Afghanistan.

Also made for domestic consumption, the glazed pottery of Quetta is hand thrown and thick walled. The red clay is dressed with a buff colored slip before it is partially glazed. The inner part is always clear glazed to allow storage of oil, pickles etc.

For several millennia, the clay mined from the riverbanks and mountainsides of Pakistan has been transformed by the intervention of the potter. With the advent of factory-produced goods, the traditional clay crafts face extinction and there is a dire need for new strategies to assimilate the skills of the craft people into sustainable production so they can earn a livelihood which is so intrinsically linked to the survival of the glazed and unglazed pottery traditions of Pakistan.

PAKISTANI STAMPS

Rabia Zafar

The history of postage stamps in the region dates back to 1852 when, under the leadership of Sir Bartle Frere, *Sindh became Asia's first region to issue its own stamps. However, with the introduction of official British Indian (see, British India) stamps in 1854 their usage ceased.

At the time of independence in 1947, the government debated upon issuing its own stamps. However, it was decided to overprint *British India, King George VI stamps with 'Pakistan' and put these into circulation. Known as the 'Nasik Overprints,' this issue consisted of 19 stamps.

The first commemorative issue was released in July 1948 for the country's first anniversary. Three of the four stamps depicted places from *West Pakistan while the fourth stamp depicted a motif. The artist, A.R. *Chughtai was amongst Pakistan's firs stamp designers.

Since its first stamps, Pakistan Post has issued over 600 different sets and singles, some 1,100 stamps. The authorities have, over the years, portrayed, commemorated and honoured various personalities, national and international organisations and events, the country's flora and fauna, its cultural and historical heritage as well as the country's development. Other themes include health, educational institutions, religion, sports and defence.

Though it has now become very common to portray a human face on stamps, for the initial 17 years this was not the case. The first issue to carry a human face was a set of three stamps released to pay homage to the country's armed forces after the War of 1965. The first incumbent head of state or government portrayed was General Ayub *Khan on the 1966 stamps for the new capital of Islamabad.

The Quaid was first pictured on his 90th birth anniversary in 1966. Earlier issues carried motifs and wordings or his mausoleum. Since then numerous stamps have been issued carrying his portrait. In 1976, authorities issued a gold stamp for his birth centenary. Each stamp carried 25 mg. of 23/24 carat gold and was valued at Rs. 10. The stamps were printed using a special silk screen printing process known as serigraphy. Besides commemorative stamps, definitive series with his portrait have also been issued.

Other personalities honoured with their own stamps include Allama Muhammad *Iqbal, *Ghalib, Kemal Attaturk, Shah of Iran, Maria Montessori, Hakim *Saeed, Liaquat Ali *Khan, Nusrat Fateh Ali, A.B.A. Haleem, Maulana Mohammad Ali Jouhar, Tipu Sultan and *Abdus Salam.

The United Nations and its agencies have been regularly depicted. Pakistan has also released stamps related to UNESCO's efforts to protect some of the world's heritage sites, including Venice (1972).

Ever since the first commemorative issue which included the *Lahore Fort, Pakistan Post has continued to depict various aspects of the country. Periodically various series have also been released on wildlife, fruits, *Moenjadaro and medicinal plants etc. Pakistan's handicrafts, dresses, mountains, sporting achievements, infrastructure including the motorway (1997) and exports (2003) have also featured.

Various educational institutions such as the National College of Arts (2001), national associations, organisations, exhibitions and conferences held within the country have also been depicted. Religious stamps depicting the *Kabah* (1977), *Masjid Nabvi* (199), advent of the 15th Century AH (1980) and Eid greetings have also been released.

Besides stamps, souvenir sheets have also been issued by the posted authorities. Sheets have been issued depicting the Quaid, Universal Postal Union and 2,500th anniversary of the Iranian Monarchy. The most recent sheet is the Rs. 30 one for the 50th Anniversary of the first ascent of K-2 mountain (2004).

Besides stamps and souvenir sheets, the Post Office also prints postal stationery and has also released specially prepared postmarks.

Three types of postmarks have been used by the postal service: slogan, special and first day cancellations. Slogan postmarks are regular postmarks but with a slogan attached to them. These have been issued in 3 languages; *Bengali, *English and *Urdu. The most famous one is 'Pakistan *Zindabad*' issued by various post offices in the late 1940's and early 1950s. Special postmarks are made to commemorate an event for which no stamp is released. Over the years these have been released for visiting heads of state and stamp and industrial exhibitions. A first day cancellation is a special cancellation prepared each time a stamp is issued and is used to tie the stamp and the cover together. It usually had the date of issue, a picture and the issue name on it.

In postal stationery; aerogrammes, presetamped enveloped and postcards have been issued. The first Pakistani aerogramme was a 'Pakistan' overprint of a 6 *anna* British India, Kig George VI one. Prestamped Envelopes have been printed for both inland and overseas mail and reflecting the current minimum postal rate.

Occassionally, these also have a slogan attached to them. The postal authorities have been regularly issuing various postcards over the years for both domestic and international usage. For official use, these are overprinted 'Service.' Special post cards have also been issued such as the set of four for the 2001 SAF Games in Islamabad.

Over the last 57 years, numerous designers have been employed with a large number affiliated with the National College of Arts, Lahore. Most Pakistani stamps have been printed within the country by the Pakistan Security Printing Corporation Limited, Karachi and since 2003, by the Pakistan Post Foundation Press (Security Division), Karachi. However, foreign printers have also been used. Thomas De La Rue and Company, UK has had the privilege of printing the first commemorative stamp of Pakistan (1948).

Over the years various errors have crept into the stamps and postal stationeries issued. Two of the most famous errors occurred in the 1960s. One of them was in the 1961-63 definitive issue. In this issue due to oversight, the country name was spelt as 'Shakistan' in Bengali. The mistake occurred when the character '*pa*' was replaced by '*sha*'. The other famous error occurred in the birth year of the famous Bengali poet, Kazi Nazarul Islam. The stamp released showed it as 1868 instead of 1869. Both errors were detected and the stamps withdrawn. The corrected stamps were later reissued but some of these stamps slipped into the hands of collectors.

PAKISTANI CURRENCY

Rabia Zafar

The first currency notes circulated in newly independent Pakistan were of British Indian (see, British India) origin, overprinted 'Government of Pakistan' in both English and *Urdu. These were supplemented by Reserve Bank of India notes issued without the inscription and holding the same value. These notes were a stop-gap effort until the new government was able to print its own notes.

1 July 1948 saw the establishment of the central bank of the country, the State Bank of Pakistan. Three months later a regular issue consisting of Rs. 5, Rs. 10 and Rs. 100 banknotes prepared by Thomas De La Rue and Company, UK were released. These were deep blue, red and rich green in colour respectively and issued without a watermark or security thread.

The first banknote issued in the name of the central bank was the Rs. 2 note issued in March 1949 and part of the first series of Pakistani banknotes. It is also the only banknote ever issued which features the bank's name transliterated in Urdu instead of 'Bank *Daulat* Pakistan'. The green Re. 1 note issued at the same time was printed for the Government of Pakistan.

Soon after the establishment of the State Bank, concerned authorities took the necessary steps for issuing permanent banknotes. Various designs were prepared and their approval taken by September 1949. Two years later, new Rs. 5 and Rs. 10 were released. However, in 1952-53 the newly established Pakistan Security Printing Corporation released Rs. 11 and Rs. 5 notes, which were the first ever notes printed by it. The Re. 1 was issued with a change in colour. The Re. 100 note, which required some design changes, was released four years later (1953) and printed by Thomas De La Rue and Company.

The first note of the second series, the Rs. 100 (1957), set the trend for future issues of featuring the *Quaid-i-Azam on the front. This note also featured Bengali text on the front for the first time. Earlier, Bengali numerals were on the front with text on the back. The note itself was predominately green with the *Badshahi Mosque on its back. The Rs. 50 note (1964) featured the promissory clause for the first time in both Urdu and Bengali. They appeared on either side of the Quaid. The note depicted jute laden boats on its back while the Rs. 500 note showed the State Bank's new building. The Rs. 500 note introduced a new security thread in banknotes with 'Pakistan' on the micro-printed thread. The Rs. 10 note (1970) featured a change from the earlier designs. Mr Jinnah's portrait appears on the front left while the promissory clauses appear in the center. The back is the same with the picture of the Shalimar Gardens.

The War of 1971 saw the introduction of the third series which was an emergency issue. Due to unrest in the Eastern wing which resulted in massive looting of the banks, as a first step, the State Bank declared the Rs. 100 and Rs. 500 note invalid. The Bank, however, allowed the public to redeemed them later provided that they had not been part of any stolen lot. In 1972, the government issued new notes. Except for the Rs. 100 notes, all other denominations; Re. 1, Rs. 5, Rs. 10 and Rs. 50, were issued with a change of colour. They were printed as brown, ochre, green and blue respectively.

The Rs. 100 was produced with a new design with the *Badshahi* Mosque on the reverse and the Quaid on the front left. Even though it was issued after the creation of Bangladesh, the presence of Bengali on the note suggests that the design was prepared before the break-up. Due to time constraints on the Pakistan Security Printing Corporation, 10 million Rs. 10 notes were printed by Thomas De La Rue, UK.

The fourth and current series of banknotes followed shortly after the third. The initial Re, 1 note, issued in 1974 with a crescent and star of the right was withdrawn soon afterwards. The note depicted the denomination in the four main regional languages of the country and was seen as promoting regionalism. The same note was reissued without the languages in April 1975. Three other denominations were introduced in 1976; Rs. 5, Rs. 10 Rs. 100. All three carried a common layout. The Rs. 5 note features the Khojak Tunnel o the Quetta to Chaman rail line. The Rs. 10 shows a view of *Moenjodaro at the back. And the Rs. 100 note shows Islamia College, Peshawar. The gates of the Lahore Fort are featured on the back of he Rs. 50 note which was issued in 1977. The Rs. 1,000 note shows Emperor Jahangir's tomb in Lahore.

The State Bank has, to date, issued only one commemorative banknote. The Rs. 5 note was issued for the country's 50th anniversary in 1997. It carries the portrait of the Quaid on the front and the tomb of Shah *Rukn-e-Alam, Multan on its back.

Circulating coins in Pakistan may be divided into two time periods: predecimal and decimal. The system of pies, pieces, *annas* and *rupees*, used until 1961, is known as predecimal coinage. The first coins were minted in 1948 and consisted of 7 pieces from 1 pice to Re. 1. In 1961, the government decided to introduce decimal coinage i.e. 100 *paisa* = Re. 1. Coins issued by the country have come in various shapes and sizes. The only coin with a hole in the centre was the 1 pice coin issue between 1948 and 1952. Other shapes minted were scalloped edged *anna* and 10 *paisa* coins and square shaped; 1/2 *anna*, 2 *paisa* and 5 *paisa* coins.

In recent years, the government has stopped minting lower denomination coins. Since 1998, Re. 1 and Rs. 2 coins have been circulating within the country. The reverse side of the Rs. 2 coin depicts the same design, *Badshahi* Masjid, as the first note. A Rs. 5 coin was released in December 2002 in preparation of the eventual withdrawal of the Rs. 5 note in 2005.

Since first issuing commemorative coins in 1976, the country has issued numerous such coins for various reasons. The government issued one gold and two silver coins in 1976 as part of its concern for the country's wild life. The Rs. 3000 gold coin depicted the Astor Markhor, while the Rs. 150 and Rs. 100 silver coins depicted the Gharial crocodile and Western Tragopan Pheasant respectively. The Rs. 150 coin was the largest ever coin (42 mm.) minted by the government. The obverse on all the coins featured the **Minar* with the crescent and star. The designer for these coins was Robert Gilmore of the Royal Mint, UK. Other commemorative coins minted include the Rs. 5 coin for the 50th Anniversary of the United Nations, Rs. 50 coin for the 50th Anniversary of the country and Rs. 100 coin for the Birth Centennial of Muhammad Ali Jinnah.

ADDENDA

Addendum No. 1

Governors-General	Dates Served
Muhammad Ali Jinnah	August 1947–September 1948
Khwaja Nazimuddin	September 1948–September 1951
Ghulam Muhammad	October 1951–September 1955
Iskander Mirza	October 1955–March 1956

Presidents	Dates Served
Iskander Mirza	March 1956–October 1958
Muhammad Ayub Khan *	October 1958–March 1969
Agha Muhammad Yahya Khan	March 1969–December 1971
Zulfikar Ali Bhutto	December 1971–August 1973
Fazal Ilahi Choudhury	15 August 1973–April 1978
Chief Justice of Pakistan, Anwar-ul-Haq**	April 1978–September 1978
Muhammad Ziaul Haq***	September 1978–August 1988
Ghulam Ishaq Khan****	August 1988–October 1993
Sardar Farooq Ahmad Khan Leghari *****	November 1993–December 1996
Mian Mohammad Rafiq Tarar	January 1997–June 2001
General Pervez Musharraf	June 2001–present

*Assumed his presidency from Iskander Mirza, who had resigned from the post; reelected in February 1960 and then again in January 1965.
** Performed presidential duties temporarily.
***Took his oath while still Chief Military Administrator after the resignation of President Choudhury, and later announced as reelected President according to the results of the referendum of 19 December 1984.
****Performed presidential duties in his capacity as Senate Chairman, after the death of President Ziaul Haq; elected President on 12 December 1988, for a term of five years.
*****Elected President of Pakistan when he secured 274 votes against Waseem Sajjad's 168 on 13 November 1993. Resigned in December 1996.

Addendum No. 2

Prime Ministers	Dates Served
Liaquat Ali Khan	August 1947–October 1951
Khwaja Nazimuddin	October 1951–April 1953
Muhammad Ali Bogra	April 1953–August 1955
Choudhry Muhammad Ali	August 1955–September 1956
Huseyn Shaheed Suhrawardy	September 1956–October 1957
Ismail Ibrahim Chundrigar	October 1957–December 1957
Malik Firoz Khan Noon	December 1957–October 1958
President was also Prime Minister*	October 1958–August 1973
Zulfikar Ali Bhutto	August 1973–July 1977
President was also the Prime Minister.	July 1977–March 1985
Mohammed Khan Junejo	March 1985–May 1987

President was also Prime Minister**	May 1988–December 1988
Benazir Bhutto	December 1988–August 1990
Ghulam Mustafa Jatoi***	August 1990–November 1990
Mian Nawaz Sharif****	November 1990–April 1993
Benazir Bhutto*****	October 1993–May 1996
Mian Nawaz Sharif	February 1997–October 1999
General Pervez Musharraf	October 1999–November 2002
Zafarullah Khan Jamali	November 2002–June 2004
Chaudhry Shujaat Hussain	June 2004–August 2004
Shaukat Aziz	August 2004–Present

*The post of Prime Minister was abolished and his duties were transferred to the President, who was simultaneously head of the government,

**Upon the dissolution of the Parliament and the government, the President assumed the duties of Prime Minister as well.

*** Appointed temporary Prime Minister by presidential decree.

**** He was removed by President Ghulam Ishaq Khan on 18 April 1993, who appointed Mir Balkh Sher Mazari as the new caretaker Prime Minister. Elections were promised within ninety days. On 26 May, the Supreme Court restored Nawaz Sharif's government to power, and reinstated the National Assembly. On 17 July President Ghulam Ishaq Khan and Nawaz Sharif agreed to step down from their positions in government, while preparations for elections were made by a neutral administration of Moeen Qureshi (a former vice president of the World Bank). His term was stipulated to last for ninety days.

***** Elected Prime Minister of Pakistan. Mian Mohammad Nawaz Sharif was re-elected in 1996. M. Nawaz Sharif was dismissed on 12 October 1999.

Addendum No. 3

List of Main Tribes

Main Pashtun Tribes Residing on Pakistan Territory

A. Yusufzai
   1. Highland Yusufzai (Main clans: Malizai, Akkozai, Isazai, Iliaszai)
   2. Lowland Yusufzai (Main clans: Utmanzai, Usmanzai, Razar)
      i. Often called by a common name, Mandan (Mandanri).

B. Tarklanri (Main clans: Ismailzai, Isazai, Mahmud, Salarzai)

C. Gadun (or Jadun)
   1. Two divisions: Salar and Mansur.

D. Nomand (or Mohmand)
   1. Highland—Bar-Momands
   2. Lowland—Kuz-Momand
      i. Part of Momands live in Afghanistan

E. Daudzai (or Dawudzai)
   1. Three divisions: Mandki, Yusaf, Mamur.

F. Khalil (Main clans: Akazai, Barozai, Ishaqzai, Mattezai, Nurzai, Taliarzai.)

G. Afridi or Apridi)
   1. Lowland Afridi (Main clan: Adam Khel),
   2. Highland Afridi (Main clans: Aka or Akka Khel, Kuki Khel, Zakka Khel, Mirahmad Khel, Sepai or Sepahi).

H. Orakzai
   1. Four divisions: Ismailzai, Lashkarzai, Daulatzai, Muhammad Khel.

I. Bangash

   1. Three divisions: Baizai, Miranzai (Malikmiri), Shamilzai.
J. Khattak
   1. Two divisions: Tari (Tarai), Balaq (Bolaq).
K. Bannuchi or Banuji
   1. Three divisions: Miri, Sami, Sarrani.
L. Waziri
   1. Darwesh Khel (Musa Darwesh Khel)
      i. Main group of clans: Utmanzail and Ahmadzai
   2. Masud (Mahsud) Waziri
      i. Main clans: Alizai (Potia Khel), Bahlolzai, Shaman Khel.
M. Marwat (Main clans: Achu Khel, Bahram Khel, Musa Khel, Tappi Khel, Khuda Khel.
N. Niazi (Niyazi)
   1. Four divisions: Isa Khel, Musa Khel, Sambal, Sarhang.
O. Khasor or Khasur
   1. Main clans: Malli Khel, Umr Khel.
P. Gandapur
   1. Five divisions: Brahimzai, Umranzai, Khubizai, Husainzai, Yakubzai.
Q. Shirani
   1. Main clans: Babar, Sian Khel, Uba Khel, Chugar Khel.
R. Mando Khel or Mandu Khel.
S. Ustarani or Ushratai
   1. Main clans: Amazai, or Ahmadzai, and Gagalzai.
T. Pani
   1. Main clans: Dephal, or Dogpal, Zmari, Isot, Musa Khel.
U. Kakar
   1. Main clans: Babi, Bayanzai, Dawi, Kibzai, Nagra, Mando Khel, Sardar Khel, Hamazai.
V. Tarin
   1. Two divisions: Spintarin, Tortarin.
W. Achakzai (or Atsakzai)
   1. One of the Durrani clans, residing in Afghanistan.

Main Balochi Tribes Residing on Pakistan Territory

Kachhi district—Rind, Magsi (Magasi), Dombki, Umrani, Buldi, Khosa, Jatoi, Kebari, Mughari, Dinari, Chalgri.
Kharran district—Nausherwani, Rakshani, Muhammadhasni.
Makrani district—Gichki, Buledi (Zikri), Sangur, Biranjani, Kilkaur.
Sibi district—Marri, Bugti, Rind.
Chagai district—Sanjrani, Jamaldini, Badini.
Loralai district—Leghari, Ghurchani, Buzdar, Kaisrani.
Las Bela district—Gadri, Sangur.
Kalat district—Zehri.

Main Brahui Tribes Residing on Pakistan Territory

Kharran district—Sasoli, Samalari.
Makran district—Bizenjo.
Quetta-Pishin district—Shahwani, Lehri, Langar, Mengal, Raisani, Kambrani, Nichari, Muhammadshahi.
Las Bela district—Bizenjo.

Kalat district—Raisani, Shahwani, Bangalzai, Lehri, Langaw, Rustamzai, Mengal, Bizenjo, Kambrani, Mirwari, Gurganari, Nichari, Sasoli, Khidrani.
Chagai district—Mengal.

YU.V. GANKOVSKY

Add to Addenda (no. 5) Section:
Months of the Muslim Year

1. Muharram
2. Safar
3. Rabi' al-awwal (Rabi' I)
4. Rabi' al-thani (Rabi' II)
5. Jumada al-awwal (Jumada I)
6. Jumada al-thani (Jumada II)
7. Rajab
8. Sha'ban
9. Ramadan
10. Shawwal
11. Dhu al-Qi'dah
12. Dhu al-Hijjah